d • ache • acroba... ...
rm-clock • alarm... ...
anda Thripp • an... ... • amble • amphibian
anklet • anniversary • announce • annoying • annual • answer •
gize • appendix • appetite • apple • approach • approve • arch •
line • asleep • assembly • astonish • astronaut • athlete • atlas •
nce • Augustus Gloop • aunt • author • autobiography • average
le • babblement • baby • backside • back-to-front • backwards
• balloon • balmy • bang • banister • banknote • bar • barber •
athtub • battle • batty • bawl • beach • beady • beak • beam
• bedroom • beetle • beg • behave • behind • belch • believe
• bewitching • BFG • bibble • bibliophile • bicirculers • bicycle •
d Pie • birthday • bish • bite • bitter • bittersweet • blabbersnitch
• bleed • end • blighter • blind • blink • blister • blithering •
• blow • wpipe • blueberry • Blue Bubbler • blurred • blush •
oggis, Bu... and Bean • boggle • bogglebox for boys • bogrotting
bomb • ... • Bonecruncher • bonnet • bony • book • boom •
n • bottle ottle-wart • bottom • bounce • bound • bow • boy
brat • br... • bread • breakfast • breath • breathe • breeches •
road • bro... • brother • browbeaten • Bruce Bogtrotter • bruise
ckle • bug... hling • buggles • bugswallop • bugwhiffle • bulge
erbluss • ... • bundongle • bungswoggle • bunk • bunkdoodle
usy • Bu... Boy • butler • butter • butterfly • butterscotch
uzzy-hum... cabbage • cacao • cackle • cage • cake • calculate
eannybully • cantankerous • captain • capture • car • caramel
• east • catapult • catasterous • catch • caterpillar • catspringer
ling • celebrate • cell • cellar • cement • Centipede • century
r • chant • chaos • character • charge • Charlie Bucket • chase
• cheek • cheeky • cheer • cheerful • cheese • chest of drawers
dchewer • childish • chilly • chimney • chin • chitter • chocolate

Oxford
ROALD
DAHL
Dictionary

Oxford ROALD DAHL Dictionary

Original text by
ROALD DAHL

Illustrated by
QUENTIN BLAKE

Compiled by
SUSAN RENNIE

OXFORD
UNIVERSITY PRESS

OXFORD
UNIVERSITY PRESS

Great Clarendon Street, Oxford OX2 6DP.
United Kingdom

Oxford University Press is a department of the University of Oxford.
It furthers the University's objective of excellence in research,
scholarship, and education by publishing worldwide

British Library Cataloguing in Publication Data
Data available

ISBN: 978-0-19-273645-1
10 9 8 7 6 5 4 3 2 1
Printed in China

Paper used in the production of this book is a natural, recyclable product made from
wood grown in sustainable forests. The manufacturing process conforms to the
environmental regulations of the country of origin.

GREETINGS TO YOU, THE LUCKY READER OF THIS DICTIONARY!

This is not an ordinary dictionary. After all, you wouldn't expect a Roald Dahl Dictionary to be ordinary, would you? Lots of dictionaries will tell you what an **alligator** is, or how to spell **balloon**, but they won't explain the difference between a **ringbeller** and a **trogglehumper**, or say why witches need **gruntles' eggs**, or suggest a word for the shape of a **Knid** (it is **oviform**, by the way), or tell you why **bobolinks** are called bobolinks. This dictionary does all those things. You will even have to read some of the definitions backwards.

ONLY REALLY INTERESTING WORDS are allowed in

this dictionary. All the words which Roald Dahl invented are here, like **biffsquiggled** and **gobblefunk**, and both **phizz-whizzing** and **whizzpopping**, to remind you which means what. But that is not all. You will find the names of Roald Dahl's characters and places, and also words to describe them, like **chocolatier** (which is not the same as a chocolate ear) and **hirsute**. You will also find words that are important in Roald Dahl's world. You might not be surprised to see **blueberry** and **elevator**, but do you know why **alarm-clock** and **anti-freeze** are in here too?

Finally, some words are simply here for fun, like **aardvark**, because just like stories, every dictionary needs a good beginning.

Susan Rennie

CHIEF EDITOR & LEXICOGRAPHER

What is a lexicographer? See page 63.

How to use this dictionary

The alphabet down the side of each page tells you where you are in the dictionary. Look for the mouse who is lost!

Headwords in blue are invented words that you can find in Roald Dahl's stories.

Thousands of example sentences show you how Roald Dahl used words in his own stories and poems.

DID YOU KNOW?
Learn about the history of words and find out how Roald Dahl created his marvellous word inventions.

LOOK IT UP!
Are you looking for names of giants or types of sweet? Find them here.

Gobblefunking with words
Roald Dahl loved to play with language. Get inspired to **gobblefunk** with words in your own writing.

LOOK UP THE WORDS **insult** AND **rude!**

---

babble **to** backwards

A B C D E F G H I J K L M N O P Q R S T U V W X Y Z

Bb

The BFG

back-to-front beastly biffsquiggled
blueberry bogthumper buzzbomb

babble verb babbles, babbling, babbled
When people babble, they chat to each other.
All around us the summer-holiday guests in this rather grand hotel were babbling away and tucking into their suppers. — THE WITCHES
DID YOU KNOW? There is an old word *conjobble* which once meant the same as *babble*, so people chatting to each other would be *conjobbling away*.

babblement noun
a friendly conversation or chat
'You is trying to change the subject,' the Giant said sternly. 'We is having an interesting babblement about the taste of the human bean.' — THE BFG

Gobblefunking with words
To make the word *babblement*, Roald Dahl added an ending or *suffix* (*-ment*) to *babble*. A *suffix* is a group of letters that you can add to some words to make others, for example *-able* in **lickable**, or *-ful* in **murderful**. The word *parliament* (from French *parler* 'to talk') originally meant the same as *babblement*, so the BFG might call the Houses of Parliament *the Houses of Babblement.*

baby noun babies
a very young child (or a very old grandparent who has taken too much Wonka-Vite)
Charlie pushed his spoon into the open mouth of the baby and tipped the drops down her throat. — CHARLIE AND THE GREAT GLASS ELEVATOR

backside noun backsides
Your backside is your bottom, the part of your body that you sit on.
'Great whistling whangdoodles!' cried Mr Wonka, leaping so high in the air that when he landed his legs gave way and he crashed on to his backside. — CHARLIE AND THE GREAT GLASS ELEVATOR
RINGBELLING RHYMES Try rhyming with *glide*, *slide* or *wide*.
SPARKY SYNONYMS You can also say **rear** or **rump** (and some other words that are too rude to print here).

back-to-front adjective
If something is back-to-front, it is the opposite way to usual. The Vicar of Nibbleswicke has **back-to-front dyslexia** which can be very *gnissarrabme*.
'You must walk backwards while you are speaking, then these back-to-front words will come out frontwards or the right way round. It's common sense.' — THE VICAR OF NIBBLESWICKE
DON'T BE BIFFSQUIGGLED! If you see a word in this dictionary that looks *railucep*, try reading it back to front. (You can also try saying it out loud while walking backwards, or reading it to a tortoise.)

backwards adverb
1 towards the place that is behind you
I watched in amazement as the top half of the Pelican's beak began to slide smoothly backwards into his head until the whole thing was almost out of sight. — THE GIRAFFE AND THE PELLY AND ME
2 in the opposite way to usual
'Esio Trot is simply tortoise spelled backwards,' Mr Hoppy said. — ESIO TROT
LOOK IT UP! You can try reading backwards in the entry for Esio Trot.

16

RINGBELLING RHYMES

Here are words to help you write your own poems or songs — or make up limericks like Matilda.

The first and the last word on each page are shown at the top. If the word you want to look up comes between these words, you are on the right page!

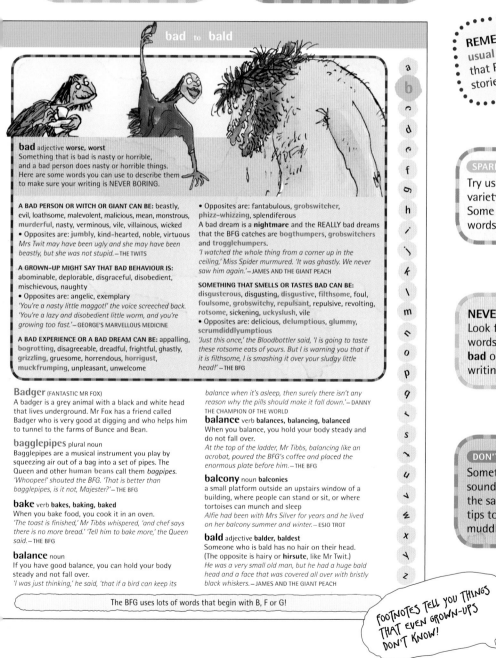

bad adjective **worse, worst**
Something that is bad is nasty or horrible, and a bad person does nasty or horrible things. Here are some words you can use to describe them to make sure your writing is NEVER BORING.

A BAD PERSON OR WITCH OR GIANT CAN BE: beastly, evil, loathsome, malevolent, malicious, mean, monstrous, murderful, nasty, verminous, vile, villainous, wicked
• Opposites are: jumbly, kind-hearted, noble, virtuous
Mrs Twit may have been ugly and she may have been beastly, but she was not stupid. — THE TWITS

A GROWN-UP MIGHT SAY THAT BAD BEHAVIOUR IS: abominable, deplorable, disgraceful, disobedient, mischievous, naughty
• Opposites are: angelic, exemplary
'You're a nasty little maggot!' the voice screeched back. 'You're a lazy and disobedient little worm, and you're growing too fast.' — GEORGE'S MARVELLOUS MEDICINE

A BAD EXPERIENCE OR A BAD DREAM CAN BE: appalling, bogrotting, disagreeable, dreadful, frightful, ghastly, grizzling, gruesome, horrendous, horrigust, muckfrumping, unpleasant, unwelcome

• Opposites are: fantabulous, grobswitcher, phizz-whizzing, splendiferous
A bad dream is a **nightmare** and the REALLY bad dreams that the BFG catches are bogthumpers, grobswitchers and trogglehumpers.
'I watched the whole thing from a corner up in the ceiling,' Miss Spider murmured. 'It was ghastly. We never saw him again.' — JAMES AND THE GIANT PEACH

SOMETHING THAT SMELLS OR TASTES BAD CAN BE: disgusterous, disgusting, disgustive, filthsome, foul, foulsome, grobswitchy, repulsant, repulsive, revolting, rotsome, sickening, uckyslush, vile
• Opposites are: delicious, delumptious, glummy, scrumdiddlyumptious
'Just this once,' the Bloodbottler said, 'I is going to taste these rotsome eats of yours. But I is warning you that if it is filthsome, I is smashing it over your sludgy little head!' — THE BFG

Badger (FANTASTIC MR FOX)
A badger is a grey animal with a black and white head that lives underground. Mr Fox has a friend called Badger who is very good at digging and who helps him to tunnel to the farms of Bunce and Bean.

bagglepipes plural noun
Bagglepipes are a musical instrument you play by squeezing air out of a bag into a set of pipes. The Queen and other human beans call them *bagpipes*.
'Whoopee!' shouted the BFG. 'That is better than bagglepipes, is it not, Majester?' — THE BFG

bake verb **bakes, baking, baked**
When you bake food, you cook it in an oven.
'The toast is finished,' Mr Tibbs whispered, 'and chef says there is no more bread.' 'Tell him to bake more,' the Queen said. — THE BFG

balance noun
If you have good balance, you can hold your body steady and not fall over.
'I was just thinking,' he said, 'that if a bird can keep its

balance when it's asleep, then surely there isn't any reason why the pills should make it fall down.' — DANNY THE CHAMPION OF THE WORLD

balance verb **balances, balancing, balanced**
When you balance, you hold your body steady and do not fall over.
At the top of the ladder, Mr Tibbs, balancing like an acrobat, poured the BFG's coffee and placed the enormous plate before him. — THE BFG

balcony noun **balconies**
a small platform outside an upstairs window of a building, where people can stand or sit, or where tortoises can munch and sleep
Alfie had been with Mrs Silver for years and he lived on her balcony summer and winter. — ESIO TROT

bald adjective **balder, baldest**
Someone who is bald has no hair on their head. (The opposite is hairy or **hirsute**, like Mr Twit.)
He was a very small old man, but he had a huge bald head and a face that was covered all over with bristly black whiskers. — JAMES AND THE GIANT PEACH

REMEMBER! This is an extra-usual dictionary. Only words that Roald Dahl used in his stories and poems are in here.

SPARKY SYNONYMS

Try using these words to add variety to your own stories. Some of these are extra-usual words invented by Roald Dahl.

NEVER A DULL WORD!
Look for really interesting words like those given at **good**, **bad** or **noise** to make your writing zippfizz along.

DON'T BE BIFFSQUIGGLED!
Sometimes words look or sound similar but don't mean the same thing. Follow these tips to avoid getting them muddled up.

a b c d e f g h i j k l m n o p q r s t u v w x y z

The BFG uses lots of words that begin with B, F or G!

FOOTNOTES TELL YOU THINGS THAT EVEN GROWN-UPS DON'T KNOW!

Aa

Alfie

ESIO TROT

alarm-clock   anklet   anti-freeze
argying   aunts

aardvark noun **aardvarks**
An aardvark is an African animal with a long snout that eats ants and termites. Roald Dahl wrote about lots of African animals, like giraffes, monkeys and crocodiles, but not about aardvarks. However, every dictionary has to start with **aardvark**; otherwise it would start with **aback**, which is just too boring.
DID YOU KNOW? *Aardvark* is an Afrikaans word which means 'earth pig', though aardvarks are not related to pigs at all.

aback adverb
If you are taken aback by something, you are surprised and slightly shocked by it.
Mrs Phelps, slightly taken aback at the arrival of such a tiny girl unaccompanied by a parent, nevertheless told her she was very welcome. – MATILDA

abbreviation noun **abbreviations**
An abbreviation is a short form of a word or group of words, so the BFG's name is an abbreviation of *Big Friendly Giant* and *BLT* is an abbreviation of *bacon, lettuce and tomato*.

abide (*rhymes with* hide) verb
You can't abide something when you detest it or can't bear it.
'I insist upon my rooms being beautiful! I can't abide ugliness in factories!' – CHARLIE AND THE CHOCOLATE FACTORY

ablaze adjective
blazing or burning brightly
The Wolf stood there, his eyes ablaze/And yellowish, like mayonnaise./His teeth were sharp, his gums were raw,/ And spit was dripping from his jaw. – REVOLTING RHYMES
RINGBELLING RHYMES Try rhyming with *amaze* (as well as *mayonnaise*, of course).

absorbed adjective
If you are absorbed in something, like reading, it means your whole mind is focused on it and you can think of nothing else.
Matilda happened to be curled up in an armchair in the corner, totally absorbed in a book. – MATILDA

absurd adjective
If something is absurd, it looks or seems silly or ridiculous.
The chicken looked perfectly absurd with its long long legs and its ordinary little body perched high up on top. It was like a chicken on stilts. – GEORGE'S MARVELLOUS MEDICINE

ache (*rhymes with* bake) verb **aches, aching, ached**
If a part of your body aches, it hurts.
Poor James was still slaving away at the chopping-block. The heat was terrible. He was sweating all over. His arm was aching. – JAMES AND THE GIANT PEACH

ache noun
aches
a dull steady pain
The medicine had done Grandma good . . . It seemed to have cured all her aches and pains, and she was suddenly as frisky as a ferret. – GEORGE'S MARVELLOUS MEDICINE

acrobat noun **acrobats**
An acrobat entertains people by doing exciting jumping and balancing tricks.
At the top of the ladder, Mr Tibbs, balancing like an acrobat, poured the BFG's coffee and placed the enormous plate before him. – THE BFG
DID YOU KNOW? The word *acrobat* comes from ancient Greek and means 'tiptoe-walker'.

address verb **addresses, addressing, addressed**
When you address someone, you speak directly to them.
'Now,' said Mr Wonka, addressing Grandpa George, Grandma Georgina and Grandma Josephine. 'Up you hop out of that bed and let's get cracking.' – CHARLIE AND THE GREAT GLASS ELEVATOR
LOOK IT UP! For other interesting ways to describe how people speak, see **say**.

admire verb admires, admiring, admired
If you admire someone, you like what they do and want to be like them.
Lavender . . . admired the older girl Hortensia to distraction for the daring deeds she had performed in the school. — MATILDA

admit verb admits, admitting, admitted
If you admit something, you tell people that it is true.
'I must admit,' said Mr Wonka, 'that for the first time in my life I find myself at a bit of a loss.' — CHARLIE AND THE GREAT GLASS ELEVATOR

adore verb adores, adoring, adored
If you adore someone, you like them a lot. Mrs Silver adores her pet tortoise, Alfie, and Miss Honey's class all adore her. Mr and Mrs Twit definitely do not adore each other.
Miss Jennifer Honey . . . possessed that rare gift for being adored by every small child under her care. — MATILDA

adult noun adults
An adult is another word for a **grown-up**.
adult adjective
An adult book is one that grown-ups think you are too young to read.
'But does it not intrigue you,' Miss Honey said, 'that a little five-year-old child is reading long adult novels by Dickens and Hemingway?' — MATILDA

adventure noun adventures
something exciting that happens to you, or that you hope will happen one day
Many of them were always begging him to tell and tell again the story of his adventures on the peach. — JAMES AND THE GIANT PEACH

aeroplane noun aeroplanes
Aeroplanes are called aeroplanes in Giant Country (and **airplanes** in North America).
'But human beans is squishing each other all the time,' the BFG said. 'They is shootling guns and going up in aeroplanes to drop their bombs on each other's heads every week.' — THE BFG

afford verb affords, affording, afforded
If you can afford something, you have enough money to pay for it.
The only meals they could afford were bread and margarine for breakfast, boiled potatoes and cabbage for lunch, and cabbage soup for supper. — CHARLIE AND THE CHOCOLATE FACTORY

afraid adjective
1 If you are afraid, you are frightened of something, such as a bonecrunching giant or a **bogthumping** nightmare, or maybe a monstrous headmistress or vicious Knid.
They were trying . . . to get away from that huge angry Vermicious Knid with the purple behind. Mr Wonka wasn't afraid of it, but Grandma Josephine was petrified. — CHARLIE AND THE GREAT GLASS ELEVATOR
2 You say *I am afraid* if you mean that you regret something.
'Ladies and gentlemen,' the Old-Green-Grasshopper said . . . 'I am afraid that we find ourselves in a rather awkward situation.' — JAMES AND THE GIANT PEACH

afraid
Try using these fearsome phrases in your writing to describe people who are afraid, or who make others afraid.

SOMEONE WHO FEELS AFRAID MIGHT: be fossilized with fear, be frozen stiff with terror, be petrified, blanch or turn pale, give a shriek of terror, quake or tremble in their boots, stand rooted to the spot, be terror-struck, tremble like a leaf in the wind
'If you'd had even the faintest idea of what horrors you were up against, the marrow would have run out of your bones! You'd have been fossilized with fear and glued to the ground!' — CHARLIE AND THE GREAT GLASS ELEVATOR

Sophie, crouching on the floor of the cave in her nightie . . . was trembling like a leaf in the wind, and a finger of ice was running up and down the length of her spine. — THE BFG

SOMETHING WHICH MAKES YOU AFRAID MIGHT: freeze your blood, give you goosebumps, make icicles in your veins, make your hair stand on end, make your knees tremble, strike fear into your heart, suck the marrow out of your bones, turn you to jelly
Little Billy glanced back quickly over his shoulder, and now, in the distance, he saw a sight that froze his blood and made icicles in his veins. — THE MINPINS

afternoon noun afternoons
The afternoon is the time from the middle of the day until the evening, when giants usually take a nap.
'Every afternoon,' the BFG said, 'all these giants is in the Land of Noddy.' — THE BFG

An old word for an alphabet is *abecedarium*, which gets its name from the letters A, B and C.

A
B C D E F G H I J K L M N O P Q R S T U V W X Y Z

aghast adjective
If something makes you aghast,
it shocks and horrifies you.
*'The Fleshlumpeater is longing
dearly to guzzle her up,' the BFG
said, smiling a little now. 'Who,
the Queen?' Sophie cried, aghast.*
— THE BFG

air noun
Air is the gas all around us, which
we breathe.
*'Dreams,' he said, 'is very mysterious
things. They is floating around in the air
like little wispy-misty bubbles.'* — THE BFG

alarm-clock noun **alarm-clocks**
An alarm-clock is a clock that you set
to wake you up in the morning when
you would rather stay in bed.
A rrroasted alarm-clock is a vital
ingredient in The Grand High Witch's
Delayed Action Mouse-Maker formula.
*'You set your alarm-clock to go off at nine
o'clock tomorrow morning. Then you rrroast
it in the oven until it is crrrisp and tender.
Are you wrrriting this down?'*
— THE WITCHES

alarmed adjective
If you are alarmed, you are afraid that
something dangerous or horrible is going
to happen.
*But don't, dear children, be alarmed;/
Augustus Gloop will not be harmed,/
Although, of course, we must admit/
He will be altered quite a bit.* — CHARLIE
AND THE CHOCOLATE FACTORY

Alfie (ESIO TROT)
Alfie is a small tortoise who belongs
to Mrs Silver and lives on her balcony.
He weighs just thirteen ounces and
Mrs Silver worries that he is not
growing very fast.

alight adjective
1 lit up or on fire
*When you have sucked a Devil's Drencher
for a minute or so, you can set your breath
alight and blow a huge column of fire
twenty feet into the air.* — THE GIRAFFE AND
THE PELLY AND ME
2 If your face is alight, you are beaming
with happiness or excitement.
*The whole face, in fact, was alight
with fun and laughter. And oh, how
clever he looked! How quick and
sharp and full of life!* — CHARLIE AND
THE CHOCOLATE FACTORY

alive adjective
1 If someone is alive, they are living and not yet dead.
*'I want a good sensible loving child, one to whom I can
tell all my most precious sweet-making secrets — while
I am still alive.'* — CHARLIE AND THE CHOCOLATE FACTORY
2 If a place is alive with something, it means it is filled
or teeming with it.
*The grass was wet with dew . . . And now suddenly, the
whole place, the whole garden seemed to be alive with
magic.* — JAMES AND THE GIANT PEACH

alligator noun **alligators**
An alligator is an animal that looks like a crocodile.
Alligators are reptiles and they live in parts of North
and South America and China.
*If you chopped off a newt's tail, the tail stayed alive and
grew into another newt ten times bigger than the first one.
It could be the size of an alligator.* — MATILDA
DID YOU KNOW? The word *alligator* comes from an old
Spanish phrase meaning 'the lizard of the Indies'.
RINGBELLING RHYMES Try rhyming with *ate her* or *elevator*.

alliteration noun
Alliteration is the use of words that begin with the
same sound to create a special effect in writing.

> **Gobblefunking with words**
> Roald Dahl loved to use alliteration and you can find lots
> of lovely alliterative lines in his splendidly spellbinding
> stories. Here are a few fantabulous examples.
> *'Here I come, you grizzly old grunion! You rotten old
> turnip! You filthy old frumpet!'* — THE TWITS
>
> *PIG PILLS, the label announced. FOR PIGS WITH PORK
> PRICKLES, TENDER TROTTERS, BRISTLE BLIGHT AND
> SWINE SICKNESS.* — GEORGE'S MARVELLOUS MEDICINE
>
> Alliteration is good for making character names
> and similes too: see more examples in the entries
> for **ghoulish** and **mad**.

allowed adjective
If you are allowed to do something, it means that
grown-ups will not try to stop you doing it.
*Little Billy's mother was always telling him exactly
what he was allowed to do . . . All the things he was
allowed to do were boring. All the things he was
not allowed to do were exciting.* — THE MINPINS
DON'T BE BIFFSQUIGGLED! The words *allowed*
and *aloud* sound the same, but they mean
different things. In a library, you wouldn't
be *allowed* to talk *aloud* (but you might be
allowed to whisper).

almighty adjective
very big or very loud
*At once, there came a blinding flash,/And then
the most almighty crash,/And sparks were
bursting all around,/And smoke was rising
from the ground.* — DIRTY BEASTS

aloft adverb
high up in the air
Matilda had never before seen a boy, or anyone else for that matter, held aloft by his ears alone. – MATILDA

alone adjective
If you are alone, there is no one with you.
Mr Hoppy lived in a small flat high up in a tall concrete building. He lived alone. – ESIO TROT

aloud adverb
If you say something aloud, you say it in a voice that can be heard (even if you are only talking to yourself).
'Well,' George said aloud to himself as he tipped in the whole bottleful, 'the old bird won't be losing any feathers after she's had a dose of this.' – GEORGE'S MARVELLOUS MEDICINE

alphabet noun **alphabets**
An alphabet is all the letters that we use in writing, arranged in a particular order. There are 26 letters in the English alphabet starting at A and ending with Z. This dictionary is arranged in alphabetical order, from **aardvark** to **zozimus**, which makes it easier to find the word you want quickly.

alter verb **alters, altering, altered**
If you alter something, you change it in some way.
'The plain fact is,' my grandmother said, 'that your son Bruno has been rather drastically altered.' 'Altered!' shouted Mr Jenkins. 'What the devil d'you mean altered?' – THE WITCHES
LOOK IT UP! When a person is altered into a mouse, it is called **metamorphosis**.

Amanda Thripp (MATILDA)
Amanda Thripp is a pupil at Crunchem Hall who makes the mistake of wearing **pigtails** to school, not realizing how much Miss Trunchbull hates them.

amaze verb **amazes, amazing, amazed**
If something amazes you, it makes you feel very surprised.
'Dear lady,' said Mr Wonka, 'you are new to the scene. When you have been with us a little longer, nothing will amaze you.' – CHARLIE AND THE GREAT GLASS ELEVATOR

amazing adjective
If something is amazing, it is both wonderful and surprising.
It was wonderful to stand there stirring this amazing mixture and to watch it smoking blue and bubbling and frothing and foaming as though it were alive. – GEORGE'S MARVELLOUS MEDICINE

ambition noun **ambitions**
something that you want to do very much
My blinding ambition, you see, my dream of dreams, was to become one day the owner of a White Mouse Circus. – THE WITCHES

amble verb **ambles, ambling, ambled**
When you amble, you walk along slowly or casually.
The Centipede . . . got down off the sofa and ambled across the room and crawled into his hammock. – JAMES AND THE GIANT PEACH

amphibian noun **amphibians**
An amphibian is an animal that lives some of its life in water and some on land. Newts are amphibians, which is why Lavender is able to transport one inside her pencil-box.
DID YOU KNOW? The word *amphibian* means literally 'having both lives' because amphibians can live both on land and in water.

amuse verb **amuses, amusing, amused**
If you amuse yourself, you do things to keep busy and not get bored.
Miss Honey said to the class, 'I think you'd all better go out to the playground and amuse yourselves until the next lesson.' – MATILDA

amusing adjective
If something is amusing, it makes you laugh or smile, like Roald Dahl's stories (or, just occasionally, a dictionary definition).
The service turned out to be an amusing business because the vicar kept peppering his sentences with the most extraordinary words. – THE VICAR OF NIBBLESWICKE

anagram noun **anagrams**
An anagram is a group of letters or words made by rearranging the letters of another word or phrase or name. For example, *inky wallow* is an anagram of *Willy Wonka*, and *a brash clashing tumult* is an anagram of *Miss Agatha Trunchbull*.

> **Gobblefunking with words**
> Anagrams are a good way of creating secret codes or messages. For example *Physician with Kit* could be a secret-code anagram for *I think I spy a witch*. For other interesting ways to jumble up words, see the entry for **Esio Trot**.

ancient adjective
An ancient person or creature is very old.
He was some sort of an elf, I used to think to myself each time I saw him, a very ancient sort of an elf with wispy white hair and steel-rimmed spectacles. – DANNY THE CHAMPION OF THE WORLD

a b c d e f g h i j k l m n o p q r s t u v w x y z

The word *alphabet* comes from *alpha* and *beta*, the first two letters of the Greek alphabet.

A
B C D E F G H I J K L M N O P Q R S T U V W X Y Z

angry adjective angrier, angriest
If you are angry, you are very annoyed or cross about something.
Aunt Spiker . . . had a screeching voice and long wet narrow lips, and whenever she got angry or excited, little flecks of spit would come shooting out of her mouth as she talked. — JAMES AND THE GIANT PEACH

Gobblefunking with words
One way to describe angry people is to use colours. People usually go *red* or *purple with rage* (unless they are turning into a blueberry and then they go purple anyway), or start to *see red*, but you can use variations on these. There are lots of angry characters (not forgetting a raging rhinoceros and a seething **grobswitcher**) in Roald Dahl's stories and many of them turn interesting colours, for example:
The Trunchbull was in such a rage that her face had taken on a boiled colour. —MATILDA

Mr Hazell's skin turned from scarlet to purple. His eyes and his cheeks were bulging so much with rage it looked as though someone was blowing up his face with a pump. —DANNY THE CHAMPION OF THE WORLD

---

animal noun animals
An animal is anything that lives and can move about. The word *animal* is normally used to mean creatures that are not **human beans** or giants.
'If an animal is very fierce and you is putting it in a cage, it will make a tremendous rumpledumpus. If it is a nice animal like a cockatootloo or a fogglefrump, it will sit quietly.' — THE BFG

ankle noun ankles
Your ankle is the thin part of your leg where it is joined to your foot.
There is no way you can become a royal footman unless you have a well-turned ankle. It is the first thing they look at when you are interviewed. — THE BFG

anklet noun anklets
An anklet is the joint that giants have between their leg and their foot. It is very similar to a human ankle.
'The teeth of the dreadly viper is still sticking into me!' he yelled. 'I is feeling the teeth sticking into my anklet!' — THE BFG

anniversary noun anniversaries
An anniversary is a day when you remember something special that happened on the same day in the past. The anniversary of Roald Dahl's birth is on 13 September, which is now celebrated as Roald Dahl Day.

announce verb announces, announcing, announced
When you announce something, you tell everyone about it.
'This is the living-room,' announced Muggle-Wump. 'The grand and glorious living-room where those two fearful frumptious freaks eat Bird Pie every week for supper!' — THE TWITS

annoying adjective
If something is annoying, it makes you angry or frustrated.
'I've tried it twenty times in the Testing Room on twenty Oompa-Loompas, and every one of them finished up as a blueberry. It's most annoying.' — CHARLIE AND THE CHOCOLATE FACTORY

annual adjective
An annual event happens once every year, like the Annual Meeting of all the witches in Inkland.
I am told that The Grand High Witch makes it a rule to fry at least one witch at each Annual Meeting. — THE WITCHES

answer noun answers
something you say or write to someone who has asked you a question
And how often did Mr Twit wash this bristly nailbrushy face of his? The answer is NEVER, not even on Sundays. — THE TWITS

answer verb answers, answering, answered
When you answer someone, you say something to them after they have asked you a question.
'What mischief are you up to in there now?' Granny screeched. 'I hear noises.' George thought it best not to answer this one. — GEORGE'S MARVELLOUS MEDICINE

ant noun ants
Ants are tiny insects that live in large groups. A group of ants is called *a colony of ants*.
'I is hearing the little ants chittering to each other as they scuddle around in the soil.' — THE BFG

LOOK IT UP! When you say *a colony of ants*, you are using a *collective noun*. You can find more examples of collective nouns in the entry for **colony**.

antenna noun antennae
another word for a **feeler** on the head of an insect such as the Old-Green-Grasshopper

anti-freeze noun
Anti-freeze is a liquid that grown-ups put in car engines to stop them freezing in cold weather. George tries it in his Marvellous Medicine to see if it will make his grandma less grumpy (it doesn't).
Back in the kitchen once again, George, with Mr Kranky watching him anxiously, tipped half a pint of engine oil and some anti-freeze into the giant saucepan. — GEORGE'S MARVELLOUS MEDICINE

antonym noun **antonyms**

An antonym is a word that means the opposite of another word. For example, **midgy** is an antonym of **gigantuous**, and **horrigust** is an antonym of **wondercrump**.

LOOK IT UP! For more examples of opposites, see the entry for **um-possible**.

anxious adjective

If you are anxious, you feel worried.
The four old people . . . propped themselves up on their pillows and stared with anxious eyes at the bar of chocolate in Charlie's hands. — CHARLIE AND THE CHOCOLATE FACTORY

apologies plural noun

You send your apologies if you are unable to accept an invitation, or unable to do something you have been asked to do.
Mr Tibbs sidled up to the Queen . . . and whispered in her ear, 'Chef sends his apologies, Your Majesty, and he says he has no more eggs in the kitchen.' — THE BFG

apologize verb **apologizes, apologizing, apologized**

When you apologize to someone, you tell them you are sorry.
'Pest!' cried the Earthworm. 'Why must you always be so rude and rambunctious to everyone? You ought to apologize to James at once.' — JAMES AND THE GIANT PEACH

appendix noun **appendixes**

Your appendix is a small tube-shaped organ inside your body.
The next day, we were allowed to inspect the appendix itself in a glass bottle. It was a longish black wormy-looking thing. — BOY

appetite noun **appetites**

If you have an appetite, you feel hungry.
'How many girls and boys are they going to eat tonight?' 'Many,' the BFG said. 'The Fleshlumpeating Giant alone has a most squackling whoppsy appetite.' — THE BFG

apple noun **apples**

An apple is a round, crisp, juicy fruit that grows on a tree. A farm of apple trees, like the one that Farmer Bean owns, is called an **orchard**.
Bean . . . never ate any food at all. Instead, he drank gallons of strong cider which he made from the apples in his orchard. — FANTASTIC MR FOX

approve verb **approves, approving, approved**

If you approve of something, you think that it is good or suitable.
'We'll mow them down with machine-guns!' cried the Head of the Army. 'I do not approve of murder,' the Queen said. — THE BFG

arch noun **arches**

a curved part of a bridge or building, or of a rainbow
They now saw a most extraordinary sight. It was a kind of arch, a colossal curvy-shaped thing that reached high up into the sky and came down again at both ends. — JAMES AND THE GIANT PEACH

argue verb **argues, arguing, argued**

When people argue, they talk in an angry way because they do not agree with each other.
Everybody gathered around the wretched Centipede and began arguing about the best way to get the paint off his body. — JAMES AND THE GIANT PEACH

argument noun **arguments**

a quarrel
'No arguments, please!' said Mr Wonka. He turned away and clicked his fingers three times in the air. — CHARLIE AND THE CHOCOLATE FACTORY

argy verb **argies, argying, argied**

If giants or **human beans** or **cattlepiddlers** are argying, they are having an argument.
'One of the biggest chatbags is the cattlepiddlers . . . They is argying all the time about who is going to be the prettiest butteryfly.' — THE BFG

arithmetic noun

When you do arithmetic, you do sums with numbers.
'Simple arithmetic,' said Mr Wonka. 'Subtract eighty from seventy-eight and what do you get?' 'Minus two!' said Charlie. — CHARLIE AND THE GREAT GLASS ELEVATOR

arm noun **arms**

Your arms are the long parts of your body that are joined to your shoulders. Giants have arms too, which they reach through bedroom windows in order to snatch human **chiddlers**.
The next moment, a huge hand with pale fingers came snaking in through the window. This was followed by an arm, an arm as thick as a tree-trunk. — THE BFG

DID YOU KNOW? An old slang word for an arm is a *smiter* (meaning something you *smite* or hit with), which sounds like a word the giants of Giant Country might use.

armadillo noun **armadillos**

a South American animal whose body is covered with bony plates
'For dinner on my birthday shall I tell you what I chose:/ Hot noodles made from poodles on a slice of garden hose/ And a rather smelly jelly/Made of armadillo's toes.' — JAMES AND THE GIANT PEACH

RINGBELLING RHYMES Try rhyming with *pillow* or *willow*.

The word *armadillo* comes from Spanish and means 'small armed creature'.

A
B
C
D
E
F
G
H
I
J
K
L
M
N
O
P
Q
R
S
T
U
V
W
X
Y
Z

army noun **armies**
a large group of people who are trained to fight on land in a war
'Hooray!' said the Chief of the Army. 'Let's blow everyone up! Bang-bang! Bang-bang!'—CHARLIE AND THE GREAT GLASS ELEVATOR

asinine adjective
extremely stupid and making no sense whatsoever
But the fact remained that any five-year-old girl in any family was always obliged to do as she was told, however asinine the orders might be.—MATILDA
DID YOU KNOW? The word *asinine* means literally 'like an ass' (i.e. a donkey) because asses were thought to be stupid and stubborn animals, rather like Matilda's parents.

asleep adjective
When you are asleep, you are sleeping. (The BFG calls it being in the *Land of Noddy*.)
'The Big Friendly Giant makes his magic powders out of the dreams that children dream when they are asleep,' he said.—DANNY THE CHAMPION OF THE WORLD

assembly noun **assemblies**
An assembly is a meeting of a large group of people, such as a whole school or a great gathering of witches.
In a matter of seconds, the entire assembly of witches had taken up the dreaded cry of dogs' droppings. 'Dogs' droppings!' they shouted.—THE WITCHES

astonish verb **astonishes, astonishing, astonished**
If something astonishes you, it surprises you a lot.
'I am preparing other surprises that are even more marvellous and . . . that will entrance, delight, intrigue, astonish, and perplex you beyond measure.'—CHARLIE AND THE CHOCOLATE FACTORY

astronaut noun **astronauts**
someone who travels in a spacecraft
The capsule they were travelling in was manned by the three famous astronauts, Shuckworth, Shanks and Showler, all of them handsome, clever and brave.—CHARLIE AND THE GREAT GLASS ELEVATOR

athlete noun **athletes**
someone who is good at athletics or other sports
Miss Trunchbull . . . was above all a most formidable female. She had once been a famous athlete, and even now the muscles were still clearly in evidence.—MATILDA

atlas noun **atlases**
a book of maps
The Head of the Air Force . . . kept staring first at the atlas, then at the ground below, trying to figure out where they were going.—THE BFG
DID YOU KNOW? *Atlas* is the name of a character in ancient Greek mythology who held up the heavens on his shoulders. His picture was used in early books of maps so people started to call them *atlases*.

atmosphere noun
1 the air around the Earth
'They're not shooting stars at all,' said Mr Wonka. 'They're Shooting Knids . . . trying to enter the Earth's atmosphere at high speed and going up in flames.'—CHARLIE AND THE GREAT GLASS ELEVATOR
2 a feeling you get in a room or at a place
In the space of thirty seconds the atmosphere in the tiny room had changed completely and now it was vibrating with awkwardness and secrets.—MATILDA

attach verb **attaches, attaching, attached**
If you attach something, you fix or fasten it onto something else.
The poor chap couldn't see where he was going without twisting his head over his shoulder . . . But by attaching a small rear-view mirror to his forehead with an elastic band, he overcame this difficulty.—THE VICAR OF NIBBLESWICKE

attack verb **attacks, attacking, attacked**
If you attack someone, you fight them and try to hurt them.
Waiters were attacking the mice with chairs and wine-bottles and anything else that came to hand.—THE WITCHES

attention noun
When you pay attention, you listen carefully to what someone is saying, or watch what they are doing.
'Veruca, darling,' said Mrs Salt, 'pay no attention to Mr Wonka! He's lying to you!' – CHARLIE AND THE CHOCOLATE FACTORY

attic noun **attics**
a room or space under the roof of a house
'That's the attic above you, Grandma!' George called out. 'I'd keep out of there! It's full of bugs and bogles!' – GEORGE'S MARVELLOUS MEDICINE

attractive adjective
An attractive thing is pleasant to look at, and an attractive person is beautiful or handsome.
This balcony belonged to an attractive middle-aged lady called Mrs Silver . . . And although she didn't know it, it was she who was the object of Mr Hoppy's secret love. – ESIO TROT

audience noun **audiences**
all the people who have come to a place to see or hear something
I would have a small stage with red curtains in front of it, and when the curtains were drawn apart, the audience would see my world-famous performing mice. – THE WITCHES

Augustus Gloop
(CHARLIE AND THE CHOCOLATE FACTORY)
Augustus Gloop is a greedy boy whose only hobby is eating. He is enormously fat, with small curranty eyes and a face like a ball of dough, and is the first child to find a Golden Ticket.

aunt noun **aunts**
Your aunt is the sister of your mother or father, or your uncle's wife.
The little boy, carrying nothing but a small suitcase containing a pair of pyjamas and a toothbrush, was sent away to live with his two aunts. – JAMES AND THE GIANT PEACH

author noun **authors**
An author is someone like Roald Dahl who writes books or stories. Charles Dickens is Matilda's favourite author.

autobiography noun **autobiographies**
the story of someone's life that they have written themselves
An autobiography is a book a person writes about his own life and it is usually full of all sorts of boring details. This is not an autobiography. – BOY

average adjective
ordinary or usual
An average tuck-box would probably contain . . . half a home-made currant cake, a packet of squashed-fly

biscuits, a couple of oranges, an apple, a banana, . . . a bar of chocolate, a bag of Liquorice Allsorts and a tin of Bassett's lemonade powder. – BOY

avoid verb **avoids, avoiding, avoided**
If you avoid something, you stay away from it, or make sure that it doesn't happen.
'Now, Violet,' Mrs Beauregarde said from a far corner of the room where she was standing on the piano to avoid being trampled by the mob. – CHARLIE AND THE CHOCOLATE FACTORY

awake adjective
When you are awake, you are not sleeping.
'Attention, please! Attention, please!/Don't dare to talk! Don't dare to sneeze!/Don't doze or daydream! Stay awake!/ Your health, your very life's at stake!' – CHARLIE AND THE GREAT GLASS ELEVATOR

awesome adjective
If something is awesome, it gives you a feeling of both fear and wonder.
Before the first week of term was up, awesome tales about the Headmistress, Miss Trunchbull, began to filter through to the newcomers. – MATILDA
DON'T BE BIFFSQUIGGLED! The word *awesome* is sometimes used now to mean 'great!' or 'brilliant!' but this is a new meaning of the word. In Roald Dahl's stories, it is always used with the original and stronger meaning.

awful adjective
Something that is awful is horrible or very bad.
The board creaked most terribly and they all ducked down, waiting for something awful to happen. Nothing did. – FANTASTIC MR FOX

awfully adverb
very or extremely
'How far d'you think he'll stretch?' asked Mr Teavee. 'Maybe miles,' said Mr Wonka. 'Who knows? But he's going to be awfully thin.' – CHARLIE AND THE CHOCOLATE FACTORY

awkward adjective
Something that is awkward is difficult to do or difficult to cope with.
Sermons were also awkward, but the congregation very soon grew accustomed to seeing their vicar walking backwards round and round the pulpit while he was preaching. – THE VICAR OF NIBBLESWICKE
DID YOU KNOW? The word *awkward* originally meant 'the wrong way round', so the Vicar of Nibbleswicke's sermons are literally 'awkward', as he delivers them while walking backwards.

axe noun **axes**
a sharp tool for chopping wood
'If I is chopping an axe into the trunk of a big tree, I is hearing a terrible sound coming from inside the heart of the tree.' – THE BFG

a
b
c
d
e
f
g
h
i
j
k
l
m
n
o
p
q
r
s
t
u
v
w
x
y
z

The word *astronaut* means literally 'star sailor'.

Bb

The BFG

back-to-front   beastly   biffsquiggled

blueberry   bogthumper   buzzbomb

babble verb **babbles, babbling, babbled**
When people babble, they chat to each other.
All around us the summer-holiday guests in this rather grand hotel were babbling away and tucking into their suppers. — THE WITCHES
DID YOU KNOW? There is an old word *conjobble* which once meant the same as *babble*, so people chatting to each other would be *conjobbling away*.

babblement noun
a friendly conversation or chat
'You is trying to change the subject,' the Giant said sternly. 'We is having an interesting babblement about the taste of the human bean.' — THE BFG

Gobblefunking with words
To make the word *babblement*, Roald Dahl added an ending or *suffix* (*-ment*) to *babble*. A *suffix* is a group of letters that you can add to some words to make others, for example *-able* in **lickable**, or *-ful* in **murderful**. The word *parliament* (from French *parler* 'to talk') originally meant the same as *babblement*, so the BFG might call the Houses of Parliament *the Houses of Babblement*.

---

baby noun **babies**
a very young child (or a very old grandparent who has taken too much Wonka-Vite)
Charlie pushed his spoon into the open mouth of the baby and tipped the drops down her throat. — CHARLIE AND THE GREAT GLASS ELEVATOR

backside noun **backsides**
Your backside is your bottom, the part of your body that you sit on.
'Great whistling whangdoodles!' cried Mr Wonka, leaping so high in the air that when he landed his legs gave way and he crashed on to his backside. — CHARLIE AND THE GREAT GLASS ELEVATOR
RINGBELLING RHYMES Try rhyming with *glide*, *slide* or *wide*.
SPARKY SYNONYMS You can also say **rear** or **rump** (and some other words that are too rude to print here).

back-to-front adjective
If something is back-to-front, it is the opposite way to usual. The Vicar of Nibbleswicke has **back-to-front dyslexia** which can be very *gnissarrabme*.
'You must walk backwards while you are speaking, then these back-to-front words will come out frontwards or the right way round. It's common sense.' — THE VICAR OF NIBBLESWICKE
DON'T BE BIFFSQUIGGLED! If you see a word in this dictionary that looks *railucep*, try reading it back to front. (You can also try saying it out loud while walking backwards, or reading it to a tortoise.)

backwards adverb
1 towards the place that is behind you
I watched in amazement as the top half of the Pelican's beak began to slide smoothly backwards into his head until the whole thing was almost out of sight.
— THE GIRAFFE AND THE PELLY AND ME
2 in the opposite way to usual
'Esio Trot is simply tortoise spelled backwards,' Mr Hoppy said. — ESIO TROT
LOOK IT UP! You can try reading backwards in the entry for **Esio Trot**.

bad adjective **worse, worst**
Something that is bad is nasty or horrible,
and a bad person does nasty or horrible things.
Here are some words you can use to describe them
to make sure your writing is NEVER BORING.

A BAD PERSON OR WITCH OR GIANT CAN BE: beastly,
evil, loathsome, malevolent, malicious, mean, monstrous,
murderful, nasty, verminous, vile, villainous, wicked
• Opposites are: **jumbly**, kind-hearted, noble, virtuous
Mrs Twit may have been ugly and she may have been
beastly, but she was not stupid. — THE TWITS

A GROWN-UP MIGHT SAY THAT BAD BEHAVIOUR IS:
abominable, deplorable, disgraceful, disobedient,
mischievous, naughty
• Opposites are: angelic, exemplary
'You're a nasty little maggot!' the voice screeched back.
'You're a lazy and disobedient little worm, and you're
growing too fast.' — GEORGE'S MARVELLOUS MEDICINE

A BAD EXPERIENCE OR A BAD DREAM CAN BE: appalling,
bogrotting, disagreeable, dreadful, frightful, ghastly,
grizzling, gruesome, horrendous, **horrigust**,
muckfrumping, unpleasant, unwelcome

• Opposites are: fantabulous, **grobswitcher**,
phizz-whizzing, splendiferous
A bad dream is a **nightmare** and the REALLY bad dreams
that the BFG catches are **bogthumpers**, **grobswitchers**
and **trogglehumpers**.
'I watched the whole thing from a corner up in the
ceiling,' Miss Spider murmured. 'It was ghastly. We never
saw him again.' — JAMES AND THE GIANT PEACH

SOMETHING THAT SMELLS OR TASTES BAD CAN BE:
disgusterous, disgusting, **disgustive**, **filthsome**, foul,
foulsome, **grobswitchy**, **repulsant**, repulsive, revolting,
rotsome, sickening, **uckyslush**, vile
• Opposites are: delicious, **delumptious**, **glummy**,
scrumdiddlyumptious
'Just this once,' the Bloodbottler said, 'I is going to taste
these rotsome eats of yours. But I is warning you that if
it is filthsome, I is smashing it over your sludgy little
head!' — THE BFG

Badger (FANTASTIC MR FOX)
A badger is a grey animal with a black and white head
that lives underground. Mr Fox has a friend called
Badger who is very good at digging and who helps him
to tunnel to the farms of Bunce and Bean.

bagglepipes plural noun
Bagglepipes are a musical instrument you play by
squeezing air out of a bag into a set of pipes. The
Queen and other **human beans** call them *bagpipes*.
'Whoopee!' shouted the BFG. 'That is better than
bagglepipes, is it not, Majester?' — THE BFG

bake verb bakes, baking, baked
When you bake food, you cook it in an oven.
'The toast is finished,' Mr Tibbs whispered, 'and chef says
there is no more bread.' 'Tell him to bake more,' the Queen
said. — THE BFG

balance noun
If you have good balance, you can hold your body
steady and not fall over.
'I was just thinking,' he said, 'that if a bird can keep its

balance when it's asleep, then surely there isn't any
reason why the pills should make it fall down.' — DANNY
THE CHAMPION OF THE WORLD

balance verb balances, balancing, balanced
When you balance, you hold your body steady and
do not fall over.
At the top of the ladder, Mr Tibbs, balancing like an
acrobat, poured the BFG's coffee and placed the
enormous plate before him. — THE BFG

balcony noun balconies
a small platform outside an upstairs window of a
building, where people can stand or sit, or where
tortoises can munch and sleep
Alfie had been with Mrs Silver for years and he lived
on her balcony summer and winter. — ESIO TROT

bald adjective balder, baldest
Someone who is bald has no hair on their head.
(The opposite is hairy or **hirsute**, like Mr Twit.)
He was a very small old man, but he had a huge bald
head and a face that was covered all over with bristly
black whiskers. — JAMES AND THE GIANT PEACH

The BFG uses lots of words that begin with B, F or G!

ball noun **balls**
1 a round object that you hit, kick or throw in games
The giant peach, with the sunlight glinting on its side, was like a massive golden ball sailing upon a silver sea.
— JAMES AND THE GIANT PEACH
2 a grand or formal party where people dance
The Ugly Sisters, jewels and all,/Departed for the Palace Ball,/While darling little Cinderella/Was locked up in a slimy cellar. — REVOLTING RHYMES

balloon noun **balloons**
A balloon is a small, colourful rubber bag that you can fill with air. Most people use balloons for playing with at parties, but Mr Twit uses them to lift his wife in the air in the hope that he will never see her again.
'How lovely all those balloons look in the sky! And what a marvellous bit of luck for me! At last the old hag is lost and gone for ever.' — THE TWITS

balmy adjective **balmier, balmiest**
very silly or slightly mad
'Be quiet, you balmy old bat!' said Grandma Josephine. 'We're in a hot enough stew already.' — CHARLIE AND THE GREAT GLASS ELEVATOR
DON'T BE BIFFSQUIGGLED! Both *balmy* and *barmy* mean 'slightly mad', but *barmy* is now used more often. The word *balmy* can also mean 'mild or pleasant'.
SPARKY SYNONYMS You can also say **batty** or **dotty**.

bang noun **bangs**
a sudden very loud noise
'Let's go inside and load our lovely new guns and then it'll be bang bang bang and Bird Pie for supper.' — THE TWITS
bang verb **bangs, banging, banged**
When you bang something, you hit it hard.
Suddenly the Trunchbull exploded. 'Eat!' she shouted, banging her thigh with the riding-crop. 'If I tell you to eat, you will eat!' — MATILDA

banister noun **banisters**
a long rail at the side of a staircase, useful for sliding down and also for grown-ups to hold on to
They came to a long flight of stairs. Mr Wonka slid down the banisters. The three children did the same. — CHARLIE AND THE CHOCOLATE FACTORY

banknote noun **banknotes**
a piece of paper money that is usually issued by a bank (although The Grand High Witch makes her own)
'I have brrrought with me six trrrunks stuffed full of Inklish

banknotes, all new and crrrisp. And all of them,' she added with a fiendish leer, 'all of them home-made.' — THE WITCHES

bar noun **bars**
a block of soap or chocolate, such as a **scrumdiddlyumptious** Wonka bar
Fully grown women were seen going into sweet shops and buying ten Wonka bars at a time, then tearing off the wrappers on the spot. — CHARLIE AND THE CHOCOLATE FACTORY

barber noun **barbers**
a hairdresser for men and boys (a place seldom visited by Mr Twit)
How often do all these hairy-faced men wash their faces? Do they go to a barber to have their hairy faces cut and trimmed? — THE TWITS
DID YOU KNOW? The word *barber* comes from *barba*, the Latin word for 'beard'. If your surname is Barber or Barbour, it probably means that one of your ancestors used to be a barber. Some other surnames that come from people's jobs are: Baker (or Baxter), Brewer, Fletcher (arrow-maker), Fowler (bird-catcher), Smith (blacksmith) and Taylor.

bare adjective **barer, barest**
1 If a part of your body is bare, it has nothing covering it.
Grandma Georgina, in her red flannel nightgown with two skinny bare legs sticking out of the bottom, was trumpeting and spitting like a rhinoceros. — CHARLIE AND THE GREAT GLASS ELEVATOR
2 A bare room or wall or floor has nothing in it or on it.
James got into his own hammock — and oh, how soft and comfortable it was compared with the hard bare boards that his aunts had always made him sleep upon at home. — JAMES AND THE GIANT PEACH

bark noun
Bark is the hard covering round the trunk and branches of a tree. The Oompa-Loompas use the bark of the bong-bong tree as a flavouring to make green caterpillars taste slightly less revolting.
bark verb **barks, barking, barked**
When a dog barks, it makes a loud, rough sound. When someone like Miss Trunchbull barks, they shout as loudly and as roughly as a barking dog.
'Bruce Bogtrotter!' the Trunchbull barked suddenly. 'Where is Bruce Bogtrotter?' — MATILDA

barmy adjective **barmier, barmiest**

very silly or slightly mad

Soon the entire village was convinced that the new vicar was completely barmy. Pleasant and harmless, they said, but completely and utterly barmy. — THE VICAR OF NIBBLESWICKE

DID YOU KNOW? The word *barmy* means literally 'frothy' and comes from *barm*, a type of yeast, so a *barmy* person is one whose head is full of frothy nonsense.

barrel noun **barrels**

1 a large container for liquids, with curved sides and flat ends

Inside Mr Twit's workshed there was an enormous barrel of HUGTIGHT sticky glue, the stuff he used for catching birds. — THE TWITS

2 The barrel of a gun is the metal tube through which the shot is fired.

Great heavens! It was the barrel of a gun! Quick as a whip, Mr Fox jumped back into his hole. — FANTASTIC MR FOX

basin noun **basins**

a large bowl

Very quickly all the blue frothy mixture in the huge basin was sucked back into the stomach of the machine. — CHARLIE AND THE CHOCOLATE FACTORY

bask verb **basks, basking, basked**

If you bask, you lie or sit (or stand if you are a tortoise) warming yourself comfortably in the sunshine.

Mr Hoppy . . . lowered the pole down on to Mrs Silver's balcony below. Alfie was basking in the pale sunlight over to one side. — ESIO TROT

bat noun **bats**

A bat is a small animal with wings that flies and hunts for food at night. It is very rude to call someone an old bat.

'Out of my way!' shouted Grandma Georgina, blowing herself back and forth. 'I'm a jumbo jet!' 'You're a balmy old bat!' said Mr Wonka. — CHARLIE AND THE GREAT GLASS ELEVATOR

bath noun **baths**

a large container which you fill with water to wash yourself, or a wash that you have in this

*'Children should **never** have baths,' my grandmother said. 'It's a dangerous habit.'* — THE WITCHES

bathroom noun **bathrooms**

A bathroom is a room with a bath, washbasin and toilet. In Prince Pondicherry's chocolate palace (created by Willy Wonka), the bathroom taps have running hot chocolate.

The bricks were chocolate, and the cement holding them together was chocolate . . . and when you turned on the taps in the bathroom, hot chocolate came pouring out. — CHARLIE AND THE CHOCOLATE FACTORY

bathtub noun **bathtubs**

A bathtub is another word for a bath. The BFG has lots of bottled dreams about bathtubs, as they are very popular things to dream about.

'If I said I wanted to dream that I was in a flying bathtub with silver wings, could you make me dream it?' 'I could,' the BFG said. — THE BFG

battle noun **battles**

A battle is a big fight, usually between two groups of people. Some hostile creatures, like giants and Knids, are fond of battles.

The giants roared and screamed and cursed, and for many minutes the noise of battle rolled across the yellow plain. — THE BFG

a
b
c
d
e
f
g
h
i
j
k
l
m
n
o
p
q
r
s
t
u
v
w
x
y
z

Words that go *bang!* are *onomatopoeic*. Find out more at **gliss**.

batty adjective **battier, battiest**
very silly or slightly mad
'He's dotty!' they cried. 'He's balmy!' 'He's batty!' 'He's nutty!' 'He's screwy!' 'He's wacky!' cried the Roly-Poly Bird. — THE TWITS
DID YOU KNOW? The word *batty* comes from an old phrase *to have bats in your belfry*, which meant 'to be mad or crazy'. A *belfry* is an old word for a bell-tower.

bawl verb **bawls, bawling, bawled**
When you bawl, you shout or cry very loudly.
'James!' bawled the Centipede. 'Please help me! Wash off this paint! Scrape it off! Anything!' — JAMES AND THE GIANT PEACH

beach noun **beaches**
an area of sand or pebbles by the edge of the sea
There are no sandy beaches on the fjord. The rocks go straight down to the water's edge and the water is immediately deep. — BOY

beady adjective **beadier, beadiest**
Beady eyes are small and bright.
The moment she entered the room, one hundred squirrels . . . turned their heads and stared at her with small black beady eyes. — CHARLIE AND THE CHOCOLATE FACTORY

beak noun **beaks**
the hard, pointed part of a bird's mouth, used for eating and (very occasionally) storing water for cleaning windows
At once the Pelican spread his huge white wings and flew down on to the road beside me. 'Hop in,' he said, opening his enormous beak. — THE GIRAFFE AND THE PELLY AND ME

beam noun **beams**
a ray of light
I switched on the torch. A brilliant beam of light reached out ahead of me like a long white arm. — DANNY THE CHAMPION OF THE WORLD

beam verb **beams, beaming, beamed**
1 When something beams, it sends out a beam of light.
2 When someone beams, they smile very happily.
'This is my private yacht!' cried Mr Wonka, beaming with pleasure. 'I made her by hollowing out an enormous boiled sweet!' — CHARLIE AND THE CHOCOLATE FACTORY

beanpole noun **beanpoles**
A beanpole is a stick used to support a bean plant. If you call someone a beanpole, you mean that they are very tall and thin, like a stick.
The ancient beanpole had already put the cup to her lips, and in one gulp she swallowed everything that was in it. — GEORGE'S MARVELLOUS MEDICINE

beanstalk noun **beanstalks**
A beanstalk is the stem of a bean plant. Giants, however, mistakenly believe it is a weapon wielded by the legendary giant-killer, Jack.
'Save me!' screamed the Fleshlumpeater. 'Have mercy on this poor little giant! The beanstalk! He is coming at me with his terrible spikesticking beanstalk!' — THE BFG

bear verb **bears, bearing, bore, borne**
1 If a tree bears fruit, it produces it.
Immediately behind the caravan was an old apple tree. It bore lovely apples that ripened in the middle of September. — DANNY THE CHAMPION OF THE WORLD
2 If you cannot bear something, you cannot put up with it.
Then suddenly, as though he couldn't bear the suspense any longer, Charlie tore the wrapper right down the middle. — CHARLIE AND THE CHOCOLATE FACTORY

beard noun **beards**
A beard is hair growing on a man's chin (or on anyone's chin after they have eaten Hair Toffee). There are many different types of beard: Willy Wonka has a neat and trim **goatee** beard, and Mr Twit has a bushy unkempt beard.
'Unfortunately the mixture is not quite right yet . . . I tried it on an Oompa-Loompa yesterday in the Testing Room and immediately a huge black beard started shooting out of his chin.' — CHARLIE AND THE CHOCOLATE FACTORY
DID YOU KNOW? Someone with a lot of facial hair, like Mr Twit, is said to be **hirsute**, which means 'hairy'. Someone who hates beards (unlike Mr Twit) has *pogonophobia*.

beastly adjective **beastlier, beastliest**
very mean and nasty
'Who did that? Oh, it's you, is it, you beastly Crocodile. Why don't you go back to the big brown muddy river where you belong?' — THE ENORMOUS CROCODILE
LOOK IT UP! For more ways to describe beastly people or creatures, see **bad**.

beat verb **beats, beating, beaten**
1 To beat someone means to hit them hard over and over, as James's beastly aunts do to him whenever they feel like it.
'Why, you lazy good-for-nothing brute!' Aunt Spiker shouted. 'Beat him!' cried Aunt Sponge. 'I certainly will!' Aunt Spiker snapped. — JAMES AND THE GIANT PEACH
2 When you beat a mixture, you stir it quickly so that it becomes thicker.

'The waterfall is most important!' Mr Wonka went on. 'It mixes the chocolate! It churns it up! It pounds it and beats it! It makes it light and frothy!' — CHARLIE AND THE CHOCOLATE FACTORY

3 When a heart beats, it makes regular movements.
'Did you know,' Matilda said suddenly, 'that the heart of a mouse beats at the rate of six hundred and fifty times a minute?' — MATILDA

4 To tell someone to *beat it* is a very rude way of telling them to go away.
'Go away!' shrieked Rat. 'Go on, beat it! This is my private pitch!' — FANTASTIC MR FOX

beautiful adjective
very pleasing to look at or listen to
It was a very beautiful thing, this Golden Ticket, having been made, so it seemed, from a sheet of pure gold hammered out almost to the thinness of paper. — CHARLIE AND THE CHOCOLATE FACTORY

bed noun **beds**
A bed is a piece of furniture that you sleep on. Charlie Bucket's four grandparents all sleep in the one bed, which is all they have space for in their tiny house.
There wasn't any question of them being able to buy a better house — or even one more bed to sleep in. They were far too poor for that. — CHARLIE AND THE CHOCOLATE FACTORY

bedroom noun **bedrooms**
a room where you sleep, and where the BFG blows dreams through the window
'Now hold on,' Sophie said. 'Listen carefully. I want you to mix a dream which you will blow into the Queen of England's bedroom when she is asleep.' — THE BFG

beetle noun **beetles**
A beetle is an insect with hard, shiny wings. The Centipede likes to douse beetles in vinegar before he eats them.
'I've eaten fresh mudburgers by the greatest cooks there are,/ . . . And pails of snails and lizards' tails,/ And beetles by the jar./(A beetle is improved by just a splash of vinegar.)' — JAMES AND THE GIANT PEACH

beg verb **begs, begging, begged**
1 If you beg someone to do something, you ask them very strongly to do it.
He wrote to every magazine/And said, 'I'm looking for a Queen.'/At least ten thousand girls replied/And begged to be the royal bride. — REVOLTING RHYMES
2 If you beg someone's pardon, you ask them to excuse you.
'I do beg your pardon,' said Muggle-Wump. 'I'm so excited I hardly know what I'm saying.' — THE TWITS

behave verb **behaves, behaving, behaved**
1 The way you behave is the way you speak and do things.
'Don't poisonous snakes kill each other?' Sophie asked. She was searching desperately for another creature that behaved as badly as the human. — THE BFG
2 If you behave yourself, you don't do anything that grown-ups do not like.
'Miss Trunchbull . . . insists upon strict discipline throughout the school, and if you take my advice you will do your very best to behave yourselves in her presence.' — MATILDA

behind noun **behinds**
Your behind is your bottom, the part of your body that you sit on.
Mrs Salt . . . was now kneeling right on the edge of the hole with her head down and her enormous behind sticking up in the air like a giant mushroom. — CHARLIE AND THE CHOCOLATE FACTORY

belch verb **belches, belching, belched**
1 When someone belches, they make a noise by letting air up from their stomach through their mouth. It is like **whizzpopping**, but at the other end.
2 If a chimney or Gruncher belches, it gives out smoke or fumes.
The Red-Hot Smoke-Belching Gruncher . . . can never see anything in front of him because of all the smoke he belches out from his nose and mouth. — THE MINPINS

belch noun **belches**
the sound of someone belching
Suddenly the boy let out a gigantic belch which rolled around the Assembly Hall like thunder. — MATILDA
RINGBELLING RHYMES Try rhyming with *squelch*.

believe verb **believes, believing, believed**
If you believe something, you feel sure that it is true.
Watch with glittering eyes the whole world around you because the greatest secrets are always hidden in the most unlikely places. Those who don't believe in magic will never find it. — THE MINPINS

bellow verb **bellows, bellowing, bellowed**
If you bellow, you shout very loudly.
'He can be armed with a machine-gun for all I care!' bellowed the Duke, his massive moustaches bristling like brushwood. — THE GIRAFFE AND THE PELLY AND ME
LOOK IT UP! For lots of ways to describe how people speak, see **say**.

belly noun **bellies**
another word for your stomach or tummy
'Some of us,' the old woman went on, 'have fire on our tongues and sparks in our bellies and wizardry in the tips of our fingers . . . ' — GEORGE'S MARVELLOUS MEDICINE

a b c d e f g h i j k l m n o p q r s t u v w x y z

You can add *-ness* to some adjectives to make nouns: *brimming with beastliness.*

bellypopper noun bellypoppers

Bellypopper is the BFG's name for a **helicopter**.
*'Of course we have helicopters.' 'Whoppsy big
bellypoppers?' asked the BFG. 'Very big ones,' the Head
of the Air Force said proudly.* — THE BFG

> **Gobblefunking with words**
> When the BFG says *bellypopper* instead of *helicopter*,
> he is using a *malapropism*. You can find more
> examples of this type of word play in the entry
> for **mudburger**.

beloved adjective

A beloved person or thing is one that you love very
much.
*The BFG's house was to have a special dream-storing
room with hundreds of shelves in it where he could put
his beloved bottles.* — THE BFG

berry noun berries

a small, round fruit with seeds in it
*'Crocodiles don't eat berries,' he said. 'We eat little boys
and girls. And sometimes we eat Roly-Poly Birds, as well.'*
— THE ENORMOUS CROCODILE

beware verb

If you tell someone to beware, you are warning them
to be careful.
*His mother's words began thrumming once again in
his head: Beware! Beware! The Forest of Sin!/None
come out, but many go in!* — THE MINPINS

bewildered adjective

If you are bewildered, you are completely **biffsquiggled**.
*The children and their parents were too flabbergasted
to speak. They were staggered. They were dumbounded.
They were bewildered and dazzled.* — CHARLIE AND THE
CHOCOLATE FACTORY

bewitching adjective

Something bewitching is so powerful and unusual that
it seems to cast a magic spell over you.
*It was a brutal and bewitching smell, spicy and staggering,
fierce and frenzied, full of wizardry and magic.* — GEORGE'S
MARVELLOUS MEDICINE

BFG (THE BFG & DANNY THE CHAMPION OF THE WORLD)

The Big Friendly Giant, or the BFG, is the only giant
in Giant Country who does not hunt and eat **human
beans**. He catches dreams which he keeps in bottles,
and later blows them into the ears of sleeping children
through his magical **dream-blower**.

bibble verb bibbles, bibbling, bibbled
When something bibbles, it makes a soft gurgling sound.
All around them lay the vast black ocean, deep and hungry. Little waves were bibbling against the side of the peach.—JAMES AND THE GIANT PEACH
RINGBELLING RHYMES Try rhyming with *dribble* or *nibble*.

bibliophile noun
bibliophiles
A bibliophile is someone who loves reading and is interested in books. It is therefore a very useful word to describe Matilda.
LOOK IT UP! A word with the same ending, which means someone who is interested in witches, is **witchophile**.

bicirculers plural noun
Bicirculers are what the BFG calls binoculars. They are a device with lenses for both eyes, which makes distant objects seem nearer.
'What a spliffling whoppsy room we is in! It is so gigantuous I is needing bicirculers and telescoops to see what is going on at the other end!'—THE BFG
DID YOU KNOW? To make this word Roald Dahl used a blend of *binoculars* and *circular*, which makes sense because binoculars have round lenses. The word *binocular* comes from Latin and means 'having or using two eyes' — so you could say that **human beans**, mice and giants are all *binocular* creatures. Miss Spider, however, has many more eyes, so she is *multiocular*.

bicycle noun bicycles
a two-wheeled vehicle that you ride by pushing down on pedals with your feet
Suddenly one of the senior twelve-year-old boys came riding full speed down the road on his bicycle about twenty yards away from me.—BOY

biffsquiggled adjective
If you feel biffsquiggled, you are confused or puzzled.
'You must not be giving up so easy,' the BFG said calmly. 'The first titchy bobsticle you meet and you begin shouting you is biffsquiggled.'—THE BFG
DID YOU KNOW? Roald Dahl made up the word *biffsquiggled* by joining together the words *biff* (meaning 'punch') and *squiggled* to make a *compound*. When you are biffsquiggled, you feel as if your brain is reeling from a punch and is as muddled as a squiggly piece of doodling.
LOOK IT UP! Some other compounds that Roald Dahl created are **icky-poo** and **zippfizz**.

big adjective bigger, biggest
Something that is big is large and not small. These words are useful for describing giants and other GIANT-SIZE THINGS.

SOMETHING BIG CAN BE: colossal, enormous, gigantic, **gigantuous**, great, huge, **jumpsquiffling**, large, mammoth, massive, **squackling**, (*informal*) ginormous, humungous, whopping
• Opposites are **midgy** and tiny
'The world is a whopping big place,' the BFG said. 'It has a hundred different countries.'—THE BFG

A BIG PERSON OR A BIG CREATURE (SUCH AS A GIANT) CAN ALSO BE: burly, giant, hefty, hulking, mighty, monstrous, towering
Then Sophie saw them. In the light of the moon, she saw all nine of those monstrous half-naked brutes thundering across the landscape together.—THE BFG

Big Dead Tree (THE TWITS)
The Big Dead Tree is a leafless tree in Mr and Mrs Twit's garden which Mr Twit uses as a bird trap. Every week he smears it with HUGTIGHT glue to trap unwary birds who land on its branches and then end up in Bird Pie.

billion noun billions
A billion is exactly a thousand million (1,000,000,000), but you can also say *billions* to mean a very large number which is too big to count.
'Where do you get these dreams?' 'I collect them,' the BFG said, waving an arm towards all the rows and rows of bottles on the shelves. 'I has billions of them.'—THE BFG

billow verb billows, billowing, billowed
When something billows, it fills with air and swells outwards.
As she floated gently down, Mrs Twit's petticoat billowed out like a parachute, showing her long knickers.—THE TWITS

Billy (THE GIRAFFE AND THE PELLY AND ME)
Billy is a boy who has always dreamed of owning a sweet-shop. He lives near an old abandoned shop which is always locked, until one day it is bought by the Ladderless Window-Cleaning Company.

The BFG is called *BFO* (*Bardzo Fajny Olbrzym*) in Polish.

a b c d e f g h i j k l m n o p q r s t u v w x

bird noun **birds**
a feathered animal with two wings, two legs and a beak, such as a duck, pelican or Roly-Poly Bird
They were surrounded by ducks, doves, pigeons, sparrows, robins, larks, and many other kinds that I did not know, and the birds were eating the barley that the boys were scattering by the handful. — THE MAGIC FINGER

Bird Pie (THE TWITS)
Bird Pie is the dish which Mr and Mrs Twit eat for supper every Wednesday. Mrs Twit makes it from the birds that Mr Twit has captured that week by smearing glue on the branches of the Big Dead Tree in their garden.

birthday noun **birthdays**
the day each year when you remember and celebrate the day you were born
Only once a year, on his birthday, did Charlie Bucket ever get to taste a bit of chocolate. — CHARLIE AND THE CHOCOLATE FACTORY

bish verb **bishes, bishing, bished**
1 If you bish something, you ruin it.
'This is it!' he whispered to himself under his breath. 'The greatest moment of my life is coming up now! I mustn't bish it. I mustn't bosh it! I must keep very calm!' — ESIO TROT
2 To bish someone also means to bash or hit them hard.
'Down vith children! Do them in! Boil their bones and fry their skin! Bish them, sqvish them, bash them, mash them! Brrreak them, shake them, slash them, smash them!' — THE WITCHES

DID YOU KNOW? *Bish* is also an informal word that means 'a mistake'.

bite noun **bites**
A bite is a mouthful cut off by biting, so a bite to a giant is as much of a **human bean** as he can gobble in one go.
'That was only one titchy little bite,' the BFG said. 'Is you having any more of this delunctious grabble in your cupboard, Majester?' — THE BFG

bite verb **bites, biting, bit, bitten**
When you bite something, you use your teeth to cut it. Vermicious Knids don't have teeth but they can still bite (just don't ask what with).
'Bite off your head with what?' said Grandma Georgina. 'I didn't see any mouth.' 'They have other things to bite with,' said Mr Wonka darkly. — CHARLIE AND THE GREAT GLASS ELEVATOR

bitter adjective
1 If something tastes bitter, it has a nasty sour taste.
*'You want to know why your spaghetti was squishy?... And why it had a nasty bitter taste?' 'Why?' he said. 'Because it was **worms**!' cried Mrs Twit* — THE TWITS
2 Bitter weather is extremely cold.
After the snow, there came a freezing gale that blew for days and days without stopping. And oh, how bitter cold it was! — CHARLIE AND THE CHOCOLATE FACTORY

bittersweet adjective

A bittersweet taste or smell is sweet with a bitter aftertaste.

The tunnel was damp and murky, and all around him there was the curious bittersweet smell of fresh peach. — JAMES AND THE GIANT PEACH

blabbersnitch noun **blabbersnitches**

The blabbersnitch is a sea-creature that is hunted by witches, who use its beak in their magic Delayed Action Mouse-Maker formula.

'We will spear the blabbersnitch and trap the crabcruncher and shoot the grobblesquirt and catch the catspringer in his burrow!' — THE WITCHES

DID YOU KNOW? To make the word *blabbersnitch*, Roald Dahl may have joined together *blabber* meaning 'chatter' and *snitch* which is a slang word for 'steal'. So perhaps a blabbersnitch makes a lot of noise and steals from other creatures, just like a magpie does.

LOOK IT UP! Some other creatures that are hunted by witches are the **crabcruncher** and the **grobblesquirt**.

blackboard noun **blackboards**

A blackboard is a smooth, dark board that you can write on with chalk, or (if you have **telekinetic** powers like Matilda) that you can make chalk write on by itself.

Nigel, at the other end of the room, jumped to his feet and started pointing excitedly at the blackboard and screaming, 'The chalk! The chalk! . . . It's moving all on its own!' — MATILDA

blancmange noun **blancmanges**

a pudding made with milk that wobbles like jelly

The Trunchbull, this mighty female giant, stood there in her green breeches, quivering like a blancmange. — MATILDA

blank adjective

A blank piece of paper or screen has nothing written, drawn or displayed on it.

The screen was quite blank. 'He's taking a heck of a long time to come across,' said Mr Teavee, wiping his brow. — CHARLIE AND THE CHOCOLATE FACTORY

blanket noun **blankets**

a thick, warm cover that you put on a bed

Sophie . . . felt strong fingers grasping hold of her, and then she was lifted up from her bed, blanket and all, and whisked out of the window. — THE BFG

blare verb **blares, blaring, blared**

If something blares, like a trumpet or a television, it makes a very loud noise.

Mr Wormwood switched on the television. The screen lit up. The programme blared. — MATILDA

blaze noun **blazes**

a large, strong fire or a very bright light

Just then, all in a blaze of light,/The Magic Fairy hove in sight,/Her Magic Wand went **swoosh** *and* **swish**!/'Cindy!' *she cried, 'come make a wish!'* — REVOLTING RHYMES

blaze verb **blazes, blazing, blazed**

When a fire or light blazes, it burns or shines brightly.

There was not a sound anywhere, not even a breath of wind, and overhead the sun blazed down upon them out of a deep blue sky. — JAMES AND THE GIANT PEACH

bleach verb **bleaches, bleaching, bleached**

When you bleach something, you make it white or lighter in colour. Matilda plays a clever trick on her father that involves bleaching his hair.

Matilda . . . had sworn her to secrecy about the parrot job she had brought off at home, and also the great hair-oil switch which had bleached her father's hair. — MATILDA

bleed verb **bleeds, bleeding, bled**

If a part of your body is bleeding, blood is coming out of it.

My tail was hurting terribly . . . About two inches of it were missing and it was bleeding quite a lot. — THE WITCHES

blend verb **blends, blending, blended**

When you blend things, you mix them together.

As he stirred and stirred, many wonderful colours rose up from the depths and blended together, pinks, blues, greens, yellows and browns. — GEORGE'S MARVELLOUS MEDICINE

blighter noun (*informal*) **blighters**

a rogue or a rascal

'What's the little blighter been up to now?' Mr Jenkins asked. 'Raiding the kitchen, I suppose.' — THE WITCHES

blind adjective

Someone who is blind, like the Earthworm, cannot see.

'Poor fellow,' the Centipede said, whispering in James's ear. 'He's blind. He can't see how splendid I look.' — JAMES AND THE GIANT PEACH

blink verb **blinks, blinking, blinked**

When you blink, you close your eyes and then open them again quickly.

A minute later, they were out in the open, standing on the very top of the peach, near the stem, blinking their eyes in the strong sunlight and peering nervously around. — JAMES AND THE GIANT PEACH

a b c d e f g h i j k l m n o p q r s t u v w x y z

Roald Dahl often *blended* words together to make new words. Find out more at **poppyrot**.

blister noun blisters

A blister is a sore spot on your skin, filled with watery liquid. If you call someone a blister, it means you find them as annoying as a sore spot on your skin.

It's a funny thing about mothers and fathers. Even when their own child is the most disgusting little blister you could ever imagine, they still think that he or she is wonderful. — MATILDA

blithering adjective (*informal*)

A blithering idiot (or bumpkin for that matter) is someone who talks complete nonsense.

'You blithering bumpkin!' screeched The Grand High Witch. 'You brrrainless bogvumper!... Never in my life am I hearing such a boshvolloping suggestion coming from a vitch!' — THE WITCHES

DID YOU KNOW? The word *blithering* comes from an Old Norse word meaning 'to talk nonsense' and is related to *blethers*, a Scottish word for 'nonsense'.

blizzard noun blizzards

a storm with a lot of snow and wind

They passed a snow machine in operation, with the Cloud-Men turning the handle and a blizzard of snowflakes blowing out of the great funnel above. — JAMES AND THE GIANT PEACH

blond or blonde adjective

Blonde hair is fair or light in colour, and someone who is blonde has light-coloured hair.

Mrs Wormwood's hair was dyed a brilliant platinum blonde, very much the same glistening silvery colour as a female tightrope-walker's tights in a circus. — MATILDA

blood (*rhymes with* mud) noun

Blood is the red liquid that is pumped round inside your body.

'We're upside down and all the blood's going to my head!' screamed Mrs Twit. 'If we don't do something quickly, I shall die, I know I will!' — THE TWITS

Bloodbottler (THE BFG)

The Bloodbottler is one of the not-so-friendly giants in Giant Country. He has a revolting appearance, with reddish-pink skin and purple lips that look like sausages.

LOOK IT UP! Some other man-gobbling giants are the **Butcher Boy** and the **Fleshlumpeater**.

bloodthirsty adjective bloodthirstier, bloodthirstiest

A bloodthirsty hunter or headmistress enjoys extreme violence. The BFG calls it **thirstbloody**.

Miss Trunchbull ... looked, in short, more like a rather eccentric and bloodthirsty follower of the stag-hounds than the headmistress of a nice school for children. — MATILDA

blossom noun blossoms

the flowers on a tree

Graceful trees and bushes were growing along the riverbanks ... and tall clumps of rhododendrons with their pink and red and mauve blossoms. — CHARLIE AND THE CHOCOLATE FACTORY

blot verb blots, blotting, blotted

If you blot something out, you cover it up so that no one can see it.

Giant trees were soon surrounding him on all sides and their branches made an almost solid roof high above his head, blotting out the sky. — THE MINPINS

blow verb blows, blowing, blew, blown

1 When you blow, you make air come out of your mouth. The BFG blows through his trumpet-like **dream-blower**, to send dreams into the ears of sleeping children.

She saw the Giant take a deep breath and whoof, he blew through the trumpet ... into the Goochey children's bedroom. — THE BFG

2 When the wind blows, it moves along.

That night, while Mr and Mrs Gregg and Philip and William were trying to get some sleep up in the high nest, a great wind began to blow. — THE MAGIC FINGER

3 If something blows up (such as a suspicious cake), it explodes like a bomb.

Perhaps it was a booby-trapped cake and the whole thing would blow up the moment it was cut, taking Bruce Bogtrotter with it. — MATILDA

4 You might say *I'll be blowed!* if you are utterly astonished.

The sergeant kept saying, 'Well I never! Well, I'll be blowed! You could knock me down with a feather! Stone the crows!' and things like that. — DANNY THE CHAMPION OF THE WORLD

blowpipe noun blowpipes

A blowpipe is a long tube for blowing through. The magical **dream-blower** that the BFG uses is a type of blowpipe.

'The BFG always carries a suitcase and a blowpipe,' my father said. 'The blowpipe is as long as a lamp-post.' — DANNY THE CHAMPION OF THE WORLD

blueberry noun blueberries

A blueberry is an edible dark blue berry that is often baked in cakes and pies. Willy Wonka makes an experimental chewing-gum that tastes of blueberry pie (among other things), which has an unfortunate effect on the champion chewer, Violet Beauregarde.

'But Mr Wonka,' said Charlie Bucket anxiously, 'will Violet Beauregarde ever be all right again or will she always be a blueberry?' — CHARLIE AND THE CHOCOLATE FACTORY

A B C D E F G H I J K L M N O P Q R S T U V W X Y Z

Blue Bubbler noun Blue Bubblers
a type of **splendiferous** sweet that is sold in the Grubber
There were Nishnobblers and Gumglotters and Blue Bubblers and Sherbet Slurpers and . . . a whole lot of splendid stuff from the great Wonka factory itself.
—THE GIRAFFE AND THE PELLY AND ME

blurred or **blurry** adjective **blurrier, blurriest**
If something is blurred or blurry, it is fuzzy and you cannot see or remember it clearly.
The landscape became blurred and again Sophie had to duck down out of the whistling gale to save her head from being blown off her shoulders. —THE BFG

blush verb **blushes, blushing, blushed**
When you blush, your face goes red because you feel shy or embarrassed.
'Those diamonds were worth millions! Millions and millions! And you have saved them!' The Monkey nodded. The Giraffe smiled. The Pelican blushed. —THE GIRAFFE AND THE PELLY AND ME

boarding-school noun **boarding-schools**
a school in which the pupils live during the term
Unless you have been to boarding-school when you are very young, it is absolutely impossible to appreciate the delights of living at home. —BOY

boast verb **boasts, boasting, boasted**
If someone boasts, they talk about how much better they are than other people.
Bruno never stopped boasting about how his father made more money than my father and that they owned three cars. —THE WITCHES

boat noun **boats**
a vehicle that floats on water and can carry people and goods over water
Out of the mist there appeared suddenly a most fantastic pink boat. It was a large open row boat with a tall front and a tall back (like a Viking boat of old). —CHARLIE AND THE CHOCOLATE FACTORY

bobolink noun **bobolinks**
The bobolink is a rare and ancient animal. Willy Wonka needs a part of the bobolink to make Vita-Wonk, but he doesn't say which part as it is a secret recipe.
'I tracked down THE WHISTLE-PIG, THE BOBOLINK, THE SKROCK, THE POLLY-FROG, THE GIANT CURLICUE, THE STINGING SLUG AND THE VENOMOUS SQUERKLE.' —CHARLIE AND THE GREAT GLASS ELEVATOR
DID YOU KNOW? A *bobolink* is also a type of a song-bird from North America, which gets its name from the sound it makes.

bobsticle noun **bobsticles**
A bobsticle is an obstacle, which is something that gets in your way or makes it difficult for you to do something.
'You must not be giving up so easy,' the BFG said calmly. 'The first titchy bobsticle you meet and you begin shouting you is biffsquiggled.' —THE BFG

body noun **bodies**
Your body is every part of you (or of a giant) that you can see and touch.
Sophie . . . saw the Fleshlumpeater's body, all fifty-four feet of it, rise up off the ground and fall back again with a thump. —THE BFG

bog noun **bogs**
A bog is a piece of soft, wet ground. It is also an informal word for a toilet.
'I put up my hand and asked to go to the bogs. But instead of going there, I sneaked into the Trunchbull's room.' —MATILDA

Boggis, Bunce and Bean (FANTASTIC MR FOX)
Boggis, Bunce and Bean are rich but mean farmers who are outwitted by the clever Mr Fox. Boggis keeps chickens, Bunce keeps ducks and geese, and Bean keeps turkeys and grows apples.
DID YOU KNOW? *Bunce* is a slang word that means 'money or profit'.

boggle verb **boggles, boggling, boggled**
If something boggles you, or boggles your brain, it leaves you utterly amazed.
The giants were all naked except for a sort of short skirt around their waists . . . But it was the sheer size of each one of them that boggled Sophie's brain most of all. —THE BFG
RINGBELLING RHYMES Try rhyming with *goggle.*

bogglebox for boys noun **boggleboxes for boys**
the name that giants give to a boys' school (a school for girls is a **gigglehouse**)
'And I knows where there is a bogglebox for boys!' shouted the Gizzardgulper. 'All I has to do is reach in and grab myself a handful!' —THE BFG

bogrotting adjective
If something is bogrotting it is very unpleasant, so a bogrotting nightmare is one where really nasty things happen.
'This one is a nasty fierce bogrotting nightmare. Just look at him splashing himself against the glass!' —THE BFG
SPARKY SYNONYMS You can also say **muckfrumping** or **rotsome**. An opposite is **splendiferous**.

bogthumper noun **bogthumpers**
A bogthumper is a truly horrible and nasty nightmare.
'A dream where you is seeing little chiddlers being eaten

You can add -ly to adjectives to make adverbs: *How bogrottingly awful!*

a b c d e f g h i j k l m n o p q r s t u v w x y z

is about the most frightsome troggle humping dream you can get. It's a kicksy bogthumper.' — THE BFG

RINGBELLING RHYMES *Bogthumper* rhymes with *trogglehumper*, which is very useful for writing poems about nightmares. It also rhymes with *jumper* which may be less useful (unless you have bad dreams about knitwear).
LOOK IT UP! Some other scary dreams are **grobswitchers** and **trogglehumpers**.

bogthumping adjective
as frightening as a **bogthumper**
'I is so upset by this trogglehumping bogthumping grobswitcher,' the BFG said, 'that I is not wishing to go on.' — THE BFG

boil verb **boils, boiling, boiled**
1 When liquid boils, it bubbles and gives off steam because it is very hot.
The place was like a witch's kitchen! All about him black metal pots were boiling and bubbling on huge stoves, and kettles were hissing and pans were sizzling. — CHARLIE AND THE CHOCOLATE FACTORY
2 When you boil food (or boys), you cook it (or them) in boiling water.
The boys were terrified. 'He's going to boil us!' cried one of them. 'He'll stew us alive!' wailed the second one. 'He'll cook us with carrots!' cried the third. — THE TWITS

boiled adjective
boiled food has been cooked in boiling water
Boggis . . . was enormously fat. This was because he ate three boiled chickens smothered with dumplings every day for breakfast, lunch and supper. — FANTASTIC MR FOX

bolt noun **bolts**
a piece of metal that you slide across to lock a door
'You see that little square door with the bolts on it?' said Mr Wonka. 'That's the docking entrance.' — CHARLIE AND THE GREAT GLASS ELEVATOR

bolt verb **bolts, bolting, bolted**
If you bolt, you run away suddenly.
James . . . glanced behind him, thinking he could bolt back into the tunnel the way he had come, but the doorway had disappeared. — JAMES AND THE GIANT PEACH

bolt upright adverb
If you stand or sit bolt upright, you stand or sit with a very straight back.
The door was opened by Miss Prewt herself, a tall, thin female who stood bolt upright and whose mouth was like the blade of a knife. — THE VICAR OF NIBBLESWICKE

bomb noun **bombs**
a weapon that explodes and hurts people or damages things
'That's not a bed, you drivelling thickwit!' yelled the President . . . 'It's a bomb. It's a bomb disguised as a bed!' — CHARLIE AND THE GREAT GLASS ELEVATOR

bone noun **bones**
Your bones are the hard white parts inside your body that make up your skeleton, and that make a crunching noise when eaten by a giant. Earthworms and Knids have no bones, which means they are *invertebrates*.
'Oh, I don't want to be eaten!' wailed the Earthworm. 'But they will take me first of all because I am so fat and juicy and I have no bones!' — JAMES AND THE GIANT PEACH

Bonecruncher or **Bonecrunching Giant**
(THE BFG)
The Bonecruncher is one of the not-so-friendly giants in Giant Country. He only eats **human beans** from Turkey because he finds them the tastiest to eat (and he wouldn't like Knids, as they have no bones).
LOOK IT UP! Some other man-gobbling giants are the **Manhugger** and the **Childchewer**.

bonnet noun **bonnets**
The bonnet is the part of a car that covers the engine. In North America it is called the *hood*.
Most of the pheasants . . . were all over the roof and the bonnet, sliding and slithering and trying to keep a grip on that beautifully polished surface. — DANNY THE CHAMPION OF THE WORLD

bony (*rhymes with* **pony**) adjective **bonier, boniest**
If someone is bony, they are so thin that you can see the bones under their skin.
James glanced up and saw Aunt Spiker standing over him, grim and tall and bony. — JAMES AND THE GIANT PEACH

book noun **books**
A book is a set of pages, usually with writing on them (like this one), which are joined together inside a cover.
The BFG . . . became a tremendous reader. He read all of Charles Dickens (whom he no longer called Dahl's Chickens) and all of Shakespeare and literally thousands of other books. — THE BFG
DID YOU KNOW? Someone who loves books and reading, like Matilda, is called a **bibliophile**, which means literally 'loving books'.

boom verb booms, booming, boomed
When someone booms, they speak in a very loud voice.
'SPEAK!' boomed the voice, getting louder and louder and ending in a fearful frightening shout that rattled Charlie's eardrums. — CHARLIE AND THE GREAT GLASS ELEVATOR

LOOK IT UP! For lots of ways to describe how people speak, see **say**.

bootboggler noun
bootbogglers
A bootboggler is the BFG's word for a soldier (especially a silly one).
'Now listen to me carefully, you two bootbogglers.' The military men began to twitch, but they stayed put. — THE BFG

bootle verb bootles, bootling, bootled
When a giant bootles, he travels from one place to another.
'Do you always know where they're going?' Sophie asked. 'Always,' the BFG said. 'Every night they is yelling at me as they go bootling past.' — THE BFG

DID YOU KNOW? The word *bootle* sounds like a mixture of *boots* and *tootle* ('to travel in a leisurely way') — although giants don't wear boots, and bootling is a bit faster than tootling.

LOOK IT UP! For other ways to describe how giants or **human beans** travel, see **move**.

bopmuggered adjective
If a giant is bopmuggered, he is in a very bad situation. It is very rude to say you are bopmuggered, which is why giants like to say it.
'I is crodsquinkled!' yowled the Bloodbottler. 'I is bopmuggered!' screeched the Butcher Boy. — THE BFG

LOOK IT UP! For other rude words that giants say, see **rude**.

bored adjective
If you are bored, you are feeling weary and uninterested because something is so dull.
This child, Miss Honey told herself, seems to be interested in everything. When one is with her it is impossible to be bored. — MATILDA

boring adjective
If you find something boring (not, of course, a dictionary), you find it dull and uninteresting.
The Hotel Magnificent . . . was an enormous white building on the sea-front and it looked to me like a pretty boring place to spend a summer holiday in. — THE WITCHES

born adjective
When a baby is born, it comes out of its mother's body and starts to live. As giants have no mothers, they are not born as babies, but arrive in the world fully grown.
'Giants isn't born,' the BFG answered. 'Giants appears and

that's all there is to it. They simply appears, the same way as the sun and the stars.' — THE BFG

bosom noun bosoms
a woman's breasts
The Trunchbull, her face more like a boiled ham than ever, was standing before the class quivering with fury. Her massive bosom was heaving in and out. — MATILDA

bottle noun bottles
1 a tall glass or plastic container for keeping liquids in, or dreams
'Here is the dream-catcher,' he said, grasping the pole in one hand. 'Every morning I is going out and snitching new dreams to put in my bottles.' — THE BFG

2 Bottle-green is a dark green colour, like some glass bottles. Willy Wonka's trousers are bottle-green, and so are Miss Trunchbull's **breeches**.

bottle-wart noun bottle-warts
The unfriendly giants call the BFG a bottle-wart as an insult, because they think it is silly to collect bottles of dreams.
The Bloodbottler pointed a finger as large as a tree-trunk at the BFG. 'Runty little scumscrewer!' he shouted. 'Piffling little swishfiggler! Squimpy little bottle-wart!' — THE BFG

LOOK IT UP! Miss Trunchbull uses the word **wart** as an insult too.

bottom noun bottoms
1 the lowest part of something
'We are probably at the bottom of a coal mine,' the Earthworm said gloomily. 'We certainly went down and down and down very suddenly at the last moment.' — JAMES AND THE GIANT PEACH
2 Your bottom is the part of your body that you sit on. Vermicious Knids have pointy bottoms which are not very good for sitting but make good weapons.
'They're coming at us backwards!' 'Backwards?' cried the President. 'Why backwards?' 'Because their bottoms are even more pointy than their tops!' — CHARLIE AND THE GREAT GLASS ELEVATOR

bounce verb bounces, bouncing, bounced
When a ball or a Knid bounces, it springs back into the air after hitting something hard.
It struck the Glass Elevator with the most enormous bang and the whole thing shivered and shook but the glass held and the Knid bounced off like a rubber ball. — CHARLIE AND THE GREAT GLASS ELEVATOR

bound verb bounds, bounding, bounded
When something bounds, it moves in a series of leaps.
The peach rolled out of the garden and began to go down the steep hill, rushing and plunging and bounding madly downward. — JAMES AND THE GIANT PEACH

bound adjective
If something is bound to happen, it will definitely happen.
Matilda felt herself getting angrier . . . and angrier . . . and

Words that Roald Dahl invented that start with *bog-* often mean unpleasant things!

29

angrier . . . so unbearably angry that something was bound to explode inside her very soon. — MATILDA

bow (rhymes with **cow**) verb **bows, bowing, bowed**
When you bow, you bend your body forwards to show respect or as a greeting.
'Wouldn't this be a perfect time for a little music?' . . .
'With pleasure, dear lady,' the Old-Green-Grasshopper answered, bowing from the waist. — JAMES AND THE GIANT PEACH

WHAT AM I DOING HERE?

boy noun **boys**
a male child
'I don't mind girls, I never 'ave no trouble with girls, but boys is 'ideous and 'orrible! I don't 'ave to tell you that, 'Eadmaster, do I?' — BOY

DID YOU KNOW? Roald Dahl used the name 'Boy' for signing the letters he wrote every week to his mother from boarding-school.

brain noun **brains**
Your brain is the part inside your head that controls your body and allows you to think and remember things.
'Dreams is not like human beans or animals. They has no brains. They is made of zozimus.' — THE BFG

brain-boggling adjective
amazing or astonishing
It was a brain-boggling sight. The giants were all naked except for a sort of short skirt around their waists, and their skins were burnt by the sun. — THE BFG

brain-power noun
Your brain-power is your ability to think, or your intelligence.
My grandmother stared at me. 'My darling child,' she said slowly, 'I do believe that turning you into a mouse has doubled your brain-power!' — THE WITCHES

brainy adjective **brainier, brainiest**
Someone who is brainy is very clever, like Matilda or Mr Fox.
This one, Piggy Number Three,/Was bright and brainy as could be./No straw for him, no twigs or sticks./This pig had built his house of BRICKS. — REVOLTING RHYMES

branch noun **branches**
a part that grows out from the trunk of a tree, where Minpins can be found
'These great trees are filled with rooms and staircases, not just in the big main trunk but in most of the other branches as well. This is a Minpin forest.' — THE MINPINS

brandish verb **brandishes, brandishing, brandished**
If you brandish something, like a sword or a frying-pan, you wave it about.
I saw a chef in a tall white hat rushing out from the kitchen brandishing a frying-pan, and another one just behind him was wielding a carving-knife above his head. — THE WITCHES

brat noun **brats**
A brat is a badly behaved child. It is also a name that badly behaved grown-ups use when they are rude to children.
'Let's make him finish chopping up the wood first. Be off with you at once, you hideous brat, and do some work!' — JAMES AND THE GIANT PEACH

brave adjective **braver, bravest**
Someone who is brave is willing to do dangerous things.
Another extremely brave little boy in the front row spoke up and said, 'But surely you were a small person once, Miss Trunchbull, weren't you?' — MATILDA

bread noun
a food made by baking flour and water, usually with yeast
The situation became desperate. Breakfast was a single slice of bread for each person now, and lunch was maybe half a boiled potato. — CHARLIE AND THE CHOCOLATE FACTORY

breakfast noun **breakfasts**
the first meal of the day, which you eat in the morning
'Everyone must be drinking frobscottle with breakfast, Majester. Then we can all be whizzpopping happily together afterwards.' — THE BFG

breath noun **breaths**
the air that you take into your body and then blow out again
When you have sucked a Devil's Drencher for a minute or so, you can set your breath alight and blow a huge column of fire twenty feet into the air. — THE GIRAFFE AND THE PELLY AND ME

breathe verb **breathes, breathing, breathed**
When you breathe, you take air into your lungs through your nose or mouth and then blow it out again.
'I'm choking!' gasped Grandma Georgina.
'I can't breathe!' 'Of course you can't,' said Mr Wonka. 'There's no air up here.' — CHARLIE AND THE GREAT GLASS ELEVATOR

breeches plural noun
short trousers that fit tightly at the knee, as sported by Miss Trunchbull in a shade of bottle-green
The massive thighs which emerged from out of the smock were encased in a pair of extraordinary breeches, bottle-green in colour and made of coarse twill. — MATILDA

breeze noun **breezes**
a gentle wind
A small breeze had taken hold of the balloon and was carrying it away in the direction of the village. — DANNY THE CHAMPION OF THE WORLD

brief adjective **briefer, briefest**
Something that is brief is short and does not last very long.
For a brief moment, the terrible Red-Hot Smoke-Belching Gruncher made the lake boil and smoke like a volcano, then the fire went out. — THE MINPINS

brigand noun **brigands**
an old word for a robber or outlaw
'A thief!' the Trunchbull screamed. 'A crook! A pirate! A brigand! A rustler!' — MATILDA

bright adjective **brighter, brightest**
1 A bright light or colour is strong and not dull.
James's little face was glowing with excitement, his eyes were as big and bright as two stars. — JAMES AND THE GIANT PEACH
2 A bright idea is clever and inspired.
Mrs Twit may have been ugly and she may have been beastly, but she was not stupid. High up there in the sky, she had a bright idea. — THE TWITS
3 Someone who is bright is clever and learns things quickly.
Matilda was moved up into the top form, where Miss Plimsoll quickly discovered that this amazing child was every bit as bright as Miss Honey had said. — MATILDA

brilliant adjective
1 A brilliant person or idea is very clever.
Muggle-Wump laid his head on one side. . . . 'Now and again,' he said, 'but not very often, I have a brilliant idea.' — THE TWITS
2 very bright and sparkling
George began to tremble. It was her face that frightened him most of all, the frosty smile, the brilliant unblinking eyes. — GEORGE'S MARVELLOUS MEDICINE

brim noun **brims**
the edge round the top of a container
The saucepan was now full to the brim. Very gently, George stirred the paint into the mixture with the long wooden spoon. — GEORGE'S MARVELLOUS MEDICINE

bristle verb **bristles, bristling, bristled**
If an animal's coat (or a person's moustache) bristles, it means the hairs rise up to show they are angry.
*'He can be armed with a **machine-gun** for all I care!' bellowed the Duke, his massive moustaches bristling like brushwood.* — THE GIRAFFE AND THE PELLY AND ME
RINGBELLING RHYMES Try rhyming with *thistle* or *whistle*.

broad adjective **broader, broadest**
A broad street, or a broad smile or grin, is wide and open.
'No more school!' said Bruno, grinning a broad and asinine mouse-grin. 'No more homework!' — THE WITCHES

brooch (*rhymes with* **coach**) noun **brooches**
A brooch is a piece of jewellery that you pin to your clothes. Brooches can also be useful for self-defence against giants.
Sophie . . . rammed the three-inch-long pin of the brooch as hard as she could into the Fleshlumpeater's right ankle. It went deep into the flesh and stayed there. — THE BFG

brother noun **brothers**
Your brother is a boy who has the same parents as you.
While Uncle Oscar was bustling around in La Rochelle, his one-armed brother Harald (my own father) was not sitting on his rump doing nothing. — BOY

browbeaten adjective
If you are browbeaten, you are bullied into doing things you do not want to do.
Miss Honey stood resolutely before the Headmistress. For once she was not going to be browbeaten. — MATILDA

Bruce Bogtrotter (MATILDA)
Bruce Bogtrotter is a greedy boy who steals a slice of Miss Trunchbull's chocolate cake and is forced to eat a whole cake in one go in as a punishment.

bruise noun **bruises**
a dark mark on your skin that you get when something hits you or when you bump into something
'Look at me!' cried the Centipede. 'Look at ME! I am freed! I am freed! Not a scratch nor a bruise nor a bleed!' — JAMES AND THE GIANT PEACH

Bruno Jenkins (THE WITCHES)
Bruno Jenkins is a boy who is always eating. The Grand High Witch decides to test her Delayed-Action Mouse-Maker formula on him by disguising it in a chocolate bar.

The BFG uses lots of words that are spelled with *-iff-*, like *bugwhiffle* and *squiffling*.

brutal adjective

savage and cruel

And there it was, cruising effortlessly alongside them, a simply colossal Vermicious Knid . . . with the most brutal vermicious look in its eye!— CHARLIE AND THE GREAT GLASS ELEVATOR

brute noun **brutes**

a cruel person or creature, such as a man-eating giant

'Your BFG is right,' the Queen said to Sophie. 'Those nine man-eating brutes did go to Sweden.'— THE BFG

bubble noun **bubbles**

Bubbles are small balls of air or gas inside a liquid, like the ones you find in fizzy drinks. Bubbles usually rise to the surface, except in **frobscottle**, where they sink downwards and so make you **whizzpop** rather than burp.

The bubbles, instead of travelling upwards and bursting on the surface, were shooting downwards and bursting at the bottom.— THE BFG

bubble verb **bubbles, bubbling, bubbled**

When a liquid bubbles, it is boiling and produces bubbles of air.

It was wonderful to stand there stirring this amazing mixture and to watch it smoking blue and bubbling and frothing and foaming as though it were alive.— GEORGE'S MARVELLOUS MEDICINE

bucket noun **buckets**

A bucket is a container with a handle used for carrying liquid. The Ladderless Window-Cleaning Company use the Pelican's beak as a bucket (so technically they are also the Bucketless Window-Cleaning Company).

'The bottom half of this glorious beak of mine is the bucket in which we carry our window-cleaning water!'
— THE GIRAFFE AND THE PELLY AND ME

Bucket, Mr (CHARLIE AND THE CHOCOLATE FACTORY & GREAT GLASS ELEVATOR)

Mr Bucket is Charlie's father. He works in a toothpaste factory, but when the factory closes down, he tries to support his starving family by shovelling snow in the streets.

buckle noun **buckles**

the part of a belt that you use to fasten the two ends together

Miss Trunchbull . . . always had on a brown cotton smock which was pinched in around the waist with a wide leather belt. The belt was fastened in front with an enormous silver buckle.— MATILDA

buckswashling noun

Buckswashling is going on a daring adventure full of action and excitement.

'You stay where you is in my pocket, huggybee,' he said. 'We is doing this lovely bit of buckswashling both together.'
— THE BFG

DID YOU KNOW? The word **buckswashling** sounds like *swashbuckling*, which is similar in meaning. A *swashbuckling adventure* is full of action and daring deeds, and comes from an old meaning of *swash* 'to clash swords'.

Gobblefunking with words
When the BFG says *buckswashling* instead of *swashbuckling*, he is using a *spoonerism*. You can find more examples of this type of word play in the entry for **mideous**.

buggles adjective

If you say that someone is buggles, you mean that they are mad or crazy.

'That is the most disgusterous taste that is ever clutching my teeth! You must be buggles to be swalloping slutch like that!'— THE BFG

DID YOU KNOW? When he invented *buggles*, Roald Dahl may have been thinking of other plural words like *bonkers* or *crackers* which mean 'mad or crazy', or of *bug-eyed*, which means 'staring with bulging eyes'. **LOOK IT UP!** For other ways to describe someone as **buggles**, see **mad**.

bugswallop noun

nonsense or lies

'I is jabbeling to myself,' the BFG answered. 'Pilfflefizz!' shouted the Bloodbottler. 'Bugswallop! . . . You is talking to a human bean, that's what I is thinking!'— THE BFG

DID YOU KNOW? Roald Dahl made up the word *bugswallop*, but he may have wanted it to sound like *codswallop*, a slang word which also means 'nonsense'.

bugwhiffle noun **bugwhiffles**

A bugwhiffle is a silly or unimportant idea.

'If you will listen carefully I will try to explain,' said the BFG. 'But your brain is so full of bugwhiffles, I doubt you will ever understand.'— THE BFG

bulge verb **bulges, bulging, bulged**

If something bulges, it sticks out because it is so full.

Mr Hazell's skin turned from scarlet to purple. His eyes and his cheeks were bulging so much with rage it looked as though someone was blowing up his face with a pump.— DANNY THE CHAMPION OF THE WORLD

bullet noun bullets

a small piece of metal that is fired from a gun
'Look!' cried the Monkey. 'That rotten burglar's bullet has made a hole in poor Pelly's beak!' — THE GIRAFFE AND THE PELLY AND ME

bullfrog noun bullfrogs

A bullfrog is a large frog with a loud deep croak. The throat of a bullfrog swells when it croaks.
At the mention of this word, Miss Trunchbull's face turned purple and her whole body seemed to swell up like a bullfrog's. — MATILDA

bump verb bumps, bumping, bumped

If you bump something, you knock against it accidentally.
Sophie crouched in the blanket, peering out. She was being bumped against the Giant's leg like a sack of potatoes. — THE BFG

bump noun bumps

1 an accidental knock or jolt
'We all felt it, didn't we, as the peach went over her? Oh, what a lovely bump that must have been for you, Miss Spider!' — JAMES AND THE GIANT PEACH
2 a swelling or lump
A purple bruisy bump the size of a small car was appearing on the pointed rear-end of the giant Knid. — CHARLIE AND THE GREAT GLASS ELEVATOR

bumper noun bumpers

a bar along the front or back of a car to protect it in a crash
But this was no ordinary whizzer. It had a brake-pedal, a steering-wheel, a comfortable seat and a strong front bumper to take the shock of a crash. — DANNY THE CHAMPION OF THE WORLD

bumplehammer noun bumplehammers

A bumplehammer is a very large type of hammer, which is bigger than a sausage.
'Why even your toes must be as big as sausages.' 'Bigger,' said the BFG, looking pleased. 'They is as big as bumplehammers.' — THE BFG

Gobblefunking with words
When the BFG says his toes are *as big as bumplehammers*, he is using a *simile*. Similes are very useful for describing giants or creatures of unusual size or features. For example, the Fleshlumpeater has a finger *as thick as a tree-trunk* and the BFG takes strides *as long as a tennis court*. You can find lots more examples of similes in the entry for **mad**.

bumpy adjective bumpier, bumpiest

A bumpy road or surface has lots of bumps in it, so it makes a car or bicycle jolt when it goes over it.
Hazell's Wood was not on the main road. To reach it you had to turn left through a gap in the hedge and go uphill over a bumpy track for about a quarter of a mile. — DANNY THE CHAMPION OF THE WORLD

bunderbluss noun bunderblusses

A bunderbluss is the BFG's name for a *blunderbuss*, which is a noisy old-fashioned type of gun.
'It sounds as though you is shootling off a bunderbluss!' 'Then how can I talk to you?' Sophie whispered. 'Don't!' cried the poor BFG. 'Please don't!' — THE BFG

DID YOU KNOW? The word *blunderbuss* comes from a Dutch word that means 'thunder gun'.

bundle noun bundles

a group of things that are tied together
Before Mr Twit had time to run away, this bundle of balloons and petticoats and fiery fury landed right on top of him, lashing out with the stick and cracking him all over his body. — THE TWITS

bundongle noun bundongles

A bundongle is something that contains only air.
'I thought all human beans is full of brains, but your head is emptier than a bundongle.' — THE BFG

bungswoggle verb bungswoggles, bungswoggling, bungswoggled

If a giant bungswoggles another giant, he thumps him very hard.
'He is swiping me right in the mouth!' yelled the Meatdripper. 'He is bungswoggling me smack in the guts!' shouted the Gizzardgulper. — THE BFG

a
b
c
d
e
f
g
h
i
j
k
l
m
n
o
p
q
r
s
t
u
v
w
x
y
z

bunk noun bunks

1 a bed that has another bed above or below it
I really loved living in that gipsy caravan. I loved it especially in the evenings when I was tucked up in my bunk and my father was telling me stories. — DANNY THE CHAMPION OF THE WORLD

2 (*informal*) If someone *does a bunk*, they leave suddenly without telling anyone.
She's done a bunk, Mr Trilby said to himself, and he went away to inform the School Governors that the Headmistress had apparently vanished. — MATILDA

bunkdoodle verb bunkdoodles, bunkdoodling, bunkdoodled

When a **bogthumper** or **trogglehumper** bunkdoodles you, it scares you by giving you a horrible nightmare.
'Ah, you wicked beastie, you! . . . Never more is you going to be bunkdoodling the poor little human-beaney tottlers!' — THE BFG

DID YOU KNOW? When he invented the word *bunkdoodle*, Roald Dahl may have been playing on the word *doodle-bug*, which is a North American beetle and also a nickname for flying bombs used in World War II.

burble verb burbles, burbling, burbled

If you burble, you speak in a way that is hard to understand.
All I could hear were the voices of the ancient witches burbling their silly sentences about 'How kind Your Grandness is' and all the rest of it. — THE WITCHES

burglar noun burglars

a thief who enters a building to steal things
'Where are my diamonds?' 'Here they are!' cried the Chief of Police, fishing great handfuls of jewellery from the burglar's pockets. — THE GIRAFFE AND THE PELLY AND ME

burn verb burns, burning, burned, burnt

1 When something burns, it catches fire.
Bruno Jenkins was focusing the sun through his magnifying-glass and roasting the ants one by one. 'I like watching them burn,' he said. — THE WITCHES

2 If you burn something, you damage it with fire or heat.
Mr Kranky . . . started jumping about as though something was burning his feet. 'Great heavens!' he cried, waving his arms. — GEORGE'S MARVELLOUS MEDICINE

burp verb burps, burping, burped

Burp is another way of saying **belch**. Remembering to burp is very important if you have drunk a Fizzy Lifting Drink, otherwise you might float upwards forever.
'But how do you come down again?' asked little Charlie. 'You do a burp, of course,' said Mr Wonka. 'You do a great big long rude burp, and up comes the gas and down comes you!' — CHARLIE AND THE CHOCOLATE FACTORY

RINGBELLING RHYMES Try rhyming with *twerp*.

burrow noun burrows

a hole in the ground that an animal lives in, such as a rabbit or a **catspringer**
'We will spear the blabbersnitch and trap the crabcruncher and shoot the grobblesquirt and catch the catspringer in his burrow!' — THE WITCHES

burrow verb burrows, burrowing, burrowed

When an animal (or a tiny green thing) burrows, it digs into the ground.
They were all sinking into the soil! He could actually see them wriggling and twisting as they burrowed their way downward into the hard earth. — JAMES AND THE GIANT PEACH

burst verb bursts, bursting, burst

If something bursts, it suddenly breaks open.
At once, there came a blinding flash,/And then the most almighty crash,/And sparks were bursting all around,/And smoke was rising from the ground. — DIRTY BEASTS

bury verb buries, burying, buried

When you bury something, you dig a hole and cover it with earth or snow, or sometimes hay.
When the colder weather came along . . . Mrs Silver would fill Alfie's house with dry hay, and the tortoise would crawl in there and bury himself deep under the hay. — ESIO TROT

bushy adjective bushier, bushiest

A bushy beard or moustache is very full and thick. Most bushy beards are just full of hairs, but Mr Twit's is full of bits of leftover food, like leaves sticking in a bush.
The pilot was a young Air Force officer with a bushy moustache. He was very proud of his moustache. — THE BFG

busy (*rhymes with* dizzy) adjective **busier, busiest**
If you are busy, you have a lot of things to do.
The Cloud-Men were much too busy with what they were doing to have noticed the great peach floating silently up behind them. — JAMES AND THE GIANT PEACH

Butcher Boy (THE BFG)
The Butcher Boy is one of the not-so-friendly giants in Giant Country. His name suggests that he chops up **human beans** before he eats them.
LOOK IT UP! Some other human-bean-eating giants are the **Bonecruncher** and the **Fleshlumpeater**.

butler noun **butlers**
the chief male servant in a palace or very grand house
Mr Tibbs skimmed into the Ballroom (butlers don't walk, they skim over the ground) followed by a whole army of footmen. — THE BFG
DID YOU KNOW? The word *butler* comes from an old French word meaning 'bottle-carrier', because butlers were in charge of wine cellars.

butter noun
Butter is a fatty yellow food made from cream that you spread on bread or toast (but don't usually stir into coffee).
'There's no waiting!' cried Mr Kranky, working himself up so much that he put butter in his coffee and milk on his toast. — GEORGE'S MARVELLOUS MEDICINE

butter verb **butters, buttering, buttered**
If you butter someone up, you try to please them by saying nice things to them.
*'We've **got** to treat these fellows gently . . . We've got to be polite to them, butter them up, make them happy.'* — CHARLIE AND THE GREAT GLASS ELEVATOR

butterfly noun **butterflies**
A butterfly is an insect with large colourful wings. If you say you have butterflies in your tummy, it means you are so nervous that you feel funny and fluttery inside.
It was the day I longed for and the day I dreaded. It was also the day of butterflies in the stomach except that they were worse than butterflies. They were snakes. — DANNY THE CHAMPION OF THE WORLD
DID YOU KNOW? Some people used to believe that witches or fairies disguised themselves as butterflies to steal butter, and that may be how they got their name; or it may just have been because some common species of butterfly are a yellow colour like butter.

butterscotch noun
Butterscotch is usually a kind of hard toffee, but Willy Wonka makes a kind of butterscotch mixed with alcohol that the Oompa-Loompas like to drink.
Shrieks of laughter and snatches of singing could be heard coming through the closed door. 'They're drunk as lords,' said Mr Wonka. 'They're drinking butterscotch and soda.' — CHARLIE AND THE CHOCOLATE FACTORY

butteryfly noun **butteryflies**
A butterfly is the BFG's name for a butterfly.
'I has a special place to go for catching dreams.' . . . 'How do you catch them?' 'The same way you is catching butteryflies,' the BFG answered. 'With a net.' — THE BFG

a
b
c
d
e
f
g
h
i
j
k
l
m
n
o
p
q
r
s
t
u
v
w
x
y
z

The BFG is called *SVK* (*Stor Vennlig Kjempe*) in Norwegian.

button noun buttons

1 A button is a flat plastic or metal disc that you use to fasten clothes. The BFG's clothing is so old and well worn that some of the buttons have fallen off.
Sophie saw that under the cloak he was wearing a sort of collarless shirt and a dirty old leather waistcoat that didn't seem to have any buttons. — THE BFG

2 A button is a small knob that you press to switch a machine on or off. Willy Wonka is very fond of pressing buttons and has lots of them in his factory.
'Now then,' cried Mr Wonka, 'which button shall we press first? Take your pick!' — CHARLIE AND THE CHOCOLATE FACTORY

RINGBELLING RHYMES Try rhyming with *glutton*.

buzz noun buzzes

1 a sharp humming sound, like bees make
2 an atmosphere of excitement
There was a buzz of excited chatter and a lot of running about and waving of arms. — CHARLIE AND THE GREAT GLASS ELEVATOR

buzzbomb noun buzzbombs

A buzzbomb is a deafening or **earbursting** sound.
'Don't!' cried the poor BFG. 'Please don't! Each word is like you is dropping buzzbombs in my earhole!' — THE BFG

buzzburger noun buzzburgers

A buzzburger is something that doesn't make sense (at least to **human beans**).
'I is brimful of buzzburgers,' the BFG said. 'If you listen to everything I am saying you will be getting earache.' — THE BFG

buzzwangle noun buzzwangles

A buzzwangle is an idea that is silly or far-fetched.
'By ringo, your head must be so full of frogsquinkers and buzzwangles, I is frittered if I know how you can think at all!' — THE BFG

buzzy-hum noun buzzy-hums

A buzzy-hum is a sound that is somewhere between a buzz and a hum.
'A dream . . . is making a tiny little buzzing-humming noise. But this little buzzy-hum is so silvery soft, it is impossible for a human bean to be hearing it.' — THE BFG

Gobblefunking with words
The word *buzzy-hum* is a *compound* word, made by joining together an adjective (*buzzy*) and a noun (*hum*). You can try this yourself, pairing up your favourite adjectives with nouns to make new words that combine their meanings. For example, a *tingly-hum* would be a kind of hum that makes your lips tingly.

Centipede

JAMES AND THE GIANT PEACH

cannybull   catasterous   cave

chiddler   chocolate

cabbage noun cabbages

A cabbage is a large, round green vegetable with layers of closely packed leaves. If you overboil a cabbage, it will start to look like Aunt Sponge.
Aunt Sponge . . . had . . . one of those white flabby faces that looked exactly as though it had been boiled. She was like a great white soggy overboiled cabbage. — JAMES AND THE GIANT PEACH

DID YOU KNOW? The word *cabbage* comes from an old French word meaning 'head', so it is quite fitting that Aunt Sponge's face resembles one.

cacao noun

Cacao beans grow on trees in tropical countries and are used to make cocoa and chocolate.
'The cacao bean,' Mr Wonka continued, 'which grows on the cacao tree, happens to be the thing from which all chocolate is made.' — CHARLIE AND THE CHOCOLATE FACTORY

DID YOU KNOW? The words *cacao*, *cocoa* and *chocolate* all come from a Mexican language called Nahuatl (which rhymes with *cattle*), because chocolate was first created and drunk in ancient Mexico.

cackle verb cackles, cackling, cackled

When someone cackles, they laugh in a loud and harsh way.
'I told you I was watching you,' cackled Mrs Twit. 'I've got eyes everywhere so you'd better be careful.' — THE TWITS

LOOK IT UP! For some other ways that people laugh, see **laugh**.

cage noun **cages**
a box or small room with bars across it that some people use for keeping animals or birds
Muggle-Wump and his family longed to escape from the cage in Mr Twit's garden and go back to the African jungle where they came from. — THE TWITS

cake noun **cakes**
A sweet food that you make with flour, fat, eggs and sugar and bake in the oven. Miss Trunchbull is particularly fond of cake.
'You do not leave this platform and nobody leaves this hall until you have eaten the entire cake that is sitting there in front of you!' — MATILDA

calculate verb **calculates, calculating, calculated**
When you calculate something, you do a sum to work it out.
The walls were perpendicular and engineers had calculated that there was no way a giant could escape once he was put in. — THE BFG

calculator noun **calculators**
a machine that you use to do sums
'The human brain is an amazing thing.' 'I think it's a lot better than a lump of metal,' Matilda said. 'That's all a calculator is.' — MATILDA

calf noun **calves**
Your calf is the back part of your leg between your knee and your ankle. Miss Trunchbull has very well-developed calves.
Below the knees her calf muscles stood out like grapefruits inside her stockings. — MATILDA

calm adjective **calmer, calmest**
If the sea or the weather is calm, it is still and not stormy.
The sun was shining brightly out of a soft blue sky and the day was calm. — JAMES AND THE GIANT PEACH

calm verb **calms, calming, calmed**
When you calm down, you become quiet and stop being noisy or excited.
'Wait!' ordered Mr Fox. 'Don't lose your heads! Stand back! Calm down! Let's do this properly!' — FANTASTIC MR FOX

candyfloss noun
Candyfloss is a fluffy mass of sugar that has been spun into fine threads.
These 'things' were actually living creatures . . . who looked as though they were made out of a mixture of cotton wool and candyfloss and thin white hairs. — JAMES AND THE GIANT PEACH

cane noun **canes**
a long, thin stick made of wood
Mr Coombes was . . . a giant of a man if ever there was one, and in his hands he held a long yellow cane which curved round the top like a walking stick. — BOY

cannybull noun **cannybulls**
A cannybull is a giant who eats **human beans** (and human bones). The BFG is the only giant in Giant Country who is not a cannybull.
'P . . . please don't eat me,' Sophie stammered. The Giant let out a bellow of laughter. 'Just because I is a giant, you think I is a man-gobbling cannybull!' he shouted. — THE BFG

DID YOU KNOW? *Cannybull* is the BFG's way of saying *cannibal*, which means 'someone who eats human flesh'. To make the word, Roald Dahl may have joined together *canny*, meaning 'shrewd', and *bull*. This type of word play is called a *malapropism* and you can find more examples in the entry for **mudburger**.

cannybully adjective
A cannybully giant likes to hunt and eat **human beans**.
'Giants is all cannybully and murderful! And they does gobble up human beans!' — THE BFG

cantankerous adjective
A cantankerous person is always grumpy and bad-tempered.
There she was again, the same cantankerous grumbling old Grandma Georgina. — CHARLIE AND THE GREAT GLASS ELEVATOR

captain noun **captains**
an officer in the army or navy, or one in charge of a ship or aircraft
Captain Lancaster . . . had been a captain in the army during the war against Hitler and that was why he still called himself Captain Lancaster instead of just plain Mister. — DANNY THE CHAMPION OF THE WORLD

capture verb **captures, capturing, captured**
When you capture a person or a dream, you catch them by force and keep hold of them.
'But you told me dreams were invisible.' 'They is always invisible until they is captured,' the BFG told her. — THE BFG

car noun **cars**
A car is a machine with four wheels and an engine which people drive along roads. Danny's father repairs cars for a living (unlike Mr Wormwood who sells people cars that don't work).
People who lived miles away used to bring their cars to him for repair rather than take them to their nearest garage. — DANNY THE CHAMPION OF THE WORLD

caramel noun **caramels**
a type of sweet made from butter, milk and sugar
'Mr Willy Wonka can make marshmallows that taste of violets, and rich caramels that change colour every ten seconds as you suck them.' — CHARLIE AND THE CHOCOLATE FACTORY

a
b
c
d
e
f
g
h
i
j
k
l
m
n
o
p
q
r
s
t
u
v
w
x
y
z

You can add *-y* to some nouns to make adjectives: a *buzzy-hummy noise.*

A B C D E F G H I J K L M N O P Q R S T U V W X Y Z

caravan noun **caravans**
A caravan is a small house on wheels that can be pulled from place to place. Danny and his father live in an old caravan behind the filling-station.
The caravan was our house and our home. It was a real old gipsy wagon with big wheels and fine patterns painted all over it in yellow and red and blue. — DANNY THE CHAMPION OF THE WORLD

carbuncle noun **carbuncles**
A carbuncle is a large swollen boil on your skin, so to call someone a carbuncle is not nice at all.
'Speak up, you clotted carbuncle!' roared the Trunchbull. 'Admit that you did it!' — MATILDA
LOOK IT UP! For other ways to insult people, see **insult**.

cardigan noun **cardigans**
a knitted jumper that has buttons down the front
'Human beans from Jersey is tasting of cardigans.' 'You mean jerseys,' Sophie said. — THE BFG

careful adjective
If you are careful, you make sure that you do things safely and well so that you do not have an accident.
'Just a minute now! Listen to me! I want everybody to be very careful in this room. There is dangerous stuff around in here and you must not tamper with it.' — CHARLIE AND THE CHOCOLATE FACTORY

careless adjective
If you are careless, you are not careful and so you make mistakes or have an accident.
'They've overstretched him on the gum-stretching machine,' said Mr Wonka. 'How very careless.' — CHARLIE AND THE CHOCOLATE FACTORY

carpet noun **carpets**
a thick, soft material that is put on a floor to cover it, and sometimes on a ceiling to confuse silly people
'Pull out the carpet!' shouted Muggle-Wump. 'Pull this huge carpet out from under the furniture and stick it on to the ceiling!' — THE TWITS

carrotty adjective
orange-red in colour, like a carrot
Captain Lancaster . . . used to sit at his desk stroking his carrotty moustache and watching us with pale watery-blue eyes, searching for trouble. — DANNY THE CHAMPION OF THE WORLD

cast verb **casts, casting, cast**
If you cast something, you throw it.
Gradually it grew darker and darker, and then a pale three-quarter moon came up over the tops of the clouds and cast an eerie light over the whole scene. — JAMES AND THE GIANT PEACH

catapult noun **catapults**
a small weapon made from a forked stick and a piece of elastic, used for shooting pellets or small stones
As well as tuck, a tuck-box would also contain all manner of treasures such as . . . a catapult, some foreign stamps, a couple of stink-bombs. — BOY

catapult verb **catapults, catapulting, catapulted**
If something is catapulted through the air, it is thrown forcefully, as if by a catapult.
My brother and one sister landed on the bonnet of the car, someone else was catapulted out on the road and at least one small sister landed in the middle of the hawthorn hedge. — BOY

catasterous adjective
A catasterous situation is very bad indeed, and a catasterous disastrophe is the worst of all.
'Catasterous!' cried the BFG. 'Upgoing bubbles is a catasterous disastrophe!' — THE BFG

Gobblefunking with words
The phrase *catasterous disastrophe* is known as a *spoonerism*, and you can find more examples of this type of word play in the entry for **mideous**.

catch verb **catches, catching, caught**
1 If you catch something, like a dream as it whiffles through the air, you get hold of it.
'You can't collect a dream,' Sophie said. 'A dream isn't something you can catch hold of.' — THE BFG
2 If you catch an illness, you get it.
'We may see a Creature with forty-nine heads/Who lives in the desolate snow,/And whenever he catches a cold (which he dreads)/He has forty-nine noses to blow.' — JAMES AND THE GIANT PEACH

caterpillar noun **caterpillars**
A caterpillar is a small animal that looks like a worm and will turn into a butterfly or moth. The BFG calls them **cattlepiddlers**.
'Cabbage doesn't taste of anything without a few boiled caterpillars in it.' — GEORGE'S MARVELLOUS MEDICINE
DID YOU KNOW? Caterpillar is thought to come from an old French word meaning 'hairy cat'.

catspringer noun catspringers
The catspringer is a fast-moving creature that lives in a burrow and is hunted by witches, who use its tongue to make Formula 86 Delayed Action Mouse-Maker.
'We will spear the blabbersnitch and trap the crabcruncher and shoot the grobblesquirt and catch the catspringer in his burrow!' – THE WITCHES

LOOK IT UP! Some other creatures that are hunted by witches are the **crabcruncher** and the **grobblesquirt**.

cattaloo noun cattaloos
The cattaloo is a rare and ancient animal from South America whose bones are an ingredient in Vita-Wonk.
'I . . . rushed all over the world collecting special items from the oldest living things . . . THE KNUCKLEBONES OF A 700-YEAR-OLD CATTALOO FROM PERU . . . ' – CHARLIE AND THE GREAT GLASS ELEVATOR

DID YOU KNOW? Roald Dahl invented the word *cattaloo* but he may have based it on *cattalo*, an animal that is a cross between a cow and a buffalo.

cattlepiddler noun cattlepiddlers
In Giant Country, cattlepiddlers grow into **butteryflies**.
'One of the biggest chatbags is the cattlepiddlers,' the BFG said . . . 'They is argying all the time about who is going to be the prettiest butterfly.' – THE BFG

DID YOU KNOW? Outside Giant Country, *cattlepiddler* sounds very funny and a bit rude. Roald Dahl probably based it on *cattle* and *piddle*, which is an informal word for 'pass urine'.

cattypiddler noun cattypiddlers
A cattypiddler is a wild creature, perhaps a kind of big cat.
'And you is absolutely sure the Queen will not put me in a zoo with all the cattypiddlers?' 'Of course she won't,' Sophie said. – THE BFG

DON'T BE BIFFSQUIGGLED! Take care not to confuse **cattypiddler** with **cattlepiddler** which is the BFG's name for a caterpillar (not usually found in zoos).

cauldron noun cauldrons
A cauldron is a large, round cooking pot, usually made of iron. The Grand High Witch does not use a cauldron, but Willy Wonka does, for making Wonka-Vite.
Place chocolate in very large cauldron and melt over red-hot furnace. When melted, lower the heat slightly so as not to burn the chocolate, but keep it boiling. – CHARLIE AND THE GREAT GLASS ELEVATOR

cavalcade noun cavalcades
a procession of vehicles or people on horseback
After a rapid breakfast, our cavalcade left the Grand Hotel in three more taxis and headed for Oslo docks. – BOY

cave noun caves
A cave is a large natural hole in the side of a hill or cliff, or under the ground. Giants and Cloud-Men live in caves, as did ancient **human beans**, and the BFG has a secret cave in which he stores his bottles of dreams.
The Giant . . . stopped and turned and rolled the great stone back into place so that the entrance to his secret cave was completely hidden from outside. – THE BFG

cavern noun caverns
A cavern is a large cave, and something as large as a cavern is said to be **cavernous**.
Sophie blinked and stared. She saw an enormous cavern with a high rocky roof. – THE BFG

ceiling noun ceilings
the part of a room above your head (or below Mr and Mrs Twits' heads, after the Great Glue Painting)
The great glue painting of the ceiling began. All the other birds who had been sitting on the roof flew in to help, carrying paint-brushes in their claws and beaks. – THE TWITS

celebrate verb celebrates, celebrating, celebrated
When you celebrate, you do something special to mark an important day or event.
Mr Twit, who thought he had seen his ugly wife for the last time, was sitting in the garden celebrating. – THE TWITS

cell noun cells
a small room in which a prisoner is kept in a prison
They certainly never gave him any toys to play with or any picture books to look at. His room was as bare as a prison cell. – JAMES AND THE GIANT PEACH

cellar noun cellars
A cellar is a room underneath a building used for storing things. Cellars are usually cold and dark, which is why the cruel Mrs Clonkers locks Sophie and other **norphans** in the cellar as a punishment.
'Bean's Secret Cider Cellar,' said Mr Fox. 'But go carefully, my dears. Don't make a noise. This cellar is right underneath the farmhouse itself.' – FANTASTIC MR FOX

cement noun
Cement is the stuff that builders use to hold bricks together. Cement is usually made from lime and clay, but Willy Wonka makes it from chocolate (of course).
The bricks were chocolate, and the cement holding them together was chocolate, and the windows were chocolate, and all the walls and ceilings were made of chocolate. – CHARLIE AND THE CHOCOLATE FACTORY

The word *caravan* originally meant 'a group of people travelling across a desert'.

Centipede (JAMES AND THE GIANT PEACH)

A centipede is a small crawling creature with a long body and many legs. The Centipede who lives in the Giant Peach has forty-two legs (not a hundred) and wears forty-two boots which take him hours to remove.

DID YOU KNOW? The word *centipede* is based on Latin and means 'a hundred feet', even though some centipedes have as few as thirty legs.

century noun centuries

a period of one hundred years
'She's going crazy!' said Mr Bucket. 'Not at all,' said Mr Wonka. 'She's going through the nineteenth century.' — CHARLIE AND THE GREAT GLASS ELEVATOR

cereal noun cereals

A breakfast cereal is a dry food made from wheat, oats or rice (not usually pencil shavings) that you eat with milk for breakfast.
'Oh, my sainted aunt!' cried Mr Wonka. '. . . Do you know what breakfast cereal is made of? It's made of all those little curly wooden shavings you find in pencil sharpeners!' — CHARLIE AND THE CHOCOLATE FACTORY

chain noun chains

a line of metal rings fastened together to form a rope
'So what you soldiers has to do is to creep up to the giants while they is still in the Land of Noddy and tie their arms and legs with mighty ropes and whunking chains.' — THE BFG

chalk noun chalks

a white or coloured stick for writing on a blackboard
Nigel . . . jumped to his feet and started pointing excitedly at the blackboard and screaming, 'The chalk! The chalk! Look at the chalk! It's moving all on its own!' — MATILDA

chambermaid noun chambermaids

a woman employed to clean bedrooms in a hotel
On the very first morning after our arrival, the chambermaid was making my bed when one of my mice poked its head out from under the sheets. — THE WITCHES

champion noun champions

the person who has won a game or competition and shown that they are the best
'Danny did it!' my father said proudly. 'My son Danny is the champion of the world.' — DANNY THE CHAMPION OF THE WORLD

chance noun chances

When something happens by chance, it just happens, with no one planning or organizing it.
If by some extraordinary chance you should one day wander into a forest and catch a glimpse of a Minpin, then hold your breath and thank your lucky stars. — THE MINPINS

chandelier noun chandeliers

a decorative light fitting with lots of bulbs which hangs from the ceiling
Crash went his head right into the chandelier. A shower of glass fell upon the poor BFG. 'Gunghummers and bogswinkles!' he cried. 'What was that?' — THE BFG

chant verb chants, chanting, chanted

If you chant words, you say them in a special rhythm.
George found himself dancing around the steaming pot, chanting strange words that came into his head out of nowhere. — GEORGE'S MARVELLOUS MEDICINE

chaos noun

When there is chaos, everything is very confused and no one knows what is happening.
'Classrooms vill all be svorrming vith mice!' shouted The Grand High Witch. 'Chaos and pandemonium vill be rrreigning in every school in Inkland!' — THE WITCHES

character noun characters

a person, animal or other creature that features in a story
The characters in this book are: HUMANS: THE QUEEN OF ENGLAND . . . SOPHIE, an orphan . . . And, of course, THE BFG. — THE BFG

charge noun

If you are in charge of something, you have the job of organizing it or looking after it.
'Something always goes wrong.' 'Not when I'm in charge of it, sir,' said Mr Wonka. — CHARLIE AND THE GREAT GLASS ELEVATOR

charge verb charges, charging, charged

1 If you charge for something, you ask for money for doing it.
'We gobble up all the nasty little insects that are gobbling up all the farmer's crops . . . and we ourselves don't charge a penny for our services.' — JAMES AND THE GIANT PEACH

2 If you charge at someone, you rush at them suddenly.
Humpy-Rumpy charged straight at the Enormous Crocodile. He caught him with his giant head and sent him tumbling and skidding over the ground. — THE ENORMOUS CROCODILE

Charlie Bucket (CHARLIE AND THE CHOCOLATE FACTORY & GREAT GLASS ELEVATOR)
Charlie Bucket lives with his parents and four elderly grandparents in a tiny house. They have very little money and Charlie dreams of one day seeing inside Willy Wonka's famous and magical Chocolate Factory.

chase verb **chases, chasing, chased**
When you chase someone, you run after them and try to catch them.
'We've absolutely got to stop them!' Sophie cried. 'Put me back in your pocket quick and we'll chase after them and warn everyone in England they're coming.' — THE BFG

chat noun **chats**
A chat is a friendly conversation.
When the Roly-Poly Bird came swooping in for an evening chat, they shouted out, 'Don't land on our cage, Roly-Poly Bird! It's covered in sticky glue!' — THE TWITS

chatbag noun **chatbags**
A chatbag is someone who never stops talking. Some creatures are chatbags, too, but only the BFG can hear them with his **extra-usual** ears.
'Who else do you hear?' Sophie asked. 'One of the biggest chatbags is the cattlepiddlers,' the BFG said. — THE BFG

chatter verb **chatters, chattering, chattered**
If you chatter, you talk a lot about things that are not very important. The BFG calls it **chittering**.

chatter noun
Chatter is the sound of people chattering.
There was a buzz of excited chatter and a lot of running about and waving of arms. — CHARLIE AND THE GREAT GLASS ELEVATOR

chatterbox noun **chatterboxes**
If someone calls you a chatterbox, it means that they think you talk too much.
The parents, instead of applauding her, called her a noisy chatterbox and told her sharply that small girls should be seen and not heard. — MATILDA

chauffeur noun **chauffeurs**
someone who is paid to drive a large smart car for someone rich or important
The chauffeur said, 'His Grace the Duke of Hampshire has instructed me to deliver this envelope to The Ladderless Window-Cleaning Company.' — THE GIRAFFE AND THE PELLY AND ME

cheap adjective **cheaper, cheapest**
Something that is cheap does not cost very much money.
'I got, I really don't know how,/A super trade-in for our cow.'/The mother said, 'You little creep,/I'll bet you sold her much too cheap.' — REVOLTING RHYMES

cheat verb **cheats, cheating, cheated**
If you cheat in a game or test, you break the rules so that you can do well.
'You may be permitted to cheat and lie and swindle in your own homes,' he went on, 'but I will not put up with it here!' — DANNY THE CHAMPION OF THE WORLD

Matilda and the BFG are *eponymous* characters. Find out more at **hero**.

cheat noun **cheats**
someone who cheats in a game or test
'You . . . you little cheat!' the father suddenly shouted, pointing at her with his finger. 'You looked at my bit of paper!' – MATILDA

cheek noun **cheeks**
1 Your cheeks are the sides of your face.
The colour was rushing to his cheeks, and his eyes were wide open, shining with joy. – CHARLIE AND THE CHOCOLATE FACTORY
2 Cheek is talking or behaving in a rude way towards a grown-up.
'Me! A baby!' shouted the Trunchbull. 'How dare you suggest such a thing! What cheek! What infernal insolence!' – MATILDA

cheeky adjective **cheekier, cheekiest**
If a grown-up calls you cheeky, they think you have done something rude, or that you do not respect them.
'Nasty cheeky lot, these little 'uns!' I heard Mrs Pratchett muttering. – BOY

cheer verb **cheers, cheering, cheered**
When you cheer, or cheer someone, you shout to show that you are pleased with what they have done.
Minpins from all over the forest had flown in on their birds to cheer the young hero, and all the branches and twigs of the great tree were crowded with tiny people. – THE MINPINS

cheerful adjective
If you are cheerful, you are happy.
'But my dear friends!' cried the Old-Green-Grasshopper, trying to be cheerful. 'We are there!' – JAMES AND THE GIANT PEACH

cheese noun **cheeses**
a food that is made from milk and has a strong, salty taste (and is therefore good for disguising the taste of worms)
The worms didn't show because everything was covered with tomato sauce and sprinkled with cheese. – THE TWITS

chest of drawers noun **chests of drawers**
a piece of furniture used for storage
For furniture, we had two chairs and a small table, and those, apart from a tiny chest of drawers, were all the home comforts we possessed. – DANNY THE CHAMPION OF THE WORLD

chew verb **chews, chewing, chewed**
When you chew food, you keep biting on it in your mouth before you swallow it.
'It's luscious, it's super,/It's mushious, it's duper,/It's better than rotten old fish./You mash it and munch it,/You chew it and crunch it!/It's lovely to hear it go squish!' – THE ENORMOUS CROCODILE

chewing-gum noun
a sticky, flavoured type of sweet for chewing, and chewing, and chewing, and chewing
Violet Beauregarde, before tasting her blade of grass, took the piece of world-record-breaking chewing-gum out of her mouth and stuck it carefully behind her ear. – CHARLIE AND THE CHOCOLATE FACTORY

chick noun **chicks**
a baby bird
In less than a minute, the hen had shrunk so much it was no bigger than a new-hatched chick. – GEORGE'S MARVELLOUS MEDICINE

chicken noun **chickens**
A chicken is a bird that is kept on farms for its meat and eggs. It is the favourite food of Mr Fox and his family.
The whole place was teeming with chickens. There were white chickens and brown chickens and black chickens by the thousand! – FANTASTIC MR FOX

chiddler noun **chiddlers**
a young **human bean**, not yet a grown-up
'Little chiddlers is not so tough to eat as old grandmamma, so says the Childchewing Giant.' – THE BFG
DID YOU KNOW? The word *chiddler* sounds a bit like *childer*, an old form of *children* which is still used in some dialects.
RINGBELLING RHYMES Try rhyming with *cattlepiddler*.

chief noun **chiefs**
a leader who is in charge of other people
The entire Cabinet was present. The Chief of the Army was there, together with four other generals. – CHARLIE AND THE GREAT GLASS ELEVATOR

child noun **children**
1 a young boy or girl
The witching hour . . . was a special moment in the middle of the night when every child and every grown-up was in a deep deep sleep. – THE BFG
2 Someone's child is their son or daughter.
Mr Fox looked at the four Small Foxes and he smiled. What fine children I have, he thought. – FANTASTIC MR FOX

Childchewer or **Childchewing Giant** (THE BFG)
The Childchewer is one of the not-so-friendly giants in Giant Country. His favourite food is young **human beans**, whose flesh he enjoys chewing.
LOOK IT UP! Some other man-gobbling giants are the **Meatdripper** and the **Gizzardgulper**.

childish adjective
Someone who is childish behaves like a young child, in a way that grown-ups think is silly.
'But I can't help it if I'm growing fast, Grandma,' George said. 'Of course you can,' she snapped. 'Growing's a nasty childish habit.' – GEORGE'S MARVELLOUS MEDICINE

A B C D E F G H I J K L M N O P Q R S T U V W X Y Z

chilly adjective **chillier, chilliest**
slightly cold
To the Duke, because the weather was a little chilly, I gave some Scarlet Scorchdroppers that had been sent to me from Iceland. — THE GIRAFFE AND THE PELLY AND ME

chimney noun **chimneys**
a tall pipe that takes smoke away from a fire inside a building
One day, early in the morning, thin columns of white smoke were seen to be coming out of the tops of the tall chimneys of the factory! — CHARLIE AND THE CHOCOLATE FACTORY

chin noun **chins**
Your chin is the part at the bottom of your face, under your mouth.
Bunce . . . was so short his chin would have been underwater in the shallow end of any swimming-pool in the world. — FANTASTIC MR FOX

chitter verb **chitters, chittering, chittered**
If you chitter, you chat or talk about unimportant things.
'Stay there please,' he said, 'and no chittering. I is needing to listen only to silence when I is mixing up such a knotty plexicated dream as this.' — THE BFG

chocolate noun **chocolates**
Chocolate is a sweet that is made from cocoa (from **cacao** beans) and sugar. It is made into bars and all sorts of other shapes for eating, drinking or baking. Willy Wonka can make anything you can imagine (and probably some things you can't) out of chocolate.

Charlie could see great slabs of chocolate piled up high in the shop windows, and he would stop and stare and press his nose against the glass. — CHARLIE AND THE CHOCOLATE FACTORY

Chocolate Factory (CHARLIE AND THE CHOCOLATE FACTORY)
The Chocolate Factory belongs to the genius confectioner Willy Wonka. It is the largest chocolate factory in the world, but no one has ever seen inside it, until the day that Mr Wonka opens it to the five lucky Golden Ticket holders.

Chocolate Room (CHARLIE AND THE CHOCOLATE FACTORY)
The Chocolate Room is the second most important room (after the **Inventing Room**) in Willy Wonka's factory. Everything in it is edible, including a frothy chocolate waterfall and a river of hot melted chocolate.

chocolatey adjective
Something that is chocolatey tastes or smells of chocolate.
On his way to and from school, little Charlie Bucket . . . would hold his nose high in the air and take long deep sniffs of the gorgeous chocolatey smell all around him. — CHARLIE AND THE CHOCOLATE FACTORY

chocolatier noun **chocolatiers**
A chocolatier is someone who makes and sells chocolate creations, like the ingenious Willy Wonka.

choke verb **chokes, choking, choked**
When you choke, you cannot breathe properly.
A fiery fearsome smell filled the kitchen. It made George choke and splutter. — GEORGE'S MARVELLOUS MEDICINE

Chokey (MATILDA)
The Chokey is a small, narrow and terrifying cupboard in which Miss Trunchbull likes to lock children as a punishment. The walls have pieces of broken glass stuck into them, and the door is covered with sharp nails.
DID YOU KNOW? *Chokey* is an Anglo-Indian word meaning 'police station' or 'prison'.

chomp verb **chomps, chomping, chomped**
When you chomp, you eat or chew noisily.
The new tortoise was still chomping away at the lettuce. 'My my, Alfie, you do seem hungry today,' Mrs Silver was saying. — ESIO TROT

chop verb **chops, chopping, chopped**
When you chop something, you cut it with a knife or axe.
He picked up the chopper and was just about to start chopping away again when he heard a shout behind him that made him stop and turn. — JAMES AND THE GIANT PEACH

chop noun **chops**
a thick slice of pork or lamb with a bone attached to it
'One giant chicken will make a hundred fried chicken dinners, and one giant pig will give you a thousand pork chops!' — GEORGE'S MARVELLOUS MEDICINE

Chopper (MATILDA)
Chopper is a talking pet parrot who belongs to Matilda's friend Fred. Matilda borrows him for a night in order to play a trick on her dim-witted parents.
DID YOU KNOW? Roald Dahl had a pet Jack Russell terrier called *Chopper*.

chortle verb **chortles, chortling, chortled**
When you chortle, you chuckle loudly.
Charlie Kinch started chuckling and chortling so much he nearly drove off the track. — DANNY THE CHAMPION OF THE WORLD
DID YOU KNOW? The word *chortle* was coined by Lewis Carroll in his poem *Jabberwocky*, perhaps as a blend of *chuckle* and *snort*.

chorus verb **choruses, chorusing, chorused**
When a group of people chorus something, they all say it at the same time.
'Children are foul and filthy!' thundered The Grand High Witch. 'They are! They are!' chorused the English witches. 'They are foul and filthy!' — THE WITCHES

Chocolate comes from the Nahuatl (Mexican) word *chocolatl*.

A B C D E F G H I J K L M N O P Q R S T U V W X Y Z

chrysalis noun **chrysalises**
the hard cover that a caterpillar makes round itself before it changes into a butterfly or moth
'Your son Wilfred has spent six years as a grub in this school and we are still waiting for him to emerge from the chrysalis.'—MATILDA

chuckle verb **chuckles, chuckling, chuckled**
When you chuckle, you laugh quietly to yourself.
'Tell Charlie about that crazy Indian prince,' said Grandma Josephine. 'He'd like to hear that.' 'You mean Prince Pondicherry?' said Grandpa Joe, and he began chuckling with laughter.—CHARLIE AND THE CHOCOLATE FACTORY
LOOK IT UP! For some other ways that people laugh, see **laugh**.

churgle verb **churgles, churgling, churgled**
When you churgle, you gurgle with laughter.
The fact that it was none other than Boggis's chickens they were going to eat made them churgle with laughter every time they thought of it.—FANTASTIC MR FOX
DID YOU KNOW? The word *churgle* is a blend of **chuckle** and **gurgle**.

chute noun **chutes**
A chute is a long open tube that you slide down for fun, or that you can throw rubbish down.
'Where are they taking her?' shrieked Mrs Salt. 'She's going where all the other bad nuts go,' said Mr Willy Wonka. 'Down the rubbish chute.'—CHARLIE AND THE CHOCOLATE FACTORY

cider noun
an alcoholic drink made from apples, much loved by Farmer Bean, who keeps gallons of it in his Secret Cider Cellar

Bean was a turkey-and-apple farmer . . .
He never ate any food at all. Instead, he drank gallons of strong cider which he made from the apples in his orchard.—FANTASTIC MR FOX

cigar noun **cigars**
a roll of compressed tobacco leaves, very rarely smoked by grandmothers
My grandmother was the only grandmother I ever met who smoked cigars. She lit one now, a long black cigar that smelt of burning rubber.—THE WITCHES

circle verb **circles, circling, circled**
When birds or Knids circle, they fly round and round in a loop.
Away in the distance, in the deep blue sky of outer space, they saw a massive cloud of Vermicious Knids wheeling and circling like a fleet of bombers.—CHARLIE AND THE GREAT GLASS ELEVATOR
RINGBELLING RHYMES Not many words rhyme with *circle*, but you can make up your own, such as *flircle* (a round flake of snow) or *gircle* (a very round girl, like Violet as a blueberry).

circus noun **circuses**
A circus is a show in which clowns, acrobats, and sometimes animals, perform in a large tent. Mr Twit used to work in a circus and dreams of owning the world's first UPSIDE DOWN MONKEY CIRCUS.
What on earth were Mr and Mrs Twit doing with monkeys in their garden? Well, in the old days, they had both worked in a circus as monkey trainers.—THE TWITS

clank verb **clanks, clanking, clanked**
When something clanks, it makes a loud sound like heavy pieces of metal banging together.
Soon, two enormous caterpillar tractors with mechanical shovels on their front ends came clanking into the wood. Bean was driving one, Bunce the other.—FANTASTIC MR FOX

class noun **classes**
a group of children who have lessons together in a school
From where I was standing I could see the whole class sitting absolutely rigid, watching Captain Lancaster. Nobody dared move.—DANNY THE CHAMPION OF THE WORLD

classroom noun **classrooms**
a room where you have lessons in a school
From the back of the classroom Miss Honey cried out, 'Miss Trunchbull! Don't! Please let him go! His ears might come off!'—MATILDA

claw noun **claws**
An animal's or a witch's claws are its sharp nails. Animals can sometimes retract their claws, but witches have to hide theirs inside gloves.
'Instead of finger-nails, she has thin curvy claws, like a cat, and she wears the gloves to hide them.'—THE WITCHES

clean adjective **cleaner, cleanest**
Something that is clean has no dirt on it.
'You even make your mother shrink/Because of your unholy stink!'/Jack answered,/'Well, if you're so clean/Why don't you climb the crazy bean.'—REVOLTING RHYMES

clean verb **cleans, cleaning, cleaned**
When you clean something, you take the dirt off it.
'We must go, too,' said the Giraffe. 'We have one hundred windows to clean before dark.'—THE GIRAFFE AND THE PELLY AND ME

clear adjective **clearer, clearest**
1 If water or glass is clear, it is not dirty and you can see through it.
'The whole lift is made of thick, clear glass!' Mr Wonka declared. 'Walls, doors, ceiling, floor, everything is made of glass so that you can see out!'—CHARLIE AND THE CHOCOLATE FACTORY
2 If something is clear, you can understand it.
'My orders are that every single child in this country shall be rrrubbed out, sqvashed, sqvirted, sqvittered and frrrittered before I come here again in vun year's time! Do I make myself clear?'—THE WITCHES
3 If a place or a view is clear, there is nothing blocking it or getting in the way.
The moon had long since disappeared but the sky was clear and a great mass of stars was wheeling above my head.—DANNY THE CHAMPION OF THE WORLD

clear verb **clears, clearing, cleared**
If you clear a place, you get rid of things that are in the way.
'Out of my way! Clear the decks! Stand back, all you miserable midgets!' – GEORGE'S MARVELLOUS MEDICINE

clench verb **clenches, clenching, clenched**
When you clench your teeth or fists, you close them tightly.
'Hey!' he cried, grabbing my left wrist. 'What's happened to your hand?' 'It's nothing,' I said, clenching the fist.
– DANNY THE CHAMPION OF THE WORLD

clever adjective **cleverer, cleverest**
Someone who is clever, or who has a clever brain, learns things quickly and easily.
Mr Wonka stood very still, and although his face looked calm, you can be quite sure his clever inventive brain was spinning like a dynamo. – CHARLIE AND THE GREAT GLASS ELEVATOR

click verb **clicks, clicking, clicked**
When something clicks, it makes a short sound like the sound of a light switch.
Mr Wonka turned around and clicked his fingers sharply, click, click, click, three times. Immediately, an Oompa-Loompa appeared. – CHARLIE AND THE CHOCOLATE FACTORY

cliff noun **cliffs**
a steep hill made of rock next to the sea
The peach was now only a hundred yards away ... and when it reached the edge of the cliff it seemed to leap up into the sky and hang there suspended for a few seconds. – JAMES AND THE GIANT PEACH

cling verb **clings, clinging, clung**
When something clings to something else, it holds on to it very tightly.
Things cling to hairs, especially food. Things like gravy go right in among the hairs and stay there. – THE TWITS

cloak noun **cloaks**
A cloak is a piece of clothing that you wrap around your shoulders and fasten round your neck. The BFG wears an old black cloak that streams out behind him as he lollops along.
I saw this tremendous tall person running along the crest of the hill. He had a queer long-striding lolloping gait and his black cloak was streaming out behind him like the wings of a bird. – DANNY THE CHAMPION OF THE WORLD

clockcoach noun **clockcoaches**
A clockcoach is a type of insect found in Giant Country that looks like a beetle. **Human beans** call them *cockroaches*.
Sophie took a small nibble ... 'It tastes of frogskins!' she gasped ... 'Worse than that!' cried the BFG, roaring with laughter. 'To me it is tasting of clockcoaches and slime-wanglers!' – THE BFG

DID YOU KNOW? The word *clock* is used in some dialects to mean 'a beetle', and there are dialect names for insects that also begin with *clock*, such as *clock-bee* for 'a flying beetle' and *clock-leddy* for 'a ladybird'.

Clonkers, Mrs (THE BFG)
Mrs Clonkers is the horrible head of the **norphanage** where Sophie lives. She dislikes children so much that she locks them in a dark cellar if they break her rules.

clot noun *(informal)* **clots**
a very stupid person
Oh, what a beastly horrid King!/The people longed to do him in!/And so a dozen brainy men/Met secretly inside a den/To formulate a subtle plot/To polish off this royal clot. – RHYME STEW

cloud noun **clouds**
Clouds are the large grey or white areas of water vapour that sometimes float high in the sky.
Clouds like mountains towered high above their heads

on all sides, mysterious, menacing, overwhelming. — JAMES AND THE GIANT PEACH

Cloud-Men (JAMES AND THE GIANT PEACH)

The Cloud-Men are wispy ghost-like creatures who live in the clouds and throw snow and hailstones down on to the world below.

clump noun clumps

A clump of trees or bushes is a group of them growing close together.

Graceful trees and bushes were growing along the riverbanks — weeping willows and alders and tall clumps of rhododendrons with their pink and red and mauve blossoms. — CHARLIE AND THE CHOCOLATE FACTORY

clump verb clumps, clumping, clumped

When a giant clumps, he moves with heavy and noisy steps (as giants usually do).

The creature came clumping into the cave and stood towering over the BFG. 'Who was you jabbeling to in here just now?' he boomed. — THE BFG

clumsy adjective clumsier, clumsiest

If you are clumsy, you are not careful and so are likely to drop things or knock them over.

'If you great clumsy brutes come messing about in here we'll all be caught!' — FANTASTIC MR FOX

clutch verb clutches, clutching, clutched

When you clutch something, you hold on to it very tightly.

George was still clutching the medicine bottle in one hand and the spoon in the other. — GEORGE'S MARVELLOUS MEDICINE

coarse adjective coarser, coarsest

Something that is coarse has a rough or hard texture.

The massive thighs which emerged from out of the smock were encased in a pair of extraordinary breeches, bottle-green in colour and made of coarse twill. — MATILDA

coast noun coasts

the land that is right next to the sea

Below them, the sea is deep and cold and hungry. Many ships have been swallowed up and lost for ever on this part of the coast. — JAMES AND THE GIANT PEACH

cockatootloo noun cockatootloos

a quiet and docile animal that lives in Giant Country

'If an animal is very fierce and you is putting it in a cage, it will make a tremendous rumpledumpus. If it is a nice animal like a cockatootloo or a fogglefrump, it will sit quietly.' — THE BFG

cockatrice noun cockatrices

The cockatrice is a legendary creature with the body of a dragon and the head of a cockerel. The tail of a cockatrice is a vital ingredient in Wonka-Vite.

THE HORN OF A COW (IT MUST BE A LOUD HORN)/THE FRONT TAIL OF A COCKATRICE/SIX OUNCES OF SPRUNGE FROM A YOUNG SLIMESCRAPER. — CHARLIE AND THE GREAT GLASS ELEVATOR

cockerel noun cockerels

a male chicken

The cockerel's body hadn't grown at all. But the neck was now about six feet long. — GEORGE'S MARVELLOUS MEDICINE

cockles adjective

completely mad

'So this is the filthing rotsome glubbage you is eating!' boomed the Bloodbottler . . . 'You must be cockles to be guzzling such rubbsquash!' — THE BFG

cocoa noun

Cocoa is a brown powder that tastes of chocolate, used for making hot chocolate drinks and chocolate cakes and biscuits.

He spooned cocoa powder and sugar into two mugs, doing it very slowly and levelling each spoonful as though he were measuring medicine. — DANNY THE CHAMPION OF THE WORLD

coconut noun coconuts

A coconut is a big, round, hard nut that grows on palm trees. It is brown and hairy on the outside and it has sweet, white flesh inside that you can eat.

The Enormous Crocodile . . . knew that children from the town often came here looking for coconuts. — THE ENORMOUS CROCODILE

coil verb coils, coiling, coiled

If you coil something (or your body, if you are an earthworm or a Knid), you wind it round and round in rings or circles.

The poor Earthworm . . . coiled himself around James's body in a panic and refused to unwind. — JAMES AND THE GIANT PEACH

coin noun coins

a piece of metal money

Charlie took the little silver coin, and slipped quickly out of the room. — CHARLIE AND THE CHOCOLATE FACTORY

cold adjective colder, coldest

1 Something that is cold is not hot.
The four old ones lay silent and huddled in their bed, trying to keep the cold out of their bones. – CHARLIE AND THE CHOCOLATE FACTORY

2 A cold look or expression is far from friendly.
The eyes of a Knid are always cold, despite being fiery red in colour.
The red pupils . . . began travelling slowly across to Charlie and Grandpa Joe and the others by the bed, settling upon them and gazing at them with a cold malevolent stare. – CHARLIE AND THE GREAT GLASS ELEVATOR

cold noun colds

an illness that makes you sneeze and gives you a runny nose
'Augustus!' shouted Mrs Gloop. 'You'll be giving that nasty cold of yours to about a million people all over the country!' – CHARLIE AND THE CHOCOLATE FACTORY

collapse verb collapses, collapsing, collapsed

1 If something collapses, it falls down.
I shone my light around the top of the pit and saw . . . how the whole thing had collapsed when my father stepped on it. – DANNY THE CHAMPION OF THE WORLD

2 If someone collapses, they fall or slump over because they are ill or tired.
'Show your father the fifth and last Golden Ticket in the world!' 'Let me see it, Charlie,' Mr Bucket said, collapsing into a chair and holding out his hand. – CHARLIE AND THE CHOCOLATE FACTORY

collect verb collects, collecting, collected

1 If you collect things, you get them and keep them together.
'Now hang on a minute,' Sophie said. 'Where do you get these dreams?' 'I collect them,' the BFG said, waving an arm towards all the rows and rows of bottles on the shelves. – THE BFG

2 When you collect someone, you go to a place and get them.
Each bird seemed to know exactly which Minpin it was collecting, and each Minpin knew exactly which bird he or she had ordered for the morning. – THE MINPINS

collection noun collections

A collection is a set of things (such as dreams or tortoises) that someone has collected.
From his enormous collection, he easily found a seventeen-ounce tortoise and once again he made sure the shells matched in colour. – ESIO TROT

colony noun colonies

a group of ants, bats, penguins or newts
There was a muddy pond at the bottom of Lavender's garden and this was the home of a colony of newts. – MATILDA

Gobblefunking with words

A *colony of newts* is an example of a *collective noun.* Collective nouns are names that are used for certain groups, especially of birds or animals. Some other collective nouns are:

a *coven of witches*
a *gaggle of geese*
a *herd* or *tower of giraffes*
a *mischief of mice*
a *murder of crows*
a *pod of dolphins* or *pelicans*
a *troop of monkeys*

Roald Dahl uses *a pack of giants* for a group of unfriendly giants. There is no collective noun for *headmistresses*, but you can always make up your own.

colossal adjective

Something colossal is absolutely enormous.
'Your name is James, isn't it? . . . Well, James, have you ever in your life seen such a marvellous colossal Centipede as me?' – JAMES AND THE GIANT PEACH
SPARKY SYNONYMS You can also say **gigantuous**.
LOOK IT UP! For other ways to describe something colossal, see **big**.

colour noun colours

Red, green, blue and yellow are different colours.
A rich blue smoke, the colour of peacocks, rose from the surface of the liquid, and a fiery fearsome smell filled the kitchen. – GEORGE'S MARVELLOUS MEDICINE

Someone who studies clouds is a *nephologist.*

comatose adjective

If someone is comatose, they are so sleepy or tired that they can barely move or speak.

Bruce Bogtrotter . . . was sitting on his chair like some huge overstuffed grub, replete, comatose, unable to move or to speak. — MATILDA

RINGBELLING RHYMES Try rhyming with *nose* or *garden hose*.

come-uppance noun

Come-uppance is what happens when nasty people get what they deserve. It is a very useful word for describing what happens to some of Roald Dahl's characters. For example, the Greggs get their come-uppance when the birds they shoot for fun start to hunt them instead.

RINGBELLING RHYMES Try rhyming with *tuppence*.

comfortable adjective

1 If something is comfortable, it is pleasant to use or to wear and does not hurt you at all.

James got into his own hammock — and oh, how soft and comfortable it was compared with the hard bare boards that his aunts had always made him sleep upon at home. — JAMES AND THE GIANT PEACH

2 If you are comfortable, you are relaxed and are not in any pain.

Sophie had not slept for a long time. She was very tired. She was also warm and comfortable. She dozed off. — THE BFG

command verb commands, commanding, commanded

If you command someone to do something, you tell them to do it.

'Fetch me a telephone,' the Queen commanded. Mr Tibbs placed the instrument on the table. — THE BFG

common adjective commoner, commonest

Something that is common is normal and ordinary.

'Back-to-Front Dyslexia . . . is very common among tortoises, who even reverse their own name and call themselves esio trots.' — THE VICAR OF NIBBLESWICKE

common sense noun

If you have common sense, you are usually sensible and make the right decisions about what to do. Some grown-ups, like Matilda's parents, have no common sense at all.

'You must walk backwards while you are speaking, then these back-to-front words will come out frontwards or the right way round. It's common sense.' — THE VICAR OF NIBBLESWICKE

commotion noun

When there is a commotion, people are making a noise and moving about all at once.

At that moment, there was a sudden commotion among the Oompa-Loompas at the far end of the Chocolate Room. — CHARLIE AND THE GREAT GLASS ELEVATOR

compare verb compares, comparing, compared

When you compare things, you try to see how they are the same and how they are different.

*'You mean you can hear things I can't hear?' Sophie said. 'You is **deaf as a dumpling** compared with me!' cried the BFG* — THE BFG

complain verb complains, complaining, complained

If you complain (as George's grandma does a lot) you say that you are not happy about something.

She spent all day and every day sitting in her chair by the window, and she was always complaining, grousing, grouching, grumbling, griping about something or other. — GEORGE'S MARVELLOUS MEDICINE

complicated adjective

Something that is complicated is difficult to understand.

Grown-ups are complicated creatures, full of quirks and secrets. — DANNY THE CHAMPION OF THE WORLD

conceal verb conceals, concealing, concealed

If you conceal something, you hide it from other people. Witches are very good at concealing the way they look.

They have claws and bald heads and queer noses and peculiar eyes, all of which they have to conceal as best they can from the rest of the world. — THE WITCHES

concentrate verb concentrates, concentrating, concentrated
When you concentrate, you think hard about the thing you are doing.
'Keep very quiet please for this final bit. I have to concentrate awfully hard, otherwise we'll come down in the wrong place.' – CHARLIE AND THE GREAT GLASS ELEVATOR

concerned adjective
If you are concerned about something, you are worried about it, or take an interest in it.
Matilda's parents, who weren't very concerned one way or the other about their daughter's education, had forgotten to make the proper arrangements in advance. – MATILDA

concert noun concerts
a show in which people (or Grasshoppers) play music for others to listen to
'Oh, hooray! He's going to play for us!' they cried, and immediately the whole company sat themselves down in a circle around the Old Green Musician — and the concert began. – JAMES AND THE GIANT PEACH

concoct verb concocts, concocting, concocted
If you concoct something, such as a plan or magic formula, you put it together.
'Attention again!' The Grand High Witch was shouting. 'I vill now give to you the rrrecipe for concocting Formula 86 Delayed Action Mouse-Maker!' – THE WITCHES

confectionery noun
Confectionery means both chocolate and sweets. It is therefore a very useful word to describe everything that Willy Wonka makes. Someone who makes confectionery is called a **confectioner**.

confess verb confesses, confessing, confessed
If you confess, you admit that you have done something wrong.
'Own up! I want the name of the filthy little boy who put down the sugar! Own up immediately! Step forward! Confess!' – BOY

confident adjective
If you are confident, you are not nervous or afraid.
Miss Honey felt confident that she would have no difficulty in convincing Mr and Mrs Wormwood that Matilda was something very special indeed. – MATILDA

congratulate verb congratulates, congratulating, congratulated
If you congratulate someone, you tell them that you are pleased that something special has happened to them. You can also say *Congratulations!*
'Oh, I do congratulate you!' he cried. 'I really do! I'm absolutely delighted! It couldn't be better! How wonderful this is! I had a hunch, you know, right from the beginning, that it was going to be you!' – CHARLIE AND THE CHOCOLATE FACTORY

consider verb considers, considering, considered
When you consider something, you think about it carefully.
'If we pulled hard enough, we could turn him inside out and he would have a new skin!' There was a pause while the others considered this interesting proposal. – JAMES AND THE GIANT PEACH

consume verb consumes, consuming, consumed
When you consume something, you eat or drink it.
When the BFG had consumed his seventy-second fried egg, Mr Tibbs sidled up to the Queen . . . 'Chef sends his apologies, Your Majesty, and he says he has no more eggs in the kitchen.' – THE BFG

contraption noun contraptions
a strange or complicated instrument or machine, such as a Great Glass Elevator
'These skyhooks,' said Grandma Josephine. 'I assume one end is hooked on to this contraption we're riding in. Right?' – CHARLIE AND THE GREAT GLASS ELEVATOR

a
b
c
d
e
f
g
h
i
j
k
l
m
n
o
p
q
r
s
t
u
v
w
x
y
z

A B C D E F G H I J K L M N O P Q R S T U V W X Y Z

control noun **controls**
The controls are the switches and buttons that you use to make a machine work.
Charlie and Mr Wonka, as cool as two cubes of ice, were up near the ceiling working the booster-rocket controls. — CHARLIE AND THE GREAT GLASS ELEVATOR

control verb **controls, controlling, controlled**
When you control someone, you make them do exactly what you want.
'You can't imagine what it's like to be completely controlled like that by a very strong personality. It turns you to jelly.' — MATILDA

conversation noun **conversations**
When people have a conversation, they talk to each other.
Every morning, Mr Hoppy and Mrs Silver exchanged polite conversation, the one looking down from above, the other looking up, but that was as far as it ever went. — ESIO TROT

convince verb **convinces, convincing, convinced**
If you convince someone about something, you make them believe it.
Some parents . . . become so blinded by adoration they manage to convince themselves their child has qualities of genius. — MATILDA

cook verb **cooks, cooking, cooked**
When you cook food, you prepare it and heat it so that it is ready to eat.
At one o'clock, she cooked spaghetti for lunch and she mixed the worms in with the spaghetti, but only on her husband's plate. — THE TWITS

cook noun **cooks**
someone whose job is to cook
There she'd got a job, unpaid,/As general cook and parlour-maid/With seven funny little men,/Each one not more than three foot ten. — REVOLTING RHYMES

cool adjective **cooler, coolest**
Something that is cool is slightly cold.
The sun had disappeared above a film of vapour. The air was becoming cooler every minute. — THE BFG

cope verb **copes, coping, coped**
If you can cope with a situation (or a Miss Trunchbull), you can manage to stay calm whatever happens.
'Oh, do shut up, Miss Honey! . . . If you can't cope in here then you can go and find a job in some cotton-wool private school for rich brats.' — MATILDA

copy verb **copies, copying, copied**
When you copy something, you do it in the same way as it has already been done before.
And of course now when Mr Wonka invents some new and marvellous sweet, neither Mr Fickelgruber nor Mr Prodnose nor Mr Slugworth nor anybody else is able to copy it. — CHARLIE AND THE CHOCOLATE FACTORY

cork noun **corks**
something that is pushed into the top of a bottle of medicine or **frobscottle** to close it
George fetched the bottle of Grandma's real medicine from the sideboard. He took out the cork and tipped it all down the sink. — GEORGE'S MARVELLOUS MEDICINE

corn noun
the seeds of plants such as wheat, which we use as food
'In the woods, the young birds . . . are guarded by keepers and fed twice a day on the best corn until they're so fat they can hardly fly.' — DANNY THE CHAMPION OF THE WORLD

cornflakes plural noun
toasted maize flakes eaten for breakfast, usually with milk (not marmalade)
'Do calm down, my dear,' Mrs Kranky said from the other end of the table. 'And stop putting marmalade on your cornflakes.' — GEORGE'S MARVELLOUS MEDICINE

correct adjective
Something that is correct is right and has no mistakes.
'Do you know what an epicure is, Matilda?' 'It is someone who is dainty with his eating,' Matilda said. 'That is correct,' Miss Honey said. — MATILDA

correct verb **corrects, correcting, corrected**
When you correct something or someone, you find the mistakes in it and put them right.
'You is a lovely little girl, but please remember that you is not exactly Miss Knoweverything yourself.' 'I'm sorry,' Sophie said. 'I really am. It is very rude of me to keep correcting you.' — THE BFG

correctly adverb
When you do something correctly, you do it right.
'You,' she said, pointing at a tiny and rather daft little girl called Prudence, 'spell "difficulty".' Amazingly, Prudence spelled it correctly and without a moment's hesitation. — MATILDA

corridor noun **corridors**
A corridor is a passage in a building with rooms leading off it. Willy Wonka's factory has long corridors with pink walls which lead to mysterious and marvellous rooms.
Charlie Bucket found himself standing in a long corridor that stretched away in front of him as far as he could see. — CHARLIE AND THE CHOCOLATE FACTORY
DID YOU KNOW? The word *corridor* comes from Latin and means 'a running place', so it is very odd that grown-ups sometimes tell you not to run in them.

cost verb **costs, costing, cost**
The amount that something costs is the amount you have to pay to buy it.
'You can sit on my back,' said the Roly-Poly Bird . . . 'You will travel by the Roly-Poly Super Jet and it won't cost you a penny!' – THE TWITS

cosy adjective **cosier, cosiest**
A cosy place is warm and comfortable.
'Is you quite cosy down there in my pocket?' 'I'm fine,' Sophie said. – THE BFG

cottage noun **cottages**
A cottage is a small house, usually in the country.
Miss Honey lives in a tiny cottage with crumbling brick walls.
Matilda saw a narrow dirt-path leading to a tiny red-brick cottage. The cottage was so small it looked more like a doll's house than a human dwelling. – MATILDA

cough (*rhymes with* off) verb **coughs, coughing, coughed**
When you cough, you make a rough sound in your throat and push air out through your mouth.
I don't know how long I had been there but it seemed like for ever. The worst part of it was not being allowed to cough or make a sound. – THE WITCHES

count verb **counts, counting, counted**
When you count things, you use numbers to say how many there are.
'Is it really true that I can tell how old a Ladybird is by counting her spots?' – JAMES AND THE GIANT PEACH

counter noun **counters**
the table where you pay for things in a shop
These five chocolate bars may be anywhere — in any shop in any street in any town in any country in the world — upon any counter where Wonka's Sweets are sold. – CHARLIE AND THE CHOCOLATE FACTORY

country noun **countries**
1 A country is a land with its own people and laws. **Inkland**, Ireland, Australia and China are all countries, as are **Dream Country** and **Giant Country**.
'Do you know how to talk to these English birds?' Muggle-Wump asked him. 'Of course I do,' said the Roly-Poly Bird. 'It's no good going to a country and not knowing the language.' – THE TWITS
2 The country is land that is not in a town.
Perhaps if I had lived in the same street . . . instead of way out in the country, things would have been different. – DANNY THE CHAMPION OF THE WORLD

couple noun **couples**
1 two people who are married or going out with each other
'Aren't we a jolly fine couple, the two of us, and isn't he a fine figure of a man, my husband the Major?' – GOING SOLO
2 A couple of things means two of them.
'And what about a couple of nice smoked hams . . . I adore smoked ham, don't you, Badger?' – FANTASTIC MR FOX

courage noun
Courage is the feeling you have when you are not afraid, and you dare to do something difficult or dangerous. Someone who shows courage is *courageous*.
'How did you pluck up the courage to tell the aunt?' 'That was tough,' Miss Honey said. – MATILDA

coward noun **cowards**
A coward is someone who is afraid when they ought to be brave. All the giants in Giant Country, except the BFG, are terrible cowards.
The BFG, knowing what a coward the Fleshlumpeater was, saw his chance. 'You is bitten by a snake!' he shouted. – THE BFG

crabcruncher noun **crabcrunchers**
The crrrabcrrruncher is an animal that is hunted by witches, who use its claws to make Formula 86 Delayed Action Mouse-Maker. It lives on rocky cliffs and its name suggests that it crunches (and then munches) crabs.
'Vun after the other you also mix in the following items: the claw of a crrrabcrrruncher, the beak of a blabbersnitch, the snout of a grrrobblesqvirt and the tongue of a catsprrringer!' – THE WITCHES

crack noun **cracks**
1 a thin line on something where it has nearly broken, or a gap in something that is normally closed
Through a crack in the door the monkeys watched. They'd jumped right out of their cage the moment the Twits had gone inside. – THE TWITS
2 a sudden loud noise
And then crack! as one of them hit the Centipede right on the nose and crack! again as another one hit him somewhere else. – JAMES AND THE GIANT PEACH

crack verb **cracks, cracking, cracked**
When you crack something, you make a crack in it, or break it open.
The Monkey took off like an arrow, and a few seconds

later he was high up in the branches of the walnut tree, cracking the nuts and guzzling what was inside.
—THE GIRAFFE AND THE PELLY AND ME

crackle verb **crackles, crackling, crackled**
If you get crackling on something, you get started on it. You can also say *get cracking*.
'What is more, I'm getting famished. I haven't had a thing to eat for twenty-four hours.' 'Then we had better get crackling,' the BFG said, moving back towards the cave.—THE BFG

craggy adjective **craggier, craggiest**
A craggy cliff or mountain is steep and rugged.
A great, craggy mountain made entirely of fudge, with Oompa-Loompas (all roped together for safety) hacking huge hunks of fudge out of its sides.—CHARLIE AND THE CHOCOLATE FACTORY

crane noun **cranes**
a large machine for lifting heavy things
Mr Kranky telephoned the Crane Company and asked them to send their biggest crane out to the house at once.—GEORGE'S MARVELLOUS MEDICINE

crash noun **crashes**
1 an accident in which a car, lorry, train or plane hits something
This was no ordinary whizzer. It had a brake-pedal, a steering-wheel, a comfortable seat and a strong front bumper to take the shock of a crash.—DANNY THE CHAMPION OF THE WORLD
2 the noise of something falling or crashing
A white porcelain lavatory pan with the wooden seat still on it came flying out of the same window and landed with a wonderful splintering crash just beside the bathtub.—THE GIRAFFE AND THE PELLY AND ME

crash verb **crashes, crashing, crashed**
If something crashes, it bumps into something else and makes a loud noise.
With the most tremendous BANG the Enormous Crocodile crashed headfirst into the hot hot sun. — THE ENORMOUS CROCODILE

crawl verb **crawls, crawling, crawled**
When you crawl, you move along on your hands and knees.
My father got down on his hands and knees and started crawling. I followed. He moved surprisingly fast on all fours. — DANNY THE CHAMPION OF THE WORLD

crazy adjective **crazier, craziest**
Someone who is crazy does very silly or strange things. Something that is crazy is very silly or strange.
'This place I am hoping to get to is so marvellous that if I described it to you now you would go crazy with excitement.' — FANTASTIC MR FOX

creak verb **creaks, creaking, creaked**
If something creaks, it makes a rough, scraping noise when it moves or opens.
Carefully, Mr Fox began pushing up one of the floorboards. The board creaked most terribly and they all ducked down, waiting for something awful to happen. — FANTASTIC MR FOX
RINGBELLING RHYMES Try rhyming with *squeak* or *Eek!* (which you might shout if you heard a door creak).

cream noun
Cream is a thick white liquid that is taken from milk. You eat cream with fruit and other sweet foods.
A real witch gets the same pleasure from squelching a child as you get from eating a plateful of strawberries and thick cream. — THE WITCHES

crease noun **creases**
a wrinkle in someone's skin, or a fold made in material by pressing it
Her tiny face was like a pickled walnut. There were such masses of creases and wrinkles that the mouth and eyes and even the nose were sunken almost out of sight. — CHARLIE AND THE GREAT GLASS ELEVATOR

creature noun **creatures**
any animal
'Even poisnowse snakes is never killing each other,' the BFG said. 'Nor is the most fearsome creatures like tigers and rhinostossterisses.' — THE BFG
LOOK IT UP! Some creatures are the **blabbersnitch**, **quodropus** and **Skillywiggler**.

creep verb **creeps, creeping, crept**
When you creep, you move along with your body very close to the ground.
Mr Fox crept up the dark tunnel to the mouth of his hole. He poked his long handsome face out into the night air and sniffed once. — FANTASTIC MR FOX

crevice noun **crevices**
a narrow opening in a rock or wall, or a recess in a giant's ear that a girl might climb into
Sophie, still wearing only her nightie, was reclining comfortably in a crevice of the BFG's right ear.
— THE BFG

cricket noun **crickets**
1 a game in which two teams hit a ball with a bat and try to score runs by running between two wickets
A Captain of any game, whether it was football, cricket, fives or squash, had many other duties. — BOY
2 an insect that makes a shrill chirping sound
'No, that's not a grasshopper, my love. It's a cricket. And did you know that crickets have their ears in their legs?' — DANNY THE CHAMPION OF THE WORLD

crikey exclamation
You might say *crikey!* if you are surprised or amazed by something.
'Oh look, Grandpa, look!' cried Charlie. 'Squirrels!' shouted Veruca Salt. 'Crikey!' said Mike Teavee. — CHARLIE AND THE CHOCOLATE FACTORY
LOOK IT UP! There are lots more exclamations in the entry for **exclamation**.

crime noun **crimes**
something bad that a person does, which is against the law
'You have put a . . . a . . . a crocodile in my drinking water!' the Trunchbull yelled back. 'There is no worse crime in the world against a Headmistress!' — MATILDA

criminal noun **criminals**
someone who has done something bad that is against the law (or that Miss Trunchbull doesn't like)
'This poisonous pustule that you see before you is none other than a disgusting criminal, a denizen of the underworld, a member of the Mafia!' 'Who, me?' Bruce Bogtrotter said. — MATILDA

crisp adjective **crisper, crispest**
Food that is crisp is dry and breaks easily.
'My mum could make toad-in-the-hole like nobody else in the world. She did it in an enormous pan with the Yorkshire pudding very brown and crisp on top.' — DANNY THE CHAMPION OF THE WORLD

a b **c** d e f g h i j k l m n o p q r s t u v w x y z

Similes can be as *crazy as a crumpet!* Read more at **mad.**

crisp noun crisps

Crisps are thin, crisp slices of fried potato that you eat as a snack.

Hortensia . . . was eating from an extra large bag of potato crisps and digging the stuff out in handfuls. — MATILDA

croak verb croaks, croaking, croaked

When someone croaks, they speak with a deep, hoarse voice.

The old woman's head jerked up off the pillow. 'That's it!' she croaked. 'You've got it, Charlie!' — CHARLIE AND THE GREAT GLASS ELEVATOR

crockadowndilly noun crockadowndillies

the BFG's name for a crocodile

'They would be putting me into the zoo or the bunkumhouse with all those squiggling hippodumplings and crockadowndillies.' — THE BFG

DID YOU KNOW? The ending of *crockadowndilly* is similar to *daffodilly* and *daffodowndilly*, which are old dialect words for 'daffodil'.

crocodile noun crocodiles

A crocodile is a large animal that lives in rivers in some hot countries. Crocodiles are reptiles, and have short legs, a long body and sharp teeth.

In the biggest brownest muddiest river in Africa, two crocodiles lay with their heads just above the water. One of the crocodiles was enormous. The other was not so big. — THE ENORMOUS CROCODILE

crodscollop noun

a food that tastes delicious

'They say the English is tasting ever so wonderfully of crodscollop.' 'I'm not sure I quite know what that means,' Sophie said. — THE BFG

DID YOU KNOW? *Crodscollop* sounds like a mixture of *cod* and *scallop* (a type of shellfish), so perhaps *crodscollop* is a delicious fishy dish. It also sounds a bit like *codswallop*, which means 'nonsense'.

crodsquinkled adjective

If a giant is crodsquinkled, he is in a hopeless situation.

'I is slopgroggled!' squawked the Gizzardgulper. 'I is crodsquinkled!' yowled the Bloodbottler. — THE BFG

crodswoggle noun

nonsense

'I've got another idea.' 'Your ideas is full of crodswoggle,' the BFG said. 'Not this one,' Sophie said. — THE BFG

DID YOU KNOW? Roald Dahl may have meant the word *crodswoggle* to sound like *codswallop*, which is an informal word for 'nonsense'.

cronking adjective

A cronking pain is very severe.

'I hope I don't fall down your earhole,' Sophie said . . . 'Be very careful not to do that,' the BFG said. 'You would be giving me a cronking earache.' — THE BFG

DID YOU KNOW? To make the word *cronking*, Roald Dahl may have started with *stonking*, which means 'huge or very great', and then changed the beginning, so that it also makes you think of a *crushing* pain.

crook noun crooks

A crook is someone who makes a living by being dishonest, like Mr Wormwood who cheats his customers by selling them worthless cars.

'He's a crook!' the Trunchbull shouted. 'A week ago he sold me a second-hand car that he said was almost new.' — MATILDA

crooked adjective

Something that is crooked is not straight.

In the silvery moonlight, the village street she knew so well seemed completely different. The houses looked bent and crooked, like houses in a fairy tale. — THE BFG

crop noun crops

1 a type of plant which farmers grow as food

'We gobble up all the nasty little insects that are gobbling up all the farmer's crops . . . and we ourselves don't charge a penny for our services.' — JAMES AND THE GIANT PEACH

2 an amount of hair on someone's head

Mr Wormwood's fine crop of black hair was now a dirty silver, the colour . . . of a tightrope-walker's tights that had not been washed for the entire circus season. — MATILDA

cross adjective crosser, crossest

If you are cross, you are angry or very annoyed.

The Grand High Witch glared around the room. 'I hope nobody else is going to make me cross today,' she remarked. — THE WITCHES

cross verb crosses, crossing, crossed

1 When you cross a road, a river or an ocean, you go across it.

Was it really possible that they were crossing oceans? It certainly felt that way to Sophie. — THE BFG

2 When you cross your arms or legs, you put one over the other.

The BFG settled himself comfortably in his chair and crossed his legs. 'Dreams,' he said, 'is very mysterious things.' — THE BFG

crotching adjective
very bad-tempered, as giants usually are
'Phew!' said the BFG. 'Phew and far between! They was in a nasty crotching mood today, was they not!'—THE BFG

DID YOU KNOW? Roald Dahl may have based the word *crotching* on *crotchety*, which means 'irritable'.

crowd noun **crowds**
a large number of people
Outside the gates of Wonka's factory, enormous crowds of people had gathered to watch the five lucky ticket holders going in.—CHARLIE AND THE CHOCOLATE FACTORY

cruel adjective **crueller, cruellest**
If someone is cruel to you, they hurt you or are very unkind to you.
'It is not needing any food,' the BFG told her. 'That's cruel,' Sophie said. 'Everything alive needs food of some sort. Even trees and plants.'—THE BFG

crumb noun **crumbs**
Crumbs are very small pieces of bread or cake, much enjoyed by pet mice.
I put William on the carpet beside me and rewarded him with some extra crumbs and a currant.—THE WITCHES

crumbly adjective **crumblier, crumbliest**
If something is crumbly, it breaks easily into very small pieces.
Mr Fox . . . saw that the cement between the bricks was old and crumbly, so he loosened a brick without much trouble and pulled it away.—FANTASTIC MR FOX

crumpet noun **crumpets**
A crumpet is a musical instrument played by giants, similar to a trumpet (but presumably a lot bigger).
'Save our souls!' bellowed the Fleshlumpeater. 'Sound the crumpets! I is bitten by a septicous venomsome vindscreen viper!'—THE BFG

DID YOU KNOW? A *crumpet* is also a type of thick pancake, which is good to eat but not so good for making music. There is an early wind instrument called a *crumhorn* which has a curved end, so perhaps musical *crumpets* are like curly trumpets.

crumpled adjective
very creased, like a piece of scrunched-up paper
That face of hers . . . was so crumpled and wizened, so shrunken and shrivelled, it looked as though it had been pickled in vinegar.—THE WITCHES

crumpscoddle noun **crumpscoddles**
The crumpscoddle is an animal that is very common in Giant Country, but which no **human bean** has ever seen.
'What about for instance . . . the wraprascal?' 'The what?' Sophie said. 'And the crumpscoddle?' 'Are they animals?' Sophie asked.—THE BFG

LOOK IT UP! Other animals commonly found in Giant Country are the **humplecrimp** and **scotch-hopper**.

crunch verb **crunches, crunching, crunched**
When you crunch food, you eat it by breaking it noisily with your teeth.
No animal is half so vile/As Crocky-Wock the crocodile./ On Saturdays he likes to crunch/Six juicy children for his lunch.—DIRTY BEASTS

crunch noun **crunches**
the noise of something breaking, or of someone crunching
Suddenly there was an especially loud crunch above their heads and the sharp end of a shovel came right through the ceiling.—FANTASTIC MR FOX

Crunchem Hall (MATILDA)
Crunchem Hall is a bleak primary school where Matilda is a pupil. It is run by the tyrannical Miss Trunchbull, who is feared by both staff and pupils. Its name sounds like *crunch 'em*, which is probably what Miss Trunchbull would like to do to her pupils.

crust noun **crusts**
the hard part around the outside of bread
The ant-eater arrived half-dead./It looked at Roy and softly said,/'I'm famished. Do you think you could/ Please give me just a little food?/A crust of bread, a bit of meat?/I haven't had a thing to eat.'—DIRTY BEASTS

cry verb **cries, crying, cried**
1 When you cry, tears come out of your eyes.
James began to cry. 'Stop that immediately and get on with your work, you nasty little beast!' Aunt Sponge ordered.—JAMES AND THE GIANT PEACH
2 When you cry, you shout something.
'Great whistling whangdoodles!' cried Mr Wonka, leaping so high in the air that when he landed his legs gave way and he crashed on to his backside.—CHARLIE AND THE GREAT GLASS ELEVATOR

crystal noun **crystals**
Crystal is a hard clear mineral rather like glass which sparkles in the light.
And what a dazzling sight it was! The moonlight was shining and glinting on its great curving sides, turning them to crystal and silver.—JAMES AND THE GIANT PEACH

cucumber noun **cucumbers**
A cucumber is a long, green vegetable that looks like a **snozzcumber** but tastes much nicer. If you cook a cucumber, it goes very limp and mushy.
'You'd have been a cooked cucumber! You'd have been rasped into a thousand tiny bits, grated like cheese and flocculated alive!'—CHARLIE AND THE GREAT GLASS ELEVATOR

culprit noun **culprits**
someone who has committed a crime or done something wrong
'The Trunchbull,' Hortensia said, 'has a nasty habit of guessing. When she doesn't know who the culprit is, she makes a guess at it, and the trouble is she's often right.'—MATILDA

a b c d e f g h i j k l m n o p q r s t u v w x y z

cupboard noun
cupboards
a piece of furniture with doors on the front, which grown-ups and giants keep things in, such as medicines or bottles of **frobscottle**

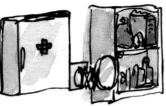

George . . . gazed longingly at the famous and dreaded medicine cupboard. But he didn't go near it. It was the only thing in the entire house he was forbidden to touch. — GEORGE'S MARVELLOUS MEDICINE

curdbloodling adjective
A curdbloodling dream (such as a **trogglehumper**) is one that terrifies you.
'I is never never letting it go!' the BFG cried. 'If I do, then some poor little tottler will be having the most curdbloodling time!' — THE BFG

> **Gobblefunking with words**
> When the BFG says *curdbloodling* instead of *bloodcurdling*, he is using a *spoonerism*. Some other examples of spoonerisms are **buckswashling** and **knack jife**.

cure verb **cures, curing, cured**
If something cures you, it makes you better after you have been ill.
Nobody had ever made a medicine like that before. If it didn't actually cure Grandma, then it would anyway cause some exciting results. — GEORGE'S MARVELLOUS MEDICINE

curious adjective
Something that is curious is strange or unusual.
The tunnel was damp and murky, and all around him there was the curious bittersweet smell of fresh peach. — JAMES AND THE GIANT PEACH

curl noun **curls**
a piece of hair that is curved, not straight
He smears the boys (to make them hot)/With mustard from the mustard pot./But mustard doesn't go with girls,/ It tastes all wrong with plaits and curls. — DIRTY BEASTS
RINGBELLING RHYMES Try rhyming with *swirl* or *twirl* (as well as *girl*).

curly adjective **curlier, curliest**
A curly tail, or curly hair, has loops or curls in it.
The skin all over her body, as well as her great big mop of curly hair, had turned a brilliant, purplish-blue, the colour of blueberry juice! — CHARLIE AND THE CHOCOLATE FACTORY

currant noun **currants**
Currants are small dried grapes used in baking biscuits and fruit cakes (and much loved by white mice).
I put William on the carpet beside me and rewarded him with some extra crumbs and a currant. — THE WITCHES

current noun **currents**
A current is an amount of water, air or electricity that is moving in one direction.
A strong current and a high wind had carried the peach so quickly away from the shore that already the land was out of sight. — JAMES AND THE GIANT PEACH
DON'T BE BIFFSQUIGGLED! Take care not to confuse a *current* of water with the kind of *currant* you get in cakes and biscuits. To help you remember, just think of curr*ants* as looking like squashed *ants*.

curse noun **curses**
If you shout curses at someone, you shout angry words saying that you hope particularly nasty things will happen to them.
Grandpa Joe, shouting war-cries and throwing curses at the Knids, was down below turning the handle that unwound the steel rope. — CHARLIE AND THE GREAT GLASS ELEVATOR

curtain noun **curtains**
Curtains are pieces of cloth that you pull together to cover a window. The BFG slides his dream-blower through the gap where curtains meet.
The BFG . . . steered the trumpet through the curtains, far into the room, aiming it at the place where he knew the bed to be. — THE BFG

curve noun **curves**
a line that is bent smoothly like the letter C
The tiny shutters of tree-bark opened wider and wider, and . . . revealed a small squarish window set neatly in the curve of the big branch. — THE MINPINS

curvy adjective **curvier, curviest**
A curvy line or body has bends or curves in it.
The creature, which had originally looked like a huge egg, now looked like a long curvy serpent standing up on its tail. — CHARLIE AND THE GREAT GLASS ELEVATOR

customer noun **customers**
A customer is someone who buys things in a shop, or who buys services from a business, such as a window-cleaning company.
On the Grand Opening Day, I decided to allow all my customers to help themselves for free, and the place was so crowded with children you could hardly move. — THE GIRAFFE AND THE PELLY AND ME

Danny

DANNY THE CHAMPION OF THE WORLD

de-juicing   disastrophe   disgusterous

dispunge   dreadly   **dreams**

dab verb **dabs, dabbing, dabbed**
When you dab something, you touch it gently to wipe away tears or a stain.
Mrs Bucket was sitting on the edge of the big bed, dabbing her eyes with a hanky. 'My poor old mum,' she kept saying. 'She's minus two and I won't see her again for months and months and months — if ever at all!'
— CHARLIE AND THE GREAT GLASS ELEVATOR

dad or **daddy** noun **dads** or **daddies**
Your dad or daddy is your father.
'Daddy says it's fine for a man to be tall,' George said. 'Don't listen to your daddy,' Grandma said. 'Listen to me.'
— GEORGE'S MARVELLOUS MEDICINE
RINGBELLING RHYMES Try rhyming with *mad* or *just a tad*.

daddle verb **daddles, daddling, daddled**
If you daddle, you run very fast.
So start to run! Oh, skid and daddle/Through the slubber slush and sossel!/Skip jump hop and try to skaddle!/ All the grobes are on the roam! — CHARLIE AND THE GREAT GLASS ELEVATOR
DON'T BE BIFFSQUIGGLED! Take care not to confuse **daddle** with **dawdle** which means the opposite.
DID YOU KNOW? Roald Dahl often joined words together to make new words, but this time he split an old word, *skedaddle*, which means 'to run away quickly', into two verbs, *skid* and a new word, *daddle*.

Dahl's Chickens (THE BFG)
Dahl's Chickens is the BFG's name for Charles Dickens. Dickens was one of Roald Dahl's favourite writers and both the BFG and Matilda read and enjoy his books. (Miss Trunchbull reads them too, but only to get ideas for how to mistreat children.)
Sophie took the book out of his hand. 'Nicholas Nickleby,' she read aloud. 'By Dahl's Chickens,' the BFG said.
— THE BFG

Gobblefunking with words
To make the phrase *Dahl's Chickens*, Roald Dahl swapped the first letters of each part of *Charles Dickens*. This type of word play is called a *spoonerism*, and you can find more examples in the entry for **mideous**.

damage verb **damages, damaging, damaged**
If you damage something, you break it or spoil it.
damage noun
Damage is injury or harm.
'You could do them permanent damage, Miss Trunchbull,' Miss Honey cried out. 'Oh, I have, I'm quite sure I have,' the Trunchbull answered, grinning. — MATILDA

damp adjective **damper, dampest**
Something that is damp is slightly wet.
Sophie nodded. The misty vapour swirled around her. It made her cheeks damp and left dewdrops in her hair. — THE BFG

dance verb **dances, dancing, danced**
When you dance, you move about in time to music.
And suddenly, George found himself dancing around the steaming pot, chanting strange words that came into his head out of nowhere. — GEORGE'S MARVELLOUS MEDICINE
dance noun **dances**
a piece of music or set of movements for dancing
The Monkey stood on the window-sill and did a jiggly little dance. — THE GIRAFFE AND THE PELLY AND ME

danger noun **dangers**
When there is danger, there is the chance that something horrible might happen and someone might get hurt.
'Keep calm!' cried Mr Wonka. 'Keep calm, my dear lady, keep calm. There is no danger! No danger whatsoever! Augustus has gone on a little journey, that's all.' — CHARLIE AND THE CHOCOLATE FACTORY

The surname *Dahl* means 'valley' and is related to the English word *dale*.

dangerous adjective

Something that is dangerous might kill or hurt you. Whangdoodles and Knids are very dangerous indeed and should be approached with extreme caution (or better still not at all).

'And oh, what a terrible country it is . . . infested by the most dangerous beasts in the world — hornswogglers and snozzwangers and those terrible wicked whangdoodles.' — CHARLIE AND THE CHOCOLATE FACTORY

dangle verb **dangles, dangling, dangled**

1 If something dangles, it swings or hangs down loosely.

Below the waterfall . . . a whole mass of enormous glass pipes were dangling down into the river from somewhere high up in the ceiling! — CHARLIE AND THE CHOCOLATE FACTORY

2 If you dangle something (such as a small child) you hold it so that it hangs or swings in the air.

It really was a quite extraordinary sight to see this giant Headmistress dangling the small boy high in the air and the boy spinning and twisting like something on the end of a string and shrieking his head off. — MATILDA

RINGBELLING RHYMES Try rhyming with *tangle* or *buzzwangle*.

Danny (DANNY THE CHAMPION OF THE WORLD)

Danny is an only child who lives with his father in an old gipsy caravan behind a filling-station. He loves helping his father to repair car engines and never gets bored.

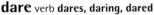

dare verb **dares, daring, dared**

1 If you dare to do something, you are brave enough to do it. Grown-ups sometimes shout *how dare you!* when they are annoyed at you for doing something.

'Just look at that beastly duck cooking at my stove!' cried Mrs Gregg as she flew past the kitchen window. 'How dare she!' — THE MAGIC FINGER

2 If you dare *not* do something, you are too scared to do it.

They dared not move. They dared hardly breathe. And Mr Wonka, who had swung quickly around to look when the first scream came, was as dumbstruck as the rest. — CHARLIE AND THE GREAT GLASS ELEVATOR

dark adjective **darker, darkest**

1 A dark place or a dark sky has little or no light in it.

Gradually it grew darker and darker, and then a pale three-quarter moon came up over the tops of the clouds and cast an eerie light over the whole scene. — JAMES AND THE GIANT PEACH

2 Something that is dark is nearly black in colour.

When Mr Wormwood arrived back from the garage that evening his face was as dark as a thunder-cloud and somebody was clearly for the high-jump pretty soon. — MATILDA

3 A dark secret is hidden and mysterious.

'Ah-ha,' said the BFG. 'Now we is getting on to the dark and dusky secrets.' — THE BFG

dark noun
The dark is the blackness of night or the gloom of a place without light.
The travellers . . . glanced up and saw an immense grey batlike creature swooping down towards them out of the dark. — JAMES AND THE GIANT PEACH

darken verb darkens, darkening, darkened
When the sky darkens, it gradually gets darker, either because night is falling or because a storm is approaching. (You can also say that someone's face darkens if they are getting more and more angry.)
It was the first of October and one of those warm windless autumn mornings with a darkening sky and a smell of thunder in the air. — DANNY THE CHAMPION OF THE WORLD

darksome adjective
dark and murky
'This one is a nasty fierce bogrotting nightmare . . . I would be hating to get this one inside me on a darksome night,' the BFG said. — THE BFG

> **Gobblefunking with words**
> To make the word *darksome*, Roald Dahl added the *suffix* or ending -*some* to *dark*. You can find -*some* at the end of other adjectives like **fearsome**, **loathsome** and **tiresome**. It means 'making or causing', so a *fearsome* Knid makes you fearful, and a *tiresome* piece of homework makes you tired just thinking about it.
>
> You could make up your own words too, like *boresome* or *yawnsome*. The BFG uses lots of words which end in -*some*, such as **filthsome**, **foulsome** and **rotsome**.

dart verb darts, darting, darted
If something darts, it moves quickly and suddenly.
Sophie saw a flash of pale red go darting towards the giant's face. For a split second it hovered above the face. Then it was gone. — THE BFG

dash verb dashes, dashing, dashed
If you dash, you run or move very quickly. You can also say that you *make a dash for it*.
George dashed upstairs to his own bedroom and there she was coming up through the floor like a mushroom. — GEORGE'S MARVELLOUS MEDICINE

daughter noun daughters
Someone's daughter is their female child.
'But I don't want a blueberry for a daughter!' yelled Mrs Beauregarde. 'Put her back to what she was this instant!' — CHARLIE AND THE CHOCOLATE FACTORY

dawdle verb dawdles, dawdling, dawdled
If you dawdle, you walk very slowly.
*'Come on!' cried Mr Wonka. 'Get a move on, please! We'll **never** get round today if you dawdle like this!'* — CHARLIE AND THE CHOCOLATE FACTORY

dawn noun
the time of day when the sun rises and it becomes light
The phone did not ring in the night and at dawn the Sergeant built his fire again and cooked us some more rice and bananas. — GOING SOLO

dawn verb dawns, dawning, dawned
When something dawns on you, it becomes clear to you.
The truth was at last beginning to dawn on the Duke. He put a cherry into his mouth and chewed it slowly. — THE GIRAFFE AND THE PELLY AND ME

dazzle verb dazzles, dazzling, dazzled
If a bright light dazzles you, you cannot see anything because it is shining in your eyes.
I put the headlamps on full . . . although actually they weren't bright enough to dazzle a cockroach. — DANNY THE CHAMPION OF THE WORLD

dead adjective
Someone who is dead is not alive. You can also say they are *dead as a dingbat*, *dead as a dumpling*, or *stone dead*.
'Listen,' he said angrily, 'I want that fox! I'm going to get that fox! I'm not giving in till I've strung him up over my front porch, dead as a dumpling!' — FANTASTIC MR FOX

> **Gobblefunking with words**
> If you describe someone as *dead as a dumpling* or *dead as a dingbat*, you are using a *simile* and you can find lots more examples in the entry for **mad**. The opposite of *dead as a dingbat* is *frisky as a ferret*.

deadly adjective deadlier, deadliest
1 A deadly poison or a deadly snake is one that can kill you.
2 If you are deadly serious it means you are very serious, as if your life depended on it.
My grandmother leaned back in her chair and sucked away contentedly at her foul black cigar . . . She was not smiling. She looked deadly serious. — THE WITCHES

> You can put *un-* before adjectives to make opposites: *some undarksome night.*

deaf adjective **deafer, deafest**
Someone who is deaf cannot hear.
'I am a little deaf in my left ear,' Mr Wonka said. 'You must forgive me if I don't hear everything you say.' — CHARLIE AND THE CHOCOLATE FACTORY

deal verb **deals, dealing, dealt**
When you deal with someone or something, you spend time sorting them out.
'All of you will be wise to remember that Miss Trunchbull deals very very severely with anyone who gets out of line in this school.' — MATILDA

deal noun
a good deal of something is a large amount of it
'I expect you will hear a good deal of singing today from time to time.' — CHARLIE AND THE CHOCOLATE FACTORY

dear adjective **dearer, dearest**
1 If someone is dear to you, you love them very much.
2 You write *Dear* before someone's name at the start of a letter to them.
As soon as father heard the news,/He quickly wrote to all the zoos./'Dear Sirs,' he said, 'My dear keepers,/Do any of you have ant-eaters?' — DIRTY BEASTS

death noun **deaths**
Death is the time when someone dies.
Astri was far and away my father's favourite. He adored her beyond measure and her sudden death left him literally speechless for days afterwards. — BOY

deathly adjective **deathlier, deathliest**
A deathly quiet or deathly stillness is absolutely quiet and still, as if there were no signs of life anywhere.
There was a new moon in the sky and across the road the big field lay pale and deserted in the moonlight. The silence was deathly. — DANNY THE CHAMPION OF THE WORLD

decide verb **decides, deciding, decided**
When you decide to do something, you choose to do it.
I, Willy Wonka, have decided to allow five children — just five, mind you, and no more — to visit my factory this year. — CHARLIE AND THE CHOCOLATE FACTORY

deck noun **decks**
a floor in a ship or bus (or on top of a giant fruit)
The Centipede was dancing around the deck and turning somersaults in the air and singing at the top of his voice. — JAMES AND THE GIANT PEACH

deep adjective **deeper, deepest**
Something that is deep goes down a long way from the top.
The tunnel began to grow longer and longer. It sloped steeply downward. Deeper and deeper below the surface of the ground it went. — FANTASTIC MR FOX

defeat verb **defeats, defeating, defeated**
If you defeat someone, you beat them in a game or battle.
This grandfather of mine was born, believe it or not, in 1820, shortly after Wellington had defeated Napoleon at Waterloo. — BOY

definite adjective
Something that is definite is certain.
Charlie began to feel cold . . . There was a very definite smell of danger in the air. — CHARLIE AND THE GREAT GLASS ELEVATOR

de-juice verb **de-juices, de-juicing, de-juiced**
If you de-juice a fruit (or a Violet), you press the juice out of it.
'They'll de-juice her in no time flat!' declared Mr Wonka. 'They'll roll her into the de-juicing machine, and she'll come out just as thin as a whistle!' — CHARLIE AND THE CHOCOLATE FACTORY

delayed adjective
Something that is delayed is late, or happens at a later time. A magic potion with delayed action (such as Formula 86 Delayed Action Mouse-Maker) is timed to take effect when you least expect it.
'Child goes to school still feeling fine . . . Formula, you understand, is delayed action, and is not vurrrking yet.' — THE WITCHES

delicate adjective
Something that is delicate will break or fall apart easily.
Bits of pale gold were flying among delicate frosty-white flakes of cloud, and over to one side the rim of the morning sun was coming up red as blood. — THE BFG

delicious adjective
Something that is delicious (such as every single thing that Willy Wonka makes) tastes very nice indeed.
'That pipe — the one Augustus went up — happens to lead directly to the room where I make a most

delicious kind of strawberry-flavoured chocolate-coated fudge.'—CHARLIE AND THE CHOCOLATE FACTORY

SPARKY SYNONYMS There are so many words that mean 'delicious' that you may never need to use the word *delicious* at all. Why not try instead **delumptious**, **delunctious**, **glumptious** or **scrumdiddlyumptious**?

delight verb delights, delighting, delighted
If something delights you, it makes you feel very happy.
'I am preparing . . . mystic and marvellous surprises that will entrance, delight, intrigue, astonish, and perplex you beyond measure.'—CHARLIE AND THE CHOCOLATE FACTORY

delight noun delights
1 a feeling of great happiness or joy
There were yells of delight from the giants below, followed by the crunching of bones.—THE BFG
2 Any chocolate bar called a *Delight* will make you feel very happy when you eat it.
'Wonka's Whipple-Scrumptious Fudgemallow Delight!' cried Grandpa George. 'It's the best of them all! You'll just love it!'—CHARLIE AND THE CHOCOLATE FACTORY

delighted adjective
When you are delighted, you feel very happy, as if you had just found a Golden Ticket in a bar of chocolate.
Mr Wonka . . . started shaking Charlie's hand so furiously it nearly came off. 'Oh, I do congratulate you!' he cried. 'I really do! I'm absolutely delighted!'—CHARLIE AND THE CHOCOLATE FACTORY

delightful adjective
Something delightful is enjoyable and makes you happy, and a delightful person is always pleasant and cheerful (unlike Aunts Spiker and Sponge, who are definitely *un*-delightful).
'I have never in my life tasted anything except those tiny little green flies that live on rosebushes. They have a perfectly delightful flavour.'—JAMES AND THE GIANT PEACH
LOOK IT UP! For other ways to describe delightful things, see **good**.

delumptious adjective
delicious or very tasty
'Where is the frobscottle?' 'The what?' the Queen asked. 'Delumptious fizzy frobscottle,' the BFG answered.—THE BFG
SPARKY SYNONYMS You can also say **glumptious** or **scrumdiddlyumptious**.

delunctious adjective
very tasty or delicious (so much the same as **delumptious**)
'Is you having any more of this delunctious grubble in your cupboard, Majester?'—THE BFG
RINGBELLING RHYMES Try rhyming with *scrumptious*.
SPARKY SYNONYMS You can also say **glumptious** or **scrumdiddlyumptious**.

demand verb demands, demanding, demanded
If you demand something, you ask for it very strongly.
'What's the matter with you?' Aunt Sponge demanded. 'It's growing!' Aunt Spiker cried. 'It's getting bigger and bigger!'—JAMES AND THE GIANT PEACH
LOOK IT UP! For lots of ways to describe how people speak, see **say**.

demon noun demons
a devil or evil spirit
'You don't seem to understand that witches are not actually women at all . . . They are demons in human shape.'—THE WITCHES

dendrochronologist noun dendrochronologists
A dendrochronologist can tell the age of a tree by counting the growth rings in its trunk.
'You can find Bristlecone Pines . . . that are over four thousand years old! . . . Ask any dendrochronologist you like (and look that word up in the dictionary when you get home, will you, please?).'—CHARLIE AND THE GREAT GLASS ELEVATOR

dent noun dents
a hollow made in a surface
'You can eat all you want,' James answered. 'It would take us weeks and weeks to make any sort of a dent in this enormous peach.'—JAMES AND THE GIANT PEACH

dentist noun dentists
A dentist is someone whose job is to check and look after your teeth. If you eat Willy Wonka's cavity-filling caramels, you won't need to go to the dentist (until they dissolve and then, sadly, you will).

deny verb denies, denying, denied
1 If you deny something, you say that it is not true.
'Do you deny it, you miserable little gumboil? Do you plead not guilty?'—MATILDA
2 If you deny someone a pleasure, you do not let them experience it.
'I do not vish to deny you the pleasure of bumping off a few thousand children each just because you have become old and feeble.'—THE WITCHES

Can you *daer sdrow sdrawkcab?* Find out more at **Esio Trot**.

depart verb **departs, departing, departed**
If you depart from a place, you leave it.
*'In case you don't know it . . . we are about to depart for
ever from the top of this ghastly hill that we've all been
living on for so long.'*—JAMES AND THE GIANT PEACH

depend verb **depends, depending, depended**
If you depend on someone or something, you rely
on them for help.
*'Get that Silkworm to work at once! Tell her to spin as
she's never spun before! Our lives depend upon it!'*
—JAMES AND THE GIANT PEACH

depth noun **depths**
1 The depth of something is how deep it is.
*The pit had been dug in the shape of a square, with each
side about six feet long. But it was the depth of it that
was so awful.*—DANNY THE CHAMPION OF THE WORLD
2 The depths of a place is its lowest or innermost
part.
*The Centipede was down there too . . . and every now and
again James could hear his voice coming up faintly from
the depths.*—JAMES AND THE GIANT PEACH

descend verb **descends, descending, descended**
If you descend, you go down to a lower level.
*Matilda, who was mesmerized by the whole crazy affair,
saw Amanda Thripp descending in a long graceful
parabola on to the playing-field beyond.*—MATILDA

describe verb **describes, describing, described**
When you describe something, you talk about it and
say what it is like.
*I cannot possibly describe to you what it felt like to be
standing alone in the pitchy blackness of that silent wood
in the small hours of the night.*—DANNY THE CHAMPION OF
THE WORLD

deserted adjective
A place that is deserted is empty, with no one in it.
*There was a new moon in the sky and across the road
the big field lay pale and deserted in the moonlight.*
—DANNY THE CHAMPION OF THE WORLD

deserve verb **deserves, deserving, deserved**
If someone deserves a punishment or reward, you think
that they should get it.
*There was no doubt in Matilda's mind that this latest
display of foulness by her father deserved severe
punishment.*—MATILDA

desk noun **desks**
A desk is a table where you can read, write or answer
a telephone. Some desks have drawers which are very
useful for keeping secret things, like sweets or newts.
*'By gum, we'll soon fix this!' snapped the President,
grabbing one of the eleven telephones on his desk.*
—CHARLIE AND THE GREAT GLASS ELEVATOR

dessert noun **desserts**
A dessert is a sweet dish that you eat at the end
of a meal (or earlier if you can't wait that long).

Willy Wonka makes a magic chewing-gum which
tastes of a whole meal, including dessert.
*'It always goes wrong when we come to the dessert,'
sighed Mr Wonka. 'It's the blueberry pie that does it.'*
—CHARLIE AND THE CHOCOLATE FACTORY

DON'T BE BIFFSQUIGGLED! Take care not to confuse
a *dessert* (which you can eat) with a *desert* (which
you can't). To avoid biffsquigglement, remember that
dessert has an extra *s* for *sugar*.

destroy verb **destroys, destroying, destroyed**
If you destroy something, you make sure that it cannot
be used again, for example by breaking, burning
or smashing it.
*'My father's will was never found,' Miss Honey said.
'It looks as though somebody destroyed it.' 'No prizes for
guessing who,' Matilda said.*—MATILDA

determined adjective
If you are determined to do something, you have made
up your mind to do it.
*Sophie felt quite ill. But this grim encounter made her more
than ever determined to go through with her mission.*
—THE BFG

develop verb **develops, developing, developed**
When something develops, it changes and grows.
*'He's developing such an appetite! I've never seen him eat
like this before! It must be the magic words.'*—ESIO TROT

Devil's Drencher noun **Devil's Drenchers**
a fiery-tasting sweet sold in the Grubber
*When you have sucked a Devil's Drencher for a minute
or so, you can set your breath alight and blow a huge
column of fire twenty feet into the air.*—THE GIRAFFE AND
THE PELLY AND ME

devour verb devours, devouring, devoured

If you devour food, you eat it hungrily, and if you devour a book, you read it enthusiastically to learn everything in it, just like Matilda.

The walk took only ten minutes and this allowed her two glorious hours sitting quietly by herself in a cosy corner devouring one book after another. — MATILDA

dew noun

Dew is tiny drops of water that form on the ground during the night. A single drop is called a *dewdrop*.

The grass was wet with dew and a million dewdrops were sparkling and twinkling like diamonds around his feet. — JAMES AND THE GIANT PEACH

dewlap noun dewlaps

a fold of loose skin on an animal's neck or throat

'That is a bullfrog calling to his wife. He does it by blowing out his dewlap and letting it go with a burp.' — DANNY THE CHAMPION OF THE WORLD

dial noun dials

a circle with numbers round it, like a clock

'Mr Wheeler has all sorts of marvellous ovens in his shop now. He's got one in there with so many dials and knobs on it, it looks like the cockpit of an airplane.' — DANNY THE CHAMPION OF THE WORLD

diameter noun diameters

the distance across the centre of a circle, such as the top of a round cake

The cake was fully eighteen inches in diameter and it was covered with dark-brown chocolate icing. — MATILDA

diamond noun diamonds

A diamond is a very hard jewel that looks like clear glass and sparkles in the light.

'Where are my diamonds?' 'Here they are!' cried the Chief of Police, fishing great handfuls of jewellery from the burglar's pockets. — THE GIRAFFE AND THE PELLY AND ME

dibbler noun dibblers

A dibbler is a part of a giant's body, but the BFG doesn't say which part, so you will just have to guess.

'Oh, save our solos!' he cried. 'Deliver us from weasels! The devil is dancing on my dibbler!' 'What are you talking about?' Sophie said. — THE BFG

dictionary noun dictionaries

A dictionary is a book like this one which explains what words mean (including, of course, **dendrochronologist**) and shows you how to spell them.

'This is fact, Charlie. Ask any dendrochronologist you like (and look that word up in the dictionary when you get home, will you, please?).' — CHARLIE AND THE GREAT GLASS ELEVATOR

DID YOU KNOW? Lots of writers use dictionaries, including Roald Dahl himself, who owned a pocket dictionary as well as a rhyming dictionary and thesaurus to help him find **ringbelling** rhymes and synonyms.

diddly adjective diddlier, diddliest

individual or distinct

'Every human bean is diddly and different. Some is scrumdiddlyumptious and some is uckyslush.' — THE BFG

die verb dies, dying, died

When a person or animal dies, they stop living.

'The only time a Gruncher dies,' Don Mini said, 'is if he falls into deep water. The water puts out the fire inside him and then he's dead.' — THE MINPINS

diet noun diets

Your diet is the kind of food that you eat.

'Am I not right in thinking that the pink and purple flowers of the tinkle-tinkle tree are your only diet?' 'Yes,' sighed the Giraffe, 'and that's been my problem ever since I arrived on these shores.' — THE GIRAFFE AND THE PELLY AND ME

difficult adjective

Something that is difficult is not easy, like shelling walnuts without breaking them.

*Nobody except squirrels can get walnuts **whole** out of walnut shells every time. It is extremely difficult.* — CHARLIE AND THE CHOCOLATE FACTORY

dig verb digs, digging, dug

When you dig, you move away soil or snow (or more rarely peach flesh) to make a hole or tunnel.

'Now, look here, Spiker. Why don't we go and get a shovel right away and dig out a great big chunk of it for you and me to eat?' — JAMES AND THE GIANT PEACH

dig noun digs

If you give someone a dig, you nudge or poke them.

'Wake up, Centipede,' whispered James, giving him a gentle dig in the stomach. 'It's time for bed.' — JAMES AND THE GIANT PEACH

dillion noun dillions

a very large number, like a million

'The human bean,' the Giant went on, 'is coming in dillions of different flavours.' — THE BFG

DID YOU KNOW? There are lots of words that mean 'a very large number' which rhyme with **dillion**, such as *zillion, squillion* and *gazillion*.

Someone who writes dictionaries is called a *lexicographer*.

dim adjective dimmer, dimmest
A dim light or a dim place is not very bright.
The filling-station was in darkness now except for a dim light coming from the caravan where the little oil-lamp was still burning. — DANNY THE CHAMPION OF THE WORLD

dingbat noun dingbats
A dingbat is someone who is very silly or slightly mad. Dingbats are not types of bat, though they may be a bit batty.
'What did I tell you!' cried Grandma Georgina. 'He's round the twist! He's bogged as a beetle! He's dotty as a dingbat!' — CHARLIE AND THE GREAT GLASS ELEVATOR
LOOK IT UP! For other ways to describe someone as *dotty as a dingbat*, see **mad**.

dinner noun dinners
the main meal of the day
'Personally, I had always thought that a big, juicy, caught-in-the-web bluebottle was the finest dinner in the world.' — JAMES AND THE GIANT PEACH

dip verb dips, dipping, dipped
When you dip something into liquid, you put it in and leave it there for a short time.
A boy at school called Ashton had had nits in his hair last term and the matron had made him dip his whole head in turpentine. — THE WITCHES

dirty adjective dirtier, dirtiest
Something that is dirty has mud or dirt on it. Staying very dirty is a good defence against witches.
'An absolutely clean child gives off the most ghastly stench to a witch,' my grandmother said. 'The dirtier you are, the less you smell.' — THE WITCHES

disappear verb disappears, disappearing, disappeared
When something disappears, it goes away and you cannot see it any more.
A moment later, the great round ball disappeared into a cloud, and the people on the ship never saw it again. — JAMES AND THE GIANT PEACH

disappointed adjective
If you are disappointed, you feel sad because something is not as good as you had hoped.
Then Mrs Bucket said gently, 'You mustn't be too disappointed, my darling, if you don't find what you're looking for underneath that wrapper.' — CHARLIE AND THE CHOCOLATE FACTORY

disapprove verb disapproves, disapproving, disapproved
If you disapprove of something, you do not like it and do not think that it is right.
The cook stood there like a shrivelled bootlace, tight-lipped, implacable, disapproving. She looked as though her mouth was full of lemon juice. — MATILDA

disaster noun disasters
something very bad that happens
'Poor Earthworm,' the Ladybird said, whispering in James's ear. 'He loves to make everything into a disaster. He hates to be happy.' — JAMES AND THE GIANT PEACH

disastrophe noun disastrophes
a terrible disaster or catastrophe
'Catasterous!' cried the BFG. 'Upgoing bubbles is a catasterous disastrophe!' — THE BFG

> **Gobblefunking with words**
> To make the phrase *catasterous disastrophe*, Roald Dahl swapped the first letters of the words *disastrous* and *catastrophe*. This type of word play is called a *spoonerism* and you can find more examples in the entry for **mideous**.

discover verb discovers, discovering, discovered
When you discover something, you find it, or find out about it.
'Witchophiles all over the world have spent their lives trying to discover the secret headquarters of The Grand High Witch.' — THE WITCHES

discuss verb discusses, discussing, discussed
When people discuss something, they talk about it.
Are you not feeling well? Are you going to faint?/ Is it something we cannot discuss?/It must be a very unpleasant complaint,/For your backside's as big as a bus! — CHARLIE AND THE GREAT GLASS ELEVATOR

disease noun diseases
an illness, such as the **Dreaded Shrinks**
*'You've got the **shrinks**, that's what you've got!... It's a terrible disease,' said Mr Twit. 'The worst in the world.'* — THE TWITS
RINGBELLING RHYMES Try rhyming with *freeze* or *sneeze*.

disguise noun disguises
If someone wears a disguise, they wear special clothes or a wig to make them look like someone else, or to hide what they really are. Witches are very good at disguises, which makes it all the more tricky to spot them.
'That's no boy, you idiot!' shouted Ground Control. 'That's an astronaut in disguise! It's a midget astronaut dressed up as a little boy!' — CHARLIE AND THE GREAT GLASS ELEVATOR

disgustable adjective
Something disgustable, like the taste of a tickly cardigan, makes you feel disgusted or ill.
'Human beans from Jersey has a most disgustable woolly tickle on the tongue,' the Giant said. 'Human beans from Jersey is tasting of cardigans.' — THE BFG

disgusterous adjective
Something disgusterous, such as a **snozzcumber** or Farmer Bunce's doughnuts, looks or tastes vile.
'You is not loving it?' the BFG asked innocently, rubbing

his head. 'Loving it!' yelled the Bloodbottler. 'That is the most **disgusterous** taste that is ever clutching my teeth!'
— THE BFG

DID YOU KNOW? To make the word *disgusterous*, Roald Dahl started with *disgusting* but gave it a different ending that makes you think of *dangerous* or *murderous*, so perhaps **snozzcumbers** taste like deadly poison.

disgusting adjective

Something disgusting is horribly unpleasant. In Giant Country, there are lots of words that mean 'disgusting', probably because there are so many disgusting things to describe. For example, the BFG says **disgustable**, **disgustive** and **disgusterous**, which all mean much the same.

My grandmother had lit up one of her disgusting black cigars and was puffing smoke over everything.
— THE WITCHES

disgustive adjective

Something disgustive, like a man-gobbling giant, is loathsome and vile.

'This is the repulsant snozzcumber, Majester, and that is all we is going to give these disgustive giants from now on!'
— THE BFG

dish noun dishes

food that has been prepared and cooked in a particular way

The Centipede . . . suddenly burst into song: 'I've eaten many strange and scrumptious dishes in my time,/ Like jellied gnats and dandyprats and earwigs cooked in slime.' — JAMES AND THE GIANT PEACH

dishonest adjective

Someone who is dishonest (like Mr Wormwood) does not tell the truth and tries to deceive people.

'But that's dishonest, Daddy,' Matilda said. 'It's cheating.' 'No one ever got rich being honest,' the father said.
— MATILDA

dislike verb dislikes, disliking, disliked

If you dislike someone or something, you do not like them.

George couldn't help disliking Grandma. She was a selfish grumpy old woman. — GEORGE'S MARVELLOUS MEDICINE

SPARKY SYNONYMS If you really dislike something, you **dispunge** it, and if you REALLY REALLY dislike it, you **mispise** it.

dismiss verb dismisses, dismissing, dismissed

If you dismiss someone, you send them away, and if a teacher says that your class is dismissed, it means that you can go home or go out to play.

'Phew!' she said. 'I think we've had enough school for one day, don't you? The class is dismissed.' — MATILDA

dispunge verb dispunges, dispunging, dispunged

If you dispunge something, you hate or loathe it.

'Here is the repulsant snozzcumber!' cried the BFG, waving it about. 'I squoggle it! I mispise it! I dispunge it!' — THE BFG

RINGBELLING RHYMES Try rhyming with *plunge* or *Aunt Sponge*.

dissolve verb dissolves, dissolving, dissolved

When something dissolves, it mixes with water or other ingredients so that you cannot see it.

Now add the following, in precisely the order given, stirring well all the time and allowing each item to dissolve before adding the next. — CHARLIE AND THE GREAT GLASS ELEVATOR

distance noun distances

1 The distance between two places is the amount of space between them.

2 If something is in the distance, it is far away.

In the distance, the mist was darker and almost black and it seemed to be swirling more fiercely than ever over there. — CHARLIE AND THE GREAT GLASS ELEVATOR

distant adjective

Something that is distant is far away.

Such wondrous, fine, fantastic tales/Of dragons, gypsies, queens, and whales/And treasure isles, and distant shores/ Where smugglers rowed with muffled oars. — CHARLIE AND THE CHOCOLATE FACTORY

a b c **d** e f g h i j k l m n o p q r s t u v w x y z

Snozzcumbers are called *snoskommers* in Dutch.

disturb verb disturbs, disturbing, disturbed

1 If you disturb someone (or a squirrel), you interrupt them and stop them from doing something.
'Whatever you do, don't go into THE NUT ROOM! If you go in, you'll disturb the squirrels!' – CHARLIE AND THE CHOCOLATE FACTORY

2 If something disturbs you, it makes you feel worried.
It was her hands, however, that disturbed us most. They were disgusting. They were black with dirt and grime. – BOY

dive verb dives, diving, dived

If you dive into water or melted chocolate, you jump in head first.
'Do something!' 'I am doing something!' said Mr Gloop, who was now taking off his jacket and getting ready to dive into the chocolate. – CHARLIE AND THE CHOCOLATE FACTORY

dizzy adjective dizzier, dizziest

If you feel dizzy, you feel as if everything is spinning round you.
Charlie hadn't moved . . . He felt quite dizzy. There was a peculiar floating sensation coming over him, as though he were floating up in the air like a balloon. – CHARLIE AND THE CHOCOLATE FACTORY

Doc Spencer (DANNY THE CHAMPION OF THE WORLD)

Doc Spencer is a kindly doctor who is much loved by his patients. He is over seventy years old but nobody wants him to retire.

doctor noun doctors

someone whose job is to give people medicines and treatment when they are ill
'He can't go round without a nose for the rest of his life!' the doctor said to my mother . . . 'I shall sew it on again.' – BOY

dodge verb dodges, dodging, dodged

If you dodge something (such as paintpots hurled by angry Cloud-Men), you move quickly to avoid it.
But for the moment everyone was far too busy dodging the things that the Cloud-Men were throwing to pay any attention to the Centipede. – JAMES AND THE GIANT PEACH

dodge noun (informal) dodges

A dodge is a trick or a clever way of doing something.
They were checking up to see if we were mixing some of our second-grade petrol in with the first-grade stuff, which is an old dodge practised by crooked filling-station owners. – DANNY THE CHAMPION OF THE WORLD

dog noun dogs

A dog is an animal often kept as a pet. The Vicar of Nibbleswicke says *Dog* when he means *God*, as he always says important words backwards.
When the service was over and 'the blessing of Dog Almighty' had been given, the vicar stepped forward to the front of the altar rail and spoke. – THE VICAR OF NIBBLESWICKE

dogswoggler noun dogswogglers

A dogswoggler is someone who is very silly and makes no sense whatsoever.
'You is only interested in guzzling human beans.' 'And you is dotty as a dogswoggler!' cried the Bloodbottler. – THE BFG

dollop noun dollops

a lump of something soft or sticky
'Now the table, the big table!' shouted Muggle-Wump. 'Turn the table upside down and put a dollop of sticky glue on to the bottom of each leg.' – THE TWITS

RINGBELLING RHYMES Try rhyming with *crash bang wallop!*

Don Mini (THE MINPINS)

Don Mini is the leader of the Minpins. He lives in a very grand but tiny room inside a tree in the Forest of Sin.

door noun doors

a movable panel that opens and closes the entrance to a room, building or cupboard
There were doors every twenty paces or so along the corridor now, and they all had something written on them . . . and delicious smells came wafting through the keyholes. – CHARLIE AND THE CHOCOLATE FACTORY

dormitory noun dormitories

A dormitory is a room with lots of beds where children sleep in a boarding-school, and where Sophie sleeps in the **norphanage**.
Once, after lights out, a brave boy called Wragg tiptoed out of our dormitory and sprinkled castor sugar all over the linoleum floor of the corridor. – BOY

DID YOU KNOW? The word *dormitory* comes from Latin and means 'a sleeping place', just like *lavatory* means 'a washing place'. You can make up your own words for places too, using the ending *-tory*. For example, if you giggle a lot in your bedroom, it could be a *gigglitory*, and if you make a lot of bubbles in the bathroom, it could be a *bubblitory*.

dory-hunky adjective dory-hunkier, dory-hunkiest

very happy or pleasant
'This dream is continuing very nice. It has a very dory-hunky ending.' – THE BFG

DID YOU KNOW? The word *dory-hunky* means the same as *hunky-dory*, but the BFG swaps the two parts of the word around. The first part of *hunky-dory* comes from a Dutch word that means 'home'.

dose noun doses

A dose of medicine is the amount that you have to take.
George looked at the kitchen clock . . . There was nearly an hour left before Grandma's next dose was due at eleven. — GEORGE'S MARVELLOUS MEDICINE

dot noun dots

a small spot that looks like a full stop
Higher and higher soared the kite. Soon it was just a small blue dot dancing in the sky miles above my head. — DANNY THE CHAMPION OF THE WORLD

doting adjective

If someone has doting parents, it means their parents love everything they do, even when they are very silly.
Occasionally one comes across parents . . . who show no interest at all in their children, and these of course are far worse than the doting ones. — MATILDA

dotty adjective dottier, dottiest

If you are dotty about something, you like it very much.
A fine currant cake is the favourite food of white mice. They are dotty about it. — THE WITCHES

double adjective

1 Something that is double the size of something else is twice as big.
'All of those man-eating giants is enormous and very fierce! They is all at least two times my wideness and double my royal highness!' — THE BFG
2 If you do something at the double, you do it very fast.
'The Trunchbull simply grabbed me by one ear and rushed me to The Chokey at the double and threw me inside and locked the door.' — MATILDA

double verb doubles, doubling, doubled

If something doubles, it becomes twice as big.
Very slowly, over seven weeks, Mrs Silver's pet had more than doubled in size and the good lady hadn't noticed a thing. — ESIO TROT

doughnut noun doughnuts

A doughnut is a fried ring of dough coated in sugar. Doughnuts are usually stuffed with **scrumdiddlyumptious** things like jam or custard, but Farmer Bunce stuffs them with mashed goose livers.
Boggis had three boiled chickens smothered in dumplings, Bunce had six doughnuts filled with disgusting goose-liver paste, and Bean had two gallons of cider. — FANTASTIC MR FOX

doze verb dozes, dozing, dozed

If you are dozing, you are nearly asleep, and if you doze off, you fall into a light sleep.
The crazy prince, who was dozing in the living room at the time, woke up to find himself swimming around in a huge brown sticky lake of chocolate. — CHARLIE AND THE CHOCOLATE FACTORY
RINGBELLING RHYMES Try rhyming with *nose* or *grows*.

dozen noun dozens

a set of twelve
'Tibbs,' the Queen said, showing true regal hospitality, 'fetch the gentleman another dozen fried eggs and a dozen sausages.' — THE BFG
RINGBELLING RHYMES Try making up a new word to rhyme, like *enfuzzen* (to make something fuzzy).

drag verb drags, dragging, dragged

When you drag something heavy, you pull it along the ground.
With the monkeys and the birds all pulling and puffing, the carpet was dragged off the floor and finally hoisted up on to the ceiling. — THE TWITS

dragon noun **dragons**
a fire-breathing monster like a giant lizard with wings and a long tail
'We may see a Dragon, and nobody knows/That we won't see a Unicorn there./We may see a terrible Monster with toes/Growing out of the tufts of his hair.' – JAMES AND THE GIANT PEACH
DID YOU KNOW? The word *dragon* comes from an ancient Greek word meaning 'serpent'. An old name for a dragon is *wyrm* which is related to *worm*, so you could describe them as *vermicious* (just like Knids).

drain verb **drains, draining, drained**
When water drains, it flows away, and when blood drains from your face, you become very pale.
Suddenly the blood seemed to have drained right out of his cheeks. His face was so pale I thought he might be going to faint. – DANNY THE CHAMPION OF THE WORLD

dramatic adjective
Something that is dramatic is very exciting.
The audience of witches was listening intently, sensing that something dramatic was about to happen. – THE WITCHES

draught (*rhymes with* **craft**) noun **draughts**
cold air that blows into a room
In the winter, freezing cold draughts blew across the floor all night long, and it was awful. – CHARLIE AND THE CHOCOLATE FACTORY

draw verb **draws, drawing, drew, drawn**
1 When you draw, you make a picture with a pen or pencil, or sometimes your finger.
'Surely you know what a minus looks like . . . Like that . . .' Mr Wonka drew a horizontal line in the air with his finger. – CHARLIE AND THE GREAT GLASS ELEVATOR
2 When you draw curtains, you open them or close them.
'Shall I draw the curtains, ma'am, then we shall all feel better. It's a lovely day.' – THE BFG
3 When you draw a weapon, you take it out to use it.
Once more the maiden's eyelid flickers./She draws the pistol from her knickers. – REVOLTING RHYMES
4 When something draws you, it seems to pull or attract you towards it.
Almost without knowing what he was doing, as though drawn by some powerful magnet, James Henry Trotter started walking slowly towards the giant peach. – JAMES AND THE GIANT PEACH

drawer noun **drawers**
a sliding compartment in a piece of furniture to store things together (or keep them hidden)
If The Grand High Witch wanted to hide something top secret, where would she put it? Certainly not in any ordinary drawer . . . It was too obvious. – THE WITCHES

dreaded adjective
If something is dreaded, like the dreaded Gruncher, people or giants or Minpins are very afraid of it.
It seemed that all the other Minpins from the big tree had turned up as well to witness the great victory over the dreaded Gruncher. – THE MINPINS

Dreaded Shrinks (THE TWITS)
The Dreaded Shrinks is a disease that Mr Twit invents to terrify Mrs Twit. If you have the Dreaded Shrinks, you get smaller and smaller until you disappear completely.
'Take a look at your stick, you old goat . . . You've got the shrinks, that's what you've got! You've got the dreaded shrinks!' – THE TWITS

dreadful adjective
Something that is dreadful is awful, or very very bad.
Charlie began to feel cold. He knew something dreadful was going to happen. – CHARLIE AND THE GREAT GLASS ELEVATOR

dreadly adjective **dreadlier, dreadliest**
A dreadly creature, such as the dreadly vindscreen-viper, is feared because it is so deadly.
'Save our souls!' bellowed the Fleshlumpeater. 'Sound the crumpets! . . . The teeth of the dreadly viper is still sticking into me!' – THE BFG

Gobblefunking with words
To make the word *dreadly*, Roald Dahl blended together *dread* and *deadly*, which works well because the two words share some letters and sounds. You can try this with other words that share letters or sounds, for example *bugly* is a blend of *ugly* and *bug*, and *sloshpan* is a blend of *saucepan* and *slosh*.

dream noun **dreams**
1 A dream is a series of pictures that you see in your mind when you are asleep. The BFG can hear dreams (both good ones and bad ones) as they flit through the air, before he captures them with his dream-catching net.

'Dreams,' he said, 'is very mysterious things. They is floating around in the air like little wispy-misty bubbles. And all the time they is searching for sleeping people.'
—THE BFG

2 A dream is also something that you want to do more than anything in the world.
Mr Twit still wanted to train monkeys. It was his dream that one day he would own the first GREAT UPSIDE DOWN MONKEY CIRCUS in the world.—THE TWITS

dream verb **dreams, dreaming, dreamed, dreamt**

1 When you dream, you see things in your mind when you are asleep.
'When I is blowing that dream into the Queen's bedroom,' the BFG said, 'she will be dreaming every single little thingalingaling you is asking me to make her dream.'—THE BFG

2 If you dream about something, you want more than anything to do it.
'Oh, I've always dreamed of going to America!' cried the Centipede.—JAMES AND THE GIANT PEACH

DID YOU KNOW? In ancient Greece, the god of dreams was called *Morpheus*. Morpheus lived in a cave, like the BFG, and could appear in people's dreams in various disguises. His name comes from Greek *morphe* 'form or shape', as in the word *metamorphose* which means 'to change shape'.

LOOK IT UP! The BFG collects all kinds of dreams, from the happy **golden phizzwizards**, **ringbellers** and **winksquifflers** to the nasty **bogthumpers**, **grobswitchers** and **trogglehumpers**.

dream-blower noun
dream-blowers
The dream-blower is a long trumpet through which the BFG blows dreams into the ears of sleeping children.
The BFG . . . picked up his long trumpet-like dream-blower. Then he turned and looked at Sophie, who was still on the table-top.—THE BFG

dream-catcher noun
dream-catchers
The dream-catcher is a long pole with a net on the end that the BFG takes with him when he goes dream-hunting.
The pole was about thirty feet long and there was a net on the end of it. 'Here is the dream-catcher,' he said.—THE BFG

Dream Country (THE BFG)
Dream Country is the place where all the dreams in the world start. It is a flat treeless land of cold air and swirling mists, where nothing grows except grey grass. The BFG goes there every day to catch dreams for his collection. Dream Country is not on any map, but you can draw it in yourself on the blank pages at the end of an **atlas**.

dressing-gown noun
dressing-gowns
A dressing-gown is a cosy coat which you wear indoors over your pyjamas or nightie (if, unlike Sophie, you are lucky enough to have one).
It was summertime in London and the night was not cold, but don't forget that Sophie was wearing only her thin nightie. She would have given anything for a dressing-gown . . . to keep her warm.—THE BFG

dribble verb **dribbles, dribbling, dribbled**
If you dribble, you let saliva trickle out of your mouth.
You had only to mention the word 'cacao' to an Oompa-Loompa and he would start dribbling at the mouth.—CHARLIE AND THE CHOCOLATE FACTORY

drift verb **drifts, drifting, drifted**
If something drifts, it is carried along gently by water or air.
They were drifting in a heavy grey mist and the mist was swirling and swishing around them as though driven by winds from many sides.—CHARLIE AND THE GREAT GLASS ELEVATOR

drill noun **drills**
A drill is a pointed tool for making holes. Matilda's father cheats his customers by using a drill to reset the mileage on the cars he sells.
Mr Wormwood . . . had to keep the hat on his head the whole day long, even

a b c **d** e f g h i j k l m n o p q r s t u v w x y z

You can add *-y* to some nouns to make adjectives: *Dreams are simply zozimussy!*

*when putting sawdust in gear-boxes and fiddling
the mileages of cars with his electric drill.* — MATILDA

drink verb **drinks, drinking, drank, drunk**
When you drink, you swallow liquid.
*The monkeys . . . had to eat and drink upside down and
that is not an easy thing to do because the food and water
has to go up your throat instead of down it.* — THE TWITS

drip verb **drips, dripping, dripped**
When water or peach juice drips, it falls in small drops.
*The floor was soggy under his knees, the walls were wet
and sticky, and peach juice was dripping from the ceiling.*
— JAMES AND THE GIANT PEACH

drop noun **drops**
A drop of liquid is a very small amount of it.
*Suddenly, as Mr Twit tipped the last drop of beer down
his throat, he caught sight of Mrs Twit's awful glass eye
staring up at him from the bottom of the mug.* — THE TWITS

drop verb **drops, dropping, dropped**
If you drop something, you let it fall out of your hands.
*The four old grandparents, who were sitting up in bed
balancing bowls of soup on their laps, all dropped their
spoons with a clatter.* — CHARLIE AND THE CHOCOLATE
FACTORY

droppings plural noun
Droppings are the dung of animals or birds. To a witch's
nostrils, human children smell like dogs' droppings.
*'What's more,' my grandmother said, speaking with
a touch of relish, 'to a witch you'd be smelling of fresh
dogs' droppings.'* — THE WITCHES

drown verb **drowns, drowning, drowned**
1 If someone drowns, they die because they are under
water and cannot breathe.
*'Save him!' screamed Mrs Gloop, going white in the face,
and waving her umbrella about. 'He'll drown! He can't
swim a yard!'* — CHARLIE AND THE CHOCOLATE FACTORY
2 If a sound is drowned, you cannot hear it because
of a louder noise.
*The giants themselves . . . never stopped bellowing, but
their howls were drowned by the noise of the engines.*
— THE BFG

drum noun **drums**
A drum is a hollow musical instrument that you bang
with a stick or with your hands. The Oompa-Loompas
are very fond of banging drums.
*At the end of the room, the Oompa-Loompas around
the giant camera were already beating their tiny drums
and beginning to jog up and down to the rhythm.*
— CHARLIE AND THE CHOCOLATE FACTORY

dry adjective **drier, driest**
Something that is dry is not wet or moist.
*A nest with eggs in it was one of the most beautiful
things in the world . . . The nest of a song-thrush, for
instance, lined inside with dry mud as smooth as polished
wood.* — DANNY THE CHAMPION OF THE WORLD

dry verb **dries, drying, dried**
When something dries, it loses its moisture and
goes hard.
*The wretched Centipede . . . was purple all over, and now
that the paint was beginning to dry and harden, he was
forced to sit very stiff and upright, as though he were
encased in cement.* — JAMES AND THE GIANT PEACH

duck noun **ducks**
A duck is a swimming bird with a flat beak that lives
near water. The Gregg family shoot ducks until one
day the ducks turn on them (thanks to a certain
Magic Finger).
*On the ground below them stood the four enormous
ducks, as tall as men, and three of them were holding
guns in their hands.* — THE MAGIC FINGER

duck verb **ducks, ducking, ducked**
If you duck, you bend down quickly so that something
will not hit you.
*The wind rushing against Sophie's face became so strong
that she had to duck down again into the blanket
to prevent her head from being blown away.* — THE BFG

Duke of Hampshire

(THE GIRAFFE AND THE PELLY AND ME)

The Duke of Hampshire is the richest man in England. He lives in a grand house with six hundred and seventy-seven windows (as well as a greenhouse), which he asks the Ladderless Window-Cleaning Company to clean.

dull adjective **duller, dullest**

1 A dull book or a dull task is boring and not at all interesting. Reading a dictionary, for example, is never dull.

'I've read all the ones that are in the public library in the High Street, Miss Honey . . . I liked some of them very much indeed,' Matilda said, 'but I thought others were fairly dull.' — MATILDA

2 A dull person has no spark or imagination, like Mike Teavee whose brain has turned to mush after watching too much television.

IT CLOGS AND CLUTTERS UP THE MIND!/IT MAKES A CHILD SO DULL AND BLIND/HE CAN NO LONGER UNDERSTAND/ A FANTASY, A FAIRYLAND! — CHARLIE AND THE CHOCOLATE FACTORY

dumbsilly adverb

If you talk dumbsilly, you are talking nonsense and not making any sense.

'How is I possibly going to get near enough to the Queen of England's bedroom to blow in my dream? You is talking dumbsilly.' — THE BFG

dumpling noun **dumplings**

a ball of dough cooked in a stew

Boggis . . . was enormously fat. This was because he ate three boiled chickens smothered with dumplings every day for breakfast, lunch and supper. — FANTASTIC MR FOX

dungeon noun **dungeons**

a prison underneath a castle

The mist came into the Elevator. It had the fusty reeky smell of an old underground dungeon. — CHARLIE AND THE GREAT GLASS ELEVATOR

dungerous adjective

very dangerous

'You is bitten by a snake!' he shouted . . . 'It was a frightsome poisnowse viper! It was a dreadly dungerous vind-screen viper!' — THE BFG

DID YOU KNOW? To make the word *dungerous*, Roald Dahl started with *dangerous* but swapped one letter so that it also makes you think of *dungeon*, which is a dark and dangerous place.

dusk noun

the dim light at the end of the day, just before it gets dark

Sophie . . . and the Big Friendly Giant sat quietly side by side on the blue rock in the gathering dusk. — THE BFG

SPARKY SYNONYMS You can also say *twilight* or **gloam**.

dusky adjective **duskier, duskiest**

rather dark and murky

'Ah-ha,' said the BFG. 'Now we is getting on to the dark and dusky secrets.' — THE BFG

dust noun

dry dirt that is like powder

I long to explore inside it but the door is always locked, and when I peer through a window all I can see is darkness and dust. — THE GIRAFFE AND THE PELLY AND ME

dustbin noun **dustbins**

a large container for putting rubbish in (but not usually pigtails)

'I want those filthy pigtails off before you come back to school tomorrow!' she barked. 'Chop 'em off and throw 'em in the dustbin, you understand?' — MATILDA

dusty adjective **dustier, dustiest**

full of dust, or covered in dust

About two hundred yards from the jetty, along a narrow dusty road, stood a simple wooden hotel painted white. — BOY

RINGBELLING RHYMES Try rhyming with *fusty* or *musty*.

duty noun **duties**

If a soldier or Oompa-Loompa is on duty, they are doing their regular work.

'"What have we here?" I cried, and I rushed it quickly to the Testing Room and gave some to the Oompa-Loompa who was on duty there at the time.' — CHARLIE AND THE GREAT GLASS ELEVATOR

dye verb **dyes, dyeing, dyed**

When you dye something, you change its colour by using a special coloured liquid.

Mrs Wormwood's hair was dyed a brilliant platinum blonde, very much the same glistening silvery colour as a female tightrope-walker's tights in a circus. — MATILDA

dyslexia noun

Someone with dyslexia finds it difficult to learn to read and write because their brain muddles up letters and words. The Vicar of Nibbleswicke has a rare form called Back-to-Front Dyslexia, which is why he muddles up Miss Prewt's name and calls her (unfortunately) *Miss Twerp.*

a
b
c
d
e
f
g
h
i
j
k
l
m
n
o
p
q
r
s
t
u
v
w
x
y
z

Ee

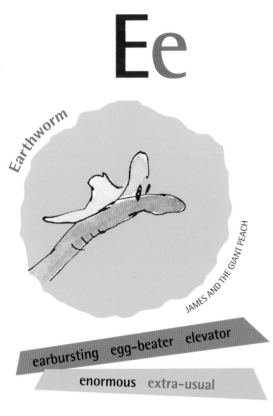

Earthworm — JAMES AND THE GIANT PEACH

earbursting   egg-beater   elevator

enormous   extra-usual

eager adjective
If you are eager to do something, you are very keen to do it.
All the children . . . were so eager to get going that their parents were having to hold them back by force to prevent them from climbing over the gates. — CHARLIE AND THE CHOCOLATE FACTORY

ear noun **ears**
Your ears are the parts of your body that you use for hearing. The BFG is very proud of his **extra-usual** ears which he can move around like a satellite dish to pick up the silvery soft sounds of dreams as they go whiffling by.
The BFG pointed up at his enormous truck-wheel ears which he now began to move in and out. He performed this exercise proudly, with a little proud smile on his face. — THE BFG
DID YOU KNOW? The word *auricular* means 'to do with ears or hearing', so the BFG is an auricular expert.

earbursting adjective
An earbursting sound is so loud that it nearly bursts your eardrums.
'Bonecrunching Giant crunches up two whoppsy-whiffling human beans for supper every night! Noise is earbursting!' — THE BFG

eardrum noun **eardrums**
a part of your ear that vibrates when sound reaches it
'SPEAK!' boomed the voice, getting louder and louder and ending in a fearful frightening shout that rattled Charlie's eardrums. — CHARLIE AND THE GREAT GLASS ELEVATOR

earth noun
1 Earth is the planet that **human beans**, giants, giraffes and all sorts of other creatures live on — but not Knids, who live on Planet Vermes.
Higher and higher rushed the Great Glass Elevator until soon they could see the countries and oceans of the Earth spread out below them like a map. — CHARLIE AND THE GREAT GLASS ELEVATOR
2 the soil in which plants grow and in which earthworms burrow
A large dining-room had been hollowed out of the earth, and in the middle of it, seated around a huge table, were no less than twenty-nine animals. — FANTASTIC MR FOX

Earthworm (JAMES AND THE GIANT PEACH)
The Earthworm is a blind worm who lives in the Giant Peach. He hates the Centipede, who teases him all the time, and always fears that the worst is going to happen.

earwig noun **earwigs**
1 a crawling garden insect with pincers at the end of its body
'A big fat earwig is very tasty,' Grandma said, licking her lips. 'But you've got to be very quick, my dear, when you put one of those in your mouth.' — GEORGE'S MARVELLOUS MEDICINE
2 The BFG calls the ears of **human beans** earwigs, as they seem so tiny compared to his.
'You is hearing only thumping loud noises with those little earwigs of yours. But I am hearing all the secret whisperings of the world.' — THE BFG
DID YOU KNOW? The *earwig* got its name because people used to think that earwigs crawled inside their ears. The second part of the word is related to *wiggle*, so an earwig is literally an 'ear wiggler'.

easily adverb
If you do something easily, you do it without any trouble.
The corridor was so wide that a car could easily have been driven along it. — CHARLIE AND THE CHOCOLATE FACTORY

easy adjective **easier, easiest**
If something is easy, you can do it or understand it without any trouble.
Mrs Twit had hidden the key to the front door under the mat and Muggle-Wump had seen her doing it, so it was easy for them to get in. — THE TWITS

eat verb **eats, eating, ate, eaten**
When you eat, you put food in your mouth and swallow it. Here are some scrumptious words to describe how someone *eats*.

TO EAT GREEDILY OR QUICKLY:
devour, gobble, gorge, gulp, guzzle, wolf or wolf down
• Someone who eats greedily, like Augustus Gloop, is a **glutton**. You can also say they are **gluttonous**.

Charlie went on wolfing the chocolate. He couldn't stop. And in less than half a minute, the whole thing had disappeared down his throat.—CHARLIE AND THE CHOCOLATE FACTORY

TO EAT NOISILY: chomp, crunch, gnash, munch, slurp
Mrs Wormwood sat munching her meal with her eyes glued to the American soap-opera on the screen.
—MATILDA

TO EAT IN SMALL AMOUNTS: nibble, peck, pick at, sup, taste
'At this moment,' continued the Ladybird, 'our Centipede, who has a pair of jaws as sharp as razors, is up there on top of the peach nibbling away at that stem.'
—JAMES AND THE GIANT PEACH

eatable adjective
If something is eatable, you can eat it without getting ill.
Charlie found himself looking out once again at the great Chocolate Room . . . where everything was eatable — the trees, the leaves, the grass, the pebbles and even the rocks.—CHARLIE AND THE GREAT GLASS ELEVATOR

eccentric adjective
An eccentric person behaves strangely all the time. Only grown-ups can be eccentric.
The service went well and was voted very jolly indeed. Everyone was pleased with the new eccentric young vicar.
—THE VICAR OF NIBBLESWICKE

echo verb **echoes, echoing, echoed**
When a sound echoes, it bounces off a wall or ceiling and you hear it repeated.
'Wait!' shrieked one of the witches in the back row. 'Hold everything!' Her shrieking voice echoed through the Ballroom like a trumpet.—THE WITCHES

educated adjective
Someone who is educated has learned things through going to school, or (like Matilda) in spite of going to school. Giants are not educated because there are no schools, and no libraries either, in Giant Country.
My father was not what you would call an educated man and I doubt if he had read twenty books in his life. But he was a marvellous story-teller.—DANNY THE CHAMPION OF THE WORLD
DID YOU KNOW? The word *educate* means 'to lead out' because education is meant to draw the best out of you (perhaps Miss Trunchbull didn't know that).

eerie adjective **eerier, eeriest**
weird and frightening
Gradually it grew darker and darker, and then a pale three-quarter moon came up over the tops of the clouds and cast an eerie light over the whole scene.—JAMES AND THE GIANT PEACH

effect noun **effects**
If something has an effect, it makes something else happen.
The effect that Medicine Number Two had on this chicken was not quite the same as the effect produced by Medicine Number One, but it was very interesting.
—GEORGE'S MARVELLOUS MEDICINE

egg noun **eggs**
An egg is an oval object with a thin shell that hens and Roly-Poly birds lay (as well as other birds, fish, reptiles and insects), and in which their offspring develop. Vermicious Knids are naturally egg-shaped, or you could say that eggs on Planet Earth are shaped like Knids.
'Old hen's laid its last egg!' Grandma shouted. 'Hens don't do any laying after they've been on fire!'—GEORGE'S MARVELLOUS MEDICINE

egg verb **eggs, egging, egged**
If you egg someone on, you encourage them to do something.
His speech was never very delicate but Matilda was used to it. She also knew that he liked to boast and she would egg him on shamelessly.—MATILDA

egg-beater noun **egg-beaters**
An egg-beater is a device with blades which you turn with a handle to whisk eggs or cream. The BFG uses an old egg-beater to whisk and mix dreams together (so he uses it as a zozimus-beater).
The BFG . . . took out a gigantic egg-beater. It was one of those that has a handle which you turn, and down below there are a lot of overlapping blades that go whizzing round.—THE BFG

elastic adjective
If something is elastic, like a Knid or a small boy, it can stretch and then go back to its usual size.
'But small boys are extremely springy and elastic. They stretch like mad. So what we'll do, we'll put him in a special machine I have for testing the stretchiness of chewing-gum!'—CHARLIE AND THE CHOCOLATE FACTORY

a b c d

I'M LOST!

e f g h i j k l m n o p q r s t u v w x y z

An old-fashioned word for an egg-beater is a *froth-stick*.

elbow noun elbows

Your elbow is the joint in the middle of your arm, where your arm can bend. Elbows are in just the right place for leaning on desks and tables, although some grown-ups frown when you do this.

Matilda, sitting in the second row about ten feet away from Miss Honey, put her elbows on the desk and cupped her face in her hands. — MATILDA

DID YOU KNOW? The word *elbow* means literally 'arm-bending'. An *ell* is an old measurement that was roughly the length of a grown-up's forearm from wrist to elbow. The second part of the word is the same as the *bow* in *bow and arrow*.

electric adjective

1 An electric light or machine is worked by electricity.
2 An electric atmosphere or effect is full of tingling excitement.

It was a brutal and bewitching smell. . . . Whenever he got a whiff of it up his nose, firecrackers went off in his skull and electric prickles ran along the backs of his legs. — GEORGE'S MARVELLOUS MEDICINE

Electric Fizzcockler noun

Electric Fizzcocklers
a hair-raising sweet that is sold in the Grubber

I can remember . . . the Electric Fizzcocklers that made every hair on your head stand straight up on end as soon as you popped one into your mouth. — THE GIRAFFE AND THE PELLY AND ME

LOOK IT UP! Some other sweet treats sold in the Grubber are **Giant Wangdoodles** and **Gumglotters**.

electricity noun

Electricity is the power or energy that is used to give light and heat and to work machines. Matilda can generate electricity in her head and use it to move objects with her **telekinetic** powers.

Very quickly this time she felt the electricity beginning to flow inside her head, gathering itself behind the eyes, and the eyes became hot and millions of tiny invisible hands began pushing out like sparks. — MATILDA

elefunt noun elefunts

the BFG's word for an elephant

'I would so much love to have a jumbly big elefunt and go riding through green forests picking peachy fruits off the trees all day long.' — THE BFG

DID YOU KNOW? The word *elephant* has been spelled many different ways in the past, including *elpend*, *olifant* and *holifant*, so the BFG's spelling is not that peculiar after all.

elephant noun elephants

a very large animal found in Africa and India, with a thick grey skin, large ears, a trunk and tusks

The Ruler of India sent the BFG a magnificent elephant,

the very thing he had been wishing for all his life. — THE BFG

elevator noun elevators

An elevator is a lift that carries people up and down the levels of a building or, in the case of the Great Glass Elevator, into Outer Space. (In North America, people say *elevator* more often than *lift*.)

Mr Wonka . . . pressed a brown button. The Elevator shuddered, and then with a fearful whooshing noise it shot vertically upward like a rocket. — CHARLIE AND THE GREAT GLASS ELEVATOR

embarrassed adjective

If you feel embarrassed, you feel shy or awkward about something.

Miss Honey paused and sipped her tea. 'I can't think why I am telling you all this,' she said, embarrassed. — MATILDA

embarrassing adjective

If something is embarrassing, it makes you feel shy or awkward.

There followed a rather long and embarrassing silence. In the space of thirty seconds the atmosphere in the tiny room had changed completely. — MATILDA

emerge verb emerges, emerging, emerged

When something emerges, it appears from somewhere.

The Giraffe, with the Monkey dancing about on her back, emerged suddenly from the bushes. — THE GIRAFFE AND THE PELLY AND ME

emergency noun emergencies

When there is an emergency, something very dangerous suddenly happens and people must act quickly so that no one gets hurt.

This was the hot line direct to the Premier of Soviet Russia in Moscow. It was always open and only used in terrible emergencies. — CHARLIE AND THE GREAT GLASS ELEVATOR

empty adjective emptier, emptiest

Something that is empty has nothing in it.

'You is not very clever,' the Giant said, moving his great ears in and out. 'I thought all human beans is full of brains, but your head is emptier than a bundongle.' — THE BFG

empty verb empties, emptying, emptied

When you empty something, you take everything out of it.

Number one was a bottle labelled GOLDEN GLOSS HAIR SHAMPOO. He emptied it into the pan. 'That ought to wash her tummy nice and clean,' he said. — GEORGE'S MARVELLOUS MEDICINE

enemy noun enemies

An enemy is someone who wants to hurt you, like a witch or Knid or headmistress (or a chicken farmer if you are a fox).

*'But who **wants** to go out, anyway; let me ask you that? We are all diggers, every one of us. We hate the outside. The outside is full of enemies.'* — FANTASTIC MR FOX

energetic adjective

If you are energetic, you have a lot of energy to do things like running or shaking hands.

The next two children . . . came forward to have their tickets examined and then to have their arms practically pumped off their shoulders by the energetic Mr Wonka. — CHARLIE AND THE CHOCOLATE FACTORY

energy noun

If you have energy, you feel strong and fit (even without taking Wonka-Vite).

'Why have they got such tiny labels?' 'That,' the BFG said, 'is because one day I is catching so many dreams I is not having the time or energy to write out long labels.' — THE BFG

engine noun engines

a machine that can make things like a car or aeroplane or **bellypopper** move

The pilots throttled back the engines and all nine helicopters landed safely on the great yellow wasteland. — THE BFG

engineer noun engineers

An engineer designs machines or plans the building of roads and bridges (or pits to imprison giants).

The walls were perpendicular and engineers had calculated that there was no way a giant could escape once he was put in. — THE BFG

enjoy verb enjoys, enjoying, enjoyed

If you enjoy something, you like doing it or watching it.

The Centipede kept on grinning. He seemed to be enjoying enormously the commotion that he was causing. — JAMES AND THE GIANT PEACH

enormous adjective

Something enormous is very VERY big.

*In the town itself, actually within **sight** of the house in which Charlie lived, there was an ENORMOUS CHOCOLATE FACTORY! Just imagine that!* — CHARLIE AND THE CHOCOLATE FACTORY

SPARKY SYNONYMS You can also say **gigantuous** or **jumpsquiffling**.

LOOK IT UP! For other ways to describe something enormous, see **big**.

a b c d e f g h i j k l m n o p q r s t u v w x y z

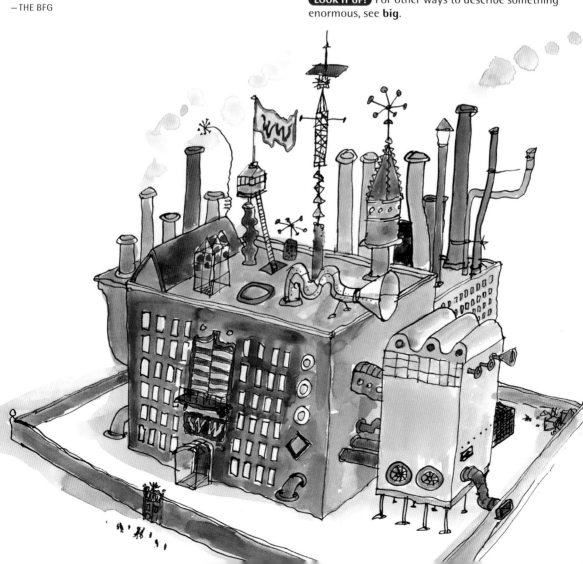

75

Enormous Crocodile (THE ENORMOUS CROCODILE)

The Enormous Crocodile lives in Africa. He has huge jaws with terrible sharp teeth and tries to trick children into coming near so that he can eat them.

enter verb enters, entering, entered

When you enter a place, you go into it.

Charlie entered the shop and laid the damp fifty pence on the counter. 'One Wonka's Whipple-Scrumptious Fudgemallow Delight,' he said. — CHARLIE AND THE CHOCOLATE FACTORY

entrance noun entrances

the way into a place

Now that the entrance had been sealed up, there was not a glint of light inside the cave. All was black. — THE BFG

envelope noun envelopes

a paper cover that you put a letter in before you send it

A single Oompa-Loompa emerged and came rushing towards Mr Wonka, carrying a huge envelope in his hands. — CHARLIE AND THE GREAT GLASS ELEVATOR

envy noun

Envy is the feeling you have when you would like to have something that someone else has. You can also say that you feel envious.

'I've seen pictures of giant tortoises that are so huge people can ride on their backs! If Alfie were to see those he'd turn green with envy.' — ESIO TROT

epicure noun epicures

An epicure is exactly what Matilda says it is.

Miss Honey said, 'Do you know what an epicure is, Matilda?' 'It is someone who is dainty with his eating,' Matilda said. 'That is correct,' Miss Honey said. — MATILDA

equal adjective

If two things are equal, they are the same size or worth the same amount. Aunt Spiker and Aunt Sponge, for example, are not equal in size, but are equal in beastliness.

'Do you know, Danny, that the cost of rearing and keeping one single pheasant up to the time when it's ready to be shot is equal to the price of one hundred loaves of bread!' — DANNY THE CHAMPION OF THE WORLD

escape verb escapes, escaping, escaped

If you escape, you get away from a horrible place, or horrible people, and become free. Sometimes you can escape in your imagination by reading books, as Matilda does.

Oh, Lord have mercy on me! These foul bald-headed females are child-killers every one of them, and here I am imprisoned in the same room and I can't escape! — THE WITCHES

Esio Trot (ESIO TROT)

Eht sdrow *Esio Trot* era trap fo a lacigam mrahc taht rM yppoH stnevni ot ekam eiflA eht esiotrot worg reggib. Eht sdrow era tsuj 'esiotrot' delleps sdrawkcab.

Mrs Silver caught the paper and held it up in front of her. This is what she read: ESIO TROT, ESIO TROT, TEG REGGIB REGGIB! — ESIO TROT

> **Gobblefunking with words**
>
> Here are some other animal names spelled backwards: *Alli Rog, Epol Etna, Olli Damra, Olaf Fub.* A word or phrase that reads the same both backwards and forwards, like *madam* or *never odd or even,* is called a *palindrome.* The word *palindrome* means literally 'running back' and is related to *dromedary,* a fast-running camel. (So a name for a camel that runs backwards would be a *Palindromic Dromedary.*)

eureka exclamation

Eureka! is something you might shout if you have discovered something brilliant and exciting.

'And all of a sudden, the answer hits me. I tell you, I felt exactly like that other brilliant fellow must have felt when he discovered penicillin. "Eureka!" I cried. "I've got it!"' — MATILDA

DID YOU KNOW? The shout *Eureka!* comes from ancient Greek and means 'I have found it'. There is a story that a famous Greek mathematician called Archimedes shouted *Eureka!* when he made an important discovery while having a bath.

evaporate verb evaporates, evaporating, evaporated

When water evaporates, it changes from liquid into steam or vapour.

Boil for a further twenty-seven days but do not stir. At the end of this time, all liquid will have evaporated and there will be left in the bottom of the cauldron only a hard brown lump. — CHARLIE AND THE GREAT GLASS ELEVATOR

evening noun evenings

the time at the end of the day before you go to bed

In the evenings, after he had finished his supper of watery cabbage soup, Charlie always went into the room of his four grandparents to listen to their stories. — CHARLIE AND THE CHOCOLATE FACTORY

everlasting adjective
An everlasting sweet (like Willy Wonka's Everlasting Gobstopper) never gets any smaller, no matter how long you chew or suck it.
'Everlasting Gobstoppers!' cried Mr Wonka proudly. 'They're completely new! I am inventing them for children who are given very little pocket money.' — CHARLIE AND THE CHOCOLATE FACTORY

evil adjective
Something evil is wicked and cruel, and an evil person does wicked and cruel things that are meant to harm you.
'Eating human beans is wrong and evil,' the BFG said. 'It is guzzly and glumptious!' shouted the Bloodbottler. — THE BFG
LOOK IT UP! For other ways to describe utterly evil characters, see **bad**.

exact adjective
completely right or accurate
'I have a lot of legs,' the Centipede answered proudly. 'And a lot of feet. One hundred, to be exact.' — JAMES AND THE GIANT PEACH

exam or examination noun exams, examinations
a test that grown-ups make you sit, to see if you have been paying attention to them
'What's so wonderful about being a little boy anyway? . . . Little boys have to go to school. Mice don't. Mice don't have to pass exams.' — THE WITCHES

examine verb examines, examining, examined
When you examine something, you look at it very carefully.
Mr Fox examined the wall carefully. He saw that the cement between the bricks was old and crumbly, so he loosened a brick without much trouble and pulled it away. — FANTASTIC MR FOX

excellent adjective
extremely good, or of the best kind
'We certainly was putting that nightmare to good use though, wasn't we?' 'Excellent use,' Sophie said. — THE BFG
SPARKY SYNONYMS You can also say **fantabulous** or **phizz-whizzing**.
LOOK IT UP! For other ways to describe fantabulousness, see **good**.

excited adjective
If you are excited, you feel as if something wonderful is going to happen and you cannot wait.
James . . . was terribly excited. He flew through the long grass and the stinging-nettles, not caring whether he got stung or not on his bare knees. — JAMES AND THE GIANT PEACH

exciting adjective
If something is exciting, it makes you interested and eager to find out more.
Nobody had ever made a medicine like that before. If it didn't actually cure Grandma, then it would anyway cause some exciting results. — GEORGE'S MARVELLOUS MEDICINE

exclaim verb exclaims, exclaiming, exclaimed
When you exclaim, you shout suddenly because you are surprised or excited.
'But what tremendous tall buildings!' exclaimed the Ladybird. 'I've never seen anything like them before in England.' — JAMES AND THE GIANT PEACH
LOOK IT UP! For lots of ways to describe how people speak, see **say**.

exclamation noun exclamations
An exclamation is something you say or shout when you are very happy, angry or surprised, such as *Oh my goodness!* or *Swipe my swoggles!*
As Little Billy went from window to window, the Minpins followed him, clustering round and smiling at his exclamations of wonder. — THE MINPINS
LOOK IT UP! Some useful exclamations are **crikey!** and **gosh!**

Gobblefunking with words
Roald Dahl liked to vary the exclamations he used for different characters. For example, Willy Wonka says *Great whistling whangdoodles!* and the US President says *Screaming scorpions!* When he is surprised, the BFG exclaims *Oh mince my maggots!* and *Oh swipe my swoggles!* and the Geraneous Giraffe says *Oh, my naked neck!* All of these examples use **alliteration** too.

excuse (rhymes with goose) noun excuses
a good reason you give to grown-ups to explain why you can't do what they have asked
You got punished if you were caught out of bed after lights-out. Even if you said you had to go to the lavatory that was not accepted as an excuse. — THE BFG

exercise noun exercises
An exercise is piece of work you have to do for homework or to practise something.
Some masters read a book while taking Prep and some corrected exercises, but not Captain Hardcastle. — BOY

exercise verb exercises, exercising, exercised
If you exercise skill or patience, you use or apply it.
Great skill would have to be exercised, Lavender told herself, and great secrecy observed if she was to come out of this exploit alive. — MATILDA

exhausted adjective
If you are exhausted, you are very tired.
Even the Silkworm, looking white and thin and completely exhausted, came creeping out of the tunnel to watch this miraculous ascent. — JAMES AND THE GIANT PEACH

exist verb exists, existing, existed
Things that exist are real, not imaginary.
'Well, first of all,' said the BFG, 'human beans is not really believing in giants, is they? Human beans is not thinking we exist.' 'I do,' Sophie said. — THE BFG

a b c d e f g h i j k l m n o p q r s t u v w x y z

A *spoonerism* is a phrase where you *lop the swetters*. Read more at **mideous**.

expect verb **expects, expecting, expected**
If you expect that something will happen, you think that it will happen.
*The pheasants that had flown up off the car **stayed up in the air**. They didn't come flapping drunkenly down as we had expected them to.* — DANNY THE CHAMPION OF THE WORLD

expel verb **expels, expelling, expelled**
If a teacher expels you from school, you are sent away and told to never come back (which is, unfortunately, not as good as it sounds).
'I can see that I'm going to have to expel as many of you as possible as soon as possible to save myself from going round the bend.' — MATILDA

expensive adjective
Something that is expensive costs a lot of money.
'A Geraneous Giraffe cannot eat anything except the pink and purple flowers of the tinkle-tinkle tree. But those, as I am sure you know, are hard to find and expensive to buy.' — THE GIRAFFE AND THE PELLY AND ME

experiment verb **experiments, experimenting, experimented**
When you experiment, you run a test to find out whether an idea works.
'I suppose you guessed,' Mr Wonka went on, 'what happened to all those Oompa-Loompas in the Testing Room when I was experimenting with Wonka-Vite.' — CHARLIE AND THE GREAT GLASS ELEVATOR

expert noun **experts**
An expert does something very well or knows a lot about it.
The BFG was an expert on windows. He had opened thousands of them over the years to blow his dreams into children's bedrooms. — THE BFG

explain verb **explains, explaining, explained**
When you explain something, you talk about it so that other people understand it.
'Exunckly,' the BFG said. 'So what I is trying to explain to you is that a human bean who says he is fifty is not fifty, he is only thirty.' — THE BFG

explode verb **explodes, exploding, exploded**
When something explodes, it bursts or blows up with a loud bang.
She was swelling! She was puffing up all over! Someone was pumping her up, that's how it looked! Was she going to explode? — GEORGE'S MARVELLOUS MEDICINE

explore verb **explores, exploring, explored**
When you explore a place, you look around it carefully to find out what it is like.
Not far from where I live there is a queer old empty wooden house standing all by itself . . . I long to explore inside it but the door is always locked. — THE GIRAFFE AND THE PELLY AND ME

explosion noun **explosions**
a loud bang that is made when something bursts or blows up
Then the old man took a deep breath, and suddenly, with no warning whatsoever, an explosion seemed to take place inside him. — CHARLIE AND THE CHOCOLATE FACTORY

express verb **expresses, expressing, expressed**
When you express your ideas or feelings, you talk about them to other people.
The BFG expressed a wish to learn how to speak properly, and Sophie herself, who loved him as she would a father, volunteered to give him lessons every day. — THE BFG

expression noun **expressions**
1 Your expression is the look on your face.
The sheet-white faces of Shuckworth, Shanks and Showler were pressed against the glass of the little windows, . . . their mouths open, their expressions frozen like fish fingers. — CHARLIE AND THE GREAT GLASS ELEVATOR
2 An expression is also a word or phrase, like *My goodness me!* or *Swipe my swoggles!*

extend verb **extends, extending, extended**
If you extend something, you make it longer, and if you extend your hand, you reach it out.
'I am Eel, Miss Twerp!' cried the vicar, extending his hand. 'I am the new rotsap, the new raciv of Nibbleswicke!' — THE VICAR OF NIBBLESWICKE

exterminate verb **exterminates, exterminating, exterminated**
If you hear a witch saying she wants to exterrrminate you, it is best to run very fast and very far, as she means to destroy you completely.
'Rrrootle it out, this small lump of dung!' screeched The Grand High Witch. 'Don't let it escape! . . . It must be exterrrminated immediately!' — THE WITCHES

extraordinary adjective

Something that is extraordinary is very unusual, like the sight of a giant chicken.

It was an extraordinary sight. The cockerel's body hadn't grown at all. But the neck was now about six feet long. — GEORGE'S MARVELLOUS MEDICINE

extra-usual adjective

Something extra-usual is extraordinarily large or extraordinarily powerful — or both, in the case of the BFG's ears.

'They maybe is looking a bit propsposterous to you,' the BFG said, 'but you must believe me when I say they is very extra-usual ears indeed.' — THE BFG

DID YOU KNOW? The word *extra-usual* is based on *extraordinary*, but Roald Dahl replaced the second part with a synonym to make a new word with a similar meaning.

extremely adverb

very, or as much or as far as possible

James . . . crawled on for several more yards, and then suddenly — bang — the top of his head bumped into something extremely hard blocking his way. — JAMES AND THE GIANT PEACH

exunckly adverb

If you say *exunckly* to someone, you are agreeing with what they have just said.

'It's a funny thought,' Sophie said. 'Exunckly,' the BFG said. — THE BFG

eye noun **eyes**

Your eyes are the parts of your body that you use for seeing. Eyes come in different colours and expressions. Mr Wonka has blue twinkling eyes, but Knids have menacing white eyes with blazing red centres.

About three-quarters of the way up, in the widest part, there were two large round eyes as big as tea-cups. The eyes were white, but each had a brilliant red pupil in the centre. — CHARLIE AND THE GREAT GLASS ELEVATOR

Gobblefunking with words

Eyes are a good way of describing the way a character looks or feels. Eyes can be *glassy* or *beady* or *sunken*. They can *shine* or *twinkle* with excitement, *blaze* with anger or menace, and *bulge* or *pop out of their sockets* in surprise. Augustus Gloop has *small greedy currant eyes* and Victor Hazell has *tiny piggy eyes*.

Mr Fox

FANTASTIC MR FOX

fantabulous   filthsome   fizzing

formula   frobscottle   frotsy

fabulous adjective

Something that is fabulous, such as drinking **frobscottle**, is very enjoyable and very exciting.

Sophie opened her mouth, and very gently the BFG tipped the bottle forward and poured some of the fabulous frobscottle down her throat. — THE BFG

SPARKY SYNONYMS You can also say **fantabulous** or **gloriumptious**.

face noun **faces**

the front part of your head, where your eyes, nose and mouth are

Mrs Twit wasn't born ugly. She'd had quite a nice face when she was young. The ugliness had grown upon her year by year as she got older. — THE TWITS

face verb **faces, facing, faced**

The direction that you are facing is the direction in which you are looking.

Then Nigel said, still balancing on one leg and facing the wall, 'Miss Honey taught us how to spell a new very long word yesterday'. — MATILDA

a b c d e f g h i j k l m n o p q r s t u v w x y z

fact noun **facts**
something that we know is true
'The plain fact is,' my grandmother said, 'that your son Bruno has been rather drastically altered.' 'Altered!' shouted Mr Jenkins. 'What the devil d'you mean altered?'
— THE WITCHES

factory noun **factories**
A factory is a large building where people make things with machines. Most factories (like the toothpaste factory where Mr Bucket works) are quite dull, but Willy Wonka's Chocolate Factory (the largest factory in the world) is as beautiful inside as one of his confectionery creations.
'This is the nerve centre of the whole factory, the heart of the whole business! And so beautiful! I insist upon my rooms being beautiful! I can't abide ugliness in factories!'
— CHARLIE AND THE CHOCOLATE FACTORY

faded adjective
Something that is faded is less bright or less distinct than it once was, like the colour of the BFG's well-worn trousers.
Under the cloak he was wearing a sort of collarless shirt and a dirty old leather waistcoat that didn't seem to have any buttons. His trousers were faded green and were far too short in the legs. — THE BFG

fail verb **fails, failing, failed**
1 If you fail, you try to do something but are not able to do it.
'They're going to dump us!' Gretel cried./'They won't succeed,' the boy replied./'We'll get back home, we cannot fail,/By following the breadcrumb trail.' — RHYME STEW
2 If you fail to do something, you do not do it when you should.
Mr and Mrs Wormwood were both so gormless and so wrapped up in their own silly little lives that they failed to notice anything unusual about their daughter.
— MATILDA

failing noun **failings**
a weakness or fault
'I think Mr C. S. Lewis is a very good writer. But he has one failing. There are no funny bits in his books.' — MATILDA

faint adjective **fainter, faintest**
If something is faint, you cannot hear or see it very clearly.
Inside the jar Sophie could see the faint scarlet outline of something that looked like a mixture between a blob of gas and a bubble of jelly. — THE BFG

faint verb **faints, fainting, fainted**
If you faint, you feel dizzy and become unconscious for a short time.
Sometimes the two small monkey children would faint with so much blood going to their heads. But Mr Twit didn't care about that. — THE TWITS

fair adjective **fairer, fairest**
1 Something that is fair treats everyone in the same way so that everyone is equal.
'There's twelve pills here! That's six for me and three each for you!' 'Hey! That's not fair!' shrilled Grandma Josephine. 'It's four for each of us!' — CHARLIE AND THE GREAT GLASS ELEVATOR
2 Fair hair is light in colour.

fairy noun **fairies**
a small creature with wings and magic powers that you read about in **fairy tales**
The Fairy said, 'Hang on a tick.'/She gave her wand a mighty flick/And quickly, in no time at all,/Cindy was at the Palace Ball! — REVOLTING RHYMES

fairy tale noun **fairy tales**
a story in which magic things happen
Could it be, George wondered, that she was a witch? He had always thought witches were only in fairy tales, but now he was not so sure. — GEORGE'S MARVELLOUS MEDICINE

faithful adjective
If you are faithful to someone, you always help them and support them.
The Queen took a deep breath. She was glad no one except her faithful old Mary was here to see what was going on. — THE BFG

fake adjective
If something is fake, it is not real or valuable, although it pretends to be.
I was glad my father was an eye-smiler. It meant he never gave me a fake smile, because it's impossible to make your eyes twinkle if you aren't feeling twinkly yourself. — DANNY THE CHAMPION OF THE WORLD

false adjective
Something that is false is not true or real.
'Where's my Chief Spy?' 'Here, sir, Mr President, sir!' said the Chief Spy. He had a false moustache, a false beard, false eyelashes, false teeth and a falsetto voice. — CHARLIE AND THE GREAT GLASS ELEVATOR

family noun **families**
Your family is all the people who are related to you, for example your parents, brothers and sisters, aunts and uncles.
The four monkeys in the cage in the garden were all one family. They were Muggle-Wump and his wife and their two small children. — THE TWITS

famished adjective
very hungry
'I'm hungry!' the Spider announced suddenly, staring hard at James. 'I'm famished!' the Old-Green-Grasshopper said. 'So am I!' the Ladybird cried. — JAMES AND THE GIANT PEACH

famous adjective

Someone or something famous is very well known. Both Willy Wonka and his Chocolate Factory are famous throughout the world.

And as for the enormous peach stone — it was set up permanently in a place of honour in Central Park and became a famous monument. — JAMES AND THE GIANT PEACH

SPARKY SYNONYMS You can also say *celebrated* or *renowned*. A famous person like Willy Wonka is a *celebrity*.

fantabulous adjective (*informal*)

fantastic and fabulous

'Whoopee!' cried the witches, clapping their hands. 'You are brilliant, O Your Grandness! You are fantabulous!' — THE WITCHES

fantastic adjective

Something that is fantastic is wonderful.

The four Small Foxes scrambled up out of the tunnel and what a fantastic sight it was that now met their eyes! — FANTASTIC MR FOX

farm noun farms

A farm is a piece of land where a farmer grows crops and keeps animals for food. Farmers Boggis, Bunce and Bean keep various kinds of poultry on their farms.

'You've had your last chicken!' yelled Boggis. 'You'll never come prowling around my farm again!' — FANTASTIC MR FOX

farmer noun farmers

A farmer is someone who has a farm, such as George's father, Mr Kranky, or the evil-minded Farmers Boggis, Bunce and Bean.

Bean was a turkey-and-apple farmer. He kept thousands of turkeys in an orchard full of apple trees. — FANTASTIC MR FOX

fascinated adjective

If you are fascinated by something, you are very interested and give it all your attention.

With thousands of fascinated spectators, including the Queen, peering down into the pit, the BFG was lowered on a rope. One by one, he released the giants. — THE BFG

fast adjective faster, fastest

For ways to describe something that moves fast, see **move**.

Someone who hates taking a bath (like Farmer Bean) has *ablutophobia*.

fat noun
the white, greasy part of meat
It was a cold meat pie. The meat was pink and tender with no fat or gristle in it, and there were hard-boiled eggs buried like treasures in several different places. — DANNY THE CHAMPION OF THE WORLD

fat adjective **fatter, fattest**
Someone who is fat has a big, round body.
'Oh, I don't want to be eaten!' wailed the Earthworm. 'But they will take me first of all because I am so fat and juicy and I have no bones!' — JAMES AND THE GIANT PEACH

father noun **fathers**
Your father is your male parent.
Mr Kranky . . . was a kind father to George, but he was not an easy person to live with because even the smallest things got him all worked up and excited. — GEORGE'S MARVELLOUS MEDICINE

faucet noun **faucets**
a tap
The faraway voice came down to them once again, this time very loud and clear. 'On with the faucets!' it shouted. 'On with the faucets!' — JAMES AND THE GIANT PEACH
DID YOU KNOW? The word *faucet* is now used mainly in North America, but it was once used in British English too. It is an old word that originally meant a kind of tap to draw liquid from a barrel.

fault noun **faults**
When something is someone's fault, they have made it happen.
'All is my fault,' the BFG said. 'I is the one who kidsnatched you.' Yet another enormous tear welled from his eye and splashed on to the floor. — THE BFG

favourite adjective
Your favourite thing is the one that you like the most. Mr Twit's favourite food is Bird Pie, Matilda's favourite author is Charles Dickens, and Miss Trunchbull's favourite punishment is to lock her pupils in the Chokey.
Mr Twit wasn't going to wait another week for his Bird Pie supper. He loved Bird Pie. It was his favourite meal. — THE TWITS

fear noun **fears**
Fear is the feeling you get when you are frightened because you think something bad is going to happen.
The Ladybird, who had been haunted all her life by the fear that her house was on fire and her children all gone, married the Head of the Fire Department and lived happily ever after. — JAMES AND THE GIANT PEACH
fear verb **fears, fearing, feared**
If you fear something, you are afraid of it.
'I fear no Knids!' said Mr Wonka. 'We've got them beaten now!' — CHARLIE AND THE GREAT GLASS ELEVATOR

Gobblefunking with words
Roald Dahl's characters often find themselves in fearful situations, so there are many ways to describe fear in his stories. For example, the passengers on the peach sit *frozen with terror* and Mrs Twit goes *white with fear* at the thought of the Dreaded Shrinks. You can also be *petrified* (which means literally 'turned to stone') or *fossilized* with fear. For other ways to describe fear see **afraid**.

fearful adjective
1 If you are fearful, you feel very afraid.
The boy stood to one side. He looked nervous . . . His plump flabby face had turned grey with fearful apprehension. — MATILDA
2 A fearful sound is terrifying.
'SPEAK!' boomed the voice, getting louder and louder and ending in a fearful frightening shout that rattled Charlie's eardrums. — CHARLIE AND THE GREAT GLASS ELEVATOR.

fearsome adjective
A fearsome creature looks or sounds menacing and very scary.
Sophie, peeping out of her spy-hole, saw all nine of the fearsome giants coming past at full gallop. — THE BFG

feast noun feasts
a grand meal for a lot of people or animals, usually
to mark a special occasion
*The feast was just beginning. A large dining-room had
been hollowed out of the earth, and in the middle of it,
seated around a huge table, were no less than twenty-nine
animals.* — FANTASTIC MR FOX

feast verb feasts, feasting, feasted
If you feast upon something, you eat it in a very grand way.
*'For my lunch today I shall feast upon a fat juicy little child
while you lie here in the river feeling hungry.'*
— THE ENORMOUS CROCODILE

feather noun feathers
the light, soft parts that grow from a bird's skin and
cover its body
*'I've come for a holiday,' said the Roly-Poly Bird . . .
He fluffed his marvellous coloured feathers and looked
down rather grandly at the monkeys.* — THE TWITS

feature noun features
Someone's features are the main parts of their face, such
as their mouth, nose and eyes. You can only see a witch's
true features when she takes off her mask (and it is not
a pretty sight).
*I was magnetized by the sheer horror of this woman's
features . . . There was a look of serpents in those eyes
of hers as they flashed around the audience.* — THE WITCHES

feed verb feeds, feeding, fed
If you feed a person or an animal, you give them food
(which is very tricky if they are less than zero years old).
*'But it's impossible to feed anything into a Minus. It's like
trying to feed one's own shadow. That's why I've got to use
a spray-gun.'* — CHARLIE AND THE GREAT GLASS ELEVATOR

feel verb feels, feeling, felt
1 When you feel something, you touch it to find out
what it is like. The way that something feels is how
it seems when you touch it.
*The giant peach . . . felt soft and warm and slightly furry,
like the skin of a baby mouse.* — JAMES AND THE GIANT PEACH

2 When you feel an emotion such as anger, fear or
happiness, you have that emotion.
*As the Great Elevator continued to streak upward further
and further away from the Earth, even Charlie began to feel
a trifle nervous.* — CHARLIE AND THE GREAT GLASS ELEVATOR

feeler noun feelers
An insect's feelers are the two long thin parts on its
head that it uses for feeling. Another word for a feeler
is an **antenna**.
*'If you want to know, I happen to be a "short-horned"
grasshopper. I have two short feelers coming out
of my head.'* — JAMES AND THE GIANT PEACH

feeling noun feelings
something that you feel inside yourself, like anger, fear
or love
*It gave Charlie a queer frightening feeling to be standing
there in the middle of this grey inhuman nothingness
— as though he were in another world altogether.*
— CHARLIE AND THE GREAT GLASS ELEVATOR

female adjective
A female animal or person can become a mother.
*The Spider (who happened to be a female spider) opened
her mouth and ran a long black tongue delicately over
her lips.* — JAMES AND THE GIANT PEACH

fence noun fences
A fence is a kind of wall made from wood or wire. Fences
are put round gardens and fields, or enclosures for
captured giants.
*The head keeper immediately put up a big notice on the
fence saying, IT IS FORBIDDEN TO FEED THE GIANTS.
And after that, there were no more disasters.* — THE BFG

festooned adjective
If something is festooned, it is decorated with ornaments
(not usually pheasants) to make it look attractive.
*The Rolls was literally festooned with pheasants, all
scratching and scrabbling and making their disgusting
runny messes over the shiny silver paint.* — DANNY THE
CHAMPION OF THE WORLD

The BFG is called *El GGB* (*Gran Gigante Bonachón*) in Spanish.

fetch verb fetches, fetching, fetched
When you fetch something, you go and get it.
'George!' Grandma yelled. 'Oh, you horrible little boy! You disgusting little worm! Fetch me a cup of tea at once and a slice of currant cake!' – GEORGE'S MARVELLOUS MEDICINE
RINGBELLING RHYMES Try rhyming with *stre-e-e-e-etch*.

fiasco noun fiascos
a very embarrassing failure
Mary, the maid, stood behind them . . . and there was a look on her face which seemed to say, 'I want no part of this fiasco.' – THE BFG

fibble verb fibbles, fibbling, fibbled
If a giant fibbles, he tells a lie.
I wouldn't ever be fibbling to you,' he said. 'I know you wouldn't,' Sophie said. 'But you must understand that it isn't easy to believe such amazing things straight away.' – THE BFG
DID YOU KNOW? Roald Dahl made up the word *fibble*, but it is based on *fib*, which is an old word that is still used to mean 'a lie'. The ending *-le* is sometimes added to words to mean 'something small', so perhaps a fibble is just a teeny tiny lie.

fibster noun fibsters
someone who fibbles
'I is stopping right here,' said the BFG sharply. 'I is not wishing to be called a fibster.' – THE BFG
DID YOU KNOW? The ending *-ster* is sometimes used to make words which mean 'someone who . . . '. For example, the surname *Webster* originally meant 'a weaver', and a *trickster* is someone who plays tricks on others.

fiction noun
stories that are made up in a writer's imagination rather than based on true events
Two hours of writing fiction leaves this particular writer absolutely drained. For those two hours he has been miles away. – BOY

fierce adjective fiercer, fiercest
A fierce animal or headmistress is dangerous because they might bite you or attack you.
Miss Trunchbull, the Headmistress . . . was a gigantic holy terror, a fierce tyrannical monster who frightened the life out of the pupils and teachers alike. – MATILDA
DON'T BE BIFFSQUIGGLED! The word **fearsome** sounds like *fierce-some*, but it is not related to *fierce* at all. However, *fiercesome* might be a very useful new word to describe something that is both *fierce* and *fearsome*.

fiery adjective
A fiery taste is very hot and burns your throat and tongue. Grown-ups with a fiery temper should be treated with caution, rather like Devil's Drenchers.
To the Monkey I gave a bag of Devil's Drenchers, those small fiery black sweets that one is not allowed to sell to children under four years old. – THE GIRAFFE AND THE PELLY AND ME

figgler noun figglers
A figgler is a finger to a giant. In Giant Country, you would say *Cross your figglers!* rather than *Cross your fingers!*
'Hold your breaths!' the BFG whispered down to her. 'Cross your figglers! Here we go!' – THE BFG

fight verb fights, fighting, fought
When people or giants fight, they hit each other or attack each other.
'Giants is never guzzling other giants,' the BFG said. 'They is fighting and squarreling a lot with each other, but never guzzling.' – THE BFG

figure noun figures
1 a number, such as 1, 2 or 3
2 Your figure is the shape of your body.
Mrs Wormwood . . . had one of those unfortunate bulging figures where the flesh appears to be strapped in all around the body to prevent it from falling out. – MATILDA

filthing adjective
Something filthing tastes or looks foul and disgusting.
'So this is the filthing rotsome glubbage you is eating!' boomed the Bloodbottler, holding up the partly eaten snozzcumber. – THE BFG

filthsome adjective
revolting or disgusting
'Burping is filthsome,' the BFG said. 'Us giants is never doing it.' – THE BFG

filthy adjective filthier, filthiest
Something that is filthy is very dirty.
'A boy!' cried the witches. 'A filthy smelly little boy! We'll swipe him! We'll swizzle him! We'll have his tripes for breakfast!' – THE WITCHES

final adjective
The final thing is the one that comes last.
There was another full day's travelling to be done before we reached our final destination, most of it by boat. – BOY

finger noun fingers
Your fingers are the parts of your body on the ends of your hands. Not many people are lucky enough to have a Magic Finger, but if you do, you will be able to perform extraordinary feats with it.
'Some of us,' the old woman went on, 'have fire on our tongues and sparks in our bellies and wizardry in the tips of our fingers.' – GEORGE'S MARVELLOUS MEDICINE

fire noun fires
Fire is the flames, heat and light that come from burning things. If something is *on fire*, it is burning.
All of a sudden, black smoke started pouring out of the hen's beak. 'It's on fire!' Grandma yelled. 'The hen's on fire!' – GEORGE'S MARVELLOUS MEDICINE

fire verb fires, firing, fired
When someone fires a gun, they make it shoot.
'Real poachers don't shoot pheasants, Danny, didn't you know that? You've only got to fire a cap-pistol up in those woods and the keepers'll be on you.' – DANNY THE CHAMPION OF THE WORLD

fire-balloon noun fire-balloons
A fire-balloon is a paper balloon with a small flame underneath that heats the air inside and makes it rise.
On a lovely still evening when there was no breath of wind anywhere, my father said to me, 'This is just the right weather for a fire-balloon.'— DANNY THE CHAMPION OF THE WORLD

firm adjective firmer, firmest
If you have a firm grip or hold on something, such as an ear or a pigtail, you hold it securely so that it will not slip away. Miss Trunchbull has a very firm grip from her days as an athlete throwing the **hammer**.
The Trunchbull . . . took a firm grip on Rupert's long golden tresses with her giant hand and then . . . she lifted the helpless boy clean out of his chair and held him aloft.— MATILDA

fish noun fishes, fish
an animal that lives and breathes in water, and that has fins to help it swim
The Pelican looked down at me and sang out: 'Oh, how I wish/For a big fat fish!/I'm as hungry as ever could be!/ A dish of fish is my only wish!/How far are we from the sea?'— THE GIRAFFE AND THE PELLY AND ME

fish verb fishes, fishing, fished
When you fish something out, you take it out from a bag or pocket.
Mrs Silver . . . fished Mr Hoppy's piece of paper out of her pocket, and holding the tortoise very close to her face, she whispered, reading from the paper: 'ESIO TROT, ESIO TROT, TEG REGGIB REGGIB!'— ESIO TROT

fist noun fists
When you make a fist, you close your hand tightly.
Just then, one of the Fleshlumpeater's flailing fists caught the still-fast-asleep Meatdripping Giant smack in the mouth.— THE BFG

fizz verb fizzes, fizzing, fizzed
When a liquid fizzes, it makes a lot of small bubbles, as when you add Wonka-Vite to water.
Mr Wonka tipped all fourteen pills into the glass. The water bubbled and frothed. 'Drink it while it's fizzing,' he said.— CHARLIE AND THE GREAT GLASS ELEVATOR

fizzlecrump noun fizzlecrumps
A fizzlecrump is a creature that can move as fast as a giant running at top speed.
'Be careful to hang on tight!' the BFG said. 'We is going fast as a fizzlecrump!'— THE BFG

fizzwiggler noun fizzwigglers
A fizzwiggler is someone who is mean and cruel. The BFG thinks that Mrs Clonkers is a real fizzwiggler because she is cruel to the children in the **norphanage**.
'The filthy old fizzwiggler!' shouted the BFG. 'That is the horridest thing I is hearing for years!'— THE BFG

fizzwinkel noun fizzwinkels
A fizzwinkel is a type of edible plant or vegetable, much smaller than a **snozzcumber**. It may be related to the **pigwinkle**, which grows outside Giant Country.
'Are you sure there's nothing else to eat around here except those disgusting smelly snozzcumbers?' she asked. 'Not even a fizzwinkel,' answered the Big Friendly Giant.— THE BFG
DON'T BE BIFFSQUIGGLED! This type of fizzwinkel is not the same as the **Fizzwinkles** that are sold in the Grubber, as there are no sweets in Giant Country.

Fizzwinkle noun Fizzwinkles
A Fizzwinkle is an exotic sweet from China that is sold in the Grubber. Its name suggests that it fizzes when you suck it, like lemonade.
There were Gumtwizzlers and Fizzwinkles from China, Frothblowers and Spitsizzlers from Africa, Tummyticklers and Gobwangles from the Fiji Islands.— THE GIRAFFE AND THE PELLY AND ME

fizzy adjective fizzier, fizziest
A fizzy drink has lots of tiny bubbles of gas in it. Fizzy Lifting Drinks and **frobscottle** are both types of fizzy drink, but they have very different effects.
'In our fizzy drinks,' Sophie said, 'the bubbles always go up and burst at the top.'— THE BFG

Fizzy Lifting Drink (CHARLIE AND THE CHOCOLATE FACTORY)
Fizzy Lifting Drinks are one of Willy Wonka's inventions. When you drink some, the bubbles make you float upwards and the only way to get down again is to burp. If you were to drink **frobscottle** and a Fizzy

---

The BFG uses lots of words that are spelled with *-igg-*, like *figglers* and *griggling*.

Lifting Drink one after the other, you would very possibly start exploding at both ends.

fjord noun fjords
a long narrow inlet of the sea between high cliffs, especially in Norway
The exciting new boat made it possible for us to go much farther afield, and every day we would travel far out into the fjord, hunting for a different island. — BOY

flabbergasted adjective
If you are flabbergasted, you are utterly astonished.
'You know where we've gone, my friends? We've gone into orbit!' They gaped, they gasped, they stared. They were too flabbergasted to speak. — CHARLIE AND THE GREAT GLASS ELEVATOR

flake noun flakes
a small piece of something
Bits of pale gold were flying among delicate frosty-white flakes of cloud, and over to one side the rim of the morning sun was coming up red as blood. — THE BFG

flame noun flames
a bright strip of fire that flickers and leaps
A witch . . . can make stones jump about like frogs and she can make tongues of flame go flickering across the surface of the water. — THE WITCHES

flap verb flaps, flapping, flapped
When a bird or bat flaps its wings, it moves them up and down in order to fly.
They glanced up and saw an immense grey batlike creature swooping down towards them out of the dark. It circled round and round the peach, flapping its great wings slowly in the moonlight. — JAMES AND THE GIANT PEACH

flash noun flashes
1 a sudden bright light, or a sudden burst of lightning or electricity
At once, there came a blinding flash,/And then the most almighty crash,/And sparks were bursting all around,/And smoke was rising from the ground. — DIRTY BEASTS
2 If something happens *quick as a flash*, it happens almost instantly.

flash verb flashes, flashing, flashed
When a light flashes, it shines brightly for a moment.
Cameras were clicking and flashbulbs were flashing and people were pushing and jostling and trying to get a bit closer to the famous girl. — CHARLIE AND THE CHOCOLATE FACTORY

flat adjective flatter, flattest
Something that is flat is smooth and level, and has no bumps on it.
Aunt Sponge and Aunt Spiker lay ironed out upon the grass as flat and thin and lifeless as a couple of paper dolls cut out of a picture book. — JAMES AND THE GIANT PEACH

flat noun flats
a set of rooms that you can live in inside a large building
Mr Hoppy lived in a small flat high up in a tall concrete building. — ESIO TROT

flatulence noun
a word that grown-ups sometimes use when they mean **whizzpopping**

flavory-savory adjective
sweet and delicious, as fresh walnuts taste to monkeys
'A walnut fresh from the tree is scrumptious-galumptious, so flavory-savory, so sweet to eat that it makes me all wobbly just thinking about it!' — THE GIRAFFE AND THE PELLY AND ME

flavour noun flavours
The flavour of something is the taste that it has when you eat it or drink it.
'What a flavour!' the Centipede cried. 'It's terrific! There's nothing like it! There never has been! And I should know because I personally have tasted all the finest foods in the world!' — JAMES AND THE GIANT PEACH

flea noun fleas
A flea is a small jumping insect that lives on larger animals and sucks their blood. Willy Wonka tracks down the oldest living flea (which is living on the oldest living cat) to add to his secret recipe for Vita-Wonk.
'I . . . rushed all over the world collecting special items from the oldest living things . . . THE WHISKERS OF A 36-YEAR-OLD CAT CALLED CRUMPETS/AN OLD FLEA WHICH HAD LIVED ON CRUMPETS FOR 36 YEARS.' — CHARLIE AND THE GREAT GLASS ELEVATOR

fleck noun flecks
a tiny piece or speck of something
Aunt Spiker . . . had a screeching voice and long wet narrow lips, and whenever she got angry or excited, little flecks of spit would come shooting out of her mouth as she talked. — JAMES AND THE GIANT PEACH

flesh noun
1 Your flesh is the soft part of your body (not the bones), which is made up of muscle and fat.
Sophie . . . rammed the three-inch-long pin of the brooch as hard as she could into the Fleshlumpeater's right ankle. It went deep into the flesh and stayed there. — THE BFG
2 The flesh of a fruit or vegetable is its soft pulpy part, which is juicy to eat. (Note that the Fleshlumpeater only eats lumps of **human beans**, not peaches.)
They all went over to the tunnel entrance and began scooping out great chunks of juicy, golden-coloured peach flesh. — JAMES AND THE GIANT PEACH
DID YOU KNOW? Some old names for a butcher are *flesher*, *flesh-hewer* (which means 'flesh-chopper') and *fleshmonger* (which means 'flesh-seller').

Fleshlumpeater or Fleshlumpeating Giant
(THE BFG)
The Fleshlumpeater is the **horriblest** of all the giants in Giant Country and he enjoys tormenting the BFG. Although he sounds scary, he is a bit of a coward and cannot withstand pain.
LOOK IT UP! Some other man-gobbling giants are the **Bonecruncher** and the **Manhugger**.

A B C D E F G H I J K L M N O P Q R S T U V W X Y Z

flick verb **flicks, flicking, flicked**
When you flick something, you knock it with your finger so that it flies through the air.
Bean picked something small and black out of his ear and flicked it away. — FANTASTIC MR FOX

flicker verb **flickers, flickering, flickered**
When a flame or light flickers, it burns or shines unsteadily.
A witch, you must understand . . . can make stones jump about like frogs and she can make tongues of flame go flickering across the surface of the water.
— THE WITCHES

flight noun **flights**
1 a journey in an aeroplane, balloon or flying peach
2 A flight of stairs is a set of stairs.
The BFG's head was level with the upper windows one flight up, and Sophie, sitting in his ear, had the same view. — THE BFG

flinch verb **flinches, flinching, flinched**
If you flinch, you move or shrink back because you are afraid.
Mr Tibbs suddenly realized that in order to serve the BFG . . . he would have to climb to the top of one of the tall step-ladders . . . A normal man would have flinched at the thought of it. But good butlers never flinch.
— THE BFG

flip verb **flips, flipping, flipped**
When you flip something over, you turn it over quickly.
Grandma's body gave a sudden sharp twist and a sudden sharp jerk and she flipped herself clear out of the chair. — GEORGE'S MARVELLOUS MEDICINE

float verb **floats, floating, floated**
When something floats, it does not sink but stays on the surface of water or in the air.
The giant peach swayed gently from side to side as it floated along, and the hundreds of silky white strings going upward from its stem were beautiful in the moonlight. — JAMES AND THE GIANT PEACH

flock noun **flocks**
A flock of sheep or birds is a large group of them.
Far above them, a single seagull was seen to come away from the rest of the flock and go flying off with a long string trailing from its neck. — JAMES AND THE GIANT PEACH

flock verb **flocks, flocking, flocked**
When people flock, they go in large numbers to see something.
Meanwhile, tourists from all over the globe came flocking to gaze down in wonder at the nine horrendous man-eating giants in the great pit. — THE BFG

flood noun **floods**
When there is a flood, a lot of water spreads over the land. If someone is in a flood of tears, they have tears pouring down their cheeks.
Very softly, the Old-Green-Grasshopper started to play the Funeral March on his violin, and by the time he had finished, everyone, including himself, was in a flood of tears. — JAMES AND THE GIANT PEACH

floor noun **floors**
The floor in a building is the part that you walk on. Muggle-Wump has a daring plan to make Mr and Mrs Twit think that the ceiling in their house is actually the floor.
The floor they were standing on was absolutely bare. What's more, it had been painted white to look like the ceiling. 'Look!' screamed Mrs Twit. 'That's the floor! The floor's up there!' — THE TWITS

flop verb **flops, flopping, flopped**
If you flop down, you sit or lie down suddenly because you are very tired.
The Fleshlumpeater . . . flopped to the ground and sat there howling his head off and clutching his ankle with both hands. — THE BFG

flow verb **flows, flowing, flowed**
When water or melted chocolate flows, it moves along like a river.
The river of chocolate was flowing very fast inside the pipe, and the Oompa-Loompas were all rowing like mad, and the boat was rocketing along at a furious pace.
— CHARLIE AND THE CHOCOLATE FACTORY

a b c d e **f** g h i j k l m n o p q r s t u v w x y z

flower noun **flowers**
the brightly coloured part of a plant
A Geraneous Giraffe cannot eat anything except the pink and purple flowers of the tinkle-tinkle tree. But those . . . are hard to find and expensive to buy. — THE GIRAFFE AND THE PELLY AND ME

fluckgungled adjective
If a giant is fluckgungled, he is in a hopeless situation. It is very rude to say you are fluckgungled, which is why giants like to say it.
'I is gunzleswiped!' shouted the Meatdripper. 'I is fluckgungled!' screamed the Maidmasher. — THE BFG
LOOK IT UP! For other rude words that giants say, see **rude**.

fluff verb **fluffs, fluffing, fluffed**
When a bird fluffs its feathers, it ruffles them.
The Roly-Poly Bird . . . fluffed his marvellous coloured feathers and looked down rather grandly at the monkeys. — THE TWITS

fluid noun **fluids**
a liquid
The entire egg-shaped body was itself moving very very slightly, pulsing and bulging gently here and there as though the skin were filled with some thick fluid. — CHARLIE AND THE GREAT GLASS ELEVATOR

flungaway adjective
A flungaway place is very far away.
'Bonecrunching Giant will be galloping to Turkey, of course,' said the BFG. 'But the others will be whiffling off to all sorts of flungaway places.' — THE BFG

flushbunk verb **flushbunks, flushbunking, flushbunked**
When giants go flushbunking, they go on a quick trip (usually to eat **human beans**).
'We is all of us flushbunking off to England tonight,' answered the Fleshlumpeater as they went galloping past. — THE BFG

flushbunking adjective
If something is flushbunking, it makes no sense whatsoever.
'Upwards is the wrong way!' cried the BFG. 'You mustn't ever be having the bubbles going upwards! That's the most flushbunking rubbish I ever is hearing!' — THE BFG
DID YOU KNOW? When he invented *flushbunking*, Roald Dahl may have had in mind the informal word *bunkum*, which means 'rubbish' or 'nonsense', and is named after *Buncombe* County in North Carolina, where it was first used in a political speech. For the verb sense of *flushbunking*, he may have been thinking of the phrase *bunking off* which means to play truant from school or work.

flushbunkled adjective
If a giant is flushbunkled, he is in a hopeless situation.
'I is flushbunkled!' roared the Fleshlumpeater. 'I is splitzwiggled!' yelled the Childchewer. — THE BFG
DON'T BE BIFFSQUIGGLED! Flushbunkled sounds very like **flushbunked**, but the two words mean different things: *The giants all flushbunked off to England.*

flussed adjective
If you are flussed, you are worried or anxious.
'Don't get so flussed,' the BFG said. 'To me that is a snitchy little jump. There's not a thingalingaling to it.' — THE BFG

flutter verb **flutters, fluttering, fluttered**
When something flutters, it flaps gently.
I caught a glimpse of something wispy-white, like a little cloud, fluttering upwards and disappearing out of the window. — THE WITCHES

fly noun **flies**
A fly is a small flying insect with two wings. Both Miss Spider and President Gilligrass catch flies: she traps them in her web and he lures them into his patented Gilligrass Fly-Catcher.
Miss Spider answered, sighing long and loud. 'I am not loved at all. And yet I do nothing but good. All day long I catch flies and mosquitoes in my webs.' — JAMES AND THE GIANT PEACH

fly verb **flies, flying, flew, flown**
When something flies, it moves along through the air. (Note that this is different from *floating*, which is what Mrs Twit does when attached to balloons.)
Every kind of wonderful bird was flying in and perching on the branches of the great tree, and as soon as one landed a Minpin would climb on to its back and off they would go. — THE MINPINS

foam noun
a thick mass of small bubbles on the top of a liquid
George loved playing with aerosols. He pressed the button and . . . a wonderful mountain of white foam built up in the giant saucepan. – GEORGE'S MARVELLOUS MEDICINE

focus verb **focuses, focusing, focused**
When you focus a camera or telescope, you move the controls to get a clear picture.
'Quick! Give me the telescope!' yelled Shuckworth. With one hand he focused the telescope and with the other he flipped the switch connecting him to Ground Control. – CHARLIE AND THE GREAT GLASS ELEVATOR

fog noun
When there is fog, there is thick cloud just above the ground, which makes it difficult to see.
The Elevator drifted on, rocking gently from side to side. The grey-black oily fog swirled around them. – CHARLIE AND THE GREAT GLASS ELEVATOR

foggiest adjective
If you do not have the foggiest idea about something, you have no idea about it at all.
'I is not having the foggiest idea where Giant Country is in the world,' the BFG said, 'but I is always able to gallop there.' – THE BFG

fogglefrump noun **fogglefrumps**
a quiet and docile animal that lives in Giant Country
'If an animal is very fierce and you is putting it in a cage, it will make a tremendous rumpledumpus. If it is a nice animal like a cockatootloo or a fogglefrump, it will sit quietly.' – THE BFG

foghorn noun **foghorns**
a loud horn used to warn ships of fog
Most of them were lying on their backs with their enormous mouths wide open, and they were snoring like foghorns. – THE BFG

fond adjective **fonder, fondest**
If you are fond of someone or something, you like them a lot.
'I am very fond of Charles Dickens,' Matilda said. 'He makes me laugh a lot. Especially Mr Pickwick.' – MATILDA

food noun **foods**
Food is anything that you eat to help you grow or give you energy.
'It must be berries,' sang the Roly-Poly Bird. 'Berries are my favourite food in the world. Is it raspberries, perhaps? Or could it be strawberries?' – THE ENORMOUS CROCODILE
LOOK IT UP! For ways to describe how you eat food, see **eat**.

foot noun **feet**
1 Your feet are the parts of your body that you stand on. Most grown-ups can reach the ground with their feet when they are sitting too, unless they have the **Dreaded Shrinks**.
As soon as Mrs Twit sat down, Mr Twit pointed at her and shouted, 'There you are! You're sitting in your old chair and you've shrunk so much your feet aren't even touching the ground!' – THE TWITS
2 Feet are used to measure how long something is, or how tall you are. One foot is about 30 centimetres.

footchel verb **footchels, footcheling, footcheled**
When giants footchel (or **moochel**), they laze around, as they do most of the daytime.
'What on earth are they doing?' Sophie asked. 'Nothing,' said the BFG. 'They is just moocheling and footcheling around and waiting for the night to come.' – THE BFG

footle verb **footles, footling, footled**
If you footle around, you play or mess about.
'Charlie,' said Grandma Josephine. 'I don't think I trust this gentleman very much.' 'Nor do I,' said Grandma Georgina. 'He footles around.' – CHARLIE AND THE GREAT GLASS ELEVATOR

footman noun **footmen**
a male servant who opens doors and serves food at tables
Footmen arrived carrying silver trays with fried eggs, bacon, sausages and fried potatoes. – THE BFG

forbid verb **forbids, forbidding, forbade, forbidden**
If a grown-up forbids you to do something, they tell you that you must not do it. If something is forbidden, you are not allowed to do it.
'A witch only knows the witches in her own country. She is strictly forbidden to communicate with any foreign witches.' – THE WITCHES

forehead noun **foreheads**
Your forehead is the part of your head that is above your eyes.
Twit was one of these very hairy-faced men. The whole of his face except for his forehead, his eyes and his nose was covered with thick hair. – THE TWITS

forest noun **forests**
a large area of trees growing close together
'These great trees are filled with rooms and staircases . . . This is a Minpin forest. And it's not the only one in England.' – THE MINPINS

Forest of Sin (THE MINPINS)
The Forest of Sin is a dark secret wood that Little Billy longs to explore. His mother tries to scare him away from it by telling him stories of the fearsome creatures that lurk there.

forget verb **forgets, forgetting, forgot, forgotten**
If you forget something (such as a vital ingredient in a magic formula), you do not remember it. Someone who often forgets things is *forgetful*.
'Wait a minute! I know what I've forgotten!' 'What?' cried Mr Kranky. 'Tell me, quick! Because if we've forgotten even one tiny thing, then it won't work!' – GEORGE'S MARVELLOUS MEDICINE

a b c d e f g h i j k l m n o p q r s t u v w x y z

Some words that start with an *f-* sound are spelled *ph-*, such as *pheasant* and *phizzwizard.*

forlorn adjective
If you look forlorn, you look sad and lonely.
The Big Friendly Giant looked suddenly so forlorn that Sophie got quite upset. — THE BFG

formula noun **formulas** or **formulae**
A formula is a recipe for a medicine or potion, or the mixture prepared from it.
'So yesterday I am personally prrree-paring a small qvantity of the magic formula in order to give to you a public demonstration. But I am making vun small change in the rrrecipe.' — THE WITCHES

Formula 86 Delayed Action Mouse-Maker (THE WITCHES)
Formula 86 Delayed Action Mouse-Maker is a magic formula invented by The Grand High Witch as part of her **giganticus** plan to turn all the children in Inkland into mice. The recipe includes fried mouse-tails, the yolk of a **gruntle's** egg and a rrroasted alarm-clock.

forthwards adverb
The BFG goes forthwards rather than forwards.
'I is galloping forthwards and backwards from Giant Country every night to blow my dreams into little chiddlers' bedrooms.' — THE BFG

fortunate adjective
If you are fortunate, you are lucky.
'On the other hand,' the Ladybird went on, 'some of my less fortunate relatives have no more than two spots altogether on their shells! Can you imagine that?' — JAMES AND THE GIANT PEACH

fortune noun **fortunes**
A fortune is a very large amount of money.
'We shall make a fortune today,' Aunt Spiker was saying. 'Just look at all those people!' — JAMES AND THE GIANT PEACH

fossilized adjective
If you are fossilized with fear, you are so afraid that you cannot move, as if you had been turned into a fossil in a rock.
'If you'd had even the faintest idea of what horrors you were up against, the marrow would have run out of your bones! You'd have been fossilized with fear and glued to the ground!' — CHARLIE AND THE GREAT GLASS ELEVATOR
SPARKY SYNONYMS You can also say **petrified**.
LOOK IT UP! For other ways to describe fear, see **afraid**.

foul adjective **fouler, foulest**
disgusting and thoroughly unpleasant
What I am trying to tell you is that Mr Twit was a foul and smelly old man. He was also an extremely horrid old man, as you will find out in a moment. — THE TWITS
SPARKY SYNONYMS You can also say **disgustable**, **maggotwise** or **rotsome**.

foulpester noun **foulpesters**
a revolting and annoying creature
The Fleshlumpeater opened his tiny piggy black eyes. 'Which of you foulpesters is wiggling my arm?' he bellowed. — THE BFG

foulsome adjective
disgusting and vile
'Try it yourself, this foulsome snozzcumber!' 'No, thank you,' Sophie said, backing away. — THE BFG

fox noun **foxes**
A fox is a wild animal that looks like a dog and has red fur and a long, furry tail. Foxes love to eat chickens and Fantastic Mr Fox is the greatest chicken-thief of them all.
DID YOU KNOW? The word *vulpine* (which comes from Latin) means 'of a fox, or like a fox', so you could describe the story of Fantastic Mr Fox as a *vulpine tale*. The name for a female fox (like Mrs Fox) is a *vixen*, and the Small Foxes are *cubs*.

Fox, Mr (FANTASTIC MR FOX)
The fantastic Mr Fox is a very clever fox who manages to outwit the evil Farmers Boggis, Bunce and Bean. He steals chickens and other birds from their farms in order to feed his family of Mrs Fox and the four Small Foxes.

fraction noun **fractions**
A fraction is a small part of something, or a small amount.
Eventually she managed to slide the lid of the pencil-box right home and the newt was hers. Then, on second thoughts, she opened the lid just the tiniest fraction so that the creature could breathe. — MATILDA

fragile adjective
Something that is fragile will break easily if you drop it.
Her body was so slim and fragile one got the feeling that if she fell over she would smash into a thousand pieces, like a porcelain figure. — MATILDA

fragment noun **fragments**
a small piece that has broken off something
The Bloodbottler ... rushed at the BFG and smashed

what was left of the snozzcumber over his head. Fragments of the filthy vegetable splashed all over the cave. — THE BFG

free adjective **freer, freest**

1 If you are free, you can go where you want and do what you want to do.
The door opened. All four monkeys leapt out together. 'We are free!' cried the two little ones. 'Where shall we go, Dad? Where shall we hide?' — THE TWITS

2 If something is free, you do not have to pay for it.
'And all the chocolate and sweets that you could eat for the rest of your life — free!' said Grandpa George. 'Just imagine that!' — CHARLIE AND THE CHOCOLATE FACTORY

free verb **frees, freeing, freed**

If you free someone, you let them go after they have been locked up.
Nobody wanted to go down . . . because the moment a giant was freed, he would be sure to turn on the wretched person who had freed him and gobble him up. — THE BFG

RINGBELLING RHYMES Try rhyming with *glee* or *Yippee!*

freeze verb **freezes, freezing, froze, frozen**

1 When something freezes, it becomes very cold and hard and changes into ice.
Little Billy glanced back quickly over his shoulder, and now, in the distance, he saw a sight that froze his blood and made icicles in his veins. — THE MINPINS

2 If you are freezing or frozen, you are very cold.
'Why hasn't he got a coat on in this cold weather?' 'Don't ask me. Maybe he can't afford to buy one.' 'Goodness me! He must be freezing!' — CHARLIE AND THE CHOCOLATE FACTORY

fresh adjective **fresher, freshest**

1 Fresh food has been made or picked only a short time ago.
'Would it be too much trouble, I wonder, if I were to ask you for a reasonably fresh piece of haddock or cod every day?' — THE GIRAFFE AND THE PELLY AND ME

2 Fresh air is clean and cool.
'Rrree-moof your vigs and get some fresh air into your spotty scalps!' she shouted, and another sigh of relief arose from the audience. — THE WITCHES

fridgy or **fridging** adjective **fridgier, fridgiest**

If you are fridgy, or fridging with cold, you are freezing.
The Big Friendly Giant sat Sophie down once again on the enormous table. 'Is you quite snuggly there in your nightie?' he asked. 'You isn't fridgy cold?' — THE BFG

'And then again, if it is a frotsy night and the giant is fridging with cold, he will probably point his nose towards the swultering hotlands to guzzle a few Hottentots to warm him up.' — THE BFG

friend noun **friends**

Your friends are the people or fellow creatures that you like and know well.
If you wish to be friends with a Giraffe, never say anything bad about its neck. Its neck is its proudest possession. — THE GIRAFFE AND THE PELLY AND ME

friendly adjective **friendlier, friendliest**

If you are friendly, you like people and are nice to them. There are lots of friendly (and some not-so-friendly) **human beans**, but only one Big Friendly Giant.
'But if you are so nice and friendly,' Sophie said, 'then why did you snatch me from my bed and run away with me?' — THE BFG

a b c d e f g h i j k l m n o p q r s t u v w x y z

fright noun **frights**
a sudden feeling of fear
Sophie opened her mouth to scream, but no sound came out. Her throat, like her whole body, was frozen with fright.
—THE BFG

frighten verb **frightens, frightening, frightened**
If something frightens you, it makes you feel scared.
George began to tremble. It was her face that frightened him most of all, the frosty smile, the brilliant unblinking eyes.—GEORGE'S MARVELLOUS MEDICINE

frightened adjective
If you are frightened of someone or something, you are scared of them.
'Jack is the only human bean all giants is frightened of,' the BFG told her. 'They is all absolutely terrified of Jack.'—THE BFG

LOOK IT UP! For some ways to describe people who are frightened, see **afraid**.

frightful adjective
horrible and shocking
That face of hers was the most frightful and frightening thing I have ever seen. Just looking at it gave me the shakes all over.—THE WITCHES

frightsome adjective
frightening and fearsome
'You is bitten by a snake!' he shouted. 'I seed it biting you! It was a frightsome poisnowse viper! It was a dreadly dangerous vind-screen viper!'—THE BFG

DID YOU KNOW? *Frightsome* is an old word that was first used hundreds of years ago. Nowadays, it is mainly used in Giant Country.

frightswiping adjective
terrifying and deadly dangerous
'It's Jack!' bellowed the Fleshlumpeater. 'It's the grueful gruncious Jack!... It is the terrible frightswiping Jack!'—THE BFG

DID YOU KNOW? The word *frightswiping* is a blend of *frightening* and *swiping*, so it makes you think of a terrifying creature that swipes at its prey.

fringe noun **fringes**
short hair that hangs down over your forehead
Lavender was exceptionally small for her age, a skinny little nymph with deep-brown eyes and with dark hair that was cut in a fringe across her forehead.—MATILDA

frisbee noun **frisbees**
a plastic disc which you skim through the air as an outdoor game
'Our classroom is one floor up and we saw Julius Rottwinkle go sailing out over the garden like a Frisbee and landing with a thump in the middle of the lettuces.'—MATILDA

frisby adjective **frisbier, frisbiest**
very cold and icy
'If it is very warm weather and a giant is feeling as hot as a sizzlepan, he will probably go galloping far up to the frisby north to get himself an Esquimo or two to cool him down.'—THE BFG

DON'T BE BIFFSQUIGGLED! Take care not to confuse **frisby** with the type of **frisbee** which you throw and try to catch.

frisk verb **frisks, frisking, frisked**
If you frisk about, you leap and run about playfully, as Cloud-Children do.
Hundreds of Cloud-Men's children were frisking about all over the place and shrieking with laughter and sliding down the billows of the cloud on toboggans.—JAMES AND THE GIANT PEACH

RINGBELLING RHYMES Try rhyming with *whisk*.

frittered adjective
If something is frittered, it is fried to a crisp like a fritter. If you say you are *frittered if you know* something, you mean you really do not know it.
'If you can't see why, you must be as quacky as a duckhound! I is frittered if I know how you can think at all!'—THE BFG

frizzle verb **frizzles, frizzling, frizzled**
If you frizzle something, you fry it until it is crisp. Frizzling Knids is one way of defeating them.
'We've done it!' cried Mr Wonka. 'They've been roasted to a crisp! They've been frizzled to a fritter! We're saved!'—CHARLIE AND THE GREAT GLASS ELEVATOR

frobscottle noun

Frobscottle is a green fizzy drink that the BFG and other giants drink instead of water. Unlike **snozzcumbers**, it tastes delicious to giants. The bubbles in frobscottle sink down rather than rise up, so if you drink a lot of it, you will soon be **whizzpopping** (even if you are the Queen).
'Here is frobscottle!' he cried, holding the bottle up proud and high, as though it contained some rare wine. 'Delumptious fizzy frobscottle!' he shouted. — THE BFG
RINGBELLING RHYMES Try rhyming with *bottle* or *axolotl* (a type of Mexican newt).

frog noun frogs

a small jumping animal that can live both in water and on land
To pay her back for the glass eye in his beer, Mr Twit decided he would put a frog in Mrs Twit's bed. — THE TWITS

frogsquinker noun frogsquinkers

A frogsquinker is just as silly as a **buzzwangle**.
'By ringo, your head must be so full of frogsquinkers and buzzwangles, I is frittered if I know how you can think at all!' — THE BFG

frost noun

Frost is ice that looks like powder and covers the ground when the weather is cold. The Cloud-Men make frost in *frost factories*.
They saw the frost factories and the wind producers and the places where cyclones and tornadoes were manufactured and sent spinning down towards the Earth. — JAMES AND THE GIANT PEACH

frosty adjective frostier, frostiest

1 Frosty weather is so cold that frost forms on the ground.
2 A frosty look or remark is very unfriendly.
Mr Jenkins . . . spoke rudely and looked very angry. My grandmother put on her frostiest look, but didn't answer him. — THE WITCHES

froth noun

a mass of tiny bubbles in a liquid
The sherbet fizzed in your mouth, and if you knew how to do it, you could make white froth come out of your nostrils and pretend you were throwing a fit. — BOY

Frothblower noun Frothblowers

A Frothblower is an exotic sweet from Africa that is sold in the Grubber. Its name suggests that it fizzes and froths, a bit like sherbet.
There were Gumtwizzlers and Fizzwinkles from China, Frothblowers and Spitsizzlers from Africa, Tummyticklers and Gobwangles from the Fiji Islands. — THE GIRAFFE AND THE PELLY AND ME

frothbungling adjective

A frothbungling idea is mind-bogglingly mad or crazy.
'But we aren't going to tell her!' Sophie said excitedly. 'We don't have to tell her! We'll make her dream it!' 'That is an even more frothbungling suggestion,' the BFG said. — THE BFG

frothy adjective frothier, frothiest

A frothy liquid is full of tiny bubbles or froth. Willy Wonka makes the frothiest chocolate in the world because of his secret waterfall method.
'The waterfall is most important!' Mr Wonka went on. 'It mixes the chocolate! It churns it up! It pounds it and beats it! It makes it light and frothy!' — CHARLIE AND THE CHOCOLATE FACTORY

frotsy adjective frotsier, frotsiest

A frotsy night or frotsy weather is very cold and frosty.
'If it is a frotsy night and the giant is fridging with cold, he will probably point his nose towards the swultering hotlands . . . to warm him up.' — THE BFG

frown verb frowns, frowning, frowned

When someone frowns, they have lines on their forehead because they are angry or worried.
Mr Jenkins looked at her over the top of his newspaper and frowned. 'Yes,' he said. 'I am Mr Jenkins. What can I do for you, madam?' — THE WITCHES

frozen adjective

1 Something that is frozen has turned to ice.
'THE TEMPERATURE IN THE SPACE HOTEL WILL DROP TO MINUS ONE HUNDRED DEGREES CENTIGRADE. ALL OF YOU WILL BE INSTANTLY DEEP FROZEN.' — CHARLIE AND THE GREAT GLASS ELEVATOR

Frobscottle is called *Blubberwasser* in German.

a b c d e f g h i j k l m n o p q r s t u v w x y z

2 If you are frozen with fear, you are so afraid that you cannot move, as if you had been turned to ice.
The passengers on the peach (all except the Centipede) sat frozen with terror, looking back at the Cloud-Men and wondering what was going to happen next. — JAMES AND THE GIANT PEACH

fruit noun **fruits** or **fruit**
A fruit is the part of a plant which contains seeds. Apples, oranges, bananas and peaches are all types of fruit that you can eat.
By lunchtime, the whole place was a seething mass of men, women, and children all pushing and shoving to get a glimpse of this miraculous fruit. — JAMES AND THE GIANT PEACH

frumpet noun **frumpets**
If you call someone a frumpet (not that you would), you mean that they are old and unattractive.
Mrs Twit . . . suddenly called out at the top of her voice, 'Here I come, you grizzly old grunion! You rotten old turnip! You filthy old frumpet!' — THE TWITS
DID YOU KNOW? Frumpet may be based on *frump*, which has a similar meaning and comes from an older word *frumple* meaning 'wrinkle'.
RINGBELLING RHYMES Try rhyming with *crumpet* or *thrumpet*.

frumpkin noun **frumpkins**
A frumpkin is a vegetable that giants use to make **frumpkin pie**. Unlike the **snozzcumber**, it is good to eat and its name suggests it looks or tastes a bit like a pumpkin.
'You would be swallowed up like a piece of frumpkin pie, all in one dollop!' — THE BFG

frumptious adjective
1 Something frumptious is marvellous or wonderful.
'Sweet-shops!' they cried. 'We are going to buy sweet-shops! What a frumptious wheeze!' — THE WITCHES
2 A frumptious freak is a complete or utter freak.
'This is the living-room,' announced Muggle-Wump. 'The grand and glorious living-room where those two fearful frumptious freaks eat Bird Pie every week for supper!' — THE TWITS

fry verb **fries, frying, fried**
1 When you fry food, you cook it in hot fat, often in a **frying-pan**.
2 If a witch gets fried, she is turned into a puff of smoke. The Grand High Witch does this to witches that annoy her by shooting fiery sparks from her eyes.
'I am told that The Grand High Witch makes it a rule to fry at least one witch at each Annual Meeting. She does it in order to keep the rest of them on their toes.' — THE WITCHES

frying-pan noun **frying-pans**
A frying-pan is a shallow pan for frying food such as eggs, bacon and snowballs. The BFG calls it a **sizzlepan**.
At the entrances to the caves the Cloud-Men's wives were crouching over little stoves with frying-pans in their hands, frying snowballs for their husbands' suppers.
— JAMES AND THE GIANT PEACH

fudge noun
a soft sweet made with milk, sugar and butter
'That pipe — the one Augustus went up — happens to lead directly to the room where I make a most delicious kind of strawberry-flavoured chocolate-coated fudge . . . '
— CHARLIE AND THE CHOCOLATE FACTORY
RINGBELLING RHYMES Try rhyming with *grimesludge*.

fun noun
When you have fun, you enjoy yourself.
'You miserable old mackerel!' said Grandma Georgina, sailing past him. 'Just when we start having a bit of fun, you want to stop it!' — CHARLIE AND THE GREAT GLASS ELEVATOR

fungus noun **fungi**
A fungus is a plant without leaves or flowers that grows best in dark, moist places. Mushrooms and toadstools are types of fungus, and Miss Trunchbull thinks that her pupils are like fungus too.
'You blithering idiot!' shouted the Trunchbull. 'You festering gumboil! You fleabitten fungus!' — MATILDA

funnel noun **funnels**
A funnel is a chimney on a ship or steam engine. It can also be a spout for blowing blizzards on a snow machine.
Once they passed a snow machine in operation, with the Cloud-Men turning the handle and a blizzard of snowflakes blowing out of the great funnel above.
— JAMES AND THE GIANT PEACH

funny adjective **funnier, funniest**
1 Something that is funny makes you laugh or smile. The Oompa-Loompas find just about everything funny.
'What's so funny?' asked Violet Beauregarde. 'Oh, don't worry about them!' cried Mr Wonka. 'They're always laughing! They think everything's a colossal joke!'
— CHARLIE AND THE CHOCOLATE FACTORY
2 Something that is funny is strange or surprising.
Last week, something very funny happened to the Gregg family. I am going to tell you about it as best I can.
— THE MAGIC FINGER

fur noun **furs**
the soft hair that covers some animals (and anyone who has taken Formula 86 Delayed Action Mouse-Maker)
'It's the Mouse-Maker!' I cried. 'Look! Some of them are growing fur on their faces!' — THE WITCHES

furious adjective
If you are furious, you are very angry.
James Henry Trotter, glancing up quickly, saw the faces of a thousand furious Cloud-Men peering down at him over the edge of the cloud. — JAMES AND THE GIANT PEACH

furnace noun **furnaces**
A furnace is a large and very hot oven.
'But . . . but . . . but . . .' shrieked Mrs Salt, 'where does the great big pipe go to in the end?' 'Why, to the furnace, of course,' Mr Wonka said calmly. 'To the incinerator.' — CHARLIE AND THE CHOCOLATE FACTORY

furniture noun
things such as tables, chairs and beds that you need inside a house
'Pull out the carpet!' shouted Muggle-Wump. 'Pull this huge carpet out from under the furniture and stick it on to the ceiling!' — THE TWITS

furry adjective **furrier, furriest**
Something furry is covered with fur.
'All they've done is to shrink you and give you four legs and a furry coat, but they haven't been able to change you into a one hundred per cent mouse.' — THE WITCHES
RINGBELLING RHYMES Try rhyming with *blurry*.
In Scotland, you can also rhyme it with *hurry* and *scurry*, which is very useful for writing poems about mice.

fury noun
violent or extreme anger
The Army General was no more used to being insulted than the Air Marshal. His face began to swell with fury and his cheeks blew out until they looked like two huge ripe tomatoes. — THE BFG

fuss noun
If you make a fuss about something, you complain or talk a lot about it because you are excited or worried.
Almost anyone else witnessing the achievements of this small child would have been tempted to make a great fuss. — MATILDA

fusty adjective **fustier, fustiest**
Fusty air smells stale and stuffy.
The mist came into the Elevator. It had the fusty reeky smell of an old underground dungeon. — CHARLIE AND THE GREAT GLASS ELEVATOR
RINGBELLING RHYMES Try rhyming with *rusty*.

future noun
The future is the time that will come.
'Listen, Bruno,' I said. 'Now that we are both mice, I think we ought to start thinking a bit about the future.' — THE WITCHES

Geraneous Giraffe — THE GIRAFFE AND THE PELLY AND ME

giants   glow-worm   glue
glumptious   golden

gait noun **gaits**
Someone's gait is the way that they walk or run.
He had a queer long-striding lolloping gait and his black cloak was streaming out behind him like the wings of a bird. — DANNY THE CHAMPION OF THE WORLD

gallon noun **gallons**
a measure for liquids equal to about 4.5 litres
One Cloud-Man, taking very careful aim, tipped a gallon of thick purple paint over the edge of the cloud right on to the Centipede himself. — JAMES AND THE GIANT PEACH

gallop verb **gallops, galloping, galloped**
When a horse or a **whangdoodle** gallops, it runs as fast as it can.
A whangdoodle would eat ten Oompa-Loompas for breakfast and come galloping back for a second helping. — CHARLIE AND THE CHOCOLATE FACTORY

game noun **games**
A game is something that you play for fun, like snakes-and-ladders or hide-and-seek.
'Ah,' he said. 'That's the fun of the whole thing. . . . It's hide-and-seek. It's the greatest game of hide-and-seek in the world.' — DANNY THE CHAMPION OF THE WORLD

gape verb **gapes, gaping, gaped**
If you gape, you stare in amazement with your mouth open.
The Queen was still staring at Sophie. Gaping at her would

a b c d e f g h i j k l m n o p q r s t u v w x y z

Answer this RIDDLE you surely shall . . . if you go to **riddle**.

be more accurate. Her mouth was slightly open, her eyes were round and wide as two saucers.—THE BFG

garden noun gardens
A garden is a piece of ground where people grow flowers, fruit or vegetables. Mrs Twit prefers to grow nettles and thistles in her garden, to keep out nosey children.
And what do you think of that ghastly garden? Mrs Twit was the gardener. She was very good at growing thistles and stinging-nettles.—THE TWITS

gas noun gases
A gas is a substance that is like air, and is not a solid or a liquid. Willy Wonka uses a special type of gas to create his Fizzy Lifting Drinks.
'Oh, those are fabulous!' cried Mr Wonka. 'They fill you with bubbles, and the bubbles are full of a special kind of gas, and this gas is so terrifically lifting that it lifts you right off the ground just like a balloon.'—CHARLIE AND THE CHOCOLATE FACTORY

gasp verb gasps, gasping, gasped
When you gasp, you breathe in quickly and noisily because you are surprised or out of breath.
The Duke . . . reeled back and his eyes popped nearly out of their sockets. 'Great Scott!' he gasped.—THE GIRAFFE AND THE PELLY AND ME

gaze verb gazes, gazing, gazed
When you gaze at something, you look at it for a long time.
Captain Lancaster sat up front at his desk, gazing suspiciously round the class with his watery-blue eyes.—DANNY THE CHAMPION OF THE WORLD

generous adjective
Someone who is generous is kind and gives or shares the things that they have.
'Thank you, thank you, O Most Generous and Thoughtful One!' chorused the ancient witches.—THE WITCHES

genius noun geniuses
A genius is someone like Matilda who is unusually clever at things like reading and maths. You can also be a genius at creating or inventing things, like Willy Wonka.
'Matilda, so far as I can gather at this early stage, is also a kind of mathematical genius. She can multiply complicated figures in her head like lightning.'—MATILDA

gentle adjective gentler, gentlest
a gentle touch or sound is light and soft, not rough
'Wake up, Centipede,' whispered James, giving him a gentle dig in the stomach. 'It's time for bed.'—JAMES AND THE GIANT PEACH

gentleman noun gentlemen
a polite name for a man or a giant
'Tibbs,' the Queen said, showing true regal hospitality, 'fetch the gentleman another dozen fried eggs and a dozen sausages.'—THE BFG

gently adverb
If you do or say something gently, you do it or say it in a careful way, and are not rough.
The BFG picked Sophie up between one finger and a thumb and placed her gently on the palm of the other hand.—THE BFG

George Kranky
(GEORGE'S MARVELLOUS MEDICINE)
George Kranky is a boy who is looked after by his mean and grumpy grandma until one day he decides to create a magical medicine to make her a better person.

DID YOU KNOW? *Kranky* sounds like *cranky*, which is an American word that means 'grumpy' or 'bad-tempered' — just like George's grumpy old grandma.

Geraneous Giraffe
(THE GIRAFFE AND THE PELLY AND ME)
The Geraneous Giraffe is one of three animals that work for the Ladderless Window-Cleaning Company. It lives on the pink and purple flowers of the **tinkle-tinkle tree** and has a neck that can extend to any length, which is very useful for cleaning hard-to-reach windows.

DID YOU KNOW? Roald Dahl made up the word *geraneous* for a type of giraffe, but he may have wanted it to sound like *geranium*, which is a plant with red, pink or white flowers (a bit like those of the tinkle-tinkle tree).

ghastly adjective ghastlier, ghastliest
A ghastly person or a ghastly experience is truly horrible and nasty.
And there they sat, these two ghastly hags, sipping their drinks, and every now and again screaming at James to chop faster and faster.—JAMES AND THE GIANT PEACH

DID YOU KNOW? The word *ghastly* is related to *ghost* and used to mean 'terrifying'.

ghost noun ghosts
the spirit of a dead person seen by a living person
'I know it's a ghost!' Matilda said. 'I've heard it here before! This room is haunted! I thought you knew that.'—MATILDA

ghoulish adjective

A ghoulish person or look is evil and cruel.

The witches gasped. They gaped. They turned and gave each other ghoulish grins of excitement. — THE WITCHES

DID YOU KNOW? The word *ghoulish* comes from *ghoul*, which was originally an Arabic word for a type of evil spirit that eats dead bodies.

Gobblefunking with words

When you put words together that start with the same sound, like *ghoulish grins*, it is called *alliteration*. Roald Dahl loved using alliteration in his stories and poems, especially for the names of characters. Some examples are *Bruce Bogtrotter*, *Willy Wonka* and the three mean and nasty farmers, *Boggis*, *Bunce* and *Bean*.

giant noun giants

A giant is a huge humanlike creature found in traditional stories like *Jack and the Beanstalk*. There are at least ten **gigantuous** giants living in Giant Country, all of them male. Most are very unfriendly, except for the BFG, who is the only one who does not hunt and eat **human beans**.

'And are all those beastly giants over there really going off again tonight to eat people?' Sophie asked. — THE BFG

LOOK IT UP! The names of the unfriendly giants are **Bloodbottler, Bonecruncher, Butcher Boy, Childchewer, Fleshlumpeater, Gizzardgulper, Maidmasher, Manhugger** and **Meatdripper**.

giant adjective

huge or enormous in size

Once again the giant peach was sailing peacefully through the mysterious moonlit sky. — JAMES AND THE GIANT PEACH

SPARKY SYNONYMS You can also say **gigantuous**.

Giant Country (THE BFG)

Giant Country is the place where all the giants in the world live, including the BFG. It is a hot and dry place where the ground is pale yellow and the rocks are blue. No one knows exactly where it is, not even the BFG, although he can always find his way back there by galloping. Giant Country is not on any map, but you can draw it in yourself on the blank pages at the end of an **atlas**.

giant curlicue noun giant curlicues

The giant curlicue is a rare and ancient animal. Part of the giant curlicue is needed to make Vita-Wonk.

'I tracked down THE WHISTLE-PIG, THE BOBOLINK, THE SKROCK, THE POLLY-FROG, THE GIANT CURLICUE, THE STINGING SLUG AND THE VENOMOUS SQUERKLE.' — CHARLIE AND THE GREAT GLASS ELEVATOR

DID YOU KNOW? A *curlicue* is also a decorative curl or scroll, so perhaps a giant curlicue gets its name because it has a curly tail or a twisted horn.

Giant Wangdoodle noun Giant Wangdoodles

a chocolate-coated strawberry sweet that is sold in the Grubber

I can remember especially the Giant Wangdoodles from Australia, every one with a huge ripe red strawberry hidden inside its crispy chocolate crust. — THE GIRAFFE AND THE PELLY AND ME

LOOK IT UP! Some other scrumptious sweets are **Gumtwizzlers** and **Mint Jujubes**.

giddy adjective giddier, giddiest

If you feel giddy, you feel unsteady or dizzy.

*'Oh, **please** why doesn't someone help us to get down from here?' Miss Spider called out. 'It's making me giddy.'* — JAMES AND THE GIANT PEACH

gift noun gifts

1 a present

2 If you have a gift for something, it means you are naturally very good at doing it.

Miss Jennifer Honey . . . possessed that rare gift for being adored by every small child under her care. — MATILDA

gigantic adjective

Something that is gigantic is very big.

The Pelican opened his gigantic beak and immediately the policemen pounced upon the burglar, who was crouching inside. — THE GIRAFFE AND THE PELLY AND ME

SPARKY SYNONYMS You can also say **gigantuous** or **jumpsquiffling**.

giganticus adjective

grand and spectacular

'So now!' barked The Grand High Witch. 'So now I am having a plan! I am having a giganticus plan for getting rrrid of every single child in the whole of Inkland!' — THE WITCHES

gigantuous adjective

absolutely huge and enormous

'What a spliffling whoppsy room we is in! It is so gigantuous I is needing bicirculers and telescoops to see what is going on at the other end.' — THE BFG

DID YOU KNOW? Roald Dahl made up the word *gigantuous* by starting with the word *gigantic* and then giving it a different ending.

Gobblefunking with words

Both *-ic* and *-ous* are often used to make adjectives, so Roald Dahl was swapping one familiar ending for another. You can try this too, using adjective endings such as *-ian*, *-ic*, *-ive*, *-ous* and *-uous*, so *magnetic* and *majestic* could become *magnetive* and *majestuous*.

LOOK IT UP! For other ways to describe something **gigantuous**, see **big** and **enormous**.

giggle verb giggles, giggling, giggled

When you giggle, you laugh in a silly way.

'I'm joking,' said Mr Wonka, giggling madly behind his beard. 'I didn't mean it. Forgive me.' — CHARLIE AND THE CHOCOLATE FACTORY

RINGBELLING RHYMES Try rhyming with *wiggle* or *wriggle* (because sometimes you *do* wriggle when you giggle).

LOOK IT UP! For some other ways that you can laugh, see **laugh**.

gigglehouse for girls noun gigglehouses for girls

the name that giants give to a girls' school (a school for boys is a **bogglebox**)

'I,' shouted the Maidmasher, 'is knowing where there is a gigglehouse for girls and I is guzzling myself full as a frothblower!' — THE BFG

Gilligrass, Lancelot R. (CHARLIE AND THE GREAT GLASS ELEVATOR)

Lancelot R. Gilligrass is the President of the United States and the most powerful man on Earth. When he hears about the Great Glass Elevator, he thinks it is a Martian spacecraft that is launching an attack on the Space Hotel.

DID YOU KNOW? Roald Dahl may have based the name *Gilligrass* on *gillyflower*, which is the name of a real plant.

gin noun

a clear alcoholic drink flavoured with juniper berries

George saw a bottle of GIN standing on the sideboard. Grandma was very fond of gin. She was allowed to have a small nip of it every evening. — GEORGE'S MARVELLOUS MEDICINE

gingerly adverb
If you do something gingerly, you do it carefully and cautiously because you are not sure about it.
Very gingerly the boy began to cut a thin slice of the vast cake. Then he levered the slice out. – MATILDA

gipsy or **gypsy** noun **gipsies** or **gypsies**
A gipsy belongs to a family that travels and traditionally lives in a caravan. They are also sometimes called **travellers**. Danny and his father live in an old caravan that used to be owned by gipsies.
We got our heat and light in much the same way as the gipsies had done years ago. – DANNY THE CHAMPION OF THE WORLD
DID YOU KNOW? The word *gipsy* comes from *Egyptian*, because gipsies were originally thought to have come from Egypt.

giraffe noun **giraffes**
A giraffe is a very tall African animal with a very long neck. Giraffes are the tallest animals in the world. A special type of giraffe is the Geraneous Giraffe.
'The moment I saw you I knew you were no ordinary giraffe. You are of the Geraneous variety, are you not?' – THE GIRAFFE AND THE PELLY AND ME
DID YOU KNOW? The word *giraffe* comes from an Arabic word that means 'fast-walker'. Another very old word for a giraffe is a *camelopard*.

girl noun **girls**
a female child and the favourite food of the Maidmasher and the Enormous Crocodile
'Crocodiles don't eat berries,' he said. 'We eat little boys and girls. And sometimes we eat Roly-Poly Birds, as well!' – THE ENORMOUS CROCODILE

Gizzardgulper or Gizzardgulping Giant
(THE BFG)
The Gizzardgulper is one of the not-so-friendly giants in Giant Country. He lies on city rooftops waiting for tasty-looking **human beans** that he can snatch up and eat.
DID YOU KNOW? A *gizzard* is a part of the stomach of birds and some animals (such as dinosaurs and crocodiles) which grinds up food to make it easier to digest.
LOOK IT UP! Some other man-gobbling giants are the **Maidmasher** and the **Bloodbottler**.

gjetost noun
a kind of goats'-milk cheese made in Norway
I had a piece of that brown Norwegian goats'-milk cheese known as gjetost which I had loved even when I was a boy. – THE WITCHES

glamourly adjective
exotic and interesting
'Bonecruncher says Turkish human beans has a glamourly flavour. He says Turks from Turkey is tasting of turkey.' – THE BFG
DID YOU KNOW? The word *glamourly* sounds a bit like *glamorous*, but the BFG gives it a different ending.

The word *glamour* was originally a Scottish word meaning 'witchcraft' or 'magic', and it is related to *grammar* (which the BFG isn't very good at).

glance verb **glances, glancing, glanced**
If you glance at something, you look at it quickly.
Little Billy glanced back quickly over his shoulder, and . . . saw a sight that froze his blood and made icicles in his veins. – THE MINPINS

glare verb **glares, glaring, glared**
If you glare at someone, you look at them angrily.
The brilliant snake's eyes that were set so deep in that dreadful rotting worm-eaten face glared unblinkingly at the witches who sat facing her. – THE WITCHES

glare noun **glares**
a very bright light
Sophie, squinting through the glare of the sun, saw several tremendous tall figures moving among the rocks. – THE BFG

glass noun **glasses**
Glass is a hard substance that you can see through, which is used to make windows, lenses and mirrors. Other things are made out of glass too, like the Great Glass Elevator and Mrs Twit's glass eye.
Because the pipe was made of glass, Augustus Gloop could be clearly seen shooting up inside it, head first, like a torpedo. – CHARLIE AND THE CHOCOLATE FACTORY

glasses plural noun
Glasses are two round pieces of glass in a frame, which some people wear over their eyes to help them to see better. Mr Bucket finds it hard to read because he cannot afford to buy glasses.
'The third ticket,' read Mr Bucket, holding the newspaper up close to his face because his eyes were bad and he couldn't afford glasses, 'the third ticket was found by a Miss Violet Beauregarde.' – CHARLIE AND THE CHOCOLATE FACTORY
SPARKY SYNONYMS You can also say *spectacles*.

gleaming adjective
A gleaming piece of metal or glass shines because it has been polished.
Mr Hazell had pulled up alongside the pumps in his glistening gleaming Rolls-Royce. – DANNY THE CHAMPION OF THE WORLD

glide verb **glides, gliding, glided**
When something glides, it moves along very smoothly. When the BFG goes dream-blowing, he glides past so softly and noiselessly that no one ever knows he is there.
There was a kind of magic in his movements . . . He would glide noiselessly from one dark place to another, always moving, always gliding forward through the streets of London, his black cloak blending with the shadows of the night. – THE BFG

Lots of words that describe light begin with *gl-*, such as *gleaming, glint, glisten* and *glitter*.

glimmer noun **glimmers**
a faint glow of light
Little glints and glimmers from the brilliant moon outside shone through the leaves and gave the place a cold eerie look. – DANNY THE CHAMPION OF THE WORLD

glimp noun **glimps**
a very quick glimpse or peek
'I is showing you now who is going to eat you up if they is ever catching even one tiny little glimp of you.' – THE BFG

glimpse noun **glimpses**
If you catch a glimpse of something, you see it for only a few seconds.
In the moonlight, Sophie caught a glimpse of an enormous long pale wrinkly face with the most enormous ears. – THE BFG

glint noun **glints**
a brief flash of light
Little glints and glimmers from the brilliant moon outside shone through the leaves and gave the place a cold eerie look. – DANNY THE CHAMPION OF THE WORLD

gliss verb **glisses, glissing, glissed**
When a **grobe** or other creature glisses, it glides slimily.
You can hear them softly slimeing,/Glissing hissing o'er the slubber,/All those oily boily bodies/Oozing onward in the gloam. – CHARLIE AND THE GREAT GLASS ELEVATOR

> **Gobblefunking with words**
> When you use words like *glissing* and *hissing* that sound like the things they describe, it is called *onomatopoeia*. Some other onomatopoeic words are *grunt*, *plop* and *splash*. Roald Dahl loved inventing new *onomatopoeic* words, such as **bibble** (for *bibbling waves*) and **quelchy** (in *quelchy quaggy sogmire*).

glisten (*rhymes with* listen) verb **glistens, glistening, glistened**
If a surface glistens, it shines or shimmers in the light.
A vast city, glistening in the early morning sunshine, lay spread out three thousand feet below them. – JAMES AND THE GIANT PEACH

glitter verb **glitters, glittering, glittered**
If something glitters, it shines and sparkles brightly.
The Trunchbull stood motionless on the platform. Her great horsy face had turned the colour of molten lava and her eyes were glittering with fury. – MATILDA

gloam noun
Gloam is a word used in poems to mean twilight, or the time just before night falls.
You can hear them softly slimeing,/Glissing hissing o'er the slubber,/All those oily boily bodies/Oozing onward in the gloam. – CHARLIE AND THE GREAT GLASS ELEVATOR
DID YOU KNOW? The word *gloam* is a short form

of *gloaming*, which also means 'twilight' and was originally a Scottish word.

glob noun **globs**
A glob is a lump of something soft, like glue or sticky mud. Miss Trunchbull uses the phrase *glob of glue* as an insult.
'You ignorant little slug!' the Trunchbull bellowed. 'You witless weed! You empty-headed hamster! You stupid glob of glue!' – MATILDA
LOOK IT UP! Some other insults that Miss Trunchbull uses are **gumboil** and **fungus**.

Globgobbler noun **Globgobblers**
an exotic sweet from the Middle East that is sold in the Grubber
The Globgobbler is an especially delicious sweet . . . and the moment you bite into it, all the perfumed juices of Arabia go squirting down your gullet. – THE GIRAFFE AND THE PELLY AND ME

gloom noun
1 deep darkness
Little Billy flicked his head round and stared into the everlasting gloom and doom of the forest. – THE MINPINS
2 a feeling of great sadness
Gloom settled upon the entire company, including for once Mr Wonka himself. – CHARLIE AND THE GREAT GLASS ELEVATOR

> **Gobblefunking with words**
> The words *gloom* and *doom* are often written together as a rhyming phrase. Some other examples are *hither and thither*, *hustle and bustle*, and *wear and tear*. You can also join two words that rhyme to make another word, like *helter-skelter*, *super-duper* and *teenie-weenie*. Roald Dahl often made up rhyming words like these, such as **flavory-savory**, **ucky-mucky** and **Oompa-Loompa**.

gloomness noun
darkness or night-time
'In the quelchy quaggy sogmire,/In the mashy mideous harshland,/At the witchy hour of gloomness,/All the grobes come oozing home.' – CHARLIE AND THE GREAT GLASS ELEVATOR
DID YOU KNOW? The word *gloomness* sounds like *gloominess* and has a similar meaning, but it fits the rhythm of the poem because it is shorter.

gloomy adjective **gloomier, gloomiest**
1 A gloomy place is dark and dismal.
They found themselves in a vast, damp, gloomy cellar. 'This is it!' cried Mr Fox. – FANTASTIC MR FOX
2 If you feel gloomy, you feel sad.
'Poor Earthworm,' the Ladybird said. . . . 'He is only happy when he is gloomy. Now isn't that odd?' – JAMES AND THE GIANT PEACH

gloop noun

Gloop is a sticky and sloppy paste. If something has the texture of gloop, such as porridge or melted marshmallows, you can say it is *gloopy*. Augustus Gloop has a name that suggests he eats lots of gloopy sticky things.

'Just imagine it! Augustus-flavoured chocolate-coated Gloop! No one would buy it.' — CHARLIE AND THE CHOCOLATE FACTORY

RINGBELLING RHYMES The Oompa-Loompas rhyme *Augustus Gloop* with *nincompoop*.

gloriumptious adjective

A gloriumptious experience is one that you find wonderful and exciting.

'I must say it's quite an experience,' Sophie said. 'It's a razztwizzler,' the BFG said. 'It's gloriumptious.' — THE BFG

RINGBELLING RHYMES Try rhyming with *frumptious*, *scrumptious* or *scrumdiddlyumptious*.

glove noun gloves

Gloves are things that you wear on your hands to keep them warm or clean (or to hide your claws if you are a witch). If you suspect someone of being a witch, it is a good idea to ask them to remove their gloves.

Instead of finger-nails, she has thin curvy claws, like a cat, and she wears the gloves to hide them. — THE WITCHES

glow verb glows, glowing, glowed

When something glows, it shines with a warm, gentle light.

James could see a mass of tiny green things . . . They were extraordinarily beautiful, and there was . . . a sort of luminous quality that made them glow and sparkle in the most wonderful way. — JAMES AND THE GIANT PEACH

glow noun glows

a soft warm light

The orange glow from the night-sky over London crept into the room and cast a glimmer of light on to its walls. — THE BFG

Glow-worm (JAMES AND THE GIANT PEACH)

A glow-worm is not a type of worm at all. It is a type of beetle with a tail that gives out a green light. The Glow-worm who lives in the Giant Peach uses her tail to provide light for all the creatures inside.

glubbage noun

something disgusting that is not fit to eat

'So this is the filthing rotsome glubbage you is eating!' boomed the Bloodbottler, holding up the partly eaten snozzcumber. — THE BFG

DID YOU KNOW? The word *glubbage* sounds a bit like *gloop* and a bit like *garbage*, so it makes you think of something sloppy and disgusting.

glue noun glues

Glue is a sticky substance that you use for sticking things together, and that Mr Twit uses to trap birds to make Bird Pie.

Inside Mr Twit's workshed there was an enormous barrel of HUGTIGHT sticky glue, the stuff he used for catching birds. — THE TWITS

glue verb glues, gluing, glued

1 If you glue something, you stick it with glue.

2 If your eyes are glued to something, you cannot stop looking at it.

Mrs Wormwood sat munching her meal with her eyes glued to the American soap-opera on the screen. — MATILDA

glum adjective glummer, glummest

If you feel glum, you are feeling sad or depressed.

'It will never grow again,' said Mr Fox. 'I shall be tail-less for the rest of my life.' He looked very glum. — FANTASTIC MR FOX

glummy adjective glummier, glummiest

Something that tastes glummy is delicious.

The BFG . . . removed the cork and took a tremendous gurgling swig. 'It's glummy!' he cried. 'I love it!' — THE BFG

RINGBELLING RHYMES Try rhyming with *tummy*.

glumptious adjective

Something that is glumptious is delicious or scrumptious.

'I is happy to let you sample it,' the BFG went on. 'But please, when you see how truly glumptious it is, do not be guzzling the whole thing.' — THE BFG

SPARKY SYNONYMS You can also say *delumptious* or *scrumdiddlyumptious*.

glutton noun gluttons

A glutton is a very greedy person, like Augustus Gloop. You can also say that they are *gluttonous*.

Gnooly noun Gnoolies

Gnoolies are invisible and deadly creatures that live under the Earth's surface in Minusland. If you are bitten by a Gnooly, you turn into one yourself after a very painful process that involves long division.

'You can't see Gnoolies, my boy. You can't even feel them . . . until they puncture your skin . . . then it's too late.' — CHARLIE AND THE GREAT GLASS ELEVATOR

goatee noun goatees

a small pointed beard, like the one that Willy Wonka has

Covering his chin, there was a small, neat, pointed black beard — a goatee. And his eyes — his eyes were most marvellously bright. — CHARLIE AND THE CHOCOLATE FACTORY

Goosegruggled or *gunzleswiped*? Find out how giants use rude words at **rude**.

DID YOU KNOW? The word *goatee* comes from *goat*, because that style of beard looks a bit like the tuft of hair under a goat's chin.

gobbit noun gobbits
a part or section of something, like a part of a long dream
'And about a Big Friendly Giant?' 'I is putting in a nice long gobbit about him,' the BFG said. — THE BFG

DID YOU KNOW? The word *gobbit* sounds like *gobbet* which means 'a lump of flesh or food'. Gobbets of **human beans** are what the Fleshlumpeater loves to eat — so another name for him could be a *Gobbetgobbler*.

gobble verb gobbles, gobbling, gobbled
If you gobble something, you eat it quickly and greedily.
'Whenever I see a live slug on a piece of lettuce,' Grandma said, 'I gobble it up quick before it crawls away. Delicious.' — GEORGE'S MARVELLOUS MEDICINE

RINGBELLING RHYMES Why not try making up your own words to rhyme with *gobble*, like *flobble* or *grobble*?

gobblefunk verb gobblefunks, gobblefunking, gobblefunked
If you gobblefunk with words, you play around with them and invent new words or meanings.
'You mean whales,' Sophie said. 'Wales is something quite different.' 'Wales is whales,' the Giant said. 'Don't gobblefunk around with words.' — THE BFG

DID YOU KNOW? Roald Dahl made up the word *gobblefunk*, but he may have wanted it to sound like *gobbledegook*, a kind of language that some grown-ups use that is full of meaningless words and is hard to understand. The BFG only uses *gobblefunk* as a verb, but you may also hear the word *gobblefunk* used as a noun, to mean all the marvellous words that Roald Dahl invented for his stories.

gobstopper noun gobstoppers
A gobstopper is a hard-boiled sweet for sucking. Willy Wonka invents the *Everlasting Gobstopper*, which never gets any smaller.

Gobwangle noun Gobwangles
an exotic type of sweet from Fiji that is sold in the Grubber
There were . . . Tummyticklers and Gobwangles from the Fiji Islands and Liplickers and Plushnuggets from the Land of the Midnight Sun. — THE GIRAFFE AND THE PELLY AND ME

LOOK IT UP! Some other scrumptious sweets are **Gumglotters** and **Giant Wangdoodles**.

goggle verb goggles, goggling, goggled
If you goggle, you stare with wide-open eyes.
This was too much for George's mother to understand. She just goggled and gaped. She looked as though she was going to faint. — GEORGE'S MARVELLOUS MEDICINE

gogglers plural noun
a word that the BFG uses for eyes
'That is why you will be coming to an ucky-mucky end if any of them should ever be getting his gogglers upon you.' — THE BFG

DID YOU KNOW? *Gogglers* is an old-fashioned slang word for 'eyes', which is based on the verb *goggle* meaning 'to stare'. Some other words for eyes are *peepers* and *blinkers*, because you peep and blink with your eyes.

goggles plural noun
Goggles are special thick glasses that you wear to protect your eyes, and that Oompa-Loompas wear as part of their uniform. The BFG says *By goggles!* when he is surprised.

They were wearing bright-red space suits, complete with helmets and goggles . . . and they were working in complete silence. — CHARLIE AND THE CHOCOLATE FACTORY
'By goggles!' he cried. 'This stuff is making snozzcumbers taste like swatchwallop!' — THE BFG

gold noun
a shiny, yellow metal that is very valuable
Jack waited till the Giant slept,/Then out along the boughs he crept/And gathered so much gold, I swear/He was an instant millionaire. — REVOLTING RHYMES

golden adjective
made of gold, or coloured like gold
The giant peach, with the sunlight glinting on its side, was like a massive golden ball sailing upon a silver sea. — JAMES AND THE GIANT PEACH

golden phizzwizard noun golden phizzwizards
A phizzwizard is a good dream, and a golden phizzwizard is the very best dream you could ever have. It is the opposite of a **trogglehumper**.
'It's a golden phizzwizard! It is not often I is getting one of these!' — THE BFG

Golden Ticket (CHARLIE AND THE CHOCOLATE FACTORY)
Only five bars of chocolate from Willy Wonka's factory have a Golden Ticket hidden inside the wrapper. Each child who finds one is invited on a special tour of the Chocolate Factory.

gollop noun gollops
a big gulp or swallow
'I'll bet if you saw a fat juicy little child paddling in the water over there at this very moment, you'd gulp him up in one gollop!' — THE ENORMOUS CROCODILE

RINGBELLING RHYMES Try rhyming with *dollop* or *wallop*.

golly exclamation
You might say *Golly!* or *By golly!* if you are surprised or amazed by something.
'By golly it is a Giant Skillywiggler!' Mr Twit said. 'It'll bite off your nose.' — THE TWITS

LOOK IT UP! For more things to say when you are surprised, see **exclamation**.

whoopsey-splunkers phizz-whizzing wondercrump squiffling

whoppsy-whiffling

good adjective **better, best**
Something good is pleasant and enjoyable, and a good person is kind and well-meaning. Try using these words to describe them to make sure your writing is **fantabulous** too.

A GOOD PERSON OR A GOOD GIANT CAN BE: honest, honourable, **jumbly**, kind, kind-hearted, noble, virtuous, worthy
• Opposites are: evil, wicked and **horrigust**
'I is a nice and jumbly Giant! I is the only nice and jumbly Giant in Giant Country! I is THE BIG FRIENDLY GIANT!'
—THE BFG

LOOK IT UP! Some truly **jumbly** characters are Grandpa Joe and Miss Honey, and some wickedly **horrigust** characters are The Grand High Witch and Mr and Mrs Twit (but there are so many more).

A GOOD EXPERIENCE OR A GOOD DREAM CAN BE: agreeable, delightful, enjoyable, pleasant

BUT IF IT IS REALLY GOOD IT IS: fantabulous, **phizz-whizzing**, splendid, splendiferous, **squiffling, whoopsey-splunkers, whoppsy-whiffling, wondercrump,** wonderful
• The good dreams that the BFG catches are **ringbellers** and **winksquifflers**, and the very best, most splendiferous dreams are **golden phizzwizards**.

'How wondercrump!' cried the BFG, still beaming. *'How whoopsey-splunkers! How absolutely squiffling! I is all of a stutter.'*—THE BFG

SOMETHING THAT TASTES GOOD CAN BE: delicious, **delumptious, lickswishy, scrumdiddlyumptious,** scrumptious, **scrumptious-galumptious,** tasty
• Opposites are: disgusting, **rotsome** and **uckyslush**
'Every human bean is diddly and different. Some is scrumdiddlyumptious and some is uckyslush.'—THE BFG

gooey adjective **gooier, gooiest**
A gooey mess or mixture is sticky or slimy.
The saucepan was full of a thick gooey purplish treacle, boiling and bubbling. — CHARLIE AND THE CHOCOLATE FACTORY
DID YOU KNOW? *Gooey* is thought to come from an old word, *burgoo*, which was a type of gooey porridge once eaten by sailors.
RINGBELLING RHYMES Try rhyming with *chewy* or *gluey*.

goose noun **geese**
A goose is a large bird that is kept on farms for its meat and eggs. A male goose is called a *gander*.
'Well, my darling, what shall it be this time? A plump chicken from Boggis? A duck or a goose from Bunce? Or a nice turkey from Bean?' — FANTASTIC MR FOX

goosegruggled adjective
If a giant is goosegruggled, he is in a hopeless situation.
'I is swogswalloped!' bellowed the Bonecruncher. 'I is goosegruggled!' howled the Manhugger. — THE BFG

gorge verb **gorges, gorging, gorged**
If you gorge yourself, you stuff yourself greedily with food.
'You can have cacao beans for every meal! You can gorge yourselves silly on them! I'll even pay your wages in cacao beans if you wish!' — CHARLIE AND THE CHOCOLATE FACTORY

gormless adjective
A gormless grown-up is foolish and has no *common sense*.
Mr and Mrs Wormwood were both so gormless and so wrapped up in their own silly little lives that they failed to notice anything unusual about their daughter. — MATILDA

gosh exclamation
You might say *Gosh!* if you are surprised or amazed by something.
'This stuff is fabulous!' said Augustus, taking not the slightest notice of his mother or Mr Wonka. 'Gosh, I need a bucket to drink it properly!' — CHARLIE AND THE CHOCOLATE FACTORY
LOOK IT UP! For more ways to show you are surprised, see **exclamation**.

gossamer noun
fine cobwebs made by small spiders
'I do hope you'll find it comfortable,' Miss Spider said . . . 'I made it as soft and silky as I possibly could. I spun it with gossamer.' — JAMES AND THE GIANT PEACH
DID YOU KNOW? The word *gossamer* comes from *goose summer*, a period of fine weather in the autumn when you see lots of gossamer about.

grab verb **grabs, grabbing, grabbed**
If you grab something, you take hold of it quickly or roughly.
Miss Spider . . . grabbed the Centipede by the waist and the two of them started dancing round and round the peach stem together. — JAMES AND THE GIANT PEACH

grabble noun
food or snacks to eat
'That was only one titchy little bite,' the BFG said. 'Is you having any more of this delunctious grabble in your cupboard, Majester?' — THE BFG

grace noun **graces**
You say *Your Grace* if you need to say something to a Duke or Duchess.
'If the Pelican is willing, perhaps he will also give me a ride in his beak now and again.' 'A pleasure, Your Grace!' cried the Pelican. — THE GIRAFFE AND THE PELLY AND ME

graceful adjective
A graceful movement is smooth and gentle.
The BFG . . . stopped and made a slow graceful bow . . . 'Your Majester,' he said. 'I is your humbug servant.' — THE BFG

> **Gobblefunking with words**
> When the BFG says the word *humbug* instead of *humble*, he is using a *malapropism*. You can find more examples of this type of word play in the entry for **mudburger**.

grammar noun
Grammar is all the rules of a language which tell us how to put the words together correctly so that they make sense. The BFG sometimes makes mistakes in grammar, as there are no schools in Giant Country where he grew up. For example, he says, *We is going fast as a fizzlecrump!* rather than *We are going fast as a fizzlecrump!*
RINGBELLING RHYMES Try rhyming with *hammer* (as Miss Trunchbull likes them both).

grand adjective **grander, grandest**
Something that is grand is very big and important (unlike Mr Twit). Important people are sometimes given a title like *Grand Duke* or *The Grand High Witch*.
Mr Twit felt that this hairiness made him look terrifically wise and grand. But in truth he was neither of these things. — THE TWITS

grandchild noun **grandchildren**
Someone's grandchild is a child of their son or daughter, so Charlie Bucket is the grandchild of Grandpa Joe. A grandchild can also be called a granddaughter or a grandson.
Grandpa Joe . . . spoke very little. But in the evenings, when Charlie, his beloved grandson, was in the room, he seemed in some marvellous way to grow quite young again. — CHARLIE AND THE CHOCOLATE FACTORY

A B C D E F G H I J K L M N O P Q R S T U V W X Y Z

grandfather or grandpa (*informal*) noun
grandfathers or **grandpas**

Your grandfather is the father of your mother or father.

Little Charlie sat very still on the edge of the bed, staring at his grandfather . . . 'Is all this really true?' he asked. 'Or are you pulling my leg?' – CHARLIE AND THE CHOCOLATE FACTORY

grandfather clock noun grandfather clocks

A grandfather clock is a clock in a tall wooden case. Mr Tibbs uses four grandfather clocks from the royal palace to make a giant table for the BFG.

'Now place the ping-pong table on top of the four grandfather clocks,' Mr Tibbs whispered. To manage this, the footmen had to stand on step-ladders. – THE BFG

Grand High Witch (THE WITCHES)

The Grand High Witch is the most important witch in the whole world. She detests children and is always thinking up evil ways to destroy them.

Grandma Georgina (CHARLIE AND THE CHOCOLATE FACTORY & GREAT GLASS ELEVATOR)

Grandma Georgina is one of Charlie's bed-ridden grandparents. She doesn't trust Willy Wonka and often calls him rude names, such as *You miserable old mackerel!*

Grandma Josephine (CHARLIE AND THE CHOCOLATE FACTORY & GREAT GLASS ELEVATOR)

Grandma Josephine is one of Charlie's bed-ridden grandparents. She is married to Grandpa Joe and is the mother of Mr Bucket.

grandmother or grandma or granny (*informal*)
noun **grandmothers** or **grandmas** or **grannies**

Your grandmother is the mother of your mother or father. Some grandmothers are lovely, but George Kranky's grandma is a bad-tempered, grizzly old **grunion**.

George sat himself down at the table in the kitchen. He was shaking a little. Oh, how he hated Grandma! He really hated that horrid old witchy woman. – GEORGE'S MARVELLOUS MEDICINE

grandness noun

Your Grandness is a polite way of addressing The Grand High Witch (and it is always a good idea to be polite to The Grand High Witch, to avoid being frrried to a frrritter).

'Whoopee!' cried the witches, clapping their hands. 'You are brilliant, O Your Grandness! You are fantabulous!' – THE WITCHES

Grandpa George (CHARLIE AND THE CHOCOLATE FACTORY & GREAT GLASS ELEVATOR)

Grandpa George is one of Charlie's bed-ridden grandparents. He is married to Grandma Georgina and is the father of Mrs Bucket.

Grandpa Joe (CHARLIE AND THE CHOCOLATE FACTORY & GREAT GLASS ELEVATOR)

Grandpa Joe is the oldest of Charlie's four grandparents. Despite being ninety-six and a half, he hasn't lost his sparkiness, and he loves telling Charlie stories about Willy Wonka and the Chocolate Factory.

grandparent noun grandparents

Your grandparents are the parents of your father or mother. All four of Charlie Bucket's grandparents sleep in the same bed, which they hardly ever leave as they are so old and tired.

Grandpa Joe was the oldest of the four grandparents. He was ninety-six and a half, and that is just about as old as anybody can be. – CHARLIE AND THE CHOCOLATE FACTORY

grasp verb grasps, grasping, grasped

If you grasp something, you get hold of it and hold it tightly.

*'Charlie!' cried Mr Wonka, grasping him by the hand. 'What **would** we do without you? You're brilliant!'* – CHARLIE AND THE GREAT GLASS ELEVATOR

a b c d e f g h i j k l m n o p q r s t u v w x y z

Roald Dahl called his Norwegian grandparents *Bestemama* and *Bestepapa*.

grass noun **grasses**
Grass is a green plant that covers the ground and is used for lawns and parks. Willy Wonka invents an edible grass made of mint-flavoured sugar.
'The grass you are standing on . . . is made of a new kind of soft, minty sugar that I've just invented! I call it swudge! Try a blade!' – CHARLIE AND THE CHOCOLATE FACTORY

Grasshopper (JAMES AND THE GIANT PEACH)
A grasshopper is an insect that has long back legs and can jump a long way. The Old-Green-Grasshopper, who lives in the Giant Peach, loves to play music by rubbing his back leg against his wing like the bow of a violin.

grateful adjective
If you are grateful for something, you are glad that you have it.
The Glow-worm became the light inside the torch on the Statue of Liberty, and thus saved a grateful City from having to pay a huge electricity bill every year. – JAMES AND THE GIANT PEACH

grave noun **graves**
a place where a dead person or animal is buried in the ground
The playground, which up to then had been filled with shrieks and the shouting of children at play, all at once became silent as the grave. – MATILDA

Gobblefunking with words
If you say that a place is *silent as the grave*, you are using a *simile*. You can find lots of similes in Roald Dahl's stories. For example, the BFG has hands *as big as wheelbarrows* and George's medicine makes his grandma *as frisky as a ferret*. For other types of simile, see **grin** and **mad**.

gravity noun
Gravity is the force that pulls things towards the Earth and that stops you from floating off into outer space. The Space Hotel is equipped with a gravity-making machine so that the guests can walk around normally inside it.
'We're outside the pull of gravity up here, Mr President. Everything floats. We'd be floating ourselves if we weren't strapped down.' – CHARLIE AND THE GREAT GLASS ELEVATOR

grease noun
thick fat or oil, such as George adds to his Marvellous Medicine mixture
Some ANTI-FREEZE — to keep her radiator from freezing up in winter. A handful of GREASE — to grease her creaking joints. – GEORGE'S MARVELLOUS MEDICINE

great adjective **greater, greatest**
For ways to say that something is fantabulously great, see **good**.

Great Glass Elevator (CHARLIE AND THE GREAT GLASS ELEVATOR)
The Great Glass Elevator is a flying lift that Willy Wonka uses to travel to and from his factory. It launches into orbit around the Earth by mistake, taking Willy Wonka, Charlie and his family with it.

greedy adjective **greedier, greediest**
Someone who is greedy wants more food or money than they need. Augustus Gloop is so greedy he cannot stop eating sweets and chocolate.
'Augustus Gloop!' chanted the Oompa-Loompas. 'Augustus Gloop! Augustus Gloop! The great big greedy nincompoop!' – CHARLIE AND THE CHOCOLATE FACTORY

green adjective **greener, greenest**
Something that is green (such as Willy Wonka's trousers) is the colour of grass or mould or **Mint Jujubes**. Grasshoppers and Knids are naturally green.
MINT JUJUBES FOR THE BOY NEXT DOOR — THEY'LL GIVE HIM GREEN TEETH FOR A MONTH. – CHARLIE AND THE CHOCOLATE FACTORY

greenish adjective
somewhat green in colour
Then a faint greenish light began to glimmer out of the Glow-worm's tail, and this gradually became stronger and stronger until it was anyway enough to see by. – JAMES AND THE GIANT PEACH

greet verb **greets, greeting, greeted**
When you greet someone, you welcome them and say hello to them.
'Toad!' I cried. 'I'm not a funk,/But ought we not to do a bunk?/These rascals haven't come to greet you./All they want to do is eat you!' – DIRTY BEASTS

Greggs (THE MAGIC FINGER)
The Greggs are a thoughtless family who live on a farm and shoot animals and birds for fun. This annoys their next-door neighbour so much that she uses the power of her Magic Finger on them.

gremlin noun **gremlins**
Gremlins are small mischievous creatures that cause problems with machines, especially aircraft. The first children's story that Roald Dahl wrote was about gremlins in Royal Air Force planes.
The gremlin . . . had a strawberry nose which looked like the moon through a telescope, and his head, with its stubby horns, was as bald as could be. – THE GREMLINS

grey adjective **greyer, greyest**
Something that is grey is the colour of ash, or of the sky on a cloudy day. The grass in Dream Country is ashy grey, and Willy Wonka wears gloves that are pearly grey.
There was some sort of grass underfoot but it was not green. It was ashy grey. – THE BFG

griggle verb **griggles, griggling, griggled**
If you griggle, you smile with a big wide grin.
Sophie couldn't stop smiling. 'What is you griggling at?' the BFG asked her, slightly nettled. – THE BFG
DID YOU KNOW? The word *griggle* sounds like *grin* and *giggle* joined together. You could make up your

own words like this, such as *sniccup* for a cross between a sneeze and a hiccup.

grim adjective grimmer, grimmest

A grim person or a grim look is not nice or cheerful.
Mr Coombes was looking grim. His hammy pink face had taken on that dangerous scowl which only appeared when he was extremely cross. — BOY

grimalkin noun grimalkins

A grimalkin is an old name for a female cat, especially one that is kept by a witch or has magical powers. The teeth of an ancient Mexican grimalkin are needed to make Vita-Wonk.
'I . . . rushed all over the world collecting special items from the oldest living things . . . THE BLACK TEETH OF A 97-YEAR OLD GRIMALKIN LIVING IN A CAVE ON MOUNT POPOCATEPETL.' — CHARLIE AND THE GREAT GLASS ELEVATOR

grimesludge noun

thick and dirty mud
'By goggles,' he said, taking the jar out of the suitcase, 'your head is not quite so full of grimesludge after all!' — THE BFG

DID YOU KNOW? To make this word Roald Dahl put together the two words *grime* and *sludge*. You could try making up your own words to mean the same thing, like *sludgegloop* or *ickymud*.

RINGBELLING RHYMES Try rhyming with *fudge* or *trudge*.

grimy adjective grimier, grimiest

Something that is grimy is covered with a layer of dirt.
The Trunchbull . . . marched back to the front of the class, dusting off her hands . . . like someone who has been handling something rather grimy. — MATILDA

RINGBELLING RHYMES Try rhyming with *slimy*.

grin verb grins, grinning, grinned

When you grin, you smile in a cheerful way.
The Enormous Crocodile grinned again, and his terrible sharp teeth sparkled like knives in the sun. — THE ENORMOUS CROCODILE

Gobblefunking with words

If you say someone (or a crocodile) has teeth which sparkle *like knives in the sun*, you are using a *simile*. Roald Dahl uses lots of similes in his stories and poems and you can see more examples in the entries for **grave** and **mad**.

grind verb grinds, grinding, ground

When a machine grinds, it rubs against a surface, making a rasping sound.
Their dreadful voices were like a chorus of dentists' drills all grinding away together. — THE WITCHES

grinksludger noun grinksludgers

A grinksludger is someone who is unpleasant or unkind.
'Grown-up human beans is not famous for their kindnesses. They is all squifflerotters and grinksludgers.' — THE BFG

grinksludging adjective

A grinksludging dream is one that is no fun at all.
'If I is giving a girl's dream to a boy . . . the boy would be waking up and thinking what a rotbungling grinksludging old dream that was.' — THE BFG

grip verb grips, gripping, gripped

When you grip something, you hold it tightly.
Mr Hoppy took Tortoise Number 2 out on to the balcony and gripped it in the claws of his tortoise-catcher. — ESIO TROT

grisly adjective grislier, grisliest

A grisly story or a grisly experience is one where horrible and unpleasant things happen.
'We shall get thinner and thinner and thirstier and thirstier, and we shall all die a slow and grisly death from starvation.' — JAMES AND THE GIANT PEACH

grittle verb grittles, grittling, grittled

If you grittle your teeth, you grit or clench them tight.
'Now close your eyes and grittle your teeth . . . while I is taking out the teeth of the venomsome viper,' the BFG said. — THE BFG

grizzling adjective

Something that is grizzling is nasty and unpleasant.
'You is a human bean and you is saying it is grizzling and horrigust for giants to be eating human beans. Right or left?' — THE BFG

SPARKY SYNONYMS You can also say **horrigust** or **muckfrumping**.

You can add -*y* to some nouns to make adjectives: *grimesludgy mud*.

grizzly adjective **grizzlier, grizzliest**
A grizzly person grumbles or complains a lot, just like George's grumbly old grandma.
George . . . was especially tired of having to live in the same house as that grizzly old grunion of a Grandma. — GEORGE'S MARVELLOUS MEDICINE
DON'T BE BIFFSQUIGGLED! Take care not to confuse *grizzly* with **grisly** which means 'horrible or ghastly', so a *grizzly* person might meet a *grim and grisly fate*.
DID YOU KNOW? *Grizzly* comes from an old dialect word *grizzle* meaning originally 'to grin with a sneer'.

groan verb **groans, groaning, groaned**
When you groan, you make a low sound because you are in pain or are disappointed about something.
'I'm a wreck!' groaned the Centipede. 'I am wounded all over!' 'It serves you right,' said the Earthworm. — JAMES AND THE GIANT PEACH

grobblesquirt noun **grobblesquirts**
The grobblesquirt is a creature that lives on moorland and is hunted by witches, who use its snout to make Formula 86 Delayed Action Mouse-Maker.
'We will spear the blabbersnitch and trap the crabcruncher and shoot the grobblesquirt and catch the catspringer in his burrow!' — THE WITCHES
LOOK IT UP! Some other creatures that are hunted by witches are the **blabbersnitch** and the **crabcruncher.**

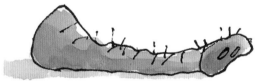

grobe noun **grobes**
A grobe is an imaginary slimy creature that Willy Wonka invents to scare the President of the United States.
'I thought they were grobes,' Charlie said. 'Those oozy-woozy grobes you were telling the President about.' — CHARLIE AND THE GREAT GLASS ELEVATOR

grobsludging adjective
A grobsludging place is unpleasant and uncomfortable.
'Why is they putting us down here in this grobsludging hole?' they shouted at the BFG. — THE BFG

grobsquiffler noun **grobsquifflers**
If you call someone a grobsquiffler, you are saying they are silly and not important.
'Now then, you little grobsquiffler!' boomed the Fleshlumpeater. — THE BFG

grobswitcher noun **grobswitchers**
A grobswitcher is one of the very worst nightmares you can have. It is the opposite of a **golden phizzwizard.**
'Is it as bad as that?' 'It's worse!' cried the BFG. 'This is a real whoppsy grobswitcher!' — THE BFG
LOOK IT UP! Some other scary dreams are **bogthumpers** and **trogglehumpers.**

grobswitchy adjective
Something that tastes grobswitchy has a nasty flavour.
'You is making the cake come out any way you want, sugary, splongy, curranty, Christmassy or grobswitchy.' — THE BFG
SPARKY SYNONYMS You can also say **maggotwise** or **rotsome.** An opposite is **scrumdiddlyumptious.**

gropefluncking adjective
Something gropefluncking is difficult to explain, like a long and complicated dream.
'I cannot be squibbling the whole gropefluncking dream on a titchy bit of paper. Of course there is more.' — THE BFG

grotesque adjective
Something that is grotesque is strange and ugly.
Nine fearsome, ugly, half-naked, fifty-feet-long brutes lay sprawled over the ground in various grotesque attitudes of sleep. — THE BFG

growl verb **growls, growling, growled**
When an animal growls, it makes a deep, angry sound in its throat.
A small black and white dog appeared between Miss Prewt's legs and began to growl. — THE VICAR OF NIBBLESWICKE

growl noun **growls**
A growl is a deep angry sound.
It was a pleasure to listen to the howls and growls of horror . . . as the giants began to chew upon the filthiest-tasting vegetable on earth. — THE BFG

grown-up noun **grown-ups**
Someone who is too old to be a child is called a grown-up.
All grown-ups appear as giants to small children. But headmasters (and policemen) are the biggest giants of all and acquire a marvellously exaggerated stature. — BOY

grub noun **grubs**
1 A baby insect, when it looks like a small fat worm, is called a grub.
Bruce Bogtrotter . . . was sitting on his chair like some huge overstuffed grub, replete, comatose, unable to move or to speak. — MATILDA
2 Grub is also an informal word for food.
'Just feast your eyes on that!' cried Mr Fox, dancing up and down. 'What d'you think of it, eh? Pretty good grub!' — FANTASTIC MR FOX

Grubber (THE GIRAFFE AND THE PELLY AND ME)
The Grubber is an old abandoned sweet-shop that Billy dreams of one day reopening. It becomes the office of the Ladderless Window-Cleaning Company.
DID YOU KNOW? The word *grubber* is an old word that used to mean a sweet-shop.

grueful adjective
horrible and scary, like a monster
'It's Jack!' bellowed the Fleshlumpeater. 'It's the grueful gruncious Jack! Jack is after me!' – THE BFG

gruesome adjective
If something is gruesome, it is horrible or disgusting to look at.
The Bloodbottler was a gruesome sight. His skin was reddish-pink. There was black hair sprouting on his chest and arms and on his stomach. – THE BFG

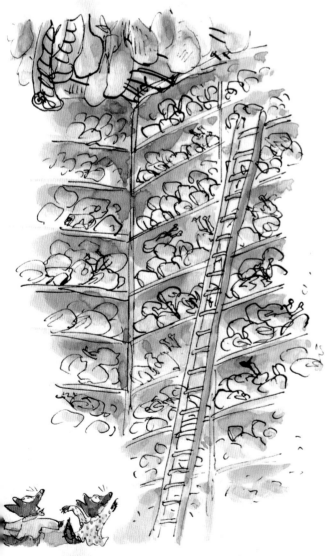

grumble verb grumbles, grumbling, grumbled
When you grumble about something, you complain about it.
Most grandmothers are lovely, kind, helpful old ladies, but not this one . . . She was always complaining, grousing, grouching, grumbling, griping about something or other. – GEORGE'S MARVELLOUS MEDICINE

grump noun grumps
A grump is a bad-tempered, grumpy person, just like George Kranky's grandma.
If you can hardly walk at all,/If living drives you up the wall,/If you're a grump and full of spite . . . THEN WHAT YOU NEED IS WONKA-VITE! – CHARLIE AND THE GREAT GLASS ELEVATOR

grumptious adjective
Someone who is grumptious is grumpy and bad-tempered.
'Oh, you horrid greedy grumptious brute!' cried Humpy-Rumpy. 'I hope you get caught and cooked and turned into crocodile soup!' – THE ENORMOUS CROCODILE
DON'T BE BIFFSQUIGGLED! Take care not to confuse *grumptious* with **glumptious**, which means 'delicious'.

grumpy adjective grumpier, grumpiest
If you are grumpy you are bad-tempered and no fun to be with.
George couldn't help disliking Grandma. She was a selfish grumpy old woman. – GEORGE'S MARVELLOUS MEDICINE
RINGBELLING RHYMES Try rhyming with *bumpy* or *lumpy* (because you *would* be grumpy if your porridge were lumpy).
SPARKY SYNONYMS You can also say **cantankerous**.

grunch verb grunches, grunching, grunched
When a Gruncher grunches, it eats its food (usually Minpins) noisily by grinding and crunching.
'The one waiting for you down there is the fearsome Gruncher, the Red-Hot Smoke-Belching Gruncher. He grunches up everything in the forest.' – THE MINPINS

Gruncher (THE MINPINS)
The Red-Hot Smoke-Belching Gruncher is a fearsome monster who lives in the Forest of Sin and terrifies the Minpins who live there.

gruncious adjective
A gruncious creature is horrible and scary, like a monster.
'It's Jack!' bellowed the Fleshlumpeater. 'It's the grueful gruncious Jack! Jack is after me!' – THE BFG

grunion noun grunions
a very mean or grumpy person
George . . . was especially tired of having to live in the same house as that grizzly old grunion of a Grandma. – GEORGE'S MARVELLOUS MEDICINE
DID YOU KNOW? A grunion is also a small thin fish found in California which lays its eggs on a beach.

Words that Roald Dahl invented that start with *grob-* or *trog-* always mean unpleasant things!

grunt noun **grunts**
A grunt is the noise a pig makes, or a noise like this made by a furious headmistress.
With a mighty grunt, the Trunchbull let go of the pigtails and Amanda went sailing like a rocket right over the wire fence of the playground. — MATILDA

gruntle noun **gruntles**
A gruntle is a type of bird that nests in tall trees. The Grand High Witch uses its eggs in her magic formula.
'I'm getting a bit old to go bird's nesting. Those ruddy gruntles always nest very high up.' — THE WITCHES
DID YOU KNOW? The word *gruntle* has some other meanings too. In some dialects, it is a verb meaning 'to grunt like a pig' or 'to grumble or complain', so you could say that the witches are *gruntling* about having to hunt for rare gruntles.

guest noun **guests**
If someone invites you to be their guest, they invite you to their home for a meal or to stay for a short time. Willy Wonka invites every Golden Ticket winner to be his guest on a special tour of his factory.
Many wonderful surprises await you! For now, I do invite you to come to my factory and be my guest for one whole day. — CHARLIE AND THE CHOCOLATE FACTORY

guilty adjective **guiltier, guiltiest**
If you feel guilty, you feel bad because you have done something wrong.
Lavender was . . . feeling a bit guilty. She hadn't intended to get her friend into trouble. On the other hand, she was certainly not about to own up. — MATILDA

gullet noun **gullets**
Your gullet is the tube that goes from your throat to your stomach. Giraffes have especially long gullets.
The Globgobbler is an especially delicious sweet . . . and the moment you bite into it, all the perfumed juices of Arabia go squirting down your gullet one after the other. — THE GIRAFFE AND THE PELLY AND ME

gulp verb **gulps, gulping, gulped**
If you gulp food or drink, you swallow it very quickly.
'Are you going to gulp it all down in one go?' George asked her. 'Or will you sip it?' — GEORGE'S MARVELLOUS MEDICINE

gulp noun **gulps**
When you take a gulp, you swallow something quickly, often making a noise.
The ancient beanpole had already put the cup to her lips, and in one gulp she swallowed everything that was in it. — GEORGE'S MARVELLOUS MEDICINE

gum noun **gums**
1 Your gums are the hard pink parts of your mouth that are around your teeth.
Bean made a sickly smile. When he smiled you saw his scarlet gums. You saw more gums than teeth. — FANTASTIC MR FOX

2 Gum is a sweet that you chew but do not swallow. Willy Wonka makes gum with magical flavours in his Great Gum Machine.
'This gum,' Mr Wonka went on, 'is my latest, my greatest, my most fascinating invention! It's a chewing-gum meal!' — CHARLIE AND THE CHOCOLATE FACTORY
3 You might say *By gum!* if you are amazed or surprised.
'By Christopher!' Jack cried. 'By gum!/The Giant's eaten up my mum!/He smelled her out! She's in his belly!/'I had a hunch that she was smelly.' — REVOLTING RHYMES

gumboil noun **gumboils**
A gumboil is a hard sweet for chewing like gum. Miss Trunchbull uses the word *gumboil* as an insult.
'You blithering idiot!' shouted the Trunchbull. 'You festering gumboil! You fleabitten fungus!' — MATILDA
LOOK IT UP! Some other sweets are **gobstoppers** and **Giant Wangdoodles**. For more ways to insult people, see **insult**.

gumdrop noun **gumdrops**
A gumdrop is a firm jelly-like sweet that you suck. The BFG says *By gumdrops!* or *By gumfrog!* when he is surprised or amazed by something.
'We're there!' Sophie whispered excitedly. 'We're in the Queen's back garden!' 'By gumdrops!' whispered the Big Friendly Giant. 'Is this really it?' — THE BFG

Gumglotter noun **Gumglotters**
a type of splendiferous sweet that is sold in the Grubber
There were Nishnobblers and Gumglotters . . . and as well as all this, there was a whole lot of splendid stuff from the great Wonka factory itself. — THE GIRAFFE AND THE PELLY AND ME

Gumtwizzler noun **Gumtwizzlers**
one of the exotic sweets from around the world that are sold in the Grubber
There were Gumtwizzlers and Fizzwinkles from China, Frothblowers and Spitsizzlers from Africa. — THE GIRAFFE AND THE PELLY AND ME
LOOK IT UP! Some other scrumptious sweets are **Giant Wangdoodles** and **Mint Jujubes**.

gunghummers exclamation
The BFG says *Gunghummers and bogswinkles!* when he is very surprised.
A shower of glass fell upon the poor BFG. 'Gunghummers and bogswinkles!' he cried. 'What was that?' — THE BFG

gungswizzled adjective
If something is gungswizzled, it is in a complete muddle or totally wrong. Matilda's homework would never be gungswizzled.
'Even when you is getting your sums all gungswizzled and muggled up, Mr Figgins is always giving you ten out of ten and writing Good Work Sophie in your exercise book.' — THE BFG

gunzleswiped adjective

If a giant is gunzleswiped, he is in a very bad situation.

'I is goosegruggled!' howled the Manhugger.
'I is gunzleswiped!' shouted the Meatdripper. — THE BFG

gurgle verb gurgles, gurgling, gurgled

When water or other liquid gurgles, it makes a bubbling sound.

The water came pouring and roaring down upon them, . . . swashing and swirling and surging and whirling and gurgling and gushing. — JAMES AND THE GIANT PEACH

gush verb gushes, gushing, gushed

If something gushes, it flows quickly and strongly. Gushing is the opposite of dribbling or trickling.

Thick smoke came gushing out of the old boy's nostrils in such quantities that I thought his moustaches were going up in flames. — THE GIRAFFE AND THE PELLY AND ME

gusto noun

If you do something with gusto, you do it with a lot of energy and enthusiasm.

Tortoise Number 2 . . . loved the lettuce and started chomping away at it with great gusto. — ESIO TROT

guts plural noun

1 Your guts are your stomach or belly.

'He is swiping me right in the mouth!' yelled the Meatdripper. 'He is bungswoggling me smack in the guts!' shouted the Gizzardgulper. — THE BFG

2 If someone has guts, it means that they are very brave.

It takes guts to do that, I thought. Terrific guts. If I'd been alone I would never have stayed there for one second. — DANNY THE CHAMPION OF THE WORLD

guzzle verb guzzles, guzzling, guzzled

If you guzzle food or drink, you eat or drink it greedily.

'Giants is never guzzling other giants,' the BFG said. 'They is fighting and squarreling a lot with each other, but never guzzling.' — THE BFG

LOOK IT UP! For lots of ways to describe how people eat, see **eat**.

guzzly adjective guzzlier, guzzliest

Something guzzly tastes good when you guzzle it.

'Eating human beans is wrong and evil,' the BFG said. 'It is guzzly and glumptious!' shouted the Bloodbottler. — THE BFG

Miss Honey

MATILDA

hippopotamus   hopscotchy   horrigust

huggybee   human bean

habit noun habits

A habit is something that you do without thinking, because you have done it so often before.

There are a number of little signals you can look out for, little quirky habits that all witches have in common. — THE WITCHES

hag noun hags

an ugly old woman

Little George stood by the door staring at the old hag in the chair . . . Could it be, George wondered, that she was a witch? — GEORGE'S MARVELLOUS MEDICINE

hail noun

Hail is made up of hailstones, small pieces of ice that Cloud-Men hurl down from the sky like rain.

'It's hailstones!' whispered James excitedly. 'They've been making hailstones and now they are showering them down on to the people in the world below!' — JAMES AND THE GIANT PEACH

A
B
C
D
E
F
G
H
I
J
K
L
M
N
O
P
Q
R
S
T
U
V
W
X
Y
Z

hail exclamation
Hail! is also an old-fashioned way of saying hello.
The Snail said, 'Hello! Greetings! Hail!/I was a Toad. Now I'm a Snail,/I had to change the way I looked/To save myself from being cooked.' – DIRTY BEASTS

hair noun **hairs**
Hair is the long, soft stuff that grows on your head, or that grows all over an animal's body.
When a man grows hair all over his face it is impossible to tell what he really looks like. Perhaps that's why he does it. – THE TWITS

Hair Toffee noun
Hair Toffee is one of Willy Wonka's latest inventions. It makes hair grow very quickly on your head and chin (which would be very useful for bald witches, if only they knew about it).
'That's Hair Toffee!' cried Mr Wonka. 'You eat just one tiny bit of that, and in exactly half an hour a brand-new luscious thick silky beautiful crop of hair will start growing out all over the top of your head!' – CHARLIE AND THE CHOCOLATE FACTORY

hairy adjective **hairier, hairiest**
A hairy person or animal has a lot of hair on their body, and someone with a hairy face has a beard and very probably a moustache too.
An ordinary unhairy face like yours or mine simply gets a bit smudgy if it is not washed . . . But a hairy face is a very different matter. Things **cling** *to hairs, especially food.* – THE TWITS
RINGBELLING RHYMES Try rhyming with *scary* or *wary*.
SPARKY SYNONYMS You can also say **hirsute**. Opposites are **bald** and *unhairy*.

halfway adverb
in the middle
George took a good look at Grandma. She certainly was a very **tiny** *person . . . Her head only came halfway up the back of the armchair.* – GEORGE'S MARVELLOUS MEDICINE

halibut noun **halibut**
a large flat sea fish that you can eat
The woman's face had turned white as snow and her mouth was opening and shutting like a halibut out of water and giving out a series of strangled gasps. – MATILDA

ham noun
Ham is meat from a pig's leg that has been salted or smoked. When you cook or boil ham, it goes pink, just like Victor Hazell's face when he drinks beer.
As he flashed by we would sometimes catch a glimpse of the great glistening beery face above the wheel, pink as a ham, all soft and inflamed from drinking too much beer. – DANNY THE CHAMPION OF THE WORLD

hammer noun **hammers**
1 a heavy tool used for hitting nails, and that Cloud-Men use to beat thunder-drums
They saw the huge drums that were used for making thunder, and the Cloud-Men beating them furiously with long hammers. – JAMES AND THE GIANT PEACH

2 A hammer is also a piece of athletic equipment, thrown as a sport. Miss Trunchbull is a former champion at throwing the hammer, which is why she is so good at throwing small children.
'You've got to remember that the Trunchbull once threw the hammer for Britain in the Olympics so she's very proud of her right arm.' – MATILDA

hammock noun hammocks
A hammock is a bed made of strong net or cloth hung up above the ground or floor. Miss Spider spins soft and silky hammocks from spider-silk.
James got into his own hammock — and oh, how soft and comfortable it was compared with the hard bare boards that his aunts had always made him sleep upon at home. — JAMES AND THE GIANT PEACH

hand noun hands
1 Your hands are the parts of your body at the ends of your arms.
Charlie smiled nervously and sat down on the edge of the bed. He was holding his present, his only present, very carefully in his two hands. — CHARLIE AND THE CHOCOLATE FACTORY
2 If you say that something is on your hands, it means that it is your responsibility.
Although he was out to give Grandma a pretty fiery mouthful, he didn't really want a dead body on his hands. — GEORGE'S MARVELLOUS MEDICINE
3 If you give or lend someone a hand, you give them some help.
'Oh, do stop shouting such rubbish and give me a hand,' said Muggle-Wump, catching hold of one corner of the carpet. — THE TWITS

handbag noun handbags
a small bag in which grandmothers carry money and hairbrushes and handkerchiefs, and even the occasional mouse
Her handbag was a large bulgy black-leather affair with a tortoise-shell clasp. She picked up Bruno and me and popped us into it. — THE WITCHES

handkerchief noun handkerchiefs
a piece of material you use for blowing your nose, or for making sure that precious things do not fall out of your pocket
Mr Teavee . . . took the tiny boy and shoved him into the breast pocket of his jacket and stuffed a handkerchief on top. — CHARLIE AND THE CHOCOLATE FACTORY

handle noun handles
the part of something that you hold in your hand
The Duke . . . pulled the handle of his walking-stick

upwards, and out of the hollow inside of the stick itself he drew a long thin sharp shining sword. — THE GIRAFFE AND THE PELLY AND ME

handle verb handles, handling, handled
1 When you handle something, you pick it up and hold it in your hands.
He brought a two-foot-long grass-snake into class and insisted every boy should handle it in order to cure us for ever . . . of a fear of snakes. — BOY
2 If you handle a tricky situation, you manage to deal with it.
'My dear Sponge,' Aunt Spiker said slowly, winking at her sister . . . 'There's a pile of money to be made out of this if only we can handle it right.' — JAMES AND THE GIANT PEACH

handsome adjective handsomer, handsomest
A handsome person is attractive to look at.
Mr Wormwood does not look at all handsome with platinum-blonde dyed hair.
'What on earth were you trying to do, make yourself look handsome or something? You look like someone's grandmother gone wrong!' — MATILDA

hang verb hangs, hanging, hung
When you hang something up, you put it on a hook or nail.
A few minutes later, Miss Spider had made the first bed. It was hanging from the ceiling, suspended by a rope of threads at either end. — JAMES AND THE GIANT PEACH
SPARKY SYNONYMS You can also say **dangle** or **suspend**.

happy adjective happier, happiest
When you are happy, you feel pleased and you are enjoying yourself.
Until he was four years old, James Henry Trotter had a happy life. He lived peacefully with his mother and father in a beautiful house beside the sea. — JAMES AND THE GIANT PEACH
SPARKY SYNONYMS You can also say **dory-hunky** or **hopscotchy**. Opposites are **gloomy** and **scrotty**.

harm verb harms, harming, harmed
If you harm someone or something, you hurt or damage them.
But don't, dear children, be alarmed;/Augustus Gloop will not be harmed,/Although, of course, we must admit/He will be altered quite a bit. — CHARLIE AND THE CHOCOLATE FACTORY

harm noun
injury or damage
'I think it's rotten that those foul giants should go off every night to eat humans. Humans have never done them any harm.' — THE BFG

harmless adjective
A harmless creature will not try to bite or hurt you. Knids and Enormous Crocodiles are definitely NOT harmless.
The newt . . . is quite harmless but doesn't look it. It is about six inches long and very slimy, with a greenish-grey skin on top. — MATILDA

a b c d e f g h i j k l m n o p q r s t u v w x y z

There are *mountains of metaphors* in Roald Dahl's stories. Read more at **mountain**.

harsh adjective harsher, harshest
Something that is harsh is not soft or gentle.
Her voice . . . had that same hard metallic quality as the voice of the witch I had met under the conker tree, only it was far louder and much much harsher. — THE WITCHES

RINGBELLING RHYMES Try rhyming with *marsh*.

harshland noun harshlands
A harshland is a hideous, **mideous** place where **grobes** are found.
'In the quelchy quaggy sogmire,/In the mashy mideous harshland,/At the witchy hour of gloomness,/All the grobes come oozing home.' — CHARLIE AND THE GREAT GLASS ELEVATOR

hat noun hats
A hat is a piece of clothing that you wear on your head. Willy Wonka always wears a magnificent black **top hat**, even indoors.
And on he rushed, down the endless pink corridors, with his black top hat perched on the top of his head. — CHARLIE AND THE CHOCOLATE FACTORY

hate verb hates, hating, hated
If you hate something or someone, you do not like them at all, not even the teeniest bit. Mr and Mrs Twit hate each other (but pretend not to, which is even worse), and the entire Muggle-Wump family hate *them*.
Muggle-Wump and his family longed to escape . . . and go back to the African jungle where they came from. They hated Mr and Mrs Twit for making their lives so miserable. — THE TWITS

haul (*rhymes with* ball) verb hauls, hauling, hauled
If you haul something, you pull it up or along.
'The rest of you hold on to Silkworm . . . and later on, if you feel three tugs on the string, start hauling me up again!' — JAMES AND THE GIANT PEACH

haunted adjective
A haunted place is one where people believe there are ghosts.
'I know it's a ghost!' Matilda said. 'I've heard it here before! This room is haunted! I thought you knew that.' — MATILDA

hawser noun hawsers
a thick rope or cable used to pull or tow a ship, or to dangle a giant from a flying **bellypopper**
Very strong steel hawsers with hooks on the ends of them were lowered from the front and rear of each helicopter. — THE BFG

Hazell, Mr Victor (DANNY THE CHAMPION OF THE WORLD)
Mr Victor Hazell is the rich and nasty owner of Hazell's Wood, where he keeps a flock of prize pheasants to shoot for fun. He made lots of money from selling beer and now drives a gleaming silver Rolls-Royce car.

head noun heads
1 the part of your body containing your brain, eyes and mouth
As the ravens whizzed over, they brushed a streak of sticky glue on to the tops of Mr and Mrs Twit's heads. — THE TWITS

2 The head is the person in charge of something.
Miss Tibbs . . . was the terror of the White House and even the Head of the Secret Service broke into a sweat when summoned to her presence. — CHARLIE AND THE GREAT GLASS ELEVATOR

head verb heads, heading, headed
If you head for somewhere, you make your way towards it.
'We is off!' cried the BFG, heading for the cave entrance. 'We is off to meet Her Majester the Queen!' — THE BFG

headline noun headlines
THE WORDS IN LARGE PRINT AT THE TOP OF A PIECE OF WRITING IN A NEWSPAPER
Mr Bucket . . . held up the paper so that they could see the huge headline. The headline said: WONKA FACTORY TO BE OPENED AT LAST TO LUCKY FEW. — CHARLIE AND THE CHOCOLATE FACTORY

headmaster noun headmasters
a male headteacher in a school
To me at that moment the Headmaster, with his black gown draped over his shoulders, was like a judge at a murder trial. — BOY

headmistress noun **headmistresses**

a female headteacher in a school, such as the tyrannical Miss Trunchbull

Miss Trunchbull, the Headmistress . . . was a gigantic holy terror, a fierce tyrannical monster who frightened the life out of the pupils and teachers alike. — MATILDA

headquarters plural noun

the place where an organization is based, and where the people in charge of it work

'In the great headquarters where The Grand High Witch lives, there is always another Grand High Witch waiting in the wings to take over should anything happen.' — THE WITCHES

healthsome adjective

Foods that are healthsome for giants are healthy or good for them (so they avoid them).

'Vegitibbles is very good for you,' he went on. 'It is not healthsome always to be eating meaty things.' — THE BFG

healthy adjective **healthier, healthiest**

1 When you are healthy, you are not ill.

'There goes Miss Violet Beauregarde, the great gum-chewer! It seems as though they managed to de-juice her after all . . . And how healthy she looks!' — CHARLIE AND THE CHOCOLATE FACTORY

2 Things that are healthy are good for you and keep you fit and well.

They retired there by the thousand because the air was so bracing and healthy it kept them, so they believed, alive for a few extra years. — THE WITCHES

heap noun **heaps**

an untidy pile of things, or a disorderly group of witches

'Useless lazy vitches! Feeble frrribbling vitches! You are a heap of idle good-for-nothing vurms!' — THE WITCHES

hear verb **hears, hearing, heard**

1 When you hear something, you notice it through your ears. The BFG is able to hear things that **human beans** can't, such as the moaning of trees and the sound of dreams whiffling through the air.

'A dream, you see, as it goes drifting through the night air, makes . . . a sound so soft and low it is impossible for ordinary people to hear it. But The BFG can hear it easily.' — DANNY THE CHAMPION OF THE WORLD

2 When you hear of something, you get news or information about it.

'A bed!' barked the President. 'Whoever heard of a bed in a spacecraft!' — CHARLIE AND THE GREAT GLASS ELEVATOR

heart noun **hearts**

Your heart is the part of your body in your chest that pumps blood all round your body.

'Did you know,' Matilda said suddenly, 'that the heart of a mouse beats at the rate of six hundred and fifty times a minute?' — MATILDA

heavens plural noun

1 The heavens is another name for the sky.

The giant peach rose up dripping out of the water and began climbing towards the heavens. — JAMES AND THE GIANT PEACH

2 You might say *heavens above!* or *Good heavens!* if you are shocked or surprised.

'Good Heavens!' cried all the monkeys together. 'It's the Roly-Poly Bird!' — THE TWITS

LOOK IT UP! For other ways to show you are surprised, see **exclamation**.

heavy adjective **heavier, heaviest**

Something that is heavy weighs a lot and is hard to lift.

George picked up the heavy three-quarters full saucepan and carried it out of the back door. — GEORGE'S MARVELLOUS MEDICINE

hedge noun **hedges**

a line of bushes growing close together at the edge of a garden or field

Hazell's Wood was not on the main road. To reach it you had to turn left through a gap in the hedge and go uphill over a bumpy track. — DANNY THE CHAMPION OF THE WORLD

You can add *-ish* to make new words: *a heavyish hippodumpling.* Read more at **jellyish**.

hedgehog noun hedgehogs

a small animal covered with prickles
'And how fast do you think a hedgehog's heart beats?'
Matilda asked. 'Tell me,' Miss Honey said, smiling again.
— MATILDA

DID YOU KNOW? *Hedgehogs* are so called because
they live near hedges and have snouts a bit like a pig.
They have also been called *thorn-hogs* and *hedge-*
pigs (perhaps the BFG would use one of those names
if he came across one). A very old word for a hedgehog
is *urchin*, which now means 'a poor or ragged child'.

heel noun heels

Your heel is the back part of your foot.
Sophie, squatting low on her heels in the pocket of the
leather waistcoat . . . saw the group of enormous giants
about three hundred yards ahead. — THE BFG

height (rhymes with bite) noun heights

The height of a person (or of a centipede on its hind
legs) is how tall they are.
The Centipede . . . stood up to his full height and started
dancing about and making insulting signs at the Cloud-Men
with all forty-two of his legs. — JAMES AND THE GIANT PEACH

helicopter noun helicopters

A helicopter is a kind of aircraft without wings, lifted
by a horizontal propeller on top. The BFG calls it a
bellypopper.
Helicopters were landing like wasps all over the hill,
and out of them poured swarms of newspaper
reporters, cameramen, and men from the television
companies. — JAMES AND THE GIANT PEACH

hello interjection

the word you say to someone when you meet them
'Oh, hello, James!' the Glow-worm said, looking down and
giving James a little wave and a smile. 'I didn't see you
come in.' — JAMES AND THE GIANT PEACH

help verb helps, helping, helped

1 When you help someone, you do something that
makes things easier for them.
The monkeys, with the birds helping them, put glue
on the bottom of each chair leg and hoisted them
up to the ceiling. — THE TWITS
2 When you help yourself to something, you take it.
It is a most marvellous thing to be able to go out and
help yourself to your own apples whenever you feel like
it. — DANNY THE CHAMPION OF THE WORLD
3 If something cannot be helped, there is nothing
anyone can do to prevent it.
Things happened to me that will probably make you
scream when you read about them. That can't be helped.
The truth must be told. — THE WITCHES

helpful adjective

If you are helpful (unlike George's grandma), you do
things to help other people.
Most grandmothers are lovely, kind, helpful old ladies, but
not this one . . . Never once, even on her best days, had
she smiled at George. — GEORGE'S MARVELLOUS MEDICINE

helping noun helpings

A helping of food is an amount that is given to one
person (or the amount that a crocodile can snatch).
'Children are bigger than fish,' said the Enormous Crocodile.
'You get bigger helpings.' — THE ENORMOUS CROCODILE

helpless adjective

If you are helpless, you cannot do things for yourself.
Mrs Twit was quite helpless now. With her feet tied to
the ground and her arms pulled upwards by the balloons,
she was unable to move. — THE TWITS

hen noun hens

a female bird that is kept on farms for the eggs that
it lays
'How about that then, eh, Mary?' Grandma shouted.
'I'll bet you've never seen a hen as big as that! That's
George's giant hen, that is!' — GEORGE'S MARVELLOUS
MEDICINE

hero noun heroes

1 a boy or man who has done something very brave
'Our saviour,' he cried out, 'our hero, our wonder-boy, is,
as you already know, our human visitor, Little Billy.'
— THE MINPINS
2 The hero of a story is the man, boy, animal or giant
who is the main character, so Charlie is the hero of
Charlie and the Chocolate Factory, and the BFG is the
hero of *The BFG*.

DID YOU KNOW? If a book is named after the main character in the story, the character is called the *eponymous* hero or heroine. So the BFG is the eponymous hero of *The BFG*.

heroine noun heroines

1 a girl or woman who has done something very brave
What a marvellously brave thing Miss Honey had done. Suddenly she was a heroine in Matilda's eyes. — MATILDA

2 The heroine of a story is the woman or girl who is the main character, so Matilda is the eponymous heroine of that book (and if you don't know what that means, just read the previous entry).

hesitate verb hesitates, hesitating, hesitated

If you hesitate, you wait for a little while before you do something because you are not sure what you should do.
Butlers never hesitate, not even when they are faced with the most impossible problems. It is their job to be totally decisive at all times. — THE BFG

hibernate verb hibernates, hibernating, hibernated

When animals hibernate, they spend the winter in a special kind of deep sleep. Bats, bears and hedgehogs all hibernate, as do Alfie and his fellow tortoises.
Alfie . . . settled down in Roberta's garden. Every day she fed him lettuce and tomato slices and crispy celery, and in the winters he hibernated in a box of dried leaves in the tool-shed. — ESIO TROT

DID YOU KNOW? The word *hibernate* comes from a Latin word that means 'wintry'. Some fish and other animals spend the summer in a kind of sleep, and there is a word for that too: you say that they *aestivate* (say **est**-i-vate).

hide verb hides, hiding, hid, hidden

1 When you hide, you go to a place where people cannot see you.
If Mr Boggis was hiding behind his Chicken House Number One, Mr Fox would smell him out from fifty yards off and quickly change direction. — FANTASTIC MR FOX

2 If you hide something, you put it in a secret place so that people cannot find it.
If The Grand High Witch wanted to hide something top secret, where would she put it? Certainly not in any ordinary drawer. — THE WITCHES

hideous adjective

very ugly or unpleasant
Aunt Sponge had a long-handled mirror on her lap, and she kept picking it up and gazing at her own hideous face. — JAMES AND THE GIANT PEACH

higgle verb higgles, higgling, higgled

If you higgle a giant, you argue with or disagree with him (which is only possible with a Big Friendly Giant, as other giants would simply eat you).
'You may think you is eight,' the BFG said, 'but you has only spent four years of your life with your little eyes open. You is only four and please stop higgling me.' — THE BFG

RINGBELLING RHYMES Try rhyming with *giggle* or *wiggle*.

high adjective higher, highest

1 far above the ground or sea
'Oweee!' shrieked the hen and it shot straight up into the air like a rocket. It went as high as the house. — GEORGE'S MARVELLOUS MEDICINE

2 measuring from top to bottom
'He is fifty-four feet high,' the BFG said softly as he jogged along. 'And he is swolloping human beans like they is sugar-lumps, two or three at a time.' — THE BFG

3 A high voice or sound is not deep or low.
'Dad!' I called out. 'Dad, are you there?' My small high voice echoed through the forest and faded away. — DANNY THE CHAMPION OF THE WORLD

hill noun hills

a bit of ground that is higher than the ground around it
The hill was so high that from almost anywhere in the garden James could look down and see for miles and miles across a marvellous landscape of woods and fields. — JAMES AND THE GIANT PEACH

hinge noun hinges

A hinge is a piece of metal on which a door, gate or lid swings when it opens.
Very slowly, with a loud creaking of rusty hinges, the great iron gates of the factory began to swing open. — CHARLIE AND THE CHOCOLATE FACTORY

hint verb hints, hinting, hinted

When you hint, you suggest something without saying exactly what you mean.
The verger hinted that if the vicar played his cards right, the lady might be good for an even larger donation in the near future. — THE VICAR OF NIBBLESWICKE

hip noun hips

Your hips are the bony parts at the sides of your body between your waist and thighs. If a grown-up stands with their hands on their hips, they are usually in a bad mood.
The Trunchbull was standing in front of the class, legs apart, hands on hips, scowling at Miss Honey, who stood silent to one side. — MATILDA

hippocampus noun hippocampi

The hippocampus is a legendary sea-creature with the front legs of a horse and the tail of a dolphin. Its hair is a vital ingredient in Wonka-Vite.
Now add the following, in precisely the order given . . . TWO HAIRS (AND ONE RABBIT) FROM THE HEAD OF A HIPPOCAMPUS. — CHARLIE AND THE GREAT GLASS ELEVATOR

DID YOU KNOW? The name *hippocampus* comes from Greek words meaning 'horse sea-monster' and is related to **hippopotamus**.

hippodumpling noun hippodumplings

Hippodumpling is the BFG's name for a hippopotamus.
'They would be putting me into the zoo or the bunkumhouse with all those squiggling hippodumplings and crockadowndillies.' — THE BFG

The word *helicopter* means literally 'spiral wing'.

DID YOU KNOW? The first part of *hippopotamus* means 'horse', so *hippodumpling* means 'horse dumpling', perhaps because it looks a bit like a horse and a bit like a doughy dumpling.

hippogriff noun **hippogriffs**
a legendary creature with the body of a horse and the wings and head of an eagle
Aladdin said, 'What if I meet/Some brute that thinks I'm good to eat?/A Gorgon or a Hippogriff?/A Doodlewhang, a Boodlesniff?' — RHYME STEW

hippopotamus noun **hippopotamuses**
A hippopotamus is a large, heavy African animal that lives near water. It is sometimes called a *hippo* for short, and in Giant Country it is a **hippodumpling**.
DID YOU KNOW? The name *hippopotamus* comes from Greek words meaning 'river horse'.

hipswitch adverb
very fast or very quickly
'If anyone is ever seeing a giant, he or she must be taken away hipswitch.' — THE BFG

hirsute adjective
Hirsute is a very useful word to describe The Twits because it means 'hairy' or 'untrimmed', so Mr Twit is hirsute and so is Mrs Twit's unweeded garden.
RINGBELLING RHYMES Try rhyming with *brute*.

hiss verb **hisses, hissing, hissed**
If something hisses, it makes a long 'sss' sound.
A tremendous hissing sound was coming from above their heads. Steam was shooting out of Grandma's mouth and nose and ears and whistling as it came. — GEORGE'S MARVELLOUS MEDICINE
DID YOU KNOW? *Hiss* is an *onomatopoeic* word, which means that it sounds like the thing it describes. You can find more words like this in the entry for **gliss** (which helpfully rhymes with *hiss*).

history noun
things that happened in the past
'This,' my father said, 'will be the first time in the history of the world that anyone has even tried to poach roosting pheasants.' — DANNY THE CHAMPION OF THE WORLD

hoarse adjective **hoarser, hoarsest**
A hoarse voice sounds rough and deep.
The next bottle he took down had about five hundred gigantic purple pills in it. FOR HORSES WITH HOARSE THROATS, it said on the label. — GEORGE'S MARVELLOUS MEDICINE
LOOK IT UP! For many more ways to describe voices, see **voice**.

hobble verb **hobbles, hobbling, hobbled**
If someone hobbles, they walk with difficulty, often because they are old or injured.
The old man hobbled a step or two nearer, and then he put a hand into the pocket of his jacket and took out a small white paper bag. — JAMES AND THE GIANT PEACH

hoist verb **hoists, hoisting, hoisted**
If you hoist something, you lift it up using ropes or pulleys.
The BFG grabbed the dangling rope and was hoisted out of the pit just in time. — THE BFG

hole noun **holes**
a gap or an empty space in something
The Giant reached out and rolled the stone to one side as easily as if it had been a football, and now, where the stone had been, there appeared a vast black hole. — THE BFG

hollow adjective
Something that is hollow has an empty space inside it.
'All the trees in this forest are hollow. Not just this one, but all of them. And inside them thousands and thousands of Minpins are living.' — THE MINPINS

home noun **homes**
Your home is the place where you live.
WARNING TO READERS: Do not try to make George's Marvellous Medicine yourselves at home. It could be dangerous. — GEORGE'S MARVELLOUS MEDICINE

Honey, Miss Jennifer (MATILDA)
Miss Jennifer Honey is a kind and mild-mannered teacher who befriends Matilda and recognizes her extraordinary talents. She lives in a tiny cottage with hardly any furniture. Her name suggests that she has a sweet nature, like the taste of honey.

honourable adjective
An honourable person or giant always behaves in a way that is good or right. The BFG is the only honourable giant in Giant Country. All the others behave very badly indeed, so they are *dishonourable* giants.
The BFG raised his great head proudly in the air. 'I is a very honourable giant,' he said. 'I would rather be chewing up rotsome snozzcumbers than snitching things from other people.' — THE BFG

hook noun **hooks**
a curved piece of metal for hanging things on (such as giants in chains) or for catching things with
The BFG quickly secured the hooks to the giants' chains, one hook near the legs and the other near the arms. — THE BFG

hook verb **hooks, hooking, hooked**
If you hook something, you fasten it with or on a hook.
Matilda . . . proceeded to squeeze a line of glue very neatly all round the inside rim of the hat. Then she carefully hooked the hat back on to the peg. — MATILDA

hoot verb **hoots, hooting, hooted**
If someone hoots with laughter, they laugh in loud bursts.
The Roly-Poly Bird was up there as well, and the monkeys were in the cage and the whole lot of them were hooting with laughter at Mr Twit. — THE TWITS

hop verb **hops, hopping, hopped**
1 When you hop, you jump on one foot.
George was hopping about from one foot to the other with excitement, pointing at the enormous hen and shouting, 'It's had the magic medicine, Grandma!' — GEORGE'S MARVELLOUS MEDICINE
2 When a bird or animal hops, it moves in jumps.
Suddenly, a second window was flung wide open and of all the crazy things a gigantic white bird hopped out and perched on the window-sill. — THE GIRAFFE AND THE PELLY AND ME

hope verb **hopes, hoping, hoped**
If you hope that something will happen, you want it to happen.
'Oh, you foul and filthy fiend! I hope you get squashed and squished and squizzled and boiled up into crocodile stew!' — THE ENORMOUS CROCODILE

Hoppy, Mr (ESIO TROT)
Mr Hoppy is a shy man who lives alone and loves growing flowers in pots on his balcony. He has been in love for years with his neighbour, Mrs Silver who, unfortunately for him, is more interested in her tortoise, Alfie.

hopscotchy adjective
If you feel hopscotchy, you feel happy and cheerful, as if you have drunk a whole bottle of **frobscottle**.
'Whenever I is feeling a bit scrotty,' the BFG said, 'a few gollops of frobscottle is always making me hopscotchy again.' — THE BFG
DID YOU KNOW? The word *hopscotchy* is based on the game *hopscotch*, perhaps because it makes people happy to play it, or because you leap about in hopscotch as if you are jumping for joy.
SPARKY SYNONYMS You can also say **dory-hunky**. Opposites are **gloomy** and **scrotty**.

horizon noun
the line in the distance where the sky and the land or sea seem to meet
They all sat in silence watching the sun as it came up slowly over the rim of the horizon for a new day. — JAMES AND THE GIANT PEACH

horn noun **horns**
1 The horns on some animals are the hard, pointed parts that grow on their heads.
The only two vitamins it doesn't have in it are vitamin S, because it makes you sick, and vitamin H, because it makes you grow horns on the top of your head, like a bull. — CHARLIE AND THE CHOCOLATE FACTORY
2 The horn on a car is the part that makes a loud noise to warn people when there is danger.
The splendid black tourer crept slowly through the village with the driver pressing the rubber bulb of the horn every time we passed a human being. — BOY

hornswoggler noun **hornswogglers**
The hornswoggler is a dangerous beast that lives in Loompaland and preys on Oompa-Loompas. Its name sounds as if it has deadly horns on its head (or maybe elsewhere).
'When I went out there, I found the little Oompa-Loompas living in tree houses . . . to escape from the whangdoodles and the hornswogglers and the snozzwangers.' — CHARLIE AND THE CHOCOLATE FACTORY

horrible adjective
Something that is horrible is very nasty or frightening, and a horrible person is particularly mean and nasty.
I saw The Grand High Witch standing over me, grinning at me in the most horrible way. — THE WITCHES
Their names were Aunt Sponge and Aunt Spiker, and I am sorry to say that they were both really horrible people. — JAMES AND THE GIANT PEACH

horrid adjective
A horrid person, or a horrid taste or smell, is very nasty and unpleasant.
Captain Lancaster, known sometimes as Lankers, was a horrid man. He had fiery carrot-coloured hair and a little clipped carrotty moustache and a fiery temper. — DANNY THE CHAMPION OF THE WORLD

horridest or horriblest adjective

as horrid or as horrible as it is possible to be

'She locked us in the dark cellar for a day and a night without anything to eat or drink' . . . 'The filthy old fizzwiggler!' shouted the BFG. 'That is the horridest thing I is hearing for years!' – THE BFG

horrigust adjective

Something horrigust is truly horrible and disgusting.

'You is saying it is grizzling and horrigust for giants to be eating human beans. Right or left?' 'Right,' Sophie said. – THE BFG

DID YOU KNOW? The word *horrigust* is a mixture of *horrible* (or *horrid*) and *disgusting*, which is exactly what it means.

horror noun

a feeling of very great fear

Mrs Teavee let out a scream of horror. 'You mean only a half of Mike is coming back to us?' she cried. – CHARLIE AND THE CHOCOLATE FACTORY

Hortensia (MATILDA)

Hortensia is a tough ten-year-old girl at Crunchem Hall who has been sent to the Chokey several times, and who thinks up ingenious ways to get revenge on Miss Trunchbull, such as using itching-powder.

hot adjective hotter, hottest

1 Something that is hot is very warm, with a high temperature.

A sizzling sound, the kind you get if you hold a hot frying-pan under a cold tap, came up from deep down in Grandma's stomach. – GEORGE'S MARVELLOUS MEDICINE

2 Hot food has a strong, spicy taste.

On Saturdays he likes to crunch/Six juicy children for his lunch, . . . /He smears the boys (to make them hot)/With mustard from the mustard pot. – DIRTY BEASTS

hotel noun hotels

A hotel is a building where guests pay to stay the night and to have meals. The Space Hotel is a hotel in space which orbits the Earth.

All around us the summer-holiday guests in this rather grand hotel were babbling away and tucking into their suppers. – THE WITCHES

hotlands plural noun

The hotlands are hot countries, far from Inkland, where the sun is always shining.

'If it is a frotsy night and the giant is fridging with cold, he will probably point his nose towards the swultering hotlands to guzzle a few Hottentots to warm him up.' – THE BFG

hour noun hours

An hour is a period of time that lasts sixty minutes. Half an hour lasts thirty minutes, which is as long as it takes for Hair Toffee to work.

'That's Hair Toffee!' cried Mr Wonka. 'You eat just one tiny bit of that, and in exactly half an hour a brand-new luscious thick silky beautiful crop of hair will start growing!' – CHARLIE AND THE CHOCOLATE FACTORY

hove (rhymes with rove) verb

Hove is an old word that means 'appeared' or 'arose'.

Just then, all in a blaze of light,/The Magic Fairy hove in sight,/Her Magic Wand went swoosh and swish!/'Cindy!' she cried, 'come make a wish!' – REVOLTING RHYMES

hover verb hovers, hovering, hovered

When something hovers, it stays in one place in the air.

Sure enough, a brand-new piece of chalk was hovering near the grey-black writing surface of the blackboard. 'It's writing something!' screamed Nigel. – MATILDA

howl verb howls, howling, howled

If someone howls, they make a long, high sound, like the sound of an animal crying or a strong wind blowing.

The Fleshlumpeater . . . flopped to the ground and sat there howling his head off and clutching his ankle with both hands. – THE BFG

howl noun howls

a long cry of pain or horror

The maid gave a howl of anguish and clasped her hands over her face. 'Control yourself, Mary,' the Queen said sharply. – THE BFG

hubbub noun

a loud confused noise of voices

Suddenly there came a great gasp from the audience. This was followed by a hubbub of shrieking and yelling. —THE WITCHES

hug verb hugs, hugging, hugged

When you hug someone, you hold them in your arms to show you love them.

'Charlie!' said Grandpa Joe, rushing forward. 'Thank heavens you're back!' Charlie hugged him. Then he hugged his mother and his father. —CHARLIE AND THE GREAT GLASS ELEVATOR

huge adjective

Something that is huge is very big.

'I don't believe that,' Sophie said. The BFG regarded her gravely with those huge eyes of his. —THE BFG

SPARKY SYNONYMS You can also say **gigantuous** or **ginormous**.

LOOK IT UP! For other ways to describe something huge, see **big**.

huggybee noun **huggybees**

If a giant calls you huggybee, he is being very friendly and affectionate. It is a bit like saying *honey* or *sugar-pie*.

'You stay where you is in my pocket, huggybee,' he said. 'We is doing this lovely bit of buckswashling both together.' —THE BFG

DID YOU KNOW? To make the word *huggybee*, Roald Dahl may have joined *honeybee* to *hug*, so the name makes you think of sweet things and friendly hugs.

HUGTIGHT (THE TWITS)

HUGTIGHT IS A VERY STRONG TYPE OF GLUE THAT MR TWIT USES TO CATCH BIRDS TO MAKE HIS WEEKLY BIRD PIE. THE NAME IS ALWAYS WRITTEN IN CAPITAL LETTERS.

hullabaloo noun **hullabaloos**

a great and noisy fuss that grown-ups make about something

If any person reported actually having seen a giant haunting the streets of a town at night, there would most certainly be a terrific hullabaloo across the world. —THE BFG

human noun **humans**

A human is a man, woman or child. A human is also called a *human being*, or in Giant Country a **human bean**.

It wasn't a human. It couldn't be. It was four times as tall

a b c d e f g h i j k l m n o p q r s t u v w x y z

as the tallest human. It was so tall its head was higher than the upstairs windows of the houses. — THE BFG

human bean noun human beans
A human bean is what the giants of Giant Country call a human. (It sounds a bit like *human being*, but tastier.)
'You is trying to change the subject,' the Giant said sternly. 'We is having an interesting babblement about the taste of the human bean. The human bean is not a vegetable.' — THE BFG

human-beaney adjective
Anything to do with **human beans** is human-beaney.
'Never more is you going to be bunkdoodling the poor little human-beaney tottlers!' — THE BFG

humplecrimp noun humplecrimps
The humplecrimp is an animal that is very common in Giant Country, but which no **human bean** has ever seen (so you will have to imagine what it looks like).
'What about for instance the great squizzly scotch-hopper?' 'I beg your pardon?' Sophie said. 'And the humplecrimp?' 'What's that?' Sophie said. — THE BFG

LOOK IT UP! Other animals commonly found in Giant Country are the **crumpscoddle** and **wraprascal**.

Humpy-Rumpy (THE ENORMOUS CROCODILE)
Humpy-Rumpy is a hippopotamus who lives on a muddy riverbank in Africa. He tries to foil the Enormous Crocodile's plans to catch children to eat.

hungry adjective hungrier, hungriest
If you are hungry (as Charlie is every day of his life until he finds a Golden Ticket), you feel that you need food.
But Charlie Bucket never got what he wanted . . . and as the cold weather went on and on, he became ravenously and desperately hungry. — CHARLIE AND THE CHOCOLATE FACTORY

hunt verb hunts, hunting, hunted
When people or giants hunt, they chase and kill animals or **human beans** for food or as a sport.
'They is always having fifty winks before they goes scumpering off to hunt human beans in the evening,' the BFG said. — THE BFG

hurl verb hurls, hurling, hurled
If you hurl something, you throw it with all your strength.
The BFG ran. What else could he do? The giants picked up rocks and hurled them after him. — THE BFG

hurry verb hurries, hurrying, hurried
When you hurry, you walk or run quickly, or try to do something quickly.
'We have to hurry, don't you understand that? Those terrible Twits will be back any moment and this time they'll have guns!' — THE TWITS

hurry noun
If you do something in a hurry, you try to do it quickly.
'Every dream is having its special label on the bottle,' the BFG said. 'How else could I be finding the one I am wanting in a hurry?' — THE BFG

RINGBELLING RHYMES Try rhyming with *scurry*.

hurt verb hurts, hurting, hurt
1 If someone hurts you, they make you feel pain.
From the back of the class, Miss Honey cried out, 'Miss Trunchbull! Please let him down! You're hurting him! All his hair might come out!' — MATILDA
2 If a part of your body hurts, it feels sore.
My tail was hurting terribly. I curled it round so as to have a look at it. About two inches of it were missing and it was bleeding quite a lot. — THE WITCHES

husband noun husbands
A husband is the man someone is married to.
The Cloud-Men's wives were crouching over little stoves with frying-pans in their hands, frying snowballs for their husbands' suppers. — JAMES AND THE GIANT PEACH

hushy quiet adjective
as quiet as quiet can be
'So you want us to proceed by jeep?' the Head of the Army said. 'Yes,' the BFG said. 'But you must all be very very hushy quiet. No roaring of motors.' — THE BFG

Ii

itching-powder

MATILDA

Inkland inky-booky

insects inventing

ice cream noun ice creams
Ice cream is a sweet frozen food made from milk or cream and often flavoured with fruit or chocolate. It usually cools you down, but Mr Wonka's hot ice cream does the opposite.
HOT ICE CREAMS FOR COLD DAYS, it said on the next door. 'Extremely useful in the winter,' said Mr Wonka, rushing on. – CHARLIE AND THE CHOCOLATE FACTORY

icky adjective ickier, ickiest
unpleasantly sticky or nasty
The shoe was long and very wide./(A normal foot got lost inside.)/Also it smelled a wee bit icky./(The owner's feet were hot and sticky.) – REVOLTING RHYMES

icky-poo adjective
If something tastes icky-poo (as all **snozzcumbers** do), it tastes really REALLY disgusting.
'In this sloshflunking Giant Country . . . Nothing is growing except for one extremely icky-poo vegetable. It is called the snozzcumber.' – THE BFG

DID YOU KNOW? To make the word *icky-poo*, Roald Dahl may have started with *icky* and then added *poo* (which is icky too).

icy adjective icier, iciest
1 Something that is icy is very cold.
As Charlie Bucket was getting dressed for school . . .
he saw the huge flakes drifting slowly down out of an icy sky that was the colour of steel. – CHARLIE AND THE CHOCOLATE FACTORY
2 An icy look or smile is very unfriendly.
Suddenly she smiled. It was a thin icy smile, the kind a snake might make just before it bites you. – GEORGE'S MARVELLOUS MEDICINE

identical adjective
Things that are identical are exactly the same.
I examined the little bottle. It was identical to the one The Grand High Witch had had in the Ballroom. – THE WITCHES

idle adjective idler, idlest
Someone who is idle is lazy. Grown-ups will sometimes call you idle if you don't have time to do everything they want you to do.
Grandma was all alone on the rooftop. 'Hey you!' she yelled. 'George! Get me a cup of tea this minute, you idle little beast!' – GEORGE'S MARVELLOUS MEDICINE

ignorant adjective
An ignorant person knows very little about anything important. Matilda knows far more interesting things than her father, but he is too ignorant to realize it.
'I don't see how sawdust can help you to sell second-hand cars, Daddy.' 'That's because you're an ignorant little twit,' the father said. – MATILDA

ignore verb ignores, ignoring, ignored
If you ignore someone, you refuse to speak to them or take any notice of them. Mr Wormwood ignores his daughter and she, in turn, ignores his television.
Mr Wormwood . . . fished a bit of paper from his pocket and studied it. 'Listen, boy,' he said, addressing the son and ignoring Matilda. – MATILDA

ill adjective iller, illest
If you are ill, you are not very well.
I felt so wonderful at being away from that dreaded school building that I very nearly forgot I was meant to be ill. – BOY

illness noun illnesses
An illness is something that makes people ill. Measles, chickenpox and the Dreaded Shrinks are all illnesses.

imagination noun
Your imagination is what you use to think up new ideas or create pictures in your head, like dreaming when you are awake.
Miss Honey . . . did not think Matilda was meaning to tell a lie. It was more likely that she was simply allowing her vivid imagination to run away with her. – MATILDA

imagine verb imagines, imagining, imagined
When you imagine something, you make a picture of it, or hear the sound of it, in your mind.
One would have expected that a mouse (if it was going to talk at all) would do so with the smallest and squeakiest voice you could imagine. – THE WITCHES

a b c d e f g h i j k l m n o p q r s t u v w x y z

Human beans are called *blodau dynol* ('human flowers') in Welsh.

immediate adjective
Something that is immediate happens straight away.
The effect was immediate. The Cloud-Men jumped round as if they had been stung by wasps. — JAMES AND THE GIANT PEACH

impatient adjective
Someone who is impatient gets bored and angry if they have to wait for something.
'Why do we have to go rushing on past all these lovely rooms?' 'We shall stop in time!' called out Mr Wonka. 'Don't be so madly impatient!' — CHARLIE AND THE CHOCOLATE FACTORY

important adjective
1 If something is important, you must think about it carefully and seriously.
But, you see, the important thing in Mr Hoppy's plan was to make sure that the new tortoise was bigger than Alfie but only a tiny bit bigger. — ESIO TROT
2 An important person has a lot of power or influence in the world of grown-ups.
THE MOST IMPORTANT PERSONS IN THE LAND WILL BE PRESENT AT THIS GATHERING TO SALUTE THE HEROES WHOSE DAZZLING DEEDS WILL BE WRITTEN FOR EVER IN THE HISTORY OF OUR NATION. — CHARLIE AND THE GREAT GLASS ELEVATOR

impossible adjective
If something is impossible, no one can do it, except in their dreams or imagination. The BFG says **um-possible**.
When a man grows hair all over his face it is impossible to tell what he really looks like. Perhaps that's why he does it. — THE TWITS

inch noun inches
Inches are used to measure how long something is, or how tall you are. One inch is about 2.5 centimetres, so an Oompa-Loompa child is about 10 centimetres tall.
A village of Oompa-Loompas, with tiny houses and streets and hundreds of Oompa-Loompa children no more than four inches high playing in the streets . . . — CHARLIE AND THE CHOCOLATE FACTORY

incinerator noun incinerators
An incinerator is a fire used for burning rubbish (not usually children and parents).
'But what about the great fiery incinerator?' asked Charlie. 'They only light it every other day,' said Mr Wonka. 'Perhaps this is one of the days when they let it go out.' — CHARLIE AND THE CHOCOLATE FACTORY

infuriate verb infuriates, infuriating, infuriated
If something infuriates you, it makes you very angry.
Mr Wormwood glared at Matilda. She hadn't moved . . . She kept right on reading, and for some reason this infuriated the father. — MATILDA

ink noun inks
Ink is the coloured liquid inside a pen. Witches never run out of ink, because they use their own blue spit to write with.
'Nobody can have blue spit!' 'Witches can,' she said. 'Is it like ink?' I asked. 'Exactly,' she said. 'They even use it to write with.' — THE WITCHES

Inkland (THE WITCHES)
Inkland is the name that the Grand High Witch gives to England. She calls English people or things **Inklish**.
'All over Inkland, in everrry school in Inkland, noise of snapping mouse-trrraps vill be heard!' — THE WITCHES

inky-booky adjective
An inky-booky taste is the taste you get from chewing a piece of paper with writing on it. **School-chiddlers** taste like this to giants, perhaps because they read more than giants do.
'I is very fond indeed of English school-chiddlers. They has a nice inky-booky flavour. Perhaps I will change my mind and go to England.' — THE BFG

> **Gobblefunking with words**
> You can add -y to lots of nouns to make adjectives like *inky-booky*. Roald Dahl often invented new words this way; for example Mr Twit has *moustachy bristles*, and the BFG talks about **human beans** who have a *booty flavour* or *hatty taste*.

innocent adjective
If you are innocent, you have not done anything wrong (such as dyeing your father's hair for fun).
'I haven't touched the flaming stuff!' Mr Wormwood shouted. He turned and looked again at Matilda, who looked back at him with large innocent brown eyes. – MATILDA

insect noun **insects**
An insect is a small animal with six legs and a body divided into three parts. Beetles, butterflies, glow-worms, grasshoppers and ladybirds are all types of insect.
The creatures, some sitting on chairs, others reclining on a sofa, were all watching him intently. Creatures? Or were they insects? – JAMES AND THE GIANT PEACH
DID YOU KNOW? The word *insect* comes from Latin and means 'cut up' because an insect's body is divided into parts.

insist verb **insists, insisting, insisted**
If you insist on something, you say very firmly that you want to do it.
There was no problem about buying the house because it was owned by the Giraffe and the Pelly and the Monkey, and they insisted upon giving it to the Duke for nothing. – THE GIRAFFE AND THE PELLY AND ME

inspect verb **inspects, inspecting, inspected**
When you inspect something, you look at it very carefully to check that it is all right.
Aunt Sponge and Aunt Spiker began walking slowly round the peach, inspecting it very cautiously from all sides. – JAMES AND THE GIANT PEACH

instant adjective
Something instant happens immediately, without delay. The opposite of Delayed Action Mouse-Maker formula would be Instant Mouse-Maker formula.
'A large overdose might even have an instant effect, and you wouldn't vont that, vould you? You wouldn't vont the children turning into mice rrright there in your sveet-shops.' – THE WITCHES

instant noun **instants**
a moment
'You see this green button. I must press it at exactly the right instant. If I'm just half a second late, then we'll go too high!' – CHARLIE AND THE GREAT GLASS ELEVATOR

instrument noun **instruments**
1 An instrument is something that you strike, pluck or blow through to make musical sounds. The Old-Green-Grasshopper uses his body as a musical instrument.
What a wonderful instrument the Old-Green-Grasshopper was playing upon . . . It was almost exactly as though he were playing upon a violin! – JAMES AND THE GIANT PEACH
2 a tool for doing a particular job
The doctor now put some water to boil in an aluminium mug . . . and into the boiling water he placed a long thin shiny steel instrument. – BOY

insult verb **insults, insulting, insulted**
If someone insults you, they upset you by saying rude or nasty things.
'Why are you insulting me? I haven't been rude to you! Why do you call me a mouse?' – THE WITCHES

insult noun **insults**
a rude or nasty remark
DID YOU KNOW? To *insult* someone means literally to 'jump on' them. It comes from Latin *salire* 'to leap' and is related to *salmon*, which means a leaping fish. It is therefore doubly *insulting* to call someone a *salmon*.

Gobblefunking with words
Roald Dahl's characters are very good at insulting each other. Grandmothers are especially good at insults, perhaps because they have had a long time to practise. George's grandmother calls him a *disgusting little worm!* and a *nasty little maggot!* and Grandma Georgina calls Willy Wonka a *miserable old mackerel!* Miss Trunchbull uses a wide range of insults. She calls her pupils:

You ignorant little slug!
You witless weed!
You empty-headed hamster!
You stupid glob of glue!
You fleabitten fungus!

Giants enjoy hurling insults too (as well as rocks). The unfriendly giants call the BFG:
Grobby little grub!
Shrivelly little shrimp!
Squaggy little squib!
Squinky little squiddler!
Pibbling little pitsqueak!

For other rude words that giants say, see **rude**.

intelligent adjective
An intelligent person or animal is clever and can learn things quickly.
It is not all that difficult to train an intelligent mouse to be an expert tight-rope walker provided you know exactly how to go about it. – THE WITCHES

intense adjective
An intense feeling or flavour is very strong.
As the rich warm creamy chocolate ran down his throat into his empty tummy . . . a feeling of intense happiness spread over him. – CHARLIE AND THE CHOCOLATE FACTORY

interesting adjective
If something is interesting, you think it is exciting and want to see it or learn about it.
BUTTERSCOTCH AND BUTTERGIN, it said on the next door they passed. 'Now that sounds a bit more interesting,' said Mr Salt, Veruca's father. – CHARLIE AND THE CHOCOLATE FACTORY

a b c d e f g h i j k l m n o p q r s t u v w x y z

There once was a word . . . Read the whole rhyme at **limerick**.

interrupt verb **interrupts, interrupting, interrupted**
If you interrupt someone, you disturb them while they are talking or working, and make them stop.
'How do you know all this, Grandmamma?' 'Don't interrupt,' she said. 'Just take it all in.' – THE WITCHES

invent verb **invents, inventing, invented**
If you invent something new, you are the first person to make it or think of it. An **inventor** is someone who invents things, like Willy Wonka who invents new sweets, or Roald Dahl who invented new words and stories.
'Now, over here,' Mr Wonka went on, skipping excitedly across the room . . . 'over here I am inventing a completely new line in toffees!' – CHARLIE AND THE CHOCOLATE FACTORY

Inventing Room (CHARLIE AND THE CHOCOLATE FACTORY)
The Inventing Room is the most important room in Willy Wonka's factory. It is where he creates his most secret new inventions, such as the Everlasting Gobstopper, and not even the Oompa-Loompas are allowed into it.

invention noun **inventions**
An invention is something new that no one has made or thought about before. Inventions begin in your imagination, which is a kind of Inventing Room in your head.
'This gum,' Mr Wonka went on, 'is my latest, my greatest,

my most fascinating invention!' – CHARLIE AND THE CHOCOLATE FACTORY

investigate verb **investigates, investigating, investigated**
If you investigate something, you find out as much as you can about it.
The following afternoon, as soon as Mrs Wormwood had departed in her car for another session of bingo, Matilda set out for Fred's house to investigate. – MATILDA

invisible adjective
If something is invisible, no one can see it, like Willy Wonka's invisible chocolate bars (for eating in class). Dreams are invisible only until they are caught and bottled.
'You told me dreams were invisible.' 'They is always invisible until they is captured,' the BFG told her. 'After that they is losing a little of their invisibility.' – THE BFG

invite verb **invites, inviting, invited**
When you invite someone, you ask them to come to your house or to go somewhere special with you.
Mr Hoppy . . . longed to invite Mrs Silver up for a cup of tea and a biscuit, but every time he was about to form the words on his lips, his courage failed him. – ESIO TROT

iron noun & adjective
a type of strong, heavy metal used to make gates and railings
WONKA'S FACTORY . . . had huge iron gates leading into it, and a high wall surrounding it, and smoke belching from its chimneys. – CHARLIE AND THE CHOCOLATE FACTORY

ironed adjective
pressed very flat
The peach rolled on. And behind it, Aunt Sponge and Aunt Spiker lay ironed out upon the grass as flat and thin and lifeless as a couple of paper dolls. – JAMES AND THE GIANT PEACH

island noun **islands**
a piece of land with water all round it
Every day, for several summers, that tiny secret sand-patch on that tiny secret island was our regular destination. – BOY

itch verb **itches, itching, itched**
When your skin itches, it is uncomfortable and feels as if you need to scratch it. You can also say that it feels **itchy**.
'The underneath of a wig is always very rough and scratchy . . . It causes nasty sores on the head. Wig-rash, the witches call it. And it doesn't half itch.' – THE WITCHES
RINGBELLING RHYMES Try rhyming with *witch* (because witches itch a lot).

itching-powder noun
a powder that makes your skin itch like mad — very good for wreaking revenge on tyrannical headmistresses
'I had sent away by post, you see, for this very powerful itching-powder,' Hortensia said. 'It cost fifty pence a packet and was called The Skin-Scorcher.' – MATILDA

A B C D E F G H I J K L M N O P Q R S T U V W X Y Z

Jj

James

JAMES AND THE GIANT PEACH

jabbeling jars jellyish
jumbly jumpsquiffling

jab verb jabs, jabbing, jabbed
When you jab something, you poke it roughly with your finger or with something sharp.
Mr Wonka jabbed a button. The doors closed and the Great Glass Elevator shot upwards for home. — CHARLIE AND THE GREAT GLASS ELEVATOR

jabbel verb jabbels, jabbeling, jabbeled
If a giant jabbels, he talks or chats (which giants don't do very often).
The creature came clumping into the cave and stood towering over the BFG. 'Who was you jabbeling to in here just now?' he boomed. — THE BFG
DID YOU KNOW? The word *jabbel* is a blend of **babble** and *jabber*, which also means 'chatter'.

jacket noun jackets
a short coat
Corkers . . . wore creaseless flannel trousers and a brown tweed jacket with patches all over it and bits of dried food on the lapels. — BOY

James Henry Trotter (JAMES AND THE GIANT PEACH)
James Henry Trotter is a boy who is sent to live with his cruel and selfish aunts, Aunt Spiker and Aunt Sponge, after his parents are eaten by an angry rhinoceros which had escaped from London Zoo.

jar noun jars
a glass container for keeping food or dreams in
The BFG was very excited. He held the jar close to one ear and listened intently. 'It's a winksquiffler!' he whispered with a thrill in his voice. — THE BFG

jaw noun jaws
Your jaws are the bones that hold your teeth in place. You move your lower jaw to open your mouth.
Violet . . . shot out a fat hand and grabbed the stick of gum . . . At once, her huge, well-trained jaws started chewing away on it like a pair of tongs. — CHARLIE AND THE CHOCOLATE FACTORY

jealous adjective
If you are jealous of someone, you are unhappy because they have something that you would like.
Every day, when Mr Hoppy looked over his balcony and saw Mrs Silver whispering endearments to Alfie and stroking his shell, he felt absurdly jealous. — ESIO TROT

jeep noun jeeps
a small sturdy vehicle for driving over rough ground
So the nine jeeps drove across to the BFG's cave and the great dream-loading operation began. — THE BFG
DID YOU KNOW? The word *jeep* comes from the abbreviation *GP* for 'General Purpose' vehicle.

a b c d e f g h i j k l m n o p q r s t u v w x y z

Old dictionaries put words starting with **i** and **j** together, so **jacket** came before **icy**!

127

jeepers exclamation
You might say *Jeepers!* if you are very surprised by something.
'There's three of them in nightshirts! Two old women and one old man!... Jeepers, they're older than Moses! They're about ninety years old!' – CHARLIE AND THE GREAT GLASS ELEVATOR

jeer verb jeers, jeering, jeered
If someone jeers at you, they laugh in a rude way.
'How are you going to do it?' 'Skyhooks, I suppose,' jeered the Centipede. 'Seagulls,' James answered calmly. – JAMES AND THE GIANT PEACH
RINGBELLING RHYMES Try rhyming with *peer* or *my dear!*

jelly noun jellies
1 a pudding made from fruit and sugar that wobbles when you shake it
Inside the jar Sophie could see the faint scarlet outline of something that looked like a mixture between a blob of gas and a bubble of jelly. – THE BFG
2 If someone turns to jelly, they feel as floppy and wobbly as a jelly because they are afraid.
'You can't imagine what it's like to be completely controlled like that by a very strong personality. It turns you to jelly.' – MATILDA
LOOK IT UP! For other ways to describe fearful people, see **afraid**.

jellyfish noun jellyfish, jellyfishes
A jellyfish is a sea animal that has a soft, clear body. It is not very nice to compare someone to a jellyfish. Some types of jellyfish can sting you (just like Aunt Sponge can sting with her words).
Aunt Sponge, fat and pulpy as a jellyfish, came waddling up behind her sister to see what was going on. – JAMES AND THE GIANT PEACH

jellyish adjective
soft and wobbly, like jelly
There it lay, this small oblong sea-green jellyish thing, at the bottom of the jar, quite peaceful, but pulsing gently. – THE BFG

Gobblefunking with words
You can add the ending *-ish* to make words that mean 'a bit' or 'a bit like', such as *greenish*, *oldish*, *stickyish* or *sweetish*. Remember to drop the *-e* at the end of words like *purple* and *square*, to make *purplish* and *squarish*:
The tiny shutters of tree-bark opened wider and wider, and when they were fully open they revealed a small squarish window set neatly in the curve of the big branch. – THE MINPINS

jerk verb jerks, jerking, jerked
When something jerks, it moves suddenly and roughly.
Captain Hardcastle was never still. His orange head twitched and jerked perpetually from side to side in the most alarming fashion. – BOY

jersey noun jerseys
A jersey is a knitted piece of clothing with long sleeves and a tickly taste. (**Human beans** from North America call it a *sweater*, which sounds like it would taste worse.)
'Human beans from Jersey has a most disgustable woolly tickle on the tongue,' the Giant said. 'Human beans from Jersey is tasting of cardigans.' 'You mean jerseys,' Sophie said. – THE BFG
DID YOU KNOW? Jerseys are named after *Jersey* in the Channel Islands, where a special kind of woollen cloth was made, so Sophie is right to connect the two words.

jet noun jets
1 a small fast-moving stream of water, steam or air
Inside the house, little jets of freezing air came rushing in through the sides of the windows and under the doors. – CHARLIE AND THE CHOCOLATE FACTORY
2 a fast aeroplane
'Out of my way!' shouted Grandma Georgina, blowing herself back and forth. 'I'm a jumbo jet!' – CHARLIE AND THE GREAT GLASS ELEVATOR
3 Jet is also a hard black mineral, and something that is *jet black* is deep black and glossy.
When the Fleshlumpeater was speaking, she got a glimpse of his tongue. It was jet black, like a slab of black steak. – THE BFG

jewel noun jewels
a beautiful and valuable stone
At this point, a lady with an enormous chest... came flying out of the house screaming, 'My jewels! Somebody's stolen my jewels!' – THE GIRAFFE AND THE PELLY AND ME

jiffy noun
If something happens in a jiffy, it happens very quickly.
'In a jiffy you would be in the garden, and in another jiffy you would be through the front gate, and in yet another jiffy you would be exploring the marvellous Forest of Sin all by yourself.' – THE MINPINS

jiggle verb jiggles, jiggling, jiggled
When something jiggles, it moves or jumps about.
Every time the Pelican spoke, the beak I was standing in jiggled madly up and down, and the more excited he got, the more it jiggled. – THE GIRAFFE AND THE PELLY AND ME
RINGBELLING RHYMES Try rhyming with *giggle* or *wiggle*.

jiggyraffe noun jiggyraffes
A jiggyraffe is what giraffes are called in Giant Country.
'I is never showing myself to human beans... If I do, they will be putting me in the zoo with all the jiggyraffes and cattypiddlers.' – THE BFG

jingle verb jingles, jingling, jingled
When something jingles, it makes a light, ringing sound.
'Have you brought money to buy the raisins?' I asked. He put a hand in his trouser pocket and made the coins jingle. – DANNY THE CHAMPION OF THE WORLD

job noun **jobs**

1 A job is the work that grown-ups do to earn money, or that Oompa-Loompas do to earn cacao beans. Mr Bucket has a horrible job working in a toothpaste factory for very little money (and no chocolate).
By the time he was twenty-seven Robert Lee had become the Reverend Lee and had been appointed to his first important job as Vicar of Nibbleswicke. — THE VICAR OF NIBBLESWICKE

2 something useful that you have to do
Hoisting the huge table upside down on to the ceiling was not an easy job, but they managed it in the end. — THE TWITS

3 (*informal*) If you have a job doing something, you find it difficult or hard to do.
The Big Friendly Giant followed behind them, but he had an awful job getting through the door. — THE BFG

jog verb **jogs, jogging, jogged**

1 When you jog, you run or bob up and down slowly.
At the end of the room, the Oompa-Loompas around the giant camera were already beating their tiny drums and beginning to jog up and down to the rhythm.
— CHARLIE AND THE CHOCOLATE FACTORY

2 When something jogs your memory, you suddenly remember.
'I can't possibly remember all the hundreds of things I put into the saucepan.'... 'Of course you can, my dear boy,' cried Mr Kranky. 'I'll help you! I'll jog your memory!'
— GEORGE'S MARVELLOUS MEDICINE

joghopper noun **joghoppers**
A joghopper is a creature that hops about.
'I always gets as jumpsy as a joghopper when the Fleshlumpeating Giant is around.' 'Keep away from him,' Sophie pleaded. — THE BFG

joint noun **joints**
Your joints are the parts of your arms and legs that you can bend and turn, and that start to creak when you get older. Your ankles, elbows and hips are all joints.
Half a pint of ENGINE OIL — to keep Grandma's engine going smoothly... A handful of GREASE — to grease her creaking joints. — GEORGE'S MARVELLOUS MEDICINE

joke noun **jokes**
A joke is something you say or do to make people laugh. The Oompa-Loompas love to play jokes on people.
'They love dancing and music. They are always making up songs... I must warn you, though, that they are rather mischievous. They like jokes.' — CHARLIE AND THE CHOCOLATE FACTORY

joke verb **jokes, joking, joked**
When you joke, you say things to make people laugh.
'Worms and slugs and beetley bugs. You don't know what's good for you.' 'You're joking, Grandma.' 'I never joke,' she said. — GEORGE'S MARVELLOUS MEDICINE

SPARKY SYNONYMS If you are joking, you can also say you are *pulling someone's leg.*

jolly adjective **jollier, jolliest**
happy and cheerful and very unlike a witch
A fat and jolly lady called Mrs Spring, who used to come and clean our house every day, also moved in and slept in the house. — THE WITCHES

jolly adverb
very or extremely
'And Rupert,' Miss Honey said, 'I am glad to see you didn't lose any of your hair after last Thursday.' 'My head was jolly sore afterwards,' Rupert said. — MATILDA

jostle verb **jostles, jostling, jostled**
If you jostle someone, you push or nudge against them roughly.
Cameras were clicking and flashbulbs were flashing and people were pushing and jostling and trying to get a bit closer to the famous girl. — CHARLIE AND THE CHOCOLATE FACTORY

journey noun **journeys**
When you go on a journey, you travel somewhere.
The BFG had made thousands of journeys to and from Giant Country over the years, but he had never in his life made one quite like this. — THE BFG

joy noun
a feeling of great happiness
The Small Fox ran back along the tunnel as fast as he could, carrying the three plump hens. He was exploding with joy. — FANTASTIC MR FOX

juice noun **juices**
the liquid that is in fruit and vegetables
'The peach is leaking!' shouted the Old-Green-Grasshopper... 'It's full of holes and the juice is dripping out everywhere!' — JAMES AND THE GIANT PEACH

juicy adjective **juicier, juiciest**
Something juicy is full of juice and is good to eat.
'Personally, I had always thought that a big, juicy, caught-in-the-web bluebottle was the finest dinner in the world — until I tasted this.' — JAMES AND THE GIANT PEACH

ju-jube tree noun **ju-jube trees**
an Asian tree with an edible fruit that is eaten fresh or dried
'So give me a bug and a jumping flea . . . And the poisonous sting of a bumblebee, And the juice from the fruit of the ju-jube tree.' — GEORGE'S MARVELLOUS MEDICINE

jumbly adjective **jumblier, jumbliest**
1 A jumbly giant is warm and friendly and will not eat you.
'I is a nice and jumbly Giant! I is the only nice and jumbly Giant in Giant Country! I is THE BIG FRIENDLY GIANT!'
— THE BFG
2 A jumbly taste is very pleasant.
'Nasty!' cried the BFG. 'Never is it nasty! Frobscottle is sweet and jumbly!' — THE BFG
RINGBELLING RHYMES Try rhyming with *crumbly*.
LOOK IT UP! For other ways to describe **jumbly** things or giants, see **good**.

jump verb **jumps, jumping, jumped**
When you jump, you move suddenly from the ground into the air.
Mr Twit jumped as though he'd been stung by a giant wasp. He dropped his beer. He looked up. He gaped. He gasped. He gurgled. — THE TWITS

jump noun **jumps**
a sudden movement into the air
Suddenly the BFG gave a jump in the air. 'By gumfrog!' he cried. — THE BFG
RINGBELLING RHYMES Try rhyming with *bump* or *Muggle-Wump*.
SPARKY SYNONYMS You can also say **jumpel**.

jumpel verb **jumpels, jumpelling, jumpelled**
If you jumpel, you jump or leap.
The BFG stared at the bare table. Sophie, where is you? he thought desperately. You cannot possibly be jumpelling off that high table. — THE BFG
RINGBELLING RHYMES Try rhyming *jumpelled* with *crumpled*.

jumpsquiffling adjective
absolutely enormous
*'Because of these jumpsquiffling ears of mine,' the BFG said, 'I is not only able to **hear** the music that dreams is making but I is **understanding** it also.'*
— THE BFG
SPARKY SYNONYMS You can also say **gigantuous**. An opposite is **midgy**.

jumpsy adjective **jumpsier, jumpsiest**
If you are jumpsy, you feel anxious and the slightest thing will make you jump.
'I is nervous myself,' the BFG whispered. 'I always gets as jumpsy as a joghopper when the Fleshlumpeating Giant is around.' — THE BFG

jungle noun **jungles**
a thick tangled forest in a tropical country
Muggle-Wump and his family longed to escape from the cage in Mr Twit's garden and go back to the African jungle where they came from. — THE TWITS

junk noun
rubbish that is not worth keeping, or not worth paying attention to
In almost every house we've been,/We've watched them gaping at the screen . . . /They sit and stare and stare and sit/Until they're hypnotized by it,/Until they're absolutely drunk/With all that shocking ghastly junk. — CHARLIE AND THE CHOCOLATE FACTORY

jut verb **juts, jutting, jutted**
If something juts out, it sticks out.
The balcony immediately below Mr Hoppy's jutted out a good bit further from the building than his own, so Mr Hoppy always had a fine view of what was going on down there. — ESIO TROT

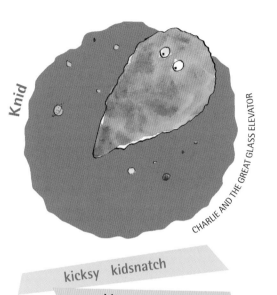

Knid

CHARLIE AND THE GREAT GLASS ELEVATOR

kicksy   kidsnatch

kite   knickers

ketchup noun
a type of thick, cold tomato sauce found in kitchen cupboards and in Mr Twit's facial hair
If you looked closely . . . you would see tiny little specks of dried-up scrambled eggs stuck to the hairs, and spinach and tomato ketchup. — THE TWITS
DID YOU KNOW? *Ketchup* is also called *catsup* in North America, though it is unlikely that a cat would ever want to sup it.

key noun keys
a piece of metal that is shaped so that it fits into a lock
At that exact moment, I heard a key turning in the lock of the door and the door burst open and The Grand High Witch swept into the room. — THE WITCHES

kick verb kicks, kicking, kicked
When you kick something, you hit it with your foot.
Soon, all nine of them were on their feet having the most almighty free-for-all. They punched and kicked and scratched and bit and butted each other as hard as they could. — THE BFG

kicksy adjective kicksier, kicksiest
very strong and powerful
'This one is a real kicksy bogthumper! I is exploding it as soon as I get home!' — THE BFG

kiddle noun kiddles
a young child
'Fleshlumpeater did that one! He went off to Baghdad to bag dad and mum and all the little kiddles!' — THE BFG
SPARKY SYNONYMS You can also say **chiddler**.

> **Gobblefunking with words**
> To make the word *kiddle* Roald Dahl added an ending or *suffix* (-*le*) to *kid*. This ending is sometimes used to make words that mean something small, for example *crumble* means literally 'small crumb' and *sparkle* is a 'small spark'. You can make up your own words using this ending too, such as *sweetle* for a small sweet, or *birdle* for a young bird or chick.

kidsnatch verb kidsnatches, kidsnatching, kidsnatched
When a giant or other creature kidsnatches a child, they take them away from their home and keep them prisoner.
'All is my fault,' the BFG said. 'I is the one who kidsnatched you.' — THE BFG
DID YOU KNOW? Roald Dahl based the word *kidsnatch* on *kidnap*, which is made up of *kid* 'child' and *nap*, an old word meaning 'seize or grab'. He swapped the second part for a synonym, *snatch*, to make a new word that has the same meaning.

kill verb kills, killing, killed
To kill a person or animal means to make them die.
'Giants isn't eating each other either,' the BFG said. 'Nor is giants killing each other. Giants is not very lovely, but they is not killing each other.' — THE BFG

king noun kings
a man who has been crowned as the ruler of a country
'Oh, what a nuisance! What a life!/Now I must find another wife!'/(It's never easy for a king/To find himself that sort of thing.) — REVOLTING RHYMES

kipper noun kippers
a smoked herring
'Eat the Earthworm first!' shouted the Centipede. 'It's no good eating me, I'm full of bones like a kipper!' — JAMES AND THE GIANT PEACH

kiss verb kisses, kissing, kissed
When you kiss someone, you touch them with your lips as a sign of affection.
Suddenly, unexpectedly, the BFG leaned forward and kissed her gently on the cheek. Sophie felt like crying. — THE BFG

kitchen noun kitchens
the room in a house in which people prepare and cook food
'Here it is!' cried Mr Killy Kranky, rushing into the kitchen. 'One carton of flea powder for dogs and one tin of brown shoe-polish!' — GEORGE'S MARVELLOUS MEDICINE

a b c d e f g h i j **k** l m n o p q r s t u v w x y z

You can put *un-* before adjectives to make opposites: *an unjumbly giant.*

A B C D E F G H I J **K** L M N O P Q R S T U V W X Y Z

kite noun kites

A kite is a light frame covered in cloth or paper, like the one that Danny and his father make. You hold a kite at the end of a long string while it flies in the wind.
I held the string while my father held the kite, and the moment he let it go, it caught the wind and soared upward like a huge blue bird. — DANNY THE CHAMPION OF THE WORLD

knack jife noun knack jives

A knack jife is what the BFG calls a jack-knife or pocket-knife. If you do something before you can say knack jife (or jack-knife), it means that you do it very quickly.
'If any one of them is waking up, he will gobble you down before you can say knack jife,' the BFG answered, grinning hugely. — THE BFG

Gobblefunking with words
When the BFG says *knack jife* instead of *jack-knife*, he is using a *spoonerism*. You can find more examples of this type of word play in the entry for **mideous**.

knee noun knees

Your knee is the part in the middle of your leg, where your leg can bend. By the time you are grown up, your knees will probably be at the same height as an adult Oompa-Loompa.
The Oompa-Loompa bowed and smiled . . . His skin was rosy-white, his long hair was golden-brown, and the top of his head came just above the height of Mr Wonka's knee. — CHARLIE AND THE CHOCOLATE FACTORY

kneel verb kneels, kneeling, kneeled

When you kneel, you go down on to your knees.
Augustus Gloop . . . was now kneeling on the riverbank, scooping hot melted chocolate into his mouth as fast as he could. — CHARLIE AND THE CHOCOLATE FACTORY

knickers plural noun

underpants for girls or women
The small girl smiles. One eyelid flickers./She whips a pistol from her knickers./She aims it at the creature's head/And bang bang bang, she shoots him dead. — REVOLTING RHYMES

DID YOU KNOW? *Knickers* is a short form (literally) of *knickerbockers*, which are a type of knee-length trousers, named after Diedrich Knickerbocker, a fictional American character.

knickle verb knickles, knickling, knickled

If a Gnooly knickles you, it does unspeakably nasty things to you (and you probably won't survive).
'I don't want to be a Minus!' croaked Grandma Georgina. *'If I ever have to go back to that beastly Minusland again, the Gnoolies will knickle me!'* — CHARLIE AND THE GREAT GLASS ELEVATOR

RINGBELLING RHYMES Try rhyming with *prickle* or *tickle*.

Knid or Vermicious Knid noun

Knids or **Vermicious Knids**
Knids are evil-minded creatures from the planet Vermes. They are sometimes called *Vermicious Knids*, which means literally 'worm-like Knids'. They have greenish-brown skin and are naturally egg-shaped but can change into any shape they want.

'From fifty yards away, a fully grown Vermicious Knid could stretch out its neck and bite your head off without even getting up!' — CHARLIE AND THE GREAT GLASS ELEVATOR

DID YOU KNOW? Roald Dahl made up the word *Knid*, but *vermicious* is a real word meaning 'worm-like' which comes from Latin *vermis* 'a worm'. When you say *Knid*, you pronounce all the letters. Some other words, like *knight* and *knee*, now have a silent *k*, but a long time ago the letters used to be pronounced as in *Knid*.

LOOK IT UP! A word to describe the egg shape of a Knid is **oviform**.

Knidproof adjective

When something is Knidproof it can't be broken by Knids, and Knids can't get inside it.
'The Great Glass Elevator is shockproof, waterproof, bombproof, bulletproof and Knidproof!'– CHARLIE AND THE GREAT GLASS ELEVATOR

knife noun knives

A knife is a tool with a long, sharp edge that you use for cutting things. If you describe something as being like a knife, you mean that it is sharp and cutting.
Everything that Charlie touched seemed to be made of ice, and each time he stepped outside the door, the wind was like a knife on his cheek.– CHARLIE AND THE CHOCOLATE FACTORY

knob noun knobs

a round button that you turn to make a machine work
There was an enormous camera on wheels, and a whole army of Oompa-Loompas was . . . adjusting its knobs and polishing its great glass lens.– CHARLIE AND THE CHOCOLATE FACTORY

knobble noun knobbles

a hard lump or bump on a surface
It was black with white stripes along its length. And it was covered all over with coarse knobbles. 'Here is the repulsant snozzcumber!' cried the BFG.– THE BFG

knock verb knocks, knocking, knocked

When you knock something, you bang it or hit it.
A witch, you must understand, does not knock children on the head or stick knives into them or shoot at them with a pistol. People who do those things get caught by the police.– THE WITCHES

knot noun knots

the twisted part where pieces of string or cloth (or the top and tail of a Vermicious Knid) have been tied together
Having curled its body twice around the Elevator, the Knid now proceeded to tie a knot with its two ends, a good strong knot, left over right, then right over left.– CHARLIE AND THE GREAT GLASS ELEVATOR

knuckle noun knuckles

Your knuckles are the parts where your fingers bend.
The one remaining squirrel . . . climbed up on to her shoulder and started tap-tap-tapping the wretched girl's head with its knuckles.– CHARLIE AND THE CHOCOLATE FACTORY

Kranky, Mr Killy (GEORGE'S MARVELLOUS MEDICINE)

Mr Killy Kranky is George's father. He is a small man with bandy legs and a huge head, and gets excited very easily.
DID YOU KNOW? *Killy Kranky* sounds like *Killecrankie*, which is a place in Scotland where a famous battle once took place. The name comes from Gaelic and means 'the Wood at the Knobbly Place'.

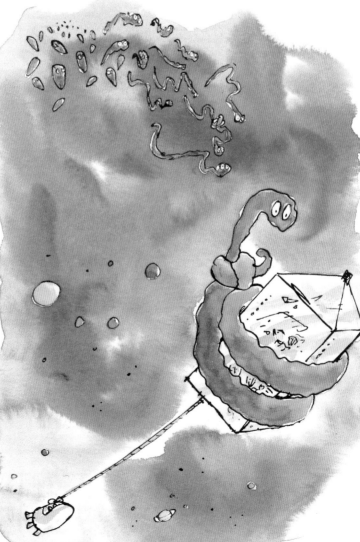

a b c d e f g h i j **k** l m n o p q r s t u v w x y z

Ll

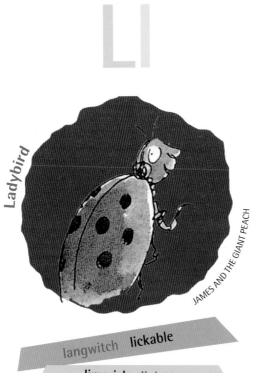

Ladybird

JAMES AND THE GIANT PEACH

langwitch lickable

limerick lixivate

label noun labels
a small piece of paper or cloth with the name or price of something on it
'Every dream is having its special label on the bottle,' the BFG said. 'How else could I be finding the one I am wanting in a hurry?' — THE BFG

laborious adjective
A laborious task is hard to do and needs a lot of effort.
The BFG gazed at her for a while longer, then he bent his head again to his slow laborious writing. — THE BFG

lace noun laces
Laces are pieces of string that you use to tie up your shoes. The Centipede has forty-two laces for his twenty-one pairs of boots.
James worked away frantically on the Centipede's boots. Each one had laces that had to be untied and loosened before it could be pulled off. — JAMES AND THE GIANT PEACH

ladder noun ladders
A ladder is a tall frame to help you climb up or down something, made of two long pieces of wood or metal with bars across them. Ladders are often used by window-cleaners, unless they happen to be a Geraneous Giraffe.
Today is Tuesday and over there you can already see the revolting Mr Twit up the ladder painting sticky glue on all the branches of The Big Dead Tree. — THE TWITS

Ladderless Window–Cleaning Company
(THE GIRAFFE AND THE PELLY AND ME)
The Ladderless Window-Cleaning Company is a group of three animals—a Giraffe, a Pelican and a Monkey—who are extraordinarily good at cleaning windows. They don't need a ladder because the Giraffe uses his extendable neck to reach high windows. Their head office is in an old sweet-shop called the Grubber.

lady noun ladies
a polite name for a woman
On one occasion the Reverend Lee walked into the village hall, where the local ladies were holding their weekly knitting session. — THE VICAR OF NIBBLESWICKE

Ladybird (JAMES AND THE GIANT PEACH)
A ladybird is a small flying beetle which is usually red with black spots on its back. Ladybirds are known as *ladybugs* in North America. The Ladybird who lives in the Giant Peach has four hundred children and becomes James's friend.

lake noun lakes
A lake is a large area of fresh water with land all around it. If a large amount of chocolate or ice cream melts, it can also form a lake (a small amount would just be a **puddle**).
The crazy prince, who was dozing in the living room at the time, woke up to find himself swimming around in a huge brown sticky lake of chocolate. — CHARLIE AND THE CHOCOLATE FACTORY

lamp noun lamps
A lamp is a light, especially one that you can hold or move around. The big lights in a street are called *street lamps.*
My father put a match to the wick of the lamp hanging from the ceiling and the little yellow flame sprang up and

A B C D E F G H I J K **L** M N O P Q R S T U V W X Y Z

filled the inside of the caravan with pale light. — DANNY THE CHAMPION OF THE WORLD

land noun lands

1 Land is the dry part of the Earth where there is no water.
A strong current and a high wind had carried the peach so quickly away from the shore that already the land was out of sight. — JAMES AND THE GIANT PEACH
2 A land is a country. The Land of the Midnight Sun is another name for the Arctic or the Antarctic, because you can still see the sun there at midnight during the summer.
There were Gumtwizzlers and Fizzwinkles from China . . . and Liplickers and Plushnuggets from the Land of the Midnight Sun. — THE GIRAFFE AND THE PELLY AND ME

land verb lands, landing, landed

When you land, you arrive on the ground (or on a roof or a tree) after being in the air.
The Roly-Poly Bird flew round and round The Big Dead Tree singing out, 'There's sticky stick stuff all over the tree! If you land in the branches, you'll never get free!' — THE TWITS

landscape noun

The landscape is everything you can see when you look out over an area of land.
Sophie peeped over the rim of the ear and watched the desolate landscape of Giant Country go whizzing by. — THE BFG

lane noun lanes

a narrow road, especially in the country
With a horse to pull it, the old caravan must have wandered for thousands of miles along the roads and lanes of England. — DANNY THE CHAMPION OF THE WORLD

language noun languages

Your language is the words that you use when you speak or write. The BFG and other giants have their own **langwitch**.
'Do you know how to talk to these English birds?' Muggle-Wump asked him. 'Of course I do,' said the Roly-Poly Bird. 'It's no good going to a country and not knowing the language.' — THE TWITS

langwitch noun langwitches

Langwitch is what the BFG and other giants call language.
'You mean you can hear ants talking?' 'Every single word,' the BFG said. 'Although I is not exactly understanding their langwitch.' — THE BFG

DID YOU KNOW? To make the word *langwitch*, Roald Dahl started with *language* but swapped the ending for a whole word (*witch*) that sounds similar. This is called a *malapropism*, and you can find more examples in the entry for **mudburger**. *Lang* is also a Scottish word meaning 'long', as in the famous song

'Auld Lang Syne', so in Scotland *langwitch* means a very tall witch.

lap noun laps

Your lap is the flat part of your legs when you are sitting down.
Charlie tore the wrapper right down the middle . . . and on to his lap, there fell . . . a light-brown creamy-coloured bar of chocolate. — CHARLIE AND THE CHOCOLATE FACTORY

lap verb laps, lapping, lapped

When an animal laps, it drinks with its tongue, as does greedy Augustus Gloop.
Augustus . . . was now lying full length on the ground with his head far out over the river, lapping up the chocolate like a dog. — CHARLIE AND THE CHOCOLATE FACTORY

large adjective larger, largest

Something that is large is big (but not quite as big as **gigantuous**).
'Come and watch this one!' he called out to Mrs Kranky. 'Come and watch us turning an ordinary chicken into a lovely great big one that lays eggs as large as footballs!' — GEORGE'S MARVELLOUS MEDICINE
LOOK IT UP! For other ways to describe something large, see **big**.

a
b
c
d
e
f
g
h
i
j
k
l
m
n
o
p
q
r
s
t
u
v
w
x
y
z

lark noun (*informal*) **larks**
something that people do for fun
It was beginning to look as though just about everybody in the entire district was in on this poaching lark. — DANNY THE CHAMPION OF THE WORLD

lark verb **larks, larking, larked**
If you lark about, you have fun.
They were all very quiet. There was no larking about. There were just a few muttered remarks about the pilots who had not come back that day.
— GOING SOLO

laugh verb **laughs, laughing, laughed**
When you laugh, you make sounds that show that you are happy or think something is funny.

Here are some ways that people *laugh* (except for Aunts Sponge and Spiker, who never EVER laugh).

TO LAUGH SOFTLY: chortle, chuckle, **churgle**, giggle
Charlie Kinch started chuckling and chortling so much he nearly drove off the track. — DANNY THE CHAMPION OF THE WORLD

TO LAUGH LOUDLY OR HARSHLY: cackle, have hysterics, hoot with laughter, roar with laughter, snort
The Roly-Poly Bird was up there as well, and the monkeys were in the cage and the whole lot of them were hooting with laughter at Mr Twit. — THE TWITS

TO LAUGH AT SOMEONE IN A MEAN WAY: jeer, mock, sneer
The people jeered and laughed. But this only made the three farmers more furious. — FANTASTIC MR FOX

SOMETHING THAT MAKES YOU LAUGH CAN BE: amusing, comical, funny, hilarious, witty
Miss Honey said . . . 'A witty limerick is very hard to write . . . They look easy but they most certainly are not.'
— MATILDA

laughter noun
Laughter is the sound you make when you laugh.
Of course the whole class started screaming with laughter, and then Mrs Winter said, 'Will you be so kind as to tell me what you find so madly funny, all of you?'
— THE MAGIC FINGER

lava noun
Lava is very hot, liquid rock that comes out of a volcano when it erupts. Molten lava is a fiery red colour, which turns dark and black as it cools.
The Trunchbull stood motionless on the platform. Her great horsy face had turned the colour of molten lava and her eyes were glittering with fury. — MATILDA
DID YOU KNOW? The word *lava* comes from Italian and is related to **lavatory**, because it originally meant a stream of water for washing.

lavatory noun **lavatories**
A lavatory is a toilet, or a room with a toilet in it.
The lavatory was a funny little wooden hut standing in the field some way behind the caravan. — DANNY THE CHAMPION OF THE WORLD
DID YOU KNOW? The word *lavatory* comes from Latin and means 'a washing place', in the same way that **dormitory** means 'a sleeping place'.

Lavender (MATILDA)
Lavender is a pupil in Miss Honey's class at Crunchem Hall who becomes Matilda's best friend. Although she is small, she is very daring and hatches a plan to scare Miss Trunchbull with a newt.

law noun **laws**
The law is all the rules that everyone in a country must obey.
The only thing he knew for certain was that the law forbade the Trunchbull to hit him with the riding-crop that she kept smacking against her thigh. — MATILDA

lawn noun **lawns**
A lawn is a piece of ground in a garden covered with short grass. Mrs Twit's garden doesn't have a lawn: just nettles and thistles.
'Our Centipede will never move again. He will turn into a statue and we shall be able to put him in the middle of the lawn with a bird-bath on the top of his head'.
— JAMES AND THE GIANT PEACH

lazy adjective **lazier, laziest**
If someone calls you lazy, they think you have not been working very hard (even if you actually have been).
'Get up at once, you lazy little beast!' a voice was suddenly shouting in James's ear . . . 'Get back over there immediately and finish chopping up those logs!' — JAMES AND THE GIANT PEACH
RINGBELLING RHYMES Try rhyming with *crazy*.

lead (*rhymes with* seed) verb **leads, leading, led**
If you lead people, you go in front of them and take them somewhere.
Mr Twit led Mrs Twit outdoors where he had everything ready for the great stretching. — THE TWITS

lead (*rhymes with* bed) noun
Lead is a type of heavy, grey metal. If something moves or falls like lead, it moves very slowly, or falls very hard, because it is so heavy.
The enormous peach, having nothing to hold it up in the air any longer, went tumbling down towards the earth like a lump of lead. — JAMES AND THE GIANT PEACH

leaf noun **leaves**
The leaves on a plant are the green parts that grow from its stem.
Doc Spencer . . . was looking at Mr Hazell rather as one would look at a slug on a leaf of lettuce in the salad. — DANNY THE CHAMPION OF THE WORLD

leak verb **leaks, leaking, leaked**
If something is leaking, it has a hole or crack in it and liquid can get through.
'The peach is leaking!' shouted the Old-Green-Grasshopper, peering over the side. 'It's full of holes and the juice is dripping out everywhere!' — JAMES AND THE GIANT PEACH

lean verb **leans, leaning, leaned, leant**
1 When you lean forwards or backwards, you bend your body that way.
My grandmother leaned back in her chair and sucked away contentedly at her foul black cigar. — THE WITCHES
2 If you lean against or on something, you rest against it.
After a while, . . . they explored further into the garden and found the ladder leaning against The Big Dead Tree. — THE TWITS

lean adjective **leaner, leanest**
Lean meat does not have any fat on it. A lean person is very thin.
Aunt Spiker . . . was lean and tall and bony, and she wore steel-rimmed spectacles that fixed on to the end of her nose with a clip. — JAMES AND THE GIANT PEACH

leap verb **leaps, leaping, leaped, leapt**
When you leap, you jump forward or up in the air.
'Great whistling whangdoodles!' cried Mr Wonka, leaping so high in the air that when he landed his legs gave way and he crashed on to his backside. — CHARLIE AND THE GREAT GLASS ELEVATOR

leap noun **leaps**
a jump forwards or up in the air
In one fantastic leap, this old fellow of ninety-six and a half . . . jumped on to the floor and started doing a dance of victory in his pyjamas. — CHARLIE AND THE CHOCOLATE FACTORY

learn verb **learns, learning, learned, learnt**
1 When you learn about something, you find out about it.

'The most important thing we've learned,/So far as children are concerned,/Is never, never, NEVER let/ Them near your television set.' — CHARLIE AND THE CHOCOLATE FACTORY
2 When you learn to do something, you find out how to do it.
The BFG expressed a wish to learn how to speak properly, and Sophie herself, who loved him as she would a father, volunteered to give him lessons every day. — THE BFG

leather noun & adjective
Leather is a strong material made from the skins of animals. Shoes and handbags are often made of leather, as is the BFG's well-worn waistcoat.
Sophie saw that under the cloak he was wearing a sort of collarless shirt and a dirty old leather waistcoat that didn't seem to have any buttons. — THE BFG

ledge noun **ledges**
a narrow shelf that sticks out from a wall or under a window, sometimes useful for sitting on
The Queen crossed over to the window and stood beside Sophie. 'Come down off that ledge,' she said. — THE BFG

leg noun **legs**
1 the parts of your body between your hips and your feet
'In my opinion,' the Earthworm said, 'the really marvellous thing is to have no legs at all and to be able to walk just the same.' — JAMES AND THE GIANT PEACH
2 the parts that a table or chair stands on
'Now the table, the big table!' shouted Muggle-Wump. 'Turn the table upside down and put a dollop of sticky glue on to the bottom of each leg.' — THE TWITS

lemonade noun
a fizzy drink made from lemons, sugar and water
Aunt Sponge and Aunt Spiker were sitting comfortably in deck-chairs near by, sipping tall glasses of fizzy lemonade. — JAMES AND THE GIANT PEACH

lend verb lends, lending, lent

1 If you lend something to someone, you let them use it or keep it for a short time.
Suddenly the parrot said, 'Hello, hello, hello.' It was exactly like a human voice . . . 'It's fabulous,' Matilda said. 'Will you lend him to me just for one night?'—MATILDA

2 If you lend someone a hand (or a paw), you help them to do something.
They dug on in silence. Badger was a great digger and the tunnel went forward at a terrific pace now that he was lending a paw.—FANTASTIC MR FOX

length noun

The length of something is how long it is.
A tingle of electricity flashed down the length of George's spine.—GEORGE'S MARVELLOUS MEDICINE

lens noun lenses

A lens is a curved piece of glass or plastic that makes things look bigger or smaller when you look through it. Glasses, cameras and telescopes all have lenses.
There was an enormous camera on wheels, and a whole army of Oompa-Loompas was clustering around it . . . polishing its great glass lens.—CHARLIE AND THE CHOCOLATE FACTORY

LOOK IT UP! Some other instruments with lenses are **biriculers** and **telescoops**.

lesson noun lessons

1 a time in school when someone is teaching you
We were having our first lesson of the day with Captain Lancaster, and he had set us a whole bunch of multiplication sums to work out in our exercise books.—DANNY THE CHAMPION OF THE WORLD

2 If someone does something to teach you a lesson, they do something very unpleasant that they think is good for you.
She was a prisoner, and Mr Twit had intended to go away and leave her like that for a couple of days and nights to teach her a lesson.—THE TWITS

letter noun letters

1 Letters are the signs that we use for writing words, such as a, b, c and x, y, z. There are twenty-six letters in the English alphabet.
The Grand High Witch . . . seemed to have trouble pronouncing the letter w. As well as that, she did something funny with the letter r.—THE WITCHES

2 A letter is a message that you write down and send to someone.
The Giraffe said, 'Be so good as to open the envelope and read us the letter.'—THE GIRAFFE AND THE PELLY AND ME

lettuce noun lettuces

a vegetable with green leaves that you eat in salads and which tortoises love to munch
Mr Hoppy . . . was leaning over his balcony-rail watching Mrs Silver serving Alfie his breakfast. 'Here's the heart of the lettuce for you, my lovely,' she was saying.
— ESIO TROT

liar noun liars

someone who tells lies
'I is never eating human beans! I swear I has never gobbled a single human bean in all my wholesome life!' 'Liar,' said the BFG.—THE BFG

librarian noun librarians

A librarian is someone who works in a library and helps you choose or borrow books to read.
Matilda . . . introduced herself to the librarian, Mrs Phelps. She asked if she might sit awhile and read a book.—MATILDA

library noun libraries

A library is a building or room with shelves full of books for people to use or borrow. The library is Matilda's favourite place to be in the whole world.
On the afternoon of the day when her father had refused to buy her a book, Matilda set out all by herself to walk to the public library in the village.—MATILDA

lick verb licks, licking, licked

When you lick something, you move your tongue over it.
'Hey, there! Mike Teavee!' shouted Mr Wonka. 'Please do not lick the boat with your tongue! It'll only make it sticky!'—CHARLIE AND THE CHOCOLATE FACTORY

lickable adjective

If something is lickable, it tastes good when you lick it. Willy Wonka invents lickable wallpaper with fruity flavours. No one has yet invented a lickable dictionary, but if they did, it would probably taste **inky-booky**.
'Lovely stuff, lickable wallpaper!' cried Mr Wonka, rushing past. 'It has pictures of fruits on it.'—CHARLIE AND THE CHOCOLATE FACTORY

Gobblefunking with words

You can add the ending *-able* to most verbs to make an adjective that means 'able to be (verb)ed'. For example, *mashable* means 'able to be mashed' and *squishable* (or *sqvishable* to the Grand High Witch) means 'able to be squished'. You can even add it to phrases to make words like *stick-upside-down-able* meaning 'able to be stuck upside down' (like Mr and Mrs Twit). Remember to drop the *-e* at the end of verbs like **lixivate** and **squoggle**, to make *lixivatable* and *squogglable*.

lickswishy adjective **lickswishier, lickswishiest**
A lickswishy taste or flavour is gloriously delicious.
'I knows where there is a bogglebox for boys!' shouted the Gizzardgulper. 'All I has to do is reach in and grab myself a handful! English boys is tasting extra lickswishy!'
— THE BFG

DID YOU KNOW? The word *lickswishy* is a mixture of **lick** and **swish**, and makes you think of licking your lips when you eat something delicious. It also sounds rather like *liquorice*, so perhaps English boys have a liquorice flavour from eating liquorice sweets.

SPARKY SYNONYMS You can also say **delumptious** or **scrumdiddlyumptious**.

lid noun **lids**
A lid is a cover on the top of a box or jar. Dream-bottles need to have tight-fitting lids so that the dreams cannot escape.
The BFG . . . quickly tipped the struggling thrashing trogglehumper out of the large jar into the small one. Then he screwed the lid tightly on to the small jar.
— THE BFG

RINGBELLING RHYMES Try rhyming with *Vermicious Knid* (because if you caught a Knid, you'd need a VERY strong lid to secure it).

lie verb **lies, lying, lied**
When you lie, you say something that you know is not true.
'You're lying as usual!' Grandma yelled. 'You're always lying!' 'I'm not lying, Grandma. I swear I'm not.'
— GEORGE'S MARVELLOUS MEDICINE

lie noun **lies**
something you say that you know is not true
'Here you are, an unhatched shrimp sitting in the lowest form there is, trying to tell me a whopping great lie like that!'— MATILDA

lie verb **lies, lying, lay, lain**
When you lie down, you rest with your body spread out on the ground or on a bed.
The four old ones lay silent and huddled in their bed, trying to keep the cold out of their bones.
— CHARLIE AND THE CHOCOLATE FACTORY

life noun **lives**
Your life is the time when you are alive.
'I shall never be the same again,' murmured the Earthworm. 'Nor I,' the Ladybird said. 'It's taken years off my life.'— JAMES AND THE GIANT PEACH

lift verb **lifts, lifting, lifted**
When you lift something, you pick it up or move it upwards.
'Can I read a boy's dream?' 'You can,' the BFG said, and he lifted her to a higher shelf.— THE BFG

lift noun **lifts**
A lift is a machine that takes people up and down inside a building (in North America, people call it an **elevator**). Most lifts just move up and down, but the lift in the Chocolate Factory can move sideways and absolutely anyways.
'This isn't just an ordinary up-and-down lift!' announced Mr Wonka proudly. 'This lift can go sideways and longways and slantways and any other way you can think of!'
— CHARLIE AND THE CHOCOLATE FACTORY

light noun **lights**
1 Light is brightness that comes from the sun and the stars, from fires and lamps, and from the tail of a Glow-worm.
Then a faint greenish light began to glimmer out of the Glow-worm's tail, and this gradually became stronger and stronger until it was anyway enough to see by.— JAMES AND THE GIANT PEACH

a
b
c
d
e
f
g
h
i
j
k
l
m
n
o
p
q
r
s
t
u
v
w
x
y
z

Insects that glow in the dark are *bioluminescent*.

2 a lamp, bulb or torch that gives out light
'Every night, after the light in your bedroom has been switched off, Swan will come to your window to see if you'd like a ride.' — THE MINPINS

light adjective **lighter, lightest**
1 Something that is light is not heavy.
'Don't forget the peach is a lot lighter now than when we started out,' James told them. 'It lost an awful lot of juice.' — JAMES AND THE GIANT PEACH
2 A place that is light is not dark, but has plenty of light in it. When it is light outside, it means that there is sunlight.
'I've got to get out of here before morning. The keepers know I'm here and they're coming back for me as soon as it gets light.' — DANNY THE CHAMPION OF THE WORLD

light verb **lights, lighting, lit**
1 If you light something, you put light in it so that you can see.
He saw a room that was lit by a pale yellow light of some sort and it was furnished with beautifully made miniature chairs and a table. — THE MINPINS
2 If you light a fire, you make it burn.
'But what about the great fiery incinerator?' asked Charlie. 'They only light it every other day,' said Mr Wonka. 'Perhaps this is one of the days when they let it go out.' — CHARLIE AND THE CHOCOLATE FACTORY

lightning noun
Lightning is a bright flash of light that you see in the sky when there is a storm. If something moves or works like lightning, it moves or works as fast as you can imagine.
'Don't you realize that Vita-Wonk acts instantly? . . . Vita-Wonk is as quick as lightning! The moment the medicine is swallowed — ping! — and it all happens!' — CHARLIE AND THE GREAT GLASS ELEVATOR

like verb **likes, liking, liked**
If you like something or someone, you think they are nice.
'I like that dream,' Sophie said. 'Of course you like it,' the BFG said. 'It is a phizzwizard.' — THE BFG
SPARKY SYNONYMS Words that mean the opposite of *like* are **dispunge** and **mispise**.

like preposition
If one thing is like another thing, it is similar to it.
The Enormous Crocodile . . . lay across the piece of wood and tucked in his feet so that he looked almost exactly like a see-saw. — THE ENORMOUS CROCODILE

Gobblefunking with words
One way to say that someone or something is like another thing is to use a *simile*. Roald Dahl uses lots of similes in his stories and poems. For example, Mrs Twit's petticoat *billows out like a parachute*, and George's grumpy grandma has *a small puckered-up mouth like a dog's bottom*. For other types of simile, see **grave** and **mad**.

---

likely adjective **likelier, likeliest**
If something is likely to happen, it will probably happen.
'If you do go back, you will be telling the world,' said the BFG, 'most likely on the telly-telly bunkum box and the radio squeaker.' — THE BFG

limb noun **limbs**
Your limbs are your arms and legs. Giants and **human beans** have four limbs, but the Centipede has a whopping forty-two limbs (all legs).
One by one, he released the giants. They stood up, stretched their stiffened limbs and started leaping about in fury. — THE BFG

limerick noun **limericks**
There once was a word with an L,
That not many people could spell.
So they checked it, you see,
In a dictionary,
Which told them the meaning as well.
(That's a limerick, in case you haven't guessed.)
'Well, Matilda, I would very much like to hear one of these limericks you say you have written. Could you try to remember one for us?' — MATILDA

limp verb **limps, limping, limped**
When you limp, you walk with uneven steps because you have hurt one of your legs or feet. (If you see someone limping in pointed shoes, they may also be a witch.)
'She must also hide her ugly witch's feet by squeezing them into pretty shoes . . . You might possibly see her limping very slightly, but only if you were watching closely.' — THE WITCHES

line noun **lines**
1 a row of people, ducks or things
The ducks were walking in a line to the door of the Greggs' house, swinging their arms and holding their beaks high in the air. — THE MAGIC FINGER

2 A fishing line is a piece of special thin string that you use for catching fish.
'Do you know how to catch a trout, Danny, without using a rod and line?' — DANNY THE CHAMPION OF THE WORLD

link noun **links**
a connection between two things
'You've got to talk to them, Mr President. Tell Houston we want another direct radio link with the Space Hotel. And hurry!' — CHARLIE AND THE GREAT GLASS ELEVATOR

I'M STILL LOST!

A B C D E F G H I J K L M N O P Q R S T U V W X Y Z

link verb links, linking, linked

When things link up, they join together in a chain.
It is a very dangerous sign if you see Vermicious Knids starting to link up.
And now all the hooks were linking up into one long chain . . . one thousand Knids . . . all joining together and curving around in the sky to make a chain of Knids half a mile long or more! — CHARLIE AND THE GREAT GLASS ELEVATOR

lip noun lips

Your lips are the parts round the edges of your mouth.
Someone licks their lips when they are looking forward to a **delumptious** meal.
'A big fat earwig is very tasty,' Grandma said, licking her lips. — GEORGE'S MARVELLOUS MEDICINE

liquid noun liquids

any substance that is like water, and is not a solid or a gas
With a slop and a gurgle, the yellow liquid splashed into the now nearly full saucepan. — GEORGE'S MARVELLOUS MEDICINE

liquorice noun

Liquorice is a soft and chewy black sweet with a strong flavour which comes from a plant root. It is sometimes made into long thin shapes to make sweets like *liquorice straws* and *liquorice bootlaces*.
You sucked the sherbet up through the straw and when it was finished you ate the liquorice. — BOY

listen verb listens, listening, listened

When you listen, you pay attention so that you can hear something.
The Enormous Crocodile grinned up at Trunky and said: 'I'm off to find a yummy child for lunch. Keep listening and you'll hear the bones go crunch!' — THE ENORMOUS CROCODILE

RINGBELLING RHYMES Try rhyming with *glisten*.

little adjective

1 Something that is little is not very big.
'Look!' Mrs Silver was shouting. 'Alfie's too big to get through the door of his little house! He must have grown enormously!' — ESIO TROT

2 A little of something is a small amount of it.
'Wouldn't this be a perfect time for a little music?' the Ladybird asked. 'How about it, Old Grasshopper?' — JAMES AND THE GIANT PEACH

SPARKY SYNONYMS You can also say midgy, snitchy or **titchy**.

Little Billy (THE MINPINS)

Little Billy is a boy who lives in a house next to the Forest of Sin which he longs to explore. He is not scared off by the tales of fearsome creatures, such as the Terrible Bloodsuckling Toothpluckling Stonechuckling Spittler, who live there.

live verb lives, living, lived

1 To live means to be alive.
Believe it or not, she lived for six months like that, upside down on the ceiling with her legs stuck permanently in the paint. — JAMES AND THE GIANT PEACH
2 If you live somewhere, that is where your home is.
Mr Hoppy lived in a small flat high up in a tall concrete building. He lived alone. — ESIO TROT

live adjective (rhymes with dive)

A live person, animal or creature is alive.
'What about people?' asked Mike Teavee. 'Could you send a real live person from one place to another in the same way?' — CHARLIE AND THE CHOCOLATE FACTORY

lixivate verb lixivates, lixivating, lixivated

If someone lixivates you, you will be squished and mushed and turned into slush.
'The man's a madman!' cried Grandma Georgina. 'Watch out, I say, or he'll lixivate the lot of us!' — CHARLIE AND THE GREAT GLASS ELEVATOR

Gobblefunking with words
You can add other endings or suffixes to *lixivate* to make new words. For example, a *lixivator* would be a machine or unfriendly creature that lixivates people.

lizard noun lizards

a reptile with a scaly skin, four legs and a long tail
'Crocodile tongues!' he cried. 'One thousand long slimy crocodile tongues boiled up in the skull of a dead witch for twenty days and nights with the eyeballs of a lizard!' — JAMES AND THE GIANT PEACH

load noun loads

1 an amount that someone can carry
2 a load of something is a large amount of it
'What a load of luck!' cried Mr Wonka. 'We've landed ourselves slap in the middle of the biggest space operation of all time!' — CHARLIE AND THE GREAT GLASS ELEVATOR

load verb loads, loading, loaded

1 When you load things into a car or lorry, you put them in.
'That's all very well,' said the Head of the Army. 'But how do we get the brutes back here? We can't load fifty-foot giants on to trucks!' — THE BFG

2 When someone loads a gun, they put bullets in it.
They were just outside the entrance to the hole, each one crouching behind a tree with his gun loaded. — FANTASTIC MR FOX

loathsome adjective
horribly unpleasant
But by far the most loathsome thing about Mrs Pratchett was the filth that clung around her. — BOY

lock noun locks
The lock on a door or gate is the part that you can open and shut with a key.
The door slammed. The key turned in the lock. Hungry and trembling, James stood alone out in the open, wondering what to do. — JAMES AND THE GIANT PEACH

lock verb locks, locking, locked
When you lock something, you shut it and fasten it with a key.
'Next time you stop before it's all finished you'll go straight into The Chokey and I shall lock the door and throw the key down the well!' — MATILDA

lofty adjective loftier, loftiest
Something lofty is very tall or very high up in the sky.
The BFG looked down from his lofty perch and said, this time to the Head of the Air Force, 'You is having bellypoppers, is you not?' — THE BFG

lolloping adjective
Lolloping strides are clumsy and not smooth.
There was an air of menace about them as they loped slowly across the plain with long lolloping strides, heading for the BFG. — THE BFG

lolly noun lollies
a sweet on a stick, for licking or nibbling
'A nice fat Esquimo to a giant is like a lovely ice-cream lolly to you.' 'I'll take your word for it,' Sophie said. — THE BFG
RINGBELLING RHYMES Try rhyming with *jolly*.

lonely adjective lonelier, loneliest
1 If you feel lonely, like Mr Hoppy, you feel sad because you are on your own.
Mr Hoppy . . . lived alone. He had always been a lonely man and now that he was retired from work he was more lonely than ever. — ESIO TROT
2 A lonely place is far away from people and houses.
To my right, going away into the blackness of the countryside, lay the lonely road that led to the dangerous wood. — DANNY THE CHAMPION OF THE WORLD

look verb looks, looking, looked
When you look at something, you use your eyes to see it. Try using these words in your writing to describe exactly *how* your characters are looking.

TO LOOK QUICKLY: glance, glimpse, peek, peep
*The Queen, sitting up in her bed with **The Times** on her lap, glanced up sharply.* — THE BFG

TO LOOK CAREFULLY OR INTENTLY: examine, gape, gaze, inspect, peer, stare, study
Aunt Sponge and Aunt Spiker began walking slowly round the peach, inspecting it very cautiously from all sides. — JAMES AND THE GIANT PEACH

TO LOOK ANGRILY: frown, glare, glower, scowl
The brilliant snake's eyes that were set so deep in that dreadful rotting worm-eaten face glared unblinkingly at the witches who sat facing her. — THE WITCHES

look noun looks
1 a look is the act of looking at something
'Take a look at your stick, you old goat, and see how much you've shrunk in comparison!' — THE TWITS
2 the look of someone or something is their appearance
Grandma didn't even hear him. The frozen pop-eyed look was back with her again now. She was miles away in another world. — GEORGE'S MARVELLOUS MEDICINE

look–see noun (informal) look–sees
a large-scale search or hunt for something, such as a search to find a real giant
'You would be scuddling around yodelling the news that you were actually SEEING a giant, and then a great giant-hunt, a mighty giant look-see, would be starting up all over the world.' — THE BFG

Loompaland (CHARLIE AND THE CHOCOLATE FACTORY)
Loompaland is the place where the Oompa-Loompas come from. It is a country full of dense jungles and dangerous beasts, such as **snozzwangers** and **hornswogglers**.

loop noun loops

a ring made in a piece of string or rope

'How on earth do you propose to get a loop of string round a seagull's neck? I suppose you're going to fly up there yourself and catch it!' – JAMES AND THE GIANT PEACH

RINGBELLING RHYMES Try rhyming with *telescoop*.

loopy adjective (*informal*) loopier, loopiest

If someone is loopy or has loopy ideas, they are mad or crazy.

'You must be loopy, Shanks,' declared the President. 'You're dotty as a doughnut!' – CHARLIE AND THE GREAT GLASS ELEVATOR

LOOK IT UP! For other ways to describe someone as loopy, see **mad**.

loose adjective looser, loosest

1 Something that is loose is not fixed firmly in place.

Crunch crunch crunch went the footsteps. It sounded as though a giant was walking on loose gravel. – BOY

2 If you cut or let something loose, you cut or set it free.

'All we'll have to do is to cut loose a few seagulls . . . Then down we shall go, slowly and gently, until we reach the ground.' – JAMES AND THE GIANT PEACH

lope verb lopes, loping, loped

If you lope, you walk with a long bounding stride.

The keeper came loping softly down the track with the dog padding quick and soft-footed at his heel. – DANNY THE CHAMPION OF THE WORLD

lose verb loses, losing, lost

If you lose something that belongs to you, you cannot find it.

'Could I please bring back here in the bellypoppers all my collection of dreams? They is taking me years and years to collect and I is not wanting to lose them.' – THE BFG

DON'T BE BIFFSQUIGGLED! Be careful not to muddle up the spelling of **lose**, which rhymes with *choose*, and **loose**, which rhymes with *goose* and means the opposite of 'tight'.

lost adjective

If you are lost, you do not know where you are or where you should go.

Mr Wonka was rushing along in front . . . and Grandpa Joe was saying, 'Keep a good hold of my hand, Charlie. It would be terrible to get lost in here.' – CHARLIE AND THE CHOCOLATE FACTORY

lot noun lots

A lot or lots of something means a large number or a large amount of it.

You can play a lot of tricks with a glass eye because you can take it out and pop it back in again any time you like. – THE TWITS

lotion noun lotions

a creamy liquid for putting on your skin or hair

Mr Wormwood kept his hair looking bright and strong . . .

by rubbing into it every morning large quantities of a lotion called OIL OF VIOLETS HAIR TONIC. – MATILDA

RINGBELLING RHYMES Try rhyming with *magic potion*.

loud adjective louder, loudest

1 Something that is loud makes a lot of noise.

Suddenly there was an especially loud crunch above their heads and the sharp end of a shovel came right through the ceiling. – FANTASTIC MR FOX

2 If you say something out loud, you say it so that other people can hear.

Very slowly and stumbling a little over the strange words, Mrs Silver read the whole message out loud in tortoise language. – ESIO TROT

3 A loud colour is bright or gaudy.

In came Mr Wormwood in a loud check suit and a yellow tie. The appalling broad orange-and-green check of the jacket and trousers almost blinded the onlooker. – MATILDA

loudspeaker noun loudspeakers

a device to broadcast messages to crowds or over a long distance

The loudspeaker began to crackle. 'Hello!' it said. 'Hello hello hello! Are you receiving me, Space Control in Houston?' – CHARLIE AND THE GREAT GLASS ELEVATOR

lousy adjective (*informal*) lousier, lousiest

very poor or very bad

'Where to?' 'Spain,' the father said. 'It's a better climate than this lousy country.' – MATILDA

love noun

the strong feeling you have when you like someone very much

Mrs Silver was a widow who also lived alone. And although she didn't know it, it was she who was the object of Mr Hoppy's secret love. – ESIO TROT

love verb loves, loving, loved
If you love someone or something, you like them a lot.
Mr Twit wasn't going to wait another week for his Bird Pie supper. He loved Bird Pie. It was his favourite meal.
—THE TWITS

lovely adjective lovelier, loveliest
Something that is lovely is beautiful or very nice. A lovely person is always nice and kind.
You can have a wonky nose and a crooked mouth . . . but if you have good thoughts they will shine out of your face like sunbeams and you will always look lovely.—THE TWITS

lower verb lowers, lowering, lowered
If you lower something, you turn or move it to a lower level.
Mr Hoppy . . . pushed the hand-lever so that the claws opened wide. Then he lowered the two claws neatly over Alfie's shell and pulled the lever.—ESIO TROT

loyal adjective
If you are loyal to someone, you always help them and support them.
'I don't know what you're talking about,' the King said, growing testy. 'It's hardly a joking matter when one's loyal subjects are being eaten like popcorn.'—THE BFG

luck noun
Luck is when something happens by chance, without anyone planning it.
'What a load of luck!' cried Mr Wonka. 'We've landed ourselves slap in the middle of the biggest space operation of all time!'—CHARLIE AND THE GREAT GLASS ELEVATOR

lucky adjective luckier, luckiest
If you are lucky, something good happens that you have not planned, such as finding a Golden Ticket, or a beetle in a stick of celery (if you like that kind of thing).
The old hag grinned, showing those pale brown teeth. 'Sometimes, if you're lucky,' she said, 'you get a beetle inside the stem of a stick of celery. That's what I like.'
—GEORGE'S MARVELLOUS MEDICINE

luctuous adjective
A luctuous place is rich and fertile and produces good things to eat (like juicy **chiddlers**).
'England is a luctuous land and we is fancying a few nice little English chiddlers.'—THE BFG
DID YOU KNOW? To make the word *luctuous*, Roald Dahl may have joined together *luscious*, meaning 'delicious', and *sumptuous*, which means 'luxurious'. (He could have said *lumptuous*, but that sounds like lumpy, which is not so good.) The beginning also makes you think of *lucky*, as you would be lucky to live in a luctuous land.

luminous adjective
Luminous things glow in the dark so that you can see them. Willy Wonka makes luminous lollies for eating at night.
Charlie started reading some of the labels alongside the buttons . . . EXPLODING SWEETS FOR YOUR ENEMIES./ LUMINOUS LOLLIES FOR EATING IN BED AT NIGHT.
—CHARLIE AND THE CHOCOLATE FACTORY

lump noun lumps
1 A lump of something is a piece of it, like the lumps of flesh the Fleshlumpeater chews.
They passed the greengrocer with his window full of apples and oranges, and the butcher with bloody lumps of meat on display and naked chickens hanging up.—MATILDA
2 a hard bump or swelling on your skin
Cried the Knid, 'What on earth am I going to do/With this painful preposterous lump?/I can't remain standing the whole summer through!/And I cannot sit down on my rump!'—CHARLIE AND THE GREAT GLASS ELEVATOR

lunch noun lunches
a meal that you eat in the middle of the day
For instance, if you were to say,/'Oh Mirror, what's for lunch today?'/The thing would answer in a trice,/'Today it's scrambled eggs and rice.'—REVOLTING RHYMES
RINGBELLING RHYMES Try rhyming with *crunch* or *munch*.

lunge verb lunges, lunging, lunged
If you lunge, you make a sudden movement forwards.
The Trunchbull . . . lunged forward and grabbed hold of Amanda's pigtails in her right fist and lifted the girl clear off the ground.—MATILDA

lurch noun lurches
If something gives a lurch, it staggers or leans over suddenly.
Rockets started firing out of the Elevator from all sides. It tilted and gave a sickening lurch and then plunged downward into the Earth's atmosphere at a simply colossal speed.—CHARLIE AND THE GREAT GLASS ELEVATOR

luscious adjective
Something luscious is rich and juicy and utterly delicious.
'The whole floor of the forest is carpeted with wild strawberries, every one of them luscious and red and juicy-ripe.'—THE MINPINS
RINGBELLING RHYMES Try rhyming with *mushious*.

Mm

Matilda

maggotwise   marshmallow   marvellous

midgy   mispise   murderful

machine noun machines

A machine is a piece of equipment with an engine and moving parts that work together. Willy Wonka's factory is full of machines that produce **splendiferous** sweets, such as the Great Gum Machine.

Mr Wonka led the party over to a gigantic machine that stood in the very centre of the Inventing Room. It was a mountain of gleaming metal that towered high above the children and their parents. — CHARLIE AND THE CHOCOLATE FACTORY

mackerel noun mackerel

A mackerel is a type of sea fish with a greenish-blue skin. It is very rude to call someone a mackerel, which is why Charlie's Grandma Georgina likes saying it.

'You miserable old mackerel!' said Grandma Georgina, sailing past him. 'Just when we start having a bit of fun, you want to stop it!' — CHARLIE AND THE GREAT GLASS ELEVATOR

LOOK IT UP! Some other insults used by grandmothers are **maggot** and **worm**.

mad adjective madder, maddest

1 Someone who is mad has something wrong with their mind.

'Wait!' she screamed. 'We must be mad! We can't go to a famous party in the White House in our nightshirts!' — CHARLIE AND THE GREAT GLASS ELEVATOR

SPARKY SYNONYMS You can also say **cockles** or **quacky**.

2 If you do something like mad, you do it with a lot of energy or enthusiasm.

Mr Twit was plotting away like mad. He was trying to think up a really nasty trick he could play on his wife that day. — THE TWITS

Gobblefunking with words

When you describe something by comparing it to something else, for example *as cold as ice* or *as hard as nails*, you are using a *simile*. Roald Dahl loved making up similes, especially ones that use **alliteration**, and there are lots of examples in his stories. Here are some similes he used to describe a character as *mad*:

*as **b**atty as a **b**ullfrog*
*as **c**razy as a **c**rumpet*
*as **d**otty as a **d**oughnut*
*as **p**otty as a **p**ilchard*
*as qua**ck**y as a du**ck**hound*

magazine noun magazines

A magazine is a collection of stories or news articles that is published every week or month. Matilda learns to read by looking at old magazines and newspapers.

By the time she was three, Matilda had taught herself to read by studying newspapers and magazines that lay around the house. — MATILDA

a b c d e f g h i j k l m n o p q r s t u v w x y z

maggot noun **maggots**
A maggot is the larva of some kinds of fly. George's grandma calls him a maggot as an insult.
'You're a nasty little maggot!' the voice screeched back. 'You're a lazy and disobedient little worm, and you're growing too fast.' — GEORGE'S MARVELLOUS MEDICINE
LOOK IT UP! For other ways to insult people, see **insult**.

maggotwise adjective
Something that looks or tastes maggotwise is rotten and disgusting, like a **snozzcumber**.
'It's disgusterous!' the BFG gurgled. 'It's sickable! It's rotsome! It's maggotwise! Try it yourself, this foulsome snozzcumber!' — THE BFG
SPARKY SYNONYMS You can also say **rotsome**.

> **Gobblefunking with words**
> The suffix -*wise* is an old word meaning 'manner' or 'way'. We still use it with this meaning in words like *otherwise* and *likewise*. You can make up your own words with this ending too, like *gloopwise* ('in the manner of gloop') or *gunkwise*.

magic noun
In stories, magic is the power that some people have to make impossible and wonderful things happen.
Several more times during the night the travellers caught glimpses of Cloud-Men moving around on the tops of these clouds, working their sinister magic upon the world below. — JAMES AND THE GIANT PEACH

magical adjective
If something is magical, it has the power to make impossible and wonderful things happen.
'Your Grace,' the Giraffe said, giving the Duke a small superior smile, 'there are no windows in the world I cannot reach with this magical neck of mine.'
— THE GIRAFFE AND THE PELLY AND ME

Magic Finger (THE MAGIC FINGER)
The Magic Finger has special powers that develop when the girl in the story gets angry, especially at her silly neighbours, the Greggs, who kill animals for fun.

magician noun **magicians**
a person who has magical, or seemingly magical, powers
'Clever!' cried the old man. 'He's more than that! He's a magician with chocolate! He can make anything — anything he wants!' — CHARLIE AND THE CHOCOLATE FACTORY

magnet noun **magnets**
a piece of metal that can attract iron or steel and that points north and south when it is hung in the air
Almost without knowing what he was doing, as though drawn by some powerful magnet, James Henry Trotter started walking slowly towards the giant peach. — JAMES AND THE GIANT PEACH

magnificent adjective
Something that is magnificent is very good or beautiful.
Then one day, a truly magnificent bird flew down out of the sky and landed on the monkey cage. 'Good heavens!' cried all the monkeys together. 'It's the Roly-Poly Bird!' — THE TWITS
SPARKY SYNONYMS You can also say **splendiferous**.

magnifying-glass noun **magnifying-glasses**
a hand-held lens which makes things look bigger
Bruno Jenkins was focusing the sun through his magnifying-glass and roasting the ants one by one. 'I like watching them burn,' he said. — THE WITCHES
LOOK IT UP! You can also magnify things with **biriculers** and **telescoops**.

Maidmasher (THE BFG)
The Maidmasher is one of the not-so-friendly giants in Giant Country. The Maidmasher loves eating human children, especially little girls.
DID YOU KNOW? *Maid* is an old word meaning 'girl', so a *Maidmasher* literally mashes up girls. Roald Dahl may have used the name *maidmasher* because of the **alliteration**. You could make up your own alliterative names for unfriendly giants, like *Maidmincer* or *Girlgrinder*.
LOOK IT UP! Some other man-gobbling giants are **Bloodbottler** and **Butcher Boy**.

majester noun **majesters**
The BFG calls the Queen *Your Majester*.
'I has great secrets to tell Your Majester,' the BFG said. 'I should be delighted to hear them,' the Queen said. 'But not in my dressing-gown.' — THE BFG

male adjective
A male person or animal produces young by fertilizing the female's egg cells. All giants are male, but there are no male witches.
*'But the fact remains that all witches **are** women. There is no such thing as a male witch.'* – THE WITCHES

malevolent adjective
A malevolent creature wishes to harm you (and might give you an evil look with its malevolent eye).
A simply colossal Vermicious Knid . . . was no more than a dozen yards away, egg-shaped, slimy, greenish-brown, with one malevolent red eye. – CHARLIE AND THE GREAT GLASS ELEVATOR

malice (*rhymes with* palace) noun
Malice is a wish to harm other people.
Yet the Reverend Lee was too nice and gentle a man for anyone to bear any deep malice towards him. – THE VICAR OF NIBBLESWICKE

malicious adjective
Someone who is malicious, or who has malicious thoughts, means to do you harm.
'You are a vile, repulsive, repellent, malicious little brute!' the Trunchbull was shouting. 'You are not fit to be in this school!' – MATILDA

mamba noun **mambas**
a venomous snake found in Africa
If a black mamba bit you, you died within the hour writhing in agony and foaming at the mouth. I couldn't wait. – BOY

mammal noun **mammals**
A mammal is an animal that gives birth to live babies and feeds its young with its own milk. Cats, dogs, whales, lions and people are all mammals, as is Fantastic Mr Fox and the Geraneous Giraffe.

man-eating or **man-gobbling** adjective
A man-eating giant or creature likes to eat **human beans** (both adults and **chiddlers**).
Tourists from all over the globe came flocking to gaze down in wonder at the nine horrendous man-eating giants in the great pit. – THE BFG

Manhugger (THE BFG)
The Manhugger is one of the not-so-friendly giants in Giant Country. The Manhugger is not as cuddly as he sounds. His name suggests he crushes his victims before he eats them, rather like a python.
LOOK IT UP! Some other man-gobbling giants are **Childchewer** and **Meatdripper**.

maniac noun **maniacs**
a person who acts in a violent and wild way
The tall skinny Bean and dwarfish pot-bellied Bunce were driving their machines like maniacs, racing the motors and making the shovels dig at a terrific speed. – FANTASTIC MR FOX

manners
plural noun
Your manners are the ways in which you behave when you are talking to people or eating your food. Mr Twit has terrible table manners.

'What an impudent fellow Rat is.' 'He has bad manners,' Badger said. 'All rats have bad manners. I've never met a polite rat yet.' – FANTASTIC MR FOX

manoeuvre verb **manoeuvres, manoeuvring, manoeuvred**
When you manoeuvre, you steer a vehicle, such as a bicycle or a flying elevator, carefully and skilfully.
'To your buttons, Charlie! You've got to help me manoeuvre! We're going right over the top of the Transport Capsule and then we'll try to hook on to it somewhere and get a firm hold!' – CHARLIE AND THE GREAT GLASS ELEVATOR

manticore noun **manticores**
The manticore is a legendary creature with the body of a lion, a human head, sharp teeth and bat-like wings. The hoof of a manticore is a vital ingredient in Wonka-Vite.
'Look out!' they cried. 'It's a Dragon!' 'It's not a Dragon! It's a Wampus!' 'It's a Gorgon!' 'It's a Sea-serpent!' 'It's a Prock!' 'It's a Manticore!' – JAMES AND THE GIANT PEACH
DID YOU KNOW? The name *manticore* comes from an old Persian word meaning 'man-eater'. Manticores have featured in stories and paintings for hundreds of years.

map noun **maps**
a drawing of a town, a country or the world
'Where is this place?' the Air Force man said to the BFG. 'I presume you can pinpoint it on the map?' 'Pinpoint?' said the BFG. 'Map? I is never hearing these words before.' – THE BFG

a
b
c
d
e
f
g
h
i
j
k
l
m
n
o
p
q
r
s
t
u
v
w
x
y
z

Another word that means 'man-eating' is *anthropophagous*.

marble noun marbles
Marbles are small glass balls that you use to play games with.
A large green marble dropped . . . into a basket on the floor. At least it looked like a marble. 'Everlasting Gobstoppers!' cried Mr Wonka proudly. — CHARLIE AND THE CHOCOLATE FACTORY

march verb marches, marching, marched
When you march, you walk with regular steps like a soldier.
A moment later, Mr and Mrs Twit came marching into the garden, each carrying a fearsome-looking gun. — THE TWITS

march noun marches
a piece of music you can march to
The Old-Green-Grasshopper started to play the Funeral March on his violin, and by the time he had finished, everyone, including himself, was in a flood of tears. — JAMES AND THE GIANT PEACH

margarine noun
Margarine is a food that looks and tastes like butter, but is made from vegetable oils. Charlie's family can only afford bread and margarine for breakfast.
The only meals they could afford were bread and margarine for breakfast, boiled potatoes and cabbage for lunch, and cabbage soup for supper. — CHARLIE AND THE CHOCOLATE FACTORY

marmalade noun
jam made from oranges or lemons
'Do calm down, my dear,' Mrs Kranky said from the other end of the table. 'And stop putting marmalade on your cornflakes.' — GEORGE'S MARVELLOUS MEDICINE

marry verb marries, marrying, married
When you marry someone, you become their husband or wife, like Mr and Mrs Twit. When you ask someone to marry you, you *propose* to them.
'Mrs Silver, please will you marry me?' 'Why, Mr Hoppy!' she cried. 'I didn't think you'd ever get round to asking me! Of course I'll marry you!'* — ESIO TROT

marsh noun marshes
a low-lying area of very wet ground, sometimes inhabited by **grobes**

marshmallow noun marshmallows
A marshmallow is a soft spongy sweet. Willy Wonka makes edible pillows made of marshmallow.
Mr Willy Wonka can make marshmallows that taste of violets . . . and little feathery sweets that melt away deliciously the moment you put them between your lips. — CHARLIE AND THE CHOCOLATE FACTORY

marvellous adjective
Something that is marvellous is wonderful and exciting.
Soon the marvellous mixture began to froth and foam. A rich blue smoke, the colour of peacocks, rose from the surface of the liquid. — GEORGE'S MARVELLOUS MEDICINE
SPARKY SYNONYMS You can also say **fantabulous**, **gloriumptious** or **wondercrump**. An opposite is **horrigust**.

Matilda Wormwood (MATILDA)

Matilda Wormwood is a five-year-old girl genius who loves reading books (including, of course, dictionaries). She is ignored by her dim-witted parents, but uses her **telekinetic** powers to get revenge on them and on her cruel headmistress, Miss Trunchbull.

DID YOU KNOW? The name *Matilda* means 'mighty in battle'. The names *Matilda* and *Honey* were also given to types of tank used in North Africa in World War II, at the time that Roald Dahl was an RAF pilot there.

mask noun masks
You wear a mask over your face to hide it or protect it. The Grand High Witch wears a face mask so that no one will recognize her and start to scream.
I saw The Grand High Witch herself reach for her face-mask and put it on over that revolting face of hers. It was astonishing how that mask transformed her. — THE WITCHES

mass noun masses
a large amount of something, or a large number of things
The moon had long since disappeared but the sky was clear and a great mass of stars was wheeling above my head. — DANNY THE CHAMPION OF THE WORLD

massive adjective
Something that is massive is very big.
The giant peach, with the sunlight glinting on its side, was like a massive golden ball sailing upon a silver sea. — JAMES AND THE GIANT PEACH
SPARKY SYNONYMS You can also say **gigantuous** or **whunking**. An opposite is **midgy**.

mast noun masts
a tall pole that holds up a ship's sails
James . . . pointed to the peach stem, which was standing up like a short thick mast in the middle of the deck. — JAMES AND THE GIANT PEACH

match noun matches
a small, thin stick that makes a flame when you rub it against something rough
I got out of my bunk and found a box of matches by the sink. I struck one and held it up to the funny old clock that hung on the wall. — DANNY THE CHAMPION OF THE WORLD

mattress noun mattresses
A mattress is the soft part of a bed that you lie on. Charlie and his parents sleep on mattresses as they only have one bed in the house, which his grandparents use.
'You think it's funny?' she cried. 'Well just you wait, Doctor Spencer, and one night I'll put a few snakes or crocodiles or something under your mattress and see how you like it!' — DANNY THE CHAMPION OF THE WORLD

mayor noun mayors
A mayor is the person in charge of the council of a town or city. A woman who is a mayor can also be called a **mayoress**.
Once more, the Queen lifted the receiver. 'Get me the Lord Mayor of Baghdad,' she said. 'If they don't have a Lord Mayor, get me the next best thing.' — THE BFG

maze noun mazes
a set of lines or paths that twist and turn so much that it is very easy to lose your way
The ground floor of the hotel was a maze of public rooms, all of them named in gold letters on the doors. — THE WITCHES

meadow noun meadows
A meadow is a field of grass and flowers. There are meadows made out of mint-flavoured sugar in Willy Wonka's chocolate factory.
'And do you like my meadows? Do you like my grass and my buttercups? The grass you are standing on, my dear little ones, is made of a new kind of soft, minty sugar that I've just invented!' — CHARLIE AND THE CHOCOLATE FACTORY

a b c d e f g h i j k l **m** n o p q r s t u v w x y z

Mattress comes from an Arabic word that means 'place where something is thrown'.

mean adjective **meaner, meanest**
A mean person is unkind and does not like sharing things.
They were rich men. They were also nasty men. All three of them were about as nasty and mean as any men you could meet.—FANTASTIC MR FOX
SPARKY SYNONYMS A word for a mean and nasty person is a **rotrasper**.
LOOK IT UP! For more words for mean people, see **bad**.

meaning noun **meanings**
The meaning of something is an explanation of what it is all about. You can find the meanings of words by looking them up in a dictionary (as you are doing). The BFG thinks that meanings are unimportant, so perhaps he doesn't use a dictionary very often.
'I'm not sure I quite know what that means,' Sophie said. 'Meanings is not important,' said the BFG. 'I cannot be right all the time. Quite often I is left instead of right.'—THE BFG

meat noun
the flesh of animals that is cooked and eaten as food
Mr Twit was furious . . . 'Boy Pie might be better than Bird Pie,' he went on, grinning horribly. 'More meat and not so many tiny little bones!'—THE TWITS

Meatdripper or **Meatdripping Giant** (THE BFG)
The Meatdripper is one of the not-so-friendly giants in Giant Country. The Meatdripper hunts **human beans** by disguising himself as a tree and luring them to picnic under the branches. Then he eats them.
LOOK IT UP! Some other man-gobbling giants are **Gizzardgulper** and **Maidmasher**.

mechanical adjective
Something that is mechanical has parts that move like a machine.
'What we need on this job,' he said, 'is machines . . . mechanical shovels. We'll have him out in five minutes with mechanical shovels.'—FANTASTIC MR FOX

medal noun **medals**
a piece of metal shaped like a coin, star or cross, given to someone who has won a competition or done something brave
'Her Majesty will be very pleased with me,' the Head of the Army said. 'I shall probably get a medal.'—THE BFG

medicine noun **medicines**
a special liquid or tablet that you take when you are ill to make you better
'I shall make her a new medicine, one that is so strong and so fierce and so fantastic it will either cure her completely or blow off the top of her head.'—GEORGE'S MARVELLOUS MEDICINE

melt verb **melts, melting, melted**
When something like chocolate or ice cream melts, it becomes liquid because it has become warm. The base ingredient in Wonka-Vite is a ton of melted chocolate.
Place chocolate in very large cauldron and melt over red-hot furnace. When melted, lower the heat slightly so as not to burn the chocolate, but keep it boiling.—CHARLIE AND THE GREAT GLASS ELEVATOR

member noun **members**
someone who belongs to a club or group
The Old-Green-Grasshopper became a member of the New York Symphony Orchestra, where his playing was greatly admired.—JAMES AND THE GIANT PEACH

memory noun **memories**
1 Your memory is your ability to remember things.
2 A memory is something that you can remember.
My father paused, and there was a gleam of pride in his eyes as he dwelt for a moment upon the memory of his own dad, the great poaching inventor.—DANNY THE CHAMPION OF THE WORLD

menacing adjective
A menacing person looks dangerous, as if they are going to hurt you.
Matilda and Lavender glanced round and saw the gigantic figure of Miss Trunchbull advancing through the crowd of boys and girls with menacing strides.—MATILDA

mercy noun
If you show mercy to someone, you are kind and do not punish them.
'Save me!' screamed the Fleshlumpeater. 'Have mercy on this poor little giant! The beanstalk! He is coming at me with his terrible spiksticking beanstalk!'—THE BFG

mesmerize verb **mesmerizes, mesmerizing, mesmerized**
If something mesmerizes you, it holds your attention completely so that you can't look away.
There are times when something is so frightful you become mesmerized by it and can't look away. I was like that now.—THE WITCHES
DID YOU KNOW? The word *mesmerize* is named after an 18th-century German doctor, Franz Anton Mesmer, who developed an early type of hypnosis.

mess noun
If something is a mess, like your room or your hair, it is very untidy.
Everyone jumped, including Mr Wormwood. 'What the heck's the matter with you, woman?' he shouted. 'Look at the mess you've made on the carpet!'—MATILDA

message noun **messages**
a question or piece of information that one person sends to another
A MESSAGE to Children Who Have Read This Book: When you grow up and have children of your own do please remember something important: a stodgy parent is no fun at all.—DANNY THE CHAMPION OF THE WORLD

messy adjective **messier, messiest**
Something messy is very untidy, like Mr Twit's facial hair.

metal noun **metals**
a hard substance that melts when it is heated, such as gold, silver, copper or iron
There was an aura of menace about her even at a distance, and when she came up close you could almost feel the dangerous heat radiating from her as from a red-hot rod of metal. — MATILDA

metamorphosis noun **metamorphoses**
Metamorphosis happens when a caterpillar turns into a butterfly, or when a boy who has taken Mouse-Maker Formula turns into a mouse. The Magic Finger can also make people **metamorphose** into other creatures.

method noun **methods**
A method is the way in which you do something. Danny's father tells him his Secret Methods for catching pheasants.
'So that's Method Number One,' he said. 'What's Number Two?' I asked. 'Ah,' he said. 'Number Two's a real beauty. It's a flash of pure brilliance.' — DANNY THE CHAMPION OF THE WORLD

micies plural noun
The BFG says *micies* instead of *mice* as the plural of **mouse**.
'From now on, we is keeping as still as winky little micies,' he whispered. — THE BFG

microphone noun **microphones**
a device that you speak into when you want to record your voice or make it sound louder
The President said a very rude word into the microphone and ten million children across the nation began repeating it gleefully and got smacked by their parents. — CHARLIE AND THE GREAT GLASS ELEVATOR

middle noun
The middle of something is the place or part that is at the same distance from all its sides or edges.
'Good heavens!' he said. 'I know what this is! I've come to the stone in the middle of the peach!' — JAMES AND THE GIANT PEACH

middle adjective
placed in the middle
There was a big hole in the floor and another in the ceiling, and sticking up like a post between the two was the middle part of Grandma. — GEORGE'S MARVELLOUS MEDICINE

mideous adjective
A mideous place is horrible and nasty (but **grobes** still love living there).
'In the quelchy quaggy sogmire,/In the mashy mideous harshland,/At the witchy hour of gloomness,/All the grobes come oozing home.' — CHARLIE AND THE GREAT GLASS ELEVATOR

> **Gobblefunking with words**
> To make the phrase *mideous harshland*, Roald Dahl swapped around the first two letters of *hideous marshland*. Roald Dahl loved this type of word play, which is called a *spoonerism*, and you can find lots of examples in his books. The BFG says *catasterous disastrophe* (for *disastrous catastrophe*), *jipping* and *skumping* (for *skipping* and *jumping*) and tells Sophie that *Nicholas Nickleby* is written by *Dahl's Chickens* (not Charles Dickens). The word *spoonerism* is named after a real person, William Spooner, who sometimes made mistakes like these.

midget noun **midgets**
A midget is someone who is unusually short. The other giants (who are very rude) call the BFG a midget, as he is so much shorter than they are.
'Ruddy little runt!' they shouted. 'Troggy little twit! Shrivelly little shrimp! Mucky little midget!' — THE BFG

An old name for a group of mice is a *mischief of mice*.

a b c d e f g h i j k l **m** n o p q r s t u v w x y z

midgy adjective **midgier, midgiest**
Something that is midgy is really small and tiny. **Human beans** look midgy to giants like the Fleshlumpeater.
'Then I is guzzling ten or twenty more of you midgy little maggots down there! You is not getting away from me.'
— THE BFG

DID YOU KNOW? The word *midgy* may be a blend of *midget* and either *tiny* or *titchy*. It could also mean 'like a midge', which is a tiny biting insect. Midges are called *midgies* in some dialects, so a very small midge would be a *midgy midgie*.

SPARKY SYNONYMS You can also say **snitchy** or **titchy**.

mightily adverb
If you do something mightily, you do it with a lot of energy or effort.
Right beneath the mountain, the Giant stopped. He was puffing mightily. His great chest was heaving in and out.
— THE BFG

mighty adjective **mightier, mightiest**
very strong or powerful
The Trunchbull, this mighty female giant, stood there in her green breeches, quivering like a blancmange. — MATILDA

Mike Teavee (CHARLIE AND THE CHOCOLATE FACTORY)
Mike Teavee is a boy who watches lots and lots of television (as his name suggests), especially shows about gangsters. He is the fourth child to find a Golden Ticket.

mild adjective **milder, mildest**
1 Something that is mild is not very strong. A mild person, like Miss Honey, has a gentle temper and does not get angry. Miss Trunchbull is not a mild person.
Miss Jennifer Honey was a mild and quiet person who never raised her voice and was seldom seen to smile.
— MATILDA
2 Mild weather is quite warm.

mile noun **miles**
a measure of distance, equal to 1,760 yards or about 1.6 kilometres
In his study two hundred and forty miles below, the President turned white as the White House. 'Jumping jack-rabbits!' he cried. — CHARLIE AND THE GREAT GLASS ELEVATOR

military adjective
Military people are part of the armed forces. The BFG calls them **bootbogglers**.
'Of course they're guns!' shouted the Head of the Army. 'I am a military man and I know a gun when I hear one!'
— THE BFG

milk noun
Milk is a white liquid that female mammals produce in their bodies to feed to their young. In Willy Wonka's factory, there are cows that produce chocolate milk.
COWS THAT GIVE CHOCOLATE MILK, it said on the next door. 'Ah, my pretty little cows!' cried Mr Wonka. 'How I love those cows!' — CHARLIE AND THE CHOCOLATE FACTORY

milky adjective **milkier, milkiest**
If something is milky, it looks pale and white like milk.
The great yellow wasteland lay dim and milky in the moonlight as the Big Friendly Giant went galloping across it. — THE BFG

million noun **millions**
A million is the number 1,000,000. Veruca Salt's father buys half a million chocolate bars to make sure she finds a Golden Ticket.
'To the planet Vermes,' gasped Grandma Josephine. 'Eighteen thousand four hundred and twenty-seven million miles from here!'—CHARLIE AND THE GREAT GLASS ELEVATOR
LOOK IT UP! Another very large number is a **dillion**.

millionaire noun **millionaires**
an extremely rich person who has at least a million pounds or dollars
'Your Aunt Spiker and I are about to become millionaires, and the last thing we want is the likes of you messing things up and getting in the way.'—JAMES AND THE GIANT PEACH

mince noun
meat that has been cut into very small pieces
mince verb **minces, mincing, minced**
To mince meat is to cut it into very small pieces. The BFG uses the phrase *mince my maggots!* when he is annoyed.
'Oh no!' he cried. 'Oh mince my maggots! Oh swipe my swoggles! . . . It's a trogglehumper!'—THE BFG

mine noun **mines**
a place where people work to dig coal, metal or stones out of the ground
'We are probably at the bottom of a coal mine,' the Earthworm said gloomily. 'We certainly went down and down and down very suddenly at the last moment.'—JAMES AND THE GIANT PEACH

Minpin noun **Minpins**
The Minpins are tiny people who live in the high branches of trees in the forest to avoid being eaten by the terrifying Gruncher.
The old Minpin said, 'All the trees in this forest are hollow. Not just this one, but all of them. And inside them thousands and thousands of Minpins are living.'—THE MINPINS

mint noun **mints**
1 a green plant that is added to food and sweets to give flavour
All the most wonderful smells in the world seemed to be mixed up in the air around them — the smell of roasting coffee and burnt sugar and melting chocolate and mint.—CHARLIE AND THE CHOCOLATE FACTORY
2 a sweet that tastes of mint

mintick noun **minticks**
a minute
'Now hang on a mintick,' the BFG said. 'How is I possibly going to get near enough to the Queen of England's bedroom to blow in my dream?'—THE BFG
DID YOU KNOW? The word *mintick* is a mixture of *minute* and *tick*, so it makes you think of a clock ticking away the minutes. Instead of saying *just a tick*, you could say *just a mintick!*

Mint Jujube noun **Mint Jujubes**
a type of sweet invented by Willy Wonka that turns your teeth green
There was a whole lot of splendid stuff from the great Wonka factory itself, for example . . . Mint Jujubes that will give the boy next door green teeth for a month.—THE GIRAFFE AND THE PELLY AND ME
DID YOU KNOW? A *jujube* is an old-fashioned type of cough sweet, originally made from the fruit of the **ju-jube tree**.
LOOK IT UP! Some other sweets invented by Willy Wonka are **Rainbow Drops** and **Wriggle-Sweets**.

Minus noun **Minuses**
A Minus is someone who is less than zero years old. If you take too much Wonka-Vite, you might become so young that you end up less than zero and living in Minusland.
'I don't want to be a Minus!' croaked Grandma Georgina. 'If I ever have to go back to that beastly Minusland again, the Gnoolies will knickle me!'—CHARLIE AND THE GREAT GLASS ELEVATOR

minus preposition
less than zero
'Subtract eighty from seventy-eight and what do you get?' 'Minus two'! said Charlie. 'Hooray!' said Mr Bucket. 'My mother-in-law's minus two years old!'—CHARLIE AND THE GREAT GLASS ELEVATOR

Minusland (CHARLIE AND THE GREAT GLASS ELEVATOR)
Minusland is a gloomy place filled with fog under the surface of the Earth. It is inhabited by invisible creatures called Gnoolies who bite their victims and turn them into Gnoolies too.

minute noun **minutes**
There are sixty seconds in one minute, and sixty minutes in one hour.
In less than a minute, the hen had shrunk so much it was no bigger than a new-hatched chick. It looked ridiculous.—GEORGE'S MARVELLOUS MEDICINE

minute (*rhymes with* newt) adjective
Something that is minute is very small, like a Minpin.
SPARKY SYNONYMS You can also say **midgy**.

miracle noun **miracles**
a wonderful or magical happening that is unexpected
'Look at me,' he said softly. 'I'm walking! It's a miracle!' 'It's Wonka-Vite!' I said.—CHARLIE AND THE GREAT GLASS ELEVATOR

mirror noun **mirrors**
a piece of glass in which you can see yourself
Aunt Sponge had a long-handled mirror on her lap, and she kept picking it up and gazing at her own hideous face.—JAMES AND THE GIANT PEACH

mischief noun
If you get into mischief, you do things that grown-ups think are silly or naughty.
George's mother said to George on Saturday morning,

'So be a good boy and don't get up to mischief.' This was a silly thing to say to a small boy at any time. — GEORGE'S MARVELLOUS MEDICINE

mischievous adjective
A mischievous person enjoys getting into mischief, rather like the Oompa-Loompas.
'I expect you will hear a good deal of singing today from time to time. I must warn you, though, that they are rather mischievous. They like jokes.' — CHARLIE AND THE CHOCOLATE FACTORY

miserable adjective
If you are miserable, you are very unhappy.
'Marvellous things will start happening to you, fabulous, unbelievable things — and you will never be miserable again in your life. Because you are miserable, aren't you?' — JAMES AND THE GIANT PEACH

mispise verb mispises, mispising, mispised
If you mispise something (like a **snozzcumber**) it means you absolutely hate and despise it.
'Here is the repulsant snozzcumber!' cried the BFG, waving it about. 'I squoggle it! I mispise it! I dispunge it!' — THE BFG

DID YOU KNOW? Roald Dahl made up the word *mispise*, but it could easily be a real word. He started with the word *despise* and swapped the first three letters for a different prefix which means 'bad' or 'wrong', as in words like *mistake* and *mishap*.

SPARKY SYNONYMS You can also say **dispunge** or **squoggle**.

missing adjective
Something that is missing is lost.
'Mike,' cried Mrs Teavee, 'are you all right? Are there any bits of you missing?' — CHARLIE AND THE CHOCOLATE FACTORY

mist noun
When there is mist, there is a lot of cloud just above the ground, which makes it difficult to see.
A steamy mist was rising up now from the great warm chocolate river, and out of the mist there appeared suddenly a most fantastic pink boat. — CHARLIE AND THE CHOCOLATE FACTORY

mistake noun mistakes
If you make a mistake, you do something wrong.
'I is telling you once before,' he said quietly, 'that I is never having a chance to go to school. I is full of mistakes. They is not my fault. I do my best.' — THE BFG

mistaken adjective
If you are mistaken about something, you are incorrect or wrong.
'I must tell you, Headmistress,' she said, 'that you are completely mistaken about Matilda putting a stink-bomb under your desk.' 'I am never mistaken, Miss Honey!' — MATILDA

mix verb mixes, mixing, mixed
When you mix things together, you put them together and stir them.
Then a giant whizzer started whizzing round inside the enormous tub, mixing up all the different coloured liquids like an ice-cream soda. — CHARLIE AND THE CHOCOLATE FACTORY

mixture noun mixtures
something that is made of different things mixed together
I'll stir them up, I'll boil them long,/A mixture tough, a mixture strong./And then, heigh-ho, and down it goes,/A nice big spoonful (hold your nose). — GEORGE'S MARVELLOUS MEDICINE

moan verb moans, moaning, moaned
When you moan, you make a low sound because you are in pain. The BFG can hear trees moaning when he chops them with an axe.
'What sort of sound?' Sophie asked. 'A soft moaning sound,' the BFG said. 'It is like the sound an old man is making when he is dying slowly.' — THE BFG

modern adjective
Something that is modern is new and up to date, not old-fashioned.
It was a modern brick house that could not have been cheap to buy and the name on the gate

said COSY NOOK. Nosey cook might have been better, Miss Honey thought. — MATILDA

modest adjective
Someone who is modest does not boast about how good they are.
Then the Queen said, 'I think we ought to get this book printed properly and published.'... This was arranged, but because the BFG was a very modest giant he wouldn't put his own name on it. — THE BFG

mole noun moles
1 a small, furry animal that digs holes and tunnels under the ground
2 A mole is also a small dark spot on the skin. Both types of mole are needed to make Wonka-Vite.
RECIPE FOR MAKING WONKA-VITE... THE SNOUT OF A PROGHOPPER/A MOLE FROM A MOLE/THE HIDE (AND THE SEEK) OF A SPOTTED WHANGDOODLE. — CHARLIE AND THE GREAT GLASS ELEVATOR

molten adjective
Molten rock or metal has been made into liquid by great heat.
The Trunchbull stood motionless on the platform. Her great horsy face had turned the colour of molten lava and her eyes were glittering with fury. — MATILDA

monkey noun monkeys
A monkey is an animal with long arms, hands with thumbs, and a tail. Mr and Mrs Twit keep a family of ex-circus monkeys, the Muggle-Wumps, in their garden.
Today, although they were retired, Mr Twit still wanted to train monkeys. It was his dream that one day he would own the first GREAT UPSIDE DOWN MONKEY CIRCUS in the world. — THE TWITS

monster noun monsters
1 a huge frightening creature, like the Gruncher or the Spittler
He glanced round again, but the Thing, the Beast, the Monster, or whatever it was, was hidden from his sight by the smoke it shot out as it galloped forward. — THE MINPINS
2 a cruel or evil-minded person
Miss Trunchbull, the Headmistress, was something else altogether. She was a gigantic holy terror, a fierce tyrannical monster who frightened the life out of the pupils and teachers alike. — MATILDA

monstrous adjective
Something monstrous is huge and horrible, like a monster.
His face was like a monstrous ball of dough with two small greedy curranty eyes peering out upon the world. — CHARLIE AND THE CHOCOLATE FACTORY

moochel verb moochels, moocheling, moocheled
When giants moochel (or **footchel**), they laze around, as they tend to do during the day.
'What on earth are they doing?' Sophie asked. 'Nothing,' said the BFG. 'They is just moocheling and footcheling around and waiting for the night to come.' — THE BFG
DID YOU KNOW? Roald Dahl may have based the word

moochel on mooch about, which is what lazy **human beans** do during the day too.

moon noun
the natural satellite which orbits the Earth and shines in the sky at night
There used to be some rather nice creatures living on the moon a long time ago. They were called Poozas. But the Vermicious Knids ate the lot. — CHARLIE AND THE GREAT GLASS ELEVATOR

moonbeam noun moonbeams
a shaft of light from the moon
Sophie couldn't sleep. A brilliant moonbeam was slanting through a gap in the curtains. It was shining right on to her pillow. — THE BFG

moonlight noun
light from the moon
The giant peach swayed gently from side to side as it floated along, and the hundreds of silky white strings going upward from its stem were beautiful in the moonlight. — JAMES AND THE GIANT PEACH

a b c d e f g h i j k l **m** n o p q r s t u v w x y z

Look for characters called *Miss* under their surname, for example **Honey**.

morsel noun **morsels**
a small piece of food
Mr Twit never went really hungry. By sticking out his tongue and curling it sideways to explore the hairy jungle around his mouth, he was always able to find a tasty morsel here and there to nibble on. – THE TWITS

mosquito noun **mosquitoes**
A mosquito is a small insect that bites people and animals.
Miss Spider answered, sighing long and loud. 'I am not loved at all. And yet I do nothing but good. All day long I catch flies and mosquitoes in my webs.' – JAMES AND THE GIANT PEACH

mother noun **mothers**
your female parent
'I don't care,' Mrs Kranky said. 'I'm not leaving my own mother sticking up through the roof for the rest of her life.' – GEORGE'S MARVELLOUS MEDICINE

mouldy adjective **mouldier, mouldiest**
Mouldy food is food that has gone bad.
If you peered deep into the moustachy bristles . . . you would probably see . . . things that had been there for months and months, like a piece of maggoty green cheese or a mouldy old cornflake. – THE TWITS
DID YOU KNOW? Some of Roald Dahl's family used to call him by the nickname *Mouldy*.
SPARKY SYNONYMS You can also say **rotsome**.

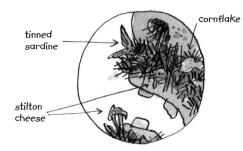

cornflake

tinned sardine

stilton cheese

mountain noun **mountains**
1 a very high hill
The Norwegians know all about witches, for Norway, with its black forests and icy mountains, is where the first witches came from. – THE WITCHES
2 a large heap of something
'From now on, you must eat cabbage three times a day. Mountains of cabbage! And if it's got caterpillars in it, so much the better!' – GEORGE'S MARVELLOUS MEDICINE

Gobblefunking with words
If you describe a pile of cabbage (or mashed potato or melted marshmallows) as a *mountain*, you are using a *metaphor*. You can find lots of metaphors in Roald Dahl's stories. For example, the Bloodbottler has *two purple frankfurter lips* and *rivers of spit* running down his chin, and the witches look like *a sea of naked scalps* without their wigs.

mouse noun **mice**
A mouse is a small furry animal with a long tail. The Grand High Witch plans to turn all the children in Inkland into mice.
Four tiny legs begin to sprrrout/From everybody rrround about./And all at vunce, all in a trrrice,/There are no children! Only mice! – THE WITCHES

moustache noun **moustaches**
a strip of hair that a man grows above his upper lip
Whenever the old Duke got excited, his enormous moustaches started to bristle and jump about. – THE GIRAFFE AND THE PELLY AND ME

mouth noun **mouths**

the part of your face that opens for eating and speaking

George couldn't help disliking Grandma. She was a selfish grumpy old woman. She had pale brown teeth and a small puckered-up mouth like a dog's bottom. — GEORGE'S MARVELLOUS MEDICINE

move verb **moves, moving, moved**

When you move, you go from one place to another. Here are some **zippfizzing** words to describe how a person, animal or giant moves.

TO MOVE QUICKLY: **bootle**, **daddle**, dash, hurry, hurtle, race, run, **scumper**, **skaddle**, skedaddle, **skiddle**, **skididdle**, speed, **splatch-winkle**, sprint, whiffle, whizz, **zippfizz**, zoom

'What's that?' Sophie cried. 'That is all the giants zippfizzing off to another country to guzzle human beans,' the BFG said. — THE BFG

TO MOVE WITH QUICK SHORT STEPS: **scuddle**, scurry, scuttle

'I is hearing the little ants chittering to each other as they scuddle around in the soil.' — THE BFG

TO MOVE WITH LONG STEPS: lollop, lope, stride

There was an air of menace about them as they loped slowly across the plain with long lolloping strides, heading for the BFG. — THE BFG

TO MOVE SLOWLY OR CASUALLY: amble, saunter, sidle, slink, stroll, toddle

The Centipede . . . got down off the sofa and ambled across the room and crawled into his hammock. — JAMES AND THE GIANT PEACH

muck noun

Muck is dirt or filth.

Bean never took a bath. He never even washed. As a result, his earholes were clogged with all kinds of muck and wax and bits of chewing-gum and dead flies and stuff like that. — FANTASTIC MR FOX

SPARKY SYNONYMS You can also say **slutch**.

muckfrumping adjective

A muckfrumping place is very unpleasant to live in.

This is a sizzling-hot muckfrumping country we is living in. Nothing grows in it except snozzcumbers. — THE BFG

muckleberry noun **muckleberries**

a type of berry that grows in the land where the Minpins live

'So now we can all go down to pick blackberries and winkleberries and puckleberries and muckleberries and twinkleberries and snozzberries to our hearts' content.' — THE MINPINS

DID YOU KNOW? When he invented *muckleberry*, Roald Dahl may have been thinking of *huckleberry*, a type of berry found in North America, and *mulberry*. The word *muckle* is also a dialect word that means 'big', so a *muckleberry* could be a huge type of berry.

LOOK IT UP! Another **mushious** fruit is the **snozzberry**.

mucky adjective **muckier, muckiest**

dirty or messy

'Troggy little twit! Shrivelly little shrimp! Mucky little midget! Squaggy little squib! Grobby little grub!' — THE BFG

SPARKY SYNONYMS You can also say **filthsome**.

mud noun

wet, sticky soil

When she lowered herself into the chair, there was a loud squelching noise similar to that made by a hippopotamus when lowering its foot into the mud on the banks of the Limpopo River. — MATILDA

mudburger noun **mudburgers**

A mudburger is a burger made with mud. Mudburgers are a great delicacy to the Centipede.

'I've eaten fresh mudburgers by the greatest cooks there are,/And scrambled dregs and stinkbugs' eggs and hornets stewed in tar.' — JAMES AND THE GIANT PEACH

Gobblefunking with words

When you say a word instead of one that sounds like it, either by mistake or to make a joke (like saying *scrambled dregs* instead of *scrambled eggs*), it is called a *malapropism*. The BFG often uses funny malapropisms, such as *skin and groans* instead of *skin and bones*. (He calls it saying things *squiggly*.) The word *malapropism* is named after Mrs Malaprop, a character in a play who made funny mistakes with words.

muddled or **muddle-headed** adjective

If you are muddled or muddle-headed, you are confused and not sure what to do or think.

'There never was a woman giant! . . . Giants is always men!' Sophie felt herself getting a little muddled. 'In that case,' she said, 'how were you born?' — THE BFG

Look for characters called *Mr* or *Mrs* under their surname, for example **Bucket**.

A B C D E F G H I J K L M N O P Q R S T U V W X Y Z

muffled adjective
A muffled sound is not clear, and is hard to hear.
And far away in the distance, from the heart of the great factory, came a muffled roar of energy as though some monstrous gigantic machine were spinning its wheels at breakneck speed. — CHARLIE AND THE CHOCOLATE FACTORY

muggled adjective
If something is muggled, or muggled up, it is in a mess or a muddle.
'Even when you is getting your sums all gungswizzled and muggled up, Mr Figgins is always giving you ten out of ten.' — THE BFG
DID YOU KNOW? To make the word *muggled*, Roald Dahl may have joined the words *muddled* and *juggled*, as sometimes when you juggle things you get them in a muddle.
RINGBELLING RHYMES Try rhyming with *goosegruggled*.
SPARKY SYNONYMS You can also say **boggled** or **squiff-squiddled**.

Muggle-Wumps (THE TWITS & THE ENORMOUS CROCODILE)
1 The Muggle-Wumps are a family of ex-circus monkeys that Mr and Mrs Twit keep in a cage overlooking the garden. They speak an African language which is understood by the Roly-Poly Bird.
2 A monkey called Muggle-Wump also has a narrow escape from the Enormous Crocodile.
DID YOU KNOW? *Muggle-Wump* sounds a bit like *mugwump*, which is a humorous American word for an important person.

multiply verb **multiplies, multiplying, multiplied**
When you multiply a number, you make it a number of times bigger. Matilda is a genius at multiplication.
*'For instance,' Miss Honey said, 'if I asked you to multiply fourteen by nineteen . . . No, that's too difficult . . . '
'It's two hundred and sixty-six,' Matilda said softly.*
— MATILDA

mum or **mummy** noun **mums, mummies**
Your mum or mummy is your mother.
'By Christopher!' Jack cried. 'By gum!/The Giant's eaten up my mum!/He smelled her out! She's in his belly!/I had a hunch that she was smelly.' — REVOLTING RHYMES
RINGBELLING RHYMES Try rhyming with *Fee Fi Fo Fum* (as well as *By gum!*).

mumble verb **mumbles, mumbling, mumbled**
When you mumble, you speak without saying the words clearly.
'I do wish you wouldn't mumble,' said Mr Wonka. 'I can't hear a word you're saying. Come on! Off we go!' — CHARLIE AND THE CHOCOLATE FACTORY
RINGBELLING RHYMES Try rhyming with *grumble* or *stumble*, or make up your own rhyming words, like *flumble* or *thumble*.

munch verb **munches, munching, munched**
When you munch something, you chew it noisily.
The floor was swarming with tortoises of different sizes, some walking slowly about and exploring, some munching cabbage leaves. — ESIO TROT
LOOK IT UP! For some other ways to munch, see **eat**.

murder verb **murders, murdering, murdered**
If someone murders another person, they kill them deliberately.
'Open your beak, bird!' 'No, no!' shouted the Duke. 'He's got a pistol! He'll murder us all!' — THE GIRAFFE AND THE PELLY AND ME

murder noun
1 Murder is killing other people (or giants) deliberately.
'We'll mow them down with machine-guns!' cried the Head of the Army. 'I do not approve of murder,' the Queen said. — THE BFG
2 If you scream *blue murder*, you scream as hard as you can because you are terrified.
Amanda was screaming blue murder and the Trunchbull was yelling, 'I'll give you pigtails, you little rat!'
— MATILDA

murderful adjective
A murderful creature has murderous thoughts and is always thinking up ways to kill people.
'Giants is all cannybully and murderful! And they does gobble up human beans!' — THE BFG
DID YOU KNOW? Roald Dahl made up the word *murderful*, but it is easy to see what it means, because he used a familiar word ending, as in *hateful* or *spiteful*. You can make up your own

words using this ending too, such as *giggleful* or *snortful*.

LOOK IT UP! Some murderful creatures are the **Fleshlumpeater** and the **Maidmasher**.

murderous adjective
A murderous creature is always thinking up ways to kill others (and is therefore best avoided).
'The murderous Gruncher, who has gobbled up so many thousands of us Minpins, has gone for ever! The forest floor is safe at last for us to walk on!' — THE MINPINS

murky adjective murkier, murkiest
Something that is murky is hard to see because it is so dark.
The newt, although fairly common in English ponds, is not often seen by ordinary people because it is a shy and murky creature. — MATILDA

RINGBELLING RHYMES Try rhyming with *quirky*.

murmur verb murmurs, murmuring, murmured
When you murmur, you speak in a very soft, low voice (unlike Miss Trunchbull).
Mr Wonka shook his head sadly and passed a hand over his eyes. Had you been standing very close to him you would have heard him murmuring softly under his breath, 'Oh, deary deary me, here we go again . . . ' — CHARLIE AND THE GREAT GLASS ELEVATOR

muscle noun muscles
Your muscles are the strong parts of your body that you use to make your body move.
The Vermicious Knid can turn itself into any shape it wants. It has no bones. Its body is really one huge muscle, enormously strong, but very stretchy and squishy. — CHARLIE AND THE GREAT GLASS ELEVATOR

mushious adjective
Something that is mushious is both mushy and delicious.
'It's luscious, it's super,/It's mushious, it's duper,/It's better than rotten old fish./You mash it and munch it,/You chew it and crunch it!/It's lovely to hear it go squish!' — THE ENORMOUS CROCODILE

DID YOU KNOW? The word *mushious* sounds like a blend of *mushy* and *delicious* or *luscious*. You can make up your own words like this too, such as *smoocious* to describe something smooth and delicious, like ice cream.

mushroom noun mushrooms
a small plant with a stem and a grey, round top that you can eat
Mrs Salt . . . was now kneeling right on the edge of the hole with her head down and her enormous behind sticking up in the air like a giant mushroom. — CHARLIE AND THE CHOCOLATE FACTORY

music noun
pleasant sounds that you make when you sing or play instruments
'Wouldn't this be a perfect time for a little music?' the Ladybird asked. 'How about it, Old Grasshopper?' 'With pleasure, dear lady,' the Old-Green-Grasshopper answered, bowing from the waist. — JAMES AND THE GIANT PEACH

musical adjective
A musical instrument is an instrument that you use to play music. Some musical instruments are the **bagglepipes** and **crumpets**.

musician noun musicians
a person or insect who plays or composes music
The Old-Green-Grasshopper . . . gave him a withering look. 'Young fellow,' he said, speaking in a deep, slow, scornful voice, 'I have never been a pest in my life. I am a musician.' — JAMES AND THE GIANT PEACH

mustard noun
a cold, yellow sauce with a hot, strong taste
He smears the boys (to make them hot)/With mustard from the mustard pot./But mustard doesn't go with girls,/It tastes all wrong with plaits and curls. — DIRTY BEASTS

musty adjective mustier, mustiest
A musty smell or musty air is stale and damp.
There was the same musty smell about the place that I had noticed in the Ballroom. It was the stench of witches. — THE WITCHES

muted adjective
A muted sound is quiet and hard to hear.
In the distance they could hear the muted sound of traffic going round Hyde Park Corner. — THE BFG

mutter verb mutters, muttering, muttered
When you mutter, you speak in a low voice to yourself.
'Nasty cheeky lot, these little 'uns!' I heard Mrs Pratchett muttering. 'They comes into my shop and they thinks they can do what they damn well likes!' — BOY

An old name for a flock of crows is a *murder of crows*.

Nn

Notsobig One

THE ENORMOUS CROCODILE

nasty   newt   nightmare

nonsense   norphan   nostrils

mysterious adjective
If something is mysterious, it is strange and difficult to understand.
'You mean she died?' I said. 'Who knows?' my grandmother said. 'Some very mysterious things go on in the world of witches.' — THE WITCHES

mystery noun **mysteries**
If something is a mystery, it is strange and puzzling and you do not understand it.
'It's all a bit beyond me,' Sophie said. 'Dreams is full of mystery and magic,' the BFG said. 'Do not try to understand them.' — THE BFG

nail noun **nails**
1 Your nails are the hard parts at the ends of your fingers and toes (unless you are a witch, in which case you will have **claws**).
'Some of us,' the old woman went on, . . . 'know how to make your nails drop off and teeth grow out of your fingers instead.' — GEORGE'S MARVELLOUS MEDICINE
2 A nail is a small thin piece of metal with a sharp point at the end. The door of the Chokey is covered with nails to stop anyone who is locked inside from leaning on it to rest.
'The door's got thousands of sharp spiky nails sticking out of it. They've been hammered through from the outside, probably by the Trunchbull herself.' — MATILDA

naked adjective
not wearing any clothes
It was a brain-boggling sight. The giants were all naked except for a sort of short skirt around their waists, and their skins were burnt by the sun. — THE BFG

name noun **names**
Your name is what people call you.
'My name is not Gregg any more,' he said. 'In honour of my feathered friends, I have changed it from Gregg to Egg.' 'And I am Mrs Egg,' said Mrs Gregg. — THE MAGIC FINGER

narrow adjective **narrower, narrowest**
Something that is narrow is not very wide.
*'The Chokey,' Hortensia went on, 'is a very tall but very
narrow cupboard. The floor is only ten inches square so
you can't sit down.* — MATILDA

nasty adjective **nastier, nastiest**
1 Something that is nasty is horribly unpleasant.
*Mr Twit was plotting away like mad. He was trying to
think up a really nasty trick he could play on his wife
that day.* — THE TWITS
2 Someone who is nasty is mean or unkind.
*'We are now underneath the farm which belongs to that
nasty little pot-bellied dwarf, Bunce.'* — FANTASTIC MR FOX
LOOK IT UP! For more ways to describe nasty people
or things, see **bad**.

nation noun **nations**
A nation is a country.
*The President said a very rude word into the microphone
and ten million children across the nation began
repeating it gleefully.* — CHARLIE AND THE GREAT GLASS
ELEVATOR

natterbox noun **natterboxes**
A natterbox is someone who cannot stop talking,
usually about nothing in particular.
*'Spiders is also talking a great deal. You might not
be thinking it but spiders is the most tremendous
natterboxes.'* — THE BFG
DID YOU KNOW? The word *natter* means the same
as *chatter*, so a *natterbox* is the same as a
chatterbox (and they rhyme with each other too).

naughty adjective **naughtier, naughtiest**
If a grown-up calls you naughty, they think you have
behaved badly.
*'Well, well, well,' sighed Mr Willy Wonka, 'two naughty
little children gone. Three good little children left.'*
— CHARLIE AND THE CHOCOLATE FACTORY
DID YOU KNOW? The word *naughty* is related
to *nought* and originally meant 'very poor' (so more
like Charlie and his family than Augustus Gloop).
It then took on the meaning of 'evil or wicked' and
later became just 'badly behaved'.

nauseating adjective
Something that is nauseating makes you feel sick
and disgusted.

*Her expression was one of utter distaste, as though she
were looking at something a dog had done in the middle
of the floor. 'What a bunch of nauseating little warts
you are.'* — MATILDA
SPARKY SYNONYMS You can also say **disgusterous**
or **sickable**.

navy noun **navies**
an army that fights at sea, in ships
*In the President's study in the White House, . . . the Chiefs
of the Army and the Navy and the Air Force . . . and
Mrs Taubsypuss the cat, all stood tense and rigid.*
— CHARLIE AND THE GREAT GLASS ELEVATOR

neat adjective **neater, neatest**
Something that is neat is clean and tidy.
*My mother, for her part, kept every one of these letters,
binding them carefully in neat bundles with green tape,
but this was her own secret.* — BOY

necessary adjective
If something is necessary, it has to be done.
*The pens we used had detachable nibs and it was
necessary to dip your nib into the ink-well every six
or seven seconds when you were writing.* — BOY

neck noun **necks**
Your neck is the part of your body that joins your head
to your shoulders. Witches have scraggy necks, but the
neck of a Geraneous Giraffe is elegant and magical.
*The Grand High Witch stretched her stringy neck forward
and grinned at the audience, showing two rows of
pointed teeth, slightly blue.* — THE WITCHES

needle noun needles

1 a thin, pointed piece of metal used for knitting or sewing

After that there came a fierce prickling sensation . . . as though tiny needles were forcing their way out through the surface of the skin from the inside. — THE WITCHES

2 a long, thin sharp object shaped like a needle

There was a squelch. The needle went in deep. And suddenly — there was the giant peach, caught and spiked upon the very pinnacle of the Empire State Building.
— JAMES AND THE GIANT PEACH

neighbour noun neighbours

Your neighbours are the people who live near you, or who sit beside you in a classroom or when you play a game.

The other giants spread out quickly in a large circle, each giant about twenty yards from his neighbour, preparing for the game they were going to play. — THE BFG

nervous adjective

If you feel nervous, you feel slightly afraid.

But as the Great Elevator continued to streak upward further and further away from the Earth, even Charlie began to feel a trifle nervous. — CHARLIE AND THE GREAT GLASS ELEVATOR

nest noun nests

A nest is a home that a bird or small animal makes for its young. The Greggs have to build a nest to sleep in after they suffer the effects of the Magic Finger.

They flew off to a tall tree, and right at the top of it Mr Gregg chose the place for the nest. 'Now we want sticks,' he said. 'Lots and lots of little sticks.'
— THE MAGIC FINGER

nest verb nests, nesting, nested

When a bird (or a Gregg) nests, it makes a home for its young.

I heard one witch in the back row saying to her neighbour, 'I'm getting a bit old to go bird's nesting. Those ruddy gruntles always nest very high up.' — THE WITCHES

net noun nets

A net is a piece of material with small holes in it, used to catch fish or dreams.

The BFG . . . strode across the cave and picked up his dream-catching net. 'I is galloping off now,' he said, 'to catch some more whoppsy-whiffling dreams for my collection.' — THE BFG

nettle noun **nettles**
a plant with leaves that can sting you if you touch them
On either side of the path there was a wilderness of nettles and blackberry thorns and long brown grass.
— MATILDA

nettled adjective
If you are nettled, you feel cross or annoyed.
Sophie couldn't stop smiling. 'What is you griggling at?' the BFG asked her, slightly nettled. — THE BFG

never adverb
Never means not ever. The BFG says, *Never in a month of Mondays!* when he means absolutely never ever EVER.
'If I went and told the Queen . . . I'm sure she'd do something about it!' The BFG looked down . . . and shook his head. 'She is never believing you,' he said. 'Never in a month of Mondays.' — THE BFG

new adjective **newer, newest**
Something that is new has just been made or bought or invented.
'Everlasting Gobstoppers!' cried Mr Wonka proudly. 'They're completely new! I am inventing them for children who are given very little pocket money.' — CHARLIE AND THE CHOCOLATE FACTORY
SPARKY SYNONYMS You can say that a new idea or invention, like one of Willy Wonka's, is a **novelty**.

newspaper noun **newspapers**
a set of large printed sheets of paper with news about things that are happening in the world
Suddenly, on the day before Charlie Bucket's birthday, the newspapers announced that the second Golden Ticket had been found. — CHARLIE AND THE CHOCOLATE FACTORY

newt noun **newts**
A newt is a small animal rather like a lizard, which lives near or in water. As newts are **amphibians**, they can survive in either a pencil-box or a glass of water, if need be.

The Trunchbull was sitting behind the teacher's table staring with a mixture of horror and fascination at the newt wriggling in the glass. — MATILDA

nibble verb **nibbles, nibbling, nibbled**
When you nibble something, you eat it by biting off a little bit at a time.
'At this moment,' continued the Ladybird, 'our Centipede, who has a pair of jaws as sharp as razors, is up there on top of the peach nibbling away at that stem.' — JAMES AND THE GIANT PEACH
LOOK IT UP! For some other ways that people nibble, see **eat**.

Nibbleswicke (VICAR OF NIBBLESWICKE)
the small village where the Reverend Robert Lee is given his first job as a vicar
DID YOU KNOW? You can find the ending *-wick* in lots of place names where it originally meant 'market' or 'trading place', so perhaps Nibbleswicke was once a place where nibbles were bought and sold.

nice adjective **nicer, nicest**
1 Something that is nice is pleasant or enjoyable.
When Mrs Twit came to, the frog had just jumped on to her face. This is not a nice thing to happen to anyone in bed at night. — THE TWITS

2 A nice person, creature or giant is kind and good-natured.
There used to be some rather nice creatures living on the moon a long time ago. They were called Poozas. But the Vermicious Knids ate the lot. — CHARLIE AND THE GREAT GLASS ELEVATOR
LOOK IT UP! For more ways to describe nice people or things, see **good** (and for not-so-nice people or things, see **bad**).

night noun **nights**
the time when it is dark outside, between sunset and sunrise
The night was very still. There was a thin yellow moon over the trees on the hill, and the sky was filled with stars. — THE MAGIC FINGER
RINGBELLING RHYMES Try rhyming with *fright* or *moonlight*.

nightgown noun **nightgowns**
a long loose garment for wearing in bed, especially by grandparents
'I can fly faster than any of you!' cried Grandpa George, whizzing round and round, his nightgown billowing out behind him like the tail of a parrot. — CHARLIE AND THE GREAT GLASS ELEVATOR

nightie noun **nighties**
a loose dress that girls or women wear in bed
'No, leave the little girl here with me,' the Queen said. 'We'll have to find something for her to put on. She can't have breakfast in her nightie.' — THE BFG

The word *nice* originally meant 'silly or foolish'—not pleasant at all!

nightingull noun nightingulls

a small brown bird like the nightingale, which sings sweetly in Giant Country

'Spiders is the most tremendous natterboxes. And when they is spinning their webs, they is singing all the time. They is singing sweeter than a nightingull.'
—THE BFG

DID YOU KNOW? *Nightingale* is a very old word that means literally 'night singer'. Roald Dahl swapped the ending for *gull*, which is funny because gulls usually squawk rather than sing. (But maybe gulls do sing sweetly in Giant Country, or perhaps the BFG is the only one who can hear their songs.)

nightmare noun nightmares

a very frightening dream, such as a **bogthumper** or a **trogglehumper**

'I is catching a frightsome trogglehumper!' he cried. 'This is a bad bad dream! It is worse than a bad dream! It is a nightmare!'—THE BFG

DID YOU KNOW? The word *nightmare* comes from an old word *mare*, which meant an evil spirit that was thought to cause bad dreams (an ancient version of a **trogglehumper** in other words).

nightshirt noun nightshirts

a long loose shirt for wearing in bed

'Wait!' she screamed. 'We must be mad! We can't go to a famous party in the White House in our nightshirts!'
—CHARLIE AND THE GREAT GLASS ELEVATOR

nincompoop noun nincompoops

a very silly person

'Augustus Gloop!' chanted the Oompa-Loompas. 'Augustus Gloop! Augustus Gloop!/The great big greedy nincompoop!'—CHARLIE AND THE CHOCOLATE FACTORY

Nishnobbler noun Nishnobblers

a type of rare and wonderful sweet that is sold in the Grubber

There were Nishnobblers and Gumglotters and Blue Bubblers . . . and as well as all this, there was a whole lot of splendid stuff from the great Wonka factory itself.
—THE GIRAFFE AND THE PELLY AND ME

LOOK IT UP! Some other **splendiferous** sweets are **Gumtwizzlers** and **Giant Wangdoodles**.

nitwit noun (*informal*) nitwits

a very silly or stupid person

Sometimes it was well nigh impossible for a teacher to convince the proud father or mother that their beloved offspring was a complete nitwit.—MATILDA

nod verb nods, nodding, nodded

When you nod, you move your head up and down to show that you agree with someone.

The other three old people nodded their heads slowly up and down, and said, 'Absolutely true. Just as true as can be.'
—CHARLIE AND THE CHOCOLATE FACTORY

noise noun noises

A noise is a sound that you can hear, especially a loud or strange one.

Roald Dahl uses these *onomatopoeic* words to make noises ring out in his writing.

banging, clanking, clinking, gurgling, hissing, humming, panting, rumbling, scraping, scrunching, sizzling, snorting, splintering, squelching, thumping, whirring, whistling, whizzing, whooshing
A tremendous banging noise was coming from inside the Pelican's beak. It sounded as though someone was using a sledgehammer against it from the inside.
—THE GIRAFFE AND THE PELLY AND ME

noisy adjective noisier, noisiest

Someone who is noisy, or a noisy engine or vehicle, makes a lot of loud sounds.

He handed the jar to Sophie and said, 'Please be still as a starfish now . . . And do kindly stop breathing. You is terribly noisy down there.'—THE BFG

nonsense noun

Nonsense is something that does not make sense (and therefore seems silly to grown-ups), but is often fun in any case.

'I have never met a man,' said Grandma Georgina, 'who talks so much absolute nonsense!' 'A little nonsense now and then, is relished by the wisest men,' Mr Wonka said.—CHARLIE AND THE GREAT GLASS ELEVATOR

nook noun nooks

1 A nook is a corner or safe place where you can find shelter. The Wormwoods call their house *Cosy Nook* (though Miss Honey, who likes making *spoonerisms*, prefers *Nosey Cook*). Matilda finds her own nook in the library, not in her home.

It was a modern brick house that could not have been cheap to buy and the name on the gate said COSY NOOK. Nosey cook might have been better, Miss Honey thought.—MATILDA

2 If something fills every *nook and cranny* of a place, it fills every single spot.

There were jars everywhere. They were piled up in the corners. They filled every nook and cranny of the cave.
— THE BFG

RINGBELLING RHYMES Try rhyming with *book* (as a nook is a very good place to read a book). You can also rhyme *nook and cranny* with *granny*.

Gobblefunking with words
There are not many words based on *nook*, which is a very good reason to make up your own.
You can use endings such as *-ful*, *-like*, and *-some* to make new adjectives (just as the BFG does). For example, a *nookful* place (like a library) would be full of nooks. You can make place names, too, like *Nookwood* (for a wood full of secret places).

normal adjective
Something that is normal is ordinary and not different or surprising.
The Giant had definitely slowed down and was now running more normally, although normal was a silly word to use to describe a galloping giant. — THE BFG

norphan noun norphans
A norphan is the BFG's word for an orphan, like Sophie.
'You is a norphan?' 'Yes.' 'How many is there in there?' 'Ten of us,' Sophie said. 'All little girls.' — THE BFG

DID YOU KNOW? The word *norphan* is made by joining up *an orphan* and then splitting it again to make a *norphan*. This is called *misdivision* and it happens with other words too. There is an old word *nuncle* meaning 'uncle' which was based on the phrase *mine uncle*, and a **newt** was originally *an ewt*.

norphanage noun norphanages
a home for norphans
'They will be sending you straight back to a norphanage,' the BFG went on. 'Grown-up human beans is not famous for their kindnesses.' — THE BFG

nose noun noses
Your nose is the part of your face that you use for breathing and smelling. The Red-Hot Smoke-Belching Gruncher has a super-sensitive nose that he uses to hunt Minpins.
'What makes him so dangerous is his amazing and magical nose. His nose can smell out a human or a Minpin or any other animal from ten miles away.' — THE MINPINS

DID YOU KNOW? There are lots of informal words for *nose*, such as *conk* and *hooter*. Some older words that once meant 'a nose' are *scent-box*, *sneezer*, *snorter* and *spectacles-seat*.

RINGBELLING RHYMES Try rhyming with *blows*.

nose-hole noun nose-holes
A nose-hole is another word for a **nostril**.
'Look for the nose-holes,' my grandmother said. 'Witches have slightly larger nose-holes than ordinary people.' — THE WITCHES

nosey or nosy adjective nosier, nosiest
Someone who is nosey is very interested in other people's business.
Mrs Twit was the gardener . . . 'I always grow plenty of spiky thistles and plenty of stinging-nettles,' she used to say. 'They keep out nasty nosey little children.' — THE TWITS

The BFG is called *Il GGG* (*Grande Gigante Gentile*) in Italian.

nostril noun nostrils

Your nostrils are the two holes at the end of your nose, which you breathe through. Witches have unusually large and sensitive nostrils which they use to sniff out children.

All the noses of all the witches in that room went up in the air, and all the nostrils began to suck and sniff. — THE WITCHES

DID YOU KNOW? The word *nostril* means 'nose hole' and is based on an old word *thirl* meaning 'hole' or 'pierce' — so a nostril is literally a 'nose piercing'.

note noun notes

1 a short letter or message

A Note about Witches. In fairy-tales, witches always wear silly black hats and black cloaks, and they ride on broomsticks. But this is not a fairy-tale. — THE WITCHES

2 A musical note is one sound in a piece of music.

From the moment that the first note was struck, the audience became completely spellbound. — JAMES AND THE GIANT PEACH

notmucher noun notmuchers

someone who doesn't do very much, or will never amount to much

'The Queen of England,' Sophie said. 'You can't call her a squifflerotter or a grinksludger . . . You can't call her a squeakpip or a notmucher either.' — THE BFG

Notsobig One (THE ENORMOUS CROCODILE)

The Notsobig One is a medium-sized crocodile who swims in the same river as the Enormous Crocodile, but eats only fish and not children.

nougat noun nougats

a chewy sweet made from nuts and sugar or honey

Then the sweets and chocs and toffees and fudges and nougats began pouring in to fill the shelves . . .

from every country in the world. — THE GIRAFFE AND THE PELLY AND ME

nought noun noughts

Nought is another name for the number 0, or zero. If you take too much Wonka-Vite, you will grow less than nought in years and will end up in Minusland.

'You must try to understand,' said Mr Wonka, 'that if she is now minus two, she's got to add two more years before she can start again from nought.' — CHARLIE AND THE GREAT GLASS ELEVATOR

novel noun novels

A novel is a book that tells a long story. A writer who writes a novel (for example, Charles Dickens) is a *novelist*.

'But does it not intrigue you,' Miss Honey said, 'that a little five-year-old child is reading long adult novels by Dickens and Hemingway?' — MATILDA

nozzle noun nozzles

the spout on the end of a hose, pipe or spray-gun

Mr Wonka . . . pumped the handle hard ONCE . . . TWICE . . . THREE TIMES! Each time, a fine black spray spurted out from the nozzle of the gun. — CHARLIE AND THE GREAT GLASS ELEVATOR

nudge verb nudges, nudging, nudged

When you nudge someone, you push them with your elbow to make them notice something.

My father was nudging me with his elbow and pointing through the branches at the pheasants. The place was absolutely stiff with them. — DANNY THE CHAMPION OF THE WORLD

nuisance noun nuisances

A nuisance is someone or something that you find annoying and that you wish would go away.
Mrs Kranky . . . calmed down quite quickly. And by lunchtime, she was saying, 'Ah well, I suppose it's all for the best, really. She was a bit of a nuisance around the house, wasn't she?' – GEORGE'S MARVELLOUS MEDICINE

nursery noun nurseries

a place where very young children go to play and be looked after
Great Scott! Gadzooks!/One half of their lives was reading books!/The nursery shelves held books galore!/Books cluttered up the nursery floor. – CHARLIE AND THE CHOCOLATE FACTORY

nut noun nuts

a hard fruit that grows on some trees and plants
The Monkey took off like an arrow, and a few seconds later he was high up in the branches of the walnut tree, cracking the nuts and guzzling what was inside. – THE GIRAFFE AND THE PELLY AND ME

nutty adjective nuttier, nuttiest

1 Nutty chocolate is full of nuts.
'Have you got it?' whispered Grandpa Joe, his eyes shining with excitement. Charlie nodded and held out the bar of chocolate. WONKA'S NUTTY CRUNCH SURPRISE, it said on the wrapper. – CHARLIE AND THE CHOCOLATE FACTORY
2 (*informal*) slightly mad
'He's nutty!' 'He's screwy!' 'He's wacky!' cried the Roly-Poly Bird. 'Poor old Muggles has gone off his wump at last!' – THE TWITS

Oo

Oompa-Loompas – CHARLIE AND THE CHOCOLATE FACTORY

Oompa-Loompish oozing orbit

orchard orphan oviform

oak noun oaks

a large tree that produces nuts called acorns
An enormous oak tree stood overshadowing the cottage. Its massive spreading branches seemed to be enfolding and embracing the tiny building. – MATILDA

oar noun oars

a pole with a flat blade at one end, used for rowing a boat
As the boat came closer, the watchers on the riverbank could see that the oars were being pulled by masses of Oompa-Loompas—at least ten of them to each oar. – CHARLIE AND THE CHOCOLATE FACTORY

obey verb obeys, obeying, obeyed

When you obey someone, you do what they tell you to do.
'I became so completely cowed and dominated by this monster of an aunt that when she gave me an order, no matter what it was, I obeyed it instantly.' – MATILDA

oblong adjective

Something oblong has the shape of a rectangle or long square.
There it lay, this small oblong sea-green jellyish thing, at the bottom of the jar, quite peaceful, but pulsing gently. – THE BFG

observe verb observes, observing, observed

When you observe something, you watch it carefully.
The finest sight of all was to observe those nine hideous

a b c d e f g h i j k l m n o p q r s t u v w x y z

A pun my word! There are lots of examples of word jokes at **pun.**

brutes squirming and twisting about on the ground like a mass of mighty snakes. — THE BFG

obvious adjective
If something is obvious, it is very easy to see or understand.
'Tortoises are very backward creatures. Therefore they can only understand words that are written backwards. That's obvious, isn't it?' — ESIO TROT

occasion noun occasions
an important event, such as a birthday or special party
Only once a year, on his birthday, did Charlie Bucket ever get to taste a bit of chocolate. The whole family saved up their money for that special occasion. — CHARLIE AND THE CHOCOLATE FACTORY

occur verb occurs, occurring, occurred
1 When something occurs, it happens.
*And this thing . . . soon caused a second thing to happen which was **very** peculiar. And then the **very** peculiar thing . . . caused a really **fantastically** peculiar thing to occur.* — JAMES AND THE GIANT PEACH
2 When something occurs to you, you think of it.
It didn't occur to Mr Twit that windows were meant mainly for looking out of, not for looking into. — THE TWITS

ocean noun oceans
the area of salt water surrounding the land of the Earth
And just beyond that, he could see the ocean itself — a long thin streak of blackish-blue, like a line of ink, beneath the rim of the sky. — JAMES AND THE GIANT PEACH

odd adjective odder, oddest
Something that is odd is strange and not normal or usual.
Miss Trunchbull . . . had an obstinate chin, a cruel mouth and small arrogant eyes. And as for her clothes . . . they were, to say the least, extremely odd. — MATILDA

offend verb offends, offending, offended
If you offend someone, you hurt their feelings.
The BFG gave her a long hard stare. Sophie looked right back at him, her face open to his. 'I believe you,' she said softly. She had offended him, she could see that. — THE BFG

offer verb offers, offering, offered
If you offer something, you hold it out so that someone can take it if they want it.
'Your cherries, Your Grace!' I said as I leaned over the edge of the Pelican's beak and offered a handful to the Duke.
—THE GIRAFFE AND THE PELLY AND ME

officer noun officers
a member of the army, navy or air force who is in charge of others and gives them orders
The pilot was a young Air Force officer with a bushy moustache. He was very proud of his moustache. He was also quite fearless and he loved adventure. — THE BFG

oily adjective oilier, oiliest
Something that is oily is thick and slippery like oil.
'Let me just say quickly that in the end, after lots of boiling and bubbling and mixing and testing in my Inventing Room, I produced one tiny cupful of oily black liquid.' — CHARLIE AND THE GREAT GLASS ELEVATOR

oinck noun oincks
An oinck is a monstrous creature that is thought to look like a giant grasshopper (so the two species are sometimes confused).
*The Old-Green-Grasshopper poked his huge green head over the side of the peach . . . 'That one's an Oinck!' screamed the Head of the Fire Department. 'I just **know** it's an Oinck!'* — JAMES AND THE GIANT PEACH

> **Gobblefunking with words**
> The word *oinck* sounds like *oink*, which is the sound that a pig makes, so perhaps **oincks** make a similar sound (which would be *very* different to the musical Old-Green-Grasshopper). Words which sound like the thing they describe are called *onomatopoeic* words, and you can find more examples in the entry for **gliss**.

old adjective older, oldest
1 Someone who is old has lived for a long time. You can also grow old in a shorter time by taking doses of Vita-Wonk.
Grandpa Joe was the oldest of the four grandparents. He was ninety-six and a half, and that is just about as old as anybody can be. — CHARLIE AND THE CHOCOLATE FACTORY
2 Something that is old was made a long time ago.
The BFG crossed the cave and opened a tiny secret door in the wall. He took out a book, very old and tattered. — THE BFG

old–fashioned adjective
Something that is old-fashioned looks old and not modern, like the clothes that the Minpins wear.

All of them were wearing these old-fashioned clothes from hundreds of years ago, and several had on very peculiar hats and bonnets. — THE MINPINS

oldish adjective
Someone who is oldish is not *very* old, just a bit old.

'Good morning, Your Majesty,' a woman was saying. It was the voice of an oldish person. There was a pause and then a slight rattle of china and silver. — THE BFG

only adjective
An only child is a child who has no brothers or sisters, like Charlie Bucket or George Kranky.

Some wealthy folks from U.S.A./Who lived near San Francisco Bay,/Possessed an only child called Roy,/A plump and unattractive boy. — DIRTY BEASTS

Oompa-Loompa noun Oompa-Loompas
Oompa-Loompas are people originally from Loompaland who work in Willy Wonka's chocolate factory in exchange for chocolate, which is their favourite food. They love music and dancing and often make up songs to sing.

The five Oompa-Loompas on the far side of the river suddenly began hopping and dancing about and beating wildly upon a number of very small drums. — CHARLIE AND THE CHOCOLATE FACTORY

DID YOU KNOW? When he invented the name *Oompa-Loompa*, Roald Dahl may have been thinking of *oompah*, the sound made by some musical instruments, as the Oompa-Loompas like to sing and make music.

Oompa-Loompish noun
Oompa-Loompish is the language that the Oompa-Loompas speak (although they can also sing and chant in English).

'Look here,' I said (speaking not in English, of course, but in Oompa-Loompish). — CHARLIE AND THE CHOCOLATE FACTORY

ooze verb oozes, oozing, oozed
When liquid oozes, it flows out slowly through a narrow opening.

'The smell that drives a witch mad actually comes right out of your own skin. It comes oozing out of your skin in waves.' — THE WITCHES

opinion noun opinions
Your opinion is what you think about something.

'It is my opinion,' Miss Honey said, 'that Matilda should be taken out of my form and placed immediately in the top form with the eleven-year-olds.' — MATILDA

orbit noun orbits
When something is in orbit, it is moving around the Earth or another planet in space.

'Too far?' cried Mr Wonka. 'Of course we went too far! You know where we've gone, my friends? We've gone into orbit!' — CHARLIE AND THE GREAT GLASS ELEVATOR

orbit verb orbits, orbiting, orbited
When something (such as a spaceship or elevator) orbits a planet, it moves around it in space.

Mr Wonka's Great Glass Elevator was orbiting the Earth at tremendous speed. Mr Wonka had all his booster-rockets firing. — CHARLIE AND THE GREAT GLASS ELEVATOR

orchard noun orchards
a piece of ground planted with fruit trees, like the one that Farmer Bean owns

Bean . . . never ate any food at all. Instead, he drank gallons of strong cider which he made from the apples in his orchard. — FANTASTIC MR FOX

order noun orders
When you give someone an order, you tell them what they must do.

'I'll give the orders,' said Mr Wonka. 'I'm the pilot. Don't fire your rockets until I tell you.' — CHARLIE AND THE GREAT GLASS ELEVATOR

order verb orders, ordering, ordered
If you order someone to do something, you tell them that they must do it.

'Now stay there till we come back!' Mr Twit ordered. 'Don't you dare to move! And don't overbalance!' — THE TWITS

ordinary adjective
Something that is ordinary is normal and not different or special.

REAL WITCHES dress in ordinary clothes and look very much like ordinary women. They live in ordinary houses and they work in ORDINARY JOBS. That is why they are so hard to catch. — THE WITCHES

a b c d e f g h i j k l m n o p q r s t u v w x y z

Roald Dahl originally called the Oompa-Loompas by the name *Whipple-Scrumpets.*

ornament noun ornaments
something that you put in a room to make it look pretty
All the furniture, the big table, . . . the ornaments, the electric fire, the carpet, everything was stuck upside down to the ceiling. — THE TWITS

orphan noun orphans
An orphan is a child like Sophie or James Henry Trotter, whose mother and father are both dead. A home for orphans is called an **orphanage**.
'No one is going to be worrying too much about me. That place you took me from was the village orphanage. We are all orphans in there.' — THE BFG

ounce noun ounces
a unit of weight equal to ¹⁄₁₆ of a pound or about 28 grams
Mr Hoppy . . . picked his way carefully through his huge collection of tortoises to find one that first of all had the same colour shell as Alfie's and secondly weighed **exactly two ounces more.** — ESIO TROT

outline noun outlines
The outline of something is its shape.
Sophie peered into the jar and there, sure enough, she saw the faint translucent outline of something about the size of a hen's egg. — THE BFG

outraged adjective
very shocked and angry
I was outraged. I simply couldn't bring myself to believe what my grandmother was telling me. — THE WITCHES

outrageous adjective
very bold and rather shocking
Matilda said, 'Never do anything by halves if you want to get away with it. Be outrageous. Go the whole hog.' — MATILDA

oval adjective
shaped like an egg, a Knid or a number 0
Inside the big jar . . . she could clearly see about fifty of those oval sea-green jellyish shapes . . . some lying on top of others, but each one still a quite separate individual dream. — THE BFG

oven noun ovens
the part of a cooker where you can bake or roast food (and alarm-clocks)
'Here is vhat you do. You set your alarm-clock to go off at nine o'clock tomorrow morning. Then you rrroast it in the oven until it is crrrisp and tender.' — THE WITCHES

overboard adverb
over the side of a boat (or peach) and into the water
'He's coming down to eat us!' wailed the Old-Green-Grasshopper. 'Jump overboard!' 'Then eat the Earthworm first!' shouted the Centipede. — JAMES AND THE GIANT PEACH

overdose noun overdoses
If you take an overdose, you take too much of a medicine or magic potion.
'An overdose of Delayed Action Mouse-Maker vill mess up the timing of the alarm-clock and cause the child to turn into a mouse too early.' — THE WITCHES

overhead adverb
above your head, in the sky
The night was all around him now, and high overhead a wild white moon was riding in the sky. — JAMES AND THE GIANT PEACH

A B C D E F G H I J K L M N O P Q R S T U V W X Y Z

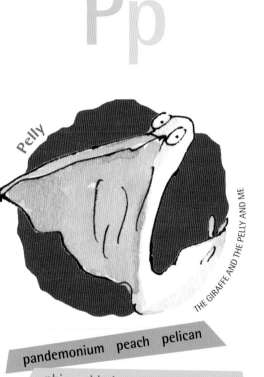

Pelly

THE GIRAFFE AND THE PELLY AND ME

overhear verb **overhears, overhearing, overheard**
If you overhear something, you hear it by accident or without the speaker knowing.
'Shut up, you little twerp!' Aunt Spiker snapped, happening to overhear him. 'It's none of your business!' — JAMES AND THE GIANT PEACH

oviform adjective
egg-shaped, as Vermicious Knids are in their natural form

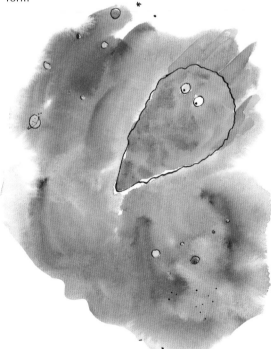

oxygen noun
a gas in the air that you need to breathe in order to stay alive
Mr Wonka . . . sort of swam across under the ceiling to a button marked OXYGEN. He pressed it. 'You'll be all right now,' he said. 'Breathe away.' — CHARLIE AND THE GREAT GLASS ELEVATOR

pandemonium   peach   pelican

phizz-whizzing   **pigtails**   plussy

pace noun **paces**
1 a step forwards or backwards
From across the street, Sophie . . . saw the Giant step back a pace and put the suitcase down on the pavement.
— THE BFG
2 the speed at which something moves
And now the peach . . . was over the edge of the hill, rolling and bouncing down the steep slope at a terrific pace.
— JAMES AND THE GIANT PEACH

pack noun **packs**
a group of wild animals or creatures that hunt together, especially wolves or man-eating giants
At last the BFG got clear of them all and in another couple of minutes the pack of giants was out of sight over the horizon. — THE BFG
DID YOU KNOW? A *pack* of giants is a *collective noun* and you can find more examples of this type of word in the entry for **colony**.
pack verb **packs, packing, packed**
When you pack things into a box, bag or suitcase, you put them in.
'We shall pack our bags and go travelling all over the world! In every country we visit, we shall seek out the houses where the witches are living!' — THE WITCHES

The word *pelecanine* means 'of a pelican' or 'to do with pelicans'.

a b c d e f g h i j k l m n o **p** q r s t u v w x y z

171

packet noun **packets**
a small box or bag that you buy things in, such as raisins, cornflakes or itching-powder
'I had sent away by post, you see, for this very powerful itching-powder,' Hortensia said. 'It cost fifty pence a packet and was called The Skin-Scorcher.'—MATILDA

paddle verb **paddles, paddling, paddled**
When you paddle, you walk about in shallow water.
'Ho, ho, ho!' cried the Enormous Crocodile. 'I'll bet if you saw a fat juicy little child paddling in the water over there at this very moment, you'd gulp him up in one gollop!'
—THE ENORMOUS CROCODILE

page noun **pages**
a piece of paper that is part of a book
'That's why they always put two blank pages at the back of the atlas. They're for new countries. You're meant to fill them in yourself.'—THE BFG

pail noun **pails**
a bucket
'I've eaten fresh mudburgers by the greatest cooks there are,/And scrambled dregs and stinkbugs' eggs and hornets stewed in tar,/And pails of snails and lizards' tails,/And beetles by the jar.' – JAMES AND THE GIANT PEACH

pain noun **pains**
1 the feeling that you have in your body when something hurts
I heard the crack first and about two seconds later I felt the pain. Never had I felt a pain such as that in my whole life.—DANNY THE CHAMPION OF THE WORLD
2 If you describe someone as a pain, or a pain in the neck (or anywhere else), you mean that you find them very annoying.
Mrs Kranky came outside and she agreed with George. 'She's my own mother,' she said. 'She's a pain in the neck,' Mr Kranky said.—GEORGE'S MARVELLOUS MEDICINE

painful adjective
If something is painful it hurts.
'What in the world has happened to your tail?'
'Don't talk about it, please,' said Mr Fox. 'It's a painful subject.'—FANTASTIC MR FOX

paint noun **paints**
Paint is a coloured liquid that you use for making pictures or putting on walls. The Cloud-Men have huge pots of paint in bright colours for painting rainbows.
Very gently, George stirred the paint into the mixture with the long wooden spoon. Ah-ha! It was all turning brown!—GEORGE'S MARVELLOUS MEDICINE

paint verb **paints, painting, painted**
When you paint something, you use paints to cover it with colour.
'That enormous arch — they seem to be painting it! They've got pots of paint and big brushes!'—JAMES AND THE GIANT PEACH

pair noun **pairs**
two things that belong together, such as shoes or boots or socks
And by the time James had pulled off the last boot of all and had lined them up in a row on the floor — twenty-one pairs altogether — the Centipede was fast asleep.—JAMES AND THE GIANT PEACH

palace noun **palaces**
a very large house where a king or queen lives
Not more than a hundred yards away . . . across the mown lawns and the tidy flower-beds, the massive shape of the Palace itself loomed through the darkness.—THE BFG

pale adjective **paler, palest**
1 If you look pale, your face looks white because you are ill or scared.
Muggle-Wump went pale and began to shake all over. 'You aren't really going to gobble up a little child, are you?' he said.—THE ENORMOUS CROCODILE
2 A pale colour or light is not bright or intense.
At eight o'clock we started walking down the road towards my school in the pale autumn sunshine, munching our apples as we strode along.—DANNY THE CHAMPION OF THE WORLD

palm noun **palms**
Your palm is the inside part of your hand.
The BFG picked Sophie up between one finger and a thumb and placed her gently on the palm of the other hand.—THE BFG

pandemonium noun
uproar and complete confusion
'Classrooms vill all be svorrming with mice!' shouted The Grand High Witch. 'Chaos and pandemonium vill be rrreigning in every school in Inkland!'—THE WITCHES
LOOK IT UP! The word pandemonium was invented by the poet John Milton over 300 years ago. It means literally 'all demon', and was the name of the capital of Hell in his poem Paradise Lost.

panic verb panics, panicking, panicked

If you panic, you suddenly feel very frightened and cannot think what to do.

Charlie . . . couldn't speak or make a sound. His throat was seized up with fright. But this time Mr Wonka didn't panic. He remained perfectly calm. — CHARLIE AND THE GREAT GLASS ELEVATOR

panic noun

sudden fear that makes people behave wildly

The peach was trapped! Panic and pandemonium broke out among the travellers. — JAMES AND THE GIANT PEACH

pant verb pants, panting, panted

When you pant, you take short, quick breaths because you have been running.

'Phew!' said Mr Fox. 'I think we've done it! They'll never get as deep as this. Well done, everyone!' They all sat down, panting for breath. — FANTASTIC MR FOX

pants plural noun

1 a piece of clothing that you wear over your bottom, underneath your other clothes

'It was pretty wonderful to be sitting there watching it all and knowing that I was the only person in the whole school who realized exactly what was going on inside the Trunchbull's pants.' — MATILDA

2 In North America, pants are trousers (and the kind of pants you wear underneath are **underpants**).

The next morning, when Mr Twit went out to collect the birds, he found four miserable little boys sitting in the tree, stuck as tight as could be by the seats of their pants to the branches. — THE TWITS

DID YOU KNOW? *Pants* used to mean 'trousers' in British English as well as in American English.

paper noun papers

1 Paper is the thin material that you use to write and draw on.

Mrs Silver caught the paper and held it up in front of her. This is what she read: ESIO TROT, ESIO TROT, TEG REGGIB REGGIB! — ESIO TROT

2 A paper is a newspaper.

'Do you think we'll all get our pictures in the papers when we get down?' the Ladybird asked. — JAMES AND THE GIANT PEACH

parabola noun parabolas

a curve like that made by an object that is thrown into the air and then falls back down

Matilda, who was mesmerized by the whole crazy affair, saw Amanda Thripp descending in a long graceful parabola on to the playing-field beyond. — MATILDA

parachute noun parachutes

a large piece of cloth that opens out and allows people or things to float slowly down to the ground from an aircraft

As she floated gently down, Mrs Twit's petticoat billowed out like a parachute, showing her long knickers. — THE TWITS

The BFG is called *MHO* (*Moc hodný obr*) in Czech.

a b c d e f g h i j k l m n o **p** q r s t u v w x y z

parallel adjective
If two lines or other things are parallel, they run side by side and the same distance apart from each other.
The BFG . . . swivelled his huge right ear until it was parallel with the ground, then he placed Sophie gently inside it. — THE BFG

parcel noun **parcels**
something wrapped up to be posted or carried
At Prep School in those days, a parcel of tuck was sent once a week by anxious mothers to their ravenous little sons. — BOY

parent noun **parents**
Your parents are your mother and father.
Occasionally one comes across parents who . . . show no interest at all in their children, and these of course are far worse than the doting ones. — MATILDA

park noun **parks**
A park is a large space with grass and trees where you can walk or play or have a picnic. If you are unlucky, you might choose to picnic under a hungry giant disguised as a tree.
'All of them is having their own special ways of catching the human bean,' the BFG said. 'The Meatdripping Giant is preferring to pretend he is a big tree growing in the park.' — THE BFG

parrot noun **parrots**
a brightly coloured bird with a curved beak that can learn to repeat words or sounds
Fred . . . led her up to his bedroom where a truly magnificent blue and yellow parrot sat in a tall cage. 'There it is,' Fred said. 'Its name is Chopper.' — MATILDA

particular adjective
only this one and no other
The chance had to be there. This particular bar of chocolate had as much chance as any other of having a Golden Ticket. — CHARLIE AND THE CHOCOLATE FACTORY

partly adverb
If something is partly done or partly eaten, you have only done or eaten some of it (probably because it is so disgusting).
'So this is the filthing rotsome glubbage you is eating!' boomed the Bloodbottler, holding up the partly eaten snozzcumber. — THE BFG

party noun **parties**
a time when people get together to have fun and celebrate something
'Let's have a party this time, Danny. We can write out invitations and I'll go into the village and buy chocolate éclairs and doughnuts and a huge birthday cake with candles on it.' — DANNY THE CHAMPION OF THE WORLD

passage noun **passages**
a corridor
The place was like a gigantic rabbit warren, with passages leading this way and that in every direction. — CHARLIE AND THE CHOCOLATE FACTORY

passenger noun **passengers**
a person who is travelling in a bus, train, boat or flying elevator
With the Oompa-Loompas rowing faster than ever, the boat shot into the pitch-dark tunnel, and all the passengers screamed with excitement. — CHARLIE AND THE CHOCOLATE FACTORY

pastry noun
a mixture of flour, fat and water that you roll flat and use for making pies
I saw before me the most enormous and beautiful pie in the world. It was covered all over, top, sides, and bottom, with a rich golden pastry. — DANNY THE CHAMPION OF THE WORLD

pat verb **pats, patting, patted**
When you pat something, you touch it gently.
'My dear boy,' the Old-Green-Grasshopper said, patting James on the back. 'I do congratulate you.' — JAMES AND THE GIANT PEACH

patch noun **patches**
1 a small piece of material that you put over a hole in your clothes, or in a tyre or beak
'Don't you worry about that, my dear Pelly,' said the Duke, patting him on the beak. 'My chauffeur will soon put a patch over it the same way he mends the tyres on the Rolls.' — THE GIRAFFE AND THE PELLY AND ME
2 a small piece of ground
All the land around us belonged to him, everything on both sides of the road, everything except the small patch of ground on which our filling-station stood. — DANNY THE CHAMPION OF THE WORLD

path noun paths
a narrow road that you can walk along but not drive along
Matilda laughed and turned away and ran up the path to her front-door, calling out as she went, 'Goodbye, Miss Honey! Thank you so much for the tea.' — MATILDA

patient noun patients
someone who is ill and being looked after by a doctor
Doc Spencer ... was over seventy now and could have retired long ago, but he didn't want to retire and his patients didn't want him to either. — DANNY THE CHAMPION OF THE WORLD

patient adjective
If you are patient, you can wait without getting cross or bored.
'Words,' he said, 'is oh such a twitch-tickling problem to me all my life. So you must simply try to be patient and stop squibbling.' — THE BFG

pattern noun patterns
a design with lines, shapes and colours
'And what about me, may I ask?' said Miss Spider. 'I can spin just as well as any Silkworm. What's more, I can spin patterns.' — JAMES AND THE GIANT PEACH

pause noun pauses
a short time when you stop what you are doing
Smoothly, without a pause and at a nice speed, Matilda began to read. — MATILDA

pause verb pauses, pausing, paused
When you pause, you stop what you are doing or saying for a short time.
The Grand High Witch paused and glared at the mass of eager faces in the audience. They waited, wanting more. — THE WITCHES

pavement noun pavements
A pavement is the path that you walk on along the side of a street. In North America, a pavement is called a *sidewalk*.
Directly in front of them, bordering the pavement, there was a brick wall with fearsome-looking spikes all along the top of it. — THE BFG

paw noun paws
An animal's paws are its feet.
I was able to move those paws. They were mine! At that moment, I realized that I was not a little boy any longer. I was a MOUSE. — THE WITCHES

pay verb pays, paying, paid
1 When you pay someone, you give them money for something they have done.
'Miss Honey,' she said suddenly, 'do they pay you very badly at our school?' — MATILDA
2 When you pay someone back, you do something bad to them in return.
To pay Mrs Twit back for the worms in his spaghetti, Mr Twit thought up a really clever nasty trick. — THE TWITS
3 When you pay out a rope or thread, you let it out by loosening it gradually.
Miss Spider ... walked calmly over to the edge of the peach and jumped off, paying out the thread behind her as she fell. — JAMES AND THE GIANT PEACH

peaceful adjective
When a place is peaceful, there is no noise or commotion there.
Miss Honey was walking slowly so that the small child could keep up with her without trotting too fast, and it was very peaceful out there on the narrow road. — MATILDA

peach noun peaches
A peach is a round, soft, juicy fruit with yellow flesh and a large stone in the middle. Peaches grow on peach trees, but giant peaches need extra magic to grow.
The garden, which covered the whole of the top of the hill, was large and desolate, and the only tree in the entire place ... was an ancient peach tree that never gave any peaches. — JAMES AND THE GIANT PEACH

peacock noun peacocks
a large bird with long, brightly coloured tail feathers
'All the dukes and lords and famous men would arrive in their big cars ... and Mr Hazell would strut about like a peacock welcoming them.' — DANNY THE CHAMPION OF THE WORLD

peck verb pecks, pecking, pecked
When a bird pecks something, it bites it or eats it with its beak.
'I don't give a hoot what the plan is!' cried the Earthworm. 'I am not going to be pecked to death by a bunch of seagulls!' — JAMES AND THE GIANT PEACH

peculiar adjective
Something that is peculiar is strange.
And this thing, which as I say was only rather peculiar, soon caused a second thing to happen which was very peculiar. — JAMES AND THE GIANT PEACH

peek noun peeks
a quick or cautious look at something
'All right,' said Mr Wonka, 'stop here for a moment and catch your breath, and take a peek through the glass panel of this door.' — CHARLIE AND THE CHOCOLATE FACTORY

peek verb peeks, peeking, peeked
If something peeks through, it sticks out just enough for you to see it.
The foxes jumped. They looked up quickly and they saw,

peeking through a small hole in the roof of the tunnel, a long black pointed furry face. — FANTASTIC MR FOX

peel noun
The peel on a fruit or vegetable is its skin.

peel verb peels, peeling, peeled
When you peel something, you take its skin or shell off.
'The shrimps were still warm from having been just cooked, and we would sit in the rowing-boat peeling them and gobbling them up.'
— THE WITCHES

peep verb peeps, peeping, peeped
If you peep at something, you look at it quickly.
Sophie peeped over the rim of the ear and watched the desolate landscape of Giant Country go whizzing by.
— THE BFG
LOOK IT UP! For other ways to describe peeping, see **look**.

peep-hole noun peep-holes
A peep-hole is a tiny hole, perhaps in a fence or a giant's pocket, just big enough for you to peep through.
Sophie crouched still as a mouse inside the BFG's pocket . . . Through the tiny peep-hole she watched the giants clustering around the poor BFG.
— THE BFG

peer verb peers, peering, peered
If you peer at something, you look at it closely.
'What is this please, Your Majester?' the BFG asked, peering down at the Queen. — THE BFG
LOOK IT UP! For other ways to look at things, see **look**.

pelican noun pelicans
Pelicans are large birds which live near rivers and the sea. They have pouches under their beaks where they store fish until they are ready to eat them.
At once the Pelican spread his huge white wings and flew down on to the road beside me. 'Hop in,' he said, opening his enormous beak.
— THE GIRAFFE AND THE PELLY AND ME

Pelly (THE GIRAFFE AND THE PELLY AND ME)
The Pelly is a pelican who works for the Ladderless Window-Cleaning Company. He has a very spacious beak with a retractable top, which he uses as a bucket to store water for washing windows.

pelt verb pelts, pelting, pelted
If a Cloud-Man or other horrible person pelts you with something, they throw it hard at you.
The infuriated Cloud-Men jumped up and ran after them along the cloud, pelting them mercilessly with all sorts of hard and horrible objects. — JAMES AND THE GIANT PEACH

pencil noun pencils
a thin stick with a lead inside that you use for writing or drawing
The BFG, with great care and patience, was printing something on a piece of paper with an enormous pencil. — THE BFG
DID YOU KNOW? The word *pencil* used to mean 'paintbrush' and comes from a Latin word meaning 'little tail'.

pencil-box noun pencil-boxes
a box for carrying pencils, rubbers, sharpeners and the occasional newt to school
Lavender . . . had lined her pencil-box with pond-weed ready to receive the creature, but she discovered that it was not easy to get the newt out of the hat and into the pencil-box. — MATILDA

penny noun pennies, pence
a British coin worth a hundredth of a pound
Mr Bucket . . . managed to earn a few pennies . . . by shovelling snow in the streets. But it wasn't enough to buy even a quarter of the food that seven people needed. — CHARLIE AND THE CHOCOLATE FACTORY

perambulator noun perambulators
an old-fashioned word for a **pram**
Slowly, almost lazily, the shark opened his mouth (which was big enough to have swallowed a perambulator) and made a lunge at the peach. — JAMES AND THE GIANT PEACH

DID YOU KNOW? *Perambulator* means 'around walker'. It comes from Latin *ambulare* 'to walk' which also gives us words like *ambulance* (because an ambulance is a 'moving' hospital). In North America, prams are called *strollers*, which means almost the same as *perambulator*.

perch noun perches
a place where a bird rests when it is not flying
I climbed into the big orange beak, and with a swoosh of wings the Pelican carried me back to his perch on the window-sill. — THE GIRAFFE AND THE PELLY AND ME

perch verb perches, perching, perched
If you perch, you sit or stand on something high or narrow, as if you were a bird.
We all perched in rows on wooden benches while the teachers sat up on the platform in armchairs, facing us. — BOY

perfect adjective
Something that is perfect is so good that it cannot be any better.
*By the age of **one and a half** her speech was perfect and she knew as many words as most grown-ups.* — MATILDA

perfectly adverb
1 Something that works perfectly works so well that it cannot be any better.
'There you are, then!' cried Mr Wonka, flashing a happy smile. 'The Wonka-Vite worked perfectly! She is now precisely three months old!' — CHARLIE AND THE GREAT GLASS ELEVATOR
2 completely or utterly
Matilda's brother Michael was a perfectly normal boy, but the sister, as I said, was something to make your eyes pop. — MATILDA

perform verb performs, performing, performed
When you perform, you do something in front of people to entertain them.
She admired the older girl Hortensia to distraction for the daring deeds she had performed in the school. — MATILDA

perfume noun perfumes
a liquid that you put on your skin that (usually) has a nice smell
There was a bottle of perfume called FLOWERS OF TURNIPS. It smelled of old cheese. In it went. — GEORGE'S MARVELLOUS MEDICINE

a b c d e f g h i j k l m n o p q r s t u v w x y z

The BFG is called *Yr CMM (Cawr Mawr Mwyn)* in Welsh.

perky adjective perkier, perkiest
If you are perky, you feel awake and full of energy.
A tiny Oompa-Loompa, looking young and perky, ran forward out of the crowd and did a marvellous little dance in front of the three old people in the big bed. — CHARLIE AND THE GREAT GLASS ELEVATOR

permanent adjective
Something that is permanent will last or remain in place for ever.
Mr Wormwood discovered that the worst thing about having a permanent hat on his head was having to sleep in it. — MATILDA

perpendicular adjective
A perpendicular wall is at right angles to the ground, so it is very hard for a giant to clamber up it.
The walls were perpendicular and engineers had calculated that there was no way a giant could escape once he was put in. — THE BFG

personality noun personalities
Your personality is the type of person you are. Someone with a strong personality is very forceful and hard to ignore or refuse, like Miss Trunchbull.
'You can't imagine what it's like to be completely controlled like that by a very strong personality. It turns you to jelly.' — MATILDA

personally adverb
If you do something personally, you do it yourself.
'These lucky five will be shown around personally by me, and they will be allowed to see all the secrets and the magic of my factory.' — CHARLIE AND THE CHOCOLATE FACTORY

persuasive adjective
If someone is persuasive, they try to get you to do or believe something.
'There you are, Bogtrotter,' the Trunchbull said, and once again her voice became soft, persuasive, even gentle. 'It's all for you, every bit of it.' — MATILDA

pest noun pests
a person, animal or plant that causes damage to things or annoys people
The Old-Green-Grasshopper . . . gave him a withering look. 'Young fellow,' he said, speaking in a deep, slow, scornful voice, 'I have never been a pest in my life. I am a musician.' — JAMES AND THE GIANT PEACH

pet noun pets
A pet is an animal which you keep and look after. Alfie the tortoise is Mrs Silver's much-loved pet.
Very slowly, over seven weeks, Mrs Silver's pet had more than doubled in size and the good lady hadn't noticed a thing. — ESIO TROT

petrified adjective
If you are petrified with fear, you are so afraid that you cannot move, as if you had been turned into rock.
Charlie climbed on to the bed and tried to calm the three old people who were still petrified with fear. — CHARLIE AND THE CHOCOLATE FACTORY

SPARKY SYNONYMS You can also say *fossilized with fear.* For other ways to describe petrified people, see **afraid**.

petrol noun
Petrol is a liquid made from petroleum which is used to make cars and engines go. Danny's father owns a filling-station where he sells petrol to motorists.
'Just imagine being able to take a thousand different bits of metal . . . and then if you feed them a little oil and petrol . . . suddenly those bits of metal will all come to life.' — DANNY THE CHAMPION OF THE WORLD

pheasant noun pheasants
A pheasant is a bird with long showy tail feathers that people like Victor Hazell like to shoot. Danny's father prefers to catch them using his own Secret Methods.
'I'll tell you something interesting about pheasants, Danny. The law says they're wild birds, so they only belong to you when they're on your own land, did you know that?' — DANNY THE CHAMPION OF THE WORLD

phenomenal adjective
Something phenomenal is remarkable or extraordinary.
Then suddenly, once again, the BFG went into that magical top gear of his. He began hurtling forward with phenomenal leaps. His speed was unbelievable. — THE BFG

phenomenon noun phenomena
something truly remarkable or extraordinary
'I am trying to explain to you,' Miss Honey said patiently, 'that we are dealing with the unknown. It is an unexplainable thing. The right word for it is a phenomenon.' — MATILDA

phizz-whizzing adjective

Something that is phizz-whizzing is excellent or splendid.

'What a phizz-whizzing flushbunking seat!' cried the BFG. 'I is going to be bug as a snug in a rug up here.' – THE BFG

DON'T BE BIFFSQUIGGLED! Take care not to confuse **phizz-whizzing** with **whizzpopping**, which is what happens when you drink too much **frobscottle**.

SPARKY SYNONYMS You can also say **spliffling**.

phizzwizard noun phizzwizards

A phizzwizard is a good dream that leaves you feeling happy when you wake up. The best kind of phizzwizard is a **golden phizzwizard**.

'Please be still as a starfish now. I is thinking there may be a whole swarm of phizzwizards up here today.' – THE BFG

DID YOU KNOW? The word *phizzwizard* sounds like something magical that *fizzes*. By spelling it this way, Roald Dahl made it look more ancient or mysterious, as lots of words which are spelled with *-ph-*, like *phobia* and *elephant*, are based on ancient Greek.

piano noun pianos

A piano is a large musical instrument with a row of black and white keys on a keyboard. If you take vitamin Wonka your toes will grow so long that they will reach a piano keyboard.

'It'll make his toes grow out until they're as long as his fingers . . . It's most useful. He'll be able to play the piano with his feet.' – CHARLIE AND THE CHOCOLATE FACTORY

pibbling adjective

very small and very unimportant

'You is not fit to be a giant! You is a squinky little squiddler! You is a pibbling little pitsqueak!' – THE BFG

RINGBELLING RHYMES Try rhyming with *dribbling* or *sibling*.

picnic noun picnics

a meal of cold food that you eat outside

'There he is waiting until some happy families is coming to have a picnic under the spreading tree. The Meatdripping Giant is watching them as they lay out their little picnic.' – THE BFG

pie noun pies

a baked dish of meat or fruit covered with pastry, such as Bird Pie or Boy Pie

Mr Twit was furious. 'As there are no birds for my pie tonight,' he shouted, 'then it'll have to be boys instead!' – THE TWITS

pierce verb pierces, piercing, pierced

When you pierce something, you make a hole through it. If a sound pierces the air, it makes a sudden, very loud noise.

The air was suddenly pierced by the most fearful roar Sophie had ever heard, and she saw the Fleshlumpeater's body . . . rise up off the ground and fall back again with a thump. – THE BFG

piffle noun (informal)

Piffle is nonsense or rubbish. If something is complete rubbish, it is **pigspiffle**.

'Cut the piffle, Shanks,' snapped the President. 'This is a national emergency!' – CHARLIE AND THE GREAT GLASS ELEVATOR

SPARKY SYNONYMS You can also say **rubbsquash** or **rommytot**.

pig noun pigs

A pig is a fat animal with short legs and a blunt snout. George's father, Mr Kranky, keeps pigs for their meat.

The last bottle on the shelf was full of pale green pills. PIG PILLS, the label announced. FOR PIGS WITH PORK PRICKLES, TENDER TROTTERS, BRISTLE BLIGHT AND SWINE SICKNESS. – GEORGE'S MARVELLOUS MEDICINE

piggery-jokery noun

Piggery-jokery means acting in a silly way and not taking things seriously.

'But you must all be very very hushy quiet. No roaring of motors. No shouting. No mucking about. No piggery-jokery.' – THE BFG

DID YOU KNOW? *Piggery-jokery* is a *spoonerism* based on *jiggery-pokery*, which means being dishonest or deceitful. You can read more about spoonerisms in the entry for **mideous**.

piggy-wig or piggy-wiggy noun piggy-wigs, piggy-wiggies

the name that the BFG (and some **chiddlers**) give to a pig or a **snipsy** piglet

'That is what the little piggy-wig is saying every day,' the BFG answered. 'He is saying, "I has never done any harm to the human bean so why should he be eating me?"' – THE BFG

pigsquibble noun

Pigsquibble is like **swigpill**, and tastes just as nasty.

'May I taste it?' the Queen asked. 'Don't, Majester, don't!' cried the BFG. 'It is tasting of trogfilth and pigsquibble!' – THE BFG

A B C D E F G H I J K L M N O **P** Q R S T U V W X Y Z

pigtail noun pigtails

A pigtail is a long plait of hair that you wear either at the back or at each side of your head. Miss Trunchbull has a deep dislike of pigtails, and it is therefore EXTREMELY RISKY to wear them to her school.
Suddenly, with a mighty grunt, the Trunchbull let go of the pigtails and Amanda went sailing like a rocket right over the wire fence of the playground and high up into the sky. — MATILDA

pigwash noun

nonsense or lies
'I fear no Knids!' said Mr Wonka. 'We've got them beaten now!' 'Poppyrot and pigwash!' said Grandma Josephine.
— CHARLIE AND THE GREAT GLASS ELEVATOR
DID YOU KNOW? Roald Dahl invented the word *pigwash*, but he may have been thinking of *hogwash*, which also means 'nonsense'. *Hogwash* originally meant pig swill or kitchen scraps fed to pigs.

pigwinkle noun pigwinkles

The pigwinkle *(Winkela porcana)* is a delicious vegetable that grows in many countries that the BFG visits, but not in Giant Country as the soil is too dry.
'In this sloshflunking Giant Country, happy eats like pineapples and pigwinkles is simply not growing.' — THE BFG
DID YOU KNOW? When he invented the word *pigwinkle*, Roald Dahl may have been thinking of *pignut*, which is a sweet-tasting root vegetable. A *pigwinkle* might be a vegetable that pigs like to eat and 'winkle' out of the ground.

pile noun piles

a number of things on top of one another
The pile of marbles beside them kept growing larger and larger. Soon there was a truckload of them there at least. — JAMES AND THE GIANT PEACH

pill noun pills

a small tablet of medicine or a magic formula that you swallow
'If I'm going to eat one of those pills, I jolly well want to know what's in it first,' said Grandma Josephine.
— CHARLIE AND THE GREAT GLASS ELEVATOR

pillow noun pillows

A pillow is a cushion that you rest your head on in bed. Willy Wonka has invented edible pillows made of marshmallow.
Propped up against the pillows at the other end of the bed was the most extraordinary-looking thing Charlie had ever seen! — CHARLIE AND THE GREAT GLASS ELEVATOR

pilot noun pilots

someone who flies an aeroplane or helicopter
Every now and then, the pilots of the helicopters would catch a glimpse of a small girl wearing glasses crouching in the giant's right ear and waving to them. — THE BFG

pimple noun pimples

a spot on our skin, such as the one on Aunt Spiker's chin
'Behold MY gorgeous curvy shape, my teeth, my charming grin!/Oh, beauteous me! . . . And please ignore/The pimple on my chin.' — JAMES AND THE GIANT PEACH

pin noun pins

A pin is a thin piece of metal with a sharp point that you use to hold pieces of cloth together. If someone is as small as a pin, they are very tiny indeed.
Grandma was the size of a match-stick and still shrinking fast. A moment later, she was no bigger than a pin . . .
— GEORGE'S MARVELLOUS MEDICINE

pin verb pins, pinning, pinned

1 When you pin something, you fasten it with a pin.
The Queen had picked up a superb sapphire brooch from her dressing-table and had pinned it on the left side of Sophie's chest. — THE BFG
2 If something pins you down, it holds you so that you cannot move.
All the time the water came pouring and roaring down upon them . . . and it was like being pinned down underneath the biggest waterfall in the world and not being able to get out. — JAMES AND THE GIANT PEACH

pinch verb pinches, pinching, pinched

1 When you pinch something, you squeeze it tightly between your finger and thumb.
Standing behind Eric, the Trunchbull reached out and took hold of the boy's two ears, one with each hand, pinching them between forefinger and thumb.
— MATILDA
2 *(informal)* If someone pinches something, they steal it.
My own father a thief! This gentle lovely man! I couldn't believe he would go creeping into the woods at night to pinch valuable birds. — DANNY THE CHAMPION OF THE WORLD

pinched adjective

Someone with a pinched look is thin and pale because they are cold or hungry.

And every day, Charlie Bucket grew thinner and thinner. His face became frighteningly white and pinched.
—CHARLIE AND THE CHOCOLATE FACTORY

pineapple noun pineapples

A pineapple is a large fruit with yellow flesh that grows in hot countries, but not in Giant Country as the soil is too dry there.

'In this sloshflunking Giant Country, happy eats like pineapples and pigwinkles is simply not growing.'
—THE BFG

DID YOU KNOW? The word *pineapple* used to mean 'pine-cone' and later came to mean a pineapple too, because it looked a bit like a pine-cone. Perhaps if pineapples grew in Giant Country, the BFG would have his own name for them, like a *pineypapple* or a *gobblefruit*.

ping-pong noun

Ping-pong is a game in which you hit a small ball over a table with bats. It is also called *table tennis*. The BFG has his breakfast at the Palace on a makeshift table made from a *ping-pong table* and four grandfather clocks.

Mr Tibbs stood back to survey the new furniture . . . He gave orders that a damask tablecloth should be draped over the ping-pong table, and in the end it looked really quite elegant after all.—THE BFG

pink adjective pinker, pinkest

Something that is pink is very pale red.

'Witches have slightly larger nose-holes than ordinary people. The rim of each nose-hole is pink and curvy, like the rim of a certain kind of sea-shell.'—THE WITCHES

Pink-Spotted Scrunch noun Pink-Spotted Scrunches

The Pink-Spotted Scrunch is a dangerous man-eating creature with a deadly bite and a huge appetite.

'We may see the venomous Pink-Spotted Scrunch/ Who can chew up a man with one bite./It likes to eat five of them roasted for lunch/And eighteen for its supper at night.'—JAMES AND THE GIANT PEACH

pint noun pints

You can measure liquids in pints. One pint is about half a litre.

George, with Mr Kranky watching him anxiously, tipped half a pint of engine oil and some anti-freeze into the giant saucepan.—GEORGE'S MARVELLOUS MEDICINE

pipe noun pipes

a hollow tube for carrying water, gas, oil or chocolate from one place to another

Charlie could see that they were indeed inside a gigantic pipe, and the great upward-curving walls of the pipe were pure white and spotlessly clean.—CHARLIE AND THE CHOCOLATE FACTORY

pipe verb pipes, piping, piped

If you pipe up, you start to say something.

'And what exactly is this magic method, Miss Honey?' asked the Headmistress. 'I'll show you,' piped up the brave Nigel again, coming to Miss Honey's rescue.—MATILDA

pirate noun pirates

a sailor who attacks and robs other ships

'Would Columbus have discovered America if he'd said "What if I sink on the way over? What if I meet pirates? What if I never come back?"'—CHARLIE AND THE GREAT GLASS ELEVATOR

RINGBELLING RHYMES Try rhyming with *fire it!* (as pirates often fire cannons).

Pishlet noun Pishlets

a type of sweet sold in the Grubber that makes a whistling noise when you suck it

Pishlets, as you probably know, are bought by children who are unable to whistle a tune as they walk along the street but long to do so.—THE GIRAFFE AND THE PELLY AND ME

pit noun pits

a deep hole in the ground

With thousands of fascinated spectators, including the Queen, peering down into the pit, the BFG was lowered on a rope.—THE BFG

pitch-black or pitch-dark adjective

as dark as the darkest moonless night

'A REAL WITCH has the most amazing powers of smell. She can actually smell out a child who is standing on the other side of the street on a pitch-black night.'
—THE WITCHES

pity noun

If something is a pity, it is unfortunate or disappointing.

Mrs Twit . . . did not, of course, have a hairy face. It was a pity she didn't because that at any rate would have hidden some of her fearful ugliness.—THE TWITS

pizzened adjective

If a giant is pizzened, he has been poisoned with deadly venom.

'I is pulling out the frightsome viper's teeth!' the BFG said as he pulled the knot tight. 'Do it quickly!' shouted the Fleshlumpeater, 'before I is pizzened to death!'
—THE BFG

plain adjective plainer, plainest

1 Something that is plain is simple and not decorated.

The walls, the ceiling and the floor of our bedrooms were made of plain unvarnished pine planks.—BOY

Don't be *a witless weed!* Read all about saying nasty things at **insult**.

a
b
c
d
e
f
g
h
i
j
k
l
m
n
o
p
q
r
s
t
u
v
w
x
y
z

2 A plain person or a plain face is neither pretty nor ugly.
Miss Honey looked at the plain plump person with the smug suet-pudding face who was sitting across the room.
—MATILDA

plain noun plains
a large area of flat ground
The giants roared and screamed and cursed, and for many minutes the noise of battle rolled across the yellow plain.
—THE BFG

plait verb plaits, plaiting, plaited
When you plait hair, you twist three pieces together by crossing them over and under each other.
'That idiot Amanda,' Hortensia said, 'has let her long hair grow even longer during the hols and her mother has plaited it into pigtails.'—MATILDA

plan noun plans
If you have a plan, you have an idea about how to do something.
Bean picked his nose delicately with a long finger. 'I have a plan,' he said. 'You've never had a decent plan yet,' said Bunce.—FANTASTIC MR FOX

plan verb plans, planning, planned
When you plan something, you decide what you are going to do and how you are going to do it.
My father . . . must have planned this one beforehand because he had already bought the four big sheets of tissue-paper and the pot of glue from Mr Witton's bookshop in the village.—DANNY THE CHAMPION OF THE WORLD

planet noun planets
A planet is a very large object in space that moves around a star or around our sun. Earth and Vermes are both planets.
'These Vermicious Knids are the terror of the Universe. They travel through space in great swarms, landing on other stars and planets and destroying everything they find.'—CHARLIE AND THE GREAT GLASS ELEVATOR

plank noun planks
a long, flat piece of wood
There were no pictures on the walls, no carpet on the floor, only rough unpolished wooden planks, and there were gaps between the planks where dust and bits of grime had gathered.—MATILDA

plant noun plants
A plant is a living thing that grows in the soil. Trees, flowers and vegetables like the **snozzcumber** are all plants.
'I is also bringing in this sack a whole bungle of snozzcumber plants which I is giving, with your permission, to the royal gardener to put in the soil.'—THE BFG

plaster noun
Plaster is a mixture of lime, sand and water, used to cover walls and ceilings.
The floorboards shake and from the wall/Some bits of paint and plaster fall./Explosions, whistles, awful bangs/

Were followed by the loudest clangs.—CHARLIE AND THE GREAT GLASS ELEVATOR

platform noun platforms
a small stage in a hall
The disgusting old Grand High Witch began to do a sort of witch's dance up and down the platform, stamping her feet and clapping her hands.—THE WITCHES

play verb plays, playing, played
1 When you play, you take part in games and have fun.
'So now we can all go down to pick blackberries and winkleberries and . . . our children can play among the wild flowers and the roots all day long.'
—THE MINPINS
2 When you play an instrument, you use it to make music.
What a wonderful instrument the Old-Green-Grasshopper was playing upon. It was like a violin!—JAMES AND THE GIANT PEACH

playground noun playgrounds
a place outside a school where you can play at break times
There was a flash of brown and something jumped into the playground and hopped up on to the top of the swings. It was Muggle-Wump, the Monkey.
—THE ENORMOUS CROCODILE

pleasant adjective **pleasanter, pleasantest**

Something that is pleasant is pleasing or enjoyable. A pleasant person is good-natured and friendly.

Soon the entire village was convinced that the new vicar was completely barmy. Pleasant and harmless, they said, but completely and utterly barmy. — THE VICAR OF NIBBLESWICKE

LOOK IT UP! For many more ways to describe pleasant things, see **good**.

please adverb

You say *please* when you want to ask for something politely.

'Please don't mention Bird Pie again,' said the Roly-Poly Bird. 'It gives me the shudders.' — THE TWITS

pleased adjective

If you are pleased, you are happy or satisfied with something.

'Why even your toes must be as big as sausages.' 'Bigger,' said the BFG, looking pleased. — THE BFG

pleasure noun

the feeling that you have when you are happy and enjoying yourself

The BFG smiled a big wide smile of absolute pleasure. 'I is loving it when they is all having a good tough and rumble,' he said. — THE BFG

plenty noun

If there is plenty of something, there is as much as you need.

'Buckets and paint-brushes!' cried Muggle-Wump. 'That's what we want next! There are plenty in the workshed!' — THE TWITS

plexicated adjective

If something is plexicated, it is complicated and difficult to do or make.

'Stay there please,' he said, 'and no chittering. I is needing to listen only to silence when I is mixing up such a knotty plexicated dream as this.' — THE BFG

plonk verb (*informal*) **plonks, plonking, plonked**

When you plonk something, you drop or throw it down carelessly.

George scooped the orange-coloured waxy stuff out of the tin and plonked it into the pan. — GEORGE'S MARVELLOUS MEDICINE

plop noun **plops**

the sound of something dropping into a liquid

Lavender . . . held the box over the neck of the jug and pulled the lid fully open and tipped the newt in. There was a plop as it landed in the water. — MATILDA

LOOK IT UP! For more examples of onomatopoeia, see **gliss**.

plot noun **plots**

a secret plan to do something

'It's a plot,' Thwaites said. 'A grown-up plot to keep us quiet.' — BOY

plot verb **plots, plotting, plotted**

If someone is plotting, they are making a secret plan to do something (often something very nasty).

'Whenever you go all quiet like that I know very well you're plotting something.' Mrs Twit was right. Mr Twit was plotting away like mad. — THE TWITS

pluck verb **plucks, plucking, plucked**

1 When someone plucks a bird, they pull its feathers off before they cook or eat it.

a b c d e f g h i j k l m n o **p** q r s t u v w x y z

'Oh, what a fantastic fox your father is! Hurry up, child, and start plucking those chickens!' – FANTASTIC MR FOX

2 If a person or giant plucks you from a place, they take you away from it suddenly.

She knew that a Monster (or Giant) with an enormous long pale wrinkly face and dangerous eyes had plucked her from her bed in the middle of the witching hour. – THE BFG

plummet verb plummets, plummeting, plummeted

When something plummets, it drops downwards quickly.

Round and round and upside down went the peach as it plummeted towards the earth, and they were all clinging desperately to the stem to save themselves from being flung into space. – JAMES AND THE GIANT PEACH

plump adjective plumper, plumpest

Someone who is plump is quite fat. A plump fruit is full and juicy.

Some wealthy folks from U.S.A./Who lived near San Francisco Bay,/Possessed an only child called Roy,/A plump and unattractive boy. – DIRTY BEASTS

'First, you take a few raisins and you soak them in water overnight to make them plump and soft and juicy.' – DANNY THE CHAMPION OF THE WORLD

plunge verb plunges, plunging, plunged

If you plunge into something, you jump or dive into it.

They plunged into a thick bank of cloud and for ten seconds they could see nothing. – CHARLIE AND THE GREAT GLASS ELEVATOR

RINGBELLING RHYMES Try rhyming with *lunge* or *Aunt Sponge*.

Plushnugget noun Plushnuggets

A Plushnugget is a sweet from the Land of the Midnight Sun (the Arctic or Antarctic) that is sold in the Grubber.

There were . . . Tummyticklers and Gobwangles from the Fiji Islands and Liplickers and Plushnuggets from the Land of the Midnight Sun. – THE GIRAFFE AND THE PELLY AND ME

plussy (rhymes with fussy) adjective plussier, plussiest

Someone who is plussy is full of life and energy. Being plussy is the opposite of being a Minus.

'She's a Minus no longer! She's a lovely Plus! She's as plussy as plussy can be!' – CHARLIE AND THE GREAT GLASS ELEVATOR

poach verb poaches, poaching, poached

When someone poaches, they hunt animals or birds illegally on someone else's land. Danny's father is an expert at poaching and has his own Secret Methods for catching pheasants.

'Is that actually what you were doing in Hazell's Wood, Dad? Poaching pheasants?' 'I was practising the art,' he said. 'The art of poaching.' – DANNY THE CHAMPION OF THE WORLD

poacher noun poachers

someone who poaches animals or birds or fish

'Your grandad,' he said, 'my own dad, was a magnificent and splendiferous poacher . . . I caught the poaching fever

from him when I was ten years old and I've never lost it since.' – DANNY THE CHAMPION OF THE WORLD

pocket noun pockets

A pocket is a small bag sewn into a piece of clothing that you can keep things in. Willy Wonka keeps a catapult, a yo-yo, a rubber fried-egg, a slice of salami, a tooth filling, a stinkbomb and a packet of itching-powder in his pockets (so they must be quite roomy). The amount that a pocket holds is a **pocketful**.

'I know it's here somewhere,' he said. 'I can't have lost it. I keep all my most valuable and important things in these pockets.' – CHARLIE AND THE GREAT GLASS ELEVATOR

pocket money noun

Pocket money is a small amount of money that your parents or other grown-ups give you to spend, usually every week. It is supposed to last for a whole week but rarely does.

'Everlasting Gobstoppers!' cried Mr Wonka proudly. 'They're completely new! I am inventing them for children who are given very little pocket money.' – CHARLIE AND THE CHOCOLATE FACTORY

poddle noun poddles

Poddle is a word that giants use to mean a pod, such as a pea-pod.

'Will he snatch them out of their beds while they're sleeping?' 'Like peas out of a poddle,' the BFG said. – THE BFG

RINGBELLING RHYMES Try rhyming with *toddle* or *waddle*.

poem noun poems

A poem is a piece of writing arranged in short lines, which often has a special rhythm and uses rhyming words. Someone who writes poems is a **poet**.

She recited a poem to him that was well-known in the district. It went like this: Beware! Beware! The Forest of Sin!/None come out, but many go in! – THE MINPINS

LOOK IT UP! For some types of poem, see **limerick**, **rhyme** and **riddle**.

poetry noun

poetry is poems as a form of literature

Matilda, who had never before heard great romantic poetry spoken aloud, was profoundly moved. 'It's like music,' she whispered. – MATILDA

pogswizzler noun pogswizzlers

A pogswizzler is a very rude name that the other giants call the BFG.

The Bloodbottler pointed a finger as large as a tree-trunk at the BFG. 'Runty little scumscrewer!' he shouted . . . 'Prunty little pogswizzler!' – THE BFG

pointed adjective

Something that is pointed has a sharp point at one end.

'There's these three old birds in nightshirts floating around in this crazy glass box and there's a funny little guy with a pointed beard wearing a black top hat.' – CHARLIE AND THE GREAT GLASS ELEVATOR

poisnowse adjective
poisonous or venomous
*'Even poisnowse snakes is never killing each other,'
the BFG said. 'Nor is the most fearsome creatures like
tigers and rhinostossterisses.'*—THE BFG

poison noun **poisons**
something that will kill you or make you ill if you
swallow it
*'If I was unlucky enough to be married to Mrs Snoddy,
I would drink something a bit stronger than gin.'
'What would you drink, Dad?' 'Poison,' he said.*
—DANNY THE CHAMPION OF THE WORLD

poisonous adjective
If something is poisonous it will kill you or make you
ill if you swallow it.
*'So give me a bug and a jumping flea,/Give me two snails
and lizards three,/And a slimy squiggler from the sea,/
And the poisonous sting of a bumblebee.'*—GEORGE'S
MARVELLOUS MEDICINE

poke verb **pokes, poking, poked**
1 If you poke something, you push it with your finger or
with something sharp, such as a stick or a stick-like aunt.
*Aunt Spiker was thin as a wire,/And dry as a bone, only
drier./She was so long and thin/If you carried her in/
You could use her for poking the fire!*—JAMES AND THE
GIANT PEACH
2 If you poke your head out, you stick it out from
somewhere.
*At that precise moment, Grandma Josephine poked her
head out from under the sheets and peered over the edge
of the bed.*—CHARLIE AND THE GREAT GLASS ELEVATOR

pole noun **poles**
a long stick, such as the long shaft of the BFG's
dream-catcher
*The pole was about thirty feet long and there was a net
on the end of it. 'Here is the dream-catcher,' he said,
grasping the pole in one hand.*—THE BFG

police noun
The police are the people whose job is to catch criminals
and make sure that people do not break the law.
*The police had taken away the fearsome burglar known
as the Cobra, and the fainting Duchess had been carried
into the house by her servants.*—THE GIRAFFE AND THE PELLY
AND ME

polish verb **polishes, polishing, polished**
When you polish something, you rub it to make it shine.
*'My goodness, I've forgotten to polish my boots!' the
Centipede said. 'Everyone must help me to polish my
boots before we arrive.'*—JAMES AND THE GIANT PEACH

polite adjective **politer, politest**
Someone who is polite has good manners and is not
rude to people.
*'What an impudent fellow Rat is.' 'He has bad manners,'
Badger said. 'All rats have bad manners. I've never met
a polite rat yet.'*—FANTASTIC MR FOX

polly–frog noun **polly-frogs**
The polly-frog is a rare and ancient animal. Part of the
polly-frog is needed to make Vita-Wonk, but only
Willy Wonka knows which part as it is a secret recipe.
*'I tracked down THE WHISTLE-PIG, THE BOBOLINK,
THE SKROCK, THE POLLY-FROG, THE GIANT CURLICUE,
THE STINGING SLUG AND THE VENOMOUS SQUERKLE.'*
—CHARLIE AND THE GREAT GLASS ELEVATOR

pond noun **ponds**
a small lake
*The newt, although fairly common in English ponds, is not
often seen by ordinary people because it is a shy and
murky creature.*—MATILDA

pony noun **ponies**
a small horse
*This ancient old hag, who was now as tall as a house,
then galloped about the farm on the gigantic pony,
jumping over trees and sheds.*—GEORGE'S MARVELLOUS
MEDICINE

poor adjective **poorer, poorest**
1 Someone who is poor does not have very much
money. Charlie Bucket and his family are desperately
poor before he finds the Golden Ticket.
*There wasn't any question of them being able to buy
a better house — or even one more bed to sleep in.
They were far too poor for that.*—CHARLIE AND THE
CHOCOLATE FACTORY
2 A poor person is unlucky or unhappy.
*Badger sat down and put a paw around his small son.
'We're done for,' he said softly. 'My poor wife up
there is so weak she can't dig another yard.'*—FANTASTIC
MR FOX

Pooza noun Poozas

A Pooza is an ancient creature that once inhabited the moon. Poozas are now extinct as every last one was hunted down and eaten by the Vermicious Knids, who found them very tasty.

There used to be some rather nice creatures living on the moon a long time ago. They were called Poozas. But the Vermicious Knids ate the lot. — CHARLIE AND THE GREAT GLASS ELEVATOR

pop verb pops, popping, popped

1 If something pops, it bursts with a loud bang.
'Don't you remember what happens when a Knid enters the Earth's atmosphere at high speed? . . . Soon these dirty beasts will start popping like popcorn!' — CHARLIE AND THE GREAT GLASS ELEVATOR

2 If your eyes pop, they bulge out because you are shocked or surprised.
The Duke was staggered. He reeled back and his eyes popped nearly out of their sockets. — THE GIRAFFE AND THE PELLY AND ME

3 If you pop something in or out, you put it in or take it out quickly.
You can play a lot of tricks with a glass eye because you can take it out and pop it back in again any time you like. — THE TWITS

4 (*informal*) If you pop somewhere, you go there quickly.
'Mrs Silver,' he said. 'Do you think I could pop down to your balcony and hold Alfie myself?' — ESIO TROT

popcorn noun

Popcorn is food that is made by heating grains of corn until they burst and become big and fluffy. When giants eat **human beans**, they stuff them in their mouths like popcorn.

'I don't know what you're talking about,' the King said, growing testy. 'It's hardly a joking matter when one's loyal subjects are being eaten like popcorn.' — THE BFG

pop-eyed adjective

If someone is pop-eyed, their eyes are bulging and staring with horror or surprise.

The girl was glued to the spot, terror-struck, pop-eyed, quivering, knowing for certain that the Day of Judgement had come for her at last. — MATILDA

poppyrot noun

nonsense or lies

'I fear no Knids!' said Mr Wonka. 'We've got them beaten now!' 'Poppyrot and pigwash!' said Grandma Josephine. — CHARLIE AND THE GREAT GLASS ELEVATOR

SPARKY SYNONYMS You can also say **crodswoggle** or **rommytot.**

Gobblefunking with words
To make the word *poppyrot* Roald Dahl may have joined together parts from two other words which mean 'nonsense': *poppycock* and *tommyrot*. This way of making a new word from parts of old ones is called *blending.* You can try making your own blends from parts of words, such as *carsnip* from *carrot* and *parsnip.*

---

population noun populations

The population of a place is the number of people who live there.

'The population of each tree looks after itself. Our large trees are like your cities and towns, and the small trees are like your villages.' — THE MINPINS

porpoise noun porpoises

A porpoise is a sea animal rather like a small whale, with a triangular fin and a blunt nose. Norwegian witches sometimes turn children into porpoises.

'When he came to the surface at last, he wasn't Leif any more.' 'What was he, Grandmamma?' 'He was a porpoise.' — THE WITCHES

DID YOU KNOW? The word *porpoise* comes from French and means literally 'pig fish', because of the porpoise's pig-like snout. The ancient Romans called it *porcus marinus* or 'pig of the sea'.

RINGBELLING RHYMES *Porpoise* is a useful rhyme for *tortoise,* but unfortunately this does not work in tortoise language (i.e. backwards), as then it would be *esio prop,* which does not quite rhyme with **Esio Trot.**

porridge noun

Porridge is a food made by boiling oatmeal or rolled oats to make a thick paste, usually eaten at breakfast. (In North America it is called *oatmeal.*) Good porridge is gloopy but not lumpy.

I could hardly believe that I didn't have to wash in cold water in the mornings . . . or eat porridge for breakfast that seemed full of little round lumpy grey sheep's-droppings. — BOY

porteedo noun **porteedoes**

A porteedo is what the BFG calls a torpedo, a long sausage-shaped missile that can be fired from a ship or a **bellypopper.**

'You do not put him inside,' the BFG said. 'You sling him underneath the belly of your bellypopper and carry him like a porteedo.' — THE BFG

possess verb possesses, possessing, possessed
If you possess something, you own it or have it.
Miss Honey . . . felt wildly excited. She had just met a
small girl who possessed, or so it seemed to her, quite
extraordinary qualities of brilliance. — MATILDA

possession noun possessions
A possession is something that you own or have.
Your proudest or prize possession is the thing that
you are most happy to own.
If you wish to be friends with a Giraffe, never say
anything bad about its neck. Its neck is its proudest
possession. — THE GIRAFFE AND THE PELLY AND ME

possible adjective
If something is possible, it might happen, or it might
be true.
'You're shrinking, woman!' said Mr Twit. 'It's not possible!'
'Oh yes it jolly well is,' said Mr Twit. — THE TWITS

post noun posts
1 A post is a pole that is fixed in the ground.
There was a big hole in the floor and another in the
ceiling, and sticking up like a post between the two was
the middle part of Grandma. — GEORGE'S MARVELLOUS
MEDICINE
2 The post is all the letters and parcels that are
delivered to people's houses.
'I had sent away by post, you see, for this very powerful
itching-powder,' Hortensia said. — MATILDA

pot–bellied adjective
A pot-bellied person, like Farmer Bunce, has a round
fat tummy.
The tall skinny Bean and dwarfish pot-bellied Bunce
were driving their machines like maniacs, racing the
motors and making the shovels dig at a terrific speed.
— FANTASTIC MR FOX

poultry plural noun
Poultry are birds such
as chickens, geese and
turkeys that are kept
on a farm for their eggs
and meat. Farmers Boggis,
Bunce and Bean are poultry
farmers.

pounce verb
pounces, pouncing,
pounced
If you pounce on something, you attack it by jumping
on it suddenly.
The Pelican opened his gigantic beak and immediately
the policemen pounced upon the burglar, who was
crouching inside. — THE GIRAFFE AND THE PELLY AND ME
RINGBELLING RHYMES Try rhyming with *bounce*.

pound noun pounds
1 You can measure weight in pounds. One pound
is about half a kilogram.
'What piffle!' said Grandma Georgina. 'I weigh one
hundred and thirty-seven pounds exactly.' 'Not now you
don't,' said Mr Wonka. 'You are completely weightless.'
— CHARLIE AND THE GREAT GLASS ELEVATOR
2 A pound is a unit of money. Pounds are used
in Britain and some other countries.
In one city, a famous gangster robbed a bank of a
thousand pounds and spent the whole lot on Wonka
bars that same afternoon. — CHARLIE AND THE CHOCOLATE
FACTORY

pound verb pounds, pounding, pounded
1 If you pound something, you hit or punch it
repeatedly.
The two of them rushed at the Fleshlumpeater and began
pounding him with their fists and feet. — THE BFG
2 If something pounds, it runs or moves with loud
heavy steps.
Then suddenly he heard another noise that was
somehow more fearsome still. It was the pounding
of gigantic galloping hooves on the floor of the forest.
— THE MINPINS

pour verb pours, pouring, poured
1 When you pour a liquid, or a dream made of **zozimus**,
you tip it into a container.
The BFG . . . unscrewed the lid. Now, very cautiously,
he poured the precious dream into the wide end of his
trumpet. — THE BFG
2 When liquid or smoke is pouring out of something,
it is coming out very quickly.

a
b
c
d
e
f
g
h
i
j
k
l
m
n
o
p
q
r
s
t
u
v
w
x
y
z

All of a sudden, black smoke started pouring out of the hen's beak. 'It's on fire!' Grandma yelled. — GEORGE'S MARVELLOUS MEDICINE

powder noun
a substance like flour that is dry and made of lots of tiny bits
There was something called BRILLIDENT FOR CLEANING FALSE TEETH. It was a white powder. In that went, too. — GEORGE'S MARVELLOUS MEDICINE

power noun powers
1 If you have power, you can do what you want, or make other people do what you want.
'You can't stop witches,' she said. 'Just look at the power that terrible Grand High Witch has in her eyes alone!' — THE WITCHES
2 If you have special powers, you are able to do magic things.
'Didn't I tell you I had magic powers! Didn't I warn you I had wizardry in the tips of my fingers!' — GEORGE'S MARVELLOUS MEDICINE
3 Power is energy that makes machines work.
'Are we all right?' cried Grandpa Joe. 'How does this thing stay up?' 'Sugar power!' said Mr Wonka. 'One million sugar power!' — CHARLIE AND THE CHOCOLATE FACTORY

powerful adjective
1 Someone who is powerful has a lot of power over other people.
In his study in the White House sat Lancelot R. Gilligrass, President of the United States of America, the most powerful man on Earth. — CHARLIE AND THE GREAT GLASS ELEVATOR
2 Something that is powerful is very strong.
As though drawn by some powerful magnet, James Henry Trotter started walking slowly towards the giant peach. — JAMES AND THE GIANT PEACH

practice noun
Practice is when you do something again and again so that you will get better at it.
Now for the practice, she told herself. It's going to be tough but I'm determined to do it. — MATILDA

practise verb practises, practising, practised
When you practise, you keep doing something over and over again so that you will get better at it.
'The children all practise learning to fly on robins. Robins are sensible and careful birds and they love the little ones.' — THE MINPINS

pram noun prams
A pram is a four-wheeled carriage for pushing a baby along. Danny's father comes up with a method for smuggling pheasants inside a pram, but sometimes the birds have other ideas.
Suddenly, out of the pram, straight up into the air, flew an enormous pheasant! — DANNY THE CHAMPION OF THE WORLD
RINGBELLING RHYMES Try rhyming with S-C-R-A-M.

precious adjective
Something that is precious is worth a lot of money, or is very special to someone.
Now the whole country, indeed, the whole world, seemed suddenly to be caught up in a mad chocolate-buying spree, everybody searching frantically for those precious remaining tickets. — CHARLIE AND THE CHOCOLATE FACTORY

precocious adjective
a precocious child is very advanced or developed for their age
'A precocious child,' Miss Honey said, 'is one that shows amazing intelligence early on. You are an unbelievably precocious child.' 'Am I really?' Matilda asked. — MATILDA

prefer verb prefers, preferring, preferred
If you prefer one thing to another, you like it more.
'That is better than bagglepipes, is it not, Majester?' It took the Queen a few seconds to get over the shock. 'I prefer the bagpipes,' she said. — THE BFG

prepare verb prepares, preparing, prepared
When you prepare something, you get it ready. When you prepare yourself, you get ready to do something.
'You vill prepare yourselves for this Great Gala Opening by filling every choc and every sveet in your shop vith my very latest and grrreatest magic formula!' — THE WITCHES
'Yesterday I am personally prrree-paring a small qvantity of the magic formula in order to give to you a public demonstration.' — THE WITCHES

present adjective
If you are present in a place, you are there.
The entire Cabinet was present. The Chief of the Army was there, together with four other generals. — CHARLIE AND THE GREAT GLASS ELEVATOR

present noun presents
something that you give to someone
'Come down out of that tree, little boy,' she said, 'and I shall give you the most exciting present you've ever had.' — THE WITCHES

present verb presents, presenting, presented
If you present something to someone, you give it to them.
The whole family saved up their money for that special occasion, and when the great day arrived, Charlie was always presented with one small chocolate bar to eat all by himself. — CHARLIE AND THE CHOCOLATE FACTORY

president noun presidents

the head of a country that is a republic, like France or the United States

Everybody heard the American President's invitation to the men from Mars to visit him in the White House. — CHARLIE AND THE GREAT GLASS ELEVATOR

press verb presses, pressing, pressed

When you press something, you push it with your finger.

'Here we go!' cried Mr Wonka, and he pressed three different buttons on the side of the machine. — CHARLIE AND THE CHOCOLATE FACTORY

pretend verb pretends, pretending, pretended

When you pretend, you say things or do things that are not really true.

All of them including The Grand High Witch herself are downstairs now! They're pretending they're the Royal Society for the Prevention of Cruelty to Children! — THE WITCHES

pretty adjective prettier, prettiest

1 Something that is pretty is pleasing to look at.
Mr Twit stood below looking up. 'What a pretty sight!' he said to himself. 'How lovely all those balloons look in the sky.' — THE TWITS
2 A pretty girl or woman has an attractive face.
She'd found it easy, being pretty,/To hitch a ride into the city,/And there she'd got a job, unpaid,/As general cook and parlour-maid. — REVOLTING RHYMES

LOOK IT UP! For other ways to describe pretty things, see **good**.

pretty adverb (informal)

fairly or moderately

Even to Mr Hoppy, peering down over his railing, Tortoise Number 8 looked pretty big. — ESIO TROT

prevent verb prevents, preventing, prevented

If you prevent something from happening, you stop it from happening.

Sophie dug her nails into the sides of the pocket, trying to prevent herself from tumbling out when she was upside down. — THE BFG

price noun prices

The price of something is the amount of money you have to pay for it.

'Roll up! Roll up!' Aunt Spiker yelled. 'Only one shilling to see the giant peach!' 'Half price for children under six weeks old!' Aunt Sponge shouted. — JAMES AND THE GIANT PEACH

prick verb pricks, pricking, pricked

When you prick something, you make a tiny hole in it with something sharp.

'You're blowing up like a balloon!' 'Like a blueberry,' said Mr Wonka. 'Call a doctor!' shouted Mr Beauregarde. 'Prick her with a pin!' said one of the other fathers. — CHARLIE AND THE CHOCOLATE FACTORY

prickle noun prickles

1 a sharp spine on an animal or plant
A hundred prickles sticking in/And puncturing my precious skin!/I ran for home. I shouted, 'Mum!/Behold the prickles in my bum!' — DIRTY BEASTS
2 a feeling that something is pricking you
It was a smell unlike any he had smelled before . . . Whenever he got a whiff of it up his nose, firecrackers went off in his skull and electric prickles ran along the backs of his legs. — GEORGE'S MARVELLOUS MEDICINE

prickly adjective pricklier, prickliest

Something that is prickly has lots of sharp points.

I think I know why porcupines/Surround themselves with prickly spines./It is to stop some silly clown/From squashing them by sitting down. — DIRTY BEASTS

RINGBELLING RHYMES Try rhyming with *quickly* or *tickly*.

pride noun

the feeling you have when you are proud

My father paused, and there was a gleam of pride in his eyes as he dwelt for a moment upon the memory of his own dad, the great poaching inventor. — DANNY THE CHAMPION OF THE WORLD

prim adjective primmer, primmest

Someone who is prim behaves in a very formal and correct way.

'Drive us to the station, please,' my grandmother said, looking prim. — THE WITCHES

prince noun princes

1 a man or boy in a royal family, especially the son of a king or queen
'Prince Pondicherry wrote a letter to Mr Willy Wonka,' said Grandpa Joe, 'and asked him to come all the way out to India and build him a colossal palace entirely out of chocolate.' — CHARLIE AND THE CHOCOLATE FACTORY
2 The Prince of Darkness is another name for the Devil.
'We are the crusaders, the gallant army fighting for our

The word *pretty* originally meant 'crafty or cunning'—just like Mr Fox!

a b c d e f g h i j k l m n o p q r s t u v w x y z

lives with hardly any weapons at all and the Trunchbull is the Prince of Darkness, the Foul Serpent, the Fiery Dragon with all the weapons at her command.'—MATILDA

princess noun princesses
a woman or girl in a royal family, especially the daughter of a king or queen
A pretty blue dress that had once belonged to one of the Princesses had been found for Sophie.—THE BFG

print verb prints, printing, printed
1 When you print words, you write them with letters that are not joined together.
The BFG, with great care and patience, was printing something on a piece of paper with an enormous pencil.
—THE BFG
2 When a machine prints words or pictures, it puts them on to paper.
Bean's face was purple with rage. Bunce was cursing the fox with dirty words that cannot be printed.—FANTASTIC MR FOX

prise verb prises, prising, prised
When you prise something, you use force to lift or open it.
The label said simply DARK BROWN GLOSS PAINT ONE QUART. He took a screwdriver and prised off the lid.
—GEORGE'S MARVELLOUS MEDICINE

prison noun prisons
A prison is a place where people are kept locked up in cells as a punishment. Most people try to avoid going to prison, but Mr and Mrs Twit live in a windowless house that looks just like a prison.
Here is a picture of Mr and Mrs Twit's house and garden. Some house! It looks like a prison. And not a window anywhere.—THE TWITS

prisoner noun prisoners
someone who is kept in a prison, or who is confined and cannot escape
Squeals and yells came from inside the pocket, and the pocket shook as the furious little prisoner fought to get out.
—CHARLIE AND THE CHOCOLATE FACTORY

private adjective
Something that is private is only for some people, not for everyone.
The Oompa-Loompas guided the boat alongside the red door. On the door it said, INVENTING ROOM — PRIVATE — KEEP OUT.—CHARLIE AND THE CHOCOLATE FACTORY

prize noun prizes
something that you get if you win a game or competition
The boy stood to one side. He looked nervous. He knew very well he wasn't up there to be presented with a prize.
—MATILDA

problem noun problems
something that is difficult to answer or deal with
'These wigs do cause a rather serious problem for witches.' 'What problem, Grandmamma?' 'They make the scalp itch most terribly.'—THE WITCHES

proboscis noun probosces
A proboscis is an animal's snout or nose. The proboscis of an elephant (which is needed to make Wonka-Vite) is called a *trunk*.

prock noun procks
The prock is a huge and terrifying creature. The Centipede is mistaken for a prock by the New York Fire and Police departments.
'It's a Dragon!' 'It's not a Dragon! It's a Wampus!' 'It's a Gorgon!' 'It's a Sea-serpent!' 'It's a Prock!'—JAMES AND THE GIANT PEACH
RINGBELLING RHYMES Try rhyming with *alarm-clock*.
LOOK IT UP! The Centipede is also mistaken for a **wampus** and a **manticore**.

prodigy noun prodigies
a young person who is exceptionally clever or talented
There was no doubt in her mind that she had met a truly extraordinary mathematical brain, and words like child-genius and prodigy went flitting through her head.
—MATILDA

produce verb produces, producing, produced
1 If you produce an effect, you make it happen.
The effect that Medicine Number Two had on this chicken was not quite the same as the effect produced by Medicine Number One.—GEORGE'S MARVELLOUS MEDICINE
2 When you produce something, you bring it out of a box or bag.
The Grand High Witch produced a mouse-trap from the folds of her dress and started to set it.—THE WITCHES

profit noun profits
If you make a profit, you sell something for more than you paid to make it or buy it.
'Well, my boy,' he said, 'your father's had a most successful day . . . He has sold no less than five cars, each one at a tidy profit.'—MATILDA

A B C D E F G H I J K L M N O **P** Q R S T U V W X Y Z

proghopper noun proghoppers
The proghopper is a rare type of animal whose snout is needed to make Wonka-Vite.
Now add the following, in precisely the order given . . .
THE HIP (AND THE PO AND THE POT) OF A HIPPOPOTAMUS/
THE SNOUT OF A PROGHOPPER. — CHARLIE AND THE GREAT GLASS ELEVATOR
DID YOU KNOW? To *prog* is a dialect word that means 'to search' or 'hunt about', so perhaps a proghopper is an animal that rootles for food with its snout, like a pig, but that also hops on its back legs, like a kangaroo.

programme noun programmes
a show on the radio or television
All radio and television programmes were interrupted with announcements that the population must go down into their cellars immediately. — JAMES AND THE GIANT PEACH

promise noun promises
A promise is a statement that you will definitely do or not do something. If you break a promise, you do not keep to it.
It was the only thing in the entire house he was forbidden to touch. He had made solemn promises to his parents about this and he wasn't going to break them. — GEORGE'S MARVELLOUS MEDICINE

promise verb promises, promising, promised
If you promise to do something, you say that you will definitely do it.
James went over and put an arm gently round the Earthworm's shoulders. 'I won't let them touch you,' he said. 'I promise I won't.' — JAMES AND THE GIANT PEACH

pronounce verb pronounces, pronouncing, pronounced
The way you pronounce a word is the way you say it. The Grand High Witch pronounces the letter *w* like *v*, so that she says *vitch*, *vindow* and *sqvishy*.
There was some sort of a foreign accent there, something harsh and guttural, and she seemed to have trouble pronouncing the letter w. — THE WITCHES

proof noun
If you have proof of something, you can show that it is true or that it definitely happened.
'I was the prime suspect this time because of the Golden Syrup job, and although I knew she didn't have any proof, nothing I said made any difference.' — MATILDA

prop verb props, propping, propped
If you prop something somewhere, you lean it there so that it does not fall over.
'Well now,' said the sergeant, propping his bicycle carefully against one of our pumps. 'This is a very hinterestin' haccusation.' — DANNY THE CHAMPION OF THE WORLD

proper adjective
1 If something is proper, it is correct or suitable.
'All I has to do is mix those dreams together in the proper way and I is very quickly making a dream where you is flying in a bathtub with silver wings.' — THE BFG
2 If you do something **good and proper**, you do it completely or thoroughly.
'You've messed it up good and proper this time, haven't you?' said Mrs Bucket. — CHARLIE AND THE GREAT GLASS ELEVATOR

properly adverb
Something that is done properly is done in the correct or right way.
'Wait!' ordered Mr Fox. 'Don't lose your heads! Stand back! Calm down! Let's do this properly! First of all, everyone have a drink of water!' — FANTASTIC MR FOX

propsposterous adjective
ridiculous or extremely silly
'They maybe is looking a bit propsposterous to you,' the BFG said, 'but you must believe me when I say they is very extra-usual ears indeed.' — THE BFG
DID YOU KNOW? The word *propsposterous* sounds a bit like *preposterous*, which also means 'ridiculous'. It comes from a Latin word meaning literally 'before after' or 'the wrong way round'.

> **Gobblefunking with words**
> *Propsposterous* and *propsposterousness* are good tongue-twisters — and are even harder to say when you add a word like **proboscis**. Try saying *propsposterous proboscis* quickly.

prospect noun prospects
The prospect of something is the possibility or hope that it will happen.
The BFG could see the greedy Bloodbottler's mouth beginning to water more than ever at the prospect of extra food. — THE BFG

prosperous adjective
successful or rich
My grandfather . . . was a fairly prosperous merchant who owned a store in Sarpsborg and traded in just about everything from cheese to chicken-wire. — BOY

a b c d e f g h i j k l m n o **p** q r s t u v w x y z

You can add *-ness* to some adjectives to make nouns: *pure propsposterousness!*

prossefor noun **prossefors**
the BFG's word for a professor
'Dreams is very mystical things,' the BFG said. 'Human beans is not understanding them at all. Not even their brainiest prossefors is understanding them.' – THE BFG

protect verb **protects, protecting, protected**
If something protects you, it keeps you safe and stops you being hurt.
'There are dangerous rays coming out of that thing! . . . That's why the Oompa-Loompas are wearing space suits! The suits protect them!' – CHARLIE AND THE CHOCOLATE FACTORY

protest verb **protests, protesting, protested**
If you protest about something, you say that you do not like it or do not agree with it.
Nigel, always ready for action, leapt up and . . . tipped the entire contents of the jug over the Trunchbull's head. No one, not even Miss Honey, protested. – MATILDA

proud adjective **prouder, proudest**
If you are proud of something, you are pleased with it and think that it is very good.
'Wait!' cried Mr Wonka, skidding suddenly to a halt. 'I am very proud of my square sweets that look round. Let's take a peek.' – CHARLIE AND THE CHOCOLATE FACTORY

prove verb **proves, proving, proved**
If you prove that something is true, you show that it is definitely true.
'She's a sort of witch,' he said. 'And to prove it, she has seven toes on each foot.' – DANNY THE CHAMPION OF THE WORLD

prowl verb **prowls, prowling, prowled**
If someone prowls, they move about quietly and secretly, as some animals do when they are hunting.
After 'lights out' the Matron would prowl the corridor like a panther trying to catch the sound of a whisper behind a dormitory door. – BOY

prunty adjective **pruntier, pruntiest**
Prunty means tiny and insignificant. It is a very great insult for one giant to call another giant prunty, and to call one a *prunty little pogswizzler* is even worse.
The Bloodbottler pointed a finger as large as a tree-trunk at the BFG. 'Runty little scumscrewer!' he shouted . . . 'Prunty little pogswizzler!' – THE BFG

LOOK IT UP! For other ways to insult giants, see **insult**.

pry verb **pries, prying, pried**
If someone pries, they look into or ask about things that do not concern them.
There is an unwritten law that no other boy, no teacher, not even the Headmaster himself has the right to pry into the contents of your tuck-box. – BOY

public adjective
Something that is public can be used by everyone.
'This happens to be a public footpath,' my father said. 'Kindly do not molest us.' – DANNY THE CHAMPION OF THE WORLD

puddle noun **puddles**
a small pool of water
A huge tear that would have filled a bucket rolled down one of the BFG's cheeks and fell with a splash on the floor. It made quite a puddle. – THE BFG

puddlenut noun **puddlenuts**
The puddlenut (*Nux puddlensis*) is a type of nut that grows in Giant Country, related to the peanut. Puddlenuts look tiny to giants, so when they say something is puddlenuts, they mean that it is small or insignificant.
'I is the titchy one. I is the runt. Twenty-four feet is puddlenuts in Giant Country.' – THE BFG

puff verb **puffs, puffing, puffed**
1 When you puff, you pant or breathe with difficulty.
Right beneath the mountain, the Giant stopped. He was puffing mightily. His great chest was heaving in and out. – THE BFG
2 If you puff out your cheeks or your chest, you make them bulge outwards by taking a deep breath.
'Well, well, well,' said Sergeant Samways at last, puffing out his chest and addressing nobody in particular. – DANNY THE CHAMPION OF THE WORLD

puff noun **puffs**
A puff is a short breath, or a short blowing of wind, air or smoke.
What he saw were two mighty puffs of orange-red smoke billowing and rolling through the trees in his direction. – THE MINPINS

pulpy adjective **pulpier, pulpiest**
Something pulpy feels soft and mushy, like mashed banana.
Aunt Sponge, fat and pulpy as a jellyfish, came waddling up behind her sister to see what was going on. – JAMES AND THE GIANT PEACH

pump noun **pumps**
a machine that forces air or liquid into or out of something, or along pipes
The picture showed a nine-year-old boy who was so enormously fat he looked as though he had been blown up with a powerful pump. – CHARLIE AND THE CHOCOLATE FACTORY

pump verb **pumps, pumping, pumped**
When you pump liquid or air, you force it into or out of something with a pump.

A Primus is a little camping-stove that you fill with paraffin and you light it at the top and then you pump it to get pressure for the flame. – MATILDA

RINGBELLING RHYMES Try rhyming with *plump* or *rump*.

pun noun puns

A pun is a joke that is funny because it uses words that sound the same but have two different meanings. (They often have different spellings too.) For example, *Why does Willy Wonka have good hearing? Because he's a chocolate-ear!*

Gobblefunking with words

Roald Dahl loved making up puns and you can find lots of examples in his stories. For example, the BFG says *Phew and far between!* (instead of *few and far between*) and Willy Wonka is using puns when he says: *'Whipped cream isn't whipped cream at all unless it's been whipped with whips. Just as a poached egg isn't a poached egg unless it's been stolen from the woods in the dead of night!'* The recipe for *Wonka-Vite* also includes several puns, such as *TWO HAIRS (AND ONE RABBIT) FROM THE HEAD OF A HIPPOCAMPUS* and *THE HIDE (AND THE SEEK) OF A SPOTTED WHANGDOODLE.*

punch verb punches, punching, punched

If you punch someone, you hit them with your fist. Giants are very fond of punching each other. When lots of people or giants are punching each other, it is called a *punch-up*.

They punched and kicked and scratched and bit and butted each other as hard as they could. Blood flowed. Noses went crunch. Teeth fell out like hailstones. – THE BFG

puncture noun punctures

a small hole in a tyre or balloon (or in an inflated Grandma)

She was puffing up all over!... Her face was turning from purple to green! But wait! She had a puncture somewhere! George could hear the hiss of escaping air. – GEORGE'S MARVELLOUS MEDICINE

puncture verb punctures, puncturing, punctured

If you puncture something, you pierce it and make a small hole.

'You can't see Gnoolies, my boy. You can't even feel them ... until they puncture your skin ... then it's too late.' – CHARLIE AND THE GREAT GLASS ELEVATOR

DID YOU KNOW? The word *puncture* comes from a Latin word meaning 'point'. It is related to *punctuation*, which used to be called 'pointing' because of the 'points' or dots used to punctuate writing.

punish verb punishes, punishing, punished

If someone punishes you, they make you suffer because they think you have done something wrong.

'How is you getting punished?' 'She locked us in the dark cellar for a day and a night without anything to eat or drink.' – THE BFG

punishment

noun **punishments**

Punishment is when someone makes you suffer because they think you have done something wrong.

'It is The Grand High Witch's most famous punishment! It is known as "getting fried", and all the other witches are petrified of having it done to them!' – THE WITCHES

pupil noun pupils

1 A pupil is a child who goes to school.

Crunchem Hall Primary School ... had about two hundred and fifty pupils aged from five to just under twelve years old. – MATILDA

2 Your pupils are the black circles in the middle of your eyes.

His eyes were wide open, shining with joy, and in the centre of each eye, right in the very centre, in the black pupil, a little spark of wild excitement was slowly dancing. – CHARLIE AND THE CHOCOLATE FACTORY

DID YOU KNOW? The word *pupil* comes from a Latin word meaning 'little girl or doll'. The circles in your eyes were called *pupils* because of the tiny images that you can see reflected in them.

pure adjective purer, purest

Something that is pure is one thing only, with nothing else mixed in.

It was a very beautiful thing, this Golden Ticket, having been made, so it seemed, from a sheet of pure gold hammered out almost to the thinness of paper. – CHARLIE AND THE CHOCOLATE FACTORY

purple adjective

Something that is purple is the colour that you make by mixing red and blue together. People sometimes go *purple in the face* when they are really angry and about to explode (or about to turn into a blueberry like Violet Beauregarde). The colour *violet* is a light shade of purple.

'Mercy! Save us!' yelled Mrs Beauregarde. 'The girl's going blue and purple all over! Even her hair is changing colour! Violet, you're turning violet, Violet!' – CHARLIE AND THE CHOCOLATE FACTORY

RINGBELLING RHYMES There are no English words which rhyme with *purple* (although there is a Scottish word *hirple* which means 'hobble'), but you can make up some new ones, like *murple* or *slurple*.

a b c d e f g h i j k l m n o p q r s t u v w x y z

In Ireland, witches were called *eye-biters* as they were thought to cast spells with their eyes.

A B C D E F G H I J K L M N O P Q R S T U V W X Y Z

purpose noun purposes
1 The purpose of something is the reason why you are doing it.
You never lost your Log Book. It contained . . . the purpose and destination of the trip and the time you had spent in the air. — GOING SOLO
2 If you do something on purpose, you do it deliberately.
'I cannot for the life of me see why children have to take so long to grow up. I think they do it on purpose.' — MATILDA

purse noun purses
a small bag that you carry money in
Under cover of the bed-clothes, the old man opened the purse and tipped it upside down. Out fell a single silver sixpence. — CHARLIE AND THE CHOCOLATE FACTORY

pustule noun pustules
an infected blister or pimple
'This clot,' boomed the Headmistress . . . 'this black-head, this foul carbuncle, this poisonous pustule that you see before you is none other than a disgusting criminal!' — MATILDA
LOOK IT UP! For more of Miss Trunchbull's favourite insults, see **insult**.

puzzle noun puzzles
A puzzle is a game in which you have to find the answer to a difficult question. A **riddle** is one type of puzzle.

puzzle verb puzzles, puzzling, puzzled
If you puzzle something out, you try to find the answer to a difficult question.
He simply couldn't puzzle out/What LIFE was really all about./What was the reason for his birth?/Why was he placed upon this earth? — DIRTY BEASTS

I'M STILL VERY LOST!

puzzled adjective
If you are puzzled, you cannot understand something or find the answer to it.
For a few minutes, Mrs Kranky kept wandering round with a puzzled look on her face, saying, 'Mother, where are you? Where've you gone?' — GEORGE'S MARVELLOUS MEDICINE

pyjamas plural noun
loose trousers and a top that you wear in bed
As she watched her skinny little husband skulking around the bedroom in his purple-striped pyjamas with a pork-pie hat on his head, she thought how stupid he looked. — MATILDA
DID YOU KNOW? The word *pyjamas* comes from Urdu and Persian words that mean 'leg clothing'.

Qq

Queen of England
THE BFG

quadropus quicksy quogwinkle

quack verb quacks, quacking, quacked
When a duck quacks, it makes a loud sound.
'Stop!' called the tiny Mr Gregg, flying down low over their heads. 'Go away! That's my house!' The ducks looked up and quacked. — THE MAGIC FINGER
LOOK IT UP! Quack is an onomatopoeic word. Read more in the entry for **gliss**.

quacky adjective quackier, quackiest
completely mad
'It is a flushbunking and a scrotty mistake to let the bubbles go upwards! If you can't see why, you must be as quacky as a duckhound!' — THE BFG
SPARKY SYNONYMS You can also say **buggles**.

quadropus noun quadropuses or quadropodes
A quadropus is a sea-creature like an octopus, but with four tentacles rather than eight. All of its tentacles are needed to make Wonka-Vite.
Now add the following, in precisely the order given . . . A CORN FROM THE TOE OF A UNICORN/THE FOUR TENTACLES OF A QUADROPUS. — CHARLIE AND THE GREAT GLASS ELEVATOR

DID YOU KNOW? Roald Dahl made the word *quadropus* by joining the first part of words like *quadrangle* and *quadruple* (from the Latin word for 'four') and the ending of *octopus* (from Greek words meaning 'eight foot'), so a *quadropus* is literally a 'four foot'.

quaggy adjective quaggier, quaggiest
A quaggy place is full of marshes or bogs.
'In the quelchy quaggy sogmire,/In the mashy mideous harshland,/At the witchy hour of gloomness,/All the grobes come oozing home.' – CHARLIE AND THE GREAT GLASS ELEVATOR

> **Gobblefunking with words**
> *Quaggy* is an old word meaning 'boggy', but the phrase *quaggy sogmire* is also a *spoonerism* (for *soggy quagmire*). You can read more about this type of word play in the entry for **mideous**.

quality noun qualities
The quality of something is how good or bad it is.
'It's all chocolate! Every drop of that river is hot melted chocolate of the finest quality. The very finest quality.' – CHARLIE AND THE CHOCOLATE FACTORY

quantity noun quantities
A quantity is an amount.
Nine jeeps, one from each helicopter, were driven down the ramps. Each jeep contained six soldiers and a vast quantity of thick rope and heavy chains. – THE BFG

quarry (rhymes with lorry) noun quarries
a place where people cut stone out of the ground so that it can be used for building
Charlie caught a glimpse of what seemed like an enormous quarry . . . and all over the rock-face there were hundreds of Oompa-Loompas working with picks and pneumatic drills. – CHARLIE AND THE GREAT GLASS ELEVATOR

quarter noun quarters
1 One quarter of something is one of four equal parts that it is divided into.
'But would a quarter of one of those pills be strong enough to put a pheasant to sleep?' I asked. – DANNY THE CHAMPION OF THE WORLD
2 Someone's quarters are the rooms where they live.
We didn't speak as we made our way down the long corridor into the Headmaster's private quarters where the dreaded study was situated. – BOY

queen noun queens
a woman who has been crowned as the ruler of a country, or who is the wife of a king
'That's it!' cried the Captain. 'It's a secret weapon! Holy cats! Send a message to the Queen at once! The country must be warned!' – JAMES AND THE GIANT PEACH

Queen of England (THE BFG)
The Queen of England (and the rest of the United Kingdom) helps the BFG and Sophie in their plan to outwit the unfriendly giants. She lives in a grand palace with a maid and other servants and prefers bagpipe music to **whizzpopping**. **Human beans** call her *Your Majesty* but the BFG says *Your Majester*.

queer adjective queerer, queerest
odd or peculiar
'This is the queerest feeling,' Charlie said, swimming about. 'I feel like a bubble.' – CHARLIE AND THE GREAT GLASS ELEVATOR

quelchy adjective quelchier, quelchiest
Something quelchy makes squelching noises when you walk on it.
'In the quelchy quaggy sogmire,/In the mashy mideous harshland,/At the witchy hour of gloomness,/All the grobes come oozing home.' – CHARLIE AND THE GREAT GLASS ELEVATOR

question noun questions
When you ask a question, you ask someone something because you want to know the answer.
'Can I ask you one special question?' 'Please do.'
'Well, is it really true that I can tell how old a Ladybird is by counting her spots?' – JAMES AND THE GIANT PEACH

quick adjective quicker, quickest
Something that is quick does not take very long.
Through the glass floor of the Elevator, Charlie caught a quick glimpse of the huge red roof and the tall chimneys of the giant factory. – CHARLIE AND THE GREAT GLASS ELEVATOR

quick adverb
If you do something quick, or quickly, you do it soon or in a very short time.
Mr Hoppy's mind was spinning like a fly-wheel. Here, surely, was his big chance! Grab it, he told himself. Grab it quick! – ESIO TROT
SPARKY SYNONYMS You can also say **quicksy**.

quicksilver noun
Quicksilver is another name for mercury, a kind of liquid silver metal that is used in thermometers.

Why is an *anagram* like *blue jam*? Find out at **anagram**.

If something moves like quicksilver, it is fast and slippery and very hard to catch.
Lavender . . . discovered that it was not easy to get the newt out of the hat and into the pencil-box. It wriggled and squirmed like quicksilver. — MATILDA

quicksy adverb
quickly or fast
'I always gets as jumpsy as a joghopper when the Fleshlumpeating Giant is around . . . He is galloping easily two times as quicksy as me.' — THE BFG

quiet adjective **quieter, quietest**
1 If a place is quiet, there is no noise there.
Oh, it was a frantic and terrible trip! But it was all over now, and the room was suddenly very still and quiet.
— JAMES AND THE GIANT PEACH
2 A quiet sound or voice is not very loud.
When she spoke again her voice was suddenly softer, quieter, more friendly, and she leaned towards the boy, smiling. — MATILDA

quirk noun **quirks**
A quirk is a peculiar habit or way of doing things that someone (usually a grown-up) has. Someone who has lots of quirks is said to be **quirky**.
Grown-ups are complicated creatures, full of quirks and secrets. Some have quirkier quirks and deeper secrets than others. — DANNY THE CHAMPION OF THE WORLD
RINGBELLING RHYMES Try rhyming *quirky* with *murky* or *turkey*.

quiver verb **quivers, quivering, quivered**
When you quiver, you shake all over because you are very excited or very afraid.
The girl was glued to the spot, terror-struck, pop-eyed, quivering, knowing for certain that the Day of Judgement had come for her at last. — MATILDA

quogwinkle noun **quogwinkles**
A quogwinkle is a creature from outer space. Quogwinkles make regular visits to Giant Country and can communicate with the BFG.
'Of course quogwinkles is existing. I is meeting them oftenly. I is even chittering to them.' — THE BFG
DID YOU KNOW? When he invented *quogwinkle*, Roald Dahl may have been thinking of the words *quagmire* (a boggy marsh) and *winkle* (a type of shellfish), so a *quogwinkle* could be an alien shellfish from a boggy planet.

Rr

Roly-Poly Bird

THE ENORMOUS CROCODILE & THE TWITS

repulsant rhinostossteriss

rhyme riddle rotsome

rabbit noun **rabbits**
A rabbit is a burrowing animal with long ears and a short furry tail. Rabbits live in holes in the ground called rabbit-holes or burrows. A network of rabbit holes is called a **warren**.
Spectators all along the way/Had come to watch and shout hooray,/The field-mice, weasels, hedgehogs, stoats/And rabbits in their furry coats. — RHYME STEW

racket noun
If people are making a racket, they are making a lot of loud noise.
I stayed there for several minutes, just listening to all the talk and the racket. By golly, what a place that kitchen was! The noise! — THE WITCHES

radio noun **radios**
A radio is a machine for receiving broadcast sound programmes, or for receiving and sending messages. The BFG calls it a **radio squeaker**.
Five hundred million people all over the world who had been listening in on their radios rushed to their television sets. — CHARLIE AND THE GREAT GLASS ELEVATOR

rage noun
a feeling of very strong anger
'I'll get you for this!' shouted Mrs Twit . . . She was purple with rage and slashing the air with her long walking-stick.
— THE TWITS

LOOK IT UP! For colourful ways to describe angry people, see **angry**.

railings plural noun
a fence made of upright metal bars
The BFG broke into a full gallop. He went scorching across the Park and just before he reached the railings that divided it from the street, he took off. — THE BFG

rain noun
Rain is drops of water that fall from the sky. A single drop of rain is a **raindrop**.
Then came the rain. It rained and rained, and the water ran into the nest and they all got as wet as could be — and oh, it was a bad, bad night! — THE MAGIC FINGER

rain verb rains, raining, rained
When it rains, drops of water fall from the sky. When something rains down, it falls from above like raindrops.
Showers of dust and broken tiles and bits of wood and cockroaches and spiders and bricks and cement went raining down on the three old ones who were lying in bed. — CHARLIE AND THE CHOCOLATE FACTORY

rainbow noun rainbows
A rainbow is a curved band of colours you see in the sky when the sun shines through rain. The Cloud-Men paint rainbows with giant brushes and then dangle them from the clouds.
In a few minutes the whole of the arch became covered with the most glorious colours — reds, blues, greens, yellows, and purples. 'It's a rainbow!' everyone said at once. 'They are making a rainbow!' — JAMES AND THE GIANT PEACH

Rainbow Drop noun Rainbow Drops
a type of sweet invented by Willy Wonka that turns your spit the colours of the rainbow
There was a whole lot of splendid stuff from the great Wonka factory itself, for example the famous Willy Wonka Rainbow Drops — suck them and you can spit in seven different colours. — THE GIRAFFE AND THE PELLY AND ME
LOOK IT UP! Some other sweets invented by Willy Wonka are **Mint Jujubes** and **Wriggle-Sweets**.

raisin noun raisins
a dried grape that is used to make fruit cakes, and that Danny's father uses to attract pheasants (who are very fond of them)
Suddenly his voice became soft and whispery and very private. 'Pheasants,' he whispered, 'are crazy about raisins.' — DANNY THE CHAMPION OF THE WORLD

rakish adjective
jaunty and dashing in appearance
The hat itself was one of those flat-topped pork-pie jobs . . . and Mr Wormwood was very proud of it. He thought it gave him a rakish daring look. — MATILDA

rambunctious adjective
A rambunctious person (or Centipede) behaves in a very wild and noisy way.
'Pest!' cried the Earthworm. 'Why must you always be so rude and rambunctious to everyone?' — JAMES AND THE GIANT PEACH
RINGBELLING RHYMES Try rhyming with *frumptious*.

ramp noun ramps
a slope that connects a higher level to the ground
All nine helicopters landed safely on the great yellow wasteland. Then each of them lowered a ramp from its belly. — THE BFG

ramshackle adjective
A ramshackle building is badly made or is in need of repair.
They lived — Aunt Sponge, Aunt Spiker, and now James as well — in a queer ramshackle house on the top of a high hill in the south of England. — JAMES AND THE GIANT PEACH

range noun ranges
A range of mountains or hills is a line of them.
He went rattling through a great forest, then down into a valley and up over a range of hills as bare as concrete. — THE BFG

A rainbow produced by moonlight is a *moonbow*.

a b c d e f g h i j k l m n o p q r s t u v w x y z

ranged adjective
If things such as books or beds, or bottles of dreams, are ranged, they are lined up in a row.
Each dormitory had about twenty beds in it. These were smallish narrow beds ranged along the walls on either side. — BOY

ransack verb **ransacks, ransacking, ransacked**
If a place is ransacked, people go through it stealing things and causing damage.
'My diamond earrings! My diamond rings! They've had the lot! My rooms have been ransacked!' — THE GIRAFFE AND THE PELLY AND ME

rapid adjective
Something that is rapid happens very quickly.
'Watch out!' the Duke shouted, taking ten rapid paces backwards. 'He's trying to shoot his way out!' — THE GIRAFFE AND THE PELLY AND ME

rapscallion noun **rapscallions**
a mischievous person who likes causing trouble
'You are scoundrels, both of you!' shouted Mr Hazell. 'You are rapscallions of the worst kind!' — DANNY THE CHAMPION OF THE WORLD

rare adjective **rarer, rarest**
If something is rare, you do not see it or find it very often.
'It does have in it a very small amount of the rarest and most magical vitamin of them all — vitamin Wonka.' — CHARLIE AND THE CHOCOLATE FACTORY

rascal noun **rascals**
a mischievous person or creature
James decided that he rather liked the Centipede. He was obviously a rascal, but what a change it was to hear somebody laughing once in a while. — JAMES AND THE GIANT PEACH

rash adjective
If you do something rash, you do something that might not be a good idea, without thinking properly about it first.
'I wouldn't do anything rash,' my grandmother said to him. 'That woman has magic powers.' — THE WITCHES

raspberry noun **raspberries**
A raspberry is a soft, sweet, red berry that you can eat.
Frobscottle tastes a bit like raspberries.
And oh gosh, how delicious it was! It was sweet and refreshing. It tasted of vanilla and cream, with just the faintest trace of raspberries on the edge of the flavour. — THE BFG
LOOK IT UP! Some other berries are **muckleberry** and **snozzberry**.

rasping adjective
A rasping voice or sound is deep and harsh, like the sound you make when you speak with a sore throat. All witches have rasping voices, but the voice of The Grand High Witch is the most rrrasping of all.
Her voice had a curious rasping quality. It made a sort of metallic sound, as though her throat was full of drawing-pins. — THE WITCHES

rat noun **rats**
A rat is an animal that looks like a large mouse. Both mice and rats are **rodents**.
'What an impudent fellow Rat is.' 'He has bad manners,' Badger said. 'All rats have bad manners. I've never met a polite rat yet.' — FANTASTIC MR FOX

rather adverb
If you would rather do something, you would prefer to do it.
*'I will **not** eat worms,' said Philip. 'I would rather die.' 'Or slugs,' said William.* — THE MAGIC FINGER

rattle verb **rattles, rattling, rattled**
When something rattles, it makes a loud noise because it is being shaken.
rattle noun **rattles**
a toy for a baby which makes a noise when you shake it
Everything and all of them were being rattled around like peas inside an enormous rattle that was being rattled by a mad giant who refused to stop. — JAMES AND THE GIANT PEACH

ratty adjective **rattier, rattiest**
1 A ratty person looks a bit like a rat, and a ratty moustache is long and stringy like a rat's tail.
The door was opened by a small ratty-looking man with a thin ratty moustache who was wearing a sports-coat that had an orange and red stripe in the material. — MATILDA

2 If someone is ratty they are feeling angry and irritable.
'This,' she said, 'was your daughter's first day at school.' 'We know that,' Mrs Wormwood said, ratty about missing her programme. — MATILDA

ravenous adjective
very hungry, like a giant who hasn't eaten for a whole day
A whole relay of footmen were kept busy hurrying to and from the kitchen carrying . . . helpings of fried eggs and sausages for the ravenous and delighted BFG. — THE BFG

raw adjective **rawer, rawest**
Food that is raw has not been cooked.
Sophie sat there in the dark, shivering with fear. He is getting ready to eat me, she told herself. He will probably eat me raw, just as I am. — THE BFG

ray noun **rays**
a strong beam of light, heat or other energy
'You there! Mike Teavee! Stand back! You're too close to the camera! There are dangerous rays coming out of that thing!' — CHARLIE AND THE CHOCOLATE FACTORY

A B C D E F G H I J K L M N O P Q R S T U V W X Y Z

razor noun **razors**
a very sharp blade that grown-ups use for shaving hair off their body (except for Mr Twit who never shaves his facial hair)
'Our Centipede, who has a pair of jaws as sharp as razors, is up there on top of the peach nibbling away at that stem.'
— JAMES AND THE GIANT PEACH

razztwizzler noun **razztwizzlers**
something wonderfully exciting or enjoyable
'I must say it's quite an experience,' Sophie said.
'It's a razztwizzler,' the BFG said. 'It's gloriumptious.'
— THE BFG

DID YOU KNOW? When he made up the word *razztwizzler*, Roald Dahl may have been thinking of *razzmatazz* or *razzle-dazzle*, which both mean 'a glamorous or showy display'.

read verb **reads, reading, read**
When you read something written or printed, you look at it and understand it or say it aloud.
Very slowly and stumbling a little over the strange words, Mrs Silver read the whole message out loud in tortoise language. — ESIO TROT

real adjective
Something that is real is true and not made up or imaginary. A real witch is the kind that lives in the real world, not in fairy stories, and so is FAR MORE SCARY.
A REAL WITCH hates children with a red-hot sizzling hatred that is more sizzling and red-hot than any hatred you could possibly imagine. — THE WITCHES

rear noun **rears**
1 The rear of something is the part at the back of it.
Very strong steel hawsers with hooks on the ends of them were lowered from the front and rear of each helicopter. — THE BFG
2 Your rear is your bottom, the part of your body that you sit on.
'So he got out a thing like an Indian spear,/With feathers all over the top,/And he lunged and he caught the Knid smack in the rear,/But alas, the balloon didn't pop.'
— CHARLIE AND THE GREAT GLASS ELEVATOR

rear verb **rears, rearing, reared**
If someone rears children or animals, they look after them while they are growing up.
Only the very rich can afford to rear pheasants just for the fun of shooting them down when they grow up.
— DANNY THE CHAMPION OF THE WORLD

reason noun **reasons**
The reason for something is why it happens.
The real reason she carried a stick was so that she could hit things with it, things like dogs and cats and small children. — THE TWITS

reasonable adjective
A reasonable argument or explanation is logical and makes sense.
'I myself,' Miss Honey said, 'am probably far more bowled over by what you did than you are, and I am trying to find some reasonable explanation.' — MATILDA

recipe noun **recipes**
a list of ingredients and instructions for preparing or cooking something, such as a cake or a magic potion
When Mr Wonka had finished reading the recipe, he carefully folded the paper and put it back into his pocket. 'A very, very complicated mixture,' he said.
— CHARLIE AND THE GREAT GLASS ELEVATOR

recite verb **recites, reciting, recited**
When you recite something, you say it out loud from memory.
She recited a poem to him that was well-known in the district. It went like this: Beware! Beware! The Forest of Sin!/None come out, but many go in!
— THE MINPINS

reckon verb **reckons, reckoning, reckoned**
If you reckon on something, you make a guess or calculation about it.
A REAL WITCH . . . reckons on doing away with one child a week. Anything less than that and she becomes grumpy. — THE WITCHES

recognize verb **recognizes, recognizing, recognized**
If you recognize someone, you know who they are because you have seen them before. If you recognize a witch, you see through her disguise (such as her **gloves** and **wig**) and can tell what she is REALLY like.

a b c d e f g h i j k l m n o p q r s t u v w x y z

Roald Dahl loved using lots of *alliteration*. Read more at **ghoulish**.

'Tonight,' the old woman said, *'I am going to tell you how to recognize a witch when you see one.'*
— THE WITCHES

recommend verb recommends, recommending, recommended

When you recommend something, you tell people that it is good.

'I am offering these pills to your grandparents. I am recommending them. And when taken according to my instructions, they are as safe as sugar-candy!' — CHARLIE AND THE GREAT GLASS ELEVATOR

record noun records

1 The record for something is the best that anyone has ever done.

*'This piece of gum I'm chewing right at this moment is one I've been working on for over **three months solid**. That's a record, that is.'* — CHARLIE AND THE CHOCOLATE FACTORY

2 A record of something is information that is written down.

'Then we shall go through the records and get the names and addresses of all the witches in the whole wide world.' — THE WITCHES

recover verb recovers, recovering, recovered

When you recover, you get better after you have been ill.

'Great Scott!' Doc Spencer cried. 'Just look at that! They've recovered! The sleeping pills have worn off at last!' — DANNY THE CHAMPION OF THE WORLD

rectangle noun rectangles

A rectangle is a shape like a long square, with four straight sides and four right angles.

'Place the four clocks in a rectangle eight feet by four alongside the grand piano,' Mr Tibbs whispered. The footmen did so. — THE BFG

DID YOU KNOW? The word *rectangle* comes from Latin and means 'straight angle'.
If you draw a rectangle with wonky or squiggly lines, you could call it a *wonkangle* or a *squiggangle*.

red adjective redder, reddest

Something that is red is the colour of blood. When someone is very cross, they *see red* (and it is best not to stand too close to them).

Well, that did it! I saw red. And before I was able to stop myself, I did something I never meant to do. I PUT THE MAGIC FINGER ON THEM ALL!
— THE MAGIC FINGER

LOOK IT UP! For more colourful ways to describe anger, see **angry**.

red-breasted wilbatross noun red-breasted wilbatrosses

The red-breasted wilbatross is a rare type of bird. Unfortunately for the wilbatross, its beak is one of the ingredients needed to make Wonka-Vite.

Now add the following, in precisely the order given . . . THE BEAK OF A RED-BREASTED WILBATROSS/A CORN FROM THE TOE OF A UNICORN. — CHARLIE AND THE GREAT GLASS ELEVATOR

DID YOU KNOW? Roald Dahl based the word *wilbatross* on *albatross*, which is a large seabird with very long wings. *Albatross* comes from a Spanish word meaning 'diver', so a *wilbatross* could be a type of diving bird which uses its beak to spear fish.

red-hot adjective

Something that is red-hot is so hot that it glows red, like the insides of the Red-Hot Smoke-Belching Gruncher.

'Why does he blow out all that smoke?' Little Billy asked. 'Because he's got a red-hot fire in his belly,' Don Mini said.
— THE MINPINS

redunculous or redunculus adjective

Something redunculous is very silly or ridiculous.

'Redunculous!' said the BFG. 'If everyone is making whizzpoppers, then why not talk about it?' — THE BFG

DID YOU KNOW? The word *redunculous* has nothing to do with red uncles — although if an uncle did something *redunculous*, he might go red in the face and become a *redunculous red uncle*.

RINGBELLING RHYMES Try making up a word to rhyme with *redunculous* — like *carbunculous* (like a carbuncle) or *great-unculous* (like a great-uncle).

reek verb reeks, reeking, reeked

If you reek of something, you smell strongly of it.

'Bunce reeks of goose-livers, and as for Bean, the fumes of apple cider hang around him like poisonous gases.'
— FANTASTIC MR FOX

LOOK IT UP! For more ways to describe nasty smells, see **bad**.

refreshing adjective
Something that is refreshing makes you feel fresh and less tired.
Every few seconds he paused and took a bite out of the wall. The peach flesh was sweet and juicy, and marvellously refreshing. — JAMES AND THE GIANT PEACH

refuse verb **refuses, refusing, refused**
If you refuse to do something, you say that you will not do it.
'Because I is refusing to gobble up human beans like the other giants, I must spend my life guzzling up icky-poo snozzcumbers instead.' — THE BFG

register noun **registers**
a book with lists of names or other important information
'But surely The Grand High Witch wouldn't have put her real name and address in the hotel register?' I said. — THE WITCHES

re-inscorched adjective
Metal that is re-inscorched has been toughened to make it extra strong.
'It's a steel rope,' said Mr Wonka. 'It's made of re-inscorched steel. If they try to bite through that their teeth will splinter like spillikins!' — CHARLIE AND THE GREAT GLASS ELEVATOR

relation or **relative** noun **relations** or **relatives**
Your relations or relatives are all the people who belong to your family.
'Didn't you have any other relations?' Matilda asked. 'Any uncles or aunts or grannies who would come and see you?' — MATILDA
'My "long-horned" relatives . . . make their music simply by rubbing the edges of their two top wings together.' — JAMES AND THE GIANT PEACH

relax verb **relaxes, relaxing, relaxed**
When you relax, you become less anxious or worried.
'The Great Glass Elevator is shockproof, waterproof, bombproof, bulletproof and Knidproof! So just relax and enjoy it.' — CHARLIE AND THE GREAT GLASS ELEVATOR

relief noun
the feeling you have when you are no longer worried or made uncomfortable by something
I heard a sigh of relief going up from all the witches in the room as they kicked off their narrow high-heeled shoes. — THE WITCHES

reluctantly adverb
If you do something reluctantly, you do it very unwillingly.
Reluctantly Matilda stood up and very slowly, very nervously, she recited her limerick. — MATILDA

remark verb **remarks, remarking, remarked**
If you remark something, you say it.
The Grand High Witch glared around the room. 'I hope nobody else is going to make me cross today,' she remarked. There was a deathly silence. — THE WITCHES
LOOK IT UP! For lots of ways to describe how people speak, see **say**.

remark noun **remarks**
something that you say
Hortensia paused to observe the effect these remarks were having on the two titchy ones. Not very much. — MATILDA

remember verb **remembers, remembering, remembered**
If you can remember something, you can think of it and have not forgotten it.
'I can't possibly remember all the hundreds of things I put into the saucepan to make the medicine,' George said. — GEORGE'S MARVELLOUS MEDICINE

remind verb **reminds, reminding, reminded**
If you remind someone about something, you tell them about it again so that they do not forget it.
'My labels is only telling bits of it,' the BFG said. 'The dreams is usually much longer. The labels is just to remind me.' — THE BFG

remote adjective **remoter, remotest**
A place that is remote is far away from towns and cities.
Matilda hung back. She was a bit frightened of this place now. It seemed so unreal and remote and fantastic and so totally away from this earth. — MATILDA

remove verb **removes, removing, removed**
When you remove something, you take it off or take it away.
The Big Friendly Giant followed behind them . . . He had removed his black cloak and got rid of his trumpet, and was now wearing his ordinary simple clothes. — THE BFG

repair verb **repairs, repairing, repaired**
When you repair something, you mend it.
'"It's a bad case of rear-ache," the medico said,/"And it's something I cannot repair./If you want to sit down, you must sit on your head,/With your bottom high up in the air!"' — CHARLIE AND THE GREAT GLASS ELEVATOR

repeat verb **repeats, repeating, repeated**
When you repeat something, you say it or do it again.
'Eight threes,' the Trunchbull shouted, swinging Wilfred from side to side by his ankle, 'eight threes is the same as three eights and three eights are twenty-four! Repeat that!' — MATILDA

replete adjective
If you are replete, you have eaten a lot and are feeling full.

The Trunchbull . . . glared at Bruce Bogtrotter, who was sitting on his chair like some huge overstuffed grub, replete, comatose, unable to move or to speak.
— MATILDA

reply verb replies, replying, replied
When you reply to someone, you answer them.

'What happens next?' 'It is all very simple, Your Grace,' the Giraffe replied. 'I am the ladder, the Pelly is the bucket and the Monkey is the cleaner.' — THE GIRAFFE AND THE PELLY AND ME

reply noun replies
an answer that you give to someone

The great moment had arrived! 'Medicine time, Grandma!' he called out. 'I should hope so, too,' came the grumpy reply. — GEORGE'S MARVELLOUS MEDICINE

LOOK IT UP! For lots of ways to describe how people speak, see **say**.

report verb reports, reporting, reported
When you report something, you describe what has happened.

If any person reported actually having seen a giant haunting the streets of a town at night, there would most certainly be a terrific hullabaloo across the world.
— THE BFG

report noun reports
1 an account of something that has happened

'For the last ten years we have been getting reports from nearly every country in the world about people disappearing mysteriously in the night.' — THE BFG

2 A school report is a description of how well you have worked at school.

I think I might enjoy writing end-of-term reports for the stinkers in my class. — MATILDA

reptile noun reptiles
A reptile is an animal that has a dry, smooth skin, and lays eggs. The Enormous Crocodile and Alfie the tortoise are both reptiles.

repulsant adjective
Something repulsant is disgusting and vile, like the taste of a **snozzcumber**.

'This is the repulsant snozzcumber, Majester, and that is all we is going to give these disgustive giants from now on!' — THE BFG

SPARKY SYNONYMS You can also say **disgusterous** or **filthsome**. An opposite is **delumptious**.

repulsive adjective
Something repulsive is disgusting or revolting, like the taste of a **snozzcumber** or the sight of a sleeping giant (except for the BFG of course).

He was thinking that if only he could get the Bloodbottler to take one bite of the repulsive vegetable, the sheer foulness of its flavour would send him bellowing out of the cave. — THE BFG

rescue verb rescues, rescuing, rescued
If you rescue someone, or come to their rescue, you save them from danger. Mr Hoppy dreams of rescuing Miss Silver, so that he can be her hero.

If only he could do something tremendous like saving her life or rescuing her from a gang of armed thugs.
— ESIO TROT

resign verb **resigns, resigning, resigned**
When someone resigns, they give up their job. If a witch resigns from her day job, it is a sign that she is about to carry out an evil plan.
'Each and every vun of you,' thundered The Grand High Witch, 'is to go back to your home towns immediately and rrree-sign from your jobs. Rrree-sign! Give notice! Rrree-tire!' — THE WITCHES

resist verb **resists, resisting, resisted**
When you resist something, you fight or struggle against it.
Sophie . . . listened again. Everywhere it was deathly still. The longing to look out became so strong she couldn't resist it. — THE BFG

resplendent adjective
If you look resplendent, you look very grand and smart.
At this point, pedalling grandly towards us on his black bicycle, came . . . Sergeant Enoch Samways, resplendent in his blue uniform and shiny silver buttons. — DANNY THE CHAMPION OF THE WORLD

rest noun **rests**
1 When you have a rest, you sleep or sit or perch for a while.
'I'll go,' said the Roly-Poly Bird. 'I'll sit on the telephone wires and keep guard. It'll give me a rest.' — THE TWITS
2 The rest of something is what remains of it.
'If the Queen is knowing that part of her dream is true, then perhaps she is believing the rest of it is true as well.' — THE BFG

rest verb **rests, resting, rested**
When you rest, you sit or lie still for a while.
And sometimes, if you were very lucky, you would find the Old-Green-Grasshopper in there as well, resting peacefully in a chair before the fire. — JAMES AND THE GIANT PEACH

result noun **results**
If something happens as a result of something else, it happens because of it.
Bean never took a bath. He never even washed. As a result, his earholes were clogged with all kinds of muck. — FANTASTIC MR FOX

retired adjective
If someone is retired, like Mr Hoppy, they have stopped working at their job because they are now quite old.
Mr Hoppy . . . had always been a lonely man and now that he was retired from work he was more lonely than ever. — ESIO TROT

reveal verb **reveals, revealing, revealed**
If you reveal something, you uncover it so that people can see it. If you reveal a secret, you tell people about it.
The tiny shutters of tree-bark opened wider and wider, and when they were fully open they revealed a small squarish window set neatly in the curve of the big branch. — THE MINPINS

reverend noun
Vicars or ministers in the Christian church are given the title of *Reverend* before their name, so Robert Lee, the Vicar of Nibbleswicke, is called the Reverend Lee.

In the end, the Reverend Robert Lee got so good at walking backwards that he never walked forwards at all. — THE VICAR OF NIBBLESWICKE

reverse verb **reverses, reversing, reversed**
When you reverse something, you make it go backwards. The Reverend Lee reverses some words when he speaks, so that the letters go backwards.
'Back-to-Front Dyslexia . . . is very common among tortoises, who even reverse their own name and call themselves esio trots.' — THE VICAR OF NIBBLESWICKE

revolting adjective
Something that is revolting is horrible and disgusting, like the stinking breath of the Red-Hot Smoke-Belching Gruncher.
Soon, below them, they began to smell the revolting hot stench of the Gruncher's breath, and the orange-red smoke was now billowing up into the lower branches in thick clouds. — THE MINPINS
SPARKY SYNONYMS You can also say **disgusterous** or **foulsome**.

reward noun **rewards**
something given to a person in return for doing something good
'No reward is too great for you,' the Duke went on. 'I am therefore going to make you an offer which I hope will give you pleasure.' — THE GIRAFFE AND THE PELLY AND ME

reward verb **rewards, rewarding, rewarded**
If you reward a person or mouse, you give them a reward for doing something good.
I put William on the carpet beside me and rewarded him with some extra crumbs and a currant. — THE WITCHES

rhinoceros noun **rhinoceroses**
A rhinoceros is a large heavy wild animal with a horn on its nose. James Henry Trotter's parents have an unfortunate encounter with a rhinoceros from London Zoo.
Mrs Salt was a great fat creature with short legs, and she was blowing like a rhinoceros. — CHARLIE AND THE CHOCOLATE FACTORY
DID YOU KNOW? The word *rhinoceros* means literally 'nose horn', and an old name for a unicorn was a *monoceros*, meaning 'single horn'.

rhinostossteriss noun **rhinostossterisses**
the name that the BFG gives to a rhinoceros
'Even poisnowse snakes is never killing each other,' the BFG said. 'Nor is the most fearsome creatures like tigers and rhinostossterisses.' — THE BFG
DID YOU KNOW? To make the word *rhinostossteriss*, Roald Dahl added *toss* in the middle of *rhinoceros*, perhaps because rhinoceroses toss things about with their massive horns.

Gobblefunking with words
Rhinostossteriss is a good *tongue-twister*. How quickly can you say *rhinostossterisses' nostrils*?

a
b
c
d
e
f
g
h
i
j
k
l
m
n
o
p
q
r
s
t
u
v
w
x
y
z

The BFG is called *De GVR* (*Grote Vriendelijke Reus*) in Dutch.

203

rhyme verb **rhymes, rhyming, rhymed**
If two words rhyme, they have the same sound at the end, like *squiggle* and *giggle*, or *gloop* and *nincompoop*.

rhyme noun **rhymes**
A rhyme is a poem,/Of one kind or other,/Where two or more lines/Rhyme with each other. Matilda is fond of **limericks**, which are a type of rhyme.
Matilda began to read: 'An epicure dining at Crewe/Found a rather large mouse in his stew./Cried the waiter, "Don't shout/And wave it about/Or the rest will be wanting one too."' Several children saw the funny side of the rhyme and laughed. — MATILDA

rhythm noun **rhythms**
the regular beat in a poem or a piece of music
At the end of the room, the Oompa-Loompas . . . were already beating their tiny drums and beginning to jog up and down to the rhythm. — CHARLIE AND THE CHOCOLATE FACTORY

rich adjective **richer, richest**
1 Someone who is rich has a lot of money, like Mr and Mrs Salt.
The second Golden Ticket had been found. The lucky person was a small girl called Veruca Salt who lived with her rich parents in a great city far away. — CHARLIE AND THE CHOCOLATE FACTORY

2 A rich colour or flavour is deep and strong.
George stirred the paint into the mixture with the long wooden spoon. Ah-ha! It was all turning brown! A lovely rich creamy brown! — GEORGE'S MARVELLOUS MEDICINE

rid verb
When you get rid of something, you throw it away or destroy it.
A REAL WITCH spends all her time plotting to get rid of the children in her particular territory. — THE WITCHES

riddle noun **riddles**
A riddle is a puzzle, a type of word game.
The answer to this one's a FOUR-letter name:
My FIRST is the head of a champion boy.
My SECOND begins a pet friend.
My THIRD is the start of a sticky glue.
My FOURTH is the Trunchbull's rear-end.
Answer this RIDDLE you surely shall,
and then you'll find, it's Mr _ _ _ _ .

riddled adjective
If dreams or other things are riddled, they are all jumbled up together.
'It is a trogglehumper!' cried the exasperated BFG. 'But it is also a bogthumper and a grobswitcher! It is all three riddled into one!' — THE BFG
DID YOU KNOW? Outside Giant Country, the word *riddled* means 'full of holes' because *riddle* is an old word for a sieve. The BFG may be thinking of the other kind of **riddle** meaning 'a puzzle', because when dreams are riddled they are as puzzling as a riddle.

ride verb **rides, riding, rode, ridden**
1 When you ride on a horse or bicycle or giant tortoise, you sit on it while it moves along.
'Why, I've seen pictures of giant tortoises that are so huge people can ride on their backs!' — ESIO TROT
2 When you ride in a car, bus or flying elevator, you sit or stand in it while it moves along.
'These skyhooks,' said Grandma Josephine. 'I assume one end is hooked on to this contraption we're riding in. Right?' — CHARLIE AND THE GREAT GLASS ELEVATOR

ride noun **rides**
When you go for a ride, you ride on or in something.
'If the Pelican is willing, perhaps he will also give me a ride in his beak now and again.' 'A pleasure, Your Grace!' cried the Pelican. — THE GIRAFFE AND THE PELLY AND ME

ridiculous adjective
Something that is ridiculous is very silly and makes you laugh.
'You're joking,' James said. 'Nobody could possibly have his ears in his legs.' 'Why not?' 'Because . . . because it's ridiculous, that's why.' — JAMES AND THE GIANT PEACH
SPARKY SYNONYMS You can also say **redunculous**.

rightful adjective
The rightful owner of something is the person to whom it really and truly belongs.
This document revealed that ever since her father's death, Miss Honey had in fact been the rightful owner of a property on the edge of the village. — MATILDA

rigid adjective
very firm or stiff
Grandma Josephine had stopped screaming now. She had gone rigid with shock. — CHARLIE AND THE GREAT GLASS ELEVATOR

A B C D E F G H I J K L M N O P Q R S T U V W X Y Z

rim noun rims

the edge around the top or outside of something
Dawn came at last, and the rim of a lemon-coloured sun rose up behind the roof-tops somewhere behind Victoria Station. — THE BFG

ring noun rings

something in the shape of a circle
Mr Twit sat there drinking the beer slowly. The froth made a white ring on the hairs around his mouth. — THE TWITS

ring verb rings, ringing, rang, rung

1 When something rings, it makes a sound like a bell.
He flung open his front door and flew down the stairs two at a time with the love-songs of a thousand cupids ringing in his ears. — ESIO TROT

2 When you say that something rings a bell, you mean that it reminds you of something.
'Plymouth . . . ' croaked the old woman. 'That rings a bell, too . . . Yes, it might easily have been Plymouth . . . ' — CHARLIE AND THE GREAT GLASS ELEVATOR

3 When you ring someone, you phone them.
An English witch, for example, will know all the other witches in England. They are all friends. They ring each other up. — THE WITCHES

ringbeller noun ringbellers

A ringbeller is a really splendid dream, the kind that makes you wake up smiling and happy.
'What a funny dream,' Sophie said. 'It's a ringbeller,' the BFG said. 'It's whoppsy.' — THE BFG

DID YOU KNOW? Sometimes people ring bells to celebrate a happy occasion like a wedding, and a *ringbeller* makes you feel so happy you could ring some bells. A person who enjoys ringing church bells (another type of ringbeller) is called a *campanologist*, from Latin *campana* 'bell'.

LOOK IT UP! You will find other names for dreams at the entries for **good**, **bad** and **dream**.

rip verb rips, ripping, ripped

If you rip something, you tear it.
The Prince cried, 'No! Alas! Alack!'/He grabbed her dress to hold her back./As Cindy shouted, 'Let me go!'/The dress was ripped from head to toe. — REVOLTING RHYMES

ripe adjective riper, ripest

Fruit that is ripe is soft and ready to eat.
'One of the nice things about a Cox's Orange Pippin,' my father said, 'is that the pips rattle when it's ripe.' — DANNY THE CHAMPION OF THE WORLD

ripple verb ripples, rippling, rippled

When water ripples, it forms lots of small waves on the surface. When something ripples on your skin, it feels as if tiny waves are passing over it.
The summer holidays! Those magic words! The mere mention of them used to send shivers of joy rippling over my skin. — BOY

ripple noun ripples

a small wave on the surface of water

rise verb rises, rising, rose, risen

1 When something rises, it moves upwards.
Very slowly, like some weird monster rising up from the deep, Grandma's head came through the roof . . . — GEORGE'S MARVELLOUS MEDICINE

a b c d e f g h i j k l m n o p q r s t u v w x y z

2 When the sun or moon rises, it moves up into the sky.
As the sun rose the next morning, Boggis and Bunce and Bean were still digging. — FANTASTIC MR FOX

risk verb risks, risking, risked
If someone risks their neck, or risks life and limb, they are doing something very dangerous that might kill them.
'Who says we can't reach them?' the Giraffe called back. 'I do,' the Duke said firmly, 'and I'm not having any of you risking your silly necks around here.' — THE GIRAFFE AND THE PELLY AND ME

river noun rivers
A river is a large stream of water that flows into the sea. In Willy Wonka's factory there is a river of molten chocolate.
'There!' cried Mr Wonka, dancing up and down and pointing his gold-topped cane at the great brown river. 'It's all chocolate!' — CHARLIE AND THE CHOCOLATE FACTORY

riveted adjective
When you are riveted by something, or your eyes are riveted on it, you are staring at it because you are fascinated.
All eyes were riveted on the TV screen as the small glass object, with its booster-rockets firing, slid smoothly up behind the giant Space Hotel. — CHARLIE AND THE GREAT GLASS ELEVATOR

roar verb roars, roaring, roared
1 When an animal or a giant roars, it makes a loud, deep and long sound.
The giants roared and screamed and cursed, and for many minutes the noise of battle rolled across the yellow plain. — THE BFG

2 When a fire or engine roars, it burns or runs noisily.
The Primus was roaring away with a powerful blue flame and already the water in the saucepan was beginning to bubble. — MATILDA

roast verb roasts, roasting, roasted
When you roast meat or vegetables or alarm-clocks, you cook them in the oven.
'Here is vhat you do. You set your alarm-clock to go off at nine o'clock tomorrow morning. Then you rrroast it in the oven until it is crrrisp and tender.' — THE WITCHES

rob verb robs, robbing, robbed
If someone robs another person or a bank, they steal money or valuable things from them.
In one city, a famous gangster robbed a bank of a thousand pounds and spent the whole lot on Wonka bars that same afternoon. — CHARLIE AND THE CHOCOLATE FACTORY

robin noun robins
a small, brown bird with a red patch on its chest
'The children all practise learning to fly on robins. Robins are sensible and careful birds and they love the little ones.' — THE MINPINS

rock noun rocks
A rock is a very big stone. Rocks come in many different colours, but the rocks in Giant Country are mainly blue.
The sun was up now and shining fiery-hot over the great yellow wasteland with its blue rocks and dead trees. — THE BFG

rock verb rocks, rocking, rocked
When something rocks, it moves gently backwards and forwards or from side to side.
The tree rocked from side to side, and everyone, even Mr Gregg, was afraid that the nest would fall down. — THE MAGIC FINGER

RINGBELLING RHYMES Try rhyming *rocks* with *Mr Fox*.

rocket noun rockets
A rocket is a pointed tube-shaped vehicle that can travel very fast through the air or into space.
Suddenly, Trunky let go of the Crocodile's tail, and the Crocodile went shooting high up into the sky like a huge green rocket. — THE ENORMOUS CROCODILE

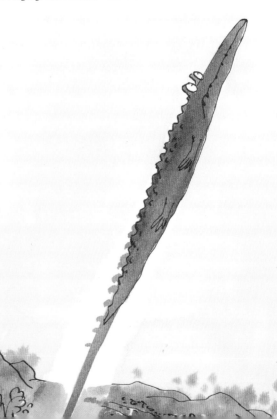

rod noun **rods**

A rod is a long, thin piece of wood or metal. Knids can turn themselves into the shape of a rod in order to form a Deadly Chain of Knids.

Each of them had turned itself into a kind of thick rod and the rod was curled around at both ends — at the tail end and at the head end — so that it made a double-ended hook. — CHARLIE AND THE GREAT GLASS ELEVATOR

rodent noun **rodents**

A rodent is an animal that has large front teeth for gnawing things. Rats and mice are rodents, as are Willy Wonka's highly skilled squirrels.

DID YOU KNOW? The word *rodent* comes from a Latin word that means 'gnawing', so a rodent is literally a 'gnawing thing'.

roll verb **rolls, rolling, rolled**

1 When something rolls, it moves along by turning over and over like a ball.

The peach rolled on. And behind it, Aunt Sponge and Aunt Spiker lay ironed out upon the grass as flat and thin and lifeless as a couple of paper dolls cut out of a picture book. — JAMES AND THE GIANT PEACH

2 When you roll something, you make it turn over and over like a ball.

The Giant reached out and rolled the stone to one side as easily as if it had been a football, and now, where the stone had been, there appeared a vast black hole. — THE BFG

Roly–Poly Bird (THE TWITS & THE ENORMOUS CROCODILE)

The Roly-Poly Bird is a magnificent bird from Africa who likes to travel. He speaks the same African language as the Muggle-Wumps.

rommytot noun

If someone talks rommytot, they are talking nonsense.

'Human beans is juicier,' the Bloodbottler said. 'You is talking rommytot,' the BFG said, growing braver by the second. — THE BFG

DID YOU KNOW? *Rommytot* is a *spoonerism* based on *tommyrot*, an old-fashioned word meaning 'nonsense' or 'rubbish'. There are more examples of spoonerisms in the entry for **mideous**.

SPARKY SYNONYMS You can also say **bugswallop** or **poppyrot**.

roof noun **roofs**

1 the sloping part on the top of a building

All the other birds who had been sitting on the roof flew in to help, carrying paint-brushes in their claws and beaks. — THE TWITS

2 the inside top part of a cave or tunnel

The foxes jumped. They looked up quickly and they saw, peeking through a small hole in the roof of the tunnel, a long black pointed furry face. — FANTASTIC MR FOX

The name *Roald* comes from an Old Norse name meaning 'famous leader'.

room noun rooms

1 The rooms in a building are the different parts inside it. Willy Wonka's factory has lots of rooms: the Fudge Room, the Nut Room, the Inventing Room, the Testing Room, and of course the CHOCOLATE ROOM.
'These rooms we are going to see are enormous! They're larger than football fields! No building in the world would be big enough to house them!'
— CHARLIE AND THE CHOCOLATE FACTORY
2 If there is room for something, there is enough space for it.
'We'll take the bed along as well, with them in it,' said Mr Wonka. 'There's plenty of room in this lift for a bed.'
— CHARLIE AND THE CHOCOLATE FACTORY

root noun roots

the part of a plant that grows under the ground
The driver was an oldish man with a thick black drooping moustache. The moustache hung over his mouth like the roots of some plant. — THE WITCHES

rootle verb rootles, rootling, rootled

If you rrrootle something out, you search and rrrummage about until you find it.
'Rrrootle it out, this small lump of dung!' screeched

The Grand High Witch. *'Don't let it escape!... It must be exterrrminated immediately!'* — THE WITCHES

rope noun ropes

a long piece of thick, strong material which you use for tying things together
'A rope's no good, Mr Wonka! The Knids will bite through a rope in one second!' 'It's a steel rope,' said Mr Wonka.
— CHARLIE AND THE GREAT GLASS ELEVATOR

rose noun roses

a flower which has a sweet smell and sharp thorns on its stem
'I look and smell,' Aunt Sponge declared, 'as lovely as a rose!/Just feast your eyes upon my face, observe my shapely nose!' — JAMES AND THE GIANT PEACH

rot verb rots, rotting, rotted

When something rots, it goes bad and soft and sometimes smells nasty.
That face of hers was the most frightful and frightening thing I have ever seen ... It seemed quite literally to be rotting away at the edges. — THE WITCHES

rot noun (*informal*)
rubbish or nonsense
'They are sharks!' cried the Earthworm ... 'What absolute rot!' the Centipede said, but his voice seemed suddenly to have become a little shaky. — JAMES AND THE GIANT PEACH

rotbungling adjective
Something that is rotbungling is very bad or very disappointing.
'If I is giving a girl's dream to a boy ... the boy would be waking up and thinking what a rotbungling grinksludging old dream that was.' — THE BFG

DID YOU KNOW? The word *rotbungling* is a **compound** made by joining *rot*, meaning something mouldy, and *bungling*, which means making silly mistakes.

rotrasper noun **rotraspers**
A rotrasper is a horribly mean and nasty person, like Mrs Clonkers or Miss Trunchbull.
'She locked us in the dark cellar for a day and a night without anything to eat or drink.' 'The rotten old rotrasper!' cried the BFG. — THE BFG

DID YOU KNOW? To make the word *rotrasper*, Roald Dahl joined together words which mean unpleasant things: *rot*, which is something that has gone bad or mouldy, and *rasp*, which is a harsh or grating sound, like the rrrasping voice of The Grand High Witch.

rotsome adjective
Something that is rotsome is rotten and mouldy with a disgusting taste.
The BFG raised his great head proudly in the air. 'I is a very honourable giant,' he said. 'I would rather be chewing up rotsome snozzcumbers than snitching things from other people.' — THE BFG

SPARKY SYNONYMS You can also say **maggotwise**.

rotten adjective
1 Something that is rotten is not fresh, but has gone bad and soft.
The Pelican cried out, 'Right now I am so hungry I could eat a stale sardine! Has anyone seen a stale sardine/Or a bucket of rotten cod?' — THE GIRAFFE AND THE PELLY AND ME

SPARKY SYNONYMS You can also say **maggotwise** or **rotsome**.

2 Someone who is rotten is bad or nasty.
'Look!' cried the Monkey. 'That rotten burglar's bullet has made a hole in poor Pelly's beak!' — THE GIRAFFE AND THE PELLY AND ME

rotten–wool noun
Rotten-wool is what the BFG calls cotton wool, a type of soft fluffy wadding. If you say someone's head is full of cotton (or rotten) wool, you mean that it is full of fluff and nonsense.
'Your brain is full of rotten-wool.' 'You mean cotton-wool,' Sophie said. 'What I mean and what I say is two different things,' the BFG announced rather grandly. — THE BFG

DID YOU KNOW? *Rotten-wool* is a *malapropism* and you can find more examples of this type of word play in the entry for **mudburger**.

rough adjective **rougher, roughest**
1 Something that is rough is not smooth or flat.
There were no pictures on the walls, no carpet on the floor, only rough unpolished wooden planks. — MATILDA
2 Rough sea or weather is wild and stormy.
The sea journey from Newcastle to Oslo took two days and a night, and if it was rough, as it often was, all of us got seasick except our dauntless mother. — BOY

round adjective **rounder, roundest**
Something that is round is shaped like a circle or ball.
Four pairs of round black glassy eyes were all fixed upon James. — JAMES AND THE GIANT PEACH

round verb **rounds, rounding, rounded**
1 When you round a corner, you go around it in a curve.
They were still singing as they rounded the final corner and burst in upon the most wonderful and amazing sight any of them had ever seen. — FANTASTIC MR FOX
2 If you round up people or animals or witches, you gather them all together in a group.
Oh, if only there were a way of telling for sure whether a woman was a witch or not, then we could round them all up and put them in the meat-grinder. — THE WITCHES

rove verb **roves, roving, roved**
When you rove, you roam or wander over a wide area. If your eyes rove around an area, they look or scan over it.
The Trunchbull's dangerous glittering eyes roved around the classroom. 'You,' she said, pointing at a tiny and rather daft little girl called Prudence, 'spell "difficulty".' — MATILDA

row (*rhymes with* toe) noun **rows**
a long, straight line of people or things
By the time James had pulled off the last boot of all and had lined them up in a row on the floor ... the Centipede was fast asleep. — JAMES AND THE GIANT PEACH

row (*rhymes with* toe) verb **rows, rowing, rowed**
When you row a boat, you use oars to make it move through water.
Such wondrous, fine, fantastic tales/Of dragons, gypsies, queens, and whales/And treasure isles, and distant shores/Where smugglers rowed with muffled oars. — CHARLIE AND THE CHOCOLATE FACTORY

row (*rhymes with* how) noun **rows**
When people have a row, they have an angry, noisy argument.
'Now now now now now!' said Mr Wonka. 'Let us not for mercy's sake have another row so late in the day.' — CHARLIE AND THE GREAT GLASS ELEVATOR

royal adjective
Something royal is used by a king or queen. A royal person belongs to a king or queen's family.
He wrote to every magazine/And said, 'I'm looking for a Queen.'/At least ten thousand girls replied/And begged to be the royal bride. — REVOLTING RHYMES

a b c d e f g h i j k l m n o p q **r** s t u v w x y z

You can add -ness to some adjectives to make nouns: *sheer rotsomeness!*

rub verb **rubs, rubbing, rubbed**
When you rub something, you move your hands backwards and forwards over it.
Bean rubbed the back of his neck with a dirty finger. He had a boil coming there and it itched.—FANTASTIC MR FOX

rubber noun **rubbers**
Rubber is a type of soft material that stretches, bends and bounces.
He started emptying the pockets and placing the contents on the bed — a homemade catapult . . . a yo-yo . . . a trick fried-egg made of rubber.—CHARLIE AND THE GREAT GLASS ELEVATOR

rubbish noun
1 things people throw away because they do not want them any more
'That particular chute,' Mr Wonka told her, 'runs directly into the great big main rubbish pipe which carries away all the rubbish from every part of the factory.'—CHARLIE AND THE CHOCOLATE FACTORY
2 If something that you say is rubbish, it is silly and not true.
'Actually, they're not shooting stars at all,' said Mr Wonka. 'They're Shooting Knids.' . . . 'What rubbish,' said Grandma Georgina.—CHARLIE AND THE GREAT GLASS ELEVATOR

rubbsquash noun
Rubbsquash is rubbish or complete nonsense.
'It is sounding such a wonky tall story, the Queen will be laughing and saying "What awful rubbsquash!"'—THE BFG

ruddy adjective (*informal*) **ruddier, ruddiest**
Ruddy is a very rude word that grown-ups sometimes say when they are annoyed at something.
'I'm getting a bit old to go bird's nesting. Those ruddy gruntles always nest very high up.'—THE WITCHES

rude adjective **ruder, rudest**
1 Someone who is rude says or does things that are not polite.
The Glow-worm slowly opened one eye and stared at the Centipede. 'There is no need to be rude,' she said coldly.—JAMES AND THE GIANT PEACH
2 A rude word is one that grown-ups do not like you to use, even if they use it themselves.
The President said a very rude word into the microphone and ten million children across the nation began repeating it gleefully and got smacked by their parents.—CHARLIE AND THE GREAT GLASS ELEVATOR
LOOK IT UP! The unfriendly giants use lots of rude words. When things are going badly, they say they are **bopmuggered** or **crodsquinkled** or **fluckgungled** or **flushbunkled** or **goosegruggled** or **gunzleswiped** or **slopgroggled** or **splitzwiggled** or **swogswalloped**.

ruin verb **ruins, ruining, ruined**
If someone ruins something, they spoil it completely.
'Get those birds off my car!' Mr Hazell bellowed. 'Can't you see they're ruining the paintwork, you madman!'—DANNY THE CHAMPION OF THE WORLD

rule noun **rules**
something that tells you what you must and must not do
'Giants is also making rules. Their rules is not suiting the human beans. Everybody is making his own rules to suit himself.'—THE BFG

rule verb **rules, ruling, ruled**
The person who rules a country or other place is in charge of it.
On the dormitory floor the Matron ruled supreme. This was her territory.—BOY

ruler noun **rulers**
1 someone who rules a country
The Ruler of India sent the BFG a magnificent elephant, the very thing he had been wishing for all his life.—THE BFG
2 a flat, straight piece of wood, metal, or plastic that you use for measuring things and drawing lines
The parting in his hair was a white line straight down the middle of the scalp, so straight it could only have been made with a ruler.—BOY

rummage verb **rummages, rummaging, rummaged**
If you rummage for something, you search for it by looking in every *crook and nanny*.
'Then a great giant-hunt . . . would be starting up all over the world, with the human beans all rummaging for the great giant you saw and getting wildly excited.'—THE BFG

rumour noun **rumours**
something that a lot of people are saying, although it might not be true
'Where do they have these meetings, Grandmamma?' 'There are all sorts of rumours,' my grandmother answered.—THE WITCHES

rump noun **rumps**
Your rump is your bottom, the part of your body that you sit on.
I sat. I screamed. I jumped a foot!/Would you believe that I had put/That tender little rump of mine/Upon a giant porcupine!—DIRTY BEASTS

rumpledumpus noun **rumpledumpuses**
a very noisy fuss or protest
'If an animal is very fierce and you is putting it in a cage, it will make a tremendous rumpledumpus . . . Dreams is exactly the same.'—THE BFG

Gobblefunking with words
To make *rumpledumpus*, Roald Dahl started with *rumpus*, which also means a noisy fuss, and made it twice as long and twice as funny by adding extra **syllables**. You can make other words this way, such as *rumblegrumble*, or even *rummedybumble*, for the noise your tummy makes when you are hungry.

run verb **runs, running, ran, run**
1 When you run, you move along quickly by taking very quick steps.
The Small Foxes went wild with excitement. They started

running around in all directions, chasing the stupid chickens. — FANTASTIC MR FOX

LOOK IT UP! For other ways to describe moving quickly, see **move**.

2 When you run something, you control it and are in charge of it.

Would he be equal to running a parish? The previous vicar, as he knew, had died in harness and there would be nobody there to guide him. — THE VICAR OF NIBBLESWICKE

runny adjective runnier, runniest
A runny mixture is thin and flows like liquid.

George . . . looked up at the medicine shelf. There were five big bottles there. Two were full of pills, two were full of runny stuff and one was full of powder. — GEORGE'S MARVELLOUS MEDICINE

runt noun runts
A runt is the smallest animal in a litter. The other giants call the BFG a runt because, although he is 24 feet tall, he is still the smallest giant in Giant Country.

Suddenly, a tremendous thumping noise came from outside the cave entrance and a voice like thunder shouted, 'Runt! Is you there, Runt?' — THE BFG

rustle verb rustles, rustling, rustled
When something rustles, it makes a soft sound like the movement of dry leaves or paper.

rustle noun rustles
a rustling sound

Just then, there was a rustle in the bushes beside the lake. Then out he came! Twenty-four feet tall, wearing his black cloak with the grace of a nobleman. — THE BFG

rusty adjective rustier, rustiest
Rusty metal has a rough, red coating because it is old and has got wet.

Very slowly, with a loud creaking of rusty hinges, the great iron gates of the factory began to swing open. — CHARLIE AND THE CHOCOLATE FACTORY

Aunt Sponge & Aunt Spiker

JAMES AND THE GIANT PEACH

sizzlepan   snozzcumber   spliffling

swashboggling   sweet-shop

sad adjective sadder, saddest
If you feel sad, you feel unhappy and the very opposite of **dory-hunky**.

James Henry Trotter, who once, if you remember, had been the saddest and loneliest little boy that you could find, now had all the friends and playmates in the world. — JAMES AND THE GIANT PEACH

safe adjective safer, safest
1 If you are safe, you are not in any danger, and if you are really safe you are *safe as sausages*.

'What did I tell you!' shouted Mr Wonka, triumphant. 'We're safe as sausages in here!' — CHARLIE AND THE GREAT GLASS ELEVATOR

2 If a place is safe, you will not get hurt or attacked by giants or Grunchers if you go there.

'The murderous Gruncher, who has gobbled up so many thousands of us Minpins, has gone for ever! The forest floor is safe at last for us to walk on!' — THE MINPINS

sail verb sails, sailing, sailed
1 When a ship or giant fruit sails, it moves through water.

Once again the giant peach was sailing peacefully through the mysterious moonlit sky. — JAMES AND THE GIANT PEACH

2 When someone sails along, they glide as if they were a ship on the sea.

'Well, I did my best,' my grandmother said, and with that

How fast can you say *redunculous rumpledumpus*? Find more tongue-twisters at **propsposterous**.

she turned and sailed out of the room, carrying Bruno with her. — THE WITCHES

salami noun salamis
A salami is a kind of strong spicy sausage.
'Do you think they would eat us?' the Earthworm asked. 'They would eat you,' the Centipede answered, grinning. 'They would cut you up like a salami and eat you in thin slices.' — JAMES AND THE GIANT PEACH

sale noun sales
If something is for sale, you can buy it. If you cannot buy it for any price, it is not for sale.
'How much d'you want for one of these squirrels? Name your price.' 'They're not for sale,' Mr Wonka answered. 'She can't have one.' — CHARLIE AND THE CHOCOLATE FACTORY

saliva noun
the natural liquid in your mouth
They were about ten feet away from the Fleshlumpeater's face . . . Every now and again a big bubble of spit formed between his two open lips and then it would burst with a splash and cover his face with saliva. — THE BFG

salmon noun salmon
A salmon is a large type of fish with pink flesh that is found in rivers. Pelicans find salmon utterly **scrumdiddlyumptious**.
The Monkey said, 'What Pelly's crazy about is salmon!' 'Yes, yes!' cried the Pelican. 'Salmon! Oh, glorious salmon! I dream about it all day long but I never get any!' — THE GIRAFFE AND THE PELLY AND ME

sample verb samples, sampling, sampled
When you sample something, you try or taste a small amount to see what it is like.
'I is happy to let you sample it,' the BFG went on. 'But please, when you see how truly glumptious it is, do not be guzzling the whole thing.' — THE BFG

sandal noun sandals
Sandals are shoes with straps that you wear in warm weather. The BFG wears sandals all the time, as the climate is very hot and dry in Giant Country.
On his bare feet he was wearing a pair of ridiculous sandals that for some reason had holes cut along each side, with a large hole at the end where his toes stuck out. — THE BFG

sap noun
Sap is the sticky liquid inside a plant. A pint of sap from an ancient pine is an essential ingredient in Vita-Wonk.
'I . . . rushed all over the world collecting special items from the oldest living things . . . A PINT OF SAP FROM A 4000-YEAR-OLD BRISTLECONE PINE.' — CHARLIE AND THE GREAT GLASS ELEVATOR

sardine noun sardines
A sardine is a small sea fish that you can buy in tins. The remains of tinned sardines are sometimes stuck in Mr Twit's facial hair.
If you peered deep into the moustachy bristles . . .

you would probably see . . . a piece of maggoty green cheese or a mouldy old cornflake or even the slimy tail of a tinned sardine. — THE TWITS

satisfy verb satisfies, satisfying, satisfied
If something satisfies you, it is good enough to make you feel happy. If food satisfies you, it fills you up so that you are no longer hungry, which is exactly what happens if you chew Wonka's magic chewing-gum.
'It's absolutely amazing! You can actually feel the food going down your throat and into your tummy! And you can taste it perfectly! And it fills you up! It satisfies you!' — CHARLIE AND THE CHOCOLATE FACTORY

sauce noun sauces
A sauce is a thick liquid that you put over food. Lots of different sauces go into making George's magical medicine.
George . . . chose the following and emptied them one by one into the saucepan: a tin of curry powder/a tin of mustard powder/a bottle of 'extra hot' chilli sauce/ a tin of black peppercorns/a bottle of horseradish sauce. — GEORGE'S MARVELLOUS MEDICINE

saucepan noun saucepans
A saucepan is a metal pan that you use for cooking. Willy Wonka's Inventing Room is full of saucepans in which his secret recipes bubble and simmer.
The saucepan was full of a thick gooey purplish treacle, boiling and bubbling. By standing on his toes, little Charlie could just see inside it. — CHARLIE AND THE CHOCOLATE FACTORY

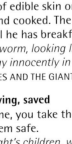

saunter verb saunters, sauntering, sauntered
When you saunter, you walk along slowly or casually.
'She's mad,' Hortensia said . . . 'I'll be seeing you some time, you two.' And with that she sauntered away. — MATILDA

sausage noun sausages
Sausages are tubes of edible skin or plastic stuffed with minced meat and cooked. The BFG has never tasted sausages until he has breakfast with the Queen.
One half of the Earthworm, looking like a great, thick, juicy, pink sausage, lay innocently in the sun for all the seagulls to see. — JAMES AND THE GIANT PEACH

save verb saves, saving, saved
1 If you save someone, you take them away from danger and make them safe.
'If we can't save tonight's children, we can anyway save tomorrow's,' Sophie said. — THE BFG
2 When you save your money or strength, you keep it so that you can use it later.
Only once a year, on his birthday, did Charlie Bucket ever

get to taste a bit of chocolate. The whole family saved up their money for that special occasion. — CHARLIE AND THE CHOCOLATE FACTORY

say verb **says, saying, said**
When you say something, you express yourself in words. If you try to describe *how* people say things, it can make your writing and characters more colourful. Here are some ideas.

TO SAY LOUDLY: bawl, bellow, boom, call, cry, exclaim, roar, scream, screech, shout, shriek, yell
'Great heavens, girl!' screeched Mrs Beauregarde. 'You're blowing up like a balloon!' — CHARLIE AND THE CHOCOLATE FACTORY

TO SAY ANGRILY: bark, growl, rant, rasp, rave, snap, snarl, thunder
'Shut up, you little twerp!' Aunt Spiker snapped, happening to overhear him. 'It's none of your business!' — JAMES AND THE GIANT PEACH

TO SAY QUIETLY OR UNCLEARLY: babble, burble, croak, mumble, murmur, mutter, stammer, stutter, whisper
The poor BFG was very nervous. 'There's n-no one in here,' he stammered. 'W-why don't you l-leave me alone?' — THE BFG

TO SAY IN SURPRISE OR ALARM: cry, gasp, squeal
'Oh, my sainted souls!' gasped the Giraffe. 'Oh, my naked neck! I cannot believe what I am seeing!' — THE GIRAFFE AND THE PELLY AND ME

TO ASK A QUESTION OR MAKE A REQUEST: beg, enquire, plead, query
'Let him go, Miss Trunchbull, please,' begged Miss Honey. 'You could damage him, you really could!' — MATILDA

TO SAY BOLDLY: announce, command, declare, demand, order
'Fetch me a telephone,' the Queen commanded. — THE BFG

scale noun **scales**
A scale, or a pair of scales, is a balance that you use for weighing things.
The whole enormous peach . . . was like a delicately balanced scale that needed only the tiniest push to tip it one way or the other. — JAMES AND THE GIANT PEACH

scamper verb **scampers, scampering, scampered**
When you scamper, you run around lightly and quickly.
Both mice crashed against the wall, and for a few moments they lay stunned. Then they got to their feet and scampered away. — THE WITCHES

scarce adjective **scarcer, scarcest**
If something is scarce, there is not very much of it. If you make yourself scarce, you leave quickly to avoid seeing someone.
When Mr Wormwood arrived back from the garage that evening his face was as dark as a thunder-cloud . . . His wife recognized the signs immediately and made herself scarce. — MATILDA

scare verb **scares, scaring, scared**
If something scares you, it makes you frightened, and if you scare someone, you make them feel afraid.
'I thought they were grobes,' Charlie said . . . 'Oh, no, I just made those up to scare the White House,' Mr Wonka answered. — CHARLIE AND THE GREAT GLASS ELEVATOR
LOOK IT UP! For other ways to describe being scared, see **afraid**.

scared adjective
If you are scared, you feel frightened, and if you are **scared to death**, you feel as if you might die from fear.
'But don't the parents complain?' Matilda asked . . . 'She treats the mothers and fathers just the same as the children and they're all scared to death of her.' — MATILDA
LOOK IT UP! For more ways to say that someone is scared, see **afraid**.

scarlet adjective
Something that is scarlet is bright red, like the colour of a ladybird's back.
And next to the Old-Green-Grasshopper, there was an enormous Spider. And next to the Spider, there was a giant Ladybird with nine black spots on her scarlet shell. — JAMES AND THE GIANT PEACH

Scarlet Scorchdropper noun **Scarlet Scorchdroppers**
a fiery sweet from Iceland that makes smoke gush from your nostrils when you suck it
To the Duke, because the weather was a little chilly, I gave some Scarlet Scorchdroppers that had been sent to me from Iceland. — THE GIRAFFE AND THE PELLY AND ME

scary adjective
Something scary makes you feel afraid.
'We did it, Danny,' he said . . . 'We pulled it off. Doesn't that make you feel good?' 'Terrific,' I said. 'But it was a bit scary while it lasted.' — DANNY THE CHAMPION OF THE WORLD

a b c d e f g h i j k l m n o p q r **s** t u v w x y z

An old-fashioned name for a sausage is a *sauserling*.

scatter verb scatters, scattering, scattered
1 When you scatter things, you throw them all around you.
'When evening comes, you creep up into the woods . . . Then you scatter the raisins. And soon, along comes a pheasant and gobbles it up.' – DANNY THE CHAMPION OF THE WORLD
2 When people scatter, they all run away in different directions.
The crowds of people who were climbing up the hill suddenly caught sight of this terrible monster plunging down upon them and they screamed and scattered to right and left as it went hurtling by. – JAMES AND THE GIANT PEACH

scent noun scents
The scent of something is its smell. The scent of danger is a warning sign that danger is coming.
There was a faint scent of danger in the air now. Each one of us had caught a whiff of it. – BOY

schnozzle noun (informal) schnozzles
Your schnozzle is your nose.
'The matter with human beans,' the BFG went on, 'is that they is absolutely refusing to believe in anything unless they is actually seeing it right in front of their own schnozzles.' – THE BFG
DID YOU KNOW? *Schnozzle* comes from a Yiddish word that means 'small snout'. Some other names that the BFG might have used are *snoutling* or *snoutkin*.

school noun schools
A school is a place where you go to learn things while you are still a child. A school for younger children, like Crunchem Hall, is a *primary school*.
The village school for younger children was a bleak brick building called Crunchem Hall Primary School. It had about two hundred and fifty pupils aged from five to just under twelve years old. – MATILDA

school–chiddler noun school-chiddlers
School-chiddlers are **chiddlers** who are old enough to go to school.
'Other giants is all saying they is wanting to gallop off to England tonight to guzzle school-chiddlers,' the Bloodbottler said. – THE BFG

scoop verb scoops, scooping, scooped
If you scoop something up, you pick it up using your hands or a spoon (or a spade if you are a giant).
The BFG grabbed the garden spade and scooped up all the eggs, sausages, bacon and potatoes in one go and shovelled them into his enormous mouth. – THE BFG

scornful adjective
If you are scornful, you disapprove strongly of someone or of what they say or believe.
'Young fellow,' he said, speaking in a deep, slow, scornful voice, 'I have never been a pest in my life. I am a musician.' – JAMES AND THE GIANT PEACH

scorpula noun scorpulas or scorpulae
A scorpula is a deadly and terrifying creature which looks a bit like a giant spider. Miss Spider is mistaken for a scorpula by the Head of the Fire Department.
'Snakes and ladders!' yelled the Head of the Fire Department. 'We are finished now! It's a giant Scorpula!' – JAMES AND THE GIANT PEACH

scotch–hopper noun scotch-hoppers
The great squizzly scotch-hopper is an animal that is very common in Giant Country, but which no **human bean** has ever seen.
'What about for instance the great squizzly scotch-hopper?' 'I beg your pardon?' Sophie said. – THE BFG
DID YOU KNOW? Roald Dahl may have based the word *scotch-hopper* on *hopscotch*, a game where you hop over squares marked on the ground. Hopscotch is a very old game and was originally called *scotch-hop*. Perhaps the scotch-hopper moves by hopping around on one leg, as if it were playing this game.
LOOK IT UP! Other animals commonly found in Giant Country are the **crumpscoddle** and **wraprascal**.

scowl (rhymes with owl) verb scowls, scowling, scowled
When someone scowls, they frown and look very cross.
The Trunchbull was standing in front of the class, legs apart, hands on hips, scowling at Miss Honey, who stood silent to one side. – MATILDA

scram exclamation
Saying *Scram!* is a rude way of telling someone to go away. The Vermicious Knids form themselves into the shape of the letters S-C-R-A-M to send a very unfriendly message to Willy Wonka.
Mr Wonka ran in front of them shouting 'Scram! Scram! Scram!' and in ten seconds flat all of them were out of the lobby and back inside the Great Glass Elevator. – CHARLIE AND THE GREAT GLASS ELEVATOR

scramble verb scrambles, scrambling, scrambled
If you scramble over things, you climb over them using your hands and feet.
The news . . . spread like wildfire across the countryside, and the next day a stream of people came scrambling up the steep hill to gaze upon this marvel. – JAMES AND THE GIANT PEACH

scrape verb scrapes, scraping, scraped
If you scrape something, you rub against it with something sharp.
'James!' bawled the Centipede. 'Please help me! Wash off this paint! Scrape it off!' – JAMES AND THE GIANT PEACH

scratch verb **scratches, scratching, scratched**
When you scratch, you rub your skin because
it is itching. Witches scratch a lot (because their
wigs make their scalps very itchy), and so do
headmistresses who have been treated with
itching-powder.
*'Well,' Hortensia said, 'a few days later, during prayers,
the Trunchbull suddenly started scratching herself like
mad down below . . . Then the scratching got worse.
She couldn't stop.'* — MATILDA

scrawny adjective **scrawnier, scrawniest**
thin and scraggy
*It was a truly fantastic sight, this ancient scrawny old
woman getting taller and taller, longer and longer,
thinner and thinner, as though she were a piece of elastic
being pulled upwards by invisible hands.* — GEORGE'S
MARVELLOUS MEDICINE

scream verb **screams, screaming, screamed**
When you scream, you shout or cry loudly because you
are frightened or hurt.
*Sophie opened her mouth to scream, but no sound came
out. Her throat, like her whole body, was frozen with fright.*
— THE BFG

scream noun **screams**
a loud cry that you give when you are frightened or hurt
*Suddenly the loudspeaker in the President's study gave
out a series of the most ghastly screams and yells.
'Ayeeee! Owwwww! Ayeeee! Hel-l-l-lp! Hel-l-l-l-lp!
Hel-l-l-l-l-l-l-lp!'* — CHARLIE AND THE GREAT GLASS
ELEVATOR

screech verb **screeches, screeching, screeched**
When you screech, you shout or cry in a loud,
high voice.
'What's the matter with you?' Aunt Spiker screeched,

glaring at him over the top of her steel spectacles.
—JAMES AND THE GIANT PEACH

screen noun screens
the part of a television where the words and pictures appear
Charlie put out his hand and touched the screen, and suddenly, miraculously, the bar of chocolate came away in his fingers.—CHARLIE AND THE CHOCOLATE FACTORY

screw verb screws, screwing, screwed
When you screw a lid on, you put it on by turning it round and round.
'The top!' he whispered. 'The jar top quick!' Sophie picked up the screw top and handed it to him. He screwed it on tight and the jar was closed.—THE BFG

scrotty adjective scrottier, scrottiest
1 If you feel scrotty, you feel sad and gloomy.
'Whenever I is feeling a bit scrotty,' the BFG said, 'a few gollops of frobscottle is always making me hopscotchy again.'—THE BFG
SPARKY SYNONYMS Opposites are **dory-hunky** and **hopscotchy**.
2 A scrotty mistake is a very silly mistake.
*'You said it was flushbunking. Now you say it's scrotty. Which is it?' Sophie asked politely. 'Both!' cried the BFG. 'It is a flushbunking **and** a scrotty mistake to let the bubbles go upwards!'*—THE BFG
RINGBELLING RHYMES Try rhyming with *dotty* or *spotty*.

scrub verb scrubs, scrubbing, scrubbed
When you scrub something, you rub it hard to clean it.
We scrubbed the floor and washed the windows and polished the grate and dusted the ledges and wiped the picture-frames and carefully tidied away all the hockey-sticks and cricket-bats and umbrellas.—BOY

scrumdiddlyumptious adjective
Scrumdiddlyumptious food is utterly delicious. Everything that Willy Wonka invents is scrumdiddlyumptious.
'Fleshlumpeater says he is never eating queen and he thinks perhaps she has an especially scrumdiddlyumptious flavour.'—THE BFG

scrumplet noun scrumplets
Scrumplet is an affectionate name that you call someone you like.
'I don't have a mother and father,' Sophie said. 'They both died when I was a baby.' 'Oh, you poor little scrumplet!' cried the BFG.—THE BFG

scrumptious adjective
Scrumptious is another way of saying **scrumdiddlyumptious**. If something is particularly scrumptious, it is **scrumptious–galumptious**.
'I've eaten many strange and scrumptious dishes in my time,/Like jellied gnats and dandyprats and earwigs cooked in slime.'—JAMES AND THE GIANT PEACH

'And I dream about walnuts!' shouted the Monkey. 'A walnut fresh from the tree is scrumptious-galumptious.'
—THE GIRAFFE AND THE PELLY AND ME

scrunch noun scrunches
1 a loud crunching noise
Scrunch, scrunch, scrunch went the shovels above their heads. Small stones and bits of earth began falling from the roof of the tunnel.—FANTASTIC MR FOX
2 For another type of scrunch, see the **Pink-Spotted Scrunch**.

scuddle verb scuddles, scuddling, scuddled
When creatures scuddle about, they scurry this way and that.
'Good gracious me!' Sophie said. 'What else can you hear?' 'I is hearing the little ants chittering to each other as they scuddle around in the soil.'—THE BFG
DID YOU KNOW? Roald Dahl may have based the word *scuddle* on *scuttle*, which also means to dash about in a hurry.
RINGBELLING RHYMES Try rhyming with *puddle*.

scuddling adjective
Scuddling weather makes you feel sticky and uncomfortable and rather grumpy.
'I is choosing Chile,' the Bloodbottler said, 'because I is fed up with the taste of Esquimos. It is important I has plenty of cold eats in this scuddling hot weather.'—THE BFG

scumper verb scumpers, scumpering, scumpered
When giants scumper, they scamper or scurry away.
'They is always having fifty winks before they goes scumpering off to hunt human beans in the evening,' the BFG said.—THE BFG

scurry verb scurries, scurrying, scurried
When you scurry, you move around lightly and quickly, like a tiny animal or insect.
Mr and Mrs Wormwood and the brother were scurrying around it like ants, piling in the suitcases, as Matilda and Miss Honey came dashing up.—MATILDA

scurry noun scurries
a frantic rush or hurry
There was a frantic scurry among the Palace servants when orders were received from the Queen that a twenty-four-foot giant must be seated with Her Majesty in the Great Ballroom within the next half-hour.—THE BFG

scuttle verb scuttles, scuttling, scuttled
If you scuttle, you hurry about with quick short steps.
'A little mouse,' I said, 'can go scuttling round the kitchen among the pots and pans, and if he's very careful no one will ever see him.'—THE WITCHES

sea noun seas
1 The sea is the salty water that covers large parts of the Earth.

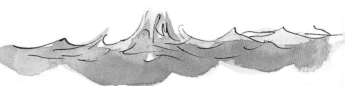

Until he was four years old, James Henry Trotter had a happy life. He lived peacefully with his mother and father in a beautiful house beside the sea. — JAMES AND THE GIANT PEACH

2 A sea of people or faces or tortoises is a great mass of them.

Mr Hoppy turned and ran from the balcony into the living-room, jumping on tip-toe like a ballet-dancer between the sea of tortoises that covered the floor. — ESIO TROT

seagull noun seagulls

A seagull is a type of seabird with long wings. It takes the flying power of 501 seagulls to lift the Giant Peach out of the sea.

Faster and faster flew the seagulls, skimming across the sky at a tremendous pace, with the peach trailing out behind them. — JAMES AND THE GIANT PEACH

seal verb seals, sealing, sealed

If you seal something, you close it tightly so that nothing can get in or out.

Now that the entrance had been sealed up, there was not a glint of light inside the cave. All was black. — THE BFG

search verb searches, searching, searched

When you search for something, you look for it very carefully.

'Dreams, my love, are very mysterious things. They float around in the night air like little clouds, searching for sleeping people.' — DANNY THE CHAMPION OF THE WORLD

seaside noun

a place by the sea where you can play in the sand and enjoy yourself

'Oh, Auntie Sponge!' James cried out. 'And Auntie Spiker! Couldn't we all — please — just for once — go down to the seaside on the bus?' — JAMES AND THE GIANT PEACH

secret adjective

A secret thing is one that not many people know about.

There is a secret place I know/Where I quite often like to go,/Beyond the wood, behind some rocks,/A super place for guzzling chocs. — DIRTY BEASTS

secret noun secrets

If something is a secret, not many people know about it and you must not tell anyone.

I was the keeper of a deep secret and a careless word from me could blow the lid off the greatest poaching expedition the world would ever see. — DANNY THE CHAMPION OF THE WORLD

secretly adverb

If you do something secretly, you do it without telling anyone.

That was the last time I had seen Bruno Jenkins . . . I doubted very much that he was about to be turned into a mouse, although I must confess that I was secretly hoping it might happen. — THE WITCHES

see verb sees, seeing, saw, seen

Take a long look at **look** for some ways to describe seeing.

seed noun seeds

A seed is a small thing that a new plant grows from. **Snozzcumbers** have many seeds inside, each of which is as large as a melon.

Sophie reached forward and scooped away half a dozen of these seeds. This left a hole in the middle of the Snozzcumber large enough for her to crouch in. — THE BFG

see-saw noun see-saws

A see-saw is a toy made of a long piece of wood that is balanced in the middle so that someone can sit on each end. The Enormous Crocodile has a clever plan to disguise himself as a see-saw to lure children to come near him.

Then, a girl who was older than the others said, 'It's rather a funny knobbly sort of a see-saw, isn't it? Do you think it'll be safe to sit on?' — THE ENORMOUS CROCODILE

seize (rhymes with sneeze) verb seizes, seizing, seized

When you seize something, you grab it roughly.

Nigel, always ready for action, leapt up and seized the big jug of water. 'My father says cold water is the best way to wake up someone who's fainted,' he said. — MATILDA

selfish adjective

Someone who is selfish thinks only about themselves and not about other people.

Mr Wonka shrugged his shoulders and turned his back on them. He hated squabbles. He hated it when people got grabby and selfish. — CHARLIE AND THE GREAT GLASS ELEVATOR

sell verb sells, selling, sold

When you sell something, you give it to someone and they give you money for it.

*'My dear sir!' cried Mr Wonka, 'when I start selling this gum in the shops it will change **everything**! It will be the end of all kitchens and all cooking!'* — CHARLIE AND THE CHOCOLATE FACTORY

sensation noun sensations

If you have a sensation in your body, you have a feeling. When you drink **frobscottle**, it gives you a wonderful sensation.

It was an amazing sensation. It felt as though hundreds of tiny people were dancing a jig inside her and tickling her with their toes. It was lovely. — THE BFG

sense noun senses

1 Your senses are your ability to see, hear, smell, feel and taste.

'A dream . . . makes . . . a sound so soft and low it is

There are 23 letters in *scrumdiddlyumptiousness.* Can you make a longer word?

impossible for ordinary people to hear it. But the BFG can hear it easily. His sense of hearing is absolutely fantastic.'—THE BFG

2 If you have good sense, you know what is the right thing to do.

The Queen, with her usual admirable tact and good sense, came to the rescue. 'BFG,' she said, 'can you tell us **more or less** *where this Giant Country is?'*—THE BFG

sensible adjective
If you are sensible, you think carefully and try to do the right thing.

Mr Wonka made a wheezing noise in his throat and a look of great sorrow came over his face. 'Why oh why can't people be more sensible?' he said sadly.—CHARLIE AND THE GREAT GLASS ELEVATOR

sensitive adjective
Something that is sensitive reacts to things around it. The BFG has super-sensitive ears that allow him to hear the tiny sounds that dreams make.

'Ah yes, my darling, there is a whole world of sound around us that we cannot hear because our ears are simply not sensitive enough.'—DANNY THE CHAMPION OF THE WORLD

sentence noun sentences
A sentence is a group of words that mean something together. A sentence begins with a capital letter and ends with a full stop.

Miss Honey went to the blackboard and wrote with her white chalk the sentence, **I have already begun to learn how to read long sentences.**—MATILDA

separate adjective
Things that are separate are not joined together or not next to each other.

'Do you have separate dreams for boys and for girls?' Sophie asked. 'Of course,' the BFG said . . . 'These here is all girls' dreams on this shelf.'—THE BFG

septicous adjective
A septicous creature is poisonous and deadly.

'Save our souls!' bellowed the Fleshlumpeater. 'Sound the crumpets! I is bitten by a septicous venomsome vindscreen viper!'—THE BFG

SPARKY SYNONYMS You can also say **venomous** or **venomsome**.

series noun series
a number of things that come one after another

Suddenly the loudspeaker in the President's study gave out a series of the most ghastly screams and yells.—CHARLIE AND THE GREAT GLASS ELEVATOR

serious adjective
1 Something that is serious is very important.

'Don't be a fool, Shuckworth!' snapped Ground Control. 'Pull yourself together, man! This is serious!'—CHARLIE AND THE GREAT GLASS ELEVATOR

2 Someone who is serious does not smile or joke, but thinks carefully about things.

My grandmother leaned back in her chair and sucked away contentedly at her foul black cigar . . . She was not smiling. She looked deadly serious.—THE WITCHES

servant noun servants
someone who works at another person's home, doing jobs such as cleaning and cooking

When . . . the fainting Duchess had been carried into the house by her servants, the old Duke stood on the lawn with the Giraffe, the Pelican, the Monkey and me.—THE GIRAFFE AND THE PELLY AND ME

serve verb serves, serving, served
1 When you serve food, you put it on people's plates or in front of them to eat.

Mr Hoppy . . . was leaning over his balcony-rail watching Mrs Silver serving Alfie his breakfast. 'Here's the heart of the lettuce for you, my lovely,' she was saying.—ESIO TROT

2 If you say that something serves someone right, you mean that they deserve it (and it is usually something bad).

'I'm a wreck!' groaned the Centipede. 'I am wounded all over!' 'It serves you right,' said the Earthworm.—JAMES AND THE GIANT PEACH

service noun services
A church service is a religious ceremony with prayers and hymns, usually held every Sunday.

Then came the first Sunday morning service, a great occasion for the village and a greater one for the vicar.—THE VICAR OF NIBBLESWICKE

settle verb settles, settling, settled
1 When you settle an argument, you agree and decide what to do about it.

'That's settled then!' said Mr Wonka . . . 'You do Grandma Josephine, the tiny one. I'll do Grandpa George, the one-year-old. Here's your spoon.'—CHARLIE AND THE GREAT GLASS ELEVATOR

2 When you settle down somewhere, you sit, perch or lie down comfortably.

The pheasants were too dopey to fly far. In a few seconds down they came again and settled themselves like a swarm of locusts all over the filling-station. — DANNY THE CHAMPION OF THE WORLD

several determiner

Several things means a number of them, or quite a few.

Outside in the yard, there were several chickens that hadn't had any of George's Marvellous Medicine Number One. — GEORGE'S MARVELLOUS MEDICINE

severe adjective severer, severest

Something that is severe is very bad or very harsh.

There was no doubt in Matilda's mind that this latest display of foulness by her father deserved severe punishment, and . . . her brain went to work on various possibilities. — MATILDA

sew verb sews, sewing, sewed, sewn

When you sew, you use a needle and thread to join pieces of cloth together.

'This Silkworm had, I'll have you know,/The honour, not so long ago,/To spin and weave and sew and press/ The Queen of England's wedding dress.' — JAMES AND THE GIANT PEACH

shade noun shades

1 an area that is dark or cool because the light of the sun cannot get to it

The eaves of the house projected far out beyond the walls to provide extra shade, and this gave the building a sort of Japanese pagoda appearance. — GOING SOLO

2 If something is a shade more or less, it is very slightly more or less.

Mr Hoppy lifted the tortoise up from her balcony and carried it inside. All he had to do now was to find one that was a shade smaller, so that it would just go through the door of the little house. — ESIO TROT

shadow noun shadows

1 a dark shape that falls on a surface when something is between it and the light

Each time they came to a road, the BFG was over it and away, and no motorist could possibly have seen anything except a quick black shadow flashing overhead. — THE BFG

2 an area that is dark because the light is blocked

'At twilight everything inside the wood becomes veiled and shady . . . And when danger threatens you can always hide in the shadows which are darker than a wolf's mouth.' — DANNY THE CHAMPION OF THE WORLD

shadowy adjective shadowier, shadowiest

A shadowy place is dark and shaded from any light.

The tall black figure was coming her way. It was keeping very close to the houses across the street, hiding in the shadowy places where there was no moonlight. — THE BFG

shake verb shakes, shaking, shook, shaken

1 When you shake something, you move it about quickly.

'Yippeeeeee!' shouted Grandpa Joe. 'What a brilliant thought, sir! What a staggering idea!' He grabbed Mr Wonka's hand and started shaking it like a thermometer. — CHARLIE AND THE GREAT GLASS ELEVATOR

2 When you shake, your body trembles because you are cold or frightened.

Muggle-Wump went pale and began to shake all over. 'You aren't really going to gobble up a little child, are you?' he said. — THE ENORMOUS CROCODILE

shallow adjective shallower, shallowest

Something that is shallow is not very deep.

Bunce . . . was so short his chin would have been underwater in the shallow end of any swimming-pool in the world. — FANTASTIC MR FOX

shambles noun

You say something is a shambles when it is in a great mess or muddle.

George stood in his bedroom gazing at the shambles. There was a big hole in the floor and another in the ceiling. — GEORGE'S MARVELLOUS MEDICINE

shame noun

the feeling you have when you are unhappy because you have done wrong

But now, my dears, we think you might/Be wondering — is it really right/That every single bit of blame/And all the scolding and the shame/Should fall upon Veruca Salt?/ Is she the only one at fault? — CHARLIE AND THE CHOCOLATE FACTORY

shampoo noun shampoos

Shampoo is liquid soap that you use to wash your hair. George adds a whole bottle of shampoo to his magical mixture for his grumpy grandma.

Number one was a bottle labelled GOLDEN GLOSS HAIR SHAMPOO. He emptied it into the pan. 'That ought to wash her tummy nice and clean,' he said. — GEORGE'S MARVELLOUS MEDICINE

shape noun shapes

The shape of something is what its outline looks like. Vermicious Knids can change into any shape they like, such as a square, round or oval. Creatures that can do this are called **shape-shifters**.

'The Vermicious Knid can turn itself into any shape it wants . . . Normally it is egg-shaped, but it can just as easily give itself two legs like a human or four legs like a horse.' — CHARLIE AND THE GREAT GLASS ELEVATOR

share verb shares, sharing, shared

When people share something, they both use it.

Charlie . . . picked up the chocolate bar and held it out to his mother, and said, 'Here, Mother, have a bit. We'll share it. I want everybody to taste it.' — CHARLIE AND THE CHOCOLATE FACTORY

a b c d e f g h i j k l m n o p q r s t u v w x y z

The BFG is called *O BGA* (*Bom Gigante Amigo*) in Brazilian Portuguese.

shark noun **sharks**
a big, fierce sea fish that has sharp teeth and hunts
and kills other fish to eat
*Slowly, almost lazily, the shark opened his mouth (which
was big enough to have swallowed a perambulator) and
made a lunge at the peach.* — JAMES AND THE GIANT PEACH

sharp adjective **sharper, sharpest**
1 Something that is sharp can cut things because it is
thin or pointed.
*The Wolf stood there, his eyes ablaze/And yellowish, like
mayonnaise./His teeth were sharp, his gums were raw,/
And spit was dripping from his jaw.* — REVOLTING RHYMES
2 If you have sharp eyes or ears, you see or hear things
easily.
*Mr Fox . . . took a last careful look around. The wood was
murky and very still . . . Just then, his sharp night-eyes
caught a glint of something bright behind a tree not far
away.* — FANTASTIC MR FOX
3 If someone speaks in a sharp voice, they say
something angrily.
*'Grandma may not have a hoarse throat,' George said,
'but she's certainly got a sharp tongue.'* — GEORGE'S
MARVELLOUS MEDICINE

shattered adjective
If you are shattered, you are exhausted and worn out.
*They dumped the poor BFG on the ground. He was dazed
and shattered. They gave him a few kicks and shouted,
'Run, you little runt! Let us be seeing how fast you is
galloping!'* — THE BFG

shave verb **shaves, shaving, shaved**
If someone shaves a part of their body, they cut all
the hair off it to make it smooth. Mr Twit never
shaves his face and chin which is why he has so
much facial hair.

sheet noun **sheets**
A sheet is a large piece of cloth that you put on a bed.
Bed sheets are often white, so if someone is very afraid,
their face might look *as white as a sheet*.
*'Is that the kind that eats fully-grown men for breakfast?'
the Head of the Fire Department asked, going white as
a sheet. 'I'm afraid it is,' the Chief of Police answered.*
— JAMES AND THE GIANT PEACH

shelf noun **shelves**
A shelf is a piece of wood fastened to a wall that you
put things on. The BFG's cave is lined with shelves that
are stacked with jars full of dreams.
*The walls on either side were lined with shelves, and
on the shelves there stood row upon row of glass jars.
There were jars everywhere.* — THE BFG

shell noun **shells**
A shell is the hard outer covering round a nut or
egg, or on the back of an animal such as a snail
or tortoise.
*Every day, when Mr Hoppy looked over his balcony and
saw Mrs Silver whispering endearments to Alfie and
stroking his shell, he felt absurdly jealous.* — ESIO TROT

sherbet noun **sherbets**
a type of fizzy sweet powder or drink
*Each Sucker consisted of a yellow cardboard tube filled
with sherbet powder, and there was a hollow liquorice
straw sticking out of it.* — BOY

shimozzle noun **shimozzles**
A shimozzle is a noisy disturbance or muddle.
*Curiously, not one of the other eight snoring giants had
woken up during this shimozzle. 'When you is only
sleeping one or two hours a day, you is sleeping extra
doubly deep,' the BFG explained.* — THE BFG
DID YOU KNOW? *Shimozzle* comes from a Yiddish word
that means 'bad luck'. It can also be spelled *shemozzle*.
SPARKY SYNONYMS You can also say **rumpledumpus**.

shine verb **shines, shining, shone**
When something shines, it gives out light or looks
very bright.
*What a dazzling sight it was! The moonlight was
shining and glinting on its great curving sides,
turning them to crystal and silver.* — JAMES AND THE
GIANT PEACH

shiny adjective shinier, shiniest
Something that is shiny looks very bright and gives out light.
Then there was a big tin of WAXWELL FLOOR POLISH. IT REMOVES FILTH AND FOUL MESSES FROM YOUR FLOOR AND LEAVES EVERYTHING SHINY BRIGHT, it said. — GEORGE'S MARVELLOUS MEDICINE

shiver verb shivers, shivering, shivered
When you shiver, you tremble because you are cold or frightened.
Poor James was backed up against the far wall, shivering with fright and much too terrified to answer. — JAMES AND THE GIANT PEACH

shiver noun shivers
a feeling of shivering or trembling
The summer holidays! Those magic words! The mere mention of them used to send shivers of joy rippling over my skin. — BOY

shock noun shocks
If something is a shock, you were not expecting it and it upsets you when it happens.
I wasn't seriously expecting that I would be able to speak at all now that I had become a mouse, so I got the shock of my life when I heard my own voice. — THE WITCHES

shock verb shocks, shocking, shocked
If something shocks you, it gives you a nasty surprise and upsets you.
I was shocked. My own father a thief! This gentle lovely man! I couldn't believe he would go creeping into the woods at night to pinch valuable birds belonging to somebody else. — DANNY THE CHAMPION OF THE WORLD

shoe noun shoes
Shoes are strong coverings you wear on your feet to keep them warm and dry. Witches wear shoes (pointed ones are best) to cover up the fact that they have no toes.
'All ladies like to wear small rather pointed shoes, but a witch, whose feet are very wide and square at the ends, has the most awful job squeezing her feet into those neat little pointed shoes.' — THE WITCHES

shoot verb shoots, shooting, shot
1 When someone shoots with a gun or other weapon, they fire it.
'Don't shoot! Please don't shoot!' 'Why not?' said one of the ducks. It was the one who wasn't holding a gun. 'You are always shooting at us.' — THE MAGIC FINGER

2 If something shoots up or out, it moves very fast.
The Roly-Poly Bird gave a shriek of terror and shot straight up into the air, leaving its tail feathers behind in the Enormous Crocodile's mouth. — THE ENORMOUS CROCODILE

shootle verb shootles, shootling, shootled
Shootling means shooting with guns, which grown-ups with no **common sense** do to each other.
'But human beans is squishing each other all the time,' the BFG said. 'They is shootling guns and going up in aerioplanes to drop their bombs on each other's heads every week.' — THE BFG
RINGBELLING RHYMES Try rhyming with *bootle*.

shop noun shops
a place where you can go to buy things, such as a bookshop or a sweetshop
I know the ground floor used once to be a shop because I can still read the faded lettering across the front which says THE GRUBBER. — THE GIRAFFE AND THE PELLY AND ME

short adjective shorter, shortest
1 Someone who is short is not very tall. Mr Twit tricks his wife into thinking she is getting shorter because of the Dreaded Shrinks.
'It's not the stick, it's you!' said Mr Twit, grinning horribly. 'It's you that's getting shorter! I've been noticing it for some time now.' — THE TWITS

2 Something that is short is not very long, or does not last long.
Mrs Salt was a great fat creature with short legs, and she was blowing like a rhinoceros. — CHARLIE AND THE CHOCOLATE FACTORY
Then the robins came in and the children began climbing onto their backs and going for short flights. — THE MINPINS

shoulder noun shoulders
Your shoulders are the parts of the body between your neck and your arms.
And then, very slowly, like some weird monster rising up from the deep, Grandma's head came through the roof . . . Then her scrawny neck . . . And the tops of her shoulders . . . — GEORGE'S MARVELLOUS MEDICINE

a b c d e f g h i j k l m n o p q r **s** t u v w x y z

The word *sherbet* comes from an Arabic word meaning 'a drink'.

shout verb **shouts, shouting, shouted**
When you shout, you speak in a very loud voice.
*'Look at me!' Grandma shouted from the rooftop.
'Never mind about the hen! What about me?'* — GEORGE'S
MARVELLOUS MEDICINE

LOOK IT UP! For ways to describe how people speak,
see **say.**

shovel noun **shovels**
a tool like a spade with the sides turned up that you
use for moving things like earth or snow
*The noise he heard now was the most frightening noise
a fox can ever hear — the scrape-scrape-scraping of
shovels digging into the soil.* — FANTASTIC MR FOX

shovel verb **shovels, shovelling, shovelled**
If you shovel things, you scoop or push them roughly,
as if you were using a shovel.
*Mr Twit started eating, twisting the long tomato-covered
strings around his fork and shovelling them into his mouth.
Soon there was tomato sauce all over his hairy chin.*
— THE TWITS

shower noun **showers**
When there is a shower, it rains or snows for a short
time. A shower of small things is a lot of them coming
or falling like rain.
*A shower of glass fell upon the poor BFG. 'Gunghummers
and bogs winkles!' he cried. 'What was that?'* — THE BFG

shower verb **showers, showering, showered**
If you shower someone with things, you give them a lot
of them.
*Kings and Presidents and Prime Ministers and Rulers of
every kind showered the enormous giant and the little girl
with compliments and thank-yous.* — THE BFG

shriek verb **shrieks, shrieking, shrieked**
If you shriek, you shout or scream in a high voice.
*The Cloud-Men . . . grabbed great handfuls of hailstones
and rushed to the edge of the cloud and started throwing
them at the peach, shrieking with fury all the time.*
— JAMES AND THE GIANT PEACH

shrill adjective **shriller, shrillest**
A shrill sound is high and loud.
*So hysterical and shrill was Nigel's scream that everyone
in the place, including the Trunchbull, looked up at the
blackboard.* — MATILDA

shrimp noun **shrimps**
A shrimp is a small shellfish. If you call someone a
shrimp, you are being very rude about how small
they are.
*'Here you are, an unhatched shrimp sitting in the lowest
form there is, trying to tell me a whopping great lie like
that!'* — MATILDA

shrink verb **shrinks, shrinking, shrank, shrunk**
When something shrinks, it gets smaller.
*Grandma was the size of a match-stick and still shrinking
fast. A moment later, she was no bigger than a pin . . .*
— GEORGE'S MARVELLOUS MEDICINE

shrivelly adjective
dried and wrinkled
*George could hear the hiss of escaping air. She was going
down. She was slowly getting thinner again, shrinking
back and back slowly to her shrivelly old self.* — GEORGE'S
MARVELLOUS MEDICINE

shrug verb **shrugs, shrugging, shrugged**
When you shrug your shoulders, you lift them slightly
as a sign that you do not care or do not know.
*Mr Wonka shrugged his shoulders and turned his back
on them. He hated squabbles.* — CHARLIE AND THE GREAT
GLASS ELEVATOR

shudder verb **shudders, shuddering, shuddered**
When a person or machine shudders, they shake
violently.
*Mr Wonka . . . pressed a brown button. The Elevator
shuddered, and then with a fearful whooshing noise it
shot vertically upward like a rocket.* — CHARLIE AND THE
GREAT GLASS ELEVATOR

shy adjective **shyer, shyest**
If you are shy, you feel frightened and nervous when
you meet people you do not know.
*The Glow-worm, who at the best of times was a very shy
and silent creature, sat glowing with pleasure near the
tunnel entrance.* — JAMES AND THE GIANT PEACH

sick adjective sicker, sickest

1 A sick person or animal is ill or unwell.
The hen got to its feet. It was rather shaky. It was making funny gurgling noises in its throat. Its beak was opening and shutting. It seemed like a pretty sick hen. — GEORGE'S MARVELLOUS MEDICINE

2 If you feel sick, you feel as if you are about to vomit.
'To talk about children is making me sick!' screamed The Grand High Witch. 'I am feeling sick even thinking about them! Fetch me a basin!' — THE WITCHES

sickable adjective

Something that is sickable looks or tastes so vile that it makes you feel instantly sick.
'It's disgusterous!' the BFG gurgled. 'It's sickable! It's rotsome! It's maggotwise! Try it yourself, this foulsome snozzcumber!' — THE BFG

SPARKY SYNONYMS You can also say **disgusterous** or **nauseating**.

> **Gobblefunking with words**
> To make this word, Roald Dahl added the ending *-able* to *sick*. This ending or *suffix* means 'making or causing': for example a *laughable* idea is so silly that it makes you laugh. It can also mean 'able to be', so that *eatable* or *edible* food is food you can eat without getting ill, and Willy Wonka's *lickable* wallpaper is meant to be licked for fun.

sidle verb sidles, sidling, sidled

If you sidle, you walk or shuffle sideways in a nervous way.
I sidled cautiously into the room. What a lovely secret silent place it was. — THE WITCHES

sigh (rhymes with by) verb sighs, sighing, sighed

When you sigh, you breathe out heavily because you are sad, tired or disappointed.
'Well, well, well,' sighed Mr Willy Wonka, 'two naughty little children gone. Three good little children left.' — CHARLIE AND THE CHOCOLATE FACTORY

sight noun sights

1 If something is in or out of sight, you can or cannot see it.
The only Knid in sight was their old friend with the purple behind, still cruising alongside in its usual place, still glaring into the Elevator. — CHARLIE AND THE GREAT GLASS ELEVATOR

2 A sight is something that you see.
It was an extraordinary sight. The cockerel's body hadn't grown at all. But the neck was now about six feet long. — GEORGE'S MARVELLOUS MEDICINE

signal noun signals

a light, sound or gesture that tells you what you should do, or that something is going to happen
And now, as though at a signal from the leader, all the other sharks came swimming in towards the peach . . . and began to attack it furiously. — JAMES AND THE GIANT PEACH

signal verb signals, signalling, signalled

If you signal to someone, you give them a signal.
Mr Wonka . . . signalled everyone to gather round close so they could whisper without being heard by the hidden microphones. — CHARLIE AND THE GREAT GLASS ELEVATOR

silence noun

When there is silence there is no sound at all.
Not the tiniest sound could be heard anywhere. Sophie had never known such a silence. — THE BFG

silent adjective

1 Something that is silent does not make any noise. Someone who is silent does not speak or make a noise.
Sophie was silent for a few moments. Then suddenly, in a voice filled with excitement, she cried out, 'I've got it! By golly, I think I've got it!' — THE BFG

2 If a place is silent, there is no noise in it.
I cannot possibly describe to you what it felt like to be standing alone in the pitchy blackness of that silent wood in the small hours of the night. — DANNY THE CHAMPION OF THE WORLD

silk noun

Silk is a fine soft thread produced by silkworms for making their cocoons.
'Silkworm says she's running out of silk!' yelled the Centipede from below. 'She says she can't keep it up much longer. Nor can Miss Spider!' — JAMES AND THE GIANT PEACH

Silkworm (JAMES AND THE GIANT PEACH)

A silkworm is a kind of caterpillar that covers itself with a cocoon of fine threads when it is ready to turn into a moth. The Silkworm who lives in the Giant Peach sleeps most of the time but she once spun and wove silk thread to make the Queen's wedding dress.

silly adjective sillier, silliest

Something that is silly is stupid, not clever or sensible.
'A witch will never do silly things like climbing up drainpipes or breaking into people's houses. You'll be quite safe in your bed.' — THE WITCHES

silver noun & adjective

Silver is a shiny, greyish-white metal that is very valuable. A silver colour is the colour of this metal.
The giant peach, with the sunlight glinting on its side, was like a massive golden ball sailing upon a silver sea. — JAMES AND THE GIANT PEACH

Silver, Mrs (ESIO TROT)

Mrs Silver is a widow who lives in a flat with her pet tortoise, Alfie. She is too busy worrying about Alfie to notice that her shy neighbour, Mr Hoppy, is hopelessly in love with her.

simple adjective **simpler, simplest**
Something that is simple is very easy.
'Simple arithmetic,' said Mr Wonka. 'Subtract eighty from seventy-eight and what do you get?' 'Minus two!' said Charlie. — CHARLIE AND THE GREAT GLASS ELEVATOR

sing verb **sings, singing, sang, sung**
When you sing, you use your voice to make music.
'Listen!' whispered Charlie. 'Listen, Grandpa! The Oompa-Loompas in the boat outside are starting to sing!'
— CHARLIE AND THE CHOCOLATE FACTORY

single adjective
only one
The old man opened the purse and tipped it upside down. Out fell a single silver sixpence. 'It's my secret hoard,' he whispered. — CHARLIE AND THE CHOCOLATE FACTORY

sink verb **sinks, sinking, sank, sunk**
1 When something sinks, it goes under water.
'That does it!' cried the Earthworm. 'If the peach is leaking then we shall surely sink!' — JAMES AND THE GIANT PEACH
2 When something sinks, it goes downwards.
There came a very hot day with a boiling sun, and the whole palace began to melt, and then it sank slowly to the ground. — CHARLIE AND THE CHOCOLATE FACTORY

sip verb **sips, sipping, sipped**
When you sip a drink, you drink it slowly, a little bit at a time.
Seated in a comfortable armchair in Mrs Silver's parlour, sipping his tea, Mr Hoppy was all of a twitter. — ESIO TROT

sir noun
a word you use when you are speaking politely to a man or a pelican
'He's got him!' cried the Monkey. 'Pelly's got the burglar in his beak!' 'Well done, sir!' shouted the Duke, hopping about with excitement. — THE GIRAFFE AND THE PELLY AND ME

sistance noun
a bit of help or assistance
'I is come here with my little friend Sophie . . . to give you a . . .' The BFG hesitated, searching for the word. 'To give me what?' the Queen said. 'A sistance,' the BFG said, beaming. — THE BFG
DID YOU KNOW? The word sistance is made by splitting assistance into two words, as if it started with the indefinite article a. The BFG often splits and recombines words in squiggly ways like this, as when he says **norphan** for an orphan.

sister noun **sisters**
Sisters are girls or women who have the same parents, like Aunts Spiker and Sponge.
Aunt Sponge, fat and pulpy as a jellyfish, came waddling up behind her sister to see what was going on. — JAMES AND THE GIANT PEACH

sizzle verb **sizzles, sizzling, sizzled**
When something sizzles, it makes a crackling and hissing sound.

The Grand High Witch went on, 'A foolish vitch without a brain/Must sizzle in the fiery flame!' — THE WITCHES

sizzlepan noun **sizzlepans**
A sizzlepan is what the BFG calls a frying-pan.
'If it is very warm weather and a giant is feeling as hot as a sizzlepan, he will probably go galloping far up to the frisby north to get himself an Esquimo or two to cool him down.' — THE BFG

Gobblefunking with words
When he calls a frying-pan a sizzlepan, the BFG is thinking of the sound that it makes (sizzling) rather than what you do with it (frying). You can try changing the names of other things to describe how they sound, so for example a saucepan or a witch's cauldron could be a bubblepan or a bubblepot.

---

skaddle verb **skaddles, skaddling, skaddled**
When you skaddle, you run away very quickly, often to avoid roaming **grobes**.
'So start to run! Oh, skid and daddle/Through the slubber slush and sossel!/Skip jump hop and try to skaddle!/All the grobes are on the roam!' — CHARLIE AND THE GREAT GLASS ELEVATOR

skeleton noun **skeletons**
Your skeleton is all the bones that are in your body.
Every one of these old people was over ninety. They were as shrivelled as prunes, and as bony as skeletons.
— CHARLIE AND THE CHOCOLATE FACTORY

skid verb **skids, skidding, skidded**
If a car skids, it slides out of control because the road is wet or slippery.
Behind the peach, skidding about all over the place in the peach juice, came the Mayor's limousine. — JAMES AND THE GIANT PEACH

skididdle verb **skididdles, skididdling, skididdled**
When giants skididdle, they dash off quickly.
'The giants is clever. They is careful not to be skididdling off to the same country too often. They is always switchfiddling around.' — THE BFG
DID YOU KNOW? Roald Dahl based the word skididdle on skedaddle, which also means 'to run away quickly'.

skill noun **skills**
If you have skill, you can do something well.
Great skill would have to be exercised, Lavender told herself, and great secrecy observed if she was to come out of this exploit alive. — MATILDA

Skillywiggler noun **Skillywigglers**
The Giant Skillywiggler is an imaginary creature that Mr Twit invents to terrify his wife. It has teeth as sharp as screwdrivers and can bite off your nose and toes.

'Help!' screamed Mrs Twit, bouncing about. 'There's something in my bed!' 'I'll bet it's that Giant Skillywiggler I saw on the floor just now,' Mr Twit said. — THE TWITS

skim verb **skims, skimming, skimmed**
When you skim, you move quickly over a surface or over the ground. The BFG skims along noiselessly when he is carrying dreams.
One or two late-night wanderers might have thought they saw a tall black shadow skimming swiftly down a murky sidestreet, but even if they had, they would never have believed their own eyes. — THE BFG

skin noun **skins**
1 Your skin is the part of you that covers all of your body.
'It's gone right through my skin!' the Earthworm groaned. 'I always thought my skin was waterproof but it isn't and now I'm full of rain!' — JAMES AND THE GIANT PEACH
2 The skin on a fruit or vegetable is the tough part on the outside of it.
The skin of the peach was very beautiful — a rich buttery yellow with patches of brilliant pink and red. — JAMES AND THE GIANT PEACH

skinny adjective **skinnier, skinniest**
Someone who is skinny is very thin.
Lavender was exceptionally small for her age, a skinny little nymph with deep-brown eyes and with dark hair that was cut in a fringe across her forehead. — MATILDA

skip verb **skips, skipping, skipped**
When you skip, you run along lightly taking a little jump with each step. Willy Wonka often skips when he is excited.
'Now, over here,' Mr Wonka went on, skipping excitedly across the room to the opposite wall, 'over here I am inventing a completely new line in toffees!' — CHARLIE AND THE CHOCOLATE FACTORY

skirt noun **skirts**
A skirt is a piece of clothing worn by a woman or girl that wraps around her waist and legs. All giants except the BFG also wear a kind of skirt as their only piece of clothing.

The giants were all naked except for a sort of short skirt around their waists, and their skins were burnt by the sun. — THE BFG

skrock noun **skrocks**
The skrock is a rare and ancient animal. Part of the skrock is needed to make Vita-Wonk, but only Willy Wonka knows which part as it is a secret recipe.
'I tracked down THE WHISTLE-PIG, THE BOBOLINK, THE SKROCK, THE POLLY-FROG, THE GIANT CURLICUE, THE STINGING SLUG AND THE VENOMOUS SQUERKLE.' — CHARLIE AND THE GREAT GLASS ELEVATOR

skulduggery noun
You practise skulduggery when you play tricks on people or cheat them deliberately.
Here was somebody who had brought the art of skulduggery to the highest point of perfection, somebody, moreover, who was willing to risk life and limb in pursuit of her calling. — MATILDA

skulk verb **skulks, skulking, skulked**
If you skulk, you move in a stealthy way, so as not to be seen.
The BFG set off across the great hot yellow wasteland where the blue rocks lay and the dead trees stood and where all the other giants were skulking about. — THE BFG

sky noun **skies**
The sky is the space above the earth where you can see the sun, moon and stars.
Once again the giant peach was sailing peacefully through the mysterious moonlit sky. — JAMES AND THE GIANT PEACH

skyhook noun **skyhooks**
Skyhooks keep the Great Glass Elevator attached to the sky so that it doesn't fall down.
'These skyhooks,' said Grandma Josephine. 'I assume one end is hooked on to this contraption we're riding in. Right?' 'Right,' said Mr Wonka. — CHARLIE AND THE GREAT GLASS ELEVATOR

a b c d e f g h i j k l m n o p q r **s** t u v w x y z

Similes can be *as scary as Skillywigglers!* Read more at **mad**.

A B C D E F G H I J K L M N O P Q R S T U V W X Y Z

skyscraper noun skyscrapers
a very tall building
It looked as though they were going to fall right in among all the tallest buildings. James could see the skyscrapers rushing up to meet them at the most awful speed. — JAMES AND THE GIANT PEACH

slab noun slabs
A slab of something is a flat, thick piece of it.
Walking to school in the mornings, Charlie could see great slabs of chocolate piled up high in the shop windows, and he would stop and stare and press his nose against the glass. — CHARLIE AND THE CHOCOLATE FACTORY

slam verb slams, slamming, slammed
If you slam a door, you push it shut so that it makes a loud bang.
'I am fed up with you useless bunch of midgets!' roared the Trunchbull . . . And with that she marched out of the classroom, slamming the door behind her. — MATILDA

slant verb slants, slanting, slanted
If something slants, it slopes and is not straight.
Sophie couldn't sleep. A brilliant moonbeam was slanting through a gap in the curtains. It was shining right on to her pillow. — THE BFG

slap verb slaps, slapping, slapped
If you slap someone, you hit them with your palm or with something flat.
The great man reeled back in his chair as though I had slapped him in the face with a plate of poached eggs. — BOY

sleek adjective sleeker, sleekest
Sleek hair or fur is smooth and shiny.
I saw plenty of giraffe and rhino and elephant and lion, and once I spotted a leopard, sleek as silk, lying along the trunk of a large tree. — GOING SOLO

sleep verb sleeps, sleeping, slept
When you sleep, you close your eyes and rest your body and your mind. Giants like to sleep or **snozzle** before they go hunting.
'How much do giants sleep?' Sophie asked. 'They is never wasting much time snozzling,' the BFG said. 'Two or three hours is enough.' — THE BFG

sleeve noun sleeves
The sleeves on a shirt, jumper or coat are the parts that cover your arms. If you have something up your sleeve, you have a secret plan or idea.
'But it isn't only chocolate bars that he makes. Oh, dear me, no! He has some really fantastic inventions up his sleeve, Mr Willy Wonka has!' — CHARLIE AND THE CHOCOLATE FACTORY

slice noun slices
A slice of something is a thin piece that has been cut off.
'Oh, you horrible little boy! You disgusting little worm! Fetch me a cup of tea at once and a slice of currant cake!' — GEORGE'S MARVELLOUS MEDICINE

slide verb slides, sliding, slid
When something slides, it moves along smoothly. The Pelly's special beak has a sliding top which allows him to use it as a bucket while washing windows.
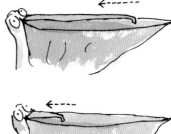
I watched in amazement as the top half of the Pelican's beak began to slide smoothly backwards into his head until the whole thing was almost out of sight. — THE GIRAFFE AND THE PELLY AND ME

slight adjective slighter, slightest
1 Something that is slight is small and not very important or noticeable.
There were slight differences in size and shape between the five, but all had the same greenish-brown wrinkled skin and the skin was rippling and pulsing. — CHARLIE AND THE GREAT GLASS ELEVATOR
2 The slightest amount of something is hardly any of it.
'This stuff is fabulous!' said Augustus, taking not the slightest notice of his mother or Mr Wonka. — CHARLIE AND THE CHOCOLATE FACTORY

slim adjective **slimmer, slimmest**
Someone who is slim, like Miss Jennifer Honey, is thin and graceful.
Her body was so slim and fragile one got the feeling that if she fell over she would smash into a thousand pieces, like a porcelain figure. – MATILDA

slime noun
Slime is unpleasantly wet, slippery stuff, sometimes used to prepare dishes for centipedes.
'I've eaten many strange and scrumptious dishes in my time,/Like jellied gnats and dandyprats and earwigs cooked in slime.' – JAMES AND THE GIANT PEACH

slime verb **slimes, slimeing, slimed**
If a **grobe** or other creature slimes, it moves around in slime, or produces slime.
'You can hear them softly slimeing,/Glissing hissing o'er the slubber,/All those oily boily bodies/Oozing onward in the gloam.' – CHARLIE AND THE GREAT GLASS ELEVATOR

slimescraper noun **slimescrapers**
The slimescraper is a rare creature which is needed to make Wonka-Vite. It thrives in slimy places, collecting (and perhaps eating) slime.
Now add the following, in precisely the order given . . . THE FRONT TAIL OF A COCKATRICE/SIX OUNCES OF SPRUNGE FROM A YOUNG SLIMESCRAPER. – CHARLIE AND THE GREAT GLASS ELEVATOR

slime-wangler noun **slime-wanglers**
The slime-wangler is a creature found in Giant Country which is edible but not pleasant to eat, as it tastes like a **snozzcumber**. It may be related to the **slimescraper** which is found outside Giant Country.
'It tastes of frogskins! . . . And rotten fish!' 'Worse than that!' cried the BFG, roaring with laughter. 'To me it is tasting of clockcoaches and slime-wanglers!' – THE BFG

slimy adjective **slimier, slimiest**
Something slimy is covered in slime, or feels like slime.
The door slid open and there, inside the second lift, was another enormous slimy wrinkled greenish-brown egg with eyes! – CHARLIE AND THE GREAT GLASS ELEVATOR

sling verb **slings, slinging, slung**
If you sling something (such as a captured giant), you hang it up or support it so that it hangs loosely.
'You do not put him inside,' the BFG said. 'You sling him underneath the belly of your bellypopper and carry him like a porteedo.' – THE BFG

slink verb **slinks, slinking, slunk**
If you slink, you move slowly and quietly because you are embarrassed or do not want people to notice you.
'Silence, you silly boy!' said Miss Tibbs, and the Chief of the Army slunk into a corner. – CHARLIE AND THE GREAT GLASS ELEVATOR

slip verb **slips, slipping, slipped**
1 If you slip, your foot accidentally slides on the ground.
Oh, if only he hadn't slipped and fallen and dropped that precious bag. All hope of a happier life had gone completely now. – JAMES AND THE GIANT PEACH
2 When you slip somewhere, you go there quickly and quietly.
Just before the father left for his beastly second-hand car garage, Matilda slipped into the cloakroom and got hold of the hat he wore each day to work. – MATILDA

slipper noun **slippers**
Slippers are soft shoes that you wear indoors.
The Queen got out of bed and put on a pale pink dressing-gown and slippers. 'You may call him now,' the Queen said. – THE BFG

slither verb **slithers, slithering, slithered**
When a worm or other creature slithers, it slips or slides along while wiggling its body.
*'You call that **walking**?' cried the Centipede. 'You're a **slitherer**, that's all you are! You just **slither** along!' 'I glide,' said the Earthworm primly.* – JAMES AND THE GIANT PEACH

slope verb **slopes, sloping, sloped**
Something that slopes is not flat but goes up or down at one end.
'Notice how all these passages are sloping downwards!' called out Mr Wonka. 'We are now going underground!' – CHARLIE AND THE CHOCOLATE FACTORY

slope noun **slopes**
a piece of ground that goes up or down like the side of a hill
'You may not have noticed it,' the Ladybird went on, 'but the whole garden, even before it reaches the steep edge of the hill, happens to be on a steep slope.' – JAMES AND THE GIANT PEACH

slopgroggled adjective
If a giant is slopgroggled, he is in a very sticky situation.
'I is fluckgungled!' screamed the Maidmasher. 'I is slopgroggled!' squawked the Gizzardgulper. – THE BFG

sloshbuckling adjective
Something that is sloshbuckling makes a lot of fuss and noise, like a whirring **bellypopper**.
'If you is taking these sloshbuckling noisy bellypoppers any closer, all the giants is waking up at once and then pop goes the weasel.' – THE BFG

DON'T BE BIFFSQUIGGLED! Sloshbuckling sounds like **buckswashling**, but they mean different things. Buckswashling is something **human beans** and giants can do, but not helicopters.

sloshflunking adjective
A sloshflunking place is barren and desolate, like Giant Country where nothing grows except **snozzcumbers**.
'In this sloshflunking Giant Country, happy eats like pineapples and pigwinkles is simply not growing.' – THE BFG

slow adjective **slower, slowest**
Something that is slow does not move or happen very quickly.
'Of course I'm right,' the Earthworm said . . . 'We shall get thinner and thinner and thirstier and thirstier, and we shall all die a slow and grisly death from starvation.' – JAMES AND THE GIANT PEACH

a b c d e f g h i j k l m n o p q r s t u v w x y z

When giants sleep, the BFG says they are *in the Land of Noddy.*

slow verb **slows, slowing, slowed**
When something slows or slows down, it starts to move or act more slowly.
The peach was still going at a tremendous speed with no sign of slowing down, and about a mile farther on it came to a village. — JAMES AND THE GIANT PEACH

slubber noun
Slubber is a kind of muddy sludge found in boggy places where **grobes** live.
'You can hear them softly slimeing,/Glissing hissing o'er the slubber,/All those oily boily bodies/Oozing onward in the gloam.' — CHARLIE AND THE GREAT GLASS ELEVATOR
DID YOU KNOW? The word *slubber* sounds like a mixture of *slime* and either *rubber* or *blubber*, which is a type of fat inside whales, so perhaps *slubber* is both slimy and bouncy like rubber, or squidgy like blubber.

slug noun **slugs**
A slug is a small, soft animal that looks like a snail but has no shell. George's grandma is fond of eating slugs and caterpillars with her greens.

'Cabbage doesn't taste of anything without a few boiled caterpillars in it. Slugs, too.' 'Not SLUGS!' George cried out. 'I couldn't eat slugs!' — GEORGE'S MARVELLOUS MEDICINE

slugburger noun **slugburgers**
a burger made with slugs
'I can mince it all up very fine and you won't know the difference. Lovely slugburgers. Delicious.' — THE MAGIC FINGER

slushbungle noun
silly nonsense or rubbish
The Air Marshal's face turned the colour of a ripe plum. He was not used to being told he was talking slushbungle. — THE BFG
SPARKY SYNONYMS You can also say **crodswoggle** or **poppyrot**.

slutch noun
Slutch is anything that looks or tastes revolting, like a bite of **snozzcumber**.
'That is the most disgusterous taste that is ever clutching my teeth! You must be buggles to be swalloping slutch like that!' — THE BFG

sly adjective **slyer, slyest**
Someone who is sly is clever at tricking people secretly to get what they want.
'My dear Sponge,' Aunt Spiker said slowly, winking at her sister and smiling a sly, thin-lipped smile. 'There's a pile of money to be made out of this.' — JAMES AND THE GIANT PEACH

smack verb **smacks, smacking, smacked**
1 To smack someone means to slap them with your hand.
The President said a very rude word into the microphone and ten million children across the nation began repeating it gleefully and got smacked by their parents. — CHARLIE AND THE GREAT GLASS ELEVATOR
2 If you smack your lips, you make a noise with them to show you are enjoying something.
'The creamiest loveliest chocolate I've ever tasted!' said Grandpa Joe, smacking his lips. — CHARLIE AND THE CHOCOLATE FACTORY

smack adverb
directly and with a lot of force
Just then, one of the Fleshlumpeater's flailing fists caught the still-fast-asleep Meatdripping Giant smack in the mouth. — THE BFG

small adjective **smaller, smallest**
Something that is small is not very big.
You can use these words in your stories or poems to describe small people or other Minpin-size things.

SOMETHING SMALL CAN BE: dainty, little, miniature, **snitchy**, teeny, tiny, **twiddly**
Opposites are **gigantuous** and **squackling**
'Don't get so flussed,' the BFG said. 'To me that is a snitchy little jump.' — THE BFG

A SMALL PERSON OR A SMALL CREATURE (SUCH AS A MINPIN) CAN ALSO BE: **midgy, snipsy,** tiddly, titchy, wee
'I know that,' Mrs Silver said. 'But I do so wish he would grow just a little bit bigger. He's such a tiny wee fellow.' — ESIO TROT

smash verb **smashes, smashing, smashed**
If you smash something, you break it into a lot of pieces with a loud noise.
The Bloodbottler . . . rushed at the BFG and smashed what was left of the snozzcumber over his head. — THE BFG

smell verb **smells, smelling, smelled, smelt**
1 You smell something when you use your nose to sense it.
Soon, below them, they began to smell the revolting hot stench of the Gruncher's breath. — THE MINPINS
2 If something smells, it gives off a smell.
The breath smelled musty and stale and slightly mildewed, like air in an old cellar. — JAMES AND THE GIANT PEACH

smell noun **smells**
A smell is something you can sense with your nose.
It was a smell unlike any he had smelled before. It was a brutal and bewitching smell, spicy and staggering, fierce and frenzied, full of wizardry and magic. — GEORGE'S MARVELLOUS MEDICINE
LOOK IT UP! For ways to describe both nice and nasty smells, see **good** and **bad**.

smile noun **smiles**
an expression on your face that shows you are pleased or amused, with your lips stretched and turning upwards at the ends
'Your Grace,' the Giraffe said, giving the Duke a small superior smile, 'there are no windows in the world I cannot reach with this magical neck of mine.' — THE GIRAFFE AND THE PELLY AND ME
smile verb **smiles, smiling, smiled**
When you smile, you give a smile.

smithereens plural noun
If you smash something to smithereens, you break it into tiny pieces so that it can never be mended.
'Come back to Earth immediately!' 'That's impossible!' cried Showler. 'They've busted our rockets! They've smashed them to smithereens!' — CHARLIE AND THE GREAT GLASS ELEVATOR

smoke noun
grey or black gas from a fire
All of a sudden, black smoke started pouring out of the hen's beak. 'It's on fire!' Grandma yelled. — GEORGE'S MARVELLOUS MEDICINE
smoke verb **smokes, smoking, smoked**
If someone smokes, they breathe in the smoke from a cigarette or cigar.
My grandmother was the only grandmother I ever met who smoked cigars. — THE WITCHES

smooth adjective **smoother, smoothest**
Something that is smooth is flat, with no bumps or rough parts.
A nest with eggs in it was one of the most beautiful things in the world . . . The nest of a song-thrush, for instance, lined inside with dry mud as smooth as polished wood. — DANNY THE CHAMPION OF THE WORLD

snack noun **snacks**
a small amount of food that you can eat between meals, like a sandwich or (for giants) a tasty **chiddler**
'I is guessing you has snitched away a human bean . . . So now I is winkling it out and guzzling it as extra snacks before my supper!' — THE BFG

snake noun **snakes**
A snake is a reptile with a long narrow body and no legs. Willy Wonka says *Holy Snakes!* when he is surprised.
Corkers . . . brought a two-foot-long grass-snake into class and insisted every boy should handle it in order to cure us for ever, as he said, of a fear of snakes. — BOY

snap verb **snaps, snapping, snapped**
1 If something snaps, it breaks suddenly.
This was followed by an awful splintering noise as the enormous rainbow snapped right across the middle and became two separate pieces. — JAMES AND THE GIANT PEACH
2 If an animal snaps at you, or snaps its jaws, it tries to bite you.
Very quickly, the Crocodile reached up and snapped his jaws at the Roly-Poly Bird. — THE ENORMOUS CROCODILE

3 If someone snaps at you, they shout at you angrily.
'It's not what you like or what you don't like,' Grandma snapped. 'It's what's good for you that counts.' — GEORGE'S MARVELLOUS MEDICINE

snapperwhipper noun **snapperwhippers**
If a grown-up calls you a snapperwhipper, they mean that you are very young compared to them.
'Titchy little snapperwhippers like you should not be higgling around with an old sage and onions who is hundreds of years more than you.' — THE BFG
DID YOU KNOW? *Snapperwhipper* is made by swapping the two parts of *whippersnapper*, a word which means the same thing.

a b c d e f g h i j k l m n o p q r **s** t u v w x y z

The word *crocodilian* means 'of or like a crocodile'.

snarl verb snarls, snarling, snarled
When an animal or witch snarls, it makes a fierce sound and shows its teeth.
'You may rrree-moof your vigs!' snarled The Grand High Witch . . . 'Rrree-moof your vigs and get some fresh air into your spotty scalps!' — THE WITCHES

snatch verb snatches, snatching, snatched
If you snatch something, you grab it quickly.
The next morning when Mr Twit came out with his huge basket to snatch all the birds from The Big Dead Tree, there wasn't a single one on it. — THE TWITS

sneak verb sneaks, sneaking, sneaked
When you sneak somewhere, you go there quietly so that people do not see or hear you.
'Yesterday morning, during break, you sneaked like a serpent into the kitchen and stole a slice of my private chocolate cake from my tea-tray!' — MATILDA

sneeze verb sneezes, sneezing, sneezed
When you sneeze, air suddenly comes out of your nose with a loud noise.
Sophie crouched still as a mouse inside the BFG's pocket. She hardly dared breathe. She was terrified she might sneeze. — THE BFG

sniff verb sniffs, sniffing, sniffed
When you sniff, you smell the air by breathing in noisily through your nose.
Mr Fox crept up the dark tunnel to the mouth of his hole. He poked his long handsome face out into the night air and sniffed once. — FANTASTIC MR FOX

snipsy adjective snipsier, snipsiest
A snipsy person is tiny, like a **chiddler** looks to a giant.
'Try it yourself, this foulsome snozzcumber! . . . Go on, you snipsy little winkle, have a go!' — THE BFG
SPARKY SYNONYMS You can also say **midgy** or **titchy**.

snitch verb snitches, snitching, snitched
When a giant snitches someone, they grab them quickly before they can run away.
'How do they actually catch the humans they eat?' Sophie asked. 'They is usually just sticking an arm in through the bedroom window and snitching them from their beds,' the BFG said. — THE BFG
DID YOU KNOW? Outside Giant Country, *snitch* is also a slang word that means 'to steal'.
RINGBELLING RHYMES Try rhyming *snitching* with *witching hour* (which is when giants go snitching).

snitchet noun snitchets
A snitchet is a snack for a giant, like a bite of **snozzcumber**.
'I is happy to let you sample it,' the BFG went on. 'But please . . . do not be guzzling the whole thing. Leave me a little snitchet for my supper.' — THE BFG

snitchy adjective snitchier, snitchiest
Something that is snitchy is tiny and insignificant.
'Don't get so flussed,' the BFG said. 'To me that is a snitchy little jump. There's not a thingalingaling to it.' — THE BFG
RINGBELLING RHYMES Try rhyming with *titchy*.

snoozle verb snoozles, snoozling, snoozled
When giants snoozle, they sleep soundly while they **snortle**.
'Exunckly!' cried the BFG. 'Every afternoon all these nine giants is lying on the ground snoozling away in a very deep sleep.' — THE BFG

snore verb snores, snoring, snored
If you snore, you breathe very noisily while you are asleep. Giants snore very loudly, which is useful as you can hear them from afar. The BFG calls it **snortling**.
Most of them were lying on their backs with their enormous mouths wide open, and they were snoring like foghorns. The noise was awful. — THE BFG

snort verb snorts, snorting, snorted
When a grandma snorts, she makes a loud noise by forcing air out through her nose, a bit like an angry rhinoceros.
The old hag bucked and shied and snorted. She gasped and gurgled. Spouts of water came shooting out of her. — GEORGE'S MARVELLOUS MEDICINE

snortle verb snortles, snortling, snortled
When giants snortle, they snore very loudly, like foghorns.
snortle noun snortles
the sound of a giant snoring
'Those is just the giants snortling in their sleep,' the BFG said. 'I is a giant myself and I know a giant's snortle when I is hearing one.' — THE BFG

snout noun snouts
An animal's snout is the front part sticking out from its head, with its nose and mouth. Aardvarks and pigs have snouts, as do **grobblesquirts** and **proghoppers**.
'You also mix in the following items: the claw of a crrrabcrrruncher, the beak of a blabbersnitch, the snout of a grrrobblesqvirt and the tongue of a catsprrringer.'
— THE WITCHES

SPARKY SYNONYMS You can also say **proboscis**.

snow noun
small, light flakes of frozen water that fall from the sky when it is very cold
Looking down through the glass floor on which he was standing, Charlie could see the small far-away houses and the streets and the snow that lay thickly over everything.
— CHARLIE AND THE CHOCOLATE FACTORY

snowball noun snowballs
A snowball is a ball of snow that you throw at someone. Cloud-Men like to eat fried snowballs for their tea.
At the entrances to the caves the Cloud-Men's wives were crouching over little stoves with frying-pans in their hands, frying snowballs for their husbands' suppers.
— JAMES AND THE GIANT PEACH

snowflake noun snowflakes
Snowflakes are small light pieces of snow that fall from the sky.
The curtains were never drawn in that house, and through the windows I could see huge snowflakes falling slowly on to an outside world that was as black as tar.
— THE WITCHES

snozzberry noun snozzberries
a type of berry that you can eat
'Lovely stuff, lickable wallpaper!' cried Mr Wonka, rushing past. 'It has pictures of fruits on it — bananas, apples, oranges, grapes, pineapples, strawberries, and snozzberries . . .'— CHARLIE AND THE CHOCOLATE FACTORY

snozzcumber noun snozzcumbers
A snozzcumber is a knobbly vegetable like an enormous cucumber with black and white stripes which grows in Giant Country. Snozzcumbers taste disgusting but they are all the BFG has to eat, as he refuses to hunt **human beans** like other giants.
The BFG was still holding the awesome snozzcumber in his right hand, and now he put one end into his mouth and bit off a huge hunk of it.— THE BFG

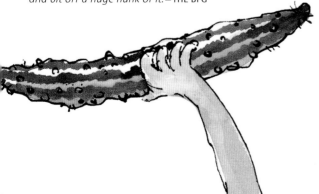

snozzle verb snozzles, snozzling, snozzled
When giants snozzle, they take a short nap.
snozzle noun snozzles
a short sleep or nap
'If we is leaving now,' the BFG said, 'we will be arriving just as the giants is having their afternoon snozzle.'
— THE BFG

DON'T BE BIFFSQUIGGLED! Take care not to confuse snozzle with **schnozzle**, which means 'a nose', so when giants have a *snozzle*, they snore through their *schnozzles*.

snozzwanger noun snozzwangers
A snozzwanger is a deadly three-footed creature that lives in Loompaland and preys on Oompa-Loompas. All three of a snozzwanger's feet are needed to make Wonka-Vite.
'When I went out there, I found the little Oompa-Loompas living in tree houses. They had to live in tree houses to escape from the whangdoodles and the hornswogglers and the snozzwangers.'— CHARLIE AND THE CHOCOLATE FACTORY

snug adjective snugger, snuggest
If you feel snug, you feel warm, cosy and comfortable. If you are *snug as a bug in a rug* (or as the BFG says, *bug as a snug in a rug*), you are as cosy as you can be.
I could see lumps of wood glowing red-hot in the old stove and wonderful it was to be lying there snug and warm in my bunk in that little room.— DANNY THE CHAMPION OF THE WORLD

snuggle verb snuggles, snuggling, snuggled
When you snuggle somewhere, you curl up there so that you are warm and comfortable. If a friendly giant snuggles you, he puts you somewhere warm and cosy, like his inside pocket.
'I is snuggling you very cosy into the pocket of my waistcoat,' the BFG said. 'Then no one is seeing you.'
— THE BFG

soak verb **soaks, soaking, soaked**
If you soak something, you put it in water or liquid until it is very wet.
'Which method did you use for pheasants?' he asked. 'Gin and raisins,' Doc Spencer said. 'I used to soak the raisins in gin for a week, then scatter them in the woods.' — DANNY THE CHAMPION OF THE WORLD

soap noun **soaps**
Soap is something that you use with water for washing yourself, and that the Ladderless Window-Cleaners use to make windows sparkle.
All your windows will glow/When we give them a go,/The Giraffe and the Pelly and me!/We use water and soap/Plus some kindness and hope,/But we never use ladders, not we. — THE GIRAFFE AND THE PELLY AND ME

soar verb **soars, soaring, soared**
When something soars, it goes high up into the air.
Higher and higher soared the kite. Soon it was just a small blue dot dancing in the sky miles above my head. — DANNY THE CHAMPION OF THE WORLD

sob verb **sobs, sobbing, sobbed**
If you sob, you cry in a noisy way.
Miss Spider, the Glow-worm, and the Ladybird all began to cry. So did the Earthworm. 'I don't care a bit about the Centipede,' the Earthworm sobbed. 'But I really did love that little boy.' — JAMES AND THE GIANT PEACH

socket noun **sockets**
Your eye sockets are the hollows in your skull that your eyes fit into. If you say that someone's eyes pop out of their sockets, you mean that they look very surprised indeed.
The Duke was staggered. He reeled back and his eyes popped nearly out of their sockets. 'Great Scott!' he gasped. — THE GIRAFFE AND THE PELLY AND ME

sofa noun **sofas**
a long, comfortable seat for more than one person
'Say two sevens are fourteen! Hurry up or I'll start jerking you up and down and then your hair really will come out and we'll have enough of it to stuff a sofa!' — MATILDA

soft adjective **softer, softest**
1 Something that is soft is not hard or stiff.
James got into his own hammock — and oh, how soft and comfortable it was compared with the hard bare boards that his aunts had always made him sleep upon at home. — JAMES AND THE GIANT PEACH
2 A soft sound is not very loud.
'Talk softer,' the tiny man said. 'If you talk too loud your voice will blow me away.' — THE MINPINS

soggy adjective **soggier, soggiest**
Something that is soggy is wet and soft.
The floor was soggy under his knees, the walls were wet and sticky, and peach juice was dripping from the ceiling. — JAMES AND THE GIANT PEACH

sogmire noun **sogmires**
an area of boggy (and very soggy) ground
'In the quelchy quaggy sogmire,/In the mashy mideous harshland,/At the witchy hour of gloomness,/All the grobes come oozing home.' — CHARLIE AND THE GREAT GLASS ELEVATOR
DID YOU KNOW? To make the new word *sogmire*, Roald Dahl blended *soggy* with the word *quagmire*, which means 'marshy or boggy ground'.

soil noun
the brown earth that plants grow in, and in which earthworms live
'Every tiny little bit of soil that you can see has actually passed through the body of an Earthworm during the last few years!' — JAMES AND THE GIANT PEACH

soldier noun **soldiers**
someone who is a member of an army
'How is I meeting the Queen?' asked the BFG. 'I is not wanting to be shooted at by her soldiers.' — THE BFG

sole noun **soles**
The sole of your foot or shoe is the part underneath it.
'You do have an interesting name, don't you? I always thought that a veruca was a sort of wart that you got on the sole of your foot!' — CHARLIE AND THE CHOCOLATE FACTORY

solid adjective
Something that is solid is hard and firm, or not hollow in the middle.
Badger's front paws hit against something flat and hard. 'What on earth is this?' he said. 'It looks like a solid stone wall.' — FANTASTIC MR FOX

somersault noun **somersaults**
When you do a somersault, you roll over forwards or backwards.
Still clutching the bottle, I gave a leap, turned a somersault in the air, and caught hold of the handle with the end of my tail. — THE WITCHES

son noun **sons**
Someone's son is their male child.
'I want you to take Mr and Mrs Gloop up to the Fudge Room and help them to find their son, Augustus. He's just gone up the pipe.' — CHARLIE AND THE CHOCOLATE FACTORY

song noun **songs**
A song is a piece of music with words that you sing.
The Oompa-Loompas are very fond of making up songs to sing.
'Ssshh!' said Grandpa Joe. 'Listen! Here comes another song!' From far away down the corridor came the beating of drums. Then the singing began. — CHARLIE AND THE CHOCOLATE FACTORY

Sophie (THE BFG)

Sophie is a very brave young girl who lives in an orphanage. One night when she cannot sleep she meets the Big Friendly Giant who **kidsnatches** her and takes her with him to Giant Country. Roald Dahl named her after his granddaughter, Sophie Dahl, who later became a writer herself.

sore adjective sorer, sorest

If a part of your body is sore, it hurts.
The label said, FOR CHICKENS WITH FOUL PEST, HEN GRIPE, SORE BEAKS, GAMMY LEGS, COCKERELITIS, EGG TROUBLE, BROODINESS OR LOSS OF FEATHERS. – GEORGE'S MARVELLOUS MEDICINE

sorry adjective sorrier, sorriest

1 If you are sorry that you did something, you are sad about it and wish that you had not done it.
'I'm joking,' said Mr Wonka, giggling madly behind his beard. 'I didn't mean it. Forgive me. I'm so sorry.' – CHARLIE AND THE CHOCOLATE FACTORY
2 If you feel sorry for someone, you feel sad because something nasty has happened to them.
Miss Spider wiped away a tear and looked sadly at the Centipede. 'You poor thing,' she murmured. 'I do feel sorry for you.' – JAMES AND THE GIANT PEACH

sossel noun

Sossel is a kind of slippery sludge found in boggy places where **grobes** live.
'So start to run! Oh, skid and daddle/Through the slubber slush and sossel!/Skip jump hop and try to skaddle!/All the grobes are on the roam!' – CHARLIE AND THE GREAT GLASS ELEVATOR

sound noun sounds

Sound is anything that you can hear. For some **spliffling** ways that Roald Dahl describes sound, see **noise**.

Gobblefunking with words

Roald Dahl loved playing with sounds when he made up new words. Certain groups of letters and sounds make you think of particular things. For example, words that start with hard sounds like *cr-* and *gr-* are often about hard or harsh things, like *crunching crashes* or *grating grunts*, and words that start with softer sounds, like *sl-* and *squ-*, are often about *slippery slimy* or *squishy squelchy* things. This is called *phonaesthesia* and it is why you can often guess what Roald Dahl's invented words mean, even if you have never heard them before. Have a look at the pages in this dictionary where words start with *sl-* and *squ-* and you will see lots of examples.

sour adjective sourer, sourest

1 Something that is sour has a sharp and bitter taste, like a lemon.
2 A sour expression is unpleasant or bad-tempered.
Her name was Mrs Pratchett. She was a small skinny old hag with a moustache on her upper lip and a mouth as sour as a green gooseberry. – BOY

space noun spaces

1 Space is the place around the Earth and far beyond the Earth, where the stars and planets are.
'These Vermicious Knids are the terror of the Universe. They travel through space in great swarms, landing on other stars and planets and destroying everything they find.' – CHARLIE AND THE GREAT GLASS ELEVATOR
2 A space is a place with nothing in it.
In the wood behind us the shadows and the spaces in between the trees were turning from grey to black. – DANNY THE CHAMPION OF THE WORLD

Space Hotel (CHARLIE AND THE GREAT GLASS ELEVATOR)

The Space Hotel is a gigantic sausage-shaped capsule which orbits the Earth. It is so huge it has a tennis court and a swimming pool inside as well as five hundred luxury bedrooms.

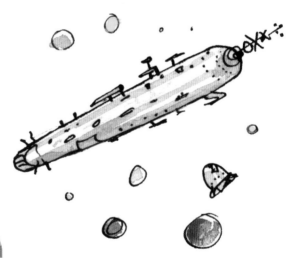

spade noun spades

A spade is a tool with a long handle and a wide blade that you use for digging. The BFG uses a spade from the royal garden to eat his breakfast at the Palace.
The BFG grabbed the garden spade and scooped up all the eggs, sausages, bacon and potatoes in one go and shovelled them into his enormous mouth. – THE BFG

spaghetti noun

Spaghetti is a type of pasta that is made in long, thin pieces. Mrs Twit (not being very nice) serves her husband *Squiggly Spaghetti* mixed with earthworms.
'Hey, my spaghetti's moving!' cried Mr Twit, poking around in it with his fork. – THE TWITS

The name *Sophie* means 'wisdom'.

spare verb **spares, sparing, spared**
If you can spare something, you have some extra that you can give to someone else.
'Couldn't you spare just one for each of us, Mother?'
'I'm afraid not,' said Grandma Georgina. 'These pills are specially reserved for us three in the bed.'– CHARLIE AND THE GREAT GLASS ELEVATOR

spare adjective
If something is spare, you are not using it at the moment but you can use it if you need it.
'I kept shouting, "How could I have done it, Miss Trunchbull? I didn't even know you kept any spare knickers at school!"'
– MATILDA

spark noun **sparks**
A spark is a tiny piece of fire or flame, or a flash of electricity. The Grand High Witch punishes other witches by frying them with white-hot sparks of fire that shoot from her eyes.
'Just look at the power that terrible Grand High Witch has in her eyes alone! She could kill any of us at any time with those white-hot sparks of hers!'– THE WITCHES

sparkle verb **sparkles, sparkling, sparkled**
When something sparkles, it shines brightly.
The Enormous Crocodile grinned again, and his terrible sharp teeth sparkled like knives in the sun.– THE ENORMOUS CROCODILE

sparky adjective **sparkier, sparkiest**
A sparky person is full of energy and fizzing with fun.
A stodgy parent is no fun at all. What a child wants and deserves is a parent who is SPARKY.– DANNY THE CHAMPION OF THE WORLD

sparrow noun **sparrows**
A sparrow is a small, brown bird that you often see in people's gardens. Any sparrows in Mr and Mrs Twits' garden, however, often meet a very sticky end.
It didn't matter what kind they were – song thrushes, blackbirds, sparrows, crows, little jenny wrens, robins, anything – they all went into the pot for Wednesday's Bird Pie supper.– THE TWITS

speak verb **speaks, speaking, spoke, spoken**
For some spliffling ways to describe speaking, see **say**.

spear noun **spears**
a long stick with a sharp point that is used as a weapon

spear verb **spears, spearing, speared**
If you spear something, you pierce it with a spear or sharp weapon.
'We will spear the blabbersnitch and trap the crabcruncher and shoot the grobblesquirt and catch the catspringer in his burrow!'– THE WITCHES

spectator noun **spectators**
Spectators are people who watch a sporting event or game.
With thousands of fascinated spectators, including the Queen, peering down into the pit, the BFG was lowered on a rope.– THE BFG

speech noun **speeches**
1 Speech is the sound of people speaking.
Suddenly I heard voices outside the Ballroom door. The sound grew louder. It swelled into a great babble of speech from many throats.– THE WITCHES
2 A speech is a talk that someone gives to a group of people.
When the cheers and the clapping had died down at last, Don Mini stood up to make a speech.– THE MINPINS

speechless adjective
If you are speechless, you cannot speak because you are so surprised, angry or afraid.
Mr and Mrs Bucket stood hugging each other, speechless with fright. Only Charlie and Grandpa Joe kept moderately cool.– CHARLIE AND THE GREAT GLASS ELEVATOR

speed noun
The speed of something is how fast it moves or how quickly it happens.
From the heart of the great factory, came a muffled roar of energy as though some monstrous gigantic machine were spinning its wheels at breakneck speed.– CHARLIE AND THE CHOCOLATE FACTORY

speed verb **speeds, speeding, sped**
When something speeds, it goes very fast, and when it speeds up, it starts to go even faster.
This extraordinary object was now speeding round and round the Earth at a height of 240 miles.– CHARLIE AND THE GREAT GLASS ELEVATOR

spell verb spells, spelling, spelled, spelt
The way in which you spell a word is the letters that you use when you write it.
Then Nigel said, still balancing on one leg and facing the wall, 'Miss Honey taught us how to spell a new very long word yesterday.' – MATILDA

spider noun spiders
A spider is a small animal with eight legs that spins sticky webs to catch insects for food. The female spider who lives inside the Giant Peach is called **Miss Spider**.
The Spider (who happened to be a female spider) opened her mouth and ran a long black tongue delicately over her lips. – JAMES AND THE GIANT PEACH

Spider, Miss (JAMES AND THE GIANT PEACH)
Miss Spider is a large female spider who lives in the peach. She spins hammock-like beds out of spider silk for her companions to sleep in.

spike noun spikes
a thin piece of metal with a sharp point
Directly in front of them, bordering the pavement, there was a brick wall with fearsome-looking spikes all along the top of it. – THE BFG

Spiker, Aunt (JAMES AND THE GIANT PEACH)
Aunt Spiker is one of James's two cruel and selfish aunts. She is tall and bony with a screeching voice and long wet narrow lips. Her sister is the flabby Aunt Sponge.

spikestick verb spikesticks, spikesticking, spikestuck
If you spikestick a giant, you stab him with a sharp weapon (so you have to be very brave).
'It's Jack!' bellowed the Fleshlumpeater. 'It's the grueful gruncious Jack! Jack is after me! Jack is wackcrackling me! Jack is spikesticking me!' – THE BFG

spill verb spills, spilling, spilled, spilt
If you spill something, you let it fall out of a container by accident (or perhaps by **telekinetic** powers).
With the power of her eyes alone she had compelled a glass of water to tip and spill its contents over the horrible Headmistress. – MATILDA

spin verb spins, spinning, spun
1 Something that spins turns round and round quickly.
Mr Hoppy's mind was spinning like a fly-wheel. Here, surely, was his big chance! – ESIO TROT

2 A spider or silkworm spins a web or cocoon when it forms one with threads from its body.
'And what about me, may I ask?' said Miss Spider. 'I can spin just as well as any Silkworm. What's more, I can spin patterns.' – JAMES AND THE GIANT PEACH

spindel noun spindels
Spindel is what the BFG calls a spine or backbone.
'Sometimes human beans is very overcome when they is hearing wonderous music. They is getting shivers down their spindels.' – THE BFG

spine noun spines
1 Your spine is the long line of bones down the middle of your back.
A tingle of electricity flashed down the length of George's spine. He began to feel frightened. – GEORGE'S MARVELLOUS MEDICINE
2 The spines on a plant or animal are sharp points on it.
I think I know why porcupines/Surround themselves with prickly spines./It is to stop some silly clown/From squashing them by sitting down. – DIRTY BEASTS

spit verb spits, spitting, spat
When you spit (not that you would), you force drops of saliva out of your mouth.
'Eeeeeowtch!' roared the Bloodbottler . . . And then he spat. All of the great lumps of snozzcumber that were in his mouth, as well as Sophie herself, went shooting out across the cave. – THE BFG

spit noun
Spit is saliva that has been spat out. Witches have blue spit, which is one way to spot them in disguise.
*'Can you **notice** the blue spit, Grandmamma? If a witch was talking to me, would I be able to notice it?' 'Only if you looked carefully,' my grandmother said.* – THE WITCHES

Spitsizzler noun Spitsizzlers
A Spitsizzler is a fiery-tasting sweet from Africa that is sold in the Grubber. It is so hot that when you suck it, it makes your saliva sizzle in your mouth.
There were Gumtwizzlers and Fizzwinkles from China, Frothblowers and Spitsizzlers from Africa . . . and Liplickers and Plushnuggets from the Land of the Midnight Sun. – THE GIRAFFE AND THE PELLY AND ME

Spittler (THE MINPINS)
The Terrible Bloodsuckling Toothpluckling Stonechuckling Spittler is a fearsome monster that Little Billy's mother invents to scare him away from the Forest of Sin.
DID YOU KNOW? The name *Spittler* may be based on *spittle* which is saliva that you spit from your mouth.

splash verb splashes, splashing, splashed
1 When you splash water or paint, you make it fly about in drops.
The Cloud-Men . . . all had huge brushes in their hands and they were splashing the paint on to the great curvy arch in a frenzy of speed. – JAMES AND THE GIANT PEACH

Someone who is afraid of spiders has *arachnophobia*.

a b c d e f g h i j k l m n o p q r **s** t u v w x y z

2 Liquid splashes when it hits a surface and makes a noise.

'All is my fault,' the BFG said. 'I is the one who kidsnatched you.' Yet another enormous tear welled from his eye and splashed on to the floor. — THE BFG

splash noun **splashes**

1 the sound of liquid splashing

Every now and again a big bubble of spit formed between his two open lips and then it would burst with a splash and cover his face with saliva. — THE BFG

2 a bright patch of colour or light

It was one of those golden autumn afternoons and there were blackberries and splashes of old man's beard in the hedges. — MATILDA

splashplunk verb **splashplunks, splashplunking, splashplunked**

If you splashplunk a giant, you attack and thump him.

'Jack is spikesticking me! Jack is splashplunking me! It is the terrible frightswiping Jack!' — THE BFG

splatch–winkle verb **splatch-winkles, splatch-winkling, splatch-winkled**

If a giant splatch-winkles, he runs or dashes off in a hurry.

'Here comes the runty one!' boomed the Fleshlumpeater. 'Ho-ho there, runty one! Where is you splatch-winkling away to in such a hefty hurry?' — THE BFG

splendiferous adjective

splendid, marvellous

'Your grandad,' he said, 'my own dad, was a magnificent and splendiferous poacher. It was he who taught me all about it.' — DANNY THE CHAMPION OF THE WORLD

> **DID YOU KNOW?** The word *splendiferous* was not invented by Roald Dahl. It is an old word that was first used more than five hundred years ago. Another old word with the same meaning is *splendacious*.

spliffling adjective

Something that is spliffling is magnificent or splendid, like a grand ballroom in a palace.

The BFG . . . gazed in wonder around the Great Ballroom. 'By gumdrops!' he cried. 'What a spliffling whoppsy room we is in!' — THE BFG

> **DID YOU KNOW?** The word *spliffling* is a blend of *splendid* and *spiffing*, an old-fashioned word meaning 'excellent'.
> **SPARKY SYNONYMS** You can also say **phizz-whizzing**.

splinter verb **splinters, splintering, splintered**

If something splinters, it breaks into small, sharp pieces.

'It's a steel rope,' said Mr Wonka. 'It's made of re-inscorched steel. If they try to bite through that their teeth will splinter like spillikins!' — CHARLIE AND THE GREAT GLASS ELEVATOR

split verb **splits, splitting, split**

When something splits, it breaks or tears.

Three seconds later, the whole underneath of the cloud seemed to split and burst open like a paper bag, and then — out came the water! — JAMES AND THE GIANT PEACH

split adjective

A split second is a fraction of a second, so hardly any time at all.

Sophie saw a flash of pale red go darting towards the giant's face. For a split second it hovered above the face. Then it was gone. — THE BFG

splitzwiggled adjective

If a giant is splitzwiggled, he is in a very bad mess.

'I is flushbunkled!' roared the Fleshlumpeater. 'I is splitzwiggled!' yelled the Childchewer. — THE BFG

splongy adjective **splongier, splongiest**

A splongy mixture is both thick and springy.

'It is a little bit like mixing a cake,' the BFG said. 'If you is putting . . . different things into it, you is making the cake come out any way you want, sugary, splongy . . . or grobswitchy.' — THE BFG

> **DID YOU KNOW?** To make the word *splongy*, Roald Dahl may have joined together *splodge*, meaning a thick smear or dollop of something, and *spongy*, which means 'as springy as a sponge cake'.

splutter verb **splutters, spluttering, spluttered**

1 If you splutter, you make little spitting or coughing sounds.

A rich blue smoke, the colour of peacocks, rose from the surface of the liquid, and a fiery fearsome smell filled the kitchen. It made George choke and splutter. — GEORGE'S MARVELLOUS MEDICINE

2 If you splutter, you say something quickly and unclearly.

Sophie took a small nibble. 'Uggggggggh!' she spluttered . . . She spat it out quickly. 'It tastes of frogskins!' she gasped. 'And rotten fish!' — THE BFG

spoil verb **spoils, spoiling, spoiled, spoilt**

1 If you spoil something, you damage it so that it is not as good or as nice as it was before.

'Now I am going to be sick!' yelled Mrs Teavee. 'No, no!' said Mr Wonka. 'Not now! We're nearly there! Don't spoil my hat!' — CHARLIE AND THE CHOCOLATE FACTORY

2 If someone spoils a child, they make them selfish by giving them everything that they want, just like Veruca Salt's silly parents.

'For though she's spoiled, and dreadfully so,/A girl can't spoil herself, you know./Who spoiled her, then? Ah, who indeed?/Who pandered to her every need?' — CHARLIE AND THE CHOCOLATE FACTORY

Sponge, Aunt (JAMES AND THE GIANT PEACH)

Aunt Sponge is one of James's two cruel and selfish aunts. She is short and fat with small piggy eyes and a face like a soggy cabbage. Her sister is the scrawny Aunt Spiker.

spooky adjective **spookier, spookiest**
A spooky voice is strange and quite scary, like the voice of a ghost. A spooky place feels like it is haunted by ghosts.
'Rattle my bones!' the parrot said, giving a wonderful imitation of a spooky voice. — MATILDA

spoon noun **spoons**
a tool with a rounded bowl on a handle, used for eating soft foods like soup and ice cream

spoon verb **spoons, spooning, spooned**
When you spoon something, you lift and move it with a spoon.
Mr Bucket was spooning something called 'Wonka's Squdgemallow Baby Food' into one-year-old Grandpa George's mouth but mostly all over his chin and chest. — CHARLIE AND THE GREAT GLASS ELEVATOR

spoonful noun **spoonfuls**
as much as a spoon will hold
'Mother!' wailed Mrs Kranky. 'You've just drunk fifty doses of George's Marvellous Medicine Number Four and look what one tiny spoonful did to that little old brown hen!' — GEORGE'S MARVELLOUS MEDICINE

Gobblefunking with words
You can use the suffix *-ful* to make words for measuring amounts. For example, a *pocketful* of sweets is as many sweets as you can fit in your pocket, and a *jarful* of dreams is as many dreams as will fit in a jar. You can make up new measurements too, like a *hatful* of mice, or a *bootful* of worms. Note that the plural of words ending in *-ful* is always *-fuls*, so the BFG carries *jarfuls* of dreams in his suitcase.

---

sport noun **sports**
A sport is a game that involves physical exercise, often outdoors.
'Poaching is such a fabulous and exciting sport that once you start doing it, it gets into your blood and you can't give it up!' — DANNY THE CHAMPION OF THE WORLD

sport verb **sports, sporting, sported**
If you sport something, you wear it in a very obvious way.
Captain Hardcastle sported a moustache that was the same colour as his hair, and oh what a moustache it was! — BOY

spot noun **spots**
a small round mark on something, such as on the back of a ladybird or the hide of a **spotted whangdoodle**
'Well, is it really true that I can tell how old a Ladybird is by counting her spots?' — JAMES AND THE GIANT PEACH

spot verb **spots, spotting, spotted**
If you spot something, you see it.
The giants had already spotted the BFG and all heads were turned, watching him as he jogged forward. — THE BFG

spotted whangdoodle noun **spotted whangdoodles**
The spotted whangdoodle is a rare species of **whangdoodle** with spots on its fur. Its patterned hide is an ingredient in Wonka-Vite.

Now add the following, in precisely the order given . . . THE SNOUT OF A PROGHOPPER/A MOLE FROM A MOLE/ THE HIDE (AND THE SEEK) OF A SPOTTED WHANGDOODLE. — CHARLIE AND THE GREAT GLASS ELEVATOR

spotty adjective **spottier, spottiest**
Something spotty is covered with spots.
Rrree-moof your vigs and get some fresh air into your spotty scalps!' she shouted, and another sigh of relief arose from the audience as . . . all the wigs (with the hats still on them) were lifted away. — THE WITCHES

DID YOU KNOW? Roald Dahl invented the idea of **spotty powder** (which makes you come out in spots so that you can miss school) for an early version of *Charlie and the Chocolate Factory*.

spray verb **sprays, spraying, sprayed**
When you spray something, you scatter tiny drops or pieces of it all about.
'It's filthing!' he spluttered, speaking with his mouth full and spraying large pieces of snozzcumber like bullets in Sophie's direction. — THE BFG

spray noun **sprays**
a device for spraying liquid, such as water, perfume or disinfectant
'We get rid of flies with fly-spray and by hanging up fly-paper. I have often thought of inventing a spray for getting rid of small children.' — MATILDA

spray-gun noun **spray-guns**
a device for spraying liquid such as paint or Vita-Wonk under pressure
Mr Wonka . . . aimed the spray-gun straight at the shadow of Grandma Georgina and he pumped the handle hard ONCE . . . TWICE . . . THREE TIMES! — CHARLIE AND THE GREAT GLASS ELEVATOR

237

spread verb spreads, spreading, spread
1 When something spreads, it starts to cover a wider area.
Then very slowly, with a slow and marvellous grin spreading all over his face, Grandpa Joe lifted his head and looked straight at Charlie.—CHARLIE AND THE CHOCOLATE FACTORY
2 When news or word spreads, more and more people find out about it.
The news that a peach almost as big as a house had suddenly appeared in someone's garden spread like wildfire across the countryside. — JAMES AND THE GIANT PEACH

spree noun sprees
If you go on a spree, you go wild doing something that is a lot of fun.
And now the whole country, indeed, the whole world, seemed suddenly to be caught up in a mad chocolate-buying spree.—CHARLIE AND THE CHOCOLATE FACTORY
RINGBELLING RHYMES Try rhyming with *Whoop*ee!

spring verb springs, springing, sprang, sprung
When you spring, you jump or move quickly or suddenly.
Suddenly the tiny doctor clapped his hands together and sprang up high in the air, hooting with laughter.—DANNY THE CHAMPION OF THE WORLD

spring noun springs
A spring is a coiled piece of metal that jumps back into shape after it has been pressed down.
The BFG changed into his famous top gear and all at once he began to fly forward as though there were springs in his legs and rockets in his toes.—THE BFG

sprint verb sprints, sprinting, sprinted
When you sprint, you run as fast as you can over a short distance.
The Giant was sprinting down the High Street. He was running so fast his black cloak was streaming out behind him like the wings of a bird.—THE BFG

sprout verb sprouts, sprouting, sprouted
When a plant sprouts, it starts to grow new parts. When hair sprouts, it grows thickly or in tufts, like a plant.
The whole of his face except for his forehead, his eyes and his nose was covered with thick hair. The stuff even sprouted in revolting tufts out of his nostrils and ear-holes. — THE TWITS

sprunge noun
Sprunge is a natural substance produced by the **slimescraper**, which is a vital ingredient in Wonka-Vite. It is probably a by-product of the slime which the creature collects.
Now add the following, in precisely the order given . . . THE FRONT TAIL OF A COCKATRICE/SIX OUNCES OF SPRUNGE FROM A YOUNG SLIMESCRAPER.—CHARLIE AND THE GREAT GLASS ELEVATOR

spy noun spies
A spy is someone who works secretly to find out information about another person or country, or about a rival chocolate factory.
'All the other chocolate makers, you see, had begun to grow jealous of the wonderful sweets that Mr Wonka was making, and they started sending in spies to steal his secret recipes.'—CHARLIE AND THE CHOCOLATE FACTORY

spy verb spies, spying, spied
When you spy something, you see it.
Watch the birds as they fly above your heads and, who knows, you might well spy a tiny creature riding high on the back of a swallow or a raven.—THE MINPINS

squackling adjective
very big or very great
'How many girls and boys are they going to eat tonight?' 'Many,' the BFG said. 'The Fleshlumpeating Giant alone has a most squackling whoppsy appetite.'—THE BFG

squarrel verb squarrels, squarreling, squarreled
When giants squarrel, they argue with each other in an angry way.
'Giants is never guzzling other giants,' the BFG said. 'They is fighting and squarreling a lot with each other, but never guzzling.'—THE BFG
DID YOU KNOW? To make the word *squarrel*, Roald Dahl may have joined together *quarrel*, meaning 'to have an argument', and *squabble*, which is like quarrelling but noisier.

squash verb squashes, squashing, squashed
When you squash something, you press it hard so that it becomes flat.
'I have discovered, Miss Honey, during my long career as a teacher that a bad girl is a far more dangerous creature than a bad boy. What's more, they're much harder to squash.'—MATILDA

squat (rhymes with hot) verb squats, squatting, squatted
When you squat, you bend your knees under you so that your bottom is almost touching the ground.
'The Chokey,' Hortensia went on, 'is a very tall but very narrow cupboard. The floor is only ten inches square so you can't sit down or squat in it. You have to stand.'—MATILDA

squawk verb squawks, squawking, squawked
When a bird squawks, it makes a loud, rough sound in its throat.
Suddenly there was the most infernal uproar inside the car as a dozen or more enormous pheasants started squawking and flapping all over the seats and round Mr Hazell's head.—DANNY THE CHAMPION OF THE WORLD

squeak verb squeaks, squeaking, squeaked
If something squeaks, it makes a very high sound, like a mouse or a bat.
'He won't be able to do anything!' cried Mrs Teavee. 'Oh, yes I will!' squeaked the tiny voice of Mike Teavee. 'I'll still be able to watch television.'—CHARLIE AND THE CHOCOLATE FACTORY

squeakpip noun squeakpips
a very unimportant and silly person
'Human beans is thinking they is very clever, but they is not. They is nearly all of them notmuchers and squeakpips.'—THE BFG
DID YOU KNOW? The word *squeakpip* is a reversal of *pipsqueak*, which means the same thing.

squeal verb **squeals, squealing, squealed**
When you squeal, you shout or cry in a high voice.
Miss Spider, who was literally squealing with excitement, grabbed the Centipede by the waist and the two of them started dancing round and round the peach stem together.
— JAMES AND THE GIANT PEACH

squeal noun **squeals**
a high-pitched shout or cry
Squeals and yells came from inside the pocket, and the pocket shook as the furious little prisoner fought to get out. — CHARLIE AND THE CHOCOLATE FACTORY

squeeze verb **squeezes, squeezing, squeezed**
When you squeeze something, you press it hard with your hands or in a machine.
'What are they going to do to her there?' 'Squeeze her,' said Mr Wonka. 'We've got to squeeze the juice out of her immediately.' — CHARLIE AND THE CHOCOLATE FACTORY

squelch verb **squelches, squelching, squelched**
When you squelch, you make a sound like a hippopotamus treading in thick mud.
'When she lowered herself into the chair, there was a loud squelching noise similar to that made by a hippopotamus when lowering its foot into the mud on the banks of the Limpopo River.' — MATILDA
RINGBELLING RHYMES Try rhyming with *belch*.

squerkle noun **squerkles**
The squerkle (also known as the **venomous squerkle**) is a rare and ancient animal with a poisonous bite. Part of the squerkle (but not its venom) is needed to make Vita-Wonk.
'I tracked down THE WHISTLE-PIG, THE BOBOLINK, THE SKROCK, THE POLLY-FROG, THE GIANT CURLICUE, THE STINGING SLUG AND THE VENOMOUS SQUERKLE.' — CHARLIE AND THE GREAT GLASS ELEVATOR

squibble verb **squibbles, squibbling, squibbled**
1 When you squibble something, you write it down quickly.
'I cannot be squibbling the whole gropefluncking dream on a titchy bit of paper. Of course there is more.' — THE BFG
2 If you squibble, you complain or find fault with something.

'Words,' he said, 'is oh such a twitch-tickling problem to me all my life. So you must simply try to be patient and stop squibbling.' — THE BFG
DID YOU KNOW? The BFG uses *squibble* to mean two different things. The first meaning is similar to *scribble* and the second is like *quibble*. Both these words sound a bit like *squibble*, so perhaps the BFG was getting **biffsquiggled**.

squifflerotter noun **squifflerotters**
a mean and nasty person
'Grown-up human beans is not famous for their kindnesses. They is all squifflerotters and grinksludgers.' — THE BFG
LOOK IT UP! For ways to describe **squifflerotters**, see **bad**.

squiffling adjective
Something that is squiffling is excellent or splendid.
'How wondercrump!' cried the BFG, still beaming. 'How whoopsey-splunkers! How absolutely squiffling!' — THE BFG
SPARKY SYNONYMS You can also say **phizz-whizzing** or **wondercrump**.

squiff-squiddle verb **squiff-squiddles, squiff-squiddling, squiff-squiddled**
When the BFG squiff-squiddles his words, he gets them in a muddle. It is the same as saying them all **squiggly**.
'As I am telling you before, I know exactly what words I am wanting to say, but somehow or other they is always getting squiff-squiddled around.' — THE BFG

squiggle verb **squiggles, squiggling, squiggled**
1 When you squiggle, you wriggle and squirm about.
The Fleshlumpeater . . . rolled and he wriggled, he fought and he figgled, he squirmed and he squiggled. But there was not a thing he could do. — THE BFG
2 If a witch squiggles you, she does unspeakably horrible things to you.
'One child a week is fifty-two a year. Squish them and squiggle them and make them disappear. That is the motto of all witches.' — THE WITCHES
RINGBELLING RHYMES Try rhyming with *giggle* or *wriggle*.

Gobblefunking with words
When you put words together that start with the same sound, like *squish* and *squiggle*, you are using **alliteration**. You can find more examples of alliteration in the entry for **ghoulish**.

squiggler noun **squigglers**
A squiggler is a creature that squirms and wriggles. You would get a very odd sensation in your tummy if you ate a live squiggler.
'You'll be all right now, Grandma.' 'ALL RIGHT?' she yelled. 'Who's ALL RIGHT? There's jacky-jumpers in my tummy! There's squigglers in my belly!' — GEORGE'S MARVELLOUS MEDICINE

a b c d e f g h i j k l m n o p q r **s** t u v w x y z

Lots of words that start with *squ-* mean squelchy things. Read more at **sound**.

A B C D E F G H I J K L M N O P R S T U V W X Y Z

squiggly adjective **squigglier, squiggliest**
Something squiggly is full of wiggly lines. Mrs Twit makes Squiggly Spaghetti which wriggles because it has live worms in it.
'It's a new kind,' Mrs Twit said, taking a mouthful from her own plate which of course had no worms. 'It's called Squiggly Spaghetti.' – THE TWITS

squiggly adverb
When the BFG says things squiggly, he gets some words in a muddle, as when he says *skin and groans* instead of *skin and bones*.
'But please understand that I cannot be helping it if I sometimes is saying things a little squiggly. I is trying my very best all the time.' – THE BFG

squimpy adjective **squimpier, squimpiest**
Something squimpy is small and weak.
The Bloodbottler pointed a finger as large as a tree-trunk at the BFG. 'Runty little scumscrewer!' he shouted . . . 'Squimpy little bottle-wart!' – THE BFG

squinker noun **squinkers**
When something happens *quicker than squinkers*, it happens so fast that no one can see it.
'Never is they seeing him . . . The Gizzardgulper has a very fast arm. His arm is going up and down quicker than squinkers.' – THE BFG
DID YOU KNOW? When he invented this phrase, Roald Dahl may have been thinking of the phrase *quick as a wink*, which also means very fast indeed.

squinky adjective **squinkier, squinkiest**
Something squinky is small and unimportant. It is very rude to call someone squinky, and even more rude to call them a *squinky squiddler*.
'You is an insult to the giant peoples!' shouted the Bloodbottler. 'You is not fit to be a giant! You is a squinky little squiddler!' – THE BFG

squint verb **squints, squinting, squinted**
If you squint, or squint at something, you peer at it with half-shut eyes.
Sophie, squinting through the glare of the sun, saw several tremendous tall figures moving among the rocks about five hundred yards away. – THE BFG

squirm verb **squirms, squirming, squirmed**
When you squirm, you wriggle about.
Sophie, by squirming around inside the blanket, managed to push the top of her head out through a little gap just below the Giant's hand. – THE BFG
RINGBELLING RHYMES Try rhyming with *worm*.

squirrel noun **squirrels**
A squirrel is a small animal with grey or red fur and a bushy tail that lives in trees and eats nuts. Willy Wonka keeps a hundred squirrels in his factory to shell walnuts for his nutty creations.
On the table, there were mounds and mounds of walnuts, and the squirrels were all working away like mad, shelling the walnuts at a tremendous speed. – CHARLIE AND THE CHOCOLATE FACTORY

squirt verb **squirts, squirting, squirted**
When water or steam squirts out of something, it shoots out quickly.
The jets of white steam kept squirting out of the skinny old hag's head, and the whistling was so high and shrill it hurt the ears. – GEORGE'S MARVELLOUS MEDICINE

squirt noun **squirts**
A squirt is a rude name for a small person. A mean grown-up might call you a squirt to make you feel very small.
'You're just an ignorant little squirt who hasn't the foggiest idea what you're talking about!' – MATILDA

squish verb **squishes, squishing, squished**
When you squish something, you press or step on it so that it becomes flat or out of shape.
'A slug is one of their favourites. Then the grown-ups step on the slug and squish it without knowing it's a child.' – THE WITCHES

squishous adjective
Something squishous is very easy to squish, like a boneless Knid.
'Oh you Knid, you are vile and vermicious,' cried Mr Wonka. 'You are slimy and soggy and squishous!/But what do we care/'Cause you can't get in here,/So hop it and don't get ambitious!' – CHARLIE AND THE GREAT GLASS ELEVATOR
RINGBELLING RHYMES As well as *ambitious*, you can rhyme **squishous** with *delicious* or *wish us*.

squizzle verb **squizzles, squizzling, squizzled**
Being squizzled is like being squished and squeezed, only worse.
'Oh, you foul and filthy fiend! I hope you get squashed and squished and squizzled and boiled up into crocodile stew!' – THE ENORMOUS CROCODILE
RINGBELLING RHYMES Try rhyming with *sizzle*.

squizzly adjective
For the great squizzly scotch-hopper, see the entry for **scotch-hopper**.

squoggle verb **squoggles, squoggling, squoggled**
If you squoggle something, you hate it and think it is **disgusterous**.
'Here is the repulsant snozzcumber!' cried the BFG, waving it about. 'I squoggle it! I mispise it! I dispunge it!' – THE BFG
RINGBELLING RHYMES Try rhyming with *boggle* or *bungswoggle*.

stagger verb **staggers, staggering, staggered**
1 When you stagger, you walk with unsteady legs, almost falling over with each step.
It took all five teachers and the matron to lift the enormous woman and stagger with her out of the room. – MATILDA
2 If something staggers you, it surprises you a lot.
The massive shape of the Palace itself loomed through the darkness. It was made of whitish stone. The sheer size of it staggered the BFG. – THE BFG

stale adjective **staler, stalest**
Something that is stale is not fresh.
The Pelican cried out, 'Right now I am so hungry I could eat a stale sardine!' — THE GIRAFFE AND THE PELLY AND ME

stalk verb **stalks, stalking, stalked**
When an animal stalks its prey, it follows it stealthily before attacking.
The Trunchbull started advancing slow and soft-footed upon Rupert in the manner of a tigress stalking a small deer. — MATILDA

stammer verb **stammers, stammering, stammered**
If you stammer, you keep repeating the sounds at the beginning of words when you speak.
'B-b-but B-B-Bruno!' stammered Mr Jenkins again. 'H-how did this happen?' — THE WITCHES

stamp noun **stamps**
A stamp is a small piece of gummed paper for sticking on a letter or parcel to show that you have paid to post it. Stamps often have a picture of a famous person, like the Queen (which is how Sophie recognizes her).
Sophie suddenly found herself looking at a face she had seen on stamps and coins and in the newspapers all her life. — THE BFG

stamp verb **stamps, stamping, stamped**
When you stamp your feet, you bang them heavily on the ground.
At this point, the disgusting old Grand High Witch began to do a sort of witch's dance up and down the platform, stamping her feet and clapping her hands. — THE WITCHES

stand verb **stands, standing, stood**
1 When you stand, you are on your feet, not sitting or lying down. If you stand on your head or your hands, you balance on your head or hands on the ground.
'I've got it!' cried Mr Twit. 'I know what we'll do! We'll stand on our heads, then anyway we'll be the right way up!' — THE TWITS

2 If you cannot stand something, you do not like it at all.
*I can't stand hunting. I just can't **stand** it. It doesn't seem right to me that men and boys should kill animals just for the fun they get out of it.* — THE MAGIC FINGER

star noun **stars**
Stars are masses of burning gas that you see as tiny, bright lights in the sky at night.
Healthy young Knids think nothing of travelling a million miles between lunch and supper . . . How else could they travel between the planet Vermes and other stars? — CHARLIE AND THE GREAT GLASS ELEVATOR
The Small Foxes crouched close, their noses twitching, their eyes shining like stars. — FANTASTIC MR FOX

stare verb **stares, staring, stared**
If you stare at something, you keep looking at it for a long time, without moving your eyes.
Mr Fox stopped digging and stared at Badger as though he had gone completely dotty. — FANTASTIC MR FOX
LOOK IT UP! For other ways to look at things, see **look**.

starve verb **starves, starving, starved**
If people starve, they become ill or die because they do not have enough food, like Charlie Bucket and his whole family.
Breakfast was a single slice of bread for each person now, and lunch was maybe half a boiled potato. Slowly but surely, everybody in the house began to starve. — CHARLIE AND THE CHOCOLATE FACTORY

statue noun **statues**
a model of a person (or a centipede) made from stone, wood or metal
'Our Centipede will never move again. He will turn into a statue and we shall be able to put him in the middle of the lawn with a bird-bath on the top of his head.' — JAMES AND THE GIANT PEACH

stature noun
Someone's stature is how tall they are.
All grown-ups appear as giants to small children. But headmasters (and policemen) are the biggest giants of all and acquire a marvellously exaggerated stature. — BOY

steak noun **steaks**
a thick slice of meat or fish
When the Fleshlumpeater was speaking, she got a glimpse of his tongue. It was jet black, like a slab of black steak. — THE BFG

steal verb **steals, stealing, stole, stolen**
To steal something means to take something that belongs to someone else.
'Yesterday morning, during break, you sneaked like a serpent into the kitchen and stole a slice of my private chocolate cake from my tea-tray!' — MATILDA

steam noun
Steam is the hot gas or vapour that comes from boiling water.
A mighty rumbling sound came from inside it, and the whole machine began to shake most frighteningly, and steam began hissing out of it all over. — CHARLIE AND THE CHOCOLATE FACTORY

a
b
c
d
e
f
g
h
i
j
k
l
m
n
o
p
q
r
s
t
u
v
w
x
y
z

Knids are *squishous* and *vermicious* — as well as *vicious!*

steep adjective **steeper, steepest**
Something that is steep slopes sharply up or down.
Through the window, Charlie caught a glimpse of what seemed like an enormous quarry with a steep craggy-brown rock-face. — CHARLIE AND THE GREAT GLASS ELEVATOR

steeplejack noun **steeplejacks**
a person who climbs tall chimneys or steeples to do repairs
One hundred steeplejacks, armed with ropes and ladders and pulleys, swarmed up to the top of the Empire State Building and lifted the giant peach off the spike and lowered it to the ground. — JAMES AND THE GIANT PEACH

stem noun **stems**
A stem is a thin part of a plant on which a leaf, flower or fruit grows. The stem of the Giant Peach sticks up from its centre like the mast of a ship.
A minute later, they were out in the open, standing on the very top of the peach, near the stem, blinking their eyes in the strong sunlight and peering nervously around. — JAMES AND THE GIANT PEACH

stench noun **stenches**
a disgustingly nasty smell
The smell was disgusting. It was the stench that comes from deep inside the tummy of a meat-eating animal. — THE MINPINS

step verb **steps, stepping, stepped**
When you step, you walk a short distance, or take a few steps in one direction.
'Come in! Come in! That's right! Step through the gates!' Mr Wonka was clearly just as excited as everybody else. — CHARLIE AND THE CHOCOLATE FACTORY

stew noun **stews**
Stew is a dish of meat or vegetables cooked slowly in liquid. If someone is in a stew, they are very upset about something.
'What on earth are they talking about?' . . . 'Search me,' the Centipede answered. 'But they seem to be in an awful stew about something.' — JAMES AND THE GIANT PEACH

stew verb **stews, stewing, stewed**
When you stew food (or boys for Boy Pie), you cook it slowly in liquid.
The boys were terrified. 'He's going to boil us!' cried one of them. 'He'll stew us alive!' wailed the second one. 'He'll cook us with carrots!' cried the third. — THE TWITS

Stickjaw noun
Stickjaw is a super-sticky toffee that Willy Wonka invents. It is so sticky and chewy that it makes your teeth stick together so that you cannot talk.
There was a whole lot of splendid stuff from the great Wonka factory itself, for example the famous Willy Wonka Rainbow Drops . . . And his Stickjaw for talkative parents. — THE GIRAFFE AND THE PELLY AND ME

sticky adjective **stickier, stickiest**
Something that is sticky will stick to things when it touches them. If you coat something with glue, it becomes sticky, and if you use HUGTIGHT glue like Mr Twit, it will become *extra-usually* sticky.

'Today is Tuesday and over there you can already see the revolting Mr Twit up the ladder painting sticky glue on all the branches of The Big Dead Tree.' — THE TWITS

stiff adjective **stiffer, stiffest**
Something that is stiff is hard and does not bend easily.
Then, all at once, they became quiet. Then they stiffened. Every single witch stood there as stiff and silent as a corpse. — THE WITCHES

stiffen verb **stiffens, stiffening, stiffened**
When something stiffens, it becomes stiff and hard.
The room became suddenly silent. I saw the tiny body of The Grand High Witch stiffen and then go rigid with rage. — THE WITCHES

sting verb **stings, stinging, stung**
1 If an insect stings you, it pierces your skin with a sharp part of its body.
Mr Twit jumped as though he'd been stung by a giant wasp. — THE TWITS
2 If something else stings you, it gives you a sharp pain on your skin.
The wind stung Sophie's cheeks. It made her eyes water. It whipped her head back and whistled in her ears. — THE BFG

stink verb **stinks, stinking, stank, stunk**
If something stinks, it smells nasty, like the foul breath of the Bloodbottler.
Sophie saw his yellow teeth clamping together, a few inches from her head . . . She caught a whiff of his evil-smelling breath. It stank of bad meat. — THE BFG

stink noun **stinks**
A stink is a foul and nasty smell. Witches (who have very sensitive nostrils) think that children give off a terrible stink, similar to fresh dogs' droppings.
'That Dining-Rrroom vill be full of filthy little children and vithout the nose-plugs the stink vill be unbearrable.' — THE WITCHES

stink–bomb noun **stink-bombs**
a small capsule that you throw on the ground to release the nasty-smelling gas inside
'I'll bet it was she who put that stink-bomb under my desk here first thing this morning. The place stank like a sewer!' — MATILDA

stir verb **stirs, stirring, stirred**
When you stir something, such as a magic potion, you move it about with a stick or spoon.
It was wonderful to stand there stirring this amazing mixture and to watch it smoking blue and bubbling and frothing and foaming as though it were alive. — GEORGE'S MARVELLOUS MEDICINE

stomach noun **stomachs**
Your stomach is the part inside your body where your food goes after you have eaten it.
I noticed my hands were shaking. And my stomach had that awful prickly feeling as though it were full of small needles. – DANNY THE CHAMPION OF THE WORLD

stone noun **stones**
1 Stone is rock, and a stone is a piece of rock. The BFG hides the entrance to his secret cave with a huge stone or boulder.
The Giant reached out and rolled the stone to one side as easily as if it had been a football, and now, where the stone had been, there appeared a vast black hole. – THE BFG
2 A stone is the hard seed in the middle of some fruits such as a cherry or peach. The stone at the centre of the Giant Peach has a door leading to the living quarters inside.
In the great stone of the peach, the Glow-worm was lighting up the room so that the two spinners, the Silkworm and Miss Spider, could see what they were doing. – JAMES AND THE GIANT PEACH

stoop verb **stoops, stooping, stooped**
When you stoop, you bend your body forwards.
The Big Friendly Giant . . . had to stoop quite a lot to avoid hitting the ceiling. Because of this he failed to notice an enormous crystal chandelier. – THE BFG

storm noun **storms**
When there is a storm, there is a strong wind and a lot of rain or snow.
*The Centipede was dancing around the deck and turning somersaults in the air and singing at the top of his voice:
'Oh, hooray for the storm and the rain!'* – JAMES AND THE GIANT PEACH

story noun **stories**
A story is an account of real or imaginary events that you read in a book or that someone tells to you. Each of Roald Dahl's books tells a story.
My father . . . used to make up a bedtime story for me every single night, and the best ones were turned into serials and went on for many nights running. – DANNY THE CHAMPION OF THE WORLD

story–teller noun **story-tellers**
A story-teller is someone who invents and writes or tells wonderful stories, just like Roald Dahl or Charles Dickens.
And a strange sight it was, this tiny dark-haired person sitting there . . . totally absorbed . . . by the spell of magic that Dickens the great story-teller had woven with his words. – MATILDA

straight adjective **straighter, straightest**
1 Something that is straight does not bend or curl.
2 If you keep a straight face, you try not to laugh or smile about something.
Sophie kept a very straight face. 'BFG,' she said, 'there is

no frobscottle here and whizzpopping is strictly forbidden!' – THE BFG

straight adverb
1 in a straight line
There was no wind at all. And because of this, Mrs Twit had gone absolutely straight up. She now began to come absolutely straight down. – THE TWITS
2 If you go straight to a place, you go there at once without delay.
'Go straight to the Fudge Room,' Mr Wonka said to the Oompa-Loompa, 'and when you get there, take a long stick and start poking around inside the big chocolate-mixing barrel.' – CHARLIE AND THE CHOCOLATE FACTORY

strange adjective **stranger, strangest**
1 Something that is strange is unusual and surprising.
Suddenly, George found himself dancing around the steaming pot, chanting strange words that came into his head out of nowhere. – GEORGE'S MARVELLOUS MEDICINE
2 A strange person is someone that you have never met or seen before.
And what was this strange woman doing in our garden anyway? – THE WITCHES

strangled adjective
If someone makes a strangled noise, they sound as if they are choking or cannot breathe.
The woman's face had turned white as snow and her mouth was opening and shutting like a halibut out of water and giving out a series of strangled gasps. – MATILDA

straw noun **straws**
1 Straw is dry cut stalks of corn or wheat.
What, for example, would you say/If strolling through the woods one day,/Right there in front of you you saw/A pig who'd built his house of STRAW? – REVOLTING RHYMES
2 A straw is a narrow tube that you can drink through, or suck through.
Each Sucker consisted of a yellow cardboard tube filled with sherbet powder, and there was a hollow liquorice straw sticking out of it. – BOY

strawberry noun **strawberries**
A strawberry is a small red juicy fruit, with its seeds on the outside. There is a strawberry hidden inside every Giant Wangdoodle.
*A REAL WITCH gets the same pleasure from squelching a child as **you** get from eating a plateful of strawberries and thick cream.* – THE WITCHES

strawbunkle noun **strawbunkles**
Strawbunkles are what the BFG calls strawberries.
'You is a human bean and human beans is like strawbunkles and cream to those giants.' – THE BFG
DID YOU KNOW? Roald Dahl made up the word *strawbunkle* by changing the ending of *strawberry*. He may having been thinking of *carbuncle*, which is a red precious stone with a similar colour to a strawberry.

stream noun **streams**
1 a small river
We would set off with the sandwiches in our pockets,

striding up over Cobblers Hill and down the other side to the small wood of larch trees with the stream running through it. — DANNY THE CHAMPION OF THE WORLD

2 A stream of things is a moving line of them.
The next day a stream of people came scrambling up the steep hill to gaze upon this marvel. — JAMES AND THE GIANT PEACH

stream verb **streams, streaming, streamed**
1 When people stream, they move in a continuous flow, like a stream.
'All factories,' said Grandpa Joe, 'have workers streaming in and out of the gates in the mornings and evenings — except Wonka's!' — CHARLIE AND THE CHOCOLATE FACTORY
2 When something streams out, it stretches out in waves or ripples.
The Giant was sprinting down the High Street. He was running so fast his black cloak was streaming out behind him like the wings of a bird. — THE BFG

strength noun
The strength of something is how strong it is.
A sense of power was brewing in those eyes of hers, a feeling of great strength was settling itself deep inside her eyes. — MATILDA

stretch verb **stretches, stretching, stretched**
1 When you stretch something, you pull it so that it becomes longer or bigger.
'Ears never come off'! the Trunchbull shouted. 'They stretch most marvellously, like these are doing now, but I can assure you they never come off'! — MATILDA
2 When you stretch, you extend your arms or legs as far as you can. When Knids stretch themselves, they become as long and thin as they can, until they look like one-eyed snakes or sausages.
Then the three remaining creatures began stretching themselves all at the same time, each one elongating itself slowly upward, growing taller and taller, thinner and thinner. — CHARLIE AND THE GREAT GLASS ELEVATOR

strict adjective **stricter, strictest**
Someone who is strict does not allow people to behave badly.
Miss Tibbs . . . stood no nonsense from anyone. Some people said she was as strict with the President now as when he was a little boy. — CHARLIE AND THE GREAT GLASS ELEVATOR

stride verb **strides, striding, strode**
When you stride along, you walk with long steps.
At eight o'clock we started walking down the road towards my school in the pale autumn sunshine, munching our apples as we strode along. — DANNY THE CHAMPION OF THE WORLD

stride noun **strides**
a long step
The BFG went bouncing off the ground as though there were rockets in his toes and each stride he took lifted him about a hundred feet into the air. — THE BFG

string noun **strings**
String is thin rope, such as Mr Twit uses to tie balloons to Mrs Twit to stretch her out.
Mr Twit tied the ends of the strings to the top half of Mrs Twit's body. Some he tied round her neck, some under her arms, some to her wrists and some even to her hair. — THE TWITS

stripe noun **stripes**
A stripe is a band of colour on something, such as the black and white stripes of a zebra or **snozzcumber**.
It was black with white stripes along its length. And it was covered all over with coarse knobbles. 'Here is the repulsant snozzcumber!' cried the BFG, waving it about. — THE BFG

stroke verb **strokes, stroking, stroked**
When you stroke something, you move your hand over it gently.
Mr Hoppy . . . wouldn't even have minded becoming a tortoise himself if it meant Mrs Silver stroking his shell each morning and whispering endearments to him. — ESIO TROT

stroll verb **strolls, strolling, strolled**
When you stroll, you walk along slowly or casually.
What, for example, would you say/If strolling through the woods one day,/Right there in front of you you saw/ A pig who'd built his house of STRAW? — REVOLTING RHYMES

strong adjective **stronger, strongest**
1 If you are strong, like Miss Trunchbull, you can lift and move heavy things, such as small children.
'She's a very strong woman. She has muscles like steel ropes.' — MATILDA
2 Something that is strong, like HUGTIGHT glue, will not break or fail easily.
'Is the glue strong enough to hold it up?' 'It's the strongest glue in the world!' Muggle-Wump replied. — THE TWITS

3 A strong taste or smell is not mild or weak.
'I'll stir them up, I'll boil them long,/A mixture tough, a mixture strong./And then, heigh-ho, and down it goes,/A nice big spoonful (hold your nose).' – GEORGE'S MARVELLOUS MEDICINE

struggle verb **struggles, struggling, struggled**
When you struggle, you fight with your arms and legs to try to get free.
The BFG didn't struggle. He simply stopped and stood quite still and said, 'Be so kind as to be letting go of my hair, Fleshlumpeater.' – THE BFG

study verb **studies, studying, studied**
1 When you study a subject, you learn about it.
'My old dad studied poaching the way a scientist studies science.' – DANNY THE CHAMPION OF THE WORLD
2 When you study something, you look at it very carefully.
Mr Wormwood . . . fished a bit of paper from his pocket and studied it. – MATILDA

study noun **studies**
a room in a house where someone works or studies
In his study in the White House sat Lancelot R. Gilligrass, President of the United States of America, the most powerful man on Earth. – CHARLIE AND THE GREAT GLASS ELEVATOR

stuff noun
Stuff is anything that you can see and touch.
Mr Wonka . . . rushed over and dipped a finger into a barrel of sticky yellow stuff and had a taste. – CHARLIE AND THE CHOCOLATE FACTORY

stuff verb **stuffs, stuffing, stuffed**
1 When you stuff something, you fill it with things.
'I have brrrought vith me six trrrunks stuffed full of Inklish banknotes, all new and crrrisp.' – THE WITCHES
2 When you stuff something somewhere, you push it there roughly.
Bunce . . . mashed the livers into a disgusting paste and then stuffed the paste into the doughnuts. – FANTASTIC MR FOX

stumble verb **stumbles, stumbling, stumbled**
1 When you stumble, you trip or walk unsteadily.
'Go and sit down, both of you!' Captain Lancaster ordered. We stumbled back to our desks and sat down. – DANNY THE CHAMPION OF THE WORLD
2 If you stumble when you are speaking, you make mistakes or hesitate.
Very slowly and stumbling a little over the strange words, Mrs Silver read the whole message out loud in tortoise language. – ESIO TROT

stump noun **stumps**
A stump is the part of something that is left after the main part has been cut (or shot) off.
Down in the hole, Mrs Fox was tenderly licking the stump of Mr Fox's tail to stop the bleeding. – FANTASTIC MR FOX

stun verb **stuns, stunning, stunned**
If something stuns you, it completely shocks or confuses you.
It was a sight that took one's breath away. Even Grandma Georgina was stunned into silence for a few seconds. – CHARLIE AND THE GREAT GLASS ELEVATOR

stupid adjective **stupider, stupidest**
1 Something that is stupid is very silly.
Bunce, the little pot-bellied dwarf, looked up at Bean and said, 'Have you got any more stupid ideas, then?' – FANTASTIC MR FOX
2 Someone who is stupid is not very clever.
Mrs Twit may have been ugly and she may have been beastly, but she was not stupid. – THE TWITS

stutter verb **stutters, stuttering, stuttered**
If you stutter, you keep repeating the sounds at the beginning of words when you speak.
'My m-m-mummy thinks I look lovely, Miss T-T-Trunchbull,' Amanda stuttered, shaking like a blancmange. – MATILDA

subtract verb **subtracts, subtracting, subtracted**
When you subtract one number from another, you take it away to make a smaller number. For each pill of Wonka-Vite that someone takes, they can subtract 20 years from their age.
'Subtract eighty from seventy-eight and what do you get?' 'Minus two!' said Charlie. 'Hooray!' said Mr Bucket. 'My mother-in-law's minus two years old!' – CHARLIE AND THE GREAT GLASS ELEVATOR

succeed verb **succeeds, succeeding, succeeded**
If you succeed, you manage to do something.
The Trunchbull . . . was especially furious that someone had succeeded in making her jump and yell like that because she prided herself on her toughness. – MATILDA

success noun **successes**
If something is a success, it works well and people like it.
The launching had been a great success and now that the Space Hotel was safely in orbit, there was a tremendous hustle and bustle to send up the first guests. – CHARLIE AND THE GREAT GLASS ELEVATOR

a b c d e f g h i j k l m n o p q r s t u v w x y z

successful adjective
1 If something is successful, it works well and is a success.
2 A successful person has done well in their job or their life.
'You chose books and I chose looks,' Mrs Wormwood said . . . 'I'm sitting pretty in a nice house with a successful businessman and you're left slaving away teaching a lot of nasty little children the ABC.' — MATILDA

succulent adjective
Succulent food is juicy and tasty.
For a while there was no conversation at all. There was only the sound of crunching and chewing as the animals attacked the succulent food. — FANTASTIC MR FOX

suck verb sucks, sucking, sucked
1 When you suck a sweet, you move it about in your mouth without chewing or swallowing it.
When you have sucked a Devil's Drencher for a minute or so, you can set your breath alight and blow a huge column of fire twenty feet into the air. — THE GIRAFFE AND THE PELLY AND ME
2 When something is sucked, it is pulled or drawn in by force.
And now there came a sort of sucking noise, and very quickly all the blue frothy mixture in the huge basin was sucked back into the stomach of the machine. — CHARLIE AND THE CHOCOLATE FACTORY

sudden adjective
Something that is sudden happens quickly without any warning. You can also say that it happens *all of a sudden* or *suddenly*.
At that moment, there was a sudden commotion among the Oompa-Loompas at the far end of the Chocolate Room. — CHARLIE AND THE GREAT GLASS ELEVATOR

sugar noun
Sugar is a sweet powder that you add to foods to make them taste sweet. Willy Wonka makes sweet confections out of sugar and also uses it to power the Great Glass Elevator.
All the most wonderful smells in the world seemed to be mixed up in the air around them — the smell of roasting coffee and burnt sugar and melting chocolate. — CHARLIE AND THE CHOCOLATE FACTORY

suggest verb suggests, suggesting, suggested
If you suggest something, you say that it would be a good idea.
'Why don't we all go down below and keep warm until tomorrow morning?' Miss Spider suggested. — JAMES AND THE GIANT PEACH

suitable adjective
Something that is suitable is just right for a particular person or occasion.
Matilda's wonderfully subtle mind was already at work devising yet another suitable punishment for the poisonous parent. — MATILDA

suitcase noun suitcases
A suitcase is a bag with stiff sides and a handle that you use for carrying clothes when you travel. The BFG uses a suitcase to carry his jars of dreams to and from Giant Country.
The BFG opened the suitcase and took out several empty glass jars. He set them ready on the ground, with their screw tops removed. — THE BFG

sum noun sums
When you do a sum, you find an answer to a question by working with numbers.
'It's two hundred and sixty-six,' Matilda said softly. Miss Honey stared at her. Then she picked up a pencil and quickly worked out the sum on a piece of paper. — MATILDA

sun noun
1 the star round which the Earth travels, and from which it gets warmth and light
With the most tremendous BANG the Enormous Crocodile crashed headfirst into the hot hot sun. And he was sizzled up like a sausage! — THE ENORMOUS CROCODILE

2 If you are in the sun, the sun is shining on you.
One half of the Earthworm, looking like a great, thick, juicy, pink sausage, lay innocently in the sun for all the seagulls to see. — JAMES AND THE GIANT PEACH

sunbeam noun sunbeams
a ray of light from the sun
If you have good thoughts they will shine out of your face like sunbeams and you will always look lovely. — THE TWITS

sunlight noun
light from the sun
The giant peach, with the sunlight glinting on its side, was like a massive golden ball sailing upon a silver sea.
—JAMES AND THE GIANT PEACH

sunny adjective sunnier, sunniest
When the weather is sunny, the sun is shining.
On this sunny summer afternoon, Little Billy was kneeling on a chair in the living-room, gazing out through the window at the wonderful world beyond.—THE MINPINS

sunshine noun
the light and heat that come from the sun
The lift had shot right up through the roof of the factory and was now rising into the sky like a rocket, and the sunshine was pouring in through the glass roof.—CHARLIE AND THE CHOCOLATE FACTORY

super adjective
Something that is super is very good.
There is a secret place I know/Where I quite often like to go,/Beyond the wood, behind some rocks,/A super place for guzzling chocs.—DIRTY BEASTS

supper noun suppers
a meal or snack that you eat in the evening
Once a week, on Wednesdays, the Twits had Bird Pie for supper. Mr Twit caught the birds and Mrs Twit cooked them.—THE TWITS

surface noun surfaces
The surface of something is the top or outside part, not the middle.
A rich blue smoke, the colour of peacocks, rose from the surface of the liquid, and a fiery fearsome smell filled the kitchen.—GEORGE'S MARVELLOUS MEDICINE

surprise noun surprises
If something is a surprise, you were not expecting it to happen.
I shake you warmly by the hand! Tremendous things are in store for you! Many wonderful surprises await you!
—CHARLIE AND THE CHOCOLATE FACTORY

surprise verb surprises, surprising, surprised
If something surprises you, you were not expecting it to happen.
The chauffeurs of very rich men are never surprised by anything they see.—THE GIRAFFE AND THE PELLY AND ME

surprising adjective
If something is surprising, you did not expect it to happen.
Then came the long silence, the waiting, the listening, and at last, with surprising suddenness came the leap and the swish of the net.—THE BFG

surround verb surrounds, surrounding, surrounded
If something surrounds you, it forms a circle all around you.
Giant trees were soon surrounding him on all sides and their branches made an almost solid roof high above his head, blotting out the sky.—THE MINPINS

survey verb surveys, surveying, surveyed
If you survey something, you take a good look at it from a distance.
Mr Tibbs stood back to survey the new furniture. 'None of it is in the classic style,' he whispered, 'but it will have to do.'—THE BFG
LOOK IT UP! For other ways to describe how people look, see **look**.

suspense noun
Suspense is a feeling of excitement that you have when you do not know what is going to happen next.
For about thirty seconds nothing happened. Nobody stirred, nobody made a sound. The silence was terrible. So was the suspense.—CHARLIE AND THE GREAT GLASS ELEVATOR

suspichy adjective
If a giant is suspichy, he is suspicious about something.
*The Fleshlumpeater turned and stared at the BFG. 'What is **you** doing here with all these grotty twiglets!' he bellowed. 'You is making me very suspichy!'*—THE BFG

suspicious adjective
1 If something looks suspicious, it makes you think there is something wrong about it.
No witch would be stupid enough to leave anything suspicious lying around for the hotel maid to see.
—THE WITCHES

2 If you are suspicious of someone, you do not trust them and think they are up to no good.
'Gimme the chocolate!' shouted Bruno, becoming suddenly suspicious. 'Gimme the chocolate and let me out of here!' – THE WITCHES

swallop verb **swallops, swalloping, swalloped**
When giants swallop something, they gobble it up. You can also spell this word as *swollop*.
'That is the most disgusterous taste that is ever clutching my teeth! You must be buggles to be swalloping slutch like that!' – THE BFG

swallow verb **swallows, swallowing, swallowed**
When you swallow something, you make it go down your throat.
The ancient beanpole had already put the cup to her lips, and in one gulp she swallowed everything that was in it. – GEORGE'S MARVELLOUS MEDICINE

swan noun **swans**
a large white water bird with a long neck and powerful wings
Little Billy could see a vast lake of water, gloriously blue, and on the surface of the lake thousands of swans were swimming slowly about. – THE MINPINS

swap verb **swaps, swapping, swapped**
When you swap something, you give it to someone and get something else in return.
'An English witch, for example, will know all the other witches in England. They are all friends. They ring each other up. They swap deadly recipes.' – THE WITCHES

swarm noun **swarms**
A swarm of insects or Knids is a lot of them all flying together.
'These Vermicious Knids . . . travel through space in great swarms, landing on other stars and planets and destroying everything they find.' – CHARLIE AND THE GREAT GLASS ELEVATOR

swarm verb **swarms, swarming, swarmed**
If a place is swarming with people or tortoises, it is full of them all moving about.
The floor was swarming with tortoises of different sizes, some walking slowly about and exploring, some munching cabbage leaves, others drinking water from a big shallow dish. – ESIO TROT

swashboggling adjective
Swashboggling ears (or anything else for that matter) are **extra-usual** and very special.
'Every dream in the world is making a different sort of buzzy-hum music. And these grand swashboggling ears of mine is able to read that music.' – THE BFG

swatchwallop noun
Swatchwallop is the most disgusting thing you can imagine eating. When the BFG first tastes sausages and eggs, everything else seems like swatchwallop to him.
The BFG . . . scooped up all the eggs, sausages, bacon and potatoes in one go . . . 'By goggles!' he cried. 'This stuff is making snozzcumbers taste like swatchwallop!' – THE BFG

sway verb **sways, swaying, swayed**
When something sways, it moves gently from side to side.
The giant peach swayed gently from side to side as it floated along, and the hundreds of silky white strings going upward from its stem were beautiful in the moonlight. – JAMES AND THE GIANT PEACH

sweat verb **sweats, sweating, sweated**
When you sweat, you give off moisture through the pores of your skin, because you are very hot, or because you are afraid.
'Nightmares are horrible,' Sophie said. 'I had one once and I woke up sweating all over.' – THE BFG

sweat noun
the moisture that you give off when you sweat
The hairs on my head were standing up like the bristles of a nail-brush and a cold sweat was breaking out all over me. – THE WITCHES

sweep verb **sweeps, sweeping, swept**
1 When you sweep something up or away, you lift or clear it away swiftly.
The Fleshlumpeater . . . made a grab at a soldier and swept him up in his hand. 'I is having early suppers today!' he shouted. – THE BFG

2 If someone sweeps into a room, they enter it very grandly, as if they were sweeping everyone else out of their way.

At that exact moment, I heard a key turning in the lock of the door and the door burst open and The Grand High Witch swept into the room. — THE WITCHES

sweet adjective **sweeter, sweetest**

1 Something that is sweet tastes of sugar.

'Nasty!' cried the BFG. 'Never is it nasty! Frobscottle is sweet and jumbly!' — THE BFG

2 A sweet person is very pleasant or charming.

And there before the cottage door/These two enraptured children saw/A sweet old dame with rosy skin/Who smiled and said, 'Oh, do come in.' — RHYME STEW

sweet noun **sweets**

A sweet is a small piece of sweet food made of sugar or chocolate. Willy Wonka makes extraordinary sweets, such as **Wriggle-Sweets** and Exploding Sweets, and sails in a boat made out of a giant pink boiled sweet.

'This is my private yacht!' cried Mr Wonka, beaming with pleasure. 'I made her by hollowing out an enormous boiled sweet!' — CHARLIE AND THE CHOCOLATE FACTORY

sweet–shop noun **sweet-shops**

a shop like the Grubber, where you can buy sweets and chocolate

In the olden days a grubber was another name for a sweet-shop, and now every time I look at it I think to myself what a lovely old sweet-shop it must have been. — THE GIRAFFE AND THE PELLY AND ME

swell verb **swells, swelling, swelled, swollen**

When something swells, it gets bigger all over.

'Matilda is a genius.' At the mention of this word, Miss Trunchbull's face turned purple and her whole body seemed to swell up like a bullfrog's. — MATILDA

swerve verb **swerves, swerving, swerved**

If a car or flying elevator swerves, it suddenly moves to the side so that it does not hit something.

The Elevator leaped forward, but swerved violently to the right. 'Hard a-port!' yelled Mr Wonka. — CHARLIE AND THE GREAT GLASS ELEVATOR

swift adjective **swifter, swiftest**

Something that is swift moves very quickly.

Except for the swift fluttering of its wings, the hawk remained absolutely motionless in the sky. It seemed

to be suspended by some invisible thread, like a toy bird hanging from the ceiling. — DANNY THE CHAMPION OF THE WORLD

swiggle noun **swiggles**

1 A swiggle is a drink or gulp of something.

'We is now having a swiggle of this delicious frobscottle and you will see the happy result.' — THE BFG

2 Swiggles of things are lots and lots of them.

'Now then, do you have dreams . . . about giants?' 'Of course,' the BFG said. 'And about giants eating people?' 'Swiggles of them,' the BFG said. — THE BFG

swiggle verb **swiggles, swiggling, swiggled**

If a giant swiggles something, he swivels it round.

'If I is swiggling my ears in the right direction . . . and the night is very clear, I is sometimes hearing faraway music coming from the stars in the sky.' — THE BFG

swigpill noun

Swigpill is what the BFG calls pigswill, which is a type of watery mush that farmers feed to pigs. The BFG thinks that coffee tastes as bad as pigswill, and nowhere near as nice as **frobscottle**.

'Please, what is this horrible swigpill I is drinking, Majester?' 'It's coffee,' the Queen told him. 'Freshly roasted.' — THE BFG

DID YOU KNOW? The word *swigpill* is one of many **spoonerisms** that the BFG uses. You can read more about this type of word play in the entry for **mideous**.

swim verb **swims, swimming, swam, swum**

When you swim, you move through water (or melted chocolate) by floating and moving your arms and legs. The BFG calls it **swimmeling**.

The whole palace began to melt . . . and the crazy prince, who was dozing in the living room at the time, woke up to find himself swimming around in a huge brown sticky lake of chocolate. — CHARLIE AND THE CHOCOLATE FACTORY

swimmel verb **swimmels, swimmeling, swimmeled**

When giants swimmel, they swim in the sea, which they do when hunting **human beans** at the seaside, like giant sharks.

'Sometimes,' the BFG said, 'they is swimmeling in from the sea like fishies with only their heads showing above the water, and then out comes a big hairy hand and grabbles someone off the beach.' — THE BFG

swinebuggler noun **swinebugglers**

a name that giants call people when they are being rude (which is most of the time)

Sophie . . . crawled under the hem of the cloak and there she crouched. 'You little swinebuggler!' roared the Bloodbottler. 'You little pigswiller!' — THE BFG

DID YOU KNOW? The word *swine* means 'pig', so both words that the Bloodbottler calls Sophie are related to pigs.

swing verb **swings, swinging, swung**

1 When something swings, it moves backwards and forwards in the air.

The ducks were walking in a line to the door of the Greggs' house, swinging their arms and holding their beaks high in the air.—THE MAGIC FINGER

2 When you swing round, you turn around quickly.
And Mr Wonka, who had swung quickly around to look when the first scream came, was as dumbstruck as the rest.—CHARLIE AND THE GREAT GLASS ELEVATOR

swirl verb **swirls, swirling, swirled**
When something swirls, it moves around quickly in circles.
They were drifting in a heavy grey mist and the mist was swirling and swishing around them as though driven by winds from many sides.—CHARLIE AND THE GREAT GLASS ELEVATOR

swirly adjective **swirlier, swirliest**
Something swirly moves around in swirls.
They stood at the open door of the Elevator, peering into the swirly grey vapours.—CHARLIE AND THE GREAT GLASS ELEVATOR

swish noun **swishes**
a hissing or rushing sound
'Here we go!' the Pelican whispered to me, and with a swish and a swoop he carried me up to the very top of the cherry tree and there he perched.—THE GIRAFFE AND THE PELLY AND ME

Gobblefunking with words
When you put words together that start with the same sound, like *swish* and *swoop*, you are using **alliteration**. You can find more examples of alliteration in the entry for **ghoulish**.

swishfiggler noun **swishfigglers**
A swishfiggler is a very rude name that giants sometimes call each other.
The Bloodbottler pointed a finger as large as a tree-trunk at the BFG. 'Runty little scumscrewer!' he shouted. 'Piffling little swishfiggler!'—THE BFG
DID YOU KNOW? In Giant Country, fingers are called **figglers**, so perhaps swishing your figglers is something that giants dislike.

swishwiffle verb **swishwiffles, swishwiffling, swishwiffled**
Swishwiffling is what bubbles do when they fizz and rise to the surface of liquid.
'And the bubbles is fizzing upwards? . . . Which means,' said the BFG, 'that they will all come swishwiffling up your throat and out of your mouth and make a foulsome belchy burp!'—THE BFG

switch noun **switches**
You press a switch to make a machine work or a light come on.
The crazy boy rushed on, and when he reached the enormous camera, he jumped straight for the switch, scattering Oompa-Loompas right and left as he went.—CHARLIE AND THE CHOCOLATE FACTORY

switch verb **switches, switching, switched**
When you switch something on or off, you turn or press a switch to make it start or stop.
When it began to get dark, the helicopters switched on powerful searchlights and trained them on to the galloping giant so as to keep him in sight.—THE BFG

switchfiddle verb **switchfiddles, switchfiddling, switchfiddled**
1 When you switchfiddle someone, you play a trick on them. The BFG tries to switchfiddle the Bloodbottler into eating a **snozzcumber**.
'You is not switchfiddling me, is you?' said the Bloodbottler.—THE BFG
2 Switchfiddling also means swapping things around, which is what giants like to do to confuse people.
'The giants is clever. They is careful not to be skididdling off to the same country too often. They is always switchfiddling around.'—THE BFG

swivel verb **swivels, swivelling, swivelled**
If you swivel something (such as an **extra-usual** ear), you turn it round.
'If you would be kind enough to swivel one of your lovely big ears so that it is lying flat like a dish, that would make a very cosy place for me to sit.'—THE BFG

swizzfiggle verb swizzfiggles, swizzfiggling, swizzfiggled

If a giant swizzfiggles you, he lies to you or tricks you. For example, if the Fleshlumpeater said he was NOT going to eat you, he would be swizzfiggling through his rotten teeth.

'Is that really true?' Sophie asked. 'You think I is swizzfiggling you?' – THE BFG

swizzle verb swizzles, swizzling, swizzled

If a witch swizzles you, she does horribly nasty things to you. Being swizzled is like being **squiggled**, only worse.

'A boy!' cried the witches. 'A filthy smelly little boy! We'll swipe him! We'll swizzle him! We'll have his tripes for breakfast!' – THE WITCHES

DID YOU KNOW? The word *swizzle* is a blend of *swipe* and *sizzle*. A *swizzle* is also an informal word that means 'something unfair or disappointing'.

swobble verb swobbles, swobbling, swobbled

When a giant swobbles a **human bean**, he swallows and gobbles them whole.

'It is guzzly and glumptious!' shouted the Bloodbottler. 'And tonight I is galloping off to Chile to swobble a few human Chile beans.' – THE BFG

swogswalloped adjective

If a giant is swogswalloped, he is in a very sticky situation.

'I is splitzwiggled!' yelled the Childchewer. 'I is swogswalloped!' bellowed the Bonecruncher. – THE BFG

swollop verb swollops, swolloping, swolloped

1 When giants like the Fleshlumpeater swollop **human beans**, they gobble them up. You can also spell this word as *swallop*.

'He is fifty-four feet high,' the BFG said softly as he jogged along. 'And he is swolloping human beans like they is sugar-lumps, two or three at a time.' – THE BFG

2 If a witch swollops someone, she destroys them completely. The Grand High Witch says *svollop*.

'Vee shall svish them and svollop them and vee shall make to disappear every single smelly little brrrat in Inkland in vun strrroke!' – THE WITCHES

RINGBELLING RHYMES Try rhyming with *dollop* or *crash bang wallop*!

swoop verb swoops, swooping, swooped

When a bird swoops down, it flies downwards quickly.

They flew in a magical world of silence, swooping and gliding over the dark world below where all the earthly people were fast asleep in their beds. – THE MINPINS

swoosh noun swooshes

a loud rushing sound

Suddenly, behind them, there was a great SWOOSH of blankets and sheets and a pinging of bedsprings as the three old people all exploded out of the bed together. – CHARLIE AND THE GREAT GLASS ELEVATOR

LOOK IT UP! For more examples of onomatopoeic words like *swish* and *swoosh*, see **gliss**.

sword noun swords

A sword is a weapon with a handle and a long, thin blade. Mr Tibbs converts a royal sword into a knife for the BFG to eat his breakfast with.

'Tell the head gardener,' he whispered, 'that I require immediately a brand-new unused garden fork and also a spade. And for a knife we shall use the great sword hanging on the wall in the morning-room.' – THE BFG

swudge noun

Swudge is a kind of soft sugar paste flavoured with mint that Willy Wonka uses to make edible grass meadows.

'The grass you are standing on, my dear little ones, is made of a new kind of soft, minty sugar that I've just invented! I call it swudge!' – CHARLIE AND THE CHOCOLATE FACTORY

DID YOU KNOW? There is an old word *sward* which means 'an area of grass', so *swudge* may be a blend of *sward* and *fudge*.

swultering adjective

swelteringly hot

'If it is a frotsy night and the giant is fridging with cold, he will probably point his nose towards the swultering hotlands to guzzle a few Hottentots to warm him up.' – THE BFG

syllable noun syllables

A syllable is one of the sounds or beats in a word. The word *choc-o-late* has three syllables, and the word *scrum-did-dly-ump-tious* has five syllables.

sympathy noun

If you have sympathy for someone, you feel sorry for them.

'Serves him right,' Sophie said. She could feel no sympathy for this great brute who ate children as though they were sugar-lumps. – THE BFG

syrup noun syrups

a very sweet, sticky liquid

'The first time,' Hortensia said, 'I poured half a tin of Golden Syrup on to the seat of the chair the Trunchbull was going to sit on at prayers. It was wonderful.' – MATILDA

a b c d e f g h i j k l m n o p q r **s** t u v w x y z

The BFG uses lots of words that are spelled with *-izz-*, like *phizzwizard* and *swizzle*.

A B C D E F G H I J K L M N O P Q R S **T** U V W X Y Z

Tt

Miss Trunchbull

MATILDA

telekinetic   ticket   top hat

trogglehumper   twits

tablet noun **tablets**
a small pill containing medicine, or sometimes Wonka-Vite
'What does it matter that the old girl has become a trifle too old? . . . Have you forgotten Wonka-Vite and how every tablet makes you twenty years younger?' — CHARLIE AND THE GREAT GLASS ELEVATOR

tail noun **tails**
An animal's tail is the long part at the end of its body. Fantastic Mr Fox has a magnificent tail, until his unfortunate encounter with Farmers Boggis, Bunce and Bean.
Down in the hole, Mrs Fox was tenderly licking the stump of Mr Fox's tail to stop the bleeding. 'It was the finest tail for miles around,' she said between licks. — FANTASTIC MR FOX

tail coat noun **tail coats**
A tail coat is a man's coat which has a long back split into two tails. Tail coats are usually worn on formal occasions, but Willy Wonka wears a velvet tail coat every day as he is a very dapper dresser.
And what an extraordinary little man he was! He had a black top hat on his head. He wore a tail coat made of a beautiful plum-coloured velvet. His trousers were bottle green. — CHARLIE AND THE CHOCOLATE FACTORY

tale noun **tales**
a story
My grandmother . . . made it very clear to me that her witch stories, unlike most of the others, were not imaginary tales. They were all true. They were the gospel truth. — THE WITCHES

talk verb **talks, talking, talked**
For some terrific ways to describe talking, see **say**.

tall adjective **taller, tallest**
1 Someone who is tall measures a lot from their head to their feet.
Because Grandma was now much too tall to get back into the house, she had to sleep that night in the hay-barn with the mice and the rats. — GEORGE'S MARVELLOUS MEDICINE

2 A tall tree or building is very high.

'But what tremendous tall buildings!' exclaimed the Ladybird. 'I've never seen anything like them before in England. Which town do you think it is?' — JAMES AND THE GIANT PEACH

tangle verb **tangles, tangling, tangled**
If you tangle something, or it gets tangled, it becomes twisted or muddled.

The ropes that the Cloud-Men had been using for lowering the rainbow got tangled up with the silk strings that went up from the peach to the seagulls! — JAMES AND THE GIANT PEACH

tangle noun **tangles**
a twisted mess of something such as hair or wire

I have a picture in my mind of a giant of a man with a face like a ham and a mass of rusty-coloured hair that sprouted in a tangle all over the top of his head. — BOY

taste verb **tastes, tasting, tasted**
1 When you taste food, you eat a small amount to see what it is like.

'Just this once,' the Bloodbottler said, 'I is going to taste these rotsome eats of yours. But I is warning you that if it is filthsome, I is smashing it over your sludgy little head!' — THE BFG

2 The way something tastes is the flavour that it has.

'Mr Willy Wonka can make marshmallows that taste of violets, and rich caramels that change colour every ten seconds as you suck them.' — CHARLIE AND THE CHOCOLATE FACTORY

taste noun
The taste of something is what it is like when you eat it.

'You want to know why your spaghetti was squishy? And why it had a nasty bitter taste? . . . Because it was worms!' cried Mrs Twit. — THE TWITS

LOOK IT UP! For ways to describe nice and nasty tastes, see **good** and **bad**.

tasty adjective **tastier, tastiest**
delicious and **scrumdiddlyumptious**

'A big fat earwig is very tasty,' Grandma said, licking her lips. — GEORGE'S MARVELLOUS MEDICINE

SPARKY SYNONYMS You can also say **delumptious** or **glumptious**.

teach verb **teaches, teaching, taught**
When someone teaches you something, they tell you about it or show you how to do it.

'There never was any schools to teach me talking in Giant Country,' the BFG said sadly. — THE BFG

teacher noun **teachers**
someone who teaches you at school

'Chaos and pandemonium vill be rrreigning in every school in Inkland! Teachers vill be hopping up and down!' — THE WITCHES

tear (*rhymes with* fair) verb **tears, tearing, tore, torn**
When you tear something, you pull it apart so that it splits or makes a hole.

Fully grown women were seen going into sweet shops and buying ten Wonka bars at a time, then tearing off the wrappers on the spot. — CHARLIE AND THE CHOCOLATE FACTORY

tear (*rhymes with* fear) noun **tears**
Tears are drops of salty water that come from your eyes when you cry.

Very softly, the Old-Green-Grasshopper started to play the Funeral March on his violin, and by the time he had finished, everyone, including himself, was in a flood of tears. — JAMES AND THE GIANT PEACH

teeter verb **teeters, teetering, teetered**
When you teeter, you stand or move unsteadily. If you teeter on the brink of something, you are dangerously close to falling over the edge.

The Centipede . . . had suddenly gone too close to the downward curving edge of the peach, and for three awful seconds he had stood teetering on the brink. — JAMES AND THE GIANT PEACH

telekinetic adjective
If you have telekinetic powers, you can make objects move just by thinking about it. Matilda develops telekinetic powers and can make a piece of chalk write on the blackboard by itself.

telescoop noun **telescoops**
A telescoop is what the BFG calls a telescope, which is a device that makes distant objects seem nearer.

'What a spliffling whoppsy room we is in! It is so gigantuous I is needing bicirculers and telescoops to see what is going on at the other end!' – THE BFG

telescope noun telescopes

A telescope is a tube with lenses at each end, through which you can see distant objects more clearly because they look closer and larger. Part of a boiled telescope is needed to make Delayed Action Mouse-Maker formula.

'Next,' said The Grand High Witch, 'you take your boiled telescope and your frrried mouse-tails and your cooked mice and your rrroasted alarm-clock and all together you put them into the mixer.' – THE WITCHES

television noun televisions

a machine that picks up radio waves and changes them into pictures and sound for viewing on a screen

Every house in the world that had a television or radio receiver heard those awful screams. There were other noises, too. Loud grunts and snortings and crunching sounds. – CHARLIE AND THE GREAT GLASS ELEVATOR

telly–telly bunkum box noun telly-telly bunkum boxes

a television

'If you do go back, you will be telling the world,' said the BFG, 'most likely on the telly-telly bunkum box and the radio squeaker.' – THE BFG

DID YOU KNOW? The word *bunkum* means 'rubbish' or 'nonsense', and you can read more about it in the entry for **flushbunking**.

temper noun

1 Someone's temper is their mood, or how angry or calm they feel.

Captain Lancaster, known sometimes as Lankers, was a horrid man. He had fiery carrot-coloured hair and a little clipped carrotty moustache and a fiery temper. – DANNY THE CHAMPION OF THE WORLD

2 If you lose your temper, you suddenly become very angry.

Miss Honey decided that if she was going to get anywhere with these people she must not lose her temper. – MATILDA

tender adjective tenderer, tenderest

Food that is tender is easy to chew and not tough or hard.

Tortoise Number 2 had never eaten tender juicy lettuce leaves before. It had only had thick old cabbage leaves. – ESIO TROT

tense adjective tenser, tensest

If you are tense, you are nervous and not able to relax.

The BFG hurried towards another shelf . . . He was becoming very tense now. Sophie could almost see the excitement bubbling inside him as he scurried back and forth among his beloved jars. – THE BFG

tentacle noun tentacles

The tentacles of a sea animal such as an octopus or **quadropus** are the long flexible parts on its body.

Now add the following, in precisely the order given . . . A CORN FROM THE TOE OF A UNICORN/THE FOUR TENTACLES OF A QUADROPUS. – CHARLIE AND THE GREAT GLASS ELEVATOR

terrible adjective

Something that is terrible is very bad.

'You've got the shrinks!' cried Mr Twit, pointing his finger at her like a pistol. 'You've got them badly! You've got the most terrible case of shrinks I've ever seen!' – THE TWITS

terrify verb terrifies, terrifying, terrified

If something terrifies you, it makes you feel very frightened.

The presence of this ancient creature seemed to have terrified not only Mr and Mrs Bucket, but Grandpa Joe as well. They stood well back, away from the bed. – CHARLIE AND THE GREAT GLASS ELEVATOR

LOOK IT UP! For other ways to be terrified, see **afraid**.

terror noun
a feeling of very great fear
The passengers on the peach (all except the Centipede) sat frozen with terror, looking back at the Cloud-Men and wondering what was going to happen next. – JAMES AND THE GIANT PEACH

testy adjective testier, testiest
Someone who is testy is very easily annoyed.
'I don't know what you're talking about,' the King said, growing testy. 'It's hardly a joking matter when one's loyal subjects are being eaten like popcorn.' – THE BFG

thank verb thanks, thanking, thanked
When you thank someone, you tell them that you are grateful for something they have given you or done for you.
'But ladies and gentlemen . . . who is it we have to thank for this great blessing that has come upon us? Who is the saviour of the Minpins?' – THE MINPINS

thermometer noun thermometers
a small glass tube for measuring temperature, which you have to shake vigorously to reset
'Yippeeeeee!' shouted Grandpa Joe. 'What a brilliant thought, sir! What a staggering idea!' He grabbed Mr Wonka's hand and started shaking it like a thermometer. – CHARLIE AND THE GREAT GLASS ELEVATOR

thickwit noun (informal) thickwits
a very stupid person
'That's not a bed, you drivelling thickwit!' yelled the President. 'Can't you understand it's a trick! It's a bomb. It's a bomb disguised as a bed!' – CHARLIE AND THE GREAT GLASS ELEVATOR

thief noun thieves
someone who steals things
'A thief!' the Trunchbull screamed. 'A crook! A pirate! A brigand! A rustler! . . . Do you deny it, you miserable little gumboil? Do you plead not guilty?' – MATILDA

thigh noun thighs
Your thighs are the top parts of your legs.
Miss Trunchbull has powerful muscles in her thighs because she was once a famous athlete.
The massive thighs which emerged from out of the smock were encased in a pair of extraordinary breeches, bottle-green in colour and made of coarse twill. – MATILDA

thin adjective thinner, thinnest
1 Something that is thin is not very thick or wide.
The night was very still. There was a thin yellow moon over the trees on the hill, and the sky was filled with stars. – THE MAGIC FINGER
2 Someone who is thin is not very fat.
The door was opened by Miss Prewt herself, a tall, thin female who stood bolt upright and whose mouth was like the blade of a knife. – THE VICAR OF NIBBLESWICKE
3 If you disappear into thin air, you vanish completely.
'Do we really have to eat it?' Sophie said. 'You do unless you is wanting to become so thin you will be disappearing into a thick ear.' 'Into thin air,' Sophie said. 'A thick ear is something quite different.' – THE BFG

Gobblefunking with words
When he says *disappearing into a thick ear* the BFG is using a *malapropism*, which means using a wrong word that sounds like the word or phrase you meant to use. You can find more examples of this type of word play in the entry for **mudburger**.

thingalingaling noun thingalingalings
a small or slight thing
'When I is blowing that dream into the Queen's bedroom,' the BFG said, 'she will be dreaming every single little thingalingaling you is asking me to make her dream.' – THE BFG

think verb thinks, thinking, thought
1 When you think, you have thoughts and ideas in your mind.
'Is there nothing we can do?' asked the Ladybird, appealing to James. 'Surely you can think of a way out of this.' Suddenly they were all looking at James. 'Think!' begged Miss Spider. 'Think, James, think!' – JAMES AND THE GIANT PEACH
2 If you think that something is true, you believe it.
'You may think you is eight,' the BFG said, 'but you has only spent four years of your life with your little eyes open. You is only four and please stop higgling me.' – THE BFG

thirstbloody adjective thirstbloodier, thirstbloodiest
the BFG's word for **bloodthirsty**
'I is also bringing in this sack a whole bungle of snozzcumber plants . . . Then we is having an everlasting supply of this repulsant food to feed these thirstbloody giants on.' – THE BFG

thistle noun thistles
a wild plant that has prickly leaves and purple flowers
And what do you think of that ghastly garden? Mrs Twit was the gardener. She was very good at growing thistles and stinging-nettles. – THE TWITS

a b c d e f g h i j k l m n o p q r s **t** u v w x y z

thought noun **thoughts**
an idea that you have
in your head
*A person who has good thoughts
cannot ever be ugly. You can have
a wonky nose and a crooked mouth . . .
but if you have good thoughts they will
shine out of your face like sunbeams.*
— THE TWITS

thoughtful adjective
1 If you look thoughtful, you look
quiet, as if you are thinking about
something.
*Matilda did not join the rush to get out of the
classroom. After the other children had all
disappeared, she remained at her desk,
quiet and thoughtful.* — MATILDA
2 If you are thoughtful, you are kind and
think about what other people want.
*'Oh, thank you, thank you!' cried the old witches.
'You are far too good to us, Your Grandness!
You are so kind and thoughtful!'* — THE WITCHES

thrash verb **thrashes, thrashing, thrashed**
If you thrash about, you fling your arms and
legs about wildly.
*'Save us!' screamed the Fleshlumpeater,
thrashing about madly. 'He is after me! He is getting
me!'* — THE BFG

thread noun **threads**
A long piece of cotton, nylon or other material
used for sewing or weaving. Miss Spider spins
thread from spider silk to make her webs.
*The Silkworm and Miss Spider, after they had both
been taught to make nylon thread instead of silk,
set up a factory together and made ropes for
tightrope walkers.* — JAMES AND THE GIANT PEACH

thrice adverb
three times
*I shouted, 'Not the dentist! No!/Oh mum, why don't
you have a go?'/I begged her twice, I begged her
thrice,/But grown-ups never take advice.*
— DIRTY BEASTS

thrill noun **thrills**
If something gives you a thrill, it is very exciting
and enjoyable.
*The BFG was very excited. He held the jar close
to one ear and listened intently. 'It's a winksquiffler!'
he whispered with a thrill in his voice.* — THE BFG

throat noun **throats**
Your throat is the part at the back of your
mouth where you swallow food and drink.
*'It's wonderful!' cried the Giraffe as a cascade of
lovely liquid flavours poured all the way down her
long long throat.* — THE GIRAFFE AND THE PELLY AND ME

thrumpet noun **thrumpets**
A thrumpet is a very loud instrument, possibly related
to the trumpet or **crumpet**.
*'You is talking too loud! . . . Your voice is sounding
like thunder and thrumpets!' 'I'm so sorry,' Sophie
whispered. 'Is that better?'* — THE BFG

thud noun **thuds**
a dull banging sound
*There was no sign of a living creature
and no sound at all except for the
soft thud of the BFG's footsteps as he
hurtled on through the fog.* — THE BFG

thump verb **thumps, thumping,
thumped**
1 If you thump something, you hit
it heavily.
*My grandmother was getting pretty worked
up herself and now she heaved herself out
of her chair and began pacing up and down
the room, thumping the carpet with her stick.*
— THE WITCHES
2 If your heart thumps, it beats so strongly
that you can feel it in your chest.
*'I'm ready!' Sophie cried. Her heart was
beginning to thump at the thought of what
they were about to do. It really was a wild and
crazy thing.* — THE BFG

thump noun **thumps**
a dull heavy sound
*At that moment there came a soft thump
from the wood behind us . . . It was a deep
muffled sound as though a bag of sand had
been dropped to the ground. Thump!*
— DANNY THE CHAMPION OF THE WORLD

thunder noun
Thunder is the loud rumbling noise that
you hear with lightning during a storm.
*It was the first of October and one of those
warm windless autumn mornings with
a darkening sky and a smell of thunder
in the air.* — DANNY THE CHAMPION OF
THE WORLD

thunder verb **thunders, thundering,
thundered**
1 If something thunders, it makes
a loud rumbling noise like thunder.
*Their speed was unbelievable. Their feet
pounded and thundered on the ground
and left a great sheet of dust behind
them.* — THE BFG
2 Someone thunders when they speak
with a loud booming voice.
*'Children are foul and filthy!' thundered
The Grand High Witch. 'They are! They are!'
chorused the English witches.*
— THE WITCHES

Tibbs, Miss Elvira (CHARLIE AND THE GREAT GLASS ELEVATOR)

Miss Elvira Tibbs is a huge lady of eighty-nine who is the Vice-President of the United States. She was President Gilligrass's nanny when he was a boy, and she still tells him (and everyone else in the White House) what to do.

Tibbs, Mr (THE BFG)

Mr Tibbs is the royal butler and is in charge of all the servants in the Palace. He never flinches and never hesitates, and can deal with any situation, however unusual, such as when a giant comes to breakfast.

ticket noun tickets

A ticket is a piece of paper that allows you to do something such as see a show or travel on a bus or train. Whoever finds the special Golden Tickets hidden inside Wonka Bars will be allowed inside the famous

Chocolate Factory for a day.
And now the whole country, indeed, the whole world, seemed suddenly to be caught up in a mad chocolate-buying spree, everybody searching frantically for those precious remaining tickets. — CHARLIE AND THE CHOCOLATE FACTORY

tickle verb tickles, tickling, tickled

When you tickle someone, you touch them lightly with your fingers to make them laugh. When you drink **frobscottle**, the bubbles tickle your insides.
It was an amazing sensation. It felt as though hundreds of tiny people were dancing a jig inside her and tickling her with their toes. It was lovely. — THE BFG

tiddly adjective (informal) tiddlier, tiddliest

slightly drunk
BUTTERSCOTCH AND BUTTERGIN, it said on the next door they passed . . . 'Glorious stuff!' said Mr Wonka.
'The Oompa-Loompas all adore it. It makes them tiddly.' — CHARLIE AND THE CHOCOLATE FACTORY

tight adjective tighter, tightest

1 A tight knot is tied very firmly and is difficult to undo.
With both the Fleshlumpeater's hands gripping his ankle, it was a simple matter for the BFG to tie the ankles and hands together with a tight knot. — THE BFG
2 fully stretched or tense
At this point Matilda noticed that Miss Honey's face had gone all tight and peculiar-looking. Her whole body had become rigid. — MATILDA

tight adverb

tightly or firmly
'Be careful to hang on tight!' the BFG said. 'We is going fast as a fizzlecrump!' — THE BFG

tights plural noun

a piece of clothing that women and girls (and tightrope-walkers) wear over their feet, legs and bottom
Mr Wormwood's fine crop of black hair was now a dirty silver, the colour this time of a tightrope-walker's tights that had not been washed for the entire circus season. — MATILDA

tilt verb tilts, tilting, tilted

When something tilts, it tips up so that it slopes.
The whole room began to tilt over and all the furniture went sliding across the floor, and crashed against the far wall. — JAMES AND THE GIANT PEACH

time-twiddler noun time-twiddlers

A time-twiddler is someone who lives for a very long time. Giants are ancient time-twiddlers who have been living for centuries.
'Giants is never dying,' the BFG answered . . . 'Mostly us giants is simply going on and on like whiffsy time-twiddlers.' — THE BFG

DID YOU KNOW? When someone *twiddles their thumbs*, they are bored because they have nothing to do, so perhaps *time-twiddlers* get bored a lot during their long lives and start twiddling their thumbs.

tingle verb tingles, tingling, tingled

Part of your body tingles when you have a slight stinging or tickling feeling there.
Charlie put the mug to his lips, and as the rich warm creamy chocolate ran down his throat into his empty tummy, his whole body from head to toe began to tingle with pleasure. — CHARLIE AND THE CHOCOLATE FACTORY

tingle noun tingles

a tingling feeling

tinkle verb tinkles, tinkling, tinkled

When something tinkles, it makes a gentle ringing sound.

tinkle noun tinkles

a tinkling sound
The chalk stopped writing. It hovered for a few moments, then suddenly it dropped to the floor with a tinkle and broke in two. — MATILDA

tired adjective
If you are tired, you feel as if you need to sleep.
The bed was given to the four old grandparents because they were so old and tired. They were so tired, they never got out of it. — CHARLIE AND THE CHOCOLATE FACTORY

titchy adjective (*informal*) **titchier, titchiest**
tiny or **midgy**
'Titchy little snapperwhippers like you should not be higgling around with an old sage and onions who is hundreds of years more than you.' — THE BFG

tinkle-tinkle tree noun tinkle-tinkle trees
The tinkle-tinkle tree (*Tinculus polyflorus*) is an exotic tree that bears pink and white blossoms. Tinkle-tinkle flowers are the only food that Geraneous Giraffes can eat.
'I am a Geraneous Giraffe and a Geraneous Giraffe cannot eat anything except the pink and purple flowers of the tinkle-tinkle tree!' — THE GIRAFFE AND THE PELLY AND ME

DID YOU KNOW? The word *tinkle* means 'to ring like a bell', so perhaps a tinkle-tinkle tree has bell-shaped blossoms that look as if they are ringing in the wind.

tiny adjective **tinier, tiniest**
A tiny thing or a tiny person is very small, like a teeny-tiny Minpin.
It was the face of an extremely old man with white hair. Little Billy could see this clearly despite the fact that the whole of the tiny man's head was no larger than a pea.
— THE MINPINS
SPARKY SYNONYMS You can also say **snitchy** or **titchy**.

tiptoe verb **tiptoes, tiptoeing, tiptoed**
When you tiptoe, you walk quietly on your toes.
'Ssshh!' whispered Grandpa Joe, and he beckoned Charlie to come closer. Charlie tiptoed over and stood beside the bed. — CHARLIE AND THE CHOCOLATE FACTORY

tip-topple verb **tip-topples, tip-toppling, tip-toppled**
If you tip-topple, you lose your balance and fall.
'Now don't you go tip-toppling backwards,' the BFG whispered. 'You must always be holding on tight with both hands to the inside of the window-sill.' — THE BFG

title noun **titles**
1 The title of a book, film or piece of music is its name, like *The BFG* or *Matilda*.
2 Someone's title is a word that describes their job or their status, such as *The Grand High Witch* or *The Palace Butler*.
The BFG's house was to have a special dream-storing room . . . where he could put his beloved bottles. What is more, he was given the title of The Royal Dream-Blower. — THE BFG

toad noun **toads**
A toad is an animal like a large frog with rough, dry skin that lives on land.
The toad said, 'Don't you think I'm fine?/Admire these lovely legs of mine,/And I am sure you've never seen/ A toad so gloriously green!' — DIRTY BEASTS

toadstool noun **toadstools**
a plant that looks like a mushroom but is poisonous to eat
Behind the wheel I could see the enormous pink beery face of Mr Victor Hazell . . . I could see the mouth hanging open, the eyes bulging out of his head like toadstools.
— DANNY THE CHAMPION OF THE WORLD

toboggan noun **toboggans**
a small sledge for sliding downhill
Hundreds of Cloud-Men's children were frisking about all over the place and shrieking with laughter and sliding down the billows of the cloud on toboggans. — JAMES AND THE GIANT PEACH

A B C D E F G H I J K L M N O P Q R S **T** U V W X Y Z

toddle verb **toddles, toddling, toddled**
When you toddle, you walk or go somewhere casually.
From then on, every afternoon, as soon as her mother had left for bingo, Matilda would toddle down to the library. — MATILDA
RINGBELLING RHYMES Try rhyming with *waddle*.

toe noun **toes**
Your toes are the parts of your body on the ends of your feet.
'Why even your toes must be as big as sausages.'
'Bigger,' said the BFG, looking pleased. 'They is as big as bumplehammers.' — THE BFG

toeless adjective
Someone who is toeless has no toes. All witches are toeless, but they wear pointed shoes to disguise this when they are with non-witches.
I got a glimpse under the chairs of several pairs of stockinged feet, square and completely toeless . . . as though the toes had been sliced away from the feet with a carving-knife. — THE WITCHES

Gobblefunking with words
You can add the suffix *-less* to make words that mean 'not having' something, for example, a *treeless* landscape, or *toothless* gums, or a trio of *ladderless* window-cleaners.

toffee noun **toffees**
Toffee is a sticky sweet made from butter and sugar, and a toffee is a piece of this made into a chewy sweet. Willy Wonka invents unusual types of toffee, such as Hair Toffee.
'Now, over here,' Mr Wonka went on, skipping excitedly across the room to the opposite wall, 'over here I am inventing a completely new line in toffees!' — CHARLIE AND THE CHOCOLATE FACTORY

toffee apple noun **toffee apples**
A toffee apple is an apple with a crispy coating of toffee that you eat on a stick like a lollipop. Willy Wonka's toffee apples grow on trees that you can plant in your garden.
Charlie started reading some of the labels alongside the buttons . . . STRAWBERRY-JUICE WATER PISTOLS/ TOFFEE-APPLE TREES FOR PLANTING OUT IN YOUR GARDEN — ALL SIZES. — CHARLIE AND THE CHOCOLATE FACTORY

tomato noun **tomatoes**
a soft round red fruit with seeds inside it, eaten as a vegetable
The Army General was no more used to being insulted than the Air Marshal. His face began to swell with fury and his cheeks blew out until they looked like two huge ripe tomatoes. — THE BFG

ton noun **tons**
1 a unit of weight equal to 2,240 pounds or about 1,016 kilograms

RECIPE FOR MAKING WONKA-VITE Take a block of finest chocolate weighing one ton (or twenty sackfuls of broken chocolate, whichever is the easier). — CHARLIE AND THE GREAT GLASS ELEVATOR
2 (*informal*) a large amount
'But why do we need more, Dad?' George asked . . .
'My dear boy,' cried Mr Killy Kranky, 'we need barrels and barrels of it! Tons and tons!' — GEORGE'S MARVELLOUS MEDICINE

tongue (*rhymes with* sung) noun **tongues**
Your tongue is the part inside your mouth that you can move about and use for speaking.
The Spider (who happened to be a female spider) opened her mouth and ran a long black tongue delicately over her lips. — JAMES AND THE GIANT PEACH

Tongue Raker noun **Tongue Rakers**
a type of sweet that is sold in the Grubber
There were . . . Sherbet Slurpers and Tongue Rakers, and as well as all this, there was a whole lot of splendid stuff from the great Wonka factory itself. — THE GIRAFFE AND THE PELLY AND ME

tooth noun **teeth**
Your teeth are the hard white bony parts that grow in your gums, and that you use for biting and chewing.
'I is hungry!' the Giant boomed. He grinned, showing massive square teeth. The teeth were very white and very square and they sat in his mouth like huge slices of white bread. — THE BFG

toothbrush noun **toothbrushes**
A toothbrush is a small brush on a long handle for brushing your teeth. James Henry Trotter takes only his toothbrush and pyjamas with him when he goes to live with his horrible aunts.
The little boy, carrying nothing but a small suitcase containing a pair of pyjamas and a toothbrush, was sent away to live with his two aunts. — JAMES AND THE GIANT PEACH

top hat noun **top hats**
A top hat is a man's tall stiff black or grey hat worn with formal clothes. Willy Wonka always wears a black top hat and a **tail coat**.
On he rushed, down the endless pink corridors, with his black top hat perched on the top of his head and his plum-coloured velvet coat-tails flying out behind him like a flag in the wind. — CHARLIE AND THE CHOCOLATE FACTORY
DID YOU KNOW? In Scotland, top hats are called *lum hats*, which means 'chimney hats', because they look a bit like small chimneys.

tornado noun **tornadoes**
a violent storm or whirlwind
They saw the frost factories and the wind producers and the places where cyclones and tornadoes were manufactured and sent spinning down towards the Earth. — JAMES AND THE GIANT PEACH

Toboggan comes from a Micmac (Native American) word for a sledge.

tortoise noun **tortoises**
A tortoise is a slow-moving animal that has four legs and a hard shell over its body. Some people, like Mrs Silver, keep tortoises as pets.
When he had finished, Mr Hoppy, in his enthusiasm, had bought no less than one hundred and forty tortoises and he carried them home in baskets, ten or fifteen at a time. — ESIO TROT

tortoise-catcher noun **tortoise-catchers**
A long pole with a claw at the end that Mr Hoppy uses to raise and lower tortoises.
Mr Hoppy took Tortoise Number 2 out on to the balcony and gripped it in the claws of his tortoise-catcher. — ESIO TROT

toss verb **tosses, tossing, tossed**
When you toss something, you throw it through the air.
The BFG . . . tossed the snozzcumber down to the giants below. 'There's your supper!' he shouted. 'Have a munch on that!' — THE BFG

tottler noun **tottlers**
a young **chiddler**
'Oh my, oh my!' he said, holding the jar in front of him. 'This will be giving some little tottler a very happy night when I is blowing it in!' — THE BFG

touch verb **touches, touching, touched**
When you touch something, you feel it with your hand, or come in contact with it.
George . . . felt quite trembly. He knew something tremendous had taken place that morning. For a few brief moments he had touched with the very tips of his fingers the edge of a magic world. — GEORGE'S MARVELLOUS MEDICINE

touch noun **touches**
the action of touching something

As the ravens whizzed over, they brushed a streak of sticky glue on to the tops of Mr and Mrs Twit's heads. They did it with the lightest touch but even so the Twits both felt it. — THE TWITS

tough adjective **tougher, toughest**
1 Something that is tough is hard or difficult.
'We really must get some sleep,' the Old-Green-Grasshopper said. 'We've got a tough day ahead of us tomorrow.' — JAMES AND THE GIANT PEACH
2 Tough food is difficult to chew.
'Little chiddlers is not so tough to eat as old grandmamma, so says the Childchewing Giant.' — THE BFG

tow (*rhymes with* low) verb **tows, towing, towed**
If you tow something, you pull it along.
The big steel rope tightened. It held! And now . . . with her booster-rockets blazing, the Elevator began to tow the huge Transport Capsule forward and away! — CHARLIE AND THE GREAT GLASS ELEVATOR

tower verb **towers, towering, towered**
If someone towers over you, they are much taller than you and seem like a giant.
In two large strides the Trunchbull was behind Eric's desk, and there she stood, a pillar of doom towering over the helpless boy. — MATILDA

trace noun **traces**
A trace is a mark or sign left by a person or thing.
The next afternoon, Mr Hoppy took all his other tortoises back to the pet-shops . . . Then he cleaned up his living-room, leaving not a leaf of cabbage nor a trace of tortoise. — ESIO TROT

tractor noun **tractors**
a strong, heavy truck with large wheels, used for pulling farm machinery or heavy loads
Soon, two enormous caterpillar tractors with mechanical shovels on their front ends came clanking into the wood. Bean was driving one, Bunce the other. — FANTASTIC MR FOX

trail noun **trails**
1 a series of marks left behind by something that has passed
But the peach rushed on across the countryside — on and on and on, leaving a trail of destruction in its wake. — JAMES AND THE GIANT PEACH
2 a long thin line stretching backwards
Soon, there was a trail of children a mile long chasing after the peach as it proceeded slowly up Fifth Avenue. — JAMES AND THE GIANT PEACH

trail verb **trails, trailing, trailed**
When something trails, it hangs down loosely or along the ground.
'The beard grew so fast that soon it was trailing all over the floor in a thick hairy carpet. It was growing faster than we could cut it!' — CHARLIE AND THE CHOCOLATE FACTORY

train verb **trains, training, trained**
If someone trains a person or animal, they teach them how to do something.
It is not all that difficult to train an intelligent mouse to be an expert tight-rope walker provided you know exactly how to go about it. — THE WITCHES

transparent adjective
If something is transparent, you can see through it. People become transparent if they take too much Wonka-Vite and end up in Minusland, like Grandma Georgina.
They could see her faintly through the mist, but oh so faintly. And they could see the mist through her as well. She was transparent. She was hardly there at all. — CHARLIE AND THE GREAT GLASS ELEVATOR

trap noun **traps**
A trap is something that is used to catch a person or an animal, such as the Gilligrass patented fly-trap.

trap verb **traps, trapping, trapped**
1 If you trap a person or animal, you catch them in a trap.
'We will spear the blabbersnitch and trap the crabcruncher and shoot the grobblesquirt and catch the catspringer in his burrow!' — THE WITCHES

A B C D E F G H I J K L M N O P Q R S T U V W X Y Z

2 If you are **trapped**, you are stuck in a dangerous situation from which you cannot escape.
Amanda Thripp stood quite still . . . and the expression on her face was one that you might find on the face of a person who is trapped in a small field with an enraged bull which is charging flat-out towards her. — MATILDA

travel verb **travels, travelling, travelled**
When you **travel**, you go from one place to another.
'You can sit on my back,' said the Roly-Poly Bird. 'I shall take you one at a time. You will travel by the Roly-Poly Super Jet and it won't cost you a penny!' — THE TWITS

tread (rhymes with bed) verb **treads, treading, trod, trodden**
If you **tread** on something, you walk on it or put your foot on it.
'He's shrunk!' said Mr Teavee . . . 'We can't send him back to school like this! He'll get trodden on! He'll get squashed!' — CHARLIE AND THE CHOCOLATE FACTORY

tread noun **treads**
the sound someone makes when they walk
'The BFG,' he said, 'can hear the tread of a ladybird's footsteps as she walks across a leaf.' — DANNY THE CHAMPION OF THE WORLD

treasure noun **treasures**
a valuable or precious thing
This, we decided, would be our secret hiding place for sweets and other small treasures such as conkers and monkey-nuts and birds' eggs. — BOY

treasure verb **treasures, treasuring, treasured**
If you **treasure** something, you think that it is very precious.
Charlie was always presented with one small chocolate bar to eat all by himself. And . . . he would place it carefully in a small wooden box that he owned, and treasure it as though it were a bar of solid gold. — CHARLIE AND THE CHOCOLATE FACTORY

tree noun **trees**
a tall plant that has a thick trunk, branches, and leaves
The big tree under which Mr Fox had dug his hole in the first place was toppled like a matchstick. On all sides, rocks were sent flying and trees were falling and the noise was deafening. — FANTASTIC MR FOX

tree-squeak noun **tree-squeaks**
The tree-squeak is an egg-laying creature that lives in trees. The whites of tree-squeak eggs are an ingredient in Wonka-Vite.
Now add the following, in precisely the order given . . . THE WHITES OF TWELVE EGGS FROM A TREE-SQUEAK/ THE THREE FEET OF A SNOZZWANGER. — CHARLIE AND THE GREAT GLASS ELEVATOR

tremble verb **trembles, trembling, trembled**
When you **tremble**, your body shakes because you are cold or nervous or frightened.
Half a minute later everybody was safely downstairs inside the stone of the peach, trembling with fright and listening to the noise of the hailstones as they came crashing against the side of the peach. — JAMES AND THE GIANT PEACH

trespass verb **trespasses, trespassing, trespassed**
To **trespass** means to go on to someone else's land, without asking them if you can.
'ATTENTION THE EIGHT FOREIGN ASTRONAUTS! THIS IS SPACE CONTROL IN HOUSTON, TEXAS, U.S.A.! YOU ARE TRESPASSING ON AMERICAN PROPERTY!' — CHARLIE AND THE GREAT GLASS ELEVATOR

trick noun **tricks**
If you play a **trick** on someone, you cheat them or make them look silly. Mr and Mrs Twit play lots of nasty tricks on each other, like making *Squiggly Spaghetti* and pretending to see *giant skillywigglers*.
You can play a lot of tricks with a glass eye because you can take it out and pop it back in again any time you like. — THE TWITS

trickle verb **trickles, trickling, trickled**
When water **trickles**, it moves very slowly.
It was beginning to rain. Water was trickling down the necks of the three men and into their shoes. — FANTASTIC MR FOX

a
b
c
d
e
f
g
h
i
j
k
l
m
n
o
p
q
r
s
t
u
v
w
x
y
z

trickle noun **trickles**
a slow gradual flow
Aunt Sponge . . . was watering at the mouth now and a thin trickle of spit was running down one side of her chin. — JAMES AND THE GIANT PEACH

tricycle noun **tricycles**
a bicycle with three wheels
Great excitement is probably the only thing that really interests a six-year-old boy and it sticks in his mind. In my case, the excitement centred around my new tricycle. — BOY

trifle noun **trifles**
1 something very small or unimportant
2 (*informal*) A trifle means very slightly or just a little bit.
'Pardon me,' murmured the Ladybird, turning a trifle pale, 'but am I wrong in thinking that we seem to be bobbing up and down?' — JAMES AND THE GIANT PEACH

trigger noun **triggers**
part of a gun that someone pulls with their finger to fire it
All the policemen were holding their guns at the ready, with their fingers on the triggers, and the firemen were clutching their hatchets. — JAMES AND THE GIANT PEACH

trim verb **trims, trimming, trimmed**
If you trim hair, you cut it so that it looks neat and tidy.
Mr Twit never bothers to trim his beard.
Do they go to a barber to have their hairy faces cut and trimmed or do they do it themselves in front of the bathroom mirror with nail-scissors? — THE TWITS

trip verb **trips, tripping, tripped**
If you trip, you catch your foot on something and nearly fall over.
Aunt Sponge, the fat one, tripped over a box that she'd brought along to keep the money in, and fell flat on her face. — JAMES AND THE GIANT PEACH

triumph noun **triumphs**
If something is a triumph, it is a great success.
'It went marvellously!' my father said, breathing heavily. 'Didn't it go absolutely marvellously?' His face was scarlet and glowing with triumph. — DANNY THE CHAMPION OF THE WORLD

trogfilth noun
Trogfilth is disgusting filth which tastes revolting. **Snozzcumbers** taste of trogfilth.
'May I taste it?' the Queen asked. 'Don't, Majester, don't!' cried the BFG. 'It is tasting of trogfilth and pigsquibble!' — THE BFG

trogglehumper noun **trogglehumpers**
A trogglehumper is one of the very worst nightmares you can have. It is the opposite of a **golden phizzwizard**.
'Of course there is something in there,' the BFG said. 'You is looking at a frightsome trogglehumper.' — THE BFG
LOOK IT UP! Some other scary dreams are **bogthumpers** and **grobswitchers**.

trogglehumping adjective
as terrifying as a **trogglehumper**
'A dream where you is seeing little chiddlers being eaten is about the most frightsome trogglehumping dream you can get.' — THE BFG

troggy adjective **troggier, troggiest**
Something troggy is vile and horrible. Troggy is a very strong word, so only troggy giants use it as an insult.
The giants picked up rocks and hurled them after him. He managed to dodge them. 'Ruddy little runt!' they shouted. 'Troggy little twit!' — THE BFG

trot verb **trots, trotting, trotted**
When a horse trots, it runs but does not gallop. When a person or giant trots, they run gently with short steps.
The BFG, with Sophie still in his ear, trotted forward and the jeeps followed close behind. — THE BFG

trousers plural noun
A pair of trousers is a piece of clothing that you wear over your legs and bottom. Both Willy Wonka and the BFG wear green trousers, but the BFG has an old faded pair which are too short in the legs. In North America, trousers are called *pants*.
Sophie saw that under the cloak he was wearing a sort of collarless shirt and a dirty old leather waistcoat . . . His trousers were faded green and were far too short in the legs. — THE BFG

trout noun **trout**
A trout is a fish that lives in rivers and lakes and can be cooked and eaten. Aunt Sponge calls her sister *dear old trout*, which is not very polite.
'My dear old trout!' Aunt Sponge cried out. 'You're only bones and skin!' — JAMES AND THE GIANT PEACH

A B C D E F G H I J K L M N O P Q R S T U V W X Y Z

trudge verb **trudges, trudging, trudged**

When you trudge along, you walk along slowly, with heavy steps.

Every day, little Charlie Bucket, trudging through the snow on his way to school, would have to pass Mr Willy Wonka's giant chocolate factory. — CHARLIE AND THE CHOCOLATE FACTORY

RINGBELLING RHYMES Try rhyming with *fudge* or *sludge.*

true adjective **truer, truest**

Something that is true is real and not made up or pretended.

Charlie's face was bright, and his eyes were stretched so wide you could see the whites all around. 'Is all this really true?' he asked. 'Or are you pulling my leg?' — CHARLIE AND THE CHOCOLATE FACTORY

trumpet noun **trumpets**

A trumpet is a brass musical instrument with a narrow tube that widens at the end. The **dream-blower** which the BFG carries is like a long trumpet.

The Giant (if that was what he was) was wearing a long BLACK CLOAK. In one hand he was holding what looked like a VERY LONG, THIN TRUMPET. — THE BFG

Trunchbull, Miss Agatha (MATILDA)

Miss Agatha Trunchbull is the tyrannical headmistress of Crunchem Hall. She despises all her pupils, but especially Matilda and her mild-mannered teacher, Miss Honey. She was once a famous athlete and still has the strength to throw her pupils as far as an Olympic hammer.

DID YOU KNOW? *Trunchbull* sounds like a mixture of *truncheon* (a type of stick for hitting people) and *bull* or *bully*, so it suits Miss Trunchbull very well, as she is a bit like a raging bull and would love using a truncheon. Writers often invent names for their characters that suit their personalities. Some other examples are: Sir Toby Belch (Shakespeare), Lady Sneerwell (Sheridan), Mr Smallweed and Inspector Stalker (both Dickens).

trunk noun **trunks**

1 The trunk of a tree is the thick stem that grows up out of the ground.

All around him, not only on the huge main trunk of the tree but also on all the big branches that grew out of it, other tiny windows were opening and tiny faces were peering out. — THE MINPINS

2 A trunk is a large box that you use for carrying things on a journey.

So off we set, my mother and I and my trunk and my tuck-box, and we boarded the paddle-steamer and went swooshing across the Bristol Channel in a shower of spray. — BOY

3 An elephant's trunk is its long nose. The trunk (and the suitcase) of an elephant is needed to make Wonka-Vite.

Trunky (THE ENORMOUS CROCODILE)

Trunky is an elephant who lives in a jungle in Africa. He has a long trunk which is very useful for swinging crocodiles round and round his head.

trust verb trusts, trusting, trusted

If you trust someone, you believe that they are good or truthful or reliable. Someone whom you can trust is **trustworthy**.

'Charlie,' said Grandma Josephine. 'I don't think I trust this gentleman very much.' 'Nor do I,' said Grandma Georgina. 'He footles around.' – CHARLIE AND THE GREAT GLASS ELEVATOR

truth noun

The truth is something that is true. Someone who tells the truth is **truthful**.

Truth is more important than modesty. I must tell you, therefore, that it was I and I alone who had the idea for the great and daring Mouse Plot. – BOY

tuck-box noun tuck-boxes

a box for storing snacks, especially at a boarding school

There is an unwritten law that no other boy, no teacher, not even the Headmaster himself has the right to pry into the contents of your tuck-box. – BOY

tuck-in noun (informal) tuck-ins

a large meal that fills you up

'I never eat anything when I get home. I have a good old tuck-in at the school lunch and that keeps me going until the next morning.' – MATILDA

tug verb tugs, tugging, tugged

When you tug something, you pull it hard.

A ghoulish snarling ghastly sound/Came up from somewhere underground,/Then slimy tendrils tugged his coat/And tried to fasten round his throat. – RHYME STEW

tug noun tugs

a hard or sudden pull

Suddenly, there came three sharp tugs on the rope. 'Pull!' shouted the Old-Green-Grasshopper. 'Everyone get behind me and pull!' – JAMES AND THE GIANT PEACH

tumble verb **tumbles, tumbling, tumbled**
If you tumble, you fall over or fall down clumsily.
Sophie dug her nails into the sides of the pocket, trying to prevent herself from tumbling out when she was upside down. She felt as though she were in a barrel going over the Niagara Falls. — THE BFG

tummy noun (*informal*) **tummies**
Your tummy is your stomach.
The bubbles were wonderful. Sophie could actually feel them bouncing and bursting all around her tummy. — THE BFG
RINGBELLING RHYMES Try rhyming with *yummy* or *glummy*.

Tummytickler noun **Tummyticklers**
an exotic type of sweet from Fiji that is sold in the Grubber
There were . . . Tummyticklers and Gobwangles from the Fiji Islands and Liplickers and Plushnuggets from the Land of the Midnight Sun. — THE GIRAFFE AND THE PELLY AND ME
LOOK IT UP! Some other scrumptious sweets are **Gumglotters** and **Giant Wangdoodles**.

tune noun **tunes**
a short piece of music
'And the Grasshopper, ladies and gents, is a boon/ In millions and millions of ways./You have only to ask him to give you a tune/And he plays and he plays and he plays.' — JAMES AND THE GIANT PEACH

tunnel noun **tunnels**
a long hole that you can walk or crawl through, either under the ground or through the centre of something solid
James . . . was crawling uphill now, as though the tunnel were leading straight towards the very centre of the gigantic fruit. — JAMES AND THE GIANT PEACH

tuppence noun
Tuppence is an old word that means two pence or two pennies. If someone *does not care tuppence*, they do not care very much at all, as tuppence is a very small amount of money.
'But what if they agreed?' Matilda cried eagerly . . . 'I honestly think they might! They don't actually care tuppence about me!' — MATILDA
RINGBELLING RHYMES Try rhyming with *come-uppance*.

turkey noun **turkeys**
a large bird that is kept on farms for its meat
Bean was a turkey-and-apple farmer. He kept thousands of turkeys in an orchard full of apple trees. — FANTASTIC MR FOX

twaddle (*rhymes with* waddle) noun (*informal*)
nonsense or rubbish
School teachers suffer a good deal from having to listen to this sort of twaddle from proud parents. — MATILDA
SPARKY SYNONYMS You can also say **rubbsquash** or **rommytot**.

twerp (*rhymes with* burp) noun (*informal*) **twerps**
A twerp is a silly or annoying person. It is very rude to call someone a *twerp*, so it is unfortunate that the Vicar of Nibbleswicke cannot help pronouncing Miss *Prewt*'s name backwards.
'Don't be a twerp, Miss Honey! You have met the little beast for only half an hour and her father has known her all her life!' — MATILDA
'My dear Miss Twerp!' cried the Reverend Lee. 'I am your new rotsap! My name is Eel, Robert Eel.' — THE VICAR OF NIBBLESWICKE

twiddle verb **twiddles, twiddling, twiddled**
If you twiddle something, you twist or turn it over and over. If you twiddle a giant's leg, you are teasing him (which you would only do to a Big Friendly Giant).
'Are you sure you is not twiddling my leg?' 'Of course not,' Sophie said. 'I just love the way you talk.' — THE BFG

twiddly adjective **twiddlier, twiddliest**
Something that is twiddly is tiny or **midgy**.
'They is very extra-usual ears indeed . . . They is allowing me to hear absolutely every single twiddly little thing.' — THE BFG

twig noun **twigs**
a very small, thin branch on a tree
Minpins from all over the forest had flown in on their birds to cheer the young hero, and all the branches and twigs of the great tree were crowded with tiny people. — THE MINPINS

twiglet noun **twiglets**
A twiglet is an insulting name that giants give to **human beans**.
The Fleshlumpeater turned and stared at the BFG. 'What is you doing here with all these grotty twiglets!' he bellowed. — THE BFG

twinkle verb **twinkles, twinkling, twinkled**
If something twinkles, it shines with little flashes of light. If someone's eyes twinkle or are **twinkly**, they are full of fun and laughter.
I was glad my father was an eye-smiler. It meant he never gave me a fake smile, because it's impossible to make your eyes twinkle if you aren't feeling twinkly yourself. — DANNY THE CHAMPION OF THE WORLD

twirl verb **twirls, twirling, twirled**
When you twirl something, you twist or spin it round and round.
'Tell me immediately who those people are in that glass capsule!' 'Ah-ha,' said the Chief Spy, twirling his false moustache. 'That is a very difficult question.' — CHARLIE AND THE GREAT GLASS ELEVATOR

twist verb **twists, twisting, twisted**
1 When you twist something, you turn it round.
Mr Twit started eating, twisting the long tomato-covered strings around his fork and shovelling them into his mouth. — THE TWITS
2 When you twist, you turn part of your body around.
Mr Twit wriggled and squirmed, and he squiggled and wormed, and he twisted and turned, and he choggled and churned, but the sticky glue held him to the floor. — THE TWITS

a
b
c
d
e
f
g
h
i
j
k
l
m
n
o
p
q
r
s
t
u
v
w
x
y
z

A trogglehumper is called *troglogoblo* in Italian.

twit noun **twits**
a very stupid person, most often a grown-up
Mr Twit was a twit. He was born a twit. And now at the age of sixty, he was a bigger twit than ever. — THE TWITS
DID YOU KNOW? *Twit* is an old word which originally meant someone who scolds or snaps at other people — just like Mr and Mrs Twit do to each other.

Twit, Mr (THE TWITS)
Mr Twit is a very hairy man with a beard that covers almost his whole face and has bits of leftover food sticking to it. He eats Bird Pie once a week on Wednesdays made from birds that he catches using HUGTIGHT glue.

Twit, Mrs (THE TWITS)
Mrs Twit used to be pretty but she has had so many ugly thoughts over the years that they have made her ugly too. She has a glass eye and carries a stick so that she can hit animals and small children.

twitch verb **twitches, twitching, twitched**
When you twitch, you make sudden jerking movements.
Captain Hardcastle was never still. His orange head twitched and jerked perpetually from side to side in the most alarming fashion. — BOY
RINGBELLING RHYMES Try rhyming with *witch* or (in the case of The Grand High Witch) *vitch*.

twitch-tickling adjective
tricky and awkward
Once again that sad winsome look came into the BFG's eyes. 'Words,' he said, 'is oh such a twitch-tickling problem to me all my life.' — THE BFG

twitter noun
If you are *all of a twitter*, you are so excited that your insides feel like jelly (making it tricky to sip a cup of tea).
Seated in a comfortable armchair in Mrs Silver's parlour, sipping his tea, Mr Hoppy was all of a twitter. — ESIO TROT

twizzler noun **twizzlers**
a difficult or unpleasant situation
'You're in a bit of a twizzler, aren't you?' the voice was saying. 'You can't go down again because if you do you'll be guzzled up at once.' — THE MINPINS

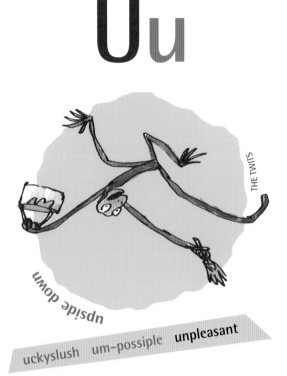

THE TWITS

upside down

uckyslush   um-possiple   unpleasant

ucky-mucky adjective **ucky-muckier, ucky-muckiest**
grisly and very unpleasant
'I am warning you not ever to go whiffling about out of this cave without I is with you or you will be coming to an ucky-mucky end!' — THE BFG

uckyslush adjective **uckyslushier, uckyslushiest**
disgusting and revolting
'Every human bean is diddly and different. Some is scrumdiddlyumptious and some is uckyslush.' — THE BFG

ugly adjective **uglier, ugliest**
Someone who is ugly is horrible to look at.
But the funny thing is that Mrs Twit wasn't born ugly. She'd had quite a nice face when she was young. The ugliness had grown upon her year by year as she got older. — THE TWITS

umbrella noun **umbrellas**
An umbrella is a waterproof cover on a folding frame that you hold above your head when it rains.
None of us, even on the sunniest days, went without his furled umbrella. The umbrella was our badge of office. — BOY
DID YOU KNOW? *Umbrella* comes from an Italian word that means 'little shadow'.

um-possiple adjective

not possible

*'We've absolutely **got** to stop them!' Sophie cried . . .
'Redunculus and **um-possiple**,' the BFG said. 'They is going
two times as fast as me.'* – THE BFG

> **Gobblefunking with words**
> The BFG adds the prefix *um-* to make a word that
> means the opposite of *possible*. There are several
> prefixes that you can use to make opposites:
> for example, *un- (unlucky)*, *im- (impossible)*,
> *in- (invisible)* and *dis- (dislike* and **dispunge**).
> You can make your own opposites, too, by adding
> these prefixes to make words such as *unjumbly* and
> *indelumptious*. To make the opposite of an opposite,
> you take off the prefix, so perhaps the opposite of
> **dispunge** would be *punge*: *I dispunge Aunt Sponge,
> but I punge sponge cake!*

underground adjective

Something that is underground is under the ground.
*'We will make,' said Mr Fox, 'a little underground village,
with streets and houses on each side — separate houses
for Badgers and Moles and Rabbits and Weasels and
Foxes.'* – FANTASTIC MR FOX

undergrowth noun

bushes and plants that grow thickly together under trees
*I had a queer feeling that the whole wood was listening
with me, the trees and the bushes, the little animals hiding
in the undergrowth and the birds roosting in the branches.*
– DANNY THE CHAMPION OF THE WORLD

unfair adjective

If a way of doing something is unfair, it does not treat
everyone (including spiders) fairly.
*'It is very unfair the way we Spiders are treated,'
Miss Spider went on. 'Why, only last week your own
horrible Aunt Sponge flushed my poor dear father down
the plug-hole in the bathtub.'* – JAMES AND THE GIANT PEACH

unfortunate adjective

You say something is unfortunate when you wish it
had not happened or did not exist.

*Mrs Wormwood . . . had one of those unfortunate
bulging figures where the flesh appears to be strapped in all
around the body to prevent it from falling out.* – MATILDA

ungrateful adjective

If you are ungrateful, you do not thank someone when
they have helped you or given you something.
*'I don't like to sound ungrateful or pushy,' murmured
the Giraffe, 'but we do have one very pressing problem.'*
– THE GIRAFFE AND THE PELLY AND ME

unicorn noun unicorns

A unicorn is a legendary creature like a horse with
a long straight horn growing out of the front of its
head. Part of a unicorn's toe is needed to make
Wonka-Vite.
*Now add the following, in precisely the order given . . .
THE BEAK OF A RED-BREASTED WILBATROSS/A CORN
FROM THE TOE OF A UNICORN.* – CHARLIE AND THE GREAT
GLASS ELEVATOR

uniform noun uniforms

a special set of clothes that everyone in the same
school, job or club wears
*'I have learnt one thing about England,' my mother went
on. 'It is a country where men love to wear uniforms and
eccentric clothes.'* – BOY

unlucky adjective unluckier, unluckiest

If you are unlucky, you have bad luck.
*'Of course it's unlucky to kill a spider!' shouted the
Centipede. 'It's about the unluckiest thing anyone can do.
Look what happened to Aunt Sponge after she'd done
that!'* – JAMES AND THE GIANT PEACH

unpleasant adjective

Something that is unpleasant is nasty or horrible.
*The Trunchbull . . . had never seen a newt before . . .
She hadn't the faintest idea what this thing was.
It certainly looked extremely unpleasant.* – MATILDA

unusual adjective

Something that is unusual is strange and not normal
or usual.
*Mr and Mrs Wormwood were both so gormless and so
wrapped up in their own silly little lives that they failed
to notice anything unusual about their daughter.*
– MATILDA

uproar noun

a loud or angry noise or disturbance
*Suddenly there was the most infernal uproar inside the
car as a dozen or more enormous pheasants started
squawking and flapping all over the seats.* – DANNY THE
CHAMPION OF THE WORLD

upset adjective

If you are upset, you are unhappy or anxious about
something.
*The Big Friendly Giant looked suddenly so forlorn that
Sophie got quite upset. 'I'm sorry,' she said. 'I didn't mean
to be rude.'* – THE BFG

> You can add *-ity* to some adjectives to make nouns: *That's an **um-possibility.***

Vv

Violet Beauregarde

CHARLIE AND THE CHOCOLATE FACTORY

vegitibble   venomsome   vermicious

vicar   viper   vitamins

in the world. — THE TWITS
own the first GREAT UPSIDE DOWN MONKEY CIRCUS
to train monkeys. It was his dream that one day he would
Today, although they were retired, Mr Twit still wanted
the bottom is at the top.
If something is upside down, it is turned over so that

upside down adjective

urge noun **urges**
a sudden strong desire or wish
*He really **hated** that horrid old witchy woman. And all
of a sudden he had a tremendous urge to do **something**
about her. Something **whopping**.* — GEORGE'S MARVELLOUS
MEDICINE

utter adjective
complete or absolute
*Sophie saw his yellow teeth clamping together, a few
inches from her head. Then there was utter darkness.
She was in his mouth.* — THE BFG

utter verb **utters, uttering, uttered**
If you utter something, you say it out loud.
*Nobody dared speak. Mr Wonka had warned them that
every word they uttered would be picked up by Space
Control in Houston.* — CHARLIE AND THE GREAT GLASS
ELEVATOR
LOOK IT UP! For other ways to utter things, see **say**.

valley noun **valleys**
A valley is an area of low land between two hills.
In Willy Wonka's factory, there is a confectionery valley
with a chocolate river running through it.
*They were looking down upon a lovely valley. There were
green meadows on either side of the valley, and along
the bottom of it there flowed a great brown river.*
— CHARLIE AND THE CHOCOLATE FACTORY

valuable adjective
Something that is valuable is worth a lot of money,
or is very useful.
*'Here it is!' cried Mr Wonka . . . holding high in one hand
a little bottle. 'The most valuable bottle of pills in the
world!'* — CHARLIE AND THE GREAT GLASS ELEVATOR

A B C D E F G H I J K L M N O P Q R S T U V W X Y Z

vanilla noun
Vanilla is a flavouring made from the pods of a tropical plant, used to flavour sweet foods like ice cream and custard. Sophie thinks that **frobscottle** tastes of vanilla.
It was sweet and refreshing. It tasted of vanilla and cream, with just the faintest trace of raspberries on the edge of the flavour. — THE BFG

vanish verb vanishes, vanishing, vanished
If something vanishes, it disappears.
'I have known no less than five children who have simply vanished off the face of this earth, never to be seen again. The witches took them.' — THE WITCHES

vapour noun vapours
A vapour is a mass of tiny drops of liquid in the air, such as steam or mist.
They were in a country of swirling mists and ghostly vapours. There was some sort of grass underfoot but it was not green. It was ashy grey. — THE BFG

varmint noun varmints
a rogue or rascal
Mrs Grace Clipstone . . . was now picking her way cautiously down the caravan steps . . . 'What a gathering!' she said, advancing towards us. 'What a gathering we have here of rogues and varmints!' — DANNY THE CHAMPION OF THE WORLD
DID YOU KNOW? The word *varmint* is related to **vermin**, so it has nothing to do with mints, but it would make a very good **pun**. For example, a new type of strong minty sweets might be called *Volcanic Varmints*.

vast adjective
Something that is vast is very large or very wide.
Already the land was out of sight. All around them lay the vast black ocean, deep and hungry. — JAMES AND THE GIANT PEACH

vegetable noun vegetables
A vegetable is a plant that can be used as food. The BFG calls them **vegitibbles**.
'Listen,' Sophie said. 'We don't have to eat snozzcumbers. In the fields around our village there are all sorts of lovely vegetables like cauliflowers and carrots.' — THE BFG

vegetarian adjective & noun vegetarians
A vegetarian is someone who does not eat meat. The BFG is a vegetarian giant, as he only eats **snozzcumbers** and not **human beans** like other giants (although the Queen later introduces him to sausages).

vegitibble noun vegitibbles
A vegitibble is what the BFG calls a *vegetable*, like the **snozzcumber**.
'Vegitibbles is very good for you,' he went on. 'It is not healthsome always to be eating meaty things.' — THE BFG
RINGBELLING RHYMES Try rhyming with *nibble*.

velvet noun
Velvet is a type of thick, soft cloth. Willy Wonka always wears a tail coat made from plum-coloured velvet.
On he rushed . . . with his black top hat perched on the top of his head and his plum-coloured velvet coat-tails flying out behind him like a flag in the wind. — CHARLIE AND THE CHOCOLATE FACTORY

venomous adjective
A venomous creature, like the **squerkle** or **Pink-Spotted Scrunch**, has a poisonous and deadly bite or sting.
'We may see the venomous Pink-Spotted Scrunch/ Who can chew up a man with one bite./It likes to eat five of them roasted for lunch/And eighteen for its supper at night.' — JAMES AND THE GIANT PEACH

venomsome adjective
poisonous and deadly
'You must grab your anklet very tight with both hands! That will stop the poisnowse juices from the venomsome viper going up your leg and into your heart!' — THE BFG

Vermes (CHARLIE AND THE GREAT GLASS ELEVATOR)
The Planet Vermes is the home of the evil-minded Vermicious Knids. It is eighteen thousand four hundred and twenty-seven million miles away from Earth.
DID YOU KNOW? *Vermes* is the plural form of Latin *vermis*, which means 'a worm'.

vermicious adjective
Something vermicious is vicious and nasty, just like a Knid.
'It's worse than that!' cried the Chief of Police. 'It's a vermicious Knid! Oh, just look at its vermicious gruesome face!' — JAMES AND THE GIANT PEACH
DID YOU KNOW? *Vermicious* is a real word meaning 'worm-like' which comes from Latin *vermis* 'a worm'.

vermin plural noun
Vermin are animals or insects that damage crops or food or carry disease, such as rats and fleas.
'All keepers have guns, Danny. It's for the vermin mostly, the foxes and stoats and weasels who go after the pheasants.' — DANNY THE CHAMPION OF THE WORLD

a b c d e f g h i j k l m n o p q r s t u **v** w x y z

Veruca Salt (CHARLIE AND THE CHOCOLATE FACTORY)

Veruca Salt is a spoilt girl whose parents buy her anything she wants, including half a million Wonka Bars to make sure that she finds a Golden Ticket. Her name sounds like *verruca*, which is a painful type of wart you can get on your foot.

vessel noun vessels

a ship or boat

The splendid little vessel with its single tall funnel would move out into the calm waters of the fjord and proceed at a leisurely pace along the coast. — BOY

vibrate verb vibrates, vibrating, vibrated

When something vibrates, it shakes with small movements from side to side.

They could all see the pills through the glass. They were brilliant yellow, shimmering and quivering inside the bottle. Vibrating is perhaps a better word. — CHARLIE AND THE GREAT GLASS ELEVATOR

vicar noun vicars

A vicar is a religious leader in the Church of England who is in charge of a parish. Vicars use the title *Reverend* before their name, like *the Reverend Robert Lee*, the new vicar of Nibbleswicke parish.

Once upon a time there lived in England a charming and God-fearing vicar called the Reverend Lee. — THE VICAR OF NIBBLESWICKE

Vicar of Nibbleswicke (THE VICAR OF NIBBLESWICKE)

The Reverend Robert Lee has suffered from dyslexia since he was a child. He causes a lot of confusion in his new job as Vicar of Nibbleswicke when he says words and phrases backwards, such as *Each of you stink* instead of 'Each of you knits'.

vicious adjective

Someone who is vicious is violent and cruel.

'I'm sure I won't meet one,' I said. 'I sincerely hope you won't . . . because those English witches are probably the most vicious in the whole world.' — THE WITCHES

victim noun victims

someone who has been, or is about to be, hurt, robbed or killed

Very carefully a victim is chosen. Then the witch stalks the wretched child like a hunter stalking a little bird in the forest. — THE WITCHES

victory noun victories

A victory is when you win a game or battle.

Back in the tree there was a tremendous celebration for Little Billy's victory over the dreaded Gruncher. — THE MINPINS

vile adjective viler, vilest

thoroughly nasty or bad

'Oh you Knid, you are vile and vermicious,' cried Mr Wonka. 'You are slimy and soggy and squishous!' — CHARLIE AND THE GREAT GLASS ELEVATOR

village noun villages

A village is a small group of houses and other buildings in the country.

Things went from bad to worse. Soon the entire village was convinced that the new vicar was completely barmy. — THE VICAR OF NIBBLESWICKE

vindscreen viper noun vindscreen vipers

The vindscreen viper is a deadly snake whose fangs are an ingredient in Wonka-Vite. Vindscreen vipers are found in Giant Country and giants are very scared of being bitten by them.

'Save our souls!' bellowed the Fleshlumpeater. 'Sound the crumpets! I is bitten by a septicous venomsome vindscreen viper!' — THE BFG

DID YOU KNOW? The name *vindscreen viper* is a pun on *windscreen wiper*, which is a device for keeping a car windscreen clear of rain. You can read more examples of this type of word play in the entry for **pun**.

vinegar noun

a sour liquid used to flavour and preserve food

That face of hers . . . was so crumpled and wizened, so shrunken and shrivelled, it looked as though it had been pickled in vinegar. — THE WITCHES

Violet Beauregarde

(CHARLIE AND THE CHOCOLATE FACTORY)

Violet Beauregarde is a girl who chews gum all day long, except for breaks at mealtimes when she puts her gum behind her ear. She is the third child to find a Golden Ticket. Her surname is French and means 'beautiful look' (although she doesn't look very beautiful when she is chewing gum).

violin noun violins

A violin is a musical instrument with four strings, played with a bow. The Old-Green-Grasshopper can play his body as though it were a violin, by rubbing his back leg against his wing.

And what a wonderful instrument the Old-Green-Grasshopper was playing upon. It was like a violin! It was almost exactly as though he were playing upon a violin! — JAMES AND THE GIANT PEACH

viper noun vipers

A viper is a type of poisonous snake. The **vindscreen viper** is a particularly deadly species of viper.

'The teeth of the dreadly viper is still sticking into me!' he yelled. 'I is feeling the teeth sticking into my anklet!' — THE BFG

A B C D E F G H I J K L M N O P Q R S T U V W X Y Z

visible adjective
If something is visible, you can see it.
There were no noses, no mouths, no ears, no chins — only the eyes were visible in each face, two small black eyes glinting malevolently through the hairs. — JAMES AND THE GIANT PEACH

vital adjective
Something that is vital is very important.
Nobody in the family gave a thought now to anything except the two vital problems of trying to keep warm and trying to get enough to eat. — CHARLIE AND THE CHOCOLATE FACTORY

vitamin noun vitamins
A vitamin is something that is found in some foods and which you need to stay healthy. Willy Wonka's Supervitamin Chocolate contains 25 vitamins: one for every letter of the alphabet (except for S and H) plus the extra-special vitamin Wonka.
'All we'll have to do is give him a triple overdose of my wonderful Supervitamin Chocolate . . . The only two vitamins it doesn't have in it are vitamin S, because it makes you sick, and vitamin H, because it makes you grow horns on the top of your head, like a bull.' — CHARLIE AND THE CHOCOLATE FACTORY

vitamin Wonka (CHARLIE AND THE CHOCOLATE FACTORY)
Vitamin Wonka is a rare and powerful vitamin that Willy Wonka adds to his Supervitamin Chocolate. If you take too much of it, it will make your toes grow as long as your fingers and do wonders for your piano playing.

'My wonderful Supervitamin Chocolate . . . does have in it a very small amount of the rarest and most magical vitamin of them all — vitamin Wonka.' — CHARLIE AND THE CHOCOLATE FACTORY

Vita-Wonk (CHARLIE AND THE GREAT GLASS ELEVATOR)
Vita-Wonk is an oily black medicine invented by Willy Wonka which makes anyone who takes it instantly older. It has the opposite effect to Wonka-Vite. The ingredients of Vita-Wonk include hairs and other parts from the oldest living creatures on Earth.

voice noun voices
Your voice is the sound you make when you speak or sing. Roald Dahl's characters have different voices, so he uses many different words to describe them. Here are some examples.

A QUIET OR PLEASANT VOICE CAN BE: distant, faint, faraway, kindly, soft, whispery
'I do have one extra special little wish.' 'And what might that be?' said the Duke in a kindly voice.
— THE GIRAFFE AND THE PELLY AND ME

A LOUD OR UNPLEASANT VOICE CAN BE: booming, high-pitched, icy, like thunder, rasping, screechy, shrill, vinegary
'The President asked you a question,' said Miss Tibbs in an icy voice. — CHARLIE AND THE GREAT GLASS ELEVATOR

volunteer noun volunteers
someone who offers to do a job they do not have to do
'I produced one tiny cupful of oily black liquid and gave four drops of it to a brave twenty-year-old Oompa-Loompa volunteer to see what happened.' — CHARLIE AND THE GREAT GLASS ELEVATOR

a
b
c
d
e
f
g
h
i
j
k
l
m
n
o
p
q
r
s
t
u
v
w
x
y
z

Vun vurd of vorning! The Grand High Witch pronounces *w* like *v.*

271

Willy Wonka

CHARLIE AND THE CHOCOLATE FACTORY

wacksey   whangdoodle   whiffle

whizzpopping   whoppsy   witches

wackcrackle verb **wackcrackles, wackcrackling, wackcrackled**
If you wackcrackle a giant, you attack him fiercely (usually by whacking him until his bones crack).
'It's the grueful gruncious Jack! Jack is after me! Jack is wackcrackling me!' — THE BFG

wacksey adjective **wacksier, wacksiest**
splendidly huge
'These wacksey big ears of mine is picking up even the noise of a man breathing the other side of this garden.'
— THE BFG
DID YOU KNOW? The word *wacksey* could be a **pun** on *waxy*, because the BFG's enormous ears would have lots of earwax in them. It also sounds a bit like *whacking* which can mean 'huge or massive'.

waddle verb **waddles, waddling, waddled**
When someone waddles, they walk with short steps, rocking from side to side, like a duck.
Aunt Sponge, fat and pulpy as a jellyfish, came waddling up behind her sister to see what was going on. — JAMES AND THE GIANT PEACH

waft verb **wafts, wafting, wafted**
If a smell or sound wafts, it floats slowly through the air.
The rich scent of chicken wafted down the tunnel to where the foxes were crouching. — FANTASTIC MR FOX

waggle verb **waggles, waggling, waggled**
When you waggle something, you move it quickly to and fro.
*'Augustus,' cried Mr Wonka, hopping up and down and waggling his stick in the air, 'you **must** come away. You are dirtying my chocolate.'* — CHARLIE AND THE CHOCOLATE FACTORY

wagon noun **wagons**
a cart with four wheels that is pulled by horses
The caravan was our house and our home. It was a real old gipsy wagon with big wheels and fine patterns painted all over it in yellow and red and blue. — DANNY THE CHAMPION OF THE WORLD

wail verb **wails, wailing, wailed**
If you wail, you give a long, sad cry.
'Give us some light!' shouted the Old-Green-Grasshopper. 'I can't!' wailed the Glow-worm. 'They've broken my bulb!'
— JAMES AND THE GIANT PEACH

waist noun **waists**
Your waist is the narrow part in the middle of your body.
Miss Spider . . . grabbed the Centipede by the waist and the two of them started dancing round and round the peach stem together. — JAMES AND THE GIANT PEACH

waistcoat noun **waistcoats**
A waistcoat is a close-fitting jacket without sleeves, worn over a shirt and under a jacket. The BFG wears an old leather waistcoat that is so well worn the buttons have fallen off.
'I is snuggling you very cosy into the pocket of my waistcoat,' the BFG said. 'Then no one is seeing you.' — THE BFG

wake verb **wakes, waking, woke, woken**
When you wake up, you stop sleeping. Tortoises like Alfie **hibernate** all winter and then wake up in the spring.
In early spring, when Alfie felt the warmer weather through his shell, he would wake up and crawl very slowly out of his house on to the balcony. — ESIO TROT

walk verb **walks, walking, walked**
For some **wondercrump** ways to describe walking, see **move**.

walking-stick noun **walking-sticks**
Some people carry or use a walking-sick as a support while walking. Mr Twit tricks his wife into thinking she has the Dreaded Shrinks by shortening her walking-stick a little bit every day.
*'What **can** have happened?' Mrs Twit said, staring at her old walking-stick. 'It must suddenly have grown longer.'*
— THE TWITS

wallet noun **wallets**
a small flat folding case for holding banknotes and bank cards
Mr Salt, Veruca's father, stepped forward. 'Very well, Wonka,' he said importantly, taking out a wallet full of

A B C D E F G H I J K L M N O P Q R S T U V **W** X Y Z

money, 'how much d'you want for one of these squirrels?'
— CHARLIE AND THE CHOCOLATE FACTORY

wallop verb wallops, walloping, walloped
If you wallop a person or giant, you punch or hit them hard.
'They'll kill each other,' Sophie said. 'Never,' the BFG answered. 'Those beasts is always bishing and walloping at one another.' — THE BFG

wallpaper noun
Wallpaper is colourful paper that is used to cover the walls of rooms. Willy Wonka makes lickable wallpaper that tastes of fruits.
'Lovely stuff, lickable wallpaper!' cried Mr Wonka, rushing past. 'It has pictures of fruits on it — bananas, apples, oranges, grapes, pineapples, strawberries, and snozzberries . . .' — CHARLIE AND THE CHOCOLATE FACTORY

wampus noun wampuses
The wampus is a legendary monster from North American folklore. The Centipede is mistaken for a wampus when he emerges from the Giant Peach in New York.
The policemen and the firemen all started shouting at once. 'Look out!' they cried. 'It's a Dragon!' 'It's not a Dragon! It's a Wampus!' — JAMES AND THE GIANT PEACH
DID YOU KNOW? In North America, the *wampus* is also called a *swamp wampus* or *whistling wampus*. A *wampus* can also be a mean and nasty person, so James Trotter's aunts are a pair of *wicked wampuses*.
LOOK IT UP! The Centipede is also mistaken for a **prock** and a **manticore**.

wander verb wanders, wandering, wandered
When you wander about, you walk about in no particular direction.
For a few minutes, Mrs Kranky kept wandering round with a puzzled look on her face, saying, 'Mother, where are you? Where've you gone?' — GEORGE'S MARVELLOUS MEDICINE

warm adjective warmer, warmest
1 Something that is warm is slightly hot.
Almost at once a great river of warm melted chocolate came pouring out of the holes in the factory wall. — JAMES AND THE GIANT PEACH
2 A warm person or smile is friendly and welcoming.
Mr Hoppy was all of a twitter . . . That smile of hers, so warm and friendly, suddenly gave him the courage he needed, and he said, 'Mrs Silver, please will you marry me?' — ESIO TROT

warn verb warns, warning, warned
If you warn someone about a danger, you tell them about it.
'This evening when the birds come in to roost, you must warn them not to perch on that tree or they will be made into Bird Pie.' — THE TWITS

warning noun warnings
something said or written to warn someone
WARNING TO READERS: Do not try to make George's Marvellous Medicine yourselves at home. It could be dangerous. — GEORGE'S MARVELLOUS MEDICINE

warren noun warrens
A warren is an underground network of rabbit holes. Willy Wonka's factory has so many rooms and corridors underground that it is like walking through a giant warren.
The place was like a gigantic rabbit warren, with passages leading this way and that in every direction. — CHARLIE AND THE CHOCOLATE FACTORY

wart noun warts
A wart is a small hard lump on your skin. Miss Trunchbull calls her pupils warts (and many other rude names) as an insult.
'What a bunch of nauseating little warts you are.' Everyone had the sense to stay silent. — MATILDA

wary adjective warier, wariest
If you are wary of something, you are slightly nervous or frightened of it.
The boy . . . was watching the Headmistress with an exceedingly wary eye and he kept edging farther and farther away from her with little shuffles of his feet. — MATILDA

wash verb washes, washing, washed
1 When you wash something, you clean it with water.
And how often did Mr Twit wash this bristly nailbrushy face of his? The answer is NEVER, not even on Sundays. He hadn't washed it for years. — THE TWITS
2 You wash when you clean yourself with water.
Bean never took a bath. He never even washed. As a result, his earholes were clogged with all kinds of muck and wax and bits of chewing-gum and dead flies and stuff like that. — FANTASTIC MR FOX
RINGBELLING RHYMES Try rhyming with *squash* or *Gosh!*

a b c d e f g h i j k l m n o p q r s t u v **W** x y z

In North America, a waistcoat is called a *vest*.

A B C D E F G H I J K L M N O P Q R S T U V W X Y Z

wasp noun **wasps**
a stinging insect with black and yellow stripes across its body
They were closer now and they could see the Knids pouring out from the tail of the Space Hotel and swarming like wasps around the Transport Capsule.
— CHARLIE AND THE GREAT GLASS ELEVATOR

watch verb **watches, watching, watched**
When you watch someone or something, you look at them for a while.
'You'd better be careful,' Mrs Twit said, 'because when I see you starting to plot, I watch you like a wombat.'
— THE TWITS
LOOK IT UP! For other ways to watch things, see **look.**

water noun
Water is the clear liquid that is in rivers and seas. All living things need water to live.
'How long can a fox go without food or water?' Boggis asked on the third day. 'Not much longer now,' Bean told him. — FANTASTIC MR FOX

water verb **waters, watering, watered**
1 When you water a plant, you pour water on to it to help it to grow.
That evening, Mr Hoppy was watering his plants on the balcony when suddenly he heard Mrs Silver's shouts from below, shrill with excitement. — ESIO TROT

2 When your eyes water, tears come into them.
The wind stung Sophie's cheeks. It made her eyes water. It whipped her head back and whistled in her ears. — THE BFG

waterfall noun **waterfalls**
A waterfall is a place where a river or stream flows over a cliff or large rock. Willy Wonka's chocolate is mixed by waterfall (or rather chocolate-fall) which makes it especially light and frothy.
'The waterfall is most important!' Mr Wonka went on. 'It mixes the chocolate! No other factory in the world mixes its chocolate by waterfall!' — CHARLIE AND THE CHOCOLATE FACTORY

water pistol noun **water pistols**
A water pistol is a toy gun with which you squirt water at people for fun. Willy Wonka makes water pistols that fire strawberry juice rather than water.
Charlie started reading some of the labels alongside the buttons . . . STRAWBERRY-JUICE WATER PISTOLS . . . EXPLODING SWEETS FOR YOUR ENEMIES. — CHARLIE AND THE CHOCOLATE FACTORY

waterproof adjective
Waterproof material or skin does not let water through.
'It's gone right through my skin!' the Earthworm groaned. 'I always thought my skin was waterproof but it isn't and now I'm full of rain!' — JAMES AND THE GIANT PEACH

watery adjective
Something watery is thin and runny, like water.
In the evenings, after he had finished his supper of watery cabbage soup, Charlie always went into the room of his four grandparents to listen to their stories. — CHARLIE AND THE CHOCOLATE FACTORY

wave verb **waves, waving, waved**
1 When you wave, you move your hand from side to side, usually to say hello or goodbye.
Charlie waved to the three astronauts in the front window. None of them waved back. They were still sitting there in a kind of shocked daze. — CHARLIE AND THE GREAT GLASS ELEVATOR

2 When you wave something, you move it from side to side or up and down.

Muggle-Wump . . . was in a frenzy of excitement now, waving his paint-brush and his bucket and leaping about all over the room. – THE TWITS

wave noun **waves**
A wave is a ridge that moves across the surface of water, especially on the sea.
All around them lay the vast black ocean, deep and hungry. Little waves were bibbling against the sides of the peach. – JAMES AND THE GIANT PEACH

wealthy adjective **wealthier, wealthiest**
Someone who is wealthy is rich.
Jack's mother said, 'We're stony broke! Go out and find some wealthy bloke/Who'll buy our cow. Just say she's sound/And worth at least a hundred pound.' – REVOLTING RHYMES

weapon noun **weapons**
A weapon is something that a person can use to hurt or kill people in a battle or fight.
'We are the crusaders, the gallant army fighting for our lives with hardly any weapons at all and the Trunchbull is the Prince of Darkness . . . with all the weapons at her command.' – MATILDA

weather noun
The weather is what it is like outside, for example, whether the sun is shining, or it is rainy or windy.
When the colder weather came along in November, Mrs Silver would fill Alfie's house with dry hay, and the tortoise would crawl in there . . . and go to sleep for months on end. – ESIO TROT

weave verb **weaves, weaving, wove, woven**
When someone weaves cloth, they make it by crossing threads under and over each other. Someone who does this (like the Silkworm) is called a **weaver**.
'This Silkworm had, I'll have you know,/The honour, not so long ago,/To spin and weave and sew and press/The Queen of England's wedding dress.' – JAMES AND THE GIANT PEACH

web noun **webs**
A web is a thin net that a spider spins to trap insects.
As for Miss Spider, she had made a lovely web for herself . . . and James could see her crouching right in the very centre of it, mumbling softly in her dreams. – JAMES AND THE GIANT PEACH

weed noun **weeds**
A weed is a wild plant that grows where it is not wanted (except by Mrs Twit, who likes growing weeds in her garden). Miss Trunchbull uses the word *weed* as an insult, as she thinks her pupils are like annoying little weeds.
'You ignorant little slug!' the Trunchbull bellowed. 'You witless weed! You empty-headed hamster! You stupid glob of glue!' – MATILDA
LOOK IT UP! Some other insults that Miss Trunchbull uses are **gumboil** and **fungus**.

weep verb **weeps, weeping, wept**
When you weep, you cry.
There she was again, the same cantankerous grumbling old Grandma Georgina . . . Mrs Bucket flung her arms around her and began weeping with joy. – CHARLIE AND THE GREAT GLASS ELEVATOR

weigh verb **weighs, weighing, weighed**
1 When you weigh something, you use a machine to find out how heavy it is.
Mr Hoppy weighed Alfie on his own kitchen scales just to make sure that Mrs Silver's figure of thirteen ounces was correct. – ESIO TROT

2 The amount that a tortoise (or anything else) weighs is how heavy it is.
'Guess what, Mr Hoppy! Guess what! He weighs twenty-seven ounces! He's twice as big as he was before!' – ESIO TROT

weight noun **weights**
The weight of something is how heavy it is.
'I once heard her say,' Hortensia went on, 'that a large boy is about the same weight as an Olympic hammer and therefore he's very useful for practising with.' – MATILDA

Great whistling whangdoodles! There are many ways to SHOUT at **exclamation**!

275

a b c d e f g h i j k l m n o p q r s t u v **w** x y z

weightless adjective
If you float in space or in orbit, you are weightless as there is no **gravity** there.
'I weigh one hundred and thirty-seven pounds exactly.'
'Not now you don't,' said Mr Wonka. 'You are completely weightless.'– CHARLIE AND THE GREAT GLASS ELEVATOR

weird adjective **weirder, weirdest**
Something that is weird is very strange or unnatural.
And then, very slowly, like some weird monster rising up from the deep, Grandma's head came through the roof.– GEORGE'S MARVELLOUS MEDICINE

welcome verb **welcomes, welcoming, welcomed**
If you welcome someone, or say welcome to them, you show that you are pleased when they arrive.
'Oh, hello, James!' the Glow-worm said, looking down and giving James a little wave and a smile. 'I didn't see you come in. Welcome, my dear boy, welcome!'– JAMES AND THE GIANT PEACH

Welly-eating Giant (THE BFG)
The Welly-eating Giant is fond of eating **human beans** from Wellington in New Zealand (who taste of boots). He is not one of the giants who bully the BFG, but he is still a **cannybully** giant.

welt noun **welts**
a raised bump on your skin, such as could be caused by a powerful **itching-powder**
The label said it was made from the powdered teeth of deadly snakes, and it was guaranteed to raise welts the size of walnuts on your skin.– MATILDA

wet adjective **wetter, wettest**
Something that is wet is covered or soaked in water or other liquid.
Then came the rain. It rained and rained, and the water ran into the nest and they all got as wet as could be — and oh, it was a bad, bad night!– THE MAGIC FINGER

whangdoodle noun **whangdoodles**
The whangdoodle is a terrifying creature that lives in Loompaland and preys on Oompa-Loompas. Whangdoodles have enormous appetites and can eat more than ten Oompa-Loompas in a single meal. Some whangdoodles, such as the rare **spotted whangdoodle**, have patterned hides.
'And oh, what a terrible country it is! Nothing but thick jungles infested by the most dangerous beasts in the world — hornswogglers and snozzwangers and those terrible wicked whangdoodles.'– CHARLIE AND THE CHOCOLATE FACTORY

DON'T BE BIFFSQUIGGLED! Take care not to confuse **whangdoodle** with **Giant Wangdoodle**, which is a type of sweet and not a creature.

wheel noun **wheels**
a round part on a car or machine that turns to make it move or go
'He'll be quite changed from what he's been,/When he goes through the fudge machine:/Slowly, the wheels go round and round,/The cogs begin to grind and pound.'
– CHARLIE AND THE CHOCOLATE FACTORY

wheel verb **wheels, wheeling, wheeled**
1 When a Knid or a bird or aircraft wheels, it flies in a wide curve or circle.
Away in the distance, in the deep blue sky of outer space, they saw a massive cloud of Vermicious Knids wheeling and circling like a fleet of bombers.
– CHARLIE AND THE GREAT GLASS ELEVATOR
2 If you wheel round, you turn round quickly to face a different direction.
Suddenly someone shouted, 'Come on, Brucie! You can make it!' The Trunchbull wheeled round and yelled, 'Silence!'– MATILDA

wheelbarrow noun **wheelbarrows**
a small cart that you push along and use for carrying things
The BFG was three times as tall as an ordinary man and his hands were as big as wheelbarrows.– DANNY THE CHAMPION OF THE WORLD

whiff noun **whiffs**
a slight smell of something
I was living in constant terror that one of the witches in the back row was going to get a whiff of my presence through those special nose-holes of hers.– THE WITCHES

whiffle verb **whiffles, whiffling, whiffled**
When something whiffles, it moves quickly and lightly, like a fluttering bird or insect.
'A dream,' he said, 'as it goes whiffling through the night air, is making a tiny little buzzing-humming noise.'– THE BFG

whiffle-bird noun whiffle-birds
The whiffle-bird is a rare bird whose eggs are an ingredient in Wonka-Vite. It probably gets its name because it darts or whiffles through the air.
Now add the following, in precisely the order given . . . THE TRUNK (AND THE SUITCASE) OF AN ELEPHANT/ THE YOLKS OF THREE EGGS FROM A WHIFFLE-BIRD. – CHARLIE AND THE GREAT GLASS ELEVATOR

whiffswiddle noun whiffswiddles
A whiffswiddle is something that moves or happens very fast.
'And if you were to put me down on the ground and I was to walk out among them now,' Sophie said, 'would they really eat me up?' 'Like a whiffswiddle!' cried the BFG. – THE BFG

whiffsy adjective whiffsier, whiffsiest
Something whiffsy is always moving.
'Giants is never dying,' the BFG answered . . . 'Mostly us giants is simply going on and on like whiffsy time-twiddlers.' – THE BFG

whip noun whips
a long piece of rope or leather that is used for hitting people or animals
whip verb whips, whipping, whipped
1 To whip a person or animal means to hit them with a whip.
2 When you whip cream, you stir it quickly until it goes thick, usually with a spoon or an egg-beater. (Only Willy Wonka's whipped cream is whipped with real whips.)
'How can you whip cream without whips? Whipped cream isn't whipped cream at all unless it's been whipped with whips.' – CHARLIE AND THE CHOCOLATE FACTORY
3 If you whip round, you turn round very quickly.
The Grand High Witch whipped round as though someone had stuck a skewer into her bottom. 'Who said that?' she snapped. – THE WITCHES

Whipple-Scrumptious Fudgemallow Delight (CHARLIE AND THE CHOCOLATE FACTORY)
The Whipple-Scrumptious Fudgemallow Delight is the most **delumptious** of all Wonka bars. The recipe is a secret but it probably includes fudge and marshmallows, as well as whipped chocolate. It is in one of these special bars that Charlie finds a Golden Ticket.

whirl verb whirls, whirling, whirled
If something whirls, it turns round and round very fast.
All the time the water came pouring and roaring down upon them . . . swashing and swirling and surging and whirling and gurgling and gushing and rushing and rushing. – JAMES AND THE GIANT PEACH
whirl noun whirls
If you are in a whirl, you feel as if you are turning or spinning around quickly.
Charlie was holding tightly on to his grandfather's bony old hand. He was in a whirl of excitement. – CHARLIE AND THE CHOCOLATE FACTORY

whirlgig adjective
If something is whirlgig, it is all topsy-turvy and higgledy-piggledy.
'They was in a nasty crotching mood today, was they not! I is sorry you was having such a whirlgig time.' – THE BFG
DID YOU KNOW? The word *whirlgig* is also an old spelling of *whirligig*, a spinning toy.

whirlpool noun whirlpools
A whirlpool is a strong current of water that goes round in a circle, pulling things towards it. Willy Wonka has a chocolate whirlpool at the bottom of his famous chocolate waterfall.
There was . . . a steep cliff over which the water curled and rolled in a solid sheet, and then went crashing down into a boiling churning whirlpool of froth and spray. – CHARLIE AND THE CHOCOLATE FACTORY

whisk verb whisks, whisking, whisked
When you whisk eggs or cream, you stir them round and round very fast. The BFG mixes dreams by whisking **zozimus** into a bubbly froth.
The BFG . . . started turning the handle very fast. Flashes of green and blue exploded inside the jar. The dreams were being whisked into a sea-green froth. – THE BFG

whisker noun whiskers
Whiskers are the long stiff hairs on the face of some animals, such as cats, mice and walruses.
I put the Magic Finger on Mrs Winter good and strong, and almost at once . . . Guess what? Whiskers began growing out of her face! – THE MAGIC FINGER

whisper verb whispers, whispering, whispered
When you whisper, you speak very quietly.
'Now what you have to do, Mrs Silver, is hold Alfie up to your face and whisper these words to him three times a day, morning, noon and night.' – ESIO TROT
whisper noun whispers
a very soft voice or sound
'Push the grand piano into the centre of the room,' Mr Tibbs whispered. Butlers never raise their voices above the softest whisper. – THE BFG

whistle verb **whistles, whistling, whistled**
When you whistle, you make a high sound by blowing air through your lips. If you can't whistle, you can try chewing **Pishlets** like Pelly the pelican.
Pishlets, as you probably know, are bought by children who are unable to whistle a tune as they walk along the street but long to do so. — THE GIRAFFE AND THE PELLY AND ME

whistle-pig noun **whistle-pigs**
The whistle-pig is a rare and ancient animal. A part of the whistle-pig is needed to make Vita-Wonk (perhaps its whistle, but only Willy Wonka knows for sure).
'I tracked down THE WHISTLE-PIG, THE BOBOLINK, THE SKROCK, THE POLLY-FROG, THE GIANT CURLICUE, THE STINGING SLUG AND THE VENOMOUS SQUERKLE.' — CHARLIE AND THE GREAT GLASS ELEVATOR

white adjective **whiter, whitest**
Something that is white is the colour of snow or milk. If someone goes white, they are very nervous or afraid, or are feeling suddenly ill.
*Mrs Twit went white with fear. 'You've got the **shrinks**!' cried Mr Twit, pointing his finger at her like a pistol.* — THE TWITS

whiz-banger noun **whiz-bangers**
A whiz-banger is something that you really enjoy, like your favourite book or television programme.
*'Didn't I **tell** you not to interrupt! This show's an absolute whiz-banger! It's terrific! I watch it every day.'* — CHARLIE AND THE CHOCOLATE FACTORY
DON'T BE BIFFSQUIGGLED! Take care not to confuse *whiz-banger* with **whizzpopper**, which is the noise you make after drinking **frobscottle**.
DID YOU KNOW? During World War I, the word *whiz-bang* meant a type of exploding shell.

whizz verb **whizzes, whizzing, whizzed**
When you whizz, or whizz along, you move very quickly.
As the ravens whizzed over, they brushed a streak of sticky glue on to the tops of Mr and Mrs Twit's heads. — THE TWITS

whizzpopper noun **whizzpoppers**
A whizzpopper is the noise you make when **whizzpopping**. Giants think whizzpoppers are very musical, like the sound of the **bagglepipes**.
'I has Her Majester's permission!' cried the BFG, and all at once he let fly with a whizzpopper that sounded as though a bomb had exploded in the room. — THE BFG

whizzpopping noun
Whizzpopping is what happens when air comes out of your bottom with a popping sound, as happens when you drink a lot of **frobscottle**.

Giants find whizzpopping more socially acceptable than burping.
'Whizzpopping is a sign of happiness. It is music in our ears! You surely is not telling me that a little whizzpopping is forbidden among human beans?' — THE BFG
DON'T BE BIFFSQUIGGLED! Take care not to confuse **whizzpopping** with **phizz-whizzing**, which is an adjective meaning 'excellent' or 'splendid'.

whole adjective
A whole thing is all of it, with nothing left out.
The Trunchbull was not a person who would give someone a whole chocolate cake to eat just out of kindness.

Many were guessing that it had been filled with pepper or castor-oil. — MATILDA

whoop noun whoops
a loud cry of joy or excitement
The little man gave a great whoop of joy and threw his bowl of mashed caterpillars right out of the tree-house window. — CHARLIE AND THE CHOCOLATE FACTORY

whoopee exclamation
People shout *Whoopee!* when they are happy and excited.
TELEVISION CHOCOLATE, it said on the tiny label beside the button. 'Whoopee!' shouted Mike Teavee. 'That's for me!' — CHARLIE AND THE CHOCOLATE FACTORY

whoopsey-splunkers adjective
wonderful or splendiferous
'How wondercrump!' cried the BFG, still beaming. 'How whoopsey-splunkers! How absolutely squiffling! I is all of a stutter.' — THE BFG
SPARKY SYNONYMS You can also say **phizz-whizzing** or **whoppsy-whiffling**.

whoosh verb whooshes, whooshing, whooshed
If something whooshes, it moves very quickly.
Sophie . . . crouched in the pocket and listened to the wind screaming past. It came knifing in through the tiny peep-hole in the pocket and whooshed around her like a hurricane. — THE BFG

whooshey adjective whooshier, whooshiest
A whooshey smell or flavour is very strong, as if the scent had whooshed into your nostrils.
'The human bean,' the Giant went on, 'is coming in dillions of different flavours. For instance, human beans from Wales is tasting very whooshey of fish.' — THE BFG

whopper noun (*informal*) whoppers
something very large
That evening Lavender went to the bottom of the garden determined to catch a newt . . . She lay on the bank for a long time waiting patiently until she spotted a whopper. — MATILDA

whoppsy adjective whoppsier, whoppsiest
very big or very great
'You is asking me to tell you whoppsy big secrets,' he said. 'Secrets that nobody is ever hearing before.' — THE BFG
DID YOU KNOW? Roald Dahl may have been thinking of **whopper** when he invented *whoppsy*. A whopper also means a lie, so a *whoppsy whopper* is a REALLY BIG lie.

whoppsy-good adjective
excellent or very good
'The Gizzardgulper is . . . watching the human beans walking on the street below, and when he sees one that looks like it has a whoppsy-good flavour, he grabs it.' — THE BFG

whoppsy-whiffling adjective
splendid or marvellous
Suddenly the BFG gave a jump in the air. 'By gumfrog!' he cried. 'I is just having the most whoppsy-whiffling idea!' — THE BFG
RINGBELLING RHYMES Try rhyming with *squiffling*.
SPARKY SYNONYMS You can also say **phizz-whizzing** or **wondercrump**.

whunking adjective
big and heavy
'So what you soldiers has to do is to creep up to the giants while they is still in the Land of Noddy and tie their arms and legs with mighty ropes and whunking chains.' — THE BFG

wicked adjective
A wicked person or creature is evil-minded and cruel.
'And oh, what a terrible country it is! Nothing but thick jungles infested by the most dangerous beasts in the world — hornswogglers and snozzwangers and those terrible wicked whangdoodles.' — CHARLIE AND THE CHOCOLATE FACTORY
LOOK IT UP! Some wicked creatures are **Gnoolies**, **Knids** and **whangdoodles**. For other ways to describe wicked people, see **bad**.

wide adjective wider, widest
Something that is wide measures a lot from one side to the other.
The Queen was still staring at Sophie. Gaping at her would be more accurate. Her mouth was slightly open, her eyes were round and wide as two saucers. — THE BFG

widow noun widows
a woman whose husband has died
This balcony belonged to an attractive middle-aged lady called Mrs Silver. Mrs Silver was a widow who also lived alone. — ESIO TROT

wife noun wives
A wife is the woman someone is married to.
The Cloud-Men's wives were crouching over little stoves with frying-pans in their hands, frying snowballs for their husbands' suppers. — JAMES AND THE GIANT PEACH

wig noun wigs
A wig is a covering of false hair that some people wear on their head, and that witches wear to hide their baldness.
'It is almost impossible to tell a really first-class wig from ordinary hair unless you give it a pull to see if it comes off.' — THE WITCHES

wiggle verb wiggles, wiggling, wiggled
1 When something wiggles, or wiggles about, it moves repeatedly from side to side.
Trogglehumpers wiggle about angrily when they are captured.

a b c d e f g h i j k l m n o p q r s t u v w x y z

Whizzpoppers are called flitspoppers *in Dutch.*

'It's wiggling all over the place!' Sophie cried. 'It's fighting to get out!' 'The nastier the dream, the angrier it is getting when it is in prison,' the BFG said. — THE BFG

2 If a giant wiggles you away, he captures and carries you away to Giant Country (so you will hope he is a friendly giant).

'I will bet you,' the BFG went on, 'that you would have been splashing the news all over the wonky world, wouldn't you, if I hadn't wiggled you away?' — THE BFG

wigglish noun

Wigglish is nonsense or words that don't make any sense.

'I know exactly what words I am wanting to say, but . . . they is always getting squiff-squiddled around . . . I is speaking the most terrible wigglish.' — THE BFG

DID YOU KNOW? When he invented the word *wigglish*, Roald Dahl may have been thinking of *wiggly English*, as the BFG sometimes gets words the wrong way round. You could also call it *squigglish*, from **squiggly** English.

wilbatross noun wilbatrosses

You can read all about wilbatrosses in the entry for **red-breasted wilbatross**.

wild adjective wilder, wildest

1 Wild animals and plants live or grow in a natural way and are not looked after by people.

'The whole floor of the forest is carpeted with wild strawberries, every one of them luscious and red and juicy-ripe. Go and see for yourself.' — THE MINPINS

2 Wild behaviour is rough and not calm.

The town in which Augustus Gloop lived, the newspaper said, had gone wild with excitement over their hero. — CHARLIE AND THE CHOCOLATE FACTORY

wild grout noun wild grouts

The wild grout is a rare type of animal. Part of its body is needed to make Wonka-Vite.

Now add the following, in precisely the order given . . . THE FANGS OF A VIPER (IT MUST BE A VINDSCREEN VIPER)/ THE CHEST (AND THE DRAWERS) OF A WILD GROUT. — CHARLIE AND THE GREAT GLASS ELEVATOR

willing adjective

If you are willing to do something, you are happy to do it.

'If the Pelican is willing, perhaps he will also give me a ride in his beak now and again.' 'A pleasure, Your Grace!' cried the Pelican. — THE GIRAFFE AND THE PELLY AND ME

willow noun willows

a tree with thin branches that bend downwards, which often grows near water

Graceful trees and bushes were growing along the riverbanks — weeping willows and alders and tall clumps of rhododendrons with their pink and red and mauve blossoms. — CHARLIE AND THE CHOCOLATE FACTORY

Willy Wonka (CHARLIE AND THE CHOCOLATE FACTORY & GREAT GLASS ELEVATOR)

Willy Wonka is a confectionery genius who owns a factory where he creates extraordinary sweets. He has a goatee beard and always wears a top hat and tail coat and carries a gold-topped walking stick.

win verb wins, winning, won

When you win a game or competition, you beat the other people or teams.

*'You mean you're the **only one left**?' Mr Wonka said, pretending to be surprised . . . 'But my **dear boy**,' he cried out, '**that means you've won!**'* — CHARLIE AND THE CHOCOLATE FACTORY

wind noun winds

Wind, or a wind, is a current of air that moves over the earth.

'The north wind is alive,' the BFG said. 'It is moving. It touches you on the cheek and on the hands. But nobody is feeding it.' — THE BFG

From far away, there came a very faint whoozing whiffling noise, like a small gusty wind blowing through the trees. — THE MINPINS

window noun windows

A window is an opening in a wall that is filled with glass to let the light in. Every night the BFG blows dreams through children's bedroom windows.

A B C D E F G H I J K L M N O P Q R S T U V W X Y Z

The BFG was an expert on windows. He had opened thousands of them over the years to blow his dreams into children's bedrooms. — THE BFG

window–sill noun window-sills
a small ledge on the bottom part of a window
She found it almost impossible to believe that she, Sophie . . . was at this moment actually sitting high above the ground on the window-sill of the Queen of England's bedroom. — THE BFG

wing noun wings
A bird's wings are the parts that it moves up and down when it is flying. The Gregg family sprout pairs of wings after the Magic Finger is turned on them.
A minute later Philip and William burst in. The same thing had happened to them. They had wings and no arms. And they were really tiny. They were about as big as robins. — THE MAGIC FINGER

wink verb winks, winking, winked
When you wink, you close and open one of your eyes quickly.
'My dear Sponge,' Aunt Spiker said slowly, winking at her sister and smiling a sly, thin-lipped smile. 'There's a pile of money to be made out of this.' — JAMES AND THE GIANT PEACH

winkle noun winkles
1 Your winkles are your eyes.
'Just because we happen not to have actually seen something with our own two little winkles, we think it is not existing.' — THE BFG
2 A winkle is also an affectionate name that you call someone you like. The BFG calls Sophie both a *winkle* and a *scrumplet.*
'Try it yourself, this foulsome snozzcumber! . . . Go on, you snipsy little winkle, have a go!' — THE BFG

winksquiffler noun winksquifflers
A winksquiffler is a thrillingly **wondercrump** type of dream.

The BFG was very excited. He held the jar close to one ear and listened intently. 'It's a winksquiffler!' he whispered with a thrill in his voice. — THE BFG

LOOK IT UP! Some other pleasant dreams are **ringbellers** and **golden phizzwizards**.

winner noun winners
The winner of a game or competition is the person or team that wins.
'I decided to invite five children to the factory, and the one I liked best at the end of the day would be the winner!' — CHARLIE AND THE CHOCOLATE FACTORY

winsome adjective
charming and appealing
Once again that sad winsome look came into the BFG's eyes. 'Words,' he said, 'is oh such a twitch-tickling problem to me all my life.' — THE BFG

wipe verb wipes, wiping, wiped
When you wipe something, you rub it gently to dry it or clean it.
Miss Spider wiped away a tear and looked sadly at the Centipede. 'You poor thing,' she murmured. 'I do feel sorry for you.' — JAMES AND THE GIANT PEACH

wise adjective wiser, wisest
Someone who is wise understands a lot of things and knows the most sensible thing to do.
'A little nonsense now and then, is relished by the wisest men,' Mr Wonka said. — CHARLIE AND THE GREAT GLASS ELEVATOR

wish verb wishes, wishing, wished
If you wish that something would happen, you think or say that you would like it to happen. Charlie wishes more than anything to win one of Willy Wonka's Golden Tickets.
Oh, how he loved that smell! And oh, how he wished he could go inside the factory and see what it was like! — CHARLIE AND THE CHOCOLATE FACTORY

wish noun wishes
A wish is something that you would like to happen.
The BFG expressed a wish to learn how to speak properly, and Sophie herself, who loved him as she would a father, volunteered to give him lessons every day. — THE BFG

wispy–misty adjective wispy-mistier, wispy-mistiest
light and floaty, like mist that you can barely see
'Dreams,' he said, 'is very mysterious things. They is floating around in the air like little wispy-misty bubbles.' — THE BFG

witch noun witches
A witch is a wicked woman who does evil things by magic. Witches in some stories have pointed hats and ride on broomsticks, but real witches (the ones in Roald Dahl's stories) go around in disguise and are FAR HARDER to spot, and also FAR NASTIER. The head of all the witches in the world (and therefore the nastiest of them all) is The Grand High Witch.
Luckily, there are not a great number of REAL WITCHES

in the world today. But there are still quite enough to make you nervous. — THE WITCHES

DID YOU KNOW? The magic that witches do is called *witchcraft* and a gathering of witches is called a *coven*.

LOOK IT UP! Some ways to spot a witch are by her **gloves**, **shoes**, **spit** and **wig**.

witching hour noun
the time around midnight when witches are active and when magical things can happen
When she reached the curtains, Sophie hesitated. She longed to duck underneath them and lean out of the window to see what the world looked like now that the witching hour was at hand. — THE BFG

witchophile noun **witchophiles**
A witchophile is an expert on witches. Witchophiles often spend a lifetime studying witches and trying to track and spot them in disguise.
'Are you a witchophile, Grandmamma?' 'I am a retired witchophile,' she said. 'I am too old to be active any longer.' — THE WITCHES

> **Gobblefunking with words**
> The ending *-phile* is used to make words that mean someone who loves, or is an expert in, something. For example, a *bibliophile* is someone like Matilda who loves books, and a *logophile* is someone who loves words (and therefore dictionaries). The opposite is *-phobe*, which means someone who hates or is afraid of something, so a *witchophobe* would be afraid of witches.

withering adjective
A withering look or remark is scornful or sarcastic.
The Old-Green-Grasshopper turned his huge black eyes upon the Centipede and gave him a withering look. — JAMES AND THE GIANT PEACH

witness verb **witnesses, witnessing, witnessed**
If you witness something, such as an accident or a battle, you are there to see it happen.

It seemed that all the other Minpins from the big tree had turned up as well to witness the great victory over the dreaded Gruncher. — THE MINPINS

wizened adjective
very old and wrinkled, like the skin of a witch or an old apple
That face of hers . . . was so crumpled and wizened, so shrunken and shrivelled, it looked as though it had been pickled in vinegar. — THE WITCHES

wobble verb **wobbles, wobbling, wobbled**
When you wobble, you move unsteadily from side to side (which can be hazardous in the Chokey).
'It's pitch dark and you have to stand up dead straight and if you wobble at all you get spiked either by the glass on the walls or the nails on the door.' — MATILDA

wolf noun **wolves**
a wild animal that is like a large, fierce dog
The Wolf stood there, his eyes ablaze/And yellowish, like mayonnaise./His teeth were sharp, his gums were raw,/ And spit was dripping from his jaw. — REVOLTING RHYMES

wolf verb **wolfs, wolfing, wolfed**
If you wolf or wolf down food, you eat it greedily.
Charlie went on wolfing the chocolate. He couldn't stop. And in less than half a minute, the whole thing had disappeared down his throat. — CHARLIE AND THE CHOCOLATE FACTORY

wonder noun
When you have a feeling of wonder, you feel pleasantly surprised and amazed.
As Little Billy went from window to window, the Minpins followed him, clustering round and smiling at his exclamations of wonder. — THE MINPINS

wonder verb **wonders, wondering, wondered**
If you wonder about something, you ask yourself about it.
Could it be, George wondered, that she was a witch? He had always thought witches were only in fairy tales, but now he was not so sure. — GEORGE'S MARVELLOUS MEDICINE

wondercrump adjective
wonderful or splendiferous
'How wondercrump!' cried the BFG, still beaming. 'How whoopsey-splunkers! How absolutely squiffling! I is all of a stutter.' — THE BFG
SPARKY SYNONYMS You can also say **phizz-whizzing** or **whoppsy-whiffling**.

wonderful adjective
Something that is wonderful will amaze and delight you at the same time. The BFG says **wondercrump**.
'We are now about to visit the most marvellous places and see the most wonderful things! Isn't that so, Centipede?' — JAMES AND THE GIANT PEACH
SPARKY SYNONYMS You can also say **phizz-whizzing** or **splendiferous**.
LOOK IT UP! For other ways to describe wonderful things, see **good**.

wonderveg noun wonderveg

A wonderveg is a delicious-tasting vegetable. The BFG pretends that **snozzcumbers** are wonderveg in order to trick the Bloodbottler.

'Take a bite and I am positive you will be shouting out oh how scrumdiddlyumptious this wonderveg is!' — THE BFG

Wonka bar noun Wonka bars

Wonka bars are bars of chocolate made in Willy Wonka's factory. There are many different types of Wonka bar, but the most **delumptious** of all is the Whipple-Scrumptious Fudgemallow Delight.

'A Wonka chocolate bar!' cried Charlie. 'It is a Wonka bar, isn't it?' 'Yes, my love,' his mother said. 'Of course it is.' — CHARLIE AND THE CHOCOLATE FACTORY

Wonka–Vite (CHARLIE AND THE GREAT GLASS ELEVATOR)

Wonka-Vite is a magical medicine invented by Willy Wonka which makes anyone who takes it younger. It has the opposite effect to Vita-Wonk. Each bright yellow pill of Wonka-Vite makes you younger by exactly twenty years. The ingredients include chocolate, the hoof of a **manticore** and the snout of a **proghopper**.

> ### Gobblefunking with words
> A word that is named after the person who invented or used it, like *Wonka-Vite* (after Willy Wonka), is called an *eponym*. Some other eponyms you might know are *cardigan* and *sandwich* (after the Earls of Cardigan and Sandwich), *leotard* (after an acrobat called Jules Leotard) and *wellingtons* (after the Duke of Wellington).

wonky adjective (*informal*) wonkier, wonkiest

If something is wonky, it is crooked and not straight.

You can have a wonky nose and a crooked mouth . . . but if you have good thoughts they will shine out of your face like sunbeams and you will always look lovely. — THE TWITS

RINGBELLING RHYMES Try rhyming with *donkey* (but not with *monkey*, which rhymes with *Trunky*).

wood noun woods

1 Wood is the hard material that trees are made of. Wood is used to make pencils and furniture, as well as walking-sticks.

'Don't be a fool!' Mr Twit said. 'How can a walking-stick possibly grow longer? It's made of dead wood, isn't it? Dead wood can't grow.' — THE TWITS

2 A wood is an area of trees growing together.

I had a queer feeling that the whole wood was listening with me, the trees and the bushes, the little animals hiding in the undergrowth and the birds roosting in the branches. — DANNY THE CHAMPION OF THE WORLD

woolly adjective woollier, woolliest

Something woolly is made of wool, or feels or tastes like wool.

'Human beans from Jersey has a most disgustable woolly tickle on the tongue,' the Giant said. — THE BFG

word noun words

A word is a group of sounds or letters that mean something. This dictionary explains the meaning of lots of words (although not the ones that Farmer Bunce says out loud).

Bean's face was purple with rage. Bunce was cursing the fox with dirty words that cannot be printed. — FANTASTIC MR FOX

worm noun worms

a small thin wriggling animal without legs, especially an **earthworm**

'Seagulls love worms, didn't you know that? And luckily for us, we have here the biggest, fattest, pinkest, juiciest Earthworm in the world.' — JAMES AND THE GIANT PEACH

Wormwood, Mr (MATILDA)

Mr Wormwood is Matilda's vain and ignorant father. He runs a secondhand-car business and cheats his customers by selling them worthless bits of junk.

Wormwood, Mrs (MATILDA)

Mrs Wormwood is Matilda's self-centred mother. She dyes her hair platinum blonde and spends all her time playing bingo and watching television.

wormy adjective wormier, wormiest

Something wormy is like a worm, or full of worms like the Squiggly Spaghetti that Mrs Twit makes for her husband.

SPARKY SYNONYMS You can also say **vermicious**.

worry verb worries, worrying, worried

When you worry, you feel upset and nervous because you think something bad might happen.

'The thing that worries me,' Sophie said, 'is having to stay in this dreadful place for the rest of my life. The orphanage was pretty awful, but I wouldn't have been there for ever, would I?' — THE BFG

Wormwood is the name of a plant that has a bitter taste.

a b c d e f g h i j k l m n o p q r s t u v **w** x y z

worse adjective

If one thing is worse than another, it is less good.

Things went from bad to worse. Soon the entire village was convinced that the new vicar was completely barmy.
—THE VICAR OF NIBBLESWICKE

worst adjective

The worst person or thing is the one that is worse than any other.

'What's worse than tigers and lions, Mummy?' 'Whangdoodles are worse,' his mother said . . . 'And worst of all is the Terrible Bloodsuckling Toothpluckling Stonechuckling Spittler.'—THE MINPINS

wounded adjective

If a person or animal is wounded, they are cut or injured on a part of their body.

'Rotten shots, most of them fellows are,' Charlie Kinch said. 'At least half the birds finish up winged and wounded.'—DANNY THE CHAMPION OF THE WORLD

wraprascal noun **wraprascals**

The wraprascal is an animal that is very common in Giant Country, but which no **human bean** has ever seen.

'What about for instance . . . the wraprascal?' 'The what?' Sophie said. 'And the crumpscoddle?' 'Are they animals?' Sophie asked.—THE BFG

DID YOU KNOW? The word *wraprascal* sounds like a mixture of *wrap* and *rascal*, so perhaps it is a rascally creature that wraps its body around things.

LOOK IT UP! Some other common animals in Giant Country are the **humplecrimp** and **scotch-hopper**.

wreck noun **wrecks**

A wreck is a badly damaged ship or car. If you say you are a wreck, you mean that you feel like a broken vehicle.

'I'm a wreck!' groaned the Centipede. 'I am wounded all over!' 'It serves you right,' said the Earthworm.—JAMES AND THE GIANT PEACH

wrestle verb **wrestles, wrestling, wrestled**

When people or giants wrestle, they fight by trying to force each other to the ground.

Charlie . . . sat quietly in the classroom during break, resting himself, while the others rushed outdoors and threw snowballs and wrestled in the snow.—CHARLIE AND THE CHOCOLATE FACTORY

wriggle verb **wriggles, wriggling, wriggled**

When you wriggle, you twist and turn with your body. Willy Wonka invents several things that wriggle, including **Wriggle-Sweets** and pills of Wonka-Vite.

'They're wriggling,' said Grandma Georgina. 'I don't like things that wriggle. How do we know they won't go on wriggling inside us after we've swallowed them?'—CHARLIE AND THE GREAT GLASS ELEVATOR

RINGBELLING RHYMES Try rhyming with *giggle*.

Wriggle-Sweet noun **Wriggle-Sweets**

a type of sweet invented by Willy Wonka that gives you a wriggly feeling in your tummy

Charlie started reading some of the labels alongside the buttons . . . WRIGGLE-SWEETS THAT WRIGGLE DELIGHTFULLY IN YOUR TUMMY AFTER SWALLOWING.
—CHARLIE AND THE CHOCOLATE FACTORY

LOOK IT UP! Some other sweets invented by Willy Wonka are **Mint Jujubes** and **Rainbow Drops**.

wrinkle noun **wrinkles**

Wrinkles are small lines in your skin that often appear as you get older (or after taking too much Vita-Wonk).

Her tiny face was like a pickled walnut. There were such masses of creases and wrinkles that the mouth and eyes and even the nose were sunken almost out of sight.
—CHARLIE AND THE GREAT GLASS ELEVATOR

wrinkled adjective

A wrinkled face or surface has lots of wrinkles in it.

The door slid open and there, inside the second lift, was another enormous slimy wrinkled greenish-brown egg with eyes!—CHARLIE AND THE GREAT GLASS ELEVATOR

wrinkly adjective **wrinklier, wrinkliest**

Something wrinkly, like the BFG's kindly face, is covered in wrinkles.

In the moonlight, Sophie caught a glimpse of an enormous long pale wrinkly face with the most enormous ears.
—THE BFG

RINGBELLING RHYMES Try rhyming with *twinkly*.

write verb **writes, writing, wrote, written**
When you write, you put letters and words on to paper so that people can read them (for tortoises, you have to write the words SDRAWKCAB).
'It's tortoise language,' Mr Hoppy said. 'Tortoises are very backward creatures. Therefore they can only understand words that are written backwards.' — ESIO TROT

Xx

GEORGE'S MARVELLOUS MEDICINE

writhe verb **writhes, writhing, writhed**
If you writhe, you twist your body about because you are uncomfortable or in pain.
The Fleshlumpeater was writhing about over the ground like some colossal tortured snake. — THE BFG

wrong adjective
1 Something that is wrong is not right or correct.
'Upwards is the wrong way!' cried the BFG. 'You mustn't ever be having the bubbles going upwards!' — THE BFG
2 Something that is wrong is bad or not fair.
'Eating human beans is wrong and evil,' the BFG said. 'It is guzzly and glumptious!' shouted the Bloodbottler. — THE BFG

wurzel noun **wurzels**
A wurzel is a yellow root vegetable that is fed to farm animals. It is very rude to call someone a wurzel.
There was no sign of Grandma . . . The old wurzel's got stuck in the attic, George thought. Thank goodness for that. — GEORGE'S MARVELLOUS MEDICINE

X, letter
There are very few words in Roald Dahl's stories that start with the letter X, but there are lots of words that *end* in X, such as *mix* and *wax*, and *moneybox* and *Mr Fox*. You can make rhymes for any of these by using words that end in *-cks*, such as *mix* and *sticks*, *wax* and *cracks*, or *fox* and *clocks*.

If this were a backwards dictionary (either for tortoise language, or for vicars with **back-to-front dyslexia**), all the words would be arranged by the last letter rather than the first one, so **Mr Fox** and **pencil-box** would be under this letter.

X-ray noun **X-rays**
An X-ray is a special photograph of the inside of your body that shows your bones. An X-ray of a Knid would therefore show that it has no bones at all.
Doc Spencer . . . called the hospital and asked for an ambulance. Then he spoke to someone else about taking X-rays and doing an operation. — DANNY THE CHAMPION OF THE WORLD

a b c d e f g h i j k l m n o p q r s t u v w **X** y z

The BFG is called *der GuRie* (*Gute Riese*) in German.

young — FANTASTIC MR FOX

yacht yippee

yacht (*rhymes with* hot) noun **yachts**
A yacht is a boat with sails that people use for racing or for pleasure. Willy Wonka builds a yacht to sail on his chocolate river out of a giant boiled sweet.
'This is my private yacht!' cried Mr Wonka, beaming with pleasure. 'I made her by hollowing out an enormous boiled sweet!' — CHARLIE AND THE CHOCOLATE FACTORY

yell verb **yells, yelling, yelled**
If you yell, you shout very loudly.
'Help me! Save me! Call a doctor!' yelled Mr Twit.
'I'm getting THE DREADED SHRINKS!' — THE TWITS
LOOK IT UP! For more ways to yell (and some quieter ways to speak), see **say**.

yellow adjective
the colour of ripe lemons and buttercups
The skin of the peach was very beautiful — a rich buttery yellow with patches of brilliant pink and red. — JAMES AND THE GIANT PEACH

yelp noun **yelps**
a shrill bark or cry, like a dog makes when it is hurt
The Cloud-Men . . . gave a yelp of surprise and dropped their shovels to the ground. — JAMES AND THE GIANT PEACH

yippee exclamation
People shout *Yippee!* to show they are happy and enjoying themselves.
Charlie could hear the whistling of the air outside as the lift went faster and faster. 'Yippee!' shouted Grandpa Joe again. 'Yippee! Here we go!' — CHARLIE AND THE CHOCOLATE FACTORY

yodel verb **yodels, yodelling, yodelled**
When someone yodels, they sing in a special way, making their voice alternate between very high and low notes.
'The first thing you would be doing, you would be scuddling around yodelling the news that you were actually SEEING a giant.' — THE BFG

yolk (*rhymes with* joke) noun **yolks**
The yolk of an egg is the yellow part inside it.
'Vhile the mixer is still mixing you must add to it the yolk of vun grrruntle's egg.' — THE WITCHES

young adjective **younger, youngest**
Someone who is young is not very old. An old person can become young again by taking Wonka-Vite (but not too much, or they might become a Minus).
'My dear young fellow,' the Old-Green-Grasshopper said gently, 'there are a whole lot of things in this world of ours that you haven't started wondering about yet.' — JAMES AND THE GIANT PEACH

yummy adjective (*informal*) **yummier, yummiest**
scrumdiddlyumptiously delicious
The Enormous Crocodile grinned up at Trunky and said: 'I'm off to find a yummy child for lunch.' — THE ENORMOUS CROCODILE

Zz

zoonk

CHARLIE AND THE GREAT GLASS ELEVATOR

zippfizzing   zoonk   zozimus

zany adjective **zanier, zaniest**
funny in a crazy kind of way
Most of the congregation found the zany word-crazy service a rather welcome change from the old routine of well-worn phrases. — THE VICAR OF NIBBLESWICKE

zippfizz verb **zippfizzes, zippfizzing, zippfizzed**
When giants zippfizz, they whizz along as fast as they can go.
'What's that?' Sophie cried. 'That is all the giants zippfizzing off to another country to guzzle human beans,' the BFG said. — THE BFG

zoo noun **zoos**
A zoo is a place where wild animals (but not usually giants) are kept so that people can look at them or study them.
*'I is **never** showing myself to human beans . . . If I do, they will be putting me in the zoo with all the jiggyraffes and cattypiddlers.'* — THE BFG

zoom verb **zooms, zooming, zoomed**
When you zoom, you move along very quickly.
So on the last day of term I zoomed joyfully away and left school behind me for ever and ever. — BOY

zoonk exclamation
Zoonk is a word that Willy Wonka says when he pretends to be speaking in Martian language.

It is probably a very rude word in Martian.
The next time Mr Wonka spoke, the words came out so fast and sharp and loud they were like bullets from a machine-gun. 'ZOONK-ZOONK-ZOONK-ZOONK-ZOONK!' he barked. — CHARLIE AND THE GREAT GLASS ELEVATOR

zozimus noun
Zozimus is what dreams are made of. The BFG whisks zozimus with an egg-beater until it forms bubbles just like soapy water.
'Dreams is not like human beans or animals. They has no brains. They is made of zozimus.' — THE BFG

AFTERWORD

This is the end of the alphabet but not the end of the book, as dictionaries never truly end. You just go back to **A**, or to any other letter that you fancy, and start again. Even if you have looked up every single word that you know from Roald Dahl's stories, there may be some that you don't yet know about — maybe even just one **extra-extra-usual** word, which might end up being your favourite word for ever and ever. Roald Dahl once said that

THE GREATEST SECRETS ARE ALWAYS HIDDEN IN THE MOST UNLIKELY PLACES

and if you don't look for them, you may never find them. Some magical words may be tucked away on a page you missed before.

THE ONLY WAY TO FIND OUT IS TO TURN BACK THE PAGES AND LOOK AGAIN . . .

a b c d e f g h i j k l m n o p q r s t u v w x y z

STORIES ARE GOOD FOR YOU.

Roald Dahl said,

'IF YOU HAVE GOOD THOUGHTS THEY WILL SHINE OUT OF YOUR FACE LIKE SUNBEAMS AND YOU WILL ALWAYS LOOK LOVELY.'

We believe in doing good things.
That's why ten percent of all Roald Dahl income* goes to our charity partners. We have supported causes including: specialist children's nurses, grants for families in need, and educational outreach programmes. Thank you for helping us to sustain this vital work.

Find out more at roalddahl.com